EDEN Dublin Annual Conference 2023

"Yes we can!" - Digital Education for Better Futures

Full Papers

Dublin, Ireland
18-20 June 2023

ISBN: 978-1-7138-9067-6

Printed from e-media with permission by:

Curran Associates, Inc.
57 Morehouse Lane
Red Hook, NY 12571

Some format issues inherent in the e-media version may also appear in this print version.

European Distance and E-Learning Network (EDEN)
Budapest University of Technology & Economics
H-1111 Budapest, Egry J. u.1.
Hungary

Phone: +36 1 463 1628
Fax: +36 1 463 1858

secretariat@eden-online.org

Additional copies of this publication are available from:

Curran Associates, Inc.
57 Morehouse Lane
Red Hook, NY 12571 USA
Phone: 845-758-0400
Fax: 845-758-2633
Email: curran@proceedings.com
Web: www.proceedings.com

TABLE OF CONTENTS

A TRANSLATIONAL APPROACH TO DIGITAL LEARNING INNOVATION: ENABLING DIGITAL INNOVATION AT DURHAM UNIVERSITY

Sam Nolan, Durham Centre for Academic Development – Durham University, UK

Correspondence: *Sam Nolan: s.j.nolan@durham.ac.uk*

Abstract

In this paper we explore how we adopted a translational approach to educational development, which incorporates educational and digital innovation, staff development and student support into a single department. Through exploring three case studies of innovative work, we highlight the key enablers that a translational approach provides such as the agility to undertake research work which can quickly feed into teaching and learning practice. By rethinking the traditional role of learning technologists and by embedding students as partners, we believe such as approach can reap dividends on allowing for meaningful digital innovation in learning and teaching.

Keywords:

Digital Learning, Digital Innovation, Students as Partners, Translational Education, Technology Enhanced Learning

Introduction

Durham University is a research-intensive university located in the city of Durham, in the north-east of England, a member of the prestigious Russell Group of leading research-intensive universities. Established in 1832, it is one of the oldest universities in England and has a long history of academic excellence. The university is organized into four faculties: Arts and Humanities, Science, Social Sciences and Health and the Durham University Business School, which offer a wide range of undergraduate and postgraduate degree and are home to around 16,000 undergraduate and 4,000 postgraduate students and 1,800 academic staff. Durham is home to a diverse student body, with students from over 130 countries, and has a strong tradition of research, with many of its departments ranked among the best in the UK.

In 2018, the University established the Durham Centre for Academic Development (DCAD), bringing together a number of areas including technology enhanced learning, educational development, innovation funding and student support into one unit. The ethos behind this was to embed a translational approach to education innovation. The notion of translational education comes from the field of translational medicine (Cohrs et al., 2015), which has revolutionised the field of applied medical research by placing research units within hospitals, so that the distance from discovery to patient is minimised.

Figure 1. Schematic showing the interlinking process of translational education. ALT: Diagram Showing Educational Innovation leads to Academic Excellence which leads to Student Success

DCAD is unique amongst its peers by minimizing the gap between pedagogical innovation, staff development, and student learning gain. This is achieved by developing and funding new approaches to teaching and learning through DCAD's Education Laboratory. These approaches are then shared with members of staff through the training provided by the academic excellence team, and introduced to students through the student success team.

The first step in this process, focussed on Educational Innovation, is achieved by DCAD's Education Laboratory. This facility, based in our £40M Teaching and Learning Centre, provides funding through three schemes for digital innovation, namely:

Collaborative Innovation Grants (CIG): This grant scheme is designed to support staff across Durham University to develop innovative and inclusive learning and teaching approaches to enhance student learning and success, and to disseminate good practice across the institution and beyond. Grants of up to £5K are available under the CIG scheme.

Enhancing Accessibility Grants (EA): These grants support the learning of students with disabilities and develop inclusive approaches to education which benefit all students at Durham. This scheme is based on Durham's allocation of the UK Government Disability Premium funding and grants of up to £40K are available.

Strategic Innovation Grants (SIG): These grants are up to £30K and are for technologies identified as addressing a strategic learning need. The outcome of each project is a recommendation to the University as to whether to deploy the technology institutionally or not ..

Each grant, regardless of category, lasts for up to one year and is co-led by a disciplinary academic member of staff, a member of the digital learning team and a student. We'll consider below some examples of successful projects as short case studies.

Case Studies

1) **The Use of Immersive Realities in Teaching**

The presence of the Education Lab at Durham has allowed for the development of research links with other universities such as Carnegie Mellon, where immersive technologies such as VR and AR are being trialled. The Education Lab ran the first national online conference on the use of VR in Learning and Teaching, which took place on 21st June 2021, with over 80 delegates joining online. This swell of interest led to several funded projects, including:

a) **Developing Virtual Field Trips in Geography (EA)**

During the Covid pandemic, field trips were difficult to run. Using funding from our Enhancing Accessibility grant scheme this project, called Project RENU (Research Expedition for Net Zero and Universal Learning) used innovative communication techniques and sustainable digital practices to produce a digital field-trip experience with the aim of making environmental learning accessible to all students in a fundamentally sustainable way. The project worked with a commercial partner to produce engaging, documentary-style, interactive resources which allow the user to experience the field trip as if they were there. The project went on to win a prestigious Green Gown award for sustainable education.

Figure 2. Screenshot from the Virtual Field Trip

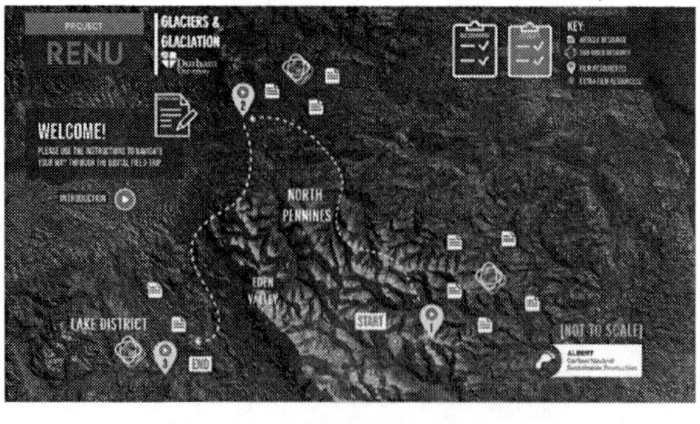

b) **Using AR in Physics Learning (CIG)**

Following the success of the Geography project, the Physics department, in partnership with our digital learning team, developed Microsoft Hololens-based resources to help explain complex invisible phenomena in Physics, such as the shape of Magnetic Fields. The work also included reaching out to a local NHS Education Centre, which itself was a hub for excellence in the use of AR, and the co-facilitation of an institutional workshop on the use of AR in teaching.

c) **Using VR in Drama (CIG)**

This project, a partnership between the English Studies department and the digital learning team, seeks to develop a more complete and nuanced understanding of how 360° video, when experienced through virtual reality (VR) technology, might support students to understand the impact of stage directions, directorial decisions, and point of view in representing dramatic texts on stage.

2) **The Transitions into HE Project (SIG and EA)**

The transition students make when leaving secondary/high school and joining a university course can be challenging (McGhie, 2017). To address this, the Education Lab funded a project to build an online course, presented through our Virtual Learning Environment, for all students to engage with prior to the commencement of their undergraduate studies. This asynchronous course includes four key elements: Preparing for Academic Study, Introducing Independent Learning, Developing Digital Literacies and Preparing to Arrive. Unique amongst other such courses, it is built by student developers and was developed using review committees comprised of students. The course is actively used by approximately 4,500 students per year, about 85% of all possible new students. A survey conducted to assess how students felt before and after using the course was conducted, and the word clouds below show indicative responses to the questions (i) 'how did you feel before undertaking this course?' and (ii) 'how do you feel after taking the course?'

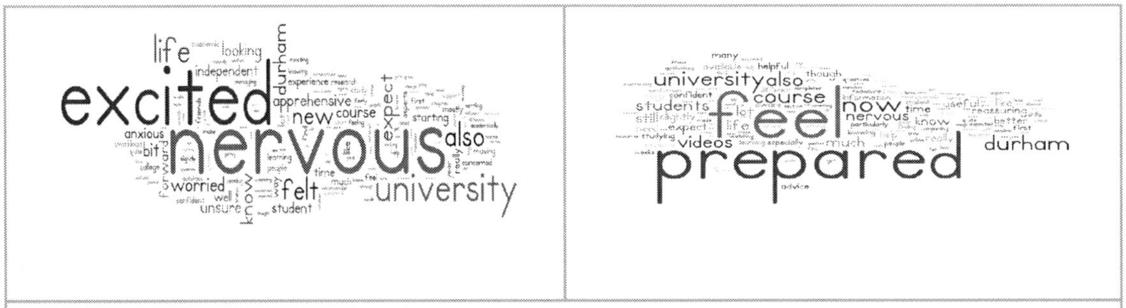

Figure 3. Word clouds indicating words used by 80 respondents in response to questions: 'How did you feel before taking the course?' (left hand side) and 'How did you feel after taking the course?' (right hand side). ALT: Word clouds indicating excited and nervous as dominant words (left hand side) and feel prepared dominant words (right hand side)

The course continues to evolve and this year an additional element exploring mental health and well-being is being developed.

3) **Building Inclusive Learning Communities during the Covid-19 Response**

Like all universities, in March 2020 Durham University needed to quickly pivot its teaching online due to the impact of the Covid-19 pandemic and the associated enforced lockdowns.

The placement of the Education Lab in DCAD and the bringing together of different elements (especially the digital learning and academic development teams), enhanced innovation significantly during this period. Initially the focus was on supporting staff to teach online and result in the production of:

- A two-week online course, 'Introducing to Learning and Teaching Online,' led by DCAD and developed by staff from DCAD and colleagues from Durham's Business School: This course gave staff a student's-eye view of the online learning experience. It was taken by over 1200 academic staff. Of the 200 who responded to an end-of-course questionnaire, over 80% agreed the course was well designed and appropriate to their needs.

- Eight asynchronous self-study courses, which covered a range of topics with a focus on active pedagogies as an underpinning framework: These are also available as Open Educational Resources (DCAD,2022a).

- Over 60 live online workshops focussed on building active learning into live online sessions through the use of breakout rooms and problem based learning.

- Establishment of a Digital Learning Community of Practice with 26 'Sharing Practice' seminars during the 20/21 academic year.

A key problem identified by academic staff during this period was the difficulty in developing inclusive communities for students when they were learning in online environments. As a result of this, a research project on Inclusive Learning Communities was quickly developed by colleagues working in the Education Lab. A team of three staff members from DCAD and eight student co-researchers undertook:

- 28 focus groups involving 103 students, recruited from across all faculties and year groups, representing a range of demographic characteristics.

- 19 staff interviews, including staff from all four faculties.

This work will be shortly published, but an open educational resource which details key findings from this work, which can be utilised in your own practice, can be found here (DCAD,2022b).

Discussion

i) Central Support

Key to this move to translational education has been a rethinking of the traditional model of the 'Learning Technologist' as instead a 'Digital Education Consultant' (DEC). Whereas, before DCAD formed, our learning technologists had supported training and development around the use of the Virtual Learning Environment, in DCAD we introduced a new role of Digital Learning Adviser to take the vast majority of VLE-related support and created the new role of Digital Education Consultant whose focus was:

- Consultation with departmental and faculty leads on the use of digital technologies in teaching.

- Advice and guidance to teaching staff on the pedagogic use of new technologies.

- Co-development and leadership of Collaborative Innovation and Enhancing Accessibility Funded projects

- Training and development on digital pedagogy in the classroom.

The role of DEC is therefore both strategy- and innovation-linked, in a way that hadn't been fully realised in the previous iteration of the role. DECs are both consultants, project managers and Co-I's, allowing projects to reach fruition and not become overly onerous to academic staff with limited time.

ii) Students as Partners

The second critical element is the involvement of students as partners throughout the projects. The four kinds of student partnership, as outlined by Mick Healey, are:

- 'Consulted' Partnership: In this form of partnership, students are consulted for their opinions and feedback on various aspects of their education. However, the ultimate decision-making power still rests with the teacher or institution.

- 'Collaborative' Partnership: This type of partnership involves joint decision-making between students and teachers, with both parties contributing equally to the design and implementation of the learning experience.

- 'Cooperative' Partnership: In this form of partnership, students take on specific roles and responsibilities within the learning environment, such as co-teaching, peer mentoring, or leading discussions.

- 'Collegial' Partnership: This highest level of partnership involves students and teachers working together as colleagues with mutual respect and shared responsibilities. This means that students are seen as active co-creators of knowledge and are given significant agency in the learning process.

The table below looks at the role of students in each of the case studies we have outlined:

Table 1: Table showing student roles from Case Studies in context of model of (Healey et al., 2014)

Case Study	Role of Student	Most Linked Element of Students as Partners Model
Use of Immersive Realities in Teaching	Students co-write the proposal for funding and act as developers on the project. Students will be co-authors on any published work.	Collaborative and Co-operative Partnership
The Transitions into HE Project	Students act as developers on the project; interviewees and students act a review committee for the project.	Collaborative and Co-operative Partnership
The Inclusive Learning Communities Project	Students act as co-investigators on the project, organising focus groups, interviewing other students and analysing the data. Students will be co-authors on any published work.	Co-operative and Collegial Partnership

Working with students as partners is central to all our work and is critical for its authenticity and impact. We continue to make for paid student involvement a mandatory requirement for all proposed projects.

Pros and Cons

The successes of the work evidenced above suggest that developing a central teaching enhancement unit built around the translational model is a powerful way of driving meaningful teaching innovation in an institution. However, this approach comes with both positive and negative aspects. Positives include:

- An agile way to develop digital resources, through a research lens, that address a particular need so that the findings can be shared quickly across the institution and the wider sector.

- A way to embed staff/student partnership as the underlying model for all strategic learning enhancement work within the institution.

- Creating pathfinder projects to explore the cutting edge in digital learning and teaching, which can be scaled up for institutional roll-out.

Whereas more negative aspects would include:

- Although not unique to this model, centres for teaching and learning such as DCAD can often end up supporting innovation with individual academic staff, which may or may not be tied to larger strategic needs of the department. We try to tackle this in Durham by having regular meetings with the leadership teams in academic departments and developing interventions focussed on improving the quality of education and the student learning experience at programme level as well as supporting individual staff.

- In a centre like DCAD, it is often easy to lose sight of the big picture. In academic year 22/23 we are developing a database system for detailing interactions with individuals and departments so that these can be actively tied to improvements in teaching and learning identified by (for example) end of module/programme questionnaires.

Conclusion

In this paper we have explored the use of a translational approach to educational digital innovation at Durham University through the development of the Durham Centre for Academic Development. The approach has allowed us to cultivate a culture of digital education innovation both within and beyond the post-pandemic period. This approach, which rethinks the role of the Learning Technologist and embeds students as partners is having a profound impact on teaching and learning within the institution. Our next steps will be to increase the impact with departments through developing closer working networks with academic and support departments.

References

Cohrs, R.J., Martin, T., Ghahramani, P., Bidaut, L., Higgins, P.J. and Shahzad, A. (2015). Translational medicine definition by the European Society for Translational Medicine.

DCAD (2022a), DCAD Online Asynchronous Teaching and Learning Courses (2022). https://dcad-resourcebank.webspace.durham.ac.uk/2022/03/17/online-teaching-and-learning-guides/

DCAD (2022b), Developing Inclusive Learning Communities (2022). https://community.dur.ac.uk/lt.team/inclusive-communities/#/

Healey, M., Flint, A., & Harrington, K. (2014). Engagement through partnership: students as partners in learning and teaching in higher education. Higher Education Academy.

McGhie, V. (2017), Entering university studies: identifying enabling factors for a successful transition from school to university, *Higher Education*, 73, pp.407-422.

Gap in pagination due to unavailable paper.

Pages 7-22

Empowering diverse learners through design-based data literacy education: the data design cycle framework

Nico Kling , University of Applied Sciences Zwickau, Germany

Chantal Kling , University of Applied Sciences Zwickau, Germany

Emelie Schwill , University of Applied Sciences Zwickau, Germany

Christian-Andreas Schumann , University of Applied Sciences Zwickau, Germany

Sajal Kabiraj , Häme University of Applied Sciences, Finland

***Correspondence**: Emelie Schwill: emelie.schwill.gfb@fh-zwickau.de*

Abstract

Data literacy is a vital life-skill that is becoming increasingly necessary in today's society. As such, public data literacy education must become a substantive component in teaching, requiring an appropriate pedagogical model. This paper aims to present a new definition for data literacy, as well as conceptual framework for public data literacy education, drawing from tenets of design-based education and synthesized principles of data literacy education from literature. The resulting framework is termed the Data Design Cycle, and emphasizes collaboration, communication, and the development of problem-solving skills. The model is highly adaptable to different educational environments and learning styles, making it easily integrable into a variety of educational settings, including traditional classroom-based learning, online learning, and experiential learning programs. Furthermore, by promoting the principles of public teaching of data literacy and a learner-centred approach, the Data Design Cycle ensures that data literacy education is accessible to heterogeneous learners from diverse educational and socioeconomical settings.

Keywords:

Data Literacy; Design-based Education; Future Competence; Life Skill; Diversity in Education

Data Literacy is a life skill

According to Einay and Levin (2014), data is now more accessible and has broader applications, including new observations and dimensions. However, despite the opportunities presented by big data analytics, there is widespread public skepticism that it threatens privacy, restricts civil liberties, and leads to increased state and corporate control (Koltay, 2015). This skepticism is heightened with the increasing complexity of data, which has led to a diminished role of human factors (Wolff et al., 2016). Therefore, the importance of understanding data has become more critical than ever, particularly in the ethical use of data (Carlson et al., 2011). Datafication, the transformation of social actions into quantifiable data, has become a new paradigm in society and science (Van Dijck, 2014), leading to data becoming a valuable commodity and emphasizing the importance of mastering data skills as a life skill. The term commonly used to describe these data skills is data literacy (Koltay, 2015). The concept of data literacy is defined in various ways, with definitions typically categorized into general and discipline-dependent, and further divided into technical and sociotechnical approaches. Technical definitions focus on the technical processes behind data literacy, emphasizing the academic skills required to handle information enriched with computer science and statistics (Raffaghelli, 2020). In contrast, sociotechnical definitions expand on technological processes and include cognitive processes such as data ethics and critical thinking. One perspective describes it as the existence of data awareness and sensitivity in order to effectively and appropriately collect, analyse, process, use and present data (Bai et al., 2021). We combined these categorizations into a new definition:

Data Literacy is a purpose-bound collection of various sociological and technical competencies, consisting of knowledge, skills and behaviour, that build on each other. The sum of the competencies allows the holistic handling of data, which in its most pronounced form encompasses the entire data lifecycle from the creation to the disposal.

Our reason for defining data literacy as a purpose-bound collection of sociological and technical competencies, rather than a list of specific knowledge, abilities, and behaviours, is that we believe this distinction is necessary for the construct to be universally valid. A purpose-bound definition recognizes that data literacy is not a fixed set of skills or knowledge, but rather a set of competencies that are developed and used in different contexts to achieve specific goals. By emphasizing the purpose-bound nature of data literacy, we hope to create a more comprehensive and flexible definition that can be applied to diverse educational settings and real-world contexts.

We believe that in a datafied society, public access to data literacy education is substantive. Only then can the citizens use their knowledge to contribute to the positive development of society. However, the current state of data literacy education in mainly done in formal educational settings, and is often inadequate, as evidenced by the low levels of proficiency demonstrated by students and professionals alike (e.g. Oguguo et al., 2020; Zhao, 2020). This highlights the need for a review of existing literature and pedagogical approaches to data literacy in education, as it allows us to identify principles that are applicable in diverse educational settings, including public education, and better equip learners with the necessary data literacy skills for the future. Additionally, due to data literacy not only being a technical skill but also a mindset and a way of thinking, traditional teaching methods may not be enough to fully equip learners with the necessary competencies, especially in the public sphere. Thus, we additionally introduce a hybrid approach that combines the problem-solving and user-centred design aspects of design-based education based on Geitz & de Geus (2019) with the technical aspects of data literacy education which could be the key to effectively teaching data literacy skills publicly. Our conceptual framework is termed Data Design Cycle.

Therefore, this paper seeks to address the question: "How can the principles of design-based education and data literacy be applied to create a comprehensive and adaptable framework for teaching data literacy in diverse educational settings?"

Five Key Principles for Fostering Data Literacy through Education

When it comes to developing a comprehensive understanding of a complex topic such as data literacy in education, an explorative approach to a literature review can be highly valuable. By reviewing a broad range of existing data literacy education research and synthesizing the key findings into five broadly applicable principles for effective data literacy education, we can develop a more nuanced and holistic understanding of the topic.

The first principle we found can be derived from the various definitions of data literacy in the existing literature, which is primarily classified as a competence, skill, or ability within an educational context. This classification is significant, as a competence is a more comprehensive term than the other two. As Marzal (2020) notes, a competence is linked to an attitude and a behaviour that allows for successful completion of an activity and efficient execution of activities, with transferability to various areas of application. However, many of the existing definitions do not fully consider the mindset aspect of data literacy (e.g. Burress et al., 2020; Bautista et al., 2017; Raffaghelli, 2020; Fraser-Arnott, 2020). As per the definition, a competent individual must be able to apply the behaviors in various interdisciplinary settings, which is also missing from many definitions. The understanding of data literacy as a competence provides a foundation for a holistic framework that includes all aspects of the term, and is crucial in determining the choice of teaching content and curriculum creation. This leads to Principle 1:

1. Principle: Understanding the concept of competence is important for teaching data literacy.

The second principle that we derived from our explorative approach is the importance of teachers being proficient in data literacy themselves in order to effectively teach the subject. The works of Starobin & Upah (2014) and Yang & Li (2020) highlight that data exists in universities and can be utilized for teaching through learning analytics and other technologies. However, the authors argue that to effectively apply these teaching-enhancing technologies, teachers must have a thorough understanding of data literacy. By becoming competent in data literacy, teachers can integrate data-driven insights into their pedagogical practices and develop innovative teaching strategies that better meet the needs of their students. Therefore, we propose the following principle:

2. Principle: Teachers need to possess a strong foundation in data literacy to deliver effective data literacy education.

The literature furthermore shows that learners are more likely to have a greater understanding of data literacy when they are actively involved in the learning process. Gläser & Spree (2022) and Werning (2020) suggest that students are more engaged and motivated when the teaching aligns with their reality. Maybee & Zilinski (2015) proposed a data-based teaching approach that can be used to achieve this alignment. The approach involves using study objects that are representative of the educational reality in the students' chosen discipline. The same idea applies to the choice of the underlying definition for the teaching intervention, which should be aligned with the learners' discipline depending on the teaching objectives (Atenas et al., 2020; Hitchcock et al., 2021; Starobin & Upah, 2014; Todorova et al., 2019; Werning, 2020). Therefore, the third principle that can be derived from these arguments is:

3. Principle: Effective data literacy education should be based on the learners' reality and aligned with their discipline.

Drawing from the literature, it is clear that the practical skills required for data literacy are just as important as knowledge and education culture. Examples of successful practical teaching methods are discussed in the literature (Schüller, 2022; Gläser & Spree, 2022; Werning, 2020; Gehrke et al., 2021; Hitchcock et al., 2021; Cheng et al., 2019), and can be virtual or analog in nature. Building practical competence not only empowers students but also encourages their involvement in the public sphere. This can be achieved through public lectures, workshops, and other initiatives that foster cooperation among learners, teachers, and society. Such engagement strengthens democracy, promotes social justice, and provides economically applicable competences (Raffaghelli, 2020; Atenas et al., 2020). In light of these findings, the fourth principle for effective data literacy education can be articulated as follows:

4. Principle: Data literacy education should be conducted in a practical and publicly engaged manner.

To synthesize effective data literacy education, it is essential to recognize that data literacy is not a skill that can be learned in isolation. Rather, it is a complex and long-term process that most likely requires a comprehensive curriculum to be taught effectively, specifically in higher education. The work of Bai et al. (2021) and Burress et al. (2020) highlights the importance of developing a structured curriculum for teaching data literacy generically. Stand-alone courses with too much content are not recommended as they do not provide students with adequate time to build the necessary competencies. Instead, entire modules that stretch the learning process and provide realistic goals are a more effective way to teach data literacy (Gläser & Spree, 2022). By understanding that data literacy is a long-term process, educators can take a more strategic and intentional approach to education, which in turn will promote better learning outcomes. This leads to the fifth and final principle:

5. Principle: The teaching and learning of data literacy should be approached as a long-term process with a comprehensive and structured curriculum.

The five principles we have developed provide a suggested foundation for effective data literacy education, both applicable for formal and informal settings. However, to implement these principles in a practical and engaging way, a suitable education approach is needed. One such approach is design-based education, which emphasizes the importance of iterative problem-solving and user-centred design. By applying the principles to a design-based education framework, we can create a pedagogical approach that has the potential to be both effective and engaging for learners. Therefore, the following chapter will explore the key tenets of design-based education and demonstrate how this approach can be used to teach data literacy in a way that promotes creativity, innovation, and problem-solving.

Design Based Education and Data Literacy

To effectively teach learners the necessary skills to work with data, a pedagogical approach that is multifaceted is needed. It is important to note that our understanding of DBE is based on the work by Gerry Geitz and Jan de Geus (2019). The DBE approach consists of six phases that can be related to the phases of self-regulated learning. Before starting a research/learning process to approach a problem, goal setting, planning, and managing one's motivational beliefs are necessary processes influencing the effectiveness of the execution of this research/learning process. During the research/learning process, the application of strategies to effectively approach and execute the research (i.e., learning) supports the intended outcome of the process. Finally, after the initial research steps resulting in a solution/prototype, self-reflection is needed to determine whether the intended outcome/performance is recognized and valued by knowledgeable others (i.e., working field and lecturers). Self-reflection leads back to the forethought phase that precedes the next learning effort. The diagram illustrating the six phases of the DBE approach can be seen in figure 1.

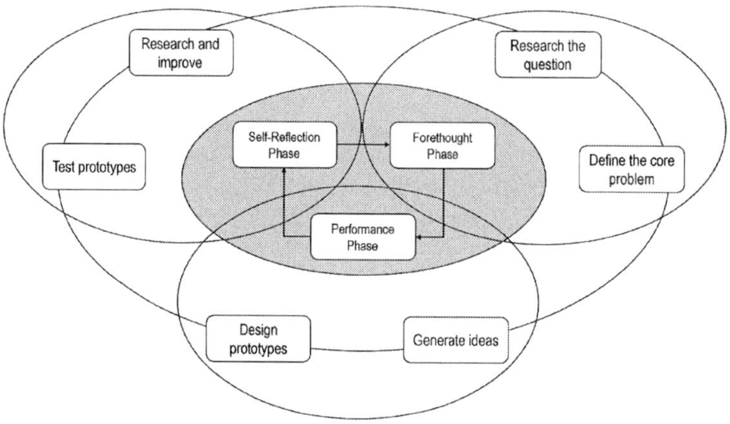

Figure 1: Geitz & de Geus (2019) Design-based education (six phases) integrated with self-regulation phases

By applying the principles of understanding the concept of competence, teaching based on the reality of the learners, practical and public teaching of data literacy, and the long-term nature of data literacy education to a DBE framework, we can create a conceptual pedagogical approach that is both effective and engaging for learners, which we named the Data Design Cycle. The results are of theoretical nature, and the application of the three different self-learning phases are still to be conceptualized.

The Data Design Cycle

The need for an effective pedagogical approach to data literacy has led to the development of the Data Design Cycle, an adaptation of the design-based education process that incorporates the principles of effective data literacy education. The Data Design Cycle is a cyclical process that allows learners to approach data-related problems from a problem-solving perspective, emphasizing collaboration, communication, and the development of problem-solving skills. By applying the principles of design-based to the Data Design Cycle, learners can develop their own solutions to complex data-related problems in a flexible and adaptable way. Ultimately, the goal of the Data Design Cycle is to equip learners with the necessary skills and mindset to succeed in a rapidly evolving field and to promote the use of data for positive change in society. As it is based on Geitz & de Geus (2019) DBE model, it consists of six different phases, as seen in figure 2:

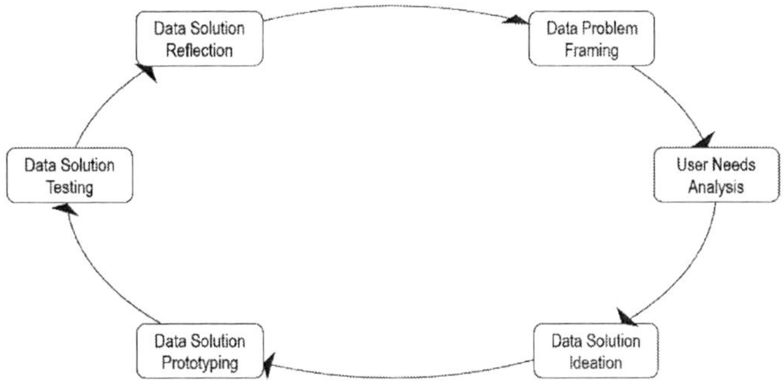

Figure 2: The Data Design cycle

1. Data Problem Framing

During the Data Problem Framing, learners identify and frame a data-related problem. This includes understanding the context, scope, and complexity of the problem. As well as considering potential stakeholders and their needs. By applying Principle 1, which emphasizes the importance of understanding the concept of competence, learners gain a clear understanding of the problem and the competencies needed to solve it. The learners should also consider the ethical and social implications of their project and ensure that their proposed solutions are grounded in responsible data use.

2. User Needs Analysis

In the User Needs Analysis, learners analyse the needs and preferences of potential users of the data-related solution they want to create. This includes considering factors such as accessibility, user-friendliness, and accuracy. By applying Principle 3, which states that teaching should be based on the reality of the learners, learners gain a deeper understanding of the practical applications of data literacy and are better equipped to design solutions that meet real-world needs. This phase helps to ensure that the final data solution will meet the needs of the intended audience.

3. Data Solution Ideation

During the Data Solution phase, learners generate ideas for potential solutions to the data-related problem they identified in the previous phase. This involves brainstorming, mind mapping, and other ideation techniques. By applying Principle 4, which advocates for practical and public teaching of data literacy, learners work to develop solutions that can be practically applied in real-world settings, while publicly discussing the social and ethical implications of their proposed solutions and ensure that their ideas are grounded in responsible data use, accepted by the community.

4. Data Solution Prototyping

During the data solution prototyping, learners create a prototype of their proposed data-related solution. This could involve creating data visualizations, developing software applications, or designing user interfaces. By applying Principle 2, which emphasizes the importance of teachers being data literate, learners develop their own data literacy skills through hands-on work.

5. Data Solution Testing

In this phase, learners test their prototype with potential users and gather feedback on its effectiveness. This feedback can be used to refine the solution and improve its usability. By applying Principle 5, which recognizes the importance of the long-term nature of data literacy education, learners are to continually refine their skills and develop a deeper understanding of data-related problem-solving.

6. Data Solution Reflection

Finally, learners reflect on their design-based data literacy experience, considering what they learned, how they could improve their approach, and how they could apply their new data literacy skills in future settings. By applying the idea of critical data literacy, learners reflect on the social and ethical implications of their work and consider how data can be used to promote positive change. This ensures that learners not only develop technical data literacy skills but also a critical perspective on data use and its implications for society.

The six phases of the Data Design Cycle provide learners with a structured approach to data literacy education, emphasizing collaboration, communication, and problem-solving skills. The framework is specifically designed to be accessible and adaptable for learners at all levels of data literacy. One of the key advantages of the Data Design Cycle is its flexibility in accommodating learners of varying levels of experience with data literacy. For beginners, the Data Design Cycle provides a structured approach to learning data literacy, with clear steps and guidance to help learners gain a foundational understanding of the key concepts and principles of data literacy. The focus on problem-solving and collaboration provides an engaging and interactive learning experience, allowing beginners to learn through hands-on experience. No-code applications, as discussed by Kling et al. (2022), could be suitable and approachable alternatives to coded solutions, and would allow beginners to test the wide range of technological possibilities for data-specific practical applications without the need for prior knowledge. For intermediate learners, the Data Design Cycle offers a platform to deepen their understanding of data literacy, building upon the foundational knowledge gained in the beginner stage. The iterative nature of the Data Design Cycle allows intermediate learners to engage with complex data-related problems and develop innovative solutions. The emphasis on collaboration and communication encourages learners to work with others, building their teamwork and leadership skills. This stage is ideal for learners who are interested in developing a deeper understanding of data literacy and its applications in real-world settings, and a switch from no-code to low-code allows to hone their data skills even more. For expert learners, the Data Design Cycle provides a space to explore cutting-edge data-related problems and develop innovative solutions to complex challenges. The flexibility of the Data Design Cycle allows expert learners to engage with data-related problems at a high level, while the emphasis on collaboration and communication provides a platform for them to share their knowledge and expertise with others. This stage is ideal for learners who have a deep understanding of data literacy and are interested in pushing the boundaries of the field, as well as users who are able to code.

Furthermore, the Data Design Cycle is highly adaptable to different educational backgrounds and learning styles. The framework can be easily integrated into a variety of public educational settings, including traditional classroom-based learning, online learning, and experiential learning programs. This adaptability ensures that the framework can be used in diverse educational contexts and can be tailored to meet the specific needs of learners in different settings. By promoting the principles of public teaching of data literacy and a learner-centred approach, the framework ensures that data literacy education is accessible to heterogeneous learners from diverse educational and socioeconomical backgrounds. Publicly teaching data literacy with the Data Design Cycle can take many forms, including workshops and community outreach programs. These programs can be tailored to meet the needs of specific groups, such as low-income communities, underrepresented groups, or marginalized populations. The focus on problem-solving and collaboration allows learners to engage with data literacy in a practical and interactive way, which increases both data literacy as well as the community spirit.

Discussion

Data literacy is becoming increasingly important in today's data-driven world, and its significance is only set to grow in the coming years. The ability to understand and work with data has become essential not just for individuals and organizations, but also for governments and society as a whole. As we become more reliant on data in various aspects of our lives, from healthcare to finance to education, being able to effectively analyse and interpret data is critical for making informed decisions and driving positive change. However, data literacy must be understood as purpose-bound. The five principles we have identified are a crucial foundation for effective data literacy education. They provide a learner-centred approach that emphasizes the importance of understanding the learners' needs, the practical applications of data literacy, and the social and ethical implications of data use. By prioritizing these principles in data literacy education, we can ensure that learners are not just developing technical skills, but also gaining a critical perspective on data use and its role in society. Our conceptual Data Design Cycle builds on these principles by providing a structured and adaptable framework for data literacy education that can be used by learners at all levels, from beginners to experts. By incorporating the principles of design-based education the framework emphasizes problem-solving, collaboration, and the development of practical, real-world solutions. The cycle also promotes the importance of reflecting on the learning process and specifically data ethics, making it a holistic and integrated approach to data literacy education. Furthermore, the Data Design Cycle's emphasis on publicly teaching data literacy ensures that the framework is accessible to learners from all backgrounds, promoting greater inclusivity and diversity in data literacy education with the goal of achieving a democratic data literacy education. However, it is important to note that the field of data literacy is constantly evolving, with new technologies and data practices emerging. As such, ongoing evaluation and improvement of the Data Design Cycle approach will be crucial to ensure that it remains effective and relevant for learners at all levels. An empirical study utilizing the framework is planned to adequately incorporate the three Self-Regulation Phases, and to validate the entire model.

To conclude and as advocates for education as a public good, we both believe and hope that our pedagogical data literacy education model can empower individuals of all backgrounds to engage critically and effectively with data, enabling them to actively participate in shaping a more equitable and just society.

References

Atenas, J., Havemann, L., & Timmermann, C., 2020, Critical literacies for a datafied society: Academic development and curriculum design in higher education. Research in Learning Technology, 28, pp. 1–14. https://doi.org/10.25304/rlt.v28.2468

Bai, Y., Zhu, M., & Chen, Z., 2021, The Reform and Construction of Computer Essential Courses in New Liberal Arts Aiming at Improving Data Literacy. In Communications in Computer and Information Science: Vol. 1385 CCIS. https://doi.org/10.1007/978-981-16-1160-5_30

Bautista, D. C., Durán, C. E. M., García-Quismondo, M. Á. M., & Álvarez, C., 2017, Constructing bridges for academic discourses the role of the information professional in the new academic literacy agenda for Latin America. European Journal of Science and Theology, 13(1), pp. 149–160.

Burress, T., Mann, E., & Neville, T., 2020, Exploring data literacy via a librarian-faculty learning community: A case study. Journal of Academic Librarianship, 46(1). https://doi.org/10.1016/j.acalib.2019.102076

Carlson, J. R., Fosmire, M., Miller, C., & Nelson, M. R. S., 2011, Determining Data Information Literacy Needs: A Study of Students and Research Faculty.

Cheng, Q., Lopez, F., & Hadjixenofontos, A., 2019, Integrating Introductory Data Science into Computer and Information Literacy through Collaborative Project-based Learning. Proceedings - Frontiers in Education Conference, FIE, 2019-October. https://doi.org/10.1109/FIE43999.2019.9028683

Einav, L., & Levin, J., 2014, The Data Revolution and Economic Analysis. Innovation Policy and the Economy, 14, pp. 1–24. https://doi.org/10.1086/674019

Fraser-Arnott, M., 2020, Academic Library COVID-19 Subject Guides. Reference Librarian, 61(3–4), pp. 165–184. https://doi.org/10.1080/02763877.2020.1862021

Gehrke, M., Kistler, T., Lübke, K., Markgraf, N., Krol, B., & Sauer, S., 2021, Statistics education from a data-centric perspective. Teaching Statistics, 43(S1), pp. 201–215. https://doi.org/10.1111/test.12264

Geitz, G., & de Geus, J. (2019). Design-based education, sustainable teaching, and learning. Cogent Education, 6(1), 1647919.

Gläser, C., & Spree, U., 2022, Finding Access Points for Data Literacy: The Example of the ERASMUS+ Project DaLiCo (Data Literacy in Context). Communications in Computer and Information Science, 1533 CCIS, pp. 109–121. https://doi.org/10.1007/978-3-030-99885-1_10

Hitchcock, C., Sullivan, J., & O'Donnell, K., 2021, Cultivating Bioliteracy, Biodiscovery, Data Literacy, and Ecological Monitoring in Undergraduate Courses with iNaturalist. Citizen Science: Theory and Practice, 6(1). https://doi.org/10.5334/CSTP.439

Kling, N., Runte, C., Kabiraj, S., & Schumann, C.-A. (2022). Harnessing Sustainable Development in Image Recognition Through No-Code AI Applications: A Comparative Analysis. In K. Santosh, R. Hegadi, & U. Pal (Eds.), Recent Trends in Image Processing and Pattern Recognition (Vol. 1576, pp. 146–155). Springer International Publishing. https://doi.org/10.1007/978-3-031-07005-1_14

Koltay, T., 2015, Data literacy: In search of a name and identity. Journal of Documentation, 71(2), pp. 401–415. https://doi.org/10.1108/JD-02-2014-0026

Marzal, M. Á., 2020, A taxonomic proposal for multiliteracies and their competences. Profesional de La Informacion, 29(4), pp. 1–16. https://doi.org/10.3145/epi.2020.jul.35

Maybee, C., & Zilinski, L., 2015, Data informed learning: A next phase data literacy framework for higher education. Proceedings of the Association for Information Science and Technology, 52(1), pp. 1–4. https://doi.org/10.1002/pra2.2015.1450520100108

Oguguo, B. C. E., Nannim, F. A., Okeke, A. O., Ezechukwu, R. I., Christopher, G. A., & Ugorji, C. O., 2020, Assessment of Students' Data Literacy Skills in Southern Nigerian Universities. Universal Journal of Educational Research, 8(6), pp. 2717–2726. https://doi.org/10.13189/ujer.2020.080658

Raffaghelli, J. E., 2020, Is data literacy a catalyst of social justice? A response from nine data literacy initiatives in higher education. Education Sciences, 10(9), pp. 1–20. https://doi.org/10.3390/educsci10090233

Schüller, K., 2022, Data and AI literacy for everyone. Statistical Journal of the IAOS, pp. 1–14. https://doi.org/10.3233/sji-220941

Starobin, S. S., & Upah, S., 2014, Educational data crossroads: Data literacy for data-driven decision making in postsecondary education. Advances in Education in Diverse Communities: Research, Policy and Praxis, 10, pp. 141–170. https://doi.org/10.1108/S1479-358X20130000010007

Todorova, T., Krasteva, R., & Tsvetkova, E., 2019, Data Literacy and Research Data Management: The Case at ULSIT. Communications in Computer and Information Science, 989, pp. 535–544. https://doi.org/10.1007/978-3-030-13472-3_50

Van Dijck, J., 2014, Datafication, dataism and dataveillance: Big Data between scientific paradigm and ideology. Surveillance & Society, 12(2), pp. 197–208. https://doi.org/10.24908/ss.v12i2.4776

Werning, S., 2020, Making data playable: A game co-creation method to promote creative data literacy. Journal of Media Literacy Education, 12(3), pp. 88–101. https://doi.org/10.23860/JMLE-2020-12-3-8

Wolff, A., Moore, J., Zdrahal, Z., Hlosta, M., & Kuzilek, J., 2016, Data literacy for learning analytics. Proceedings of the Sixth International Conference on Learning Analytics & Knowledge - LAK '16, pp. 500–501. https://doi.org/10.1145/2883851.2883864

Yang, N., & Li, T, 2020, How stakeholders' data literacy contributes to student success in higher education: A goal-oriented analysis. International Journal of Educational Technology in Higher Education, 17(1). https://doi.org/10.1186/s41239-020-00220-3

Zhao, Y., Sánchez Gómez, M. C., Pinto Llorente, A. M., & Zhao, L, 2021, Digital competence in higher education: Students' perception and personal factors. Sustainability (Switzerland), 13(21). https://doi.org/10.3390/su132112184

CO-CREATING VISIONS WITH HIGHER EDUCATION INSTITUTIONS: A CASE STUDY IN THE GERMAN HIGHER EDUCATION LANDSCAPE

Johannes Schleiss, Otto von Guericke University Magdeburg, Germany

Lea Bachus, Bielefeld University, Germany

Yasmin Djabarian, Hochschulforum Digitalisierung/Stifterverband, Germany

***Correspondence**: Johannes Schleiss: johannes.schleiss@ovgu.de*

Abstract

Higher education institutions (HEIs) must navigate diverse stakeholder interests and align their efforts towards a common goal to sustainably fulfill their missions. Co-creating visions is a promising approach to developing shared visions and thus aligning stakeholders' interests. However, there is a lack of methodological guidance to support individual institutions during these co-creation processes. To address this gap, this paper aims to understand the impact of providing external methodological support to co-create visions with a multi-stakeholder approach. It investigates the perceived benefits and challenges of the co-creation process, the key factors that contribute to its success, and how student participation is perceived in the process. The co-creation program was evaluated with 30 participants from 11 institutions that took part in the program. The results show that a systematic and moderated co-creation of visions supports stakeholders in clarifying their contribution to achieving a better future for higher education.

Keywords:

Vision Building, Futures Thinking, Co-Creation, Participation, Educational Leadership

Introduction

Higher education institutions (HEIs) are put under pressure by digital transformation in governance and learning, the changing expectations of students, and decreasing enrolment numbers (Pucciarelli, & Kaplan, 2016; Benavides et al., 2020). Given their complex organizational constructs and high diversity in status groups, goals, and needs, HEIs have to face various requirements to sustainably fulfill their mission in a changing and volatile world (Ewing, 2021). To align institutions and move forward, many HEIs already publish strategy papers (e.g., for teaching and learning) or negotiate target agreements with ministries. Moreover, third-party funding projects are often acquired to implement innovative projects, especially in the area of digital learning, and third-mission teams are set up to increase efforts in contributing to society at large.

From this abbreviated presentation of the HEI organizational construct, it is already apparent that HEIs are dealing with diverse goals and requirements. Moreover, decision-making power and responsibilities are distributed among different levels that have varying degrees of autonomy (e.g., leadership, faculties, administration, research institutes), and a range of stakeholders have differing interests in steering and developing the institution (Ewing, 2021). At the same time, participation becomes more and more important for HEIs. The diversity of interests, perspectives, and goals within an HEI poses a challenge to developing and aligning it towards a common vision and mission. This strengthens the need for approaching the development of visions and strategies as a systematic co-creation process (Pucciarelli, & Kaplan, 2016; Doten-Snitker et al., 2021).

Several approaches and tools for co-creation in businesses (Rajan and Read, 2016) as well as experiences with vision building in higher education (HE) already exist (Doten-Snitker et al., 2021). In particular, vision building is often used as an approach in broader foresight studies for the future HE landscape (HolonIQ, 2018; Orr et al., 2020; Sabzalieva et al., 2021; Pelletier et al., 2022). The studies indicate that the co-creation of visions can support the development of HEIs and align the efforts of heterogeneous stakeholders toward a common goal. At the same time, there seems to be a lack of methodological approaches that can guide individual institutions through such a co-creation process.

This case study aims to understand the impact of providing external methodological support and facilitation to vision co-creation with a multi-stakeholder approach. It investigates the perceived benefits and challenges of implementing a co-creation process for vision building for HEIs and explores the key factors that contribute to its successful implementation. Moreover, it explores how the participation of students is perceived during the process.

The paper is structured as follows: First, we introduce related work on vision building in HEIs and describe the methodology. Next, we present a program for co-creating visions for HEIs and report its evaluation. Last, we discuss the results and implications, and then conclude with a summary and outlook on future work.

Related Work

Vision Building in HEIs

Vision building is a creative and aspirational approach to strategic planning and focuses on what an organization wants to achieve in the future (Collins & Porras, 1996). It typically involves creating inspiring narratives and open innovation sessions to generate ideas and build consensus on long-term goals, values, and purpose. Moreover, it is often combined with methods from futures thinking which is a more analytical and data-driven approach to design possibility spaces and create projections about how the future may unfold.

In the context of HEIs, vision building approaches can be used to create future scenarios in strategic planning (Ahmad, 2020). Moreover, methods of vision building and futures thinking are commonly used in foresight studies to create future scenarios that inform political and leadership decisions. Examples in the context of HE are mapping out the UK HE landscape 2035 (Blass et al., 2010), a trend analysis for the HE landscape 2030 (Orr et al., 2020), or an analysis of the impact of technology on HE (HolonIQ, 2018). Accordingly, the UNESCO report on the future of HE (Sabzalieva et al., 2021) and the Horizon Report (Pelletier et al., 2022) are built upon methods from this area.

Co-Creation of Visions as a Participation Tool in HE

Next to strategic planning and foresight studies, vision building approaches are commonly used to align multiple stakeholders and foster participation within an institution. In the context of business organization, this is called co-creation and includes concepts of co-production (multiple stakeholders working together) and value-in-use (how participants create individual value from co-creation activities) (Rajan and Read, 2016).

This also reflects in HE research where studies focus mostly on participation between students and staff, e.g., through approaches like students-as-partners (Mercer-Mapstone et al., 2016). In the context of visions for HE, Géring et al. (2018) explored the use of participatory backcasting to study the future of HE. Similarly, Doten-Snitker et al. (2021) investigated the co-creation of shared visions in 13 change projects and a collaborative approach as a means to support empowerment and inclusion. Inclusion and empowerment were also studied by Dollinger & Lodge (2020), who analyzed ten case studies of student-staff co-creation and found that co-creation activities tend to not only produce greater output value but also reward the participating individuals. They report that student-staff co-creation is a broad category of activities and highlight the importance to reflect on individual and environmental considerations in the design of co-creation activities to ensure authenticity and remove potential barriers.

Methodology

With the aim to develop and test educational innovations in real-world contexts, this study uses a design-based research (DBR) approach (Barab & Squire, 2004). DBR involves iterative cycles of designing, implementing, and evaluating interventions in practice and improving them based on feedback. In this case study, we developed a prototype of a program to co-create visions with HEIs working with small groups of relevant representatives from the institutions including students. The program was then implemented in two cohorts of HEIs. We describe the program in the following section.

Data Collection

To evaluate and iteratively improve the approach in practice, we surveyed the participants on their expectations and experiences before the program, the experience with the program components, the participation of students, and the outlook on future activities.

The first cohort was surveyed at the end of the program, with a response rate of 16 answers. Out of the 16 survey participants, ten were working in service or support structures, three were lecturers, and the rest considered themselves as students or others. Two-thirds (n=10) were in the age group between 30-45, and the rest were distributed among the other age groups.

The second cohort was surveyed after the fourth workshop, with a response rate of 14 answers. Half of the survey participants were working in service or support structures, the rest were distributed among students (3), HEI leadership (2), and lecturers and others (2). Age groups were distributed as follows: five persons between 36-45, four between 18-25, two persons each between 26-35 and 46-55, and one above 55.

Data Analysis

For the closed questions in the survey, the quantitative responses were reported directly or with descriptive statistics. The open items were independently analyzed and coded by two raters using qualitative content analysis (Mayring, 2004) to identify common themes in the answers.

Case Study: Co-creating Visions with HEIs

The case study describes the implementation of a program set-up to co-create visions with teams from German HEIs. The program - a joint initiative by the German think & do tank Hochschulforum Digitalisierung (German Forum for Higher Education in the Digital Age) and its student future working group "DigitalChangeMaker" - ran in two cohorts and consisted of five workshops spread over 4-5 months with integrated remote working phases including take-home tasks for the teams.

The conceptual approach of both cohorts was the same. However, some slight changes in methods and workshop designs were implemented based on the feedback from the first cohort. These include, for example, extending the workshop length to 4 hours instead of 3 hours, starting a regular cross-university student check-in call, and allowing for more flexibility regarding the methods used.

The first cohort consisted of Germany-based 6 HEIs, each providing a heterogeneous team of 3-6 people, and ran between June and October 2022. The second cohort consisted of 4 HEIs and one HEI network and ran between October 2022 and March 2023.

Beside collaborating in cross-HEI workshops, the participating teams formed tandems within their cohort for a more in-depth interaction during and beyond the workshops, e.g., in shorter tandem check-in meetings in between the workshops and a dedicated communication channel. Moreover, each tandem had designated student mentors guiding and facilitating the discussions as well as coaching the teams during the workshop sessions. An overview of the program is shown in Figure 1.

Overall, the program can be divided into three phases: understanding futures, designing futures, and getting futures off the ground. The first phase aims to collect, describe and understand future images. The second phase focuses on the development of future scenarios by the participating teams for their HEI in 2035. The third phase sets out to pave the way to proactively achieving these desirable futures by developing a roadmap, backcasting the next steps, and communicating visions. The components and exercises of the program were built based on relevant literature as well as strongly inspired by approaches and methods used by futures facilitator organizations and competence centers KNOWEAUX Applied Futures (n.d.), Berliner Ideenlabor (2020) and Zukunftsinstitut (n.d.).

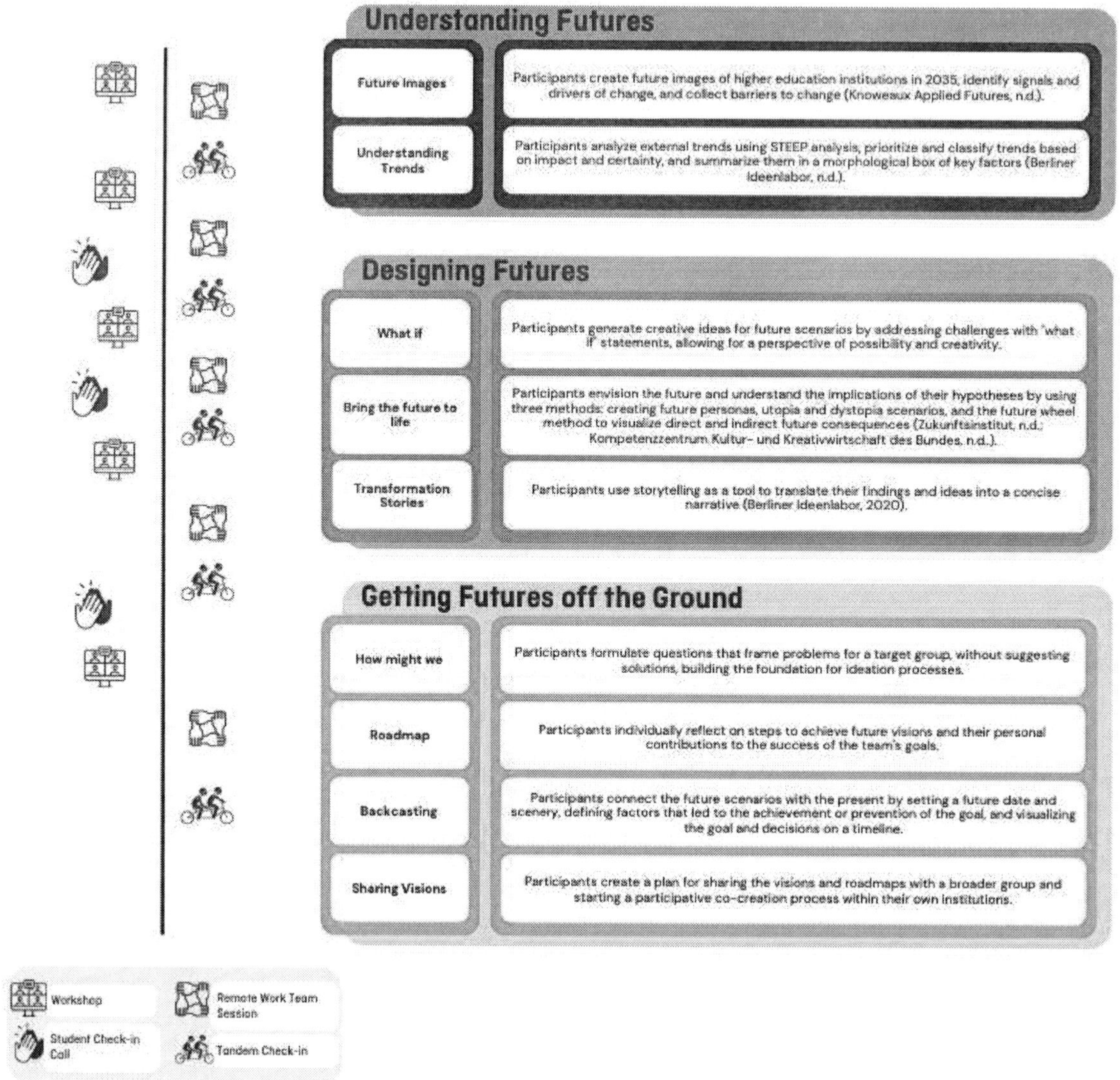

Figure 1. Overview of the program time line (left) and phases of the co-creation program with respective exercises (right).

Results

The following section reports the results of the survey of 30 participants distributed among two cohorts and 11 institutions.

Prior Experiences and Expectations

In the first cohort, 50 % (n=8) mentioned that they had at least one prior experience with vision building or futures thinking, 31.3 % (n=5) had no experience, and 18.8 % (n=3) considered themselves as experienced. Two-thirds of the participants of the first cohort (n=10) were "excited about what awaits me" and the rest (n=6) were "open and curious."

In the second cohort, 35.7 % (n=5) mentioned that they had at least one prior experience with vision building or futures thinking, 35.7 % (n=5) had no experience, and 28.6 % (n=4) considered themselves as experienced. Half of the participants (n=7) reported being "open and curious," and the other half were "excited about what awaits me."

Regarding expectations the participants had when starting the program, participants of the first cohort mentioned aspects like "impulses" (n=8), "(methodological) support and structure" (n=5), "room for exchange" (n=4), and "getting to know new methods" (n=3). The second cohort reported, "concrete visions and plans" (n=5), "(methodological) support and structure" (n=5), and "getting to know new methods" (n=4).

Program Components

Table 1 illustrates the perceived benefit of the participants regarding the different program components, each rated on a scale from 1 (not helpful at all) to 5 (very helpful). Both cohorts rated the remote work phases as most helpful, followed by the support through mentors and cross-HEI workshops.

Table 1: Perception of program components on a scale from 1 (not helpful at all) to 5 (very helpful).

	Cohort 1 Mean (Std)	**Cohort 2** Mean (Std)
Cross-HEI workshops	3.50 (0.73)	3.07 (0.83)
Remote work phases	4.06 (1.12)	3.86 (0.95)
Support through mentors	3.44 (0.81)	3.43 (0.85)
Exchange in tandems	2.88 (0.89)	2.50 (0.76)

Overall Program Evaluation

In the first cohort, 75 % (n=12) would recommend the program to a friend or colleague at another university, 25 % (n=4) were unsure, and one would not recommend it (multiple answers were possible). In the second cohort, 64 % (n=9) would further recommend the program, 21 % (n=3) were unsure and two would not recommend it.

Highlights and Improvements

When asked about their highlight of the program, participants of the first cohort reported: "workshops/methods" (n=4), "network and exchange" (n=4), "working on transformation story/own vision" (n=3), "documentation of process" (n=3), and "work in their team" (n=2). Accordingly, participants in cohort two highlighted the "work in their team" (n=6), "workshops /methods" (n=5), "in-person workshop" (n=3), and "working on transformation story/own vision" (n=2).

To the open question of what changes would lead to a ten percent improvement of the program, the first cohort reported: "working more concretely on own vision" (n=5), "overview over program" (n=3), and "more time" (n=3). Participants of the second cohort mentioned "working more concretely on own vision" (n=4), "individualizing the support" (n=4), "reducing process reflexion" (n=3), "more time" (n=2), and "focus on results" (n=2).

Participation

Table 2 reports the perception of participation of students during the different program components, showing an overall good perception of participation.

Table 2: Perception of student participation in the program on a scale from 1 (not good at all) to 5 (excellent).

	Cohort 1 Mean (Std)	**Cohort 2** Mean (Std)
Cross-HEI workshops	4.00 (0.89)	3.64 (1.28)
Remote work phases	3.94 (1.29)	4.29 (0.83)
Exchange in tandems	3.44 (1.03)	3.07 (0.62)

Participation in own team	3.19 (1.60)	4.43 (0.85)

To the question of measures to strengthen student participation in the future, participants of the first cohort mentioned: "support with the recruitment of students" (n=3), "expectation management" (n=2), "incentives (credit points, monetary)" (n=2), and "guidelines/obligation" (n=2). The second cohort mentioned "strengthening the role of the students" (n=4), "inclusive participation" (n=2), and also "guidelines/obligation" (n=2).

Future Steps

On the question of what the next steps would be, participants of the first cohort reported aiming to "bring vision/process into institutions" (n=12), "get more specific" (n=5), and "initiate measures for implementation" (n=4). Correspondingly, the next steps of the second cohort were to "get more specific" (n=8), and "initiate measures for implementation" (n=8), "bring vision/process into institutions" (n=3). However, it is important to note that the second cohort was surveyed with one workshop to come.

When asked what support measures and conditions would be needed to implement their next steps, participants of the first cohort mentioned, "external moderation" (n=4), "time" (n=3), "acceptance in the institution" (n=3), and a "participative process" (n=2). Participants of the second cohort reported the need for "external support (politics/funding)" (n=4), "motivation/commitment in their team" (n=4), "acceptance in the institution" (n=4), and "further exchange" (n=2).

Discussion and Implications

Concerning our question about the perceived benefits and challenges of implementing a co-creation process for vision building for HEIs, the results show that more than two-thirds of both cohorts would recommend the program, highlighting the methods and the structured time to work with their team as beneficial. Moreover, exchange and networking between institutions was helpful. At the same time, the question of improvements indicates that working on visions is a highly individualized process and might require customized support and supervision. Moreover, participants of both cohorts mentioned "working more concretely on own vision" indicating a desire to spend more time on the later phases of designing and getting futures off the ground, and less on understanding futures at the beginning.

The results indicate that the key factors that contribute to the successful implementation are (1) the structure of the program, (2) the methodological support, and (3) the network and exchange among the participants. First, the structure of the program combining workshops and remote working phases seemed to be an important factor. On average, the remote working phase was rated as the most helpful (see Table 1). Moreover, multiple participants highlighted "working in their teams" as their highlight. This hints at the fact that providing a structure and clear take-home tasks helped the teams to move forward. Second, the results show that providing methodological support is an important success factor for participants. Multiple participants mention "workshops /methods" as a highlight and the support through mentors is perceived as rather helpful (see Table 1). This also aligns with the initial expectations of multiple participants to learn new methods and get methodological support in the process. Third, the aspect of network and exchange played an important role. The cross-HEI workshops were perceived as rather helpful and multiple participants highlighted the aspect of "network and exchange." At the same time, the exchange in tandems between two HEIs in the current offered form seemed to not contribute that much.

The reported participation was relatively high throughout the program components, which support the benefits of co-creation found in literature (Doten-Snitker et al., 2021). At the same time, we find that participation needs to be actively pursued and willed.

Conclusion and Outlook

This case study has investigated the impact of providing external methodological support for co-creating visions with a multi-stakeholder approach, focusing on the perceived benefits and challenges, key success factors, and student participation. The results indicate that the key factors that contribute to the successful implementation are the structure of the program, methodological support, and network and exchange.

Based on the results, we can conclude that providing methodological support to co-creating visions with a multi-stakeholder approach can be an important tool in supporting institutions in the development of visions and underlying strategies. In this context, a co-creation process supports team building as well as the alignment, engagement, and sense of ownership of different stakeholders in the process. This underlines that participation is an important aspect of creating better visions for the future. Overall, this case study provides valuable insights into the potential of co-creation of visions for HEIs on their way to creating better futures and offers practical guidance for institutions seeking to implement this approach.

Future research should continue to explore the long-term impact of the intervention of a systematic co-creation process for vision building within HEIs. Moreover, it can examine the contribution of (student-)participation to vision building as well as aim to investigate if the findings generalize in an international context.

References

Ahmad, T. (2020). Scenario based approach to re-imagining future of higher education which prepares students for the future of work. *Higher Education, Skills and Work-Based Learning, 10*(1), 217-238.

Barab, S., & Squire, K. (2004). Design-based research: Putting a stake in the ground. *The Journal of the Learning Sciences, 13*(1), 1-14.

Benavides, L. M. C., et al. (2020). Digital Transformation in Higher Education Institutions: A systematic literature review. *Sensors, 20*(11), 3291.

Berliner Ideenlabor (2020). Wünschbare Zukünfte entwerfen [08.-22.05.20] - Berliner Ideenlabor. Retrieved March 2, 2023, from https://berliner-ideenlabor.de/dsg_wuenschbare_zukuenfte_entwerfen

Berliner Ideenlabor (n.d.). Zukunftstrends – Das Kartenset. Retrieved March 3, 2023, from https://berliner-ideenlabor.de/zukunftstrends

Blass, E., Jasman, A., & Shelley, S. (2010). Visioning 2035: The future of the higher education sector in the UK. *Futures, 42*(5), 445-453.

Collins, J. C., & Porras, J. I. (1996). Building your company's vision. *Harvard Business Review, 74*(5), 65.

Dollinger, M., & Lodge, J. (2020). Student-staff co-creation in higher education: an evidence-informed model to support future design and implementation. *Journal of Higher Education Policy and Management, 42*(5), 532-546.

Doten-Snitker, K., et al. (2021). Developing a shared vision for change: Moving toward inclusive empowerment. *Research in Higher Education, 62*, 206-229.

Ewing, L. A. (2021). Rethinking higher education post COVID-19. *The Future of Service Post-COVID-19 Pandemic, Volume 1*, 37-54.

Géring, Z., et al. (2018). Applying participatory backcasting to study the future of higher education. *Journal of Futures Studies, 22*(4), 61-82.

Holon, I. Q. (2018). Education in 2030—Five scenarios for the future of learning and talent. Retrieved March 3, 2023 https://www.holoniq.com/2030.

KNOWEAUX Applied Futures. (n.d.). Future Modeling Framework. Retrieved March 3, 2023, from https://www.knoweaux.com/en/futuremodeling

Kompetenzzentrum Kultur- und Kreativwirtschaft des Bundes. "Wie die Kreativwirtschaft eine Post-Corona-Welt entwirft."

Mayring, P. (2004). Qualitative content analysis. A companion to qualitative research, 1(2), 159-176.

Mercer-Mapstone, L., et al. (2017). A systematic literature review of students as partners in higher education. *International Journal for Students as Partners.*

Orr, D., et al. (2020). *Higher education landscape 2030: A trend analysis based on the ahead international horizon scanning*. Springer Nature.

Pelletier, K., et al. (2022). *2022 EDUCAUSE Horizon Report, Teaching and Learning Edition.* Educase.

Pucciarelli, F., & Kaplan, A. (2016). Competition and strategy in higher education: Managing complexity and uncertainty. *Business Horizons, 59*(3), 311-320.

Ranjan, K.R., & Read, S. (2016). Value co-creation: Concept and measurement. *Journal of the Academy of Marketing Science*, *44*, 290–315.

Sabzalieva, E., et al. (2021). Thinking Higher and Beyond Perspectives on the Futures of Higher Education to 2050. *Extraído el*, 5.

Zukunftsinstitut (n.d.). Future Persona. Retrieved March 1, 2023, from https://www.zukunftsinstitut.de/format/future-persona/

This page intentionally left blank.

CHALLENGES FOR INNOVATION AND EDUCATIONAL CHANGE IN DIGITAL EDUCATION IN LOW RESOURCED SETTINGS: A KENYAN EXAMPLE

Fereshte Goshtasbpour, Beck Pitt, Simon Cross, Rebecca Ferguson and Denise Whitelock, The Open University, UK

Correspondence: *Fereshte Goshtasbpour: fereshte.goshtasbpour@open.ac.uk*

Abstract

Many governments invest in digital education and deliver multi-faceted initiatives to develop the capacity of educational institutions and staff confidence in use of technology for enhanced learning and better student outcomes. However, the impact of these initiatives does not always result in improved technology-supported learning or successful digital educational products. Research shows many factors impede the achievement of such objectives. Yet, they are not well understood particularly in low-resourced educational settings. Thus, this paper as part of a larger study aimed to explore barriers to implementing TEL for higher education in low-resourced contexts and potential solutions from the perspective of educators, managers and support staff. The unique inclusion of support staff and management in this research provides a deeper understanding of current barriers to TEL, and the value of multi-stakeholder engagement to develop meaningful context-driven solutions. Using a qualitative oriented mixed-method approach underpinned by Beyond Prototypes conceptual model of TEL complex, the study found that most barriers and enablers of effective TEL implementation are related to the ecology in which it is practised, together with the influence of the salient communities. Findings also suggest that most stakeholders are aware and prioritise barriers related to their role, but have limited awareness of barriers faced by other stakeholders or how others perceived their role in supporting TEL. While the study supports findings of previous research, it adds further insight by considering the views of all implementing stakeholders and the relationships between them.

Keywords:

Technology-enhanced learning (TEL), Educational change, innovation, LMIC

1. Introduction and background

Many governments invest in digital education through staff capacity building to enhance learning and teaching and contribute to better student outcomes (McCowan et al., 2022; Kings, 2014). Governments plan and deliver multi-faceted initiatives to develop the capacity of educational institutions and staff confidence in use of technology (Gabriel et al., 2022). The impact of these initiatives does not always result in improved technology-supported learning and teaching or successful digital educational products (Scanlon et al., 2013; Darling-Hammond et al., 2017). Factors including lack of shared vision, resourcing issues, limited opportunities for reflection or transformative learning (McCowan et al., 2022), little contextual fit, and staff agency (McChesney and Aldridge, 2021) impede the achievement of objectives. In low-resourced settings, additional factors influence the extent and nature of uptake and implementation of Technology-enhanced learning (TEL) initiatives and educational change. These include lack of policy at national and institutional levels, inadequate ICT infrastructure, conflicting goals and priorities, heavy staff workload, and limited funding (Agava et al., 2021; Hudson, 2017). According to McCrowan et al. (2022:2) these factors "are not well understood" in low-income countries particularly Sub-Saharan Africa and "consequently national policies and local initiatives struggle to move beyond rhetorical impact".

After studying nearly 100 TEL initiatives and relevant stakeholders, Scanlon et al. (2013) conclude that the ways in which TEL innovation is designed, funded and implemented must be changed in order to radically improve the quality of learning and teaching. They suggest a move from short-term initiatives to sustained ways of building capacity in TEL. Responding to this call and considering limited understanding of factors influencing TEL implantation in a low-resourced context (McCowan et al., 2022), this paper focuses on a nationwide TEL capacity building initiative in a low-resourced context (Kenya) and reports part of a longitudinal study. This paper presents the barriers and identifies changes needed to support delivery and management of TEL initiatives in higher education from the perspective of three stakeholders (educators, support staff and institutional managers) and reports proposed solutions. It addresses two questions:

1. What problems did participants of Skills for Prosperity Kenya programme face in supporting, delivering or managing TEL in their institutions?

2. What solutions did participants propose for the problems identified by question 1?

1.1 Skills for Prosperity Kenya programme

Skills for Prosperity Kenya (SFPK) is an FCDO-funded TEL initiative to develop capacity of public universities in Kenya to offer digital education, with the longer-term goal of increasing access to university education. The Open University (UK) designed and offered a 2.5-year capacity development programme for university staff at all levels and varied roles. This ran 2020-2023, based on Beyond Prototypes model of TEL innovation (see 2.1) and JISC Digital Capabilities Framework. Over 300 teaching, support and management staff (selected by Kenya Ministry of Education) from 37 public universities participated in the open, online course Digital Education for Universities in Kenya. Table 1 outlines the programme's two strands.

Table 1: Skills for Prosperity Kenya TEL capacity building initiative

Skills for Prosperity Kenya (2020-23)	
Fundamental Capacity Building (Aug 2021- Mar 2022)	**Mastery Capacity Building (May 2021- Jan 2023)**
• 29 public universities, 254 staff • 8-session self-study online course (Level 2, 30 hours of study) • Wraparound webinars • Online community of practice	• 8 public universities, 80 staff • Thought-leader training (32 leaders completed a 150-hr microcredential course) • 8-block online course (Level 3, 72 hours of study) with moderated discussions • Expert webinars with moderated discussions • Practical workshops • University capacity building projects supported by expert mentors

2. Methodology

To design the Skills for Prosperity Kenya initiative and evaluate its short and medium-term impact, a mixed-method study with a continuous data collection procedure (Figure 1) was designed. It included data collection at four points using different tools. The study adopted a problem-based approach to identify problems in TEL implementation and the areas of practice and/or behaviour that require improvement. Understanding the problems was crucial in enhancing academic and practical knowledge and addressing the knowledge and practice gap (Van de Ven, 2007).

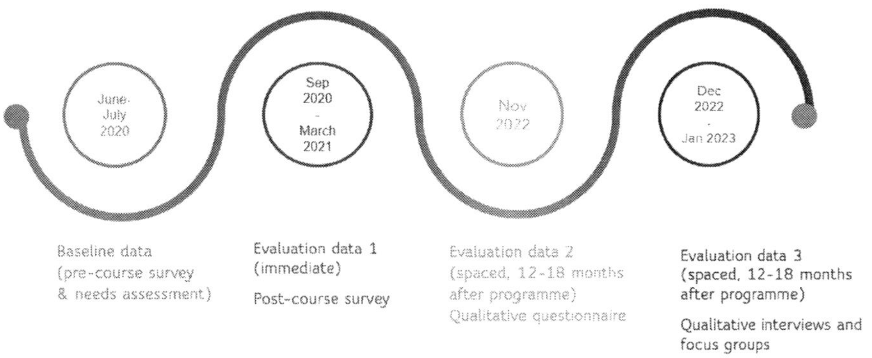

Figure 1. Skills for Prosperity Kenya evaluation timeline and data collection tools

2.1 Conceptual framework Beyond Prototypes model of the TEL complex

TEL is a complex system (Scanlon et al, 2013) which cannot be fully understood without consideration of all its interconnected elements. Figure 2 sets out Scanlon et al.'s (2013) model of the TEL complex. All elements must be addressed if innovation is to be successfully implemented, leading to sustained impact.

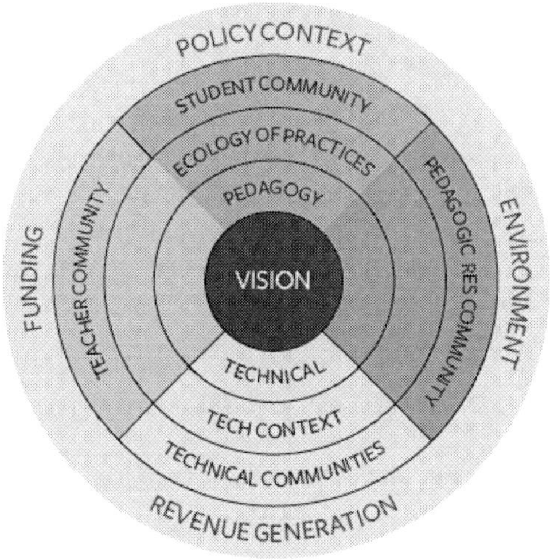

Figure 2. The *Beyond Prototypes* model of TEL complex (Scanlon et al., 2013:29)

These main elements of the TEL complex are:

- *Vision:* Initiatives are unlikely to succeed if it is not clear what they are intended to achieve.
- *Pedagogy:* a successful TEL initiative must support learning. This requires both teacher and learner engagement in educational activities
- *Technical components:* the most visible element of the TEL complex, technologies that support pedagogy with the aim of enhancing learning and achieving the vision
- *Ecology of practice and technical context:* including both existing teacher and learner practices and technical considerations such as local infrastructure
- *Communities:* includes stakeholders such as learners, researchers, teachers and technical staff. Engagement with the wider community (e.g. learners' families) should also be considered
- *Policy, funding and revenue generation: the wider context for implementing a TEL initiative including* financial support for initiation, delivering, innovation and sustainability. (Scanlon et al, 2013).

The Beyond Prototypes model is the conceptual framework for this study because of its comprehensive view of factors contributing to successful implementation of a TEL initiative. In addition, it supports coding and analysing data through classification of barriers (and relevant solutions) to TEL implementation in a low-resourced context while enabling the relationship between several factors to be unpacked.

2.2. Participants

Most studies that examine TEL initiatives at tertiary level in Kenya involve teaching staff (e.g. Agava et al. 2021; Makokha and Mutisya, 2016) with few studies including educational leaders and managers (e.g. McCowan et al. 2022). To our knowledge no study has considered support staff (for example, librarians and learning designers). Since TEL is multidisciplinary and requires a combination of expertise including subject matter experts, learning designers, production and support teams (Dalton et al., 2019; Scanlon et al., 2013), this study involved participants in various roles, revealing factors related to teaching and learning (educators and support staff) and the management of TEL (managers).

Participants completed both the pre- and post-course surveys for the SFPK programme and had a 12-18-month gap following completion. 120 of the programme's 300 participating staff were invited to participate. 92 participants from 25 universities including 45 educators, 28 managers and 19 support staff completed the relevant survey. 20 different departments and a range of disciplines are represented.

2.3 Data collection and data analysis

A two-staged approach to data collection was used. First, participants completed a survey comprising eight questions about the focal area(s), scope and context of the barriers and their significance in relation to factors that affect educational changes, as well as potential solutions to address them. Thirty educators, support staff and managers and four university teams (including 12 participants) were then selected for semi-structured interviews and focus groups respectively. This combination of approaches provided a rich dataset to understand barriers to TEL implementation after our capacity development programme and potential ways to address them. Two questions from the survey are the focus of this paper.

Applying a directed content analysis (using NVivo), answers to survey questions were coded and analysed based on the Beyond the Protypes Complex of TEL model. All sub-components of the model were considered to avoid limited insight. The coding process was open to new codes to ensure new variables were not excluded. Results are reported in the next section, based on number of references in each code using descriptive statistics. These are then discussed in more depth and differences between different stakeholder groups and their proposed solutions explored further.

3. Findings

3.1 Barriers to implementation of TEL in low-resourced settings

The most cited barriers to TEL implementation (Figure 3) relate to the ecology of practice (56%), followed by challenges related to involved communities (33%), pedagogy (4%) and technical components (4%).

Each group of participants emphasised a different group of barriers. Educators mostly cited barriers related to the ecology of practice (49%), communities involved (47%) and pedagogy (46%) while managers' most cited barriesr were pedagogy (54%), communities (34%) and issues related to the ecology of practice (31%). Technical barriers (30%) were considered of equal importance. Support staff emphasised technical components (60%) and technologies required for TEL implementation and referred to the ecology of practice (20%) and communities involved (19%) to a lesser extent. This can be largely attributed to most support staff being based in Open and Distance Learning and ICT departments.

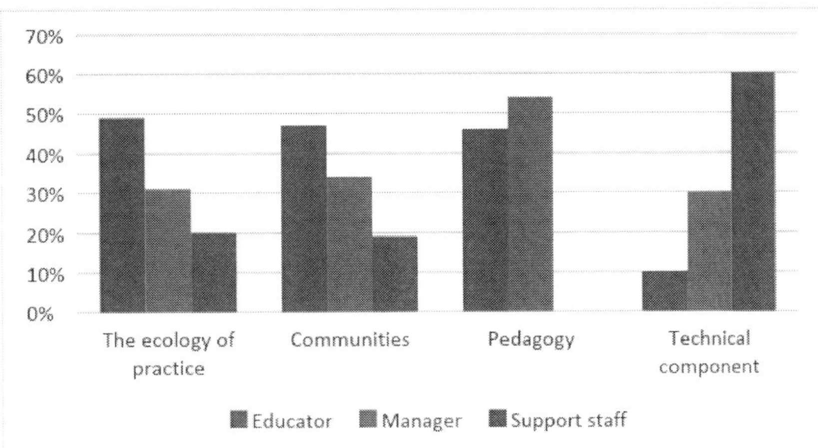

Figure 3. Cited barriers to implementing digital education based on participant roles

3.1.1 The ecology of practice and technical context

The main local and contextual barriers raised related to physical infrastructure and resources, for students and teachers. All groups of participants cited limited internet services, cuts in electricity, inadequate ICT infrastructure, lack of software for learning and teaching (particularly online assessments), and limited e-resources as barriers. Perceived barriers for students were access to appropriate technologies and the internet. For both educators and support staff "class size" was considered a barrier. Support staff stated that university facilities are often overwhelmed when large number of students use them, and they cannot manage student requests. Educators were more concerned about the pedagogical implications of large cohorts particularly in terms of individual interaction.

When teachers' practices were considered, all participant groups referred to the perceived limited knowledge and skills of teachers to design and deliver TEL. Both educators and managers put more emphasis on this aspect than support staff.

3.1.2 Communities

Most reported barriers related to students' perception or responses to TEL, although barriers related to teachers and support staff were also noted. Students' resistance and negative attitudes towards TEL, low motivation/engagement with TEL, and limited digital literacies were the major reported barriers. Again, the groups had different perspectives on these barriers. Managers referred to students' perceived low/limited digital literacies while educators and support staff highlighted negative attitudes and resistance to acceptance.

Several barriers were attributed to teachers by the three groups. The most cited barrier by educators was teachers' heavy workload and time constraints to engage meaningfully with TEL or develop and deliver online content. However, managers and support staff believed teachers' resistance to, and fear of change and their low motivation and willingness, were the main factors to lack of engagement.

A very small number of managers and support staff referred to a third stakeholder group, i.e. professional support staff, stating that one barrier is this group's limited and ineffective professional support to teaching staff particularly when creating digital content. Some support staff reported uncertainty around how best to support educators, particularly in the creation of interactive content.

3.1.3 Pedagogy

Pedagogical issues were a barrier reported only by educators and managers. Educators found choosing appropriate pedagogy for TEL, the rigidity of existing curriculum and not having a curriculum for open and distance learning challenging. Managers, on the other hand, mainly reported challenges related to teaching practical subjects such as STEM, ineffective facilitation and online assessment.

3.1.4 Technical components

Technical barriers to supporting TEL were mostly reported by support staff and focused largely on tools. A very small number of managers also emphasised lack of appropriate technologies for online examination and attendance monitoring tools. Educators did not report any barriers related to digital technologies.

3.1.5 Wider context of TEL

Managers and a small number of support staff were the only participant groups that highlighted the importance of funding and the scale of investment required. They found limited funding for developing TEL content and programmes and providing internet on campus is a major barrier to implementing and sustaining TEL activities. No educators involved in the study reported lack of funding or policies as a barrier to TEL.

3.2 Proposed solutions to reported barrier to implementation of TEL in low-resourced settings

Participants were asked to propose ways of overcoming barriers they faced in implementing TEL. These were analysed using the Beyond Prototypes model. Results show that the majority of solutions can be provided by changes in the ecology of TEL (51%) and the TEL wider context (27%), i.e. funding and policies. A smaller number of proposed solutions related to communities (14%), technical components (5%) and pedagogy (3%). The top three solution groups are reported here.

3.2.1 Solutions related to the ecology of practice and technical context

For barriers related to physical infrastructure and resources, particularly those of the internet and power, regional and national co-ordinated action is needed. Participants also suggested telecommunication providers boosting regional networks and back-up internet and electricity supplies. Solutions were proposed for increasing students' access to resources, including loan schemes, institutional and county-level financial support, and student sponsorship.

For teachers' existing practices and limited knowledge and skills to offer TEL, all groups proposed continuous capacity building and training. Managers also suggested more exposure to TEL through conferences, workshops and mentorship programmes. Although "class size" was identified as a barrier by educators and support staff, no solution was proposed.

3.2.1 Solutions related to the wider context: funding and policy

The second largest group of solutions related to funding and policies connected to the wider context. Managers believed many barriers would be removed through increased funding for TEL and university senior management lobbying for enhanced financial support. They also emphasised funding models for students and for departments needs to be re-addressed to capture the cost of technology-supported courses. Educators proposed universities monitor priorities and the use of public funds to enable managers provide essential resources for TEL. They also suggested more investment in university infrastructure and student sponsorships. Support staff proposed similar solutions whilst highlighting the role of government and relevant ministries.

Another proposed solution to address many TEL implementation challenges is the introduction of institutional policies for technology-supported learning and teaching or making TEL part of the university learning policy.

> *"We could alter University practices and policies, make new policies to support new ways of teaching and learning and to persuade students to engage in online learning. We should allow teaching and learning policies be contributed to by the learners themselves so that an ideal mechanism of delivery is found".* (Support staff, ICT department)

In addition, several participants highlighted the role of government support:

> *"The government needs to ensure that universities have appropriate and adequate infrastructure in terms of fibre optic cables, bandwidth and other ICT needs. If the government of Kenya must charge universities, the costs should be subsidized otherwise the cost is passed to parents and guardians making education only accessible to a few.* (Manager, DVC Academics, Research & Outreach)

3.2.3 Solutions related to communities

When participants discussed barriers related to communities involved in TEL, three communities of teachers, students and professional services were mentioned. However, to minimise barriers to TEL implementation, results suggest involvement from an additional community stakeholder (institutional managers) is needed. Educators and support staff believed more institutional management involvement in TEL, e.g. advocacy and providing essential resources, could support TEL implementation. Managers did not identify any solution their community could provide.

Proposed solutions to support the teacher community included introducing a reward and incentive system to motivate staff, and providing continuous professional training. While these proposed solutions can address barriers related to attitude and motivation, they will not address the main challenge of time constraints highlighted by participants. Solutions related to the student community mostly focused on raising students' awareness about TEL (e.g. through orientation and sensitisation) and providing access to affordable devices.

4. Discussion and conclusions

This study explored barriers to implementing TEL for higher education in low-resourced settings from the perspectives of educators, managers and support staff. It addressed three gaps: firstly, scholars' poor understanding of the factors that affect implementation of TEL and educational change in low-resourced contexts (McCowan et al., 2022) and the absence of support staff's perspectives from recent related literature. It also sought to explore potential solutions to minimise identified barriers.

The study shows most barriers and enablers of effective implementation of TEL are related to the ecology in which it is practised, together with the influence of the salient communities. This supports findings of previous studies such as Makokha and Mutisya (2016), Newton et al., (2021) and McCowan et al., (2022). This study adds further insight by considering the views of all implementing stakeholders and the relationships between them. Findings suggest most stakeholders are aware and prioritise barriers related to their role, but have limited awareness of barriers faced by other stakeholders or how others perceived their role in supporting TEL. For example, technical issues were only identified by support staff and managers; educators did not report them. A holistic approach, which engages with a range of stakeholders, can identify different perspectives on similar barriers or solutions. For example, cohort size was viewed as a barrier by both educators and support staff, who outlined different but interconnected aspects. This shows how collaborative working processes to design and implement TEL (Dalton et al., 2019) and opportunities for stakeholder communication and reflection could reduce or remove barriers (McCowan et al., 2022).

Some barriers (e.g. cohort size) were identified without possible solutions. Ensuring that all barriers and solutions proposed by the participants are mapped, then the complexity and multi-stakeholder approach needed is captured but also this method ensures no aspect is overlooked. This approach could also be used to support engagement with various stakeholders, especially those who appear unaware of their potential role in removing barriers from key aspects of their work. For example, educators and support staff emphasised the role of institutional managers in overcoming many barriers. However, managers did not identify themselves as one of the communities that could resolve these difficulties. This may be due to what Neuman (2014) describes as unconscious non-reporting as managers know their role is to remove barriers and assume it is not important to report this work.

Overall, the main implication of these finding is that there are key barriers to implementing TEL which can be more effectively addressed if the perspectives and expertise of all stakeholders are considered, solution(s) associated to different aspects of each barrier are considered within a collaborative working process together with enough time and opportunity for collective reflection.

References

Agava, S., Selvam, S.G. and Pete, J. (2021), University Preparedness for Online Teaching and Learning amid COVID-19 in Kenya. In Sengupta, E. and Blessinger, P. (Ed.) *New Student Literacies amid COVID-19: International Case Studies*. Emerald Publishing Limited, Bingley, pp. 83-100. https://doi.org/10.1108/S2055-364120210000041012

Dalton EM, Lyner-Cleophas M, Ferguson BT, McKenzie J. (2019). Inclusion, universal design and universal design for learning in higher education: South Africa and the United States. *African Journal of Disability.* (9) https://doi.org/10.4102/ajod.v8i0.519

Darling-Hammond, L., Hyler, M. E., & Gardner, M. (2017). Effective teacher professional development (project report). Palo Alto, CA: Learning Policy Institute. https://doi.org/10.54300/122.311

Gabriel, F., Marrone, R., Van Sebille, Y., Kovanovic, V., & de Laat, M. (2022). Digital education strategies around the world: practices and policies. Irish Educational Studies, 41(1), 85-106. https://doi.org/10.1080/03323315.2021.2022513

Hudson, K.E. (2017). Faculty development in developing countries: Introduction and overview. In: Smith, C., Hudson, K.E. (Eds.), *Faculty development in developing countries: Improving teaching quality in higher education.* Routledge, New York, pp. 3-5.

King, F. (2014). Evaluating the impact of teacher professional development: an evidence-based framework. Professional Development in Education, 40(1), 89–111. https://doi.org/10.1080/19415257.2013.823099

McChesney, & Aldridge, J. M. (2021). What gets in the way? A new conceptual model for the trajectory from teacher professional development to impact. Professional Development in Education, 47(5): 834–852. https://doi.org/10.1080/19415257.2019.1667412

McCowan, T., Omingo, M., Schendel, R., Adu-Yeboah, C., & Tabulawa, R. (2022). Enablers of pedagogical change within universities: Evidence from Kenya, Ghana and Botswana. *International Journal of Educational Development*, 90: 102558. https://doi.org/10.1016/j.ijedudev.2022.102558

Mutisya, D. N., & Makokha, G. L. (2016). Challenges affecting adoption of e-learning in public universities in Kenya. *E-Learning and Digital Media*, 13(3–4): 140–157. https://doi.org/10.1177/2042753016672902

Newton, M. A., Oduor, A and Kiplaga, S. J. (2021). Opportunities and challenges of remote teaching and learning in university education during the covid19 pandemic lockdown periods: the case of Maasai Mara University, Narok, Kenya. *International Society for the Study of Behavioural Development.* Bulletin 79 (1): 7-15

Neuman, W. L. (2014). Social Research Methods: Qualitative and Quantitative Approaches (International-7th ed.). London: Pearson.

Scanlon, E., Sharples, M., Fenton-O'Creevy, M., Fleck, J., Cooban, C, Ferguson, R., Cross, S. and Waterhouse, P. (2013). Beyond Prototypes: Enabling Innovation in Technology-enhanced Learning (Project report). Open University, Milton Keynes. [online] http://oro.open.ac.uk/41119/1/BeyondPrototypes.pdf

Van de Ven, A. H. (2007). *Engaged scholarship: A guide for organizational and social research.* Oxford: Oxford University Press.

EXPLORING LEARNERS' MOTIVATIONS AND PREFERENCES FOR MICRO-CREDENTIALS: A MIXED-METHOD STUDY

Carles Bruguera, Universitat Oberta De Catalunya, Spain

Àngels Fitó, Universitat Oberta De Catalunya, Spain

Carmen Pagés, Universitat Oberta De Catalunya, Spain

***Correspondence**: Carles Bruguera: cbruguerat@uoc.edu*

Abstract

As professionals aim to stay abreast of their ever-changing disciplines and global challenges, and universities reframe their offerings, the popularity of micro-credentials continues to grow. Without replacing traditional qualifications, micro-credentials offer the potential for short, flexible learning experiences that support learners in achieving their career or life goals. Universities, providers, employers, and students are all important stakeholders in the micro-credentials ecosystem. However, there is a significant dearth of academic research on students' perspectives towards micro-credentials. This gap represents a crucial challenge that universities must tackle when developing training options. This study aims to investigate learners´ motivations and preferences for micro-credentials employing a mixed-method methodology. The research sample comprises 37 adult learners, alumni of continuous education programs at the Open University of Catalonia. After reviewing the research data, results revealed a multitude of factors driving diverse learners towards pursuing micro-credentials. Among these factors, personal interests and career objectives appear to be the primary motivators, followed by social and academic motivations, which play a secondary role. Additionally, the study indicates that there is a notable preference for short courses that last between two to three months, requiring a part-time dedication of between six to fifteen hours per week. Students have a stronger inclination towards micro-credentials that are applicable, as opposed to the theoretical knowledge emphasized in college or master's programs. Courses delivered in online and asynchronous formats are particularly demanded, although some learners appreciate the opportunity for synchronous Q&A sessions with instructors. Learners highly value the modularization of micro-credentials into different levels and prefer courses that offer credentials, although not all of them consider official credentials to be essential, particularly those that pursue micro-credentials for personal reasons. This research supports universities in their efforts to develop and align short learning courses that respond to actual learners' demands.

Keywords:

Micro-credentials, certification, short learning experiences, learners, higher education, learners´ motivations, learners´ preferences.

Introduction

The current global transformation, driven by multiple factors such as the pandemic (Tamoliune et al., 2023), digital and green transitions (Cedefop, 2022), and the changing nature of work (Brown & Michil, 2022), has led to significant life and job disruption and changing skills needs. This prompts the need for periodic, just-in-time reskilling and upskilling of the workforce (World Economic Forum's, 2020). As a result, there is a growing demand for short, flexible, and personalized learning options that can address emerging labor market and societal needs (Leong et al., 2020). Micro-credentials have emerged as an adaptive response for universities to offer more flexible learning pathways to adult learners (Gauthier, 2020; McGreal & Olcott, 2022), without necessarily replacing traditional credentials (Shapiro et al., 2021). Therefore, micro-credentials can be a complement, substitute, or component of traditional qualifications (Brown & Michil, 2022) and provide a way to certify competencies acquired through life experience, work, or study (Cedefop, 2023).

Micro-credentials have emerged as a global trend that is expected to continue growing in the post-pandemic years (Brown et al., 2021; Leong et al., 2020). However, the lack of a shared definition and the use of multiple forms has led to ambiguity about its definition among universities, employers, providers, policymakers, and learners (Oliver, 2019). To reduce it, the Council of the European Union recommended the adoption of a European approach for micro-credentials, defining them as "the record of the learning outcomes that a learner has acquired following a small volume of learning. These learning outcomes will have been assessed against transparent and clearly defined criteria. Learning experiences leading to micro-credentials are designed to provide the learner with specific knowledge, skills and competencies that respond to societal, personal, cultural or labour market needs" (European Union, 2022, p.27).

In recent years, a significant body of literature has explored the potential opportunities raised by micro-credentials, including their use in post-COVID-19 recovery and higher education (Selvaratnam & Sankey, 2021; Tamoliune et al., 2023; Thi Ngoc Ha et al., 2022). Research has focused on multiple perspectives, such as employers, higher education leaders, students, and providers (Gauthier, 2020; Oliver 2019; McGreal & Olcott, 2022) but overall the voice of learners has been mostly scarce (Brown & Michil, 2022; Bruguera et al., 2022), although micro-credentials are primarily intended to fulfil the learning needs of individuals (Saphiro et al. 2021). To understand the value and benefits of micro-credentials for learners, more learner-based empirical data is needed (Thi Ngoc Ha et al., 2022). The objective of this paper is to identify what learners expect from micro-credentials. The study seeks to answer two main research questions: 1) What motivates learners to pursue micro-credentials? and 2) What are learners' preferences for micro-credentials?. Exploring what learners want and expect from short learning experiences will enable universities and policymakers to provide and promote better learner-centric offerings.

Methodology

This research employs a mixed-method methodology to assess students' perspectives on micro-credentials. A concurrent embedded design, which combines quantitative and qualitative data collection, is employed (Creswell, 2009). Qualitative research was conducted through a synchronous online focus group, enabling an open discussion designed to obtain rich qualitative data from learners' views (Fàbregues et al., 2016). The quantitative research was implemented through an online survey, which collected quantitative data about the motivations and preferences of focus group participants (Fink, 2017). Qualitative data was given priority in interpreting participants' view on micro-credentials, while the survey provided additional numerical data on socio-demographics and specific opinions of participants. The interview script and questionnaire items were based on a sound conceptual foundation derived from a systematic review of the literature on learners' perspectives developed by the authors as an output of the Erasmus + project "Modularisation for Continuing Education and Microcredentials" (Bruguera et al. 2022), which serves as the framework for this research.

Participants for this study were selected through intentional sampling (Babbie, 2013) from a population consisting of adult learners who had taken short courses at the Open University of Catalonia (UOC) between 2017-2021, including seminars and professional courses. The UOC is a fully online university that utilizes innovative teaching methodologies and technology to deliver high-quality education. A total of 37 alumni from continuous education programs at UOC were included as participants. The researchers ensured the privacy and anonymity of the participants, and participants signed a consent for their anonymized data to be used for research purposes. Jointly with the consent form, they received a brief questionnaire to be filled out before the interviews. Focus group sessions were conducted through the Zoom platform during the second semester of 2022. Interview transcriptions were analysed using thematic analysis (Given, 2008, p.868). ATLAS.ti 22 was used for the qualitative analysis, following Friese et al. (2018) recommended steps and the iterative validation process of Creswell (2009) to ensure reliability. Descriptive statistics were used to present the survey data.

Results

Results are presented below, categorized by themes identified in the qualitative analysis.

Socio-demographic information of participants

Most of the participants were middle-aged workers with completed university degrees or master's degrees (Table 1). More women than men took part in the study. The participants came from a diverse range of professions including health workers, computer scientists, civil servants, or secondary school teachers. Most of them were working, either full or part time, and a significant share were studying while working. All participants had experience with online education.

Table 1: Participants socio-demographics

Age (years)	Recount	%
25 or less	0	0%
26-35	5	12,2%
36-45	11	26,8%
46-55	21	51,2%
56-65	4	9,8%
66 or more	0	0%
Gender	Recount	%
Men	13	31,7%
Woman	26	63,4%
Other	2	4,8%
I prefer not to say	1	2,4%
Highest degree of training achieved	Recount	%
Primary	0	0%
Secondary	0	0%
Baccalaureate	4	9,8%
Bachelor degree	21	51,2%
Master degree	12	29,3%
Doctorate / PhD	0	0%
Vocational training	4	9,8%
Professional status	Recount	%
Studying full time without working	1	2,4%
Studying part-time while working	16	39,0%
Working	19	46,3%
Unemployed	3	7,3%
Inactive	2	4,9%

Learners' motivations for micro-credentials

Table 2 provides a summary of participants' level of familiarity with micro-credentials and their main reasons for enrolling in them.

Table 2: Learners' motivations for micro-credentials (* percentage of total responses)

Are you familiar with micro-credentials?	Recount	%

No	22	55%
Yes	18	45%
Motivations to participate in micro-credentials	Recount	% *
For the pleasure of learning new things	25	17,9%
Keep up with my occupation	23	16,4%
Improve my employment situation	20	14,3%
Make my skills more visible to employers	19	13,6%
Explore new fields	17	12,1%
For personal curiosity	12	8,6%
Change job	11	7,9%
Find a job	4	2,9%
Meet new people	4	2,9%
Enter a "long" training	4	2,9%

Over half of the participants were unaware of the term "micro-credentials" prior to their participation in the study. However, upon being presented with its definition, several participants were able to relate the term to the short, accredited courses they had completed previously. To provide further illustration, opinions from the learners have been included in quotation marks.

"I came across the term 'micro-credentials' in your email and decided to search for its meaning. From my understanding, micro-credentials refer to short courses that can be accredited. However, I was initially confused as some short courses may not have certification."

A large majority of answers are related to professional career advancement, professional development, and employability. However, the primary drivers for learners to pursue micro-credentials are motivated by personal curiosity, learning something new or exploring an unfamiliar field.

"My main motivation for continuing my training throughout my life, as long as my skills allow it, is personal satisfaction. I am a curious person who enjoys learning."

Many adult learners enrol in micro-credentials to fill the gaps in knowledge and skills required in their professional disciplines that were not covered in their initial training.

"Both for me personally and for my profession, lifelong learning is very important. It is essential to stay updated because those who fall behind lose their jobs quickly."

Senior learners, that is, professionals with several years of experience in their professional fields, see micro-credentials as a good solution for their career progression, being a way to gain essential expertise and skills that can help them promote or gain greater recognition in their current positions.

"For any type of promotion at work, it is essential that my training is accredited. This increases my chances of being considered for higher positions than the one I currently hold."

Junior learners, meaning professionals with little or no experience in their professional fields, view the certification aspect of micro-credentials as a useful way to demonstrate their skills to potential employers and companies.

"Often, even if you possess certain skills or competencies, they may not be valued unless you have a document that proves you have been taught by a recognized institution."

Micro-credentials can also serve as a means for senior learners to experiment and venture into new fields or professional areas, enabling them to assess their level of interest. This could potentially serve as a gateway to longer training opportunities.

"The motivation behind taking these short-duration training courses for me is like taking a pill, a way to test my level of interest in the subject. If it meets my expectations, then I can decide to delve further into the subject."

Learners' preferences for micro-credentials

Research participants' preferences for micro-credentials are summarized in Table 4

Do you prefer a course...	Recount	%
Online	31	70,5%
Face-to-face	1	2,3%
mixed	12	27,3%
If online, do you prefer a course...	Recount	%
Asynchronous: you connect when you have availability	23	63,9%
Synchronous: you connect at the same time as your teachers / classmates	7	19,4%
Mixed	6	16,7%
Ideal length (months)	Recount	%
Less than 1	6	13,3%
From 1 to 2	8	17,8%
From 2 to 3	17	37,8%
From 3 to 4	4	8,9%
From 4 to 5	2	4,4%
From 5 to 6	5	11,1%
More than 6	3	6,7%
Ideal schedule	Recount	%
Morning	3	7,7%
Afternoon	16	41,0%
Night	10	25,6%
Weekend	10	25,6%
Ideal dedication	Recount	%
Full time	2	5,3%
Part time	36	94,7%
Hours a week dedication	Recount	%
1-5	11	27,5%
6-10	10	25,0%
11-15	12	30,0%

16-20	6	15,0%
21-25	1	2,5%
Preference for credentials	Recount	%
Credentials are preferred / crucial	35	94,6%
Credentials are not essential	2	5,4%

Most participants have positive prior experiences with online learning, so they tend to prefer online micro-credentials. This allows adult learners to study at their own pace, enabling them to balance their studies with other commitments such as work, family, and personal time. For senior learners, face-to-face courses are seen as time-consuming and conflicting with their schedules.

"At times in my life, I may have preferred in-person interactions, but once virtual options became available, I embraced them. This allowed me to overcome time, travel, work, family, and other obstacles that previously hindered my participation."

While asynchronous modalities are typically preferred, especially among older learners, many participants also value a blended approach that incorporates both asynchronous course material and occasional synchronous sessions. This allows for real-time resolution of doubts and fosters interaction with instructors or peers.

"I believe that online training is ideal for this type of learning, with a synchronous component that allows for real-time interaction with teachers to address questions and delve deeper into the material. In my experience, synchronous learning enables participants to express their opinions and discuss topics that may not come up in pre-recorded masterclasses."

Most learners prefer shorter courses that last 3 months or less, with an ideal duration of 1-2 months. However, if a course is interesting for them, learners may opt to do another one or even a longer-term training like a degree.

"In my opinion, short courses should not last longer than 2 or 3 months. I have specific needs that require quick solutions."

The majority of participants view the option to modularise micro-credentials into basic, intermediate, and advanced levels positively. It enables them to select a suitable level based on their profile and skill level and allows them to build knowledge and skills incrementally towards their desired level of expertise.

"I prefer a program with continuity, where completing each course would lead to a degree or credential. This way, you can work towards a global degree gradually. I prefer this to a Master or Postgraduate program where you have to complete all courses at once."

Different learners value official course credentials for various reasons. Junior learners often prioritize certification to boost their employability,

"I believe that certification is important because it guarantees to the companies the level of knowledge that has been acquired, among other things."

Senior learners may use credentials for promoting or improving their working conditions. Generally, they are willing to pay more for courses that offer official credentials, relative to courses without them, although some of them find micro-credentials expensive in the long run.

"I understand that there is a clear drawback with micro-credentials, such as the pricing per credit. However, I value the specialized and targeted nature of the training, and therefore don't mind paying more. Because that system is also very respectful of my career and my needs."

In contrast, adult learners who want to explore different topics, disciplines or learn for personal reasons may not necessarily require a course that comes with official credentials

“I don't place much importance on accreditation for my current professional situation. However, as life is unpredictable, my priorities may change. As the head of a unit, the opportunity to advance to a higher position as the head of a department requires a degree, which I currently do not possess due to my previous diploma-level training. I see value in accreditation, as it may enhance my opportunities.”

Conclusions

This study uses both qualitative and quantitative methods to gather data on learners´ motivations and preferences for micro-credentials, addressing a gap in the literature for empirical qualitative data (Bruguera et al., 2022; Tamoliune et al., 2023).Through focus groups and questionnaires, our findings reveal the following conclusions. First, despite several efforts made by organizations such as the Council of the European Union (2022), the term “micro-credential” remains relatively unknown or ambiguous among students (Laryea et al., 2021).

Second, results highlight that adult learners have diverse drivers for seeking micro-credentials, emphasising the need and opportunity for universities to offer micro-credentials that cater to these various needs. There are two distinct and complementary groups of motivations for adult learners to pursue micro-credentials, namely: personal and professional, in that order, with social and academic motivations, playing a much smaller role. While the debate on micro-credentials has been mostly framed in the context of labour market objectives (Gauthier, 2020), intrinsic drivers, such as the pleasure of learning new things, appear as the most cited driver in our study.

Third, this research sheds some light on learners' preferred formats for micro-credentials, a topic for which a dearth of literature exists (Thi Ngoc Ha et al., 2022). Results indicate that learners tend to prefer online, asynchronous, short (2-3 months), specific learning experiences, requiring between 6-15 hours of dedication, and that provide a credential. Nevertheless, due to the specific characteristics of the sample, prudence should be exercised in extending the findings to a broader population. This research contributes to positioning the learner's perspective at the centre of the ongoing debate on micro-credentials among employers, policymakers and learning providers, and it offers valuable insights for educational institutions seeking to create more learner-centric offerings.

References

Babbie, E. (2013). *The Practice of Social Research* (13th ed). Wadsworth Cengage Learning.

Brown, M., Mhichíl, M. N. G., Beirne, E., & Mac Lochlainn, C. (2021). The global microcredential landscape: charting a new credential ecology for lifelong learning. *Journal of Learning for Development*, *8*(2), 228-254.

Brown, M., & Nic-Giolla-Mhichil, M. (2022). Unboxing micro-credentials: an inside, upside and downside view. *Culture and Education*, 34(4), 938-973

Bruguera, C., Fitó, A., Pagés, C., & Antonaci, A. (2022). Meta-research on the learner perspective on micro-credential formats and learning services for continuing education and professional development. Zenodo. doi: https://doi.org/10.5281/zenodo.7356761

Cedefop. (2023). Microcredentials for labour market education and training: microcredentials and evolving qualifications Systems. *Cedefop Research Paper*, 89, 1-164

Creswell, J. (2009). *Research design : qualitative, quantitative, and mixed methods approaches.* Sage Publications.

Council of the European Union (2022). *Proposal for a Council Recommendation on a European approach to micro-credentials for lifelong learning and employability – Adoption.* Brussels: General Secretariat of the Council.

Fàbregues, S., Meneses, J., Rodríguez-Gómez, D., & Paré, M. (2016). *Técnicas de investigación social y educativa.* Oberta UOC Publishing, SL.

Fink, A. (2017). *How to conduct surveys : A step-by-step guide (6th ed.).* SAGE Publications.

Friese, S., Soratto, J., & Pires, D. (2018). Carrying out a computer-aided thematic content analysis with ATLAS.ti. *MMG Working Paper,* (18-02).

Gauthier, T. (2020). The value of microcredentials: The employer's perspective. *The Journal of Competency-Based Education*, *5*(2), 1-6.

Given, L. M. (Ed.). (2008). *The Sage encyclopedia of qualitative research methods*. SAGE publications.

Leong, K., Sung, A., Au, D., & Blanchard, C. (2021). A review of the trend of microlearning. *Journal of Work-Applied Management*, *13*(1), 88-102.

McGreal, R., & Olcott Jr, D. (2022). A strategic reset: micro-credentials for higher education leaders. *Smart Learning Environments*, *9*(1), 9.

Oliver, B. (2019). *Making micro-credentials work for learners, employers and providers*. Deakin University.

Selvaratnam, R. M., & Sankey, M. D. (2021). An integrative literature review of the implementation of micro-credentials in higher education: Implications for practice in Australasia. *Journal of Teaching and Learning for Graduate Employability*, *12*(1), 1-17.

Shapiro, F. Andersen A. & Nedergaard L. (2021) *A European approach to micro-credentials : output of the micro-credentials higher education consultation group : final report*. Publications Office of the European Union.

Tamoliune, G., Greenspon, R., Tereseviciene, M., Volungeviciene, A., Trepule, E., & Dauksiene, E. (2023). Exploring the potential of micro-credentials: A systematic literature review. *In Frontiers in Education*, 7, 1-15.

Thi Ngoc Ha, N., Spittle, M., Watt, A., & Van Dyke, N. (2022). A systematic literature review of micro-credentials in higher education: a non-zero-sum game. *Higher Education Research & Development*, 1-22.

Pouliakas, K., & Souto-Otero, M. (2022). *Setting Europe on course for a human digital transition: new evidence from Cedefop's second European skills and jobs survey*. Publications Office of the European Union.

World Economic Forum. (2020). *The future of jobs report 2020*. World Economic Forum.

CASE STUDY OF THE ROLE OF THE DISTANCE LEARNING STUDY COURSE "PERSONAL DEVELOPMENT" ON THE STUDENT PERSONAL DEVELOPMENT AT THE COLLEGE OF BUSINESS ADMINISTRATION

Signe Enkuzena, College of Business Administration, Latvia

Jana Roze, College of Business Administration, Latvia

Janis Supe, College of Business Administration, Latvia

Correspondence: *Janis Supe: janis.supe@bvk.lv*

Abstract

An important aim of higher education is not only to equip people with new skills, knowledge, and competencies but also the personal development of students. In the past decades, personal development planning is becoming more popular. Personal development planning is a method of recording achievements, identifying strengths and areas for improvement, reflecting on progress, and setting clear goals and action plans

The purpose of the article is to analyze the implementation of the new E-learning course "Professional development" for the short-cycle higher education study program students at the College of Business Administration. Sample: 24 students of the study program "Law".

Method: a thematic analysis of the achieved study results by evaluating the feedback provided by 24 students who completed the course on the progress and benefits of the course.

Results: The thematic analysis of student reviews showed that the purpose and the results of the study course have been achieved. Although the reviews of some students indicate resistance to the awareness of the personality situation, the structure and organizational form of the course contribute to the successful overcoming of resistance and help to solve the issues of personal growth at the level of "depth" and complexity appropriate for the student.

Keywords:

Personal development, distance learning study course

Theoretical background for personal development planning

Higher education has different aims. The most important ones are to equip people with new skills, knowledge and competencies, also according to the needs of the job market (Cheng et.al., 2021). But very important aim that is not mentioned so often is also the personal development of the students, with "personal development" understanding not only developing academic and professional knowledge but improving the personality of the student. This aspect of higher education has been analysed in several research papers so far. Edmunds and Richardson have developed the heuristic model of learning and development in university students (Figure 1). This model shows that different concepts of learning and approaches to studying (study activities carried out by students) lead not only to acquiring academic knowledge but also to personal development and changes in their personalities.

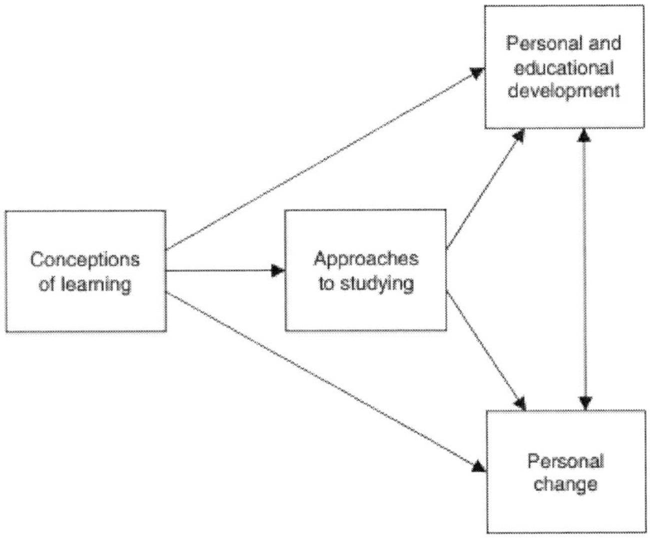

Figure 1. Heuristic model of learning and development in university students (Edmunds & Richardson, 2009).

More and more higher education institutions nowadays come to the conclusion that personal development planning is an integral tool in placing the responsibility to analyze, track, and continuously develop academic skills as well as soft skills directly in the hands of the students (Kahl & Sundram, 2014). Personal development planning is a method of recording achievements, identifying strengths and areas for improvement, reflecting on progress and setting clear goals and action plans (Kumar, 2009). Previous research has shown positive impact of personal development planning on the achievements of the students (Strivens & Ward, 2010). Personal development planning is connected with soft skills. Stek emphasizes the importance of soft skills in higher education - in order to thrive in the twenty-first century, students need more than traditional academic learning. They must be adept at collaboration, communication and problem solving, which are some of the skills developed through social and emotional learning. Coupled with mastery of traditional skills, social and emotional proficiency will equip students to succeed in the swiftly evolving digital economy (Stek, 2022).

Case study: implementation of the E-learning study course "Personal development"

The study course "Personal development" was created and implemented in the short-cycle professional higher education study program "Law" from March 1, 2021 to February 28, 2023 at the College of Business Administration. Its total amount is 1.5 ECTS or 80 academic hours, the implementation of which is divided evenly into 4 modules from the first to fourth semester and the volume of each module is 20 academic hours.

The structure and content of the study course was developed in accordance with the "Quality Matters" international e-study environment and content quality standards (Quality Matters, 2023), and in this process, the study course instructor (with education and experience in psychology and pedagogy) cooperated with the e-study methodologist. In order to ensure acquiring of the planned learning outcomes, each study module included:

1. an introduction to the study course;
2. two online lessons,
3. theoretical materials,
4. individual, pair and group exercises and their descriptions,
5. video clips with exercise rationale and sample demonstrations.

During the course, throughout the study semester as an additional resource, the students were provided with the opportunity to receive individual counselling by writing their questions to the course instructor by e-mail.

In order to pass the study course, students had to complete 3 consecutive tasks in each module and submit a self-reflection work according to the defined criteria.

In the first module "My goals, my ideal self", students had to complete:

1. the task "My goals in personality development" with the following learning outcomes: understand how the human psyche works; identify and define their goals for the next year and beyond, integrating their knowledge about positive personality thinking; carry out self-reflection of their feelings, thoughts, goals;
2. the task "My goals and my strengths", with the following learning outcomes: evaluate the experience of the manifestation of one's strengths in various challenging situations; to be aware of the positive resources of one's character when faced with challenges; to define new goals for the coming year; to self-reflect on one's feelings, thoughts, goals;
3. the task "My Ideal ME", with the following learning outcomes: plan the development of themselves in a certain period of time according to the auxiliary scheme, connecting it with their understanding of personal development, strengths, and existing and planned resources.

In the second module of the study course "Positive thinking", students had to complete:

1. the task "Positive past - positive future". Planned learning outcomes: to identify and define their strengths, transforming future concerns; to recognize how past positive experiences can be applied to future events; make a real future situation-oriented, group-supported story of their own experience;
2. task: "Positive focus" with the following planned learning outcomes: select and modify perceived information by sorting it; connect the perceived negative, disturbing information with the filter of positive thinking; evaluate and vary different types of objects of focus of attention, which allow forming a positive focus; adapt surrounding objects or memory images as objects for their perception; organize their positive thinking process;
3. task: "Re-framing, or paraphrasing of thinking and speech" with the following planned learning outcomes: choose the new style of thinking - positive or at least transformative; identify what is and is not a positive way of thinking and how to work with it; modify their speech from negative to positive or at least understand the transformative method; demonstrate transformative thinking-speech in real situations.

In the third module of the study course "Social and emotional competence", students had to complete:

1. the task "My emotional self-regulation" with the following learning outcomes: concentrate and maintain attention; plan and make a responsible decision about one's behaviour; regulate one's emotional expression in contact with other people in the group; suppress impulses long enough to consider what to do in the next moment, action, being able to find a suitable alternative to one's actions; choose constructive actions that take into account issues such as ethics, safety and other people's social and cultural expectations;
2. the task "Strengths of internal conflict prevention", with the following learning outcomes: apply and analytically evaluate the experience of one's conflict prevention strengths in various conflict challenge situations; to be aware of the positive resources of one's character when faced with a conflict, when internal anger or irritation can develop into an open conflict; be able to choose specific strengths from the list based on the experience gained in the exercise; to self-reflect on one's feelings, thoughts, goals;
3. the task "Non-violent or respectful communication", with the following learning outcomes: better engage in positive communication; create a dialogue according to the 4-step non-violent communication method, being able to provoke positive reactions from other people; develop their empathy abilities, feeling the needs of the other conversation partner and their own emotions; manage conflicts using the ability to understand the other's feelings in a given situation.

In the fourth module of the study course "Vitality", students had to complete:

1. the task "Vitality and my values", planned learning outcomes: determine values that help overcome challenges; to understand the solution of the problem situation according to the value approach; integrate the positive thinking skills learned so far in the context of values; to create a new focus for self-reflection - a hierarchy of values;
2. exercise "Vitality in thinking: 7-step skills", planned learning outcomes: use the "Life force in thinking" exercise and creatively use the 7-step approach to solving difficult situations; understand the connection

between positive thinking and vitality - the ability to overcome difficulties and accept challenges; focus and sustain attention and focus persistence; to plan and make a responsible decision about one's behaviour; choose constructive actions;

3. task "Conclusions about the entire course as a whole", planned learning outcomes: create a balanced and analytical summary of the knowledge and skills acquired in the tasks of all 4 modules; evaluate the change in their emotions and attitude towards certain tasks and the growth of their personality, the usefulness of the given tasks in the context of their goals and professional career; identify their positive thinking and personal growth resources in summary; analytically and concentratedly connect their experience in the practice of personal development with life goals that are currently important in their life; to conclude the most important thing about the growth of certain aspects of one's personality during the course.

By providing the students with the opportunity to model the quality of their work and the transparency of the tasks, task assessment criteria were developed and explained to the students. The self-reflection submitted by the students after completing each task was evaluated according to the following criteria: volume (weight 15%); message (weight 15%); discussion of concepts (weight 30%), and understanding of the topic included in the task (weight 40%).

The analysis of the impact and role of the course

The thematic analysis of the achieved study results was carried out by evaluating the feedback provided by 24 students from study program "Law" who completed the course between March 2021 and February 2023. At the end of the course, students wrote an assignment where they gave their subjective opinion about the knowledge and skills acquired during the course, illustrated examples of how the knowledge and skills learned in the course affected their lives: relationships, behaviour, thinking, professional field. The answers were divided into four large groups: acquired knowledge, acquired skills, the impact of taking the course on the future, and others. The "other" section included analysis of students' comments on the structure and form of the course and evaluation of the instructor's work.

Collecting information about how the students acquired new knowledge during the learning experience, it can be concluded that most students emphasized that they had already encountered psychology literature earlier in their lives, both about setting goals, positive thinking and recognizing emotions, and determining the strengths of their personality. However, several students emphasized that for the first time, they managed to connect this literature directly with their lives. Students wrote: "you hear about it at every step, but this course made me stop and listen to myself, made me make this transformation in myself", "the information about respectful communication and the steps of the conversation structure improved my understanding of effective communication". Students who had previously studied psychology or pedagogy indicated that this course updated and supplemented their previous knowledge. None of the students expressed the opinion that the knowledge to be learned in the course was not relevant.

Despite the fact that the course is designed as a standard course, each student has found exactly the topic, exercise, and explanation necessary for their personal development. Common in the feedback about the benefits of the course is the conclusion of each student about identifying an important individual situation for him, which is characterized by the words "I understood": "I realized that I am not so crazy, I am aware that I have many positive qualities and strengths", "I realized that I was emotionally unstable after giving birth, and I worked with it", "I have always looked for confidence in myself and my abilities - I have understood the most important thing, that in interaction with this course it gradually emerges, only this path requires a continuous learning process", "I understood, I am emotionally exhausted, tired and unhappy", "I understood that working with myself is difficult, but the time devoted to yourself, to organizing yourself, to understanding yourself is important and should not be "thrown" aside".

The quotes show that the topics and form of implementation of the course have promoted situational awareness among students, and within the course they were offered not only to read literature, but also to use practical methods, tools and exercises, and the instructor gave advice for identifying their own resources and solving situations. Different students highlighted different exercises for development tasks, the learning and use of which have given them useful skills and led to important conclusions. Students mentioned very different things as their practical benefits: skills in setting goals, developing positive thinking, building relationships and getting to know themselves. The feedback confirms the fact that each student has found a method or tool suitable for his individual situation: "knowing the current situation and my resources has increased my productivity", "I used the method of deep analysis, made lists of goals and described the course of action in detail to make it easier to achieve the goal", "I want to note Seligman's optimistic way of thinking as a lifestyle habit - I have also implemented it in my everyday life", "I learned to listen to my in the body and understand emotions better in a moment", "I have become aware of my strengths, which are also appreciated by my colleagues at my workplace, because I can do everything I set my mind to".

A thematic analysis of students' comments about whether and how taking the course has an impact on their future clearly shows that it is positive. The reviews mention that the acquired competencies will help to navigate various difficult life situations, they will be used to understand and accept other people's behaviour and reactions. Students noted that what they have learned will help them build more successful relationships, avoid conflicts, manage their emotions in difficult situations, and constructively approach the goals they have achieved. Many noted the role of identifying and realizing the values of their life in making future decisions and defining their life position: "it will definitely help in leading teams, because motivation and psychological support are a priority in the workplace", "the change in the way of thinking, the learned positivity, which I am still learning little by little, makes me feel myself and helps me understand that priorities in life tend to be very different from society "affixed" seal".

Although some students mentioned in their reviews that at first they perceived the exercises as an easy way to pass the time and did not understand the meaning of the exercises, later they often resisted the execution of various exercises and performed them carelessly, however, during the course of the first module, the resistance was overcome: "I have two higher educations and more than 20 years of work experience, and I have also studied psychology, but none of the studies had such a well-modelled system for self-knowledge and personal growth". Often, students mention the support of other students and the opportunity to get acquainted with their life situation and its reasons as a factor that successfully overcomes resistance and motivates them to complete the course: "group work made me understand and feel in unfamiliar situations and understand that not only I see my problems in such a pessimistic light, the experience of others makes you look at yourself from a different point of view".

The students admit that this course has stimulated their personal development and "gave the 'drive' to read more and more deeply and to learn in practice various possibilities and ways of self-development". Many write that they are aware of personal development as a continuous process, and the course has been a good incentive to actualize it: "my personal growth must be continuous. You have to find strength in yourself, the desire to transform yourself, develop and never give up". Students often note the important role of the course instructor's personal experience and professional teaching in stimulating learning motivation for successful course completion.

During the course, the students' attitude towards soft skills and the importance of their development in the field of professional activity has changed. The acquired skills and conclusions will help to make decisions not only in private living space and relationships but most mention the fact that the competencies learned in the course will help to build harmonious relationships and a career at work. The students' comments create confidence that the promotion of personal development during higher education is an essential factor that also contributes to the recognition and purposeful use and development of professional competencies: "we expect from formal education knowledge of external affairs in our chosen professional field. However, multifaceted self-understanding is necessary for the effective application of professional competences. Thank you for allowing me to come to such an important conclusion".

Conclusions and discussion

The authors conclude that the form of a distance learning course is also suitable for promoting personal development, and despite the fact that the course is designed in a standard form, each student can individually find and work with materials in accordance with their personal relevance and readiness. The thematic analysis of students' reviews showed that the purpose of the study course has been met and the results of the study course have been achieved.

Positive thinking, managing emotions, setting goals, identifying one's strengths, developing concentration, identifying and prioritizing one's values, understanding and accepting diversity are the main skills that students indicate as benefits of taking the course.

Although the reviews of some students indicate resistance to the awareness of the personality situation, the structure and organizational form of the course contribute to the successful overcoming of resistance and help to solve issues of personal development at the level of "depth" and complexity appropriate for the student.

Promotion of students' personal development, using the content and form of the specific study course, helps to successfully implement the mission of the College of Business Administration by improving not only the quality of students' professional, but also personal life.

The course instructor's professional competence and personal charisma are of critical importance in the implementation of the "Personal development" study course, which is made up of both knowledge in psychology and successful practical experience in group and individual counselling and life activities.

During the research, the authors identified two key elements where further research and analysis is necessary. At first, it is necessary to analyse the ethical aspects of this study course, taking into account that students with different previous experiences and also possible psychological diagnosis can take part in the course, and it is important to draw a boundary not to intervene too much in the personal life of the student. Secondly, it would be necessary to make a longitudinal study, for example, to make a survey for these students 2 or more years after finishing this course. It would give a possibility to evaluate the long-term impact of this study course on the professional careers and lives of the students.

References

Cheng, M., Adekola, O., Albia, J. and Cai, S. (2022), "Employability in higher education: a review of key stakeholders' perspectives", Higher Education Evaluation and Development, Vol. 16 No. 1, pp. 16-31. https://doi.org/10.1108/HEED-03-2021-0025

Edmunds, R., & Richardson, J. T. (2009). Conceptions of learning, approaches to studying and personal development in UK higher education. British Journal of Educational Psychology, 79(2), 295-309.

Kahl, C., Sundram, G.R. (2015). Are Students Pursuing Higher Education Aware of Personal Development Planning and Its Importance? A Pilot Study at Taylor's University. In: Tang, S., Logonnathan, L. (eds) Taylor's 7th Teaching and Learning Conference 2014 Proceedings. Springer, Singapore. https://doi.org/10.1007/978-981-287-399-6_13

Kumar, A. (2009). Personal, academic and career development in higher education: SOARing to success. Routledge.

Stek, K. (2022), "Personality Development in Higher Education in the Era of Industry 4.0: Comparing Educational Practices and Philosophies in Industry 1.0 and Industry 4.0", Bondarouk, T. and Olivas-Luján, M.R. (Ed.) Smart Industry – Better Management (Advanced Series in Management, Vol. 28), Emerald Publishing Limited, Bingley, pp. 35-50. https://doi.org/10.1108/S1877-636120220000028005

Strivens, J., & Ward, R. (2010). An overview of the development of Personal Development Planning (PDP) and e-Portfolio practice in UK higher education. Journal of Learning Development in Higher Education.

Quality Matters (2023). https://www.qualitymatters.org/

BUILDING COMMUNITIES OF TEACHERS; STORIES FROM THE CLASSROOM, HOW TO SCAFFOLD LEARNING ADVENTURES THROUGH TRUST

Zeta Dooly, South East Technological University, Ireland

Correspondence: *Zeta Dooly: zdooly@wit.ie*

Abstract

Education is recognised as a viable pathway to a better future. It is not a linear rite of passage but a meandering recognition of learning along the way. The advocacy of education for all, internationally, has led to education policy implementation across our global citizenship albeit at differing levels of accessibility and quality. It is widely recognised that the seminal work of Freire, Rousseau and Dewey have embedded the importance of active learning and critical pedagogy in our modern society. But have our leaders of education sufficiently recognised the need to promote education as a sustainable, complementary activity to social and caring aspects of our society.

This paper focuses on strategies used to build a sense of community in a classroom of educationalists who through their own learning experiences gain empowerment. Drawing on 3 iterations of delivering a module in synchronous virtual classroom, the strategies adopted are outlined, the overall theme is to enable the building of trustworthy relationships and to teach educationalists to embed beliefs and values into their teaching practice. Aspects of the induction period are designed to foster resilience and wellbeing in the teacher cohort for digital and physical life so that students feel nurtured and gain confidence to grow and empower others within the learning lifecycle.

Following on from the global pandemic, most formal education ecosystems had to temporarily pivot to digital education. Reflection and critical thinking beyond COVID position digital education at a juncture that needs careful consideration to understand the giant leap required to utilise advancements in technology in a classroom. This paper presents a pedagogical approach that tightly couples classroom dialogue with the application of existing technology for teaching and learning at level 9 (Masters) to surmount a sense of uncomfortableness encountered for teachers when faced with moving from a whole group, self-contained classroom approach to a multi-faceted learning ecosystem. Furthermore, the case studies described here address complexity in the classroom, acknowledging the 'valley of death' approach used in transitioning research into practice, and furthering our understanding how innovative technologies only make a difference when deployed and used in line with user needs and requirements (Maughan et. al, 2018).

Students describe how they overcome fear from one's own comfort zone toward recognising the power of teachers as change agents using an array of community communication platforms to equip and enhance their toolkit with engagement tools tailored for their subject expert domain needs.

Technology is a critical enabler to access knowledge, resources and people and has empowered those unable to engage with traditional educational settings to gain formal and informal knowledge whilst making learning more fun and engaging alongside other life responsibilities. Education as a career has expanded, teachers, tutors, lecturers, instructional designers, social and community enterprises, data analysts, database architects, facilitators all contribute to a complex education ecosystems that aspire to equality, inclusion and diversity. The population in this study includes diverse educationalists contexts and demonstrates the use of ice-breakers (Eggleston and Smith, 2004). This paper details examples of community building over a number of semesters delivering the same module to different cohorts. It illuminates the difficult induction period whilst students gain trust within small groups and overcome challenges that are presented. The results identify mechanisms that foster a sense of urgency to advocate for change, overcome complacency in classroom and introduce experimentation as a lever to learning in a failsafe ecosystem. Fear is identified as a concept that prevents the use of some technology due to its unpredictability and teacher legacy for being the person at the top of the class with all the knowledge. Times have changed, creativity is key and teachers are realising that they must prepare their students for failure in addition to success and that they need to model experimentation and failure to demonstrate that recovery and problem based learning prevails in a knowledge economy. As educator's compliance is a critical factor to meet the quality standards of our trade, meeting learning outcomes is just one part of the learning journey, gaining trust, delivery of engaging content and the realisation that students need an education ecosystem that promotes a nurture environment, self-actualisation and phronesis.

Keywords:

Trust, education, flipped classroom, innovative pedagogies, online learning, transformative learning, experiential learning

Introduction

This paper uses a novel approach to innovative pedagogy, introducing challenge-based learning and problem-based learning to actively engage students to use group work and individual work in an iterative approach to building their own virtual learning environment as assessment.

Design and planning are critical elements of education provision, the literature is rich with models and frameworks to aid educationalists. We start calss with a picture of snakes and ladders under the understanding that all learning starts somewhere and will have ups and downs.

The context for this research is a Masters of Education programme (level 9) which attracts a diverse group of higher education lecturers, instructional designers, primary and post primary teachers and tutors from Irish Education and Training Boards (ETBs). The sharing of context and experience in the classroom is promoted and regarded as essential to the ethos of this learning environment. Student's motivation to register for level 9 in a module on Blended and online learning can be diverse, it's an elective module, also offered to staff for continuous professional development (CPD). Initially, pre-covid it was redesigned to become an 80% online course and is now delivered fully online using a mix of blended learning frameworks and leveraging the use of Gilly Salmon's Carpe Diem model and etivity design guidelines (Salmon, 2013). This paper details the delivery of the module over a semester, the design, implementation and assessment considerations are embedded within the story. Building trust is achieved through transparency of grading and feedback, co-creation of curriculum and discussion of alignment of etivities to marks and value of group work (Wang, 2014).

Playing the game

Students are initially introduced to an ice-breaker exercise using a two-pronged communication approach, the virtual learning environment and MS Teams a week before class with accessibility at the fore of design using principles of universal design for learning (UDL). Sub-themes are introduced here and discussed at each of the synchronous classes. A flipped classroom approach is adopted and a strict approach to consistency enables a standard approach that the students can become familiar with fast (Tucker, 2012).

The lecturer spends time in the first hour of class to establish the netiquette and adopt elements promoted by Maha Bali through the intentionally equitable hospitality model (Bali and Zamora, 2022). Messages to assure students that life provides enablers, barriers and complexities for learning and reality can be challenging. Its sometimes the little things, students are encouraged to help each catch up if they need to pop out of class for an interruption and facilitate working in group by leaving messages on the platform for others to pick up at times suitable for them. Another tip is to edit your status online to indicate that whilst your listening you are unable to actively participate in a break-out room activity. This flexibility eliminates some of the professional guilt associated with not being able to reach to a high standard all the time.

Padlet and google slides are used for ice-breakers before and during the kick-off class with clear instructions to gain familiarity with different platforms, whilst students recommend places to visit, job contexts, image retrieval. Students are given a wide array of resources for this class to 'set the scene', these include introducing students to gurus in the teaching and learning space, advocating the use of networking theory to enable weak ties in addition to strong ties (Granovetter, 1973). Technology to support this approach is demonstrated, using linkedIn and twitter as gateways to people, research, conferences and good practice for teaching and learning. The approach is again recommending students to move outside of their comfort zone and contact people that have similar professional interests toward immersive learning environments and events. The design adopts elements of digital marketing to create a hook, Gravells (2014) and call to action language. Students discuss this in groups and use their zone of proximal development, peer learning techniques and scaffolding to enact this (Vygotsky, 1980 and Boud and Lee, 2005). Groups are advised to develop a group logo and name and area within MS teams to collaborate and use their creativity to experiment.

The use of ice-breakers cannot be underestimated both in the physical classroom and online and whilst we operate more and more in an online, flipped classroom arena the evidence and practice is pointing us to novel and innovative ways to engage students, motivate and encourage students to get involved and take ownership toward empowerment and transformative learning experiences (Chlup and Collins, 2010, West, 1999 and Cornell Univeristy 2022).

The course design has the usual boundaries of compliance to quality and module and programme learning outcomes. For this module though, the emphasis is on engagement, collaboration, transformative and innovative learning as promoted by Freire and UNESCO (Darder, 2014, Groff, 2013, Kitchenham, 2008, Perales and McCowan, 2021). This is further enhanced where learning is socially constructed within the social constructivism paradigm and group work (Kim, 200, Biggs and Tang, 2015).

Meat in the sandwich

Peer learning is facilitated through the continuation of the same groups for the duration of the semester, the incubation of communities of practice approach to experiment with technology and cross-discipline to iteratively develop new curriculum and pedagogical approaches is promoted. Students are building their own curriculum through the prioritisation of available options. This fosters a digital education ecosystem that the students thrive in and flourish.

During the semester discussions surround the use of technology enhanced learning and students are empowered to be advocates of education that have adequate knowledge to inform policy-makers and leaders in education on priorities and challenges to nurture and enact phronesis in their own contexts and toward the national and global agenda. This is further accentuated with the ongoing priority that nations sustainable developmental goals (SDGs) and in particular SDG4

Whilst much of the practical lab tutorial work focusses on off the shelf software that includes mind maps, quizzes, multiple choice question banks, polling apps, video and audio recording apps, gamestorming, metaverse platforms, VLE/MS Teams integrated and non-integrated applications learners generally observed that they quickly adopted the UDL theme of +1 and when required they had to adopt, evaluate and demonstrate a 'new to them' application. This approach was hugely successful as peer learning opportunity across multiple disciplines illuminated the opportunities for adopting pedagogies and approaches not evident within the students own sphere of education ecosystem. This further supports the network theory concept of structural holes and its applicability to education community building, knowledge acquisition and knowledge transfer (Burt, 1995).

A simple online checklist of etivities, where progress is self-managed by the student, aids motivation and gives ownership to the student in relation to progress. This is coupled with no deadline for etivities during semester but a recommendation to aim to complete them in line with the sub-themes, additionally an extra 2 weeks at the end of semester facilitates this catch up period. However, the results showed that students were motivated and incentivised by each other and the learning process to engage and in majority of cases etivities were completed on a weekly basis.

The potential for VR and AR in education has long been vaunted but limitations imposed by access to the technology, ease of use and software requirements have presented barriers to this potential been realised. A rapid decline in hardware cost, increased availability and ease of use, coupled with availability of low cost or open source software has mitigated many of the limitations highlighted in earlier studies. Whilst these cohorts of students were simply reading publications and case studies in this space with some exposure to 3D the time is ripe for more physical experimentation using education research labs as detailed in the further research section below.

The intent for introducing state of the art EdTech to cohorts of educators is to promote the concepts to early adopters and reduce the lag time to general adoption and implementation. A significant benefit of adopting advanced technologies to facilitate agreater eco-system of learning tools to facilitate truly personalised learning (Humble and Mozelius, 2019). It is clear that there is a lack of understanding of how these extended reality technologies can be effectively deployed in a higher education environment, their net contribution to learning, the risks associated with their uptake, and their potential to enhance the learning environment.

There are a number of studies that examine the use of previous iterations of extended reality (XR) in education, and it is postulated that this technology could benefit in areas, such as complex data visualisation, design visualisation, digital twins, increased immersion and enhanced cognitive states. Using future literacy techniques students looked at emerging technology in addition to current technology to further move and voluntarily jump into zones of instability, questioning the ethics of artificial intelligence use in the classroom and in government (Miller, 2007 and Nemorin et al, 2023).

The results from the student surveys and their reflective logs have not yet been fully analysed and collated and will inform this research further gaining knowledge in the student partnership model adopted and the emotions felt by the students in the zone of instability. The students that described the impact of the teaching and learning on their own personal learning journey to date have used the term transformative often and it is clear that sharing of course design, curriculum and implementation and open education communities are not the current trend with these education contexts in Ireland. Furthermore, concepts such as trust and transparency are not explicitly clear in the relationship between student and educator and between students, often further complicated by the dis-jointed nature of education in this context. However, there are National policy[1] changes underfoot that may start to address these challenges to optimised learning ecosystems 'Policy Platform: Progressing A Unified Tertiary System for Learning, Skills and Knowledge'.

Further research

It is planned to offer this course in a blended delivery mode to include physical face to face classroom, it is currently fully online, moving to blended will facilitate the use of experimenting with physical hardware such as meta quests for students to evaluate experiences and learning adventures using mixed reality, extended reality, virtual reality and augmented reality. This testbed environment can facilitate a greater eco-system of learning tools that can enable truly personalised learning (Humble and Mozelius, 2019).

Known to help with student learning (Flink et al., 2019), immersive learning environments (ILEs) are learning situations that are constructed using a variety of techniques and software tools, including game-based learning, simulation-based learning and virtual 3D worlds. ILEs are distinguished from other learning methods by their ability to simulate realistic scenarios and environments that give learners the opportunity to practice skills and interact with other learners on their own terms by engaging their optimum learning style. Applying adaptive learning techniques can further accentuate the teacher or lecturers toolkit and increate the potential to be inclusive, flexible, personalised and engaging for students (Holmes et al., 2019).

Furthermore, there is an opportunity to experiment with forest and beach classrooms, our university is regional and there is capacity to utilise our surroundings to enhance the learning experience for the students and continue the virtual classroom discussions, dialogue debate outside. This approach will complement the adopted social constructivist and experiential learning approaches (Kim, 2001 and Kolbe, 2014). As purported by Hawxwell et al, 2019, through adopting a learning outside of the classroom (LOtC) approach it will not only enrich the educational experience of the learner, but also be a viable and robustly tested method of pedagogy. This research intends to test this approach to further move students outside of their comfort zones into zones of managed instability to enable their coping mechanisms to extend and thus manage our societys integration of disruptive technologies.

[1] https://www.gov.ie/pdf/?file=https://assets.gov.ie/225165/fff8a843-0df6-436a-ade1-ae060deadd45.pdf#page=null

References

Bali, M., & Zamora, M. (2022). Intentionally Equitable Hospitality as critical instructional design. *Designing for Care.*

Biggs, J. and Tang, C., 2015. Constructive alignment: An outcomes-based approach to teaching anatomy. In *Teaching anatomy* (pp. 31-38). Springer, Cham.

Burt, R. S. (1995). *Structural holes: The social structure of competition.* Harvard university press.

CAST, accessed online May, 2022, Universal Design for Learning Framework, https://www.cast.org/impact/universal-design-for-learning-udl

Chlup, D. T., & Collins, T. E. (2010). Breaking the ice: Using icebreakers and re-energizers with adult learners. *Adult Learning, 21*(3-4), 34-39.

Cornell University 'Icebreaker', accessed online at; https://teaching.cornell.edu/teaching-resources/building-inclusive-classrooms/icebreakers.

Darder, A., 2014. *Freire and education.* Routledge.

Eggleston, T., & Smith, G. (2004). Building community in the classroom through ice-breakers and parting ways. *Office of Teaching Resources in Psychology Online.* Retrieved from http://teachpsych.org/resources/Documents/otrp/resources/eggleston04.pdf

Flink, P. (2019) 'Second Life and Virtual Learning: an Educational Alternative for Neurodiverse Students in College', *College Student Journal,* Vol. 53, No. 1, pp. 33-41.

Garrison, D. R. *E-Learning in the 21st Century.* 3rd. Abingdon, Oxon: Routledge, 2017. Community of inquiry model and 2008 social presence

Hawxwell, L., O'Shaughnessy, M., Russell, C., & Shortt, D. (2019). 'Do you need a kayak to learn outside?': a literature review into learning outside the classroom. *Education 3-13, 47*(3), 322-332.

Holmes, W., Bialik, M. and Fadel, C. (2019) *Artificial intelligence in education: Promises and implications for teaching and learning,* Center for Curriculum Redesign Boston, MA.

Humble, N. and Mozelius, P. (2019) 'Artificial Intelligence in Education - a Promise, a Threat or a Hype?' European Conference on the Impact of Artificial Intelligence and Robotics, Oxford, UK, Oct.

Kim, B. (2001). Social constructivism. *Emerging perspectives on learning, teaching, and technology, 1*(1), 16.

Groff, J., 2013. Technology-rich innovative learning environments. *OCED CERI Innovative Learning Environment project, 2013,* pp.1-30.

Kitchenham, A., 2008. The evolution of John Mezirow's transformative learning theory. *Journal of transformative education, 6*(2), pp.104-123.

Kolb, D. A., Boyatzis, R. E., & Mainemelis, C. (2014). Experiential learning theory: Previous research and new directions. In *Perspectives on thinking, learning, and cognitive styles* (pp. 227-248). Routledge.

Maughan, D., Balenson, D., Lindqvist, U., & Tudor, Z. (2013). Crossing the" Valley of Death": Transitioning cybersecurity research into practice. IEEE Security & Privacy, 11(2), 14-23.

Nemorin, S., Vlachidis, A., Ayerakwa, H. M., & Andriotis, P. (2023). AI hyped? A horizon scan of discourse on artificial intelligence in education (AIED) and development. *Learning, Media and Technology, 48*(1), 38-51.

Rose, D. H., & Meyer, A. (2002). *Teaching every student in the digital age: Universal design for learning.* Association for Supervision and Curriculum Development, 1703 N. Beauregard St., Alexandria, VA 22311-1714

Salmon, G. (2013). *E-tivities: The key to active online learning.* Routledge.

Tucker, B. (2012). The flipped classroom. *Education next, 12*(1), 82-83.

Wang, Y. D. (2014). Building student trust in online learning environments. *Distance Education, 35*(3), 345-359.

West, E. (1999). *The big book of icebreakers: Quick, fun activities for energizing meetings and workshops.* New York, NY: McGraw-Hill.

THE GLOBAL OER GRADUATE NETWORK: AN EXAMPLE OF A COMMUNITY OF CARE

Martin Weller, the Open University, The UK,

Francisco Iniesto, The Open University, The UK

Beck Pitt, The Open University, The UK

Rob Farrow, The Open University, The UK

Carina Bossu, The Open University, The UK

***Correspondence**: Martin Weller: edtechie@gmail.com*

Abstract

The Global OER (Open Educational Resources) Graduate Network (GO-GN) was founded in 2013 to support and connect doctoral researchers on OER worldwide and to promote open education research and its potential impact on society. In its ten-year history GO-GN has brought together doctoral students, experts, and educators from all five continents. GO-GN organises face-to-face events, online webinars and other activities that promote support and collaboration among its members. The pandemic impacted on GO-GN members and the network; this research shows how the network moved from a community of practice to a community of care.

Keywords:

Open education, OER, research, collaboration

Introduction

This research focuses on informal networks of support for higher education doctoral researchers and explores the extent to which these constitute communities of care due to open educational practices. The Covid-19 pandemic has challenged traditional models and structures in higher education, often removing the support structures that exist for the benefit of research students and doctoral candidates. In many contexts, higher education practices have adapted rapidly and in response to immediate needs. This paper examines the extent to which open values and practices can empower those who are potentially isolated or in need of community support. Our approach is effectively that of a 'community of care' which draws on open values to support and enable its members to achieve their immediate goals, move in the direction of open practices, and give and receive emotional support.

GO-GN

The Global OER Graduate Network (GO-GN) is a network of PhD candidates around the world whose research projects include a focus on open education, Open Educational Resources (OER), Open Educational Practices (OEP) or Massive Open Online Courses (MOOC). These doctoral researchers are at the core of the network; around them, over two hundred experts, supervisors, mentors and interested parties connect to form a community of practice. GO-GN started in 2013 as an initiative from Fred Mulder, in collaboration with Rory McGreal. GO-GN is currently administered by the Open Education Research Hub from the Institute of Educational Technology at The Open University, UK. GO-GN aims to raise the profile of research into open education, offer support for those conducting PhD research in this area, promote equity and inclusion in the field of open education research, and develop openness as a process of research.

GO-GN exists in parallel to formal educational systems rather than being integrated with them. In a typical year, GO-GN engagement takes place online through monthly webinars and other online events and activities (social media, newsletters, etc.) with the main interaction being a face-to-face workshop which is organised in collaboration with one of the major international conferences in open education. After a two-day intensive workshop, doctoral candidates in the GO-GN network are supported in attending the conference and presenting their research.

Due to the Covid-19 pandemic, the core feature of GO-GN activity - an annual face-to-face workshop to bring together members from around the world - became impossible. Aside from the disruption caused, it soon became apparent that doctoral students, who often feel isolated and in need of pastoral support at the best of times, were particularly vulnerable to the effects of institutional closures and the impact of lockdowns and other Covid measures. Consequently, GO-GN network activity shifted to a range of online interactions intended to provide a higher level of support.

There were several ways in which the GO-GN pandemic response was coordinated around the concept of developing an informal, yet supportive, community of care, based on open values and practices. This included:

1. In encouraging members to explore openness in their own context.
2. Co-production of community resources.
3. A continuing focus on Equity, Diversity & Inclusion.
4. Developing a Fellowship scheme.
5. Facilitating the participating in online conferences and co-chairing the OER22 conference.

The innovation exploring these activities has characterised GO-GN in its aspect of a 'community of care'.

Openness as a function of research and educational practice

GO-GN has a longstanding commitment to advocating for open values and open practices, many of which have an explicitly normative dimension. In encouraging members to explore openness in their own context, GO-GN has promoted moral values including autonomy, criticality, representation, equity, and commitment to sharing (Farrow, 2016; Jordan & Weller, 2017). The pandemic has affected GO-GN members, friends and experts, in several ways, and active support has been provided from the network including personalised support with 1:2:1 sessions and an interactive WhatsApp group.

Co-production of community resources

One focus for the GO-GN community was the co-production of resources through inclusive authoring and editorial practices. Outputs produced by the community during the pandemic included:

- The GO-GN Research Methods Handbook (Farrow et al., 2020) which was written through an open editorial process and has found an international audience, being downloaded more than 12,500 times, and being recognised with a prestigious award for excellence
- The GO-GN Conceptual Frameworks Guide (Farrow et al., 2021) which was again produced collectively and offered network members the chance to openly share insights into their work which would typically be concealed under 'closed' approaches
- A special issue of the Journal of Interactive Media in Education which shared a range of international perspectives on open education with a global audience (Weller et al., 2021)
- Participating in community events such as the GO-GN Gasta session at the ALT Summer Summit in 2020, or collectively training to be Wikipedia editors, and improve open education articles on Wikipedia, with Wiki Education
- Reviewing the state-of-the-art research relevant to open education published recently in the yearly published "Research review" (Farrow et al., 2021).

Equity, Diversity & Inclusion

Equity, diversity and inclusion (EDI) have been a growing topic within the Open Education community, although some would argue that it has been underpinning the open education discourse since the beginning (Lapum et al., 2022). However, access to free and online resources alone cannot be considered equitable, diverse, and inclusive. For example, most open resources are only available in English, which limits access and reach for many learners around the world (Willems & Bossu, 2012).

EDI has been driving the GO-GN agenda since its foundation, but it was only in 2018 when GO-GN's first project directly related to DEI was developed. the nature of this work involved GO-GN members working with the team. he first phase of the GO-GN EDI project focused on EDI practices in Open Education in Africa. Findings at this first stage informed the initial GO-GN guidelines for EDI (Bossu et al., 2019). The findings of phase 1 have also been used as a foundation for phase 2, which focused on EDI in Latin America (Bossu & Vladimirschi, 2020).

Phase 2 was conducted during the pandemic, which has created some challenges, but also opportunities for participant engagement. GO-GN currently supports 125 doctoral candidates and alumni registered at universities in 35 countries, however, of these members, only 30% conduct their research in the Global South (Weller et al., 2021). The concern is that, even with all the efforts put into place to be open and a willingness to be diverse, the Global South is still under-represented within this community, which means that GO-GN is not reaching those who could potentially benefit the most from being part of the network (Rodés & Iniesto, 2021).

To address this gap and assist the fulfilment of its mission, GO-GN has embarked on a quest to push the EDI agenda by implementing some of the recommendations suggested by the participants of the above projects, which will encourage further equitable, diverse, and inclusive collaboration between Global South and North colleagues and in turn foster open higher education for good. For this purpose, an EDI handbook in open education is being created, and includes research findings and recommendations from both phases and input from experts in the area.

Fellowship Programme

The GO-GN Fellowship scheme has been designed for three years (2020-2022) to foster connections to other networks, to promote GO-GN at strategic events and to encourage applications from the Global South. The latter aimed at incorporating some of the recommendations of GO-GN Diversity, Equity and Inclusion (DEI) project. The motivation for this fellowship scheme is to provide formal recognition to members after they have formally finished their doctoral studies to become an alumnus of the network in the format of a post-doctoral scholarship. The Fellowship scheme provides visibility and recognition in return for specific contributions to the network. This presents a means by which alumni can stay involved and share their expertise with the wider GO-GN membership.

The first cohort included four alumni, the second cohort of GO-GN fellows comprised two alumni, while the ongoing third one includes three alumni. Fellowships exemplify the diversity of the scheme, with fellows further developing doctoral research (two of them), while another focused-on network expansion in the Global South (one fellow). Fellowships also centred on the development of OERs (a book and a set of podcasts) through community co-creation (two fellows). Other fellowships have explored OER opportunities in their local and national communities (two fellows). Finally, fellowships also supported ongoing research in social justice and open textbooks (one fellow) or investigating the use of frameworks such as TPACK for teachers' use of OERs in their professional development (one fellow).

While the fellowship scheme was designed before the pandemic, Covid-19 impacted the first cohort, and required an agile response from fellows. For example, one fellow had to promote the network in the online environment instead of travelling to visit partners, and another fellow used the opportunity to research the Uruguayan context during the worst moment of the pandemic. In the case of a fellow who is currently researching in 2022, the experience of the pandemic is being used to inform and understand the impact of OER on teachers from public schools with low resources within the Brazilian context.

Dissemination and chairing conferences

During the pandemic support for members to submit and present their research at online conferences, such as UK OER, OE Global and OpenEd, was increased. This has enabled members to both network with, and receive feedback from, the wider open education community.

GO-GN were co-chairs for the last OER conference which took place face-to-face in London, UK and online 26-28 April 2022 (Pitt, 2022). The network had eight GO-GN members and alumni from around the world join for the first face-to-face workshop in over two years. The one-day workshop provided an opportunity for participants to share their current or doctoral research in a supportive space. GO-GN had presence across OER22 including a total of 29 sessions which featured GO-GN team and members, 25 non-team sessions including the conference plenary and GO-GN showcase, and 20 individual members listed as (co-)authors on presentations.

Member Feedback

Every year GO-GN invites members to participate in a survey. The GO-GN survey is an opportunity for members to share feedback and ideas on what we are doing as a network, how we could improve and how GO-GN can better serve the wider open education community. We had 27 respondents in 2021's survey (Weller et al., 2021). Members felt GO-GN has supported them during the pandemic very well (81%) with the features of GO-GN most important to members reported as: (1) community of peers, (2) research communications and (3) Research advice on open practices. Throughout the survey members shared a range of comments that highlight the different ways in which GO-GN is important and impactful. For example, GO-GN's open, collegiate community and support network, offering an alternative to their regular supervisory team:

"Hugely valuable emotional support and affirmation of our area of research was available from mentors throughout the journey. More so during my time as a graduate student but continued opportunities to connect and give back are welcomed, and strengths that provided psychosocial support during Covid tough times." (GO-GN alumni)

Presenting their work in front of the community:

"I love that you reached out to me about presenting at one of the webinars. I don't think that I would have volunteered at this point in my research, but it was a wonderful opportunity to talk about my interests and allowed me to network and hone my skills." (Current GO-GN member)

Fighting the loneliness in pandemic times:

"I suddenly do not feel alone in my doctoral journey. It has encouraged me to submit more academic writing for consideration and nudged me along in my studies" (GO-GN member)

Or, creating relationships among diverse international members:

"I believe that GO-GN has done an excellent job in creating strong human bonds among its diverse international members and that is the strongest asset it has. That is for me what makes it unique and incredibly powerful." (Current GO-GN member)

Conclusion

In summary, the GO-GN pandemic response was coordinated around the concept of developing an informal, yet supportive, community of care, based on open values and practices. Going forward GO-GN will continue to support members in a variety of different ways, both online and face-to-face, and offer an increased range of activities to support its membership in the future.

References

Bossu, C., Pete, J., Prinsloo, P., & Agbu, J. F. (2019). How to tame a dragon: Scoping diversity, inclusion and equity in the context of an OER project. http://oasis.col.org/handle/11599/3349

Bossu, C. & Vladimirschi, V. (2020). Diversity, Equity and Inclusion in Latin America in the Context of an Open Education Initiative, presented at the Open Education Global 2020.

Farrow, R. (2017). Open education and critical pedagogy. Learning, Media and Technology 42 (2): 130-146. https://doi.org/10.1080/17439884.2016.1113991

Farrow, R., Cardoso, P., Chtena, N., Cox, G., Czerwonogora, A., DeWaard, H., Iniesto, F., Kuhn, C., Peramunugamage, A., Pitt, R., Vladimirschi, V. & Weller, M. (2021). GO-GN Research Review (Winter 2021). Global OER Graduate Network. https://go-gn.net/gogn_outputs/research-review-winter-2021/

Farrow, R., Iniesto, F., Weller, M., Pitt., R., Algers, A., Baas, M., Bozkurt, A., Cox, G., Czerwonogora, A., Elias, T., Essmiller, K., Funk, J., Mittelmeier, J., Nagashima, T., Rabin, E., Rets, I., Spica, E., Vladimirschi, V. & Witthaus, G. (2021). The GO-GN Guide to Conceptual Frameworks. Open Education Research Hub. The Open University, UK. CC-BY 4.0. http://go-gn.net/gogn_outputs/conceptual-frameworks/

Farrow, R., Iniesto, F., Weller, M. & Pitt., R. (2020). The GO-GN Research Methods Handbook. Open Education Research Hub. The Open University, UK. CC-BY 4.0. http://go-gn.net/gogn_outputs/research-methods-handbook/

Jordan, K. & Weller, M. (2017) Openness and Education: A beginner's guide. Global OER Graduate Network. http://oro.open.ac.uk/53028/

Lapum, J., Bailey, A., St-Amant, O., Garmaise-Yee, J., Hughes, M., & Mistry, S. (2022). Equity, diversity, and inclusion in open educational resources: An interpretive description of students' perspectives. *Nurse Education Today*, 105459.

Pitt, R. (2022). GO-GN Workshop and #OER22. https://go-gn.net/gogn/go-gn-workshop-and-oer22/

Rodés, V., & Iniesto, F. (2021). Research in Open Education in Latin America: towards an agenda of collaboration between networks. In *2021 XVI Latin American Conference on Learning Technologies (LACLO)* (pp. 462-465). IEEE.

Weller, M., Pitt, R., Iniesto, F., Farrow, R., Bossu, C. and Vladimirschi, V. (2021). Annual Review 2021. Global OER Graduate Network. https://go-gn.net/gogn_outputs/2021-in-review/

Weller, M., Farrow, R., Iniesto, F. & Pitt, R. (eds.) (2021). Special Collection: Global OER Graduate Network. Journal of Interactive Media in Education. https://jime.open.ac.uk/collections/special/global-oer-graduate-network-go-gn/

Willems, J., & Bossu, C. (2012). Equity considerations for open educational resources in the glocalization of education. *Distance Education, 33*(2), 185–199. Author, A. A., Author, B. B., & Author, C. C. (yyyy). Title of article in sentence-style capitalization. *Title of Journal in Italics and Heading-style Capitalization, vol*(issue), pp-pp. :xxx

Bannan-Ritland, B. (2003). The role of design in research: The integrative learning design framework. *Educational Researcher, 32*(1), 21-24. :10.3102/0013189X032001021

Koehler, M. J., & Mishra, P. (2009). What is technological pedagogical content knowledge? *Contemporary Issues in Technology and Teacher Education, 9*(1), 60-70.

Wilson, G., & Stacey, E. (2004). Online interaction impacts on learning: Teaching the teachers to teach online. *Australasian Journal of Educational Technology, 20*(1), 33-48. Retrieved from http://www.ascilite.org.au/ajet/ajet20/wilson.html [where there is no DOI you can refer to the URL, but do not include both]

SKILLS ALIGNMENT FOR LIFELONG LEARNERS IN HIGHER EDUCATION: SMART CATALOGUES FOR RESKILLING AND UPSKILLING PATHWAYS

Mitchell Peters, Universitat Oberta de Catalunya, Spain

Corinne Aubert, Sorbonne University, France

François Vincent Rochet, Sorbonne University, France

Carmen Pagés, Universitat Oberta de Catalunya, Spain

Francesco Bullini, Bullini Enterprise, France

***Correspondence**: Mitchell Peters: mjosephp@uoc.edu*

Abstract

The future of work and the ever-changing skills demand in the labour market has been a constant debate and pressing challenge for higher education institutions (HEI's), governments and industry. In the current context, HEI's must increase the transformational effect of education on people's employability, on organizations' competitiveness and on society's progress. This paper presents the design and development of a mock-up career guidance tool to empower lifelong learners through digital reskilling and upskilling. We discuss the methods used for designing a skills alignment tool and a smart catalogue for identifying stackable training pathways in two specific disciplinary domains. The skills alignment methodology features a skill gap analysis (SGA) in the occupational domains of Data Science and Chemistry, linked to the evolution and demand of the European labour market through an ESCO compatible tool. The smart program catalog presents the necessary program information to facilitate the creation of stackable training pathways. Considerations are made for the importance of virtual career guidance tools for lifelong learners as we face the ever-changing demand of the labor market and as we continue to embrace online education, micro-credentialing and the digital transformation of higher education.

Keywords

Lifelong learning, Agile Continuous Education, Skills Alignment, Skills Gap, Skills Mapping, Upskilling, Reskilling

Introduction

The future of work and the ever-changing skills demand in the labour market has been a constant debate and a pressing challenge for higher education institutions (HEI's). Economic growth across all sectors has been driven by the digitalization of public organizations and private enterprise. According to a report from Gartner (2020) digitalization-driven skills shifts can be described by three central tendencies; (a) new skills are emerging driven by accelerating technological advancements; (b) skills are evolving through shifts toward big-data oriented tools and artificial intelligence; and (c) yesterday's skills are expiring as technology performs more and more tasks faster and cheaper than humans, exemplified by the enormous influence of ChatGPT at the beginning of 2023. Educational leaders need to interpret the current higher education zeitgeist and strategically respond to the need for agile continuous education and lifelong learning for new and working professionals.

In this dynamic context, lifelong learners need insights into the new and different skills they will need for career growth and the potential offerings that could support their goalsProviding guidance for lifelong learners in a labour market in continuous evolution has become a clear goal for governments and educational organizations. HEI's have a key role for empowering lifelong learning, and the development of novel forms of career guidance leveraged by data on skills demand. By implementing skills alignment methodologies, that is, methodologies that ensure that learners 'skills are well matched to current skill needs in their desired roles or occupations HEIs can help individuals identify their skills, match them with relevant career paths, and make more informed decisions about their educational and professional development..

This paper presents the results of an Erasmus + project, D-Reskill, whose objective is developing the prototype of a learner-centric career guidance tool to support digital reskilling and upskilling for employability. To that end, the D-Reskill project consortium has put together a team of practitioners, educational leaders, labor market experts, policy-makers, technologists and innovators. The core motivations behind this work relate to empowering individuals to make informed career decisions; and create new learning and career pathways using digital career guidance tools, while ensuring that the qualifications and training pathways offered by HEIs match the evolving demands of the labour market.

D-Reskill responds to the "European Skills Agenda", which prioritizes equity and inclusivity as a key instrument of socioeconomic development and excellence. The Skills agenda assumes that public universities can play a pivotal role in providing innovative lifelong learning pathways and agile continuous education solutions to support employability in key economic sectors. The project aim is to be accessible, readily applicable, and responsive, thanks to its alignment with the European Skills, Competences, and Occupations (ESCO) database (European Commission, 2022) and the European Learning Model (ELM) (2023).

In this article we intend to contribute to the existing literature on skills alignment technologies for career guidance in HE in three ways: (1) by offering conceptual and methodological guidelines for a mock-up career guidance tool; (2) by emphasizing a user-centered design and UX research approach; and (3) by presenting two use cases for skills alignment in the field of Data Science and Chemistry.

Project Objectives and Justification

The D-Reskill project is based on the premise that individuals aiming to enter the workforce or grow their careers need effective and timely opportunities for reskilling or upskilling supported by novel forms of career guidance tools. Such tools should enable individuals to identify their skills, match them with relevant training pathways and career opportunities, and make informed decisions about their educational and professional development. Following a user-centred design approach, the project aims to:

- Design a proof of concept (mock-up) of a career guidance tool to support agile continuous education through digital reskilling and upskilling.
- Design the proof of concept of a tool for identifying stackable micro-credential compatible training pathways, based on an identified Skill Gap Analysis (SGA) in the occupational domains of Data Science and Chemistry and linked to the evolution and demand of the European labour market.
- Develop the conceptual, methodological, and technical guidelines for designing an ESCO-compatible smart digital course catalogue that can support skills alignment and the identification of training pathways through micro-credentialing for users.
- Maximize impact via an active dissemination plan to ensure visibility and continued project sustainability.

The DRESKILL@U project builds on the most recent policy agenda for the European Higher Education Area (EHEA), with a particular emphasis on the alignment between education and training systems and the labour market. It is based on and complements ongoing policy discussions related to lifelong learning and employability established in the July 2020 Skills Agenda and the 2022 Council Recommendation on a European Approach to Micro-credentialing (European Council, 2022), including the role of micro-credentialing for transformation and change management in higher education (Brown et al., 2023). D-Reskill also uses the multilingual classification of European Skills, Competences, and Occupations (ESCO) developed by the European Union (EU) to describe and categorize skills in a common format across EU countries. D-Reskill follows the ESCO handbook use case of supporting and improving career guidance services through competence assessment and by matching skill profiles to new learning opportunities through micro-credentials (European Union, 2017).

As a collaboration across 4 distinct national education systems (France, Budapest, Italy, and Spain), D-Reskill uses policy tools developed for the EHEA, including the European Qualifications Framework (EQF), and the European Credit Transfer and Accumulation System (ECTS). According to Europass (2022), the EQF "is an 8-level, learning outcomes-based framework for all types of qualifications that serves as a translation tool between different national qualifications frameworks. This framework helps improve transparency, comparability and portability of people's qualifications and makes it possible to compare qualifications from different countries and institutions"(Europass, 2022). By using such EHEA policy mechanisms, D-Reskill can operate in a transparent and comparable way across distinct education systems.

Conceptual and Methodological Guidelines

D-Reskill proposes a mock-up of a career guidance tool, that following a skills alignment methodology, is able to do the following:

Skill Assessment: First, the tool begins by assessing the skills of the user. Various methods can be used, such as self-assessment questionnaires, online tests such as the ELM digital skills test, interactive exercises, or inferring the user´s skills based on work experience and occupation. The assessment should cover a wide range of skills, including technical, and transferable. This step recognizes that a lifelong learner has previous education and work experience and that this needs to be expressed as a standardised set of knowledge and skills, classified, as previously mentioned according to ESCO.

Occupation/Skills Database: Based on ESCO, the tool provides a comprehensive database of skills required in various occupations and sectors. To reflect the evolving nature of job roles and emerging skills in the labor market, the database should be updated regularly. The skills database allows the user to choose a targeted occupation and be assessed against the benchmarked knowledge and skills to perform it.

Skills Mapping: The tool compares users' skill assessment results with the skills needs in a targeted occupation or role. Based on the user skill profile, it would identify the skills that closely match the individual's proficiency and highlight areas where skill development may be needed.

Career Exploration: The tool allows to explore different occupations and roles and provides personalized career suggestions based on the skills mapping. Recommendations for specific occupations or industries would be made that align with the individual's skills and interests.

Learning Opportunities: Using a digital "smart catalogue" and advanced algorithms, the tool recommends relevant learning opportunities to bridge any skills gaps identified during the skills assessment and mapping process.

Figure 1 below provides a conceptual overview of the D-Reskill skills alignment methodology.

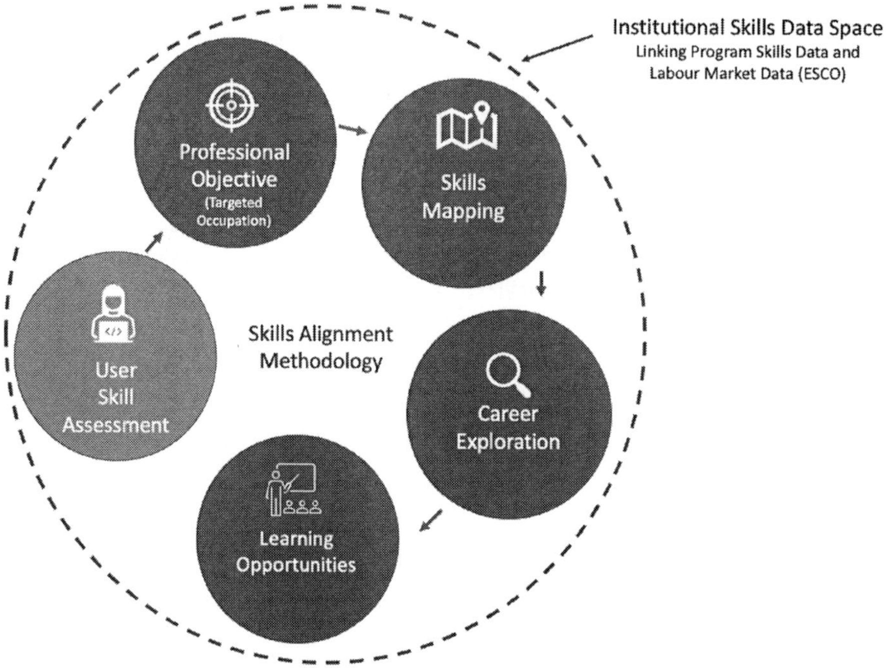

Figure 1 Conceptual overview of the D-Reskill skills alignment methodology

The core conceptual features of this system are as follows (See also Figure 2):.

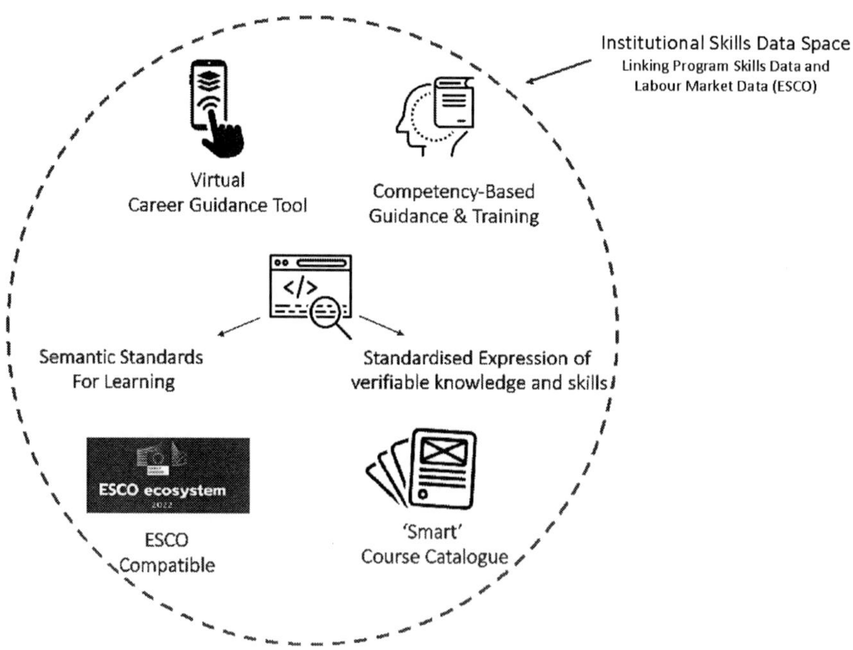

Figure 2 Core Conceptual Features of D-Reskill System

A *competency-based career guidance and training* approach focuses on developing and assessing specific skills and abilities required for success in a particular occupational domain or job role. It emphasizes the practical application of knowledge and the demonstration of specific competencies, rather than solely relying on traditional measures like educational qualifications or years of experience. The tool will be *ESCO* compatible, in line with the objective of serving as a common and interoperable tool across European countries to connect employment and education. While there are other skills ontologies, such as *ONET, or those from Lightcast or the World Economic Forum that could be used, ESCO has the desirable characteristics of being: European created, open source, well documented and updated regularly. Finally, *a smart catalogue of offerings* aligned with the objectives of the ELM. This includes implementing semantic standards for learning; i.e. standardized frameworks and formats used to organize and describe learning contents and outcomes and a standardized expression of verifiable skills and knowledge linked to academic programs and training pathways.

Skills Mapping and Defining Skills Gaps

Skills mapping is a process of identifying and assessing the skills possessed by individuals or organizations. It includes mapping out the specific skills and competencies required for various job roles or occupations and then benchmarking the skills of individuals or teams against common requirements. For individuals, skills mapping provides a comprehensive overview of an individual's professional profile, highlighting strengths, gaps, and areas for development. Thus, a major motivation for the "Skills Agenda" is the existence of a skills gaps for individuals throughout their careers, which has been described as:

"a fundamental mismatch between the skills that employers rely upon in their employees, and the skills that job seekers possess. This mismatch makes it difficult for individuals to find jobs and for employers to find appropriately trained workers" (Brookings Institute, 2022).

A Skill Gap Analysis (SGA) is a procedure central to the skills alignment methodological and technical specifications of the D-Reskill software, is defined as the disparity between a user´s current skills profile and the skill profile required to perform in the target occupation.

Skill Gap Analysis	The process of identifying the disparity between a user's: (a) current skill profile based on a skills assessment -skill self-assessment survey, online test, interactive exercises -inferred from current educational level, -inferred from current occupation and associated skill profile AND (b) a desired target occupation and associated skill profile

A core goal has been to develop methodological guidelines for identifying user skill gaps, most examples of SGA's come from the world of work and human resources development. SGA's are not commonly used in higher education and therefore we have developed two specific use cases for career transitions in the occupation of Data Scientist and Chemistry, as is throughout this article.

Core users of the D-Reskill system

The core users of the DRSKILL@U system are lifelong learners, teachers learning providers and industry partners (see Figure 3) The central user is a lifelong learner in need of agile continuous education to meet short- and long-term professional goals.

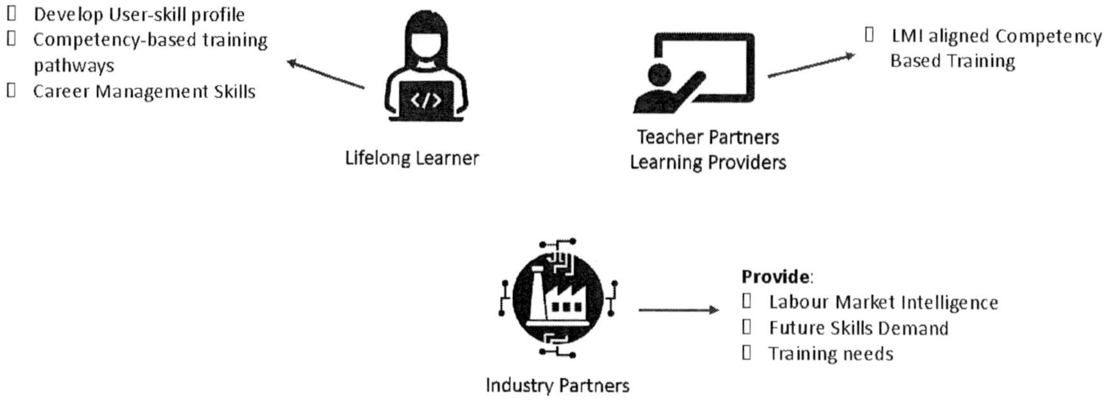

Figure 3 Core users of D-Reskill

Lifelong learners engage with the tool to perform skills assessment, career exploration in relation to their professional objectives, and to access relevant learning opportunities that can address their skill gap. Teachers and learning providers use the system to upload training opportunities using a competency based approach. including relevant metadata such as learning outcomes, length and depth of learning etc., which can allow the tool to recommend learning opportunities in specific occupational domains. Finally, industry partners may use the system to provide real-time data on the skills demand in specific industries, for example data science or chemistry, based on current or extended ESCO skill profiles.

A User-Centered Design Approach

In line with project goals, D-Reskill follows a a user-centered design approach, incorporating some generative user-experience research techniques, including a user experience mapping technique (Gibbons, 2018) which is presented in Figure 4 below through user journey mapping. This serves to visualize the tasks and experiences that a learner goes through to accomplish the overall goal of using the D-Reskill system for receiving virtual career guidance.

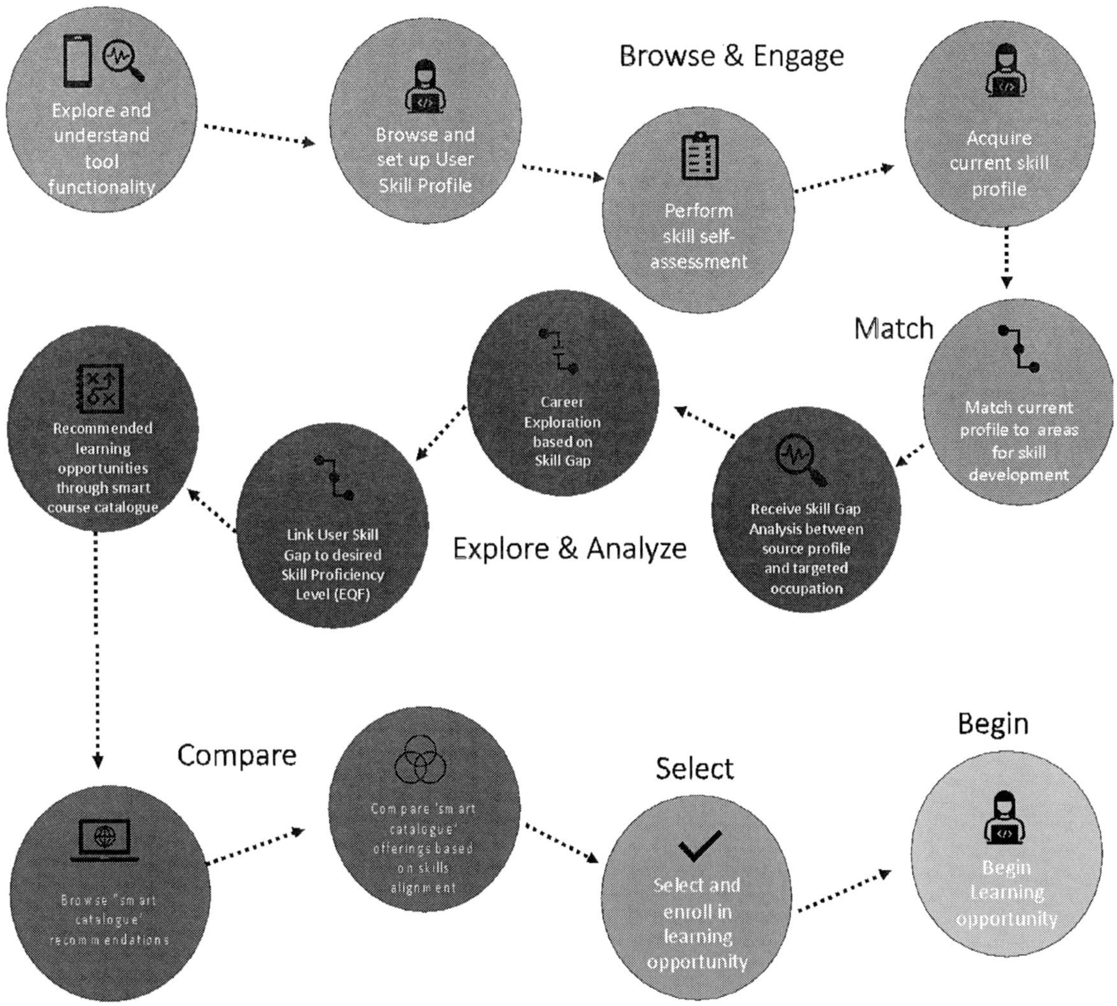

Figure 4 D-Reskill User Journey Mapping

Determining skill proficiency levels

Whether the skill alignment procedure allows identifying the skills that a learner requires to achieve a determined career goal, it does not provide an assessment of the level of proficiency needed for each skill.: Therefore, determining skill proficiency levels was a a core challenge of the project. The project proposed a Skill Proficiency Scale (see Table 1), avital feature for the internal algorithms of the career guidance software. This scale has been adapted for precision and clarity from previous European projects, namely OpenSkimr (MCI, 2017), which aimed to match learners with in-demand skill development for career transitions, as well as from Entrepreneurship competence framework (Bacigalupo et al., 2016). The scale rates skill proficiency levels at different qualification levels and their associated educational levels, according to the European Qualification Framework. This proficiency scale is used for the learners´ skill-assessment, for the skills mapping exercise (stating at what level of proficiency each skill needed to carry out a given occupation or role needs to be performed) and for the course catalog (stating the level of skills proficiency achieved after undertaking a given program or course).

Table 1 D-Reskill Skill Proficiency Scale

D-Reskill Skill Proficiency Scale					
EQF Level	N/A	EQF-5 <------------------------EQF6------------------------EQF7--------------□EQF-8			
Example Educational Level	N/A	Undergraduate <--------------------- Masters -----------------------□Doctoral			
Skill Proficiency Scale	No Experience/ Competence Level 0	Novice Level 1	Experienced Level 2	Advanced Level 3	Specialized Expert Level 4
Self-Assessment Survey Scale	N/A	User has limited skill/knowledge experience	User has some skill/knowledge autonomy, although some help may be required	User has full skill/knowledge autonomy, and is capable of coaching others	User is a recognized authority

Use Case I: Career transitions in Data Science

In Use Case I, we used ESCO's skills classification for Statistician and Data Scientist to conduct a SGA to analyze the disparity between the two skill profiles, as shown in Tables 2 and 3. Table 2 represents the skill profiles of target and source occupation. Many skills are common between the two occupations. Which implies that a person that makes this transition, will be able to reuse many of their existing skills. Table 3 presents the skill gap between source and target occupation.

Table 2 Skill pillar based on target and source occupation, based on ESCO's skills classification

Target Occupation: Data Scientist Skills/Competencies	Source Occupation: Statistician Skills/Competencies
apply research ethics and scientific integrity principles in research activities	apply for research funding
build recommender systems	apply research ethics and scientific integrity principles in research activities
collect ICT data	apply scientific methods
communicate with a non-scientific audience	apply statistical analysis techniques
conduct research across disciplines	communicate with a non-scientific audience
deliver visual presentation of data	conduct quantitative research
demonstrate disciplinary expertise	conduct research across disciplines
design database scheme	demonstrate disciplinary expertise
develop data processing applications	develop professional network with researchers and scientists
develop professional network with researchers and scientists	disseminate results to the scientific community
disseminate results to the scientific community	draft scientific or academic papers and technical documentation
draft scientific or academic papers and technical documentation	evaluate research activities
establish data processes	execute analytical mathematical calculations
evaluate research activities	gather data
execute analytical mathematical calculations	identify statistical patterns
handle data samples	increase the impact of science on policy and society
implement data quality processes	interact professionally in research and professional environments
increase the impact of science on policy and society	manage findable accessible interoperable and reusable data

interact professionally in research and professional environments	manage intellectual property rights
interpret current data	manage open publications
manage data collection systems	manage personal professional development
manage findable accessible interoperable and reusable data	manage research data
manage intellectual property rights	mentor individuals
manage open publications	operate open source software
manage personal professional development	perform data analysis
manage research data	perform project management
mentor individuals	perform scientific research
normalise data	process data
operate open source software	promote inclusion in research
perform data cleansing	promote open innovation in research
perform project management	promote the participation of citizens in scientific and research activities
perform scientific research	promote the transfer of knowledge
promote inclusion in research	publish academic research
promote open innovation in research	speak different languages
promote the participation of citizens in scientific and research activities	synthesise information
promote the transfer of knowledge	think abstractly
publish academic research	think analytically
report analysis results	write scientific publications
speak different languages	
synthesise information	
think abstractly	
think analytically	
use data processing techniques	
use databases	
write scientific publications	

Table 3 Results of SGA between Statistician and Data Scientist

Skill gap between target and source occupation
build recommender systems
collect ICT data
deliver visual presentation of data
design database scheme
develop data processing applications
establish data processes
handle data samples
implement data quality processes
interpret current data
manage data collection systems
normalize data
perform data cleansing
report analysis results
use data processing techniques
use databases

Use Case II: Career transitions in Chemistry

Similar to Use Case I, in order to measure a skill gap between two occupations in the chemistry domain, a source and target occupation were considered. Use Case II included the source occupation of Chemistry

Technician (ESCO ID 3111.1) and the target occupation of Analytical Chemist (ESCO ID 2113.1.1). This is a typical case of upskilling frequently encountered in industry, corresponding to a transition from a junior role to a more senior role at the masters level.

A data table was produced with several columns in Excel, shown in Figure 6. For "chemistry technician" and "analytical chemist" w two columns collecting "essential or optional skills/knowledge" provided by the ESCO database. Each skill or knowledge (e. g. "handle chemicals") was assigned an "industry-ready proficiency level" defined on a scale from 1 to 4, as discussed before. Considering that the aim of the project is the design of a career guidance software, the industry-ready proficiency level was determined through consensus among a focus group of participating professors. The scale, and the measured skill-gaps seemed reasonable and sufficient for the exercise.

Chemistry Technician				Analytical Chemist			Skill gap	
essential skills required for the occupation	analyse chemical substances	sector	3	analyse chemical substances	sector	4	analyse chemical substances	1
	apply safety procedures in lab	sector	4	apply safety procedures in laboratory	sector	4	apply safety procedures in laboratory	0
	handle chemicals	cross-sector	4	handle chemicals	cross-sector	4	handle chemicals	0
				apply statistical analysis techniques	cross-sector	4	apply statistical analysis techniques	4
				apply scientific methods	cross-sector	4	apply scientific methods	4
				execute analytical mathematical calculations	cross-sector	4	execute analytical mathematical calculations	4
				perform scientific research	cross-sector	3	perform scientific research	3
				perform laboratory tests	cross-sector	4	perform laboratory tests	4
				use chemical analysis equipment	cross-sector	4	use chemical analysis equipment	4
				identify purpose of analysis	cross-sector	4	identify purpose of analysis	4
	use chemical analysis equipme	cross-sector	2	use chemical analysis equipment	cross-sector	4	use chemical analysis equipment	2
	write work-related reports	cross-sector	2	write work-related reports	cross-sector	4	write work-related reports	2
		sector	2	analyse experimental laboratory data	sector	4	analyse experimental laboratory data	2
				develop scientific research protocols	cross-sector	4	**develop scientific research protocols**	4
	mentor individuals	cross-sector	1	mentor individuals	cross-sector	3	mentor individuals	2
	promote inclusion in research	cross-sector	2	promote inclusion in research	cross-sector	3	promote inclusion in research	1
	perform project management	cross-sector	1	perform project management	cross-sector	3	perform project management	2
				disseminate results to the scientific community	cross-sector	3	disseminate results to the scientific community	3
				publish academic research	cross-sector	2	publish academic research	2
				manage personal professional development	cross-sector	3	manage personal professional development	3
				think abstractly	cross-sector	3	think abstractly	3
				think analytically	transversal	3	think analytically	3
essential knowledge required for the occupation								
	basic chemicals		4	basic chemicals	cross-sector	4	basic chemicals	0
				analytical chemistry	cross-sector	4	analytical chemistry	4
				chemical processes	sector	4	chemical processes	4

Figure 6 Chemistry use case Skill-gap EXCEL Table

Discussion and Conclusion

This paper describes the design and guiding principles of a novel form of career guidance tool in higher education in the context of rapidly changing work and training environments. It argues that facilitating the matching of individuals skills and competencies with industry needs through the creation of skills alignment technologies can greatly enhance the effectiveness of career guidance and student support in HE. In addition to the development of the tool itself, this process requires significant organizational and educational change on the part of institutions and professors, by creating competency-based, semantic standards for learning contents and outcomes, This is essential to be able to match learners skills gaps to appropriate learning pathways. An emerging literature on institutional transformation and strategic responses to micro-credentialing (Brown et al., 2023; Olcott, 2022; Olcott et al., 2023) encourages educational leaders to interpret the current zeitgeist to set decision-action priorities, making strategic decisions about how they engage with digital transformations. We argue that one such strategic response is designing career guidance tools which incorporate skills alignment technologies and smart catalogues capable of identifying and recommending personalized and flexible training pathways through reskilling and upskilling.

There continues to be a strong debate about the need for embedding employability skills in higher education (Kornelakis & Petrakaki, 2020) and calls for more integrated approaches to studying employability (Römgens et al., 2020), including competency-based methods for teaching and career guidance. Our paper contributes to the debate for integrating skills alignment technologies for lifelong learners in higher education by; offering conceptual and methodological guidelines for a mock-up career guidance tool; by integrating this tool with EU policy agenda initiatives, such as the ESCO database and the ELM; by highlighting the need for UX research and design; and by presenting two illustrative cases of how to integrate this methodology to reskill and upskill in the field of Data Science and Chemistry.

As we continue to embrace online education, micro-credentialing and the digital transformation of higher education, the importance of virtual career guidance tools for empowering lifelong learners will only increase. It is crucial for institutional leaders, policymakers, educators, and industry partners to invest in the development and implementation of innovative career guidance tools and agile training pathways to ensure that everyone has access to the support they need to manage career growth and development. Research and development in this area can help advance our understanding of how best to support lifelong learners and their career trajectories through skills alignment technologies. As the labour market faces unprecedented challenges and shifting job market demands, the need for reskilling and upskilling has become more critical. Virtual career guidance tools can provide an effective solution to empower individuals when navigating these changes and remain competitive in the job market. By providing personalized guidance, ESCO compatible skill profiles, semantic standards for learning, up-to-date industry insights, and access to relevant training pathways, skills alignment tools can help individuals make informed career decisions and develop the necessary skills to thrive in their chosen field.

References

Bacigalupo, M., Kampylis, P., Punie, Y., & Van den Brande, G. (2016). EntreComp: The entrepreneurship competence framework. Luxembourg: Publication Office of the European Union, 10, 593884. https://eige.europa.eu/resources/lfna27939enn.pdf

Brookings Institute. (2022) Understanding the skills gap—and what employers can do about it. Available at: https://www.brookings.edu/research/understanding-the-skills-gap-and-what-employers-can-do-about-it/

Brown, M., McGreal, R., & Peters, M. (2023 in press). A Strategic Institutional Response to Micro-credentials: Key Questions for Educational Leaders. Journal of Interactive Media in Education, 2023(1). https://doi.org/10.5334/jime.801

Chiarello, F., Fantoni, G., Hogarth, T., Giordano, V., Baltina, L., & Spada, I. (2021). Towards ESCO 4.0–Is the European classification of skills in line with Industry 4.0? A text mining approach. Technological Forecasting and Social Change, 173, 121177.

Europass (2022) [online] [accessed: 19 October 2022]. Available at: https://europa.eu/europass/en/europass-tools/european-qualifications-framework

European Commission. (2022) [online] [accessed: 19 October 2022]. European Skills, Competences, and Occupations (ESCO). Available at: https://ec.europa.eu/social/main.jsp?catId=1223

European Commission. (2022) [online] [accessed: 19 October 2022]. European Skills Agenda. Employment, Social Affairs and Inclusion Available at: https://ec.europa.eu/social/main.jsp?catId=1223

European Council. (2022) Council recommends European approach to micro-credentials. https://www.consilium.europa.eu/en/press/press-releases/2022/06/16/council-recommends-european-approach-to-micro-credentials/

European Learning Model. (2023) [online] [accessed: 14 June 2023]. https://europa.eu/europass/en/news/launch-european-learning-model

European Training Foundation. (2023) [online] [accessed: 14 June 2023]. https://www.etf.europa.eu/en/what-we-do/skills-demand-analysis

European Union (2017). ESCO Handbook. European Commission. doi:10.2767/934956

Gartner (2020). Do More With Data to Close Critical Skill Gap. Available at: https://www.gartner.com/en

Gibbons, S., (2018) Journey Mapping 101. Neilson Norman Group. Retrieved: https://www.nngroup.com/articles/journey-mapping-101/

Kornelakis, A., & Petrakaki, D. (2020). Embedding employability skills in UK higher education: Between digitalization and marketization. Industry and Higher Education, 34(5), 290-297.

MCI. (2017). Annotation Guide Learnings Supporting learning providers and integrating learnings in the OpenSKIMR Annotation. Dept. Management , Communication & IT OpenSKIMR. Retrieved: https://openskimr.eu/pdf/Deliverable_2-2_learning.pdf

Olcott, D. (2022). Micro-credentials: A catalyst for strategic reset and change in U.S. higher education. American Journal of Distance Education, 36(1): 19–35. DOI: https://doi.org/10.1080/08923647.2021.1997537

Olcott, , Arnold, D. & Blaschke, L. (2023) "Leadership 2030: Renewed visions and empowered choices for European university leaders" European Journal of Open, Distance and E-Learning, vol.25, no.1, pp.74-92. https://doi.org/10.2478/eurodl-2023-0006

Römgens, I., Scoupe, R., & Beausaert, S. (2020). Unraveling the concept of employability, bringing together research on employability in higher education and the workplace. Studies in Higher Education, 45(12), 2588-2603.

DO LIVE WRITING/ STUDY SESSIONS FOR AT-RISK STUDENTS, IN AN ONLINE, DISTANCE LEARNING ENVIRONMENT, DEMONSTRATE THE SAME BENEFITS DOCUMENTED FOR FACE-TO-FACE SHARED WRITING EVENTS?

Hannah Lavery, The Open University, United Kingdom
Debbie Parker Kinch, The Open University, United Kingdom
Jennifer Hillman, The Open University, United Kingdom

***Correspondence**: Hannah Lavery: hannah.lavery@open.ac.uk*

Abstract

A recent project focussing on students studying an Arts and Humanities Access module at the Open University revealed that students in IMD Q1 are disproportionately more likely to 'passively' withdraw than their peers (i.e. not submit an assignment, not register with the university their intention to defer, ultimately leading to a 'fail' grade for that module: Lavery & Padley, 2022). Recent data shows a significant award gap for students studying Arts and Humanities modules who have a mental health need registered with the university. Colleagues were therefore motivated to assess whether the inclusion of synchronous, online, study and support opportunities, training students in the use of the Pomodoro technique, might support success for participants. This paper outlines the approach of two projects that applied techniques associated with group writing sessions, reflecting on whether their findings demonstrate similar benefits for participants in an online, distance learning environment as for those traditionally run in the physical space (i.e. writing retreats).

Keywords:

Academic writing support; arts and humanities; synchronous online delivery; coach-mentor; low socio-economic; mental health; retention; student success; writing retreats; writing communities.

Research tools and methodology

Scholarship on the use of writing retreats for supporting academic colleagues' development of writing skills talks of the numerous ways in which attendance at shared, live writing experiences can benefit the attendee. Kornhaber et al.'s (2016, p. 1210) survey of scholarship in this area enabled them to define the characteristics of writing retreats that make them 'conducive to increasing publication output': these are, protected time and space; development of a community of practice; development of academic writing competence; intra-personal benefits; and organisational investment. There is further evidence that study groups or academic writing groups can have a positive impact on wellbeing (Eardley, et al., 2021), which could have beneficial outcomes when supporting students with mental health needs, as well as for students from non-traditional backgrounds studying at a distance. Although much of the literature focuses on the use of writing retreats to support teachers and academics, we produced this paper, bringing together findings from two current projects focusing on student support, to explore whether the same benefits could be seen to apply to groups of adult learners at a distance learning organisation, where the live writing/ study sessions are provided online and at a distance.

The project follows an action research methodology, as the development of our projects' support sessions utilising the Pomodoro time management technique (Cirillo, n.d.) arose in response to student feedback as well as the respective teams' reflection on earlier support interventions focussed on other pedagogical approaches (respectively, direct teaching in the form of 'catch up' sessions; and 'Learn – Grow – Connect' group coach-mentoring approaches). Additional support was therefore added to existing provision in the form of group live writing/study sessions. Evaluation was completed via survey of participants, with plans to follow up with quantitative analysis regarding the impact on student outcomes for these cohorts of students. (A limitation of the current approach is that, in the absence of an RTC evaluation, causal 'impact' cannot be definitively shown because there may be a self-selection bias).

Approach and content

'Catch up and Write' sessions

In response to earlier findings regarding the higher likelihood of IMD Q1 students passively withdrawing having not submitted an assignment, we implemented a series of 'catch up' sessions after each Tutor Marked Assignment (TMA) on our three Arts and Humanities Level 1 modules (February 2022 cohort. NB this followed similar pilots on a Social Sciences module DD218 and English Literature module A233). Students who had not submitted their TMA within 10-14 days of the deadline, and had not recorded an extension with their tutor, were invited by email to attend. Each session ran for c. 30-45 mins (depending on level of student participation), with an additional 15 minutes allocated for welcome and final Q&A, and were hosted in Adobe Connect. We organised for an experienced tutor to provide each session, with two iterations scheduled to run over two weeks.

Suggested content for the 'catch up' session included:

- standard skills support (e.g. time management; contacts when students face challenges; how to plan and draft a piece of written work)
- focus on both the relevant module materials and specific TMA task that had been missed
- activities focussing on unpacking the question and how to use the guidance notes
- preparing students to catch up with work toward the next assignment.

From October 2022, building on previous work undertaken on the Level 2 Literature module A233 (2021), an additional 30-45 minute live writing session ('Write Now') was added to the series of catch-up sessions running across 12 x 60 credit undergraduate modules: 3 x Level 1, 2 x Level 2 English, 1 x Level 2 Classical Studies, 1 x Level 2 History, 2 x Level 3 English, 2 x Level 3 Classical Studies. The rationale for this part of the session was to encourage attendees to immediately build on the support and encouragement they had gained from the catch-up session, by staying online for a further 30-45 minutes to make progress with a specific aspect of their TMA planning or writing, and gain practice in using the Pomodoro technique introduced in the session.

The aim for this part of the session was to encourage students to feel that they were not alone in falling behind and that they had the support they needed to help them move forward and complete the TMA. Influenced by feedback from the A233 pilot, we allocated two tutors to each session, and encouraged tutors to engage in dialogue for their delivery. They were also asked to share with students the writing task they were completing during the 'write now' part of the session, to reinforce the idea that this approach to goal setting, planning, and writing is valuable for all writers, not just students.

Given that these students are at most risk of passive withdrawal, attendance figures are heartening for the first phase of this initiative (Figure 1). In addition to this, there are high numbers of viewings of the 'empty room recordings' for each session.

Figure 1: Attendance at 'Catch up and write' sessions, October 2022 cohort.

Attendance rate (as a % of students invited)	Number of sessions	Total number of students invited (per band)	Total attendees (per band)	Average attendance rate (per band)
0-5%	59 (70%)	12421	209	2%
5-12%	22 (26%)	1938	152	8%
Over 12%	3 (4%)	197	85	43%

Similarly, attendance at a 'Catch up' session does appear to have positive student outcomes in relation to submission of the missed TMA, with an average submission rate of 94% for attendees (for the missed assignment), compared to an average of 75% for the overall module submission rate.

'Study Together' with the Open University's Personal Learning Advisory (PLA) Service

'Study Together' sessions were designed in response to student feedback on a programme of group coaching workshops aimed at OU students with mental health declarations. The programme was entitled 'Learn, Grow, Connect' and aimed to provide a forum for sharing study successes, challenges and the intersections with lived experience. Of a potential target population of 283 students on A&H modules, we had a 17.7% response rate. (This response rate to the group sessions was higher in the current academic year - 17.75% - than the response to the one-to-one offer in the 21-22 academic year - 15.2%).

Student feedback gathered in response to a regular survey on the Learn, Grow, Connect programme demonstrated demand for a space to study and connect with other students – to help motivation and sense of connection. The context of distance learning and mental health is important here as students told us that they:

- Feel alone in their studies
- Struggle with internal motivation to study and procrastination
- Want techniques to develop study habits
- Value opportunities to focus on study

'Study Together' sessions for Level 1 students in Arts, Humanities and Social Sciences were therefore launched by the centralised coaching and mentoring service (PLA) in March 2023 as a follow-on intervention. These sessions are exclusively for students with a declared mental health condition who also have a pass probability prediction of less than 70%.

'Study Together' creates a quiet study space online for students to focus on their studies in a facilitated way. Students sign up for an 80-minute session hosted by the PLA service in MS Teams. Using the structure of the Pomodoro technique, students are invited to set their own study goals for the session, work quietly online with other students, and then share their achievements. PLAs hold the space for students to develop their focus (as they do in coaching and mentoring) but the study is the student's own. Study Together also gives space to connect with other students.

Analysis

Scholarship has shown that barriers to writing can be overcome through the 'legitimisation of time and space for writing' offered by participation in a shared, live writing experience clearly demarcated from attendees' usual working environment (Girardeau et al., 2014; Grant, 2006; Moore, 2003; Murray & Newton, 2009; Pololi et al., 2004). The common model for a writing retreat involves participants physically travelling to a location, separate from the usual work environment, which therefore offers attendees associated benefits in terms of removal from caring responsibilities in the home, for instance. As a distance-learning organisation, at the Open University we rely on synchronous online software to ensure our teaching and support sessions are delivered to the largest group possible. The majority of students at our sessions were therefore likely to be participating in our live writing sessions in their 'usual' study environment. Nevertheless, some initial feedback from surveys from the 'Catch up and write' sessions records:

I am often called upon at home to 'put of [sic] fires' and so it is nice to have a reason to say no, now I am looking at this.

The online delivery of these sessions therefore still enables students to take 'legitimate time away from conflicting demands and priorities' (Kornhaber et al., 2016, p. 1217); and once students have reflected on the value of this legitimate space for writing they may be able to better embed this within standard study time.

Physical space is also implied by Moore's notion of a writing retreat as a 'sanctuary', connoting a safe, supportive, secure and comfortable space (2003). In the PLA-led Learn, Grow, Connect sessions, which targeted students with mental health needs, meetings were held in Microsoft Teams but not recorded. A stripped-back, accessible version of session materials was sent to students in advance of each session. Students were required to register with their Personal Identifier so hosts were able to identify them in the event of any safeguarding issues; however, students were able to join the sessions with their initials/alias so they did not have to (implicitly) declare their mental health condition to other students if they chose not to. There was the option for 1-2-1 follow ups and/or check-ins where issues were raised in the group setting. Additionally, there was a named contact in the institutional mental health casework team to discuss possible referrals into mental health support from a caseworker. This time spent constructing a safe space online is reflected in the feedback comments received from the follow on 'Study Together' sessions attended by students who had engaged in Learn, Grow, Connect. Students referenced feeling being with others and the value of 'seeing' facilitators with video camera functionality, as well as feeling 'accepted':

Being in a virtual room with others who were doing the same thing as me made me feel settled within myself, so it helped with my concentration and focus.
It made a massive difference to my mood and concentration being involved in a group activity.
Nice to see friendly faces with the people running the session. They were all pleasant and professional.
I really liked the way it was run. I felt welcomed and accepted.

Note is made in the scholarship of the need to help participants develop follow-up strategies, to maintain momentum when back in the work (study) environment. This appears to be a particularly effective part of the current delivery of the 'Catch Up and Write' sessions (Figure 2).

Figure 2 'Catch Up and Write' student feedback survey (n=91)

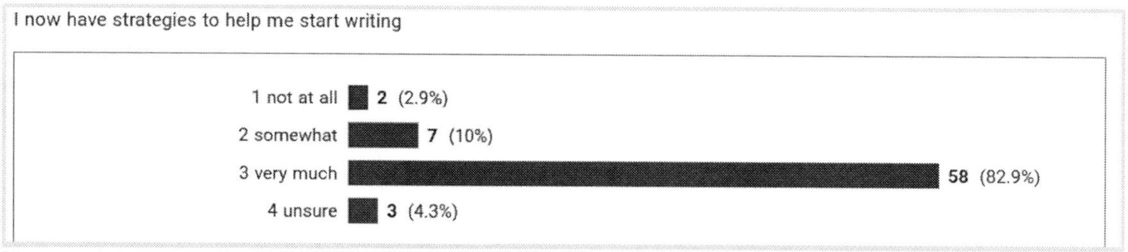

The development of a 'community of practice' model in relation to the face-to-face writing retreat notes positive outcomes for participants in terms of providing a shared vision, collegial support, mentorship and social interaction (Cable et al., 2013; Jackson 2009; Murray & Newton 2009; Rickard et al., 2009). Again, previous studies generally focus on retreats that enabled the building of communities of practice over a longer time period (i.e. a day or weekend), and in a space where colleagues would be physically present together. Instead, our projects are based on the principle that by creating opportunities for students to learn actively together we also create a community of practice – defined as people "joined together by shared interests and a mutual participation in a particular practice" (Chavez et al., 2021), in an online, distance space. Student feedback survey data for A233 'Write Now' sessions (n=72) shows that 69% of respondents found it useful to talk with other students and share experiences in the sessions.

With a particular focus on supporting students with mental health needs, studies have shown that the act of working on something synchronously with others (even in silence) helps to forge a 'we-community' with associated positive emotions – 'including sense of belongings, mutual support and dependence, and satisfaction' (Koulaxi & Kong, 2022, p. 13). Furthermore, a recent study (2019) which surveyed c.2800 Australian students found that regular interaction with peers and staff for students with mental health needs is a 'protective' factor for student wellbeing (Baik et al., 2019, p. 10). In the Study Together session feedback to date students have identified wellbeing and mood, as well as sense of connection, as something positively impacted by attending guided study sessions (Figure 3).

Figure 3: Student Feedback Survey: Areas of positive impact following attendance at a Study Together session

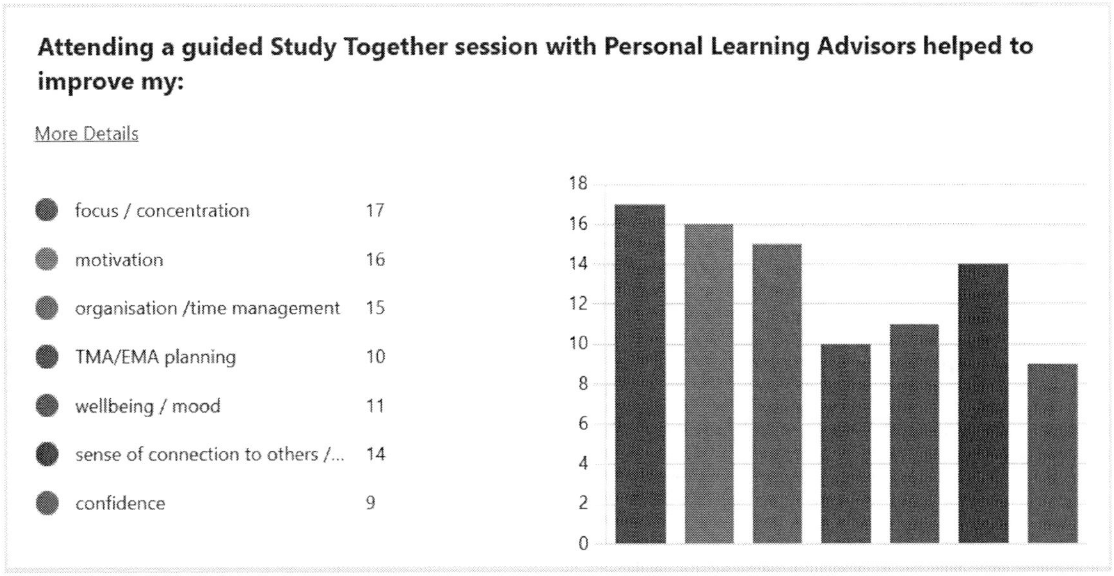

Recent case studies have highlighted a significant role for student support teams in combating loneliness and isolation in the context of online learning (Morley & Aston, 2023; Chakma & Kahuhung, 2021). From the A233 Catch up and write sessions, 9 from 47 respondents to the survey register that they appreciated finding that they are 'not alone' in their struggles with academic writing and assignment preparation. There is also evidence that study groups or academic writing groups can have a positive impact on wellbeing (Eardley et al., 2021), as well as helping to maintain productivity. Intrapersonal benefits of participation in writing retreats, noted in Kornhaber et al.'s analysis (2016, p. 1223), include increased self-awareness, confidence and motivation; and reduced writing-related anxiety. Evidence from the 'Study Together' sessions so far record that 87% of attendees feel that they are able to achieve their goals in this setting (Figure 4).

Figure 4: Student Feedback Survey: Study Together Session Attendees

I achieved the goals I set for myself in this session

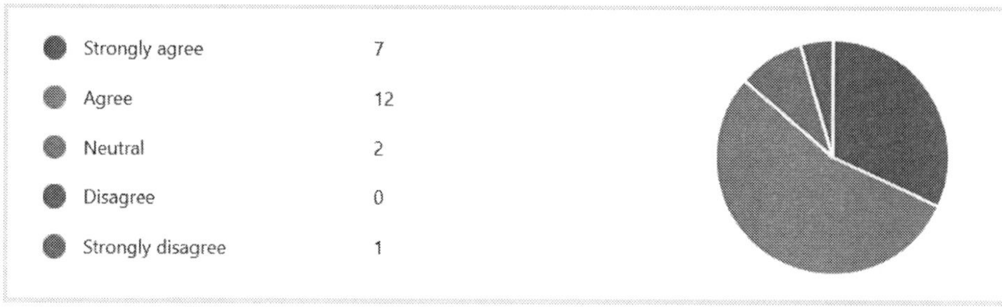

Study Together students also stated the benefits in terms of a sense of accountability:

By being held accountable with my studies, I was able to achieve more than I expected
I am normally quite last minute with things and have to cram in hours of study but the 25 minute bursts are helpful , i [sic] can try and fit them in at work

Similarly, attendees at A233 'Write Now' sessions, when asked if the session had made them think or feel differently about any aspect of their writing process, responded positively:

Yes, made me calmer when writing.
Yes, it's given me the tools to be more confident approaching essay writing and not feel so over whelmed.

In terms of the specific content and approaches that had an impact on attendees, Murray and Newton (2009) note that the 'proximity and balance of experienced and inexperienced writers provided a forum for constructive synchronous feedback that was instrumental to building confidence and writing capacity and alleviating writing-related anxiety'. Our decision to include two tutors to co-facilitate the 'Catch Up and Write' sessions was positively received by attendees, with one student noting that they appreciated the mix of student and tutor input to the sessions:

I[t] makes you realise that you are not alone in experiencing difficulties and that others have the same issues - no idea what to write, procrastination etc. The tutors were also great at sharing their ideas on how to tackle some of these issues. It also helped to reaffirm that I am doing some things right which helps to build confidence.

We also noted the positive adaptations our respective projects made to this approach, bringing in pedagogy of care. Particularly in the sessions organised for students with mental health needs, the use of 'holding silence' for students can show 'care, attention and respect to students who prefer to join in conversation through the text chat, to allow them the necessary time to think and type their thoughts and ideas, without unintentionally excluding them from the community or prioritising those on microphone and camera' (Morley & Aston, 2023). Both the case studies discussed in this paper used software that allowed participants to elect whether to participate using video, microphone, chat, or any combination of those. Arguably, this could mean that shared study/writing sessions delivered online and at a distance might better serve inclusivity and accessibility for the students we are targeting.

Conclusion

During a time of financial constraints, it is heartening to see that students attending online, distance live writing/study sessions appear to receive many of the same or similar benefits as experienced through attendance at face-to-face writing events. There are additional challenges, but with thought and attention it is possible to create safe spaces (or 'sanctuary'), in which students report the value of sharing experiences, receiving support from both tutors and peers, reduction in writing-relating anxiety, and the development of strategies for on-going management and development of their own academic writing skills.

Some of the aspects of face-to-face delivery that are missed include benefits associated with repeat participation, which has not been explicitly encouraged in the format of existing projects. Colleagues are aware that "identifying a group of people as a community of practice does not make them one": the community has to be actively cultivated (Li et al. 2009; Wenger et al., 2002, in Benvenuti, 2017, p. 103). Furthermore, success of that depends on "knowledge of participants' needs... skillful engagement by participants" with benefits seen from "repeat participation". (Benvenuti, 2017, p. 105). This is an area for further exploration in the online, distance learning space.

References

Baik, C., Larcombe, W., & Brooker, A. (2019). How universities can enhance student mental wellbeing: The student perspective. *Higher Education Research & Development, 38*(4). https://doi.org/10.1080/07294360.2019.1576596

Benvenuti, S. (2017). Pedagogy of peers: Cultivating writing retreats as communities of academic writing practice. *South African Journal of Higher Education*, *45*(2), 89-107. https://doi.org/10.20853/31-2-1340

Cable, C.T., Boyer, D., Colbert, C.Y,. & Boyer, E.W. (2013). The writing retreat: A high-yield clinical faculty development opportunity in academic writing. *Journal of Graduate Medical Education*, *5*(2), 299–302.

Chavez, M., Watson, D., & Treharne, R. (2021). A spotlight on learning communities. University of Liverpool Centre of Innovation in Education. https://www.liverpool.ac.uk/media/livacuk/centre-for-innovation-in-education/staff-guides/learning-communities/learning-communities.pdf

Chakma, U., Li, B., & Kabuhung, G. (2021), Creating online metacognitive spaces: Graduate research writing during the COVID-19 pandemic. *Issues in Educational Research, 31*(1), 37-55. http://www.iier.org.au/iier31/chakma.pdf

Cirillo, F. (n.d.). The Pomodoro Technique. https://francescocirillo.com/products/the-pomodoro-technique

Eardley, A.F., Banister, E., & Fletcher, M. (2021). Can academic writing retreats function as wellbeing interventions? *Journal of Further and Higher Education*, *45*(2),183–196. https://doi.org/10.1080/0309877X.2020.1744542

Girardeau, L., Rud, A., & Trevisan, M. (2014). Jumpstarting junior faculty motivation and performance with focused writing retreats. *Journal of Faculty Development, 28*(1), 33–40.

Grant, B.M. (2006). Writing in the company of other women: Exceeding the boundaries. *Studies in Higher Education*, *31*(4), 483–495.

Jackson, D. (2009). Mentored residential writing retreats: A leadership strategy to develop skills and generate outcomes in writing for publication. *Nurse Education Today*, *29*(1), 9–15.

Kornhaber, R., Cross, M., Betihavas, V., & Bridgman, H. (2016). The benefits and challenges of academic writing retreats: An integrative review. *Higher Education Research & Development*, *35*(6) 1210-1227. https://doi.org/10.1080/07294360.2016.1144572

Koulaxi, A. and Kong, J. (2022). Re-thinking virtual writing retreats in the Covid-19 higher education environment. *Journal of Applied Learning & Teaching JALT.* https://doi.org/10.37074/jalt.2022.5.s1.2

Lavery, H. & Padley, S. (2022). Improving student success for global majority and low socio-economic status students through additional synchronous support and information embedded on a distance learning access module. *European Distance and E-Learning Network (EDEN) Conference Proceedings* (in press).

Moore, S. (2003). Writers' retreats for academics: exploring and increasing the motivation to write. *Journal of Further & Higher Education*, *27*(3), 333–342.

Morley, C., & Aston, S. (2023). Overcoming isolation with community based digital writing initiatives. *Journal of University Teaching & Learning Practice, 20*(2). https://doi.org/10.53761/1.20.02.03

Murray, R., & Newton, M. (2009). Writing retreat as structured intervention: Margin or main-stream? *Higher Education Research & Development*, *28*(5), 541–553.

Pololi, L., Knight, S., & Dunn, K. (2004). Facilitating scholarly writing in academic medicine. *Journal of General Internal Medicine*,19(1), 64–68.

Rickard, C.M., McGrail, M.R., Jones, R., O'Meara, P., Robinson, A., Burley, M., & Ray-Barruel, G. (2009). Supporting academic publication: Evaluation of a writing course combined with writers' support group. *Nurse Education Today*, *29*(5), 516–52.

A LETTER TO MY FORMER SELF: THE ONLINE PHD AS A TRANSFORMATIVE JOURNEY

Efrem Melián and Julio Meneses, Universitat Oberta de Catalunya, Spain

Correspondence: *Efrem Melián: emelian@uoc.edu*

Abstract

Online doctoral programmes have become increasingly popular, allowing adult professionals to pursue their academic goals while carrying on with their lives. This research inquired into a seldom-explored aspect of the online PhD experience: its transformative nature. Through in-depth interviews, we investigated the impact of online doctorates on candidates' lives and perspectives, as well as the retrospective advice they would give to their past selves at the beginning of the programme. Findings indicate that a sense of empowerment and agency is frequently rekindled in online graduate students as they rediscover their own unique voices and perspectives. The PhD also opens them up to new networks and worldviews, promoting personal and professional growth. Students' advice emphasises the importance of having a support network to turn to in times of need, cultivating grit and time-management skills, and learning to cope with constant rejection. This paper offers insights into the lived experience of online graduate students that might interest both prospective students and programme administrators.

Keywords:

Online PhD programmes, non-traditional students, mature doctoral students, students' voices, lived experiences.

Introduction

Online doctoral degrees are gaining traction worldwide, particularly in the wake of the pandemic (Seyri & Rezaee, 2022). The non-traditional profile of students is now dominant in these research degrees (Lee, 2022b). These doctoral candidates are mostly mature-aged, working professionals juggling part-time academic life with paid work and family responsibilities (Lee, 2022b). They choose to do a PhD online for its flexibility and convenience, but at the probable cost of compromised supervision, increased loneliness, and strained personal lives (Melián et al., 2023). Compared to traditional face-to-face PhD programmes, online delivery also places greater demands on students' self-regulation, self-motivation, and time management skills (Xavier & Meneses, 2021). While stubbornly high dropout rates have been a concern in this educational stage for decades (Baltes, 2018; Marston, 2019), recent literature has also raised concerns about unprecedented low well-being (Boone et al., 2022) and mental health vulnerabilities (Naumann et al., 2022) among this student population.

Beyond this situation, pursuing a PhD can also be regarded as an intimate journey that is closely tied to life goals, professional expectations, and personal aspirations (Lee, 2022a; Stanley, 2015). The online doctoral journey is far from a homogeneous experience with predictable outcomes, however. The vast range of experiences among the students correlates with their diverse professional, financial, familial, and cultural backgrounds. In addition, the diverse life circumstances that are expected of an adult during an academic journey that lasts several years are blended into this. As a consequence, embarking on such academic pursuits might necessarily bring about personal transformations and identity transitions (Savva & Nygaard, 2021; Seyri & Rezaee, 2022).

Altogether, non-traditional doctoral students live in an in-between space (Bhabha, 1994), with their often long professional expertise in one particular field on one side and their novice status as academics on the other. This position often results in a changed self-image and identity upon completing the doctorate, compared to when they first entered the program (Nygaard & Savva, 2021). The transformative aspect of belonging and becoming in academia (Nygaard & Savva, 2021), as well as the interplay between candidates' lives and the process of doing a PhD from an experiential point of view, have received scarce attention in the literature (Stanley, 2015).

This is even more so for the online modality, which is the focus of our study.

Therefore, this research examines the effects of pursuing a doctoral degree at the Open University of Catalonia on students' lives. This fully online university offers several PhD programs in fields such as social sciences, humanities, and technical subjects. Most students in these doctoral programs are enrolled in the distance and part-time mode, which is expected to last for five years (Open University of Catalonia, 2018).

Methods

This study is qualitative and exploratory following a single case study approach (Yin, 2002). We collected data through in-depth semi-structured interviews with 24 online, part-time doctoral students at the Open University of Catalonia. The interviews lasted around one hour and were held either online or face-to-face. Participants came from various PhD programmes (from both the social sciences and technical fields); stages in the programmes (first year, mid-phase, thesis deposited or recently graduated); countries (from Europe, Latin America, North America, and Africa); ages (27 to 63 years old); and backgrounds (working either in the public or private sector, outside or inside academia). Half of the participants were female.

Transcription and coding of the interviews were assisted by the qualitative analysis software atlas.ti. The researchers then employed thematic analysis to develop the codes and themes, following the stages described in Braun and Clark (2006). The coding process was primarily inductive, listening to the participants' narratives, and pragmatic, developing themes as domain summaries (see Tables 1 and 2). We then used the observed patterns of meaning across the dataset (Clarke & Braun, 2021) to structure the textual analysis.

Preliminary Results

Next, we present the research questions (RQ) of the study and its preliminary findings.

RQ1: How does pursuing a PhD program online affect students' life?

The students' narratives revealed impacts in three different domains of their lives, such as internal and relational changes, as well as in the professional sphere. Table 1 displays the primary effects in each of these areas.

Table 1: Perceived impacts of the online PhD experience on students' lives.

Domain	Perceived effect
Internal	I am more critical and open-minded.
	I have found my voice: I speak up more and feel heard.
	I have improved my time-management skills.
	I am more conscientious and patient.
	I have experienced self-growth.
Relational	It has changed the way I interact with people.
	It has opened me up to whole different types of connections.
Professional	It has enriched and facilitated my work.

Overall, most students felt the doctoral program exerted remarkable effects on their lives. On the one hand, the very process of training to become an independent researcher, with its constant evaluation and emphasis on critical thinking and academic writing, positively impacts candidates' self-regulation, persistence, and time-management skills. Most importantly, as the candidates advance in the programme from the initial courses to the dissertation stage, a sense of discovering one's voice becomes apparent. This often newfound voice grows gradually in both quality and quantity, uniqueness and strength. Most students note how they have gained along the way a type of confidence in their judgement and authority in how their messages are received in their personal, work, or academic environments. As an illustration, one participant observed how the PhD had "shaped how I engage and I do speak up more because I feel like I've got the credentials" and she now feels she is able to present arguments "in a way that's a bit more thoughtful, that is kinder".

On the other hand, immersion for several years in the particular topic of the dissertation often affects doctoral students' points of view and worldviews. Some find nuances and contradictions in their most previously well-established takes, while others —particularly in the social sciences— find a new sense of empathy and compassion towards the persons or groups they have studied.

Lastly, PhD students also noted how the doctoral training had enriched their professional lives and future job prospects. Both by allowing them to perform at a higher level, which, interestingly, is often noticed by their coworkers, and by allowing them to access a whole new network of people in their academic fields.

Notwithstanding, few students felt unchanged by the online doctoral experience. The most identifiable reasons were either being in the early stages of the programme, usually in their first year, or having previous or current experience working in academic settings. Indeed, being already familiar with the academic environment and the skills involved, generally having collaborated as a research assistant in group projects, lessens the PhD programme impact in both the positive and negative aspects.

RQ2: Considering the experience undergone, what advice would students give to their past selves beginning the doctorate?

After reviewing their entire doctoral journey, we asked students to provide a piece of advice to their inexperienced, beginner selves. Although the question was directed at the individual level and rooted in personal experiences, our goal was to extract a lived piece of advice that could be transferable and beneficial for all doctoral students given the common challenges they typically face. In this regard, online graduate students' advice (Table 2) ranged from relational and internal aspects to practicalities.

Table 2: Advice given by students to their past selves beginning the doctorate.

Domain	Piece of advice
Relational	Reach out for support when in need, do not postpone it.
	You are not responsible for your supervisor's feelings and behaviours.
Internal	When a crisis hits, rely on your passion, and trust your gut.
	Work on your time-management skills and be persistent.
	Get used to dealing with rejection, that's a big part of academia.
	Do not let your guard down, online is (also) tough.
Practicalities	Secure funding first so that you can enjoy the journey.
	Get informed about regulations and be prepared for bureaucracy.

The most recurrent topic concerned the importance of having a support network to rely on during such a long and often lonely pursuit. As one of our participants noted, "the enthusiasm with which you start is great, but a PhD can affect your mental health". Seeking assistance from friends, family, or mental health services helps alleviate the hardships of the journey.

Another frequent source of concern for online doctoral students is the relationship with the supervisors. In this respect, a participant experiencing erratic and neglectful supervision lucidly advised to take responsibility for your own behaviours and emotions, but not for those of your supervisor. Indeed, instances of blurred boundaries and self-blame arising from the internalization of others' shortcomings are common in power-imbalanced relationships such as the supervisory one (Tröster & Van Quaquebeke, 2021).

Separately, online doctoral candidates must restore to internal qualities such as passion, grit, and self-organization to navigate the hardships of the programme. Their advice stressed the importance of self-reliance when everything else in the programme, particularly supervision and institutional support, seems to be falling apart.

Finally, PhD students also noted the importance of being financially secure. For many, having a permanent job contract is a necessary means of financing their parallel academic endeavours, making a stable income a prerequisite for success. Furthermore, they pointed out that one simple method to avoid unpleasant surprises related to academic bureaucracy is to carefully read the regulations that are in effect.

Conclusions and Implications

According to our participants' narratives, pursuing a PhD online is just as daunting as it is transformative. Most students perceived significant changes in various domains, including shifts in worldview, self-value, and skill development. The most prominent self-reported effect, however, had to do with the discovery and growth of their own voices. Drawing on their experiences, participants engaged in a retrospective revision of the doctoral journey and offered advice emphasising the significance of having a varied support network, cultivating internal strengths like passion and grit, and being financially secured.

Non-traditional doctoral students face unique challenges related to distance, being mature-aged, coming from diverse cultural backgrounds, combining academic life with personal and professional duties, and navigating unexpected life circumstances. Nevertheless, they are valuable assets bringing a wealth of professional skills and outsider perspectives to doctoral programmes and universities. For this reason, both programme administrators and faculty must take into account online doctoral candidates' unique challenges in the design and development of online PhD programmes. As has been shown, promoting the integration and success of online doctoral students can result in significant transformative effects on their personal and professional trajectories. Furthermore, future online doctoral students can derive valuable insights from this ongoing line of research, especially in terms of adjusting their expectations of what undertaking such an endeavour entails. It is important to note that pursuing an online doctoral degree while managing an already complex adult life can result in blurred boundaries between studying and personal life, and can lead to personal strain.

The subjective, first-hand experiences of non-traditional doctoral candidates pursuing distance research doctorates are an underexplored topic. Therefore, future research must aim to deepen our understanding of the experiential changes and identity transformations brought about by the online PhD, with a focus on how gender, age, and cultural background influence these changes.

References

Bhabha, H. K. (1994). *The location of culture*. Routledge.

Baltes, B., & Brown, M. (2018*). Impact of additional early feedback on doctoral capstone proposal approval. International Journal of Online Graduate Education, 1*(2), 2–11. https://ijoge.org/index.php/IJOGE/article/view/21

Boone, A., Vander Elst, T., Vandenbroeck, S., & Godderis, L. (2022). *Burnout profiles among young researchers: A latent profile analysis. Frontiers in Psychology, 13*, 839728. https://doi.org/10.3389/fpsyg.2022.839728

Braun, V., & Clarke, V. (2006). Using thematic analysis in psychology. *Qualitative Research in Psychology, 3*(2), 77–101. https://doi.org/10.1191/1478088706qp063oa

Clarke, V., & Braun, V. (2021). *Thematic analysis: a practical guide*. Sage Publications.

Lee, K. (2022a). Introducing 16 doctoral autoethnographers in an online PhD programme. *Studies in Technology Enhanced Learning, 2*(3), 329–338. https://doi.org/10.21428/8c225f6e.6757685c

Lee, K. (2022b). Online doctoral education: A synthesis of literature. In *Handbook of open, distance and digital education* (pp. 1–21). Springer Nature Singapore. https://doi.org/10.1007/978-981-19-0351-9_66-1

Marston, D., Gopaul, M., & Kenney, J. (2019). Issues to consider for online doctoral candidates utilizing meta-analysis for dissertations. *International Journal of Online Graduate Education,* 2(1), 2–16. http://ijoge.org/index.php/IJOGE/article/download/30/10

Melián, E., Reyes, J. I., & Meneses, J. (2023). The online PhD experience: A qualitative systematic review. *The International Review of Research in Open and Distributed Learning, 24*(1), 137–158. https://doi.org/10.19173/irrodl.v24i1.6780

Naumann, S., Matyjek, M., Bögl, K., & Dziobek, I. (2022). Doctoral researchers' mental health and PhD training satisfaction during the german COVID-19 lockdown: Results from an international research sample. *Scientific Reports, 12,* 22176. https://doi.org/10.1038/s41598-022-26601-4

Nygaard, L. P. & Savva, M. (2021). Belonging and becoming in academia: A conceptual framework. In M. Savva & L. P. Nygaard (Eds.), *Becoming a scholar. Cross-cultural reflections on identity and agency in an education doctorate* (pp. 10–26). UCL Press. https://doi.org/10.14324/111.9781787357662

Open University of Catalonia. (2018). *Autoinforme para la acreditación. Doctorado de Educación y TIC (E-learning).* https://www.uoc.edu/portal/_resources/CA/documents/qualitat/qualitat-titulacions/escola-doctorat/Autoinforme_EducacioTIC_ES.pdf

Savva, M., & Nygaard, L. P. (2021). The 'peripheral' student in academia: An analysis. In M. Savva & L. P. Nygaard (Eds.), *Becoming a scholar. Cross-cultural reflections on identity and agency in an education doctorate* (pp. 154–171). UCL Press. https://doi.org/10.14324/111.9781787357662

Seyri, H., & Rezaee, A. A. (2022). PhD students' identity construction in face-to-face and online contexts. *Research in Post-Compulsory Education, 27*(1), 48–65. https://doi.org/10.1080/13596748.2021.2011507

Stanley, P. (2015). Writing the PhD journey(s): An autoethnography of zine-writing, angst, embodiment, and backpacker travels. *Journal of Contemporary Ethnography, 44*(2), 143–168. https://doi.org/10.1177/0891241614528708

Tröster, C., & Van Quaquebeke, N. (2021). When victims help their abusive supervisors: The role of LMX, self-blame, and guilt. *Academy of Management Journal, 64*(6), 1793–1815. https://doi.org/10.5465/amj.2019.0559

Xavier, M., & Meneses, J. (2021). The tensions between student dropout and flexibility in learning design: The voices of professors in open online higher education. *The International Review of Research in Open and Distributed Learning, 22*(4), 72–88. https://doi.org/10.19173/irrodl.v23i1.5652

Yin, R. (2002). *Case study research. Design and Methods.* (3rd ed.). SAGE.

FUTURE PROSPECTS OF ARTIFICIAL INTELLIGENCE IN EDUCATION: A PRELIMINARY ANALYSIS OF EDUCATOR PERSPECTIVES FROM FOCUS GROUPS IN JAPAN, SPAIN, AND GERMANY

John Y. H. Bai, Carl von Ossietzky University of Oldenburg, Germany

Victoria I. Marín, Universitat de Lleida, Spain

Insung Jung, International Christian University, Japan (Retired)

Olaf Zawacki-Richter, Carl von Ossietzky University of Oldenburg, Germany

Correspondence: *John Y. H. Bai: john.yihao.bai@uni-oldenburg.de*

Abstract

Artificial intelligence in education (AIEd) is a growing field of research that has the potential to transform learning and teaching practices. The process of developing ethical AIEd applications that are fit-for-purpose requires ongoing multi-stakeholder dialogues that include students and teachers. The present study sought to explore the perspectives of teachers in higher education on the possible futures of AIEd. Using qualitative methods, we conducted focus-group discussions in three countries (Japan, Spain, and Germany) with educators working in the social sciences. We presented participants with four scenarios that each described the implementation of a hypothetical AIEd application. A descriptive thematic analysis of the focus-group transcripts identified two key themes regarding possible future AIEd applications: 1) concerns about the validity of input variables and the accuracy of output variables, and 2) the importance of students having an active role in the integration of AI in education. These contributions highlight the importance of including teachers and students in multi-stakeholder discussions to shape the future of education.

Keywords:

artificial intelligence in education, higher education, teachers, students, focus groups, thematic analysis

Introduction

The recent discourse on ChatGPT (e.g., Bai et al., in press; Kasneci et al., 2023; Rudolph et al., 2023) and an increasing rate of research on artificial intelligence in education (AIEd; see Zawacki-Richter et al., 2019, for review) demonstrate a growing interest in the potential for AI to transform teaching and learning (Tuomi, 2018). However, the prohibitive costs to developing cutting-edge AI tools, combined with resource disparities between stakeholders, can result in AI applications that further entrench existing inequalities (see Bender et al., 2021; Facer & Selwyn, 2021; Hu et al., 2019, for critical discussions). In response, efforts to develop policy for ethical AI have identified multi-stakeholder dialogue as one method to mitigate the risk of exacerbating societal inequities (e.g., IEEE, 2018; OECD, 2022; UNESCO, 2021).

The present project aims to contribute to this multi-stakeholder dialogue by responding to Zawacki-Richter et al.'s (2019) call "for educational perspectives on these technological developments" (p. 22). We invited educators from multiple countries to a series of online focus groups to share their views on four scenarios that each describe the implementation of a hypothetical AIEd application. These scenarios correspond to four areas of AIEd research identified in Zawacki-Richter et al.'s review and were designed to capture possible outcomes of some key macro and meso variables (see Bai et al., 2022, for discussion of how scenarios were developed). While data collection for the overall project is still ongoing, the present paper takes the opportunity to explore educator perspectives from a subset of the data from educators working in the social sciences in Japan, Spain, and Germany.

Methods

We conducted a qualitative, focus-group study using scenarios or "vignettes" as the basis for discussions. As noted by Kitzinger (1995, p. 300), the focus group is "a method that facilitates the expression of criticism and the exploration of different types of solutions"; this makes focus groups well-suited for gathering perspectives on the potential benefits and challenges of AIEd applications. Using the scenarios enabled us to present potential future outcomes of AIEd in concrete terms and allowed participants to highlight the variables that they found most important. One potential disadvantage of our design is that particular details in the scenario descriptions may unduly influence participant responses and constrain the scope of the discussions. However, the use of focus groups generally allows participants more control over the direction of the discussions compared with individual interviews (Morgan, 1997).

Ethics approval for the study was granted by the University of Oldenburg and University of Lleida Ethics Committees. The development of Participant Information Sheets and Consent Forms was guided by Tolich's (2009) discussion on focus-group ethics.

Participants

The present paper analyses data from 15 educators working in social-science subjects in Japan (five participants), Spain (seven participants), and Germany (three participants). Fourteen participants completed an optional post-discussion questionnaire. The participants were diverse in terms of gender (nine identified as female and five as male), age (three between 30-39, five between 40-49, three between 50-59, and three between 60-69), and experience, with the number of years working in higher education ranging from 3-30 years (*M* = 16.71, *SD* = 9.30) and roles ranging from Research Assistant to Professor. Two participants indicated direct experience working with AIEd applications in the questionnaire, and others indicated familiarity with various AI applications and techniques in the discussions.

Materials

During each focus group, we presented participants with four scenarios that each describe the implementation of a hypothetical AIEd application. These scenarios were developed to capture some possible outcomes of key variables and correspond to four areas of AIEd applications identified in Zawacki-Richter et al.'s (2019) review. The full texts of the scenarios are presented in Table 1.

Table 1: Text of four hypothetical scenarios used in the focus groups

Scenario	Text (in English)
S1. Profiling and prediction	A prediction system is implemented in your institution to predict students' performance and their risk of dropout. The system collects a range of data from each student (for example, assignment grades, attendance, and interactions with the institution's online systems) to calculate the probability of the student achieving a particular grade in each of their courses. Teachers can view the tracked data and the system's predictions via a dashboard on the institution's virtual platforms. In addition, when a student is classified as "at risk", the system sends student support a notification and a personalized list of suggested interventions. The support staff make the final decision about which intervention to implement. The system was developed by a joint collaboration between academic researchers and a private company. It is provided to your institution for a reduced subscription cost in exchange for pseudonymized student data that the company uses to improve the system's performance.
S2. Assessment and evaluation	An automated essay scoring system is implemented in an introductory course in your field. The system is recommended for courses with large classes and is trained with a subset of essays that are hand marked by teachers. These hand-marked essays can be randomly sampled from the submitted essays or reused from a previous year. The system then analyses the remaining unmarked essays and automatically assigns a grade to each essay, along with a confidence rating. Essays marked low confidence are flagged for teachers to review. The system was developed by a private company. It is provided to your institution for a reduced subscription cost in exchange for pseudonymized student essays that the company uses to improve the system's performance.

S3. Adaptive systems and personalisation	As part of a pilot study, a multi-function learning management platform is implemented in your institution. The system collects a range of data from each student (for example, assignment grades, interactions with the institution's online and learning systems, and use of campus facilities) to monitor their performance and development and make recommendations for personalized learning paths, student support services, and future courses. Teachers can monitor students' progress via a dashboard and override the system's recommendations if they disagree. At the end of each semester, teachers and developers conduct a review of the system's performance and adjust the system's settings in a quasi-experimental design. In addition, students may opt-out and withdraw their data at any point. The system is being developed by a joint collaboration between academic researchers and a private company. During its development, the system is provided to your institution free of charge in exchange for pseudonymized student data that the company uses to improve the system's performance.
S4. Intelligent tutoring system	An intelligent tutoring system is implemented in an introductory (first-year) course in your field. The system includes a range of inbuilt learning tasks that cover basic and advanced concepts. The system analyses student performance on each task (for example, time taken to complete task, types of errors made, and performance in similar tasks) to give personalized feedback and decide on the next appropriate task. The system sends teachers a notification if the student is stuck or struggling with a particular task or concept. The system was developed by a university research group, and trained with data collected from the researchers' institution. It is provided to your institution free of charge as open-source software (i.e., an Open Educational Resource) and no student data is sent outside of your institution to improve the system's performance.

Procedure

Focus groups started with a brief introduction, the collection of informed consent, and two warm-up questions. Participants were then presented with the scenarios and asked to share their perspectives on the possible benefits and challenges of each AIEd application, and what they would change if they were involved in implementing such a system. The scenarios served as the basis for discussion and participants were free to deviate and discuss aspects of AIEd that they found most important. We then invited participants to share their general thoughts on AIEd and, after the focus group, to complete a brief questionnaire to provide basic demographic information.

All focus-group discussions were conducted online and lasted between 80 and 120 min. The focus group in Spain was conducted in Spanish and the focus groups in Japan and Germany were conducted in English. All discussions were recorded and transcribed using arbitrary labels to de-identify participants. The discussion in Japan was transcribed by hand. The other discussions were first transcribed by speech-to-text models (Microsoft Teams in Spain, vosk-model-en-us-0.22[1] in Germany) and then checked and corrected manually; the Spanish transcript was then translated to English by the second author. As the present analysis focuses on what participants said, rather than how they said it, the extracts below were lightly cleaned to correct grammar and remove false starts and non-semantic sounds (e.g., "um", "ah").

Data analysis

We used thematic analysis (Braun & Clarke, 2013) as it allowed us flexibility in identifying and interpreting patterns from the transcripts. As we wanted to focus on what the participants found most important (i.e., what elements they chose to highlight during the discussions), we chose a descriptive approach that allowed for disjuncture between the questions posed to the participants and the themes identified from the transcripts (Braun & Clarke, 2006).

Results

The focus-group discussions generated rich data and covered a range of different issues. In the present paper, we limit ourselves to exploring two of the central themes identified in the data: 1) input and output variables in the hypothetical AIEd applications, and 2) student agency. Participant contributions are identified below by country (NH, ES, and DE for Japan, Spain, and Germany, respectively), participant (n), and scenario (S1-4; see Table 1).

---

[1] See https://alphacephei.com/vosk/models

Inputs and Outputs

Participants expressed concern about the validity of input variables used in the AI systems and the possible effects of confounding variables. The following contribution succinctly captures the question of whether the input variables can accurately measure constructs that are pedagogically meaningful:

> ES6-S4: What I still find a little bit creaky, and hence my scepticism about artificial intelligence, is the variables that we use, right? The time it takes to complete a task: how can you assess whether the student has been devoting all their time to completing the task or whether they have gone for a coffee and then come back?

In addition to concerns about the variables used as inputs, participants also expressed concern that other relevant variables would be overlooked. For example, the following contribution contrasted human and AI decision making, and specifically their ability to seek and integrate contextual information:

> NH1-S1: I mean the AI won't care that the person had COVID or whatever, but I would care, and I said "OK now I'll give you something else to make up that". So you can't really just leave it up to the AI because the AI is not going to find out what was wrong, why the student missed those assignments or didn't come to class and things like that.

Another participant further problematised the issue of validity by critiquing the use of historical data to predict outcomes in a dynamic environment:

> DE1-S3: I would be sceptical about the output of it. Like, it is influenced from past data and maybe students reacted like to... kind of a labour market that is different than the next year and it recommends maybe things that are not as relevant anymore.

The response above also raises questions about the accuracy and value of the output of AI systems, a point developed further in the following:

> DE2-S4: The question is how do you interpret it? And how do you put meaning into it? And I have huge doubts if you get something meaningful from the system, or if it's reduced to "well he didn't work today". And then how do you actually draw conclusions, and what do you do with that?

In exploring how the outputs of AI could be used, and misused, participants expressed concern about the effects on their teaching practices. For examples:

> ES6-S2: We have to be careful, also, with the amount of information that can come to us. We can be overloaded by this information.

> NH4-S1: I also find it problematic in the sense that these data may kind of relax advisors [who] have less interaction with students and too much dependency on data and give some bias for decision making on the university side.

Student Agency

Participants also expressed concern about how the AI systems might affect students and argued that students should have a more active role in the future of AIEd. This theme encompasses the issues of informed consent and how students control whether their data are used to train and fine-tune AI systems:

> ES2-S1: I am concerned that the idea of... well, is there informed consent on the part of the student body? Are they just passive actors who are subjected to this technological intervention or are they somehow counted on? Can I, as an individual agent, decide to say "no", that my data will not be collected?

Other participants echoed this sentiment and questioned whether it was possible for students to withdraw their consent:

DE3-S3: If the student... chooses to opt out at a certain point, but his data is already gone to the company in this anonymised [form], there's no way of getting it back and opting out of being a part of the product development, even though it's anonymised.

Furthermore, another participant argued that some AIEd applications may lead students to feel implicitly coerced to provide private, personal data:

DE1-S4: I thought about how... how maybe vulnerable it makes students, because when such a system is in place, they would maybe feel coerced to disclose personal information to me, about why they are not performing well. They should not be encouraged to tell me, for example, that they struggle with something, that they have kids, maybe they don't want to disclose, but struggle because of that and it's their right and their privacy not to tell me. They don't have to give up that information, and I would hate if such a system, makes them think they have to explain to me why they're not performing.

In addition to concerns about data privacy and informed consent, participants also expressed concern that the use of AIEd applications could result in unintended, negative effects on student behaviour. This was especially salient in the discussions of Scenario 1 (profiling and prediction):

NH1-S1: The disadvantage of that is that it would actually make students focus on outcome rather than doing the work to reach the goal.

DE3-S1: It runs the risk of becoming a self-fulfilling prophecy because students [...] maybe they didn't feel like they were at risk of failing the class because they learn in a different pace, or whatever, and because an AI tells them "You're at risk of failing" they might fail or, might see it as an actual prediction.

Part of this concern relates to a broader issue of how AI-informed decisions may influence or constrain a student's pedagogical journey. For example:

NH3-S3: It may hinder the creativity, you know, some other interests may arise or by having conversation with students, great ideas might pop up. But by having substantive information that suggests future courses and learning path that may confine the creative mind of students as well as you know us as a mentor of that process.

Similarly, other participants highlighted the inherent variation between different students and argued that AIEd applications designed to optimize student performance may only be tailored for students who "follow the model path" (NH4). This sentiment is further articulated by:

DE2-S4: It always boils down for me to having this kind of optimal student picture, and again there's so many premises that we put into it and how should a student of today be? [...] I have seen quite a couple of students who basically failed a semester, but then woke up and realized "okay I've now done this part of my life experience and now I can really sit down [...] and do my studies" and get really, really good marks, and this is all kind of equalled out in such a system because it's simply this kind of Bilderbuch, idealized student who, from the first day just learns hard.

In contrast to the concerns raised above, participants were more positive when considering possibilities for students to be active participants in the scenarios. This included the potential for students to use the AIEd applications as self-monitoring tools or aids to making their own decisions. For examples:

DE3-S1: One of the options could be that students would have to opt in to use it, so that the students who feel "I need someone to track my progress, or I need that extra little bit of help, or the push in the right direction if I'm close to failing the class", they can opt into using it.

ES4-S3: In terms of scenarios, it [S3, adaptive systems and personalisation] seems to me to be the model that is the most respectful, above all with the issue of the students' agency, right? And well, I would just like to emphasise that, of course, this type of situation makes sense insofar as it can complement or help students' decision-making.

Discussion

Across focus groups conducted in three countries, educators working in the social sciences articulated rich and nuanced views on possible applications of AI in education. Two of the major themes in the discussions can be summarised as: 1) concerns about the validity of variables that are fed into AI systems and the accuracy of information produced by AI, and 2) the importance of students taking an active role in deciding how they interface with, and provide data to, the AI systems. Together, these themes highlight the importance of engaging students and teachers in participatory AI research (Prabhakaran et al., 2022) and multi-stakeholder discussions during the design, development, and implementation of AI technologies (Bai et al., 2022, in press).

While the two themes explored in the present paper highlight educator concerns about AIEd, it would be misleading to portray their perspectives as overall negative towards AIEd. Indeed, participants frequently expressed enthusiastic and nuanced views on the benefits and affordances of the AIEd applications, including the hope that AIEd applications can be used to ensure fairer assessment, encourage individualised learning pathways, and provide better access to support systems. These and other themes will be explored further once data collection for the project is completed.

While the present analysis takes a descriptive approach to foreground the perspectives of our participants, future analyses of the completed dataset can adopt a more theoretically informed approach (Braun & Clarke, 2006, 2013) to explore directly how educators perceive the variables that informed the scenarios (Bai et al., 2022, in press). Even within the limited data reported here, the discussions have made contact with issues such as AI ethics (see e.g., du Boulay, 2022), accountability (e.g., Porayska-Pomsta & Rajendran, 2019), automation bias (e.g., Skitka et al., 2000), and construct validity (e.g., Perelman, 2020). However, more data are required to represent accurately the diversity of educator perspectives. Therefore, the present project is gathering more data from educators working in other subjects (e.g., Science, Technology, Engineering, and Mathematics) and in three additional countries (Turkey, Korea, and the USA).

As we argued previously, "the activities involved in shaping the future are collective and require an ongoing exchange of ideas" (Bai et al., 2022, p. 63). To further these collective efforts, we provide the full text of the scenario descriptions in Table 1 and invite interested readers to use and/or modify these scenarios for their own research. We hope that these and future discussions with students and teachers will contribute to ongoing multi-stakeholder dialogues and help to shape a more-inclusive future.

Authors' note: This project is funded by the Volkswagen Foundation and the Ministry of Science and Culture in Lower Saxony (2N3743). We thank Cengiz Hakan Aydin, Aras Bozkurt, Junhong Xiao, and Patricia Slagter van Tryon for their active collaboration and contributions to the scenarios in Table 1. We also thank Andrea Broens for insightful discussions on qualitative research, and Wolfgang Müskens and Sreekari Vogeti for valuable feedback on previous versions of this paper.

References

Bai, J. Y. H., Zawacki-Richter, O., & Müskens, W. (2022). Developing strategic scenarios for artificial intelligence applications in higher education. In *5th International Open and Distance Learning Conference Proceedings Book* (pp. 47-70). Eskişehir, Turkey. https://iodl.anadolu.edu.tr/proceedings-iodl-2022

Bai, J. Y. H., Zawacki-Richter, O., & Müskens, W. (in press). Re-examining the future prospects of artificial intelligence in education (AIEd) in light of the GDPR and ChatGPT. *Turkish Online Journal of Distance Education*.

Bender, E. M., Gebru, T., McMillan-Major, A., & Shmitchell, S. (2021). On the dangers of stochastic parrots: Can language models be too big?. In *Proceedings of the 2021 ACM Conference on Fairness, Accountability, and Transparency* (pp. 610-623). https://doi.org/10.1145/3442188.3445922

Braun, V., & Clarke, V. (2006). Using thematic analysis in psychology. *Qualitative Research in Psychology*, *3*, 77-101. https://doi.org/10.1191/1478088706qp063oa

Braun, V., & Clarke, V. (2013). *Successful qualitative research: A practical guide for beginners.* SAGE Publications.

du Boulay, B. (2022). Artificial Intelligence in Education and Ethics. In O. Zawacki-Richter & I. Jung (Eds.), *Handbook of Open, Distance and Digital Education.* Springer Nature Singapore. https://doi.org/10.1007/978-981-19-0351-9_6-1

Facer, K., & Selwyn, N. (2021). *Digital technology and the futures of education: Towards 'Non-Stupid' optimism.* Paper commissioned for the UNESCO Futures of Education report. https://unesdoc.unesco.org/ark:/48223/pf0000377071.locale=en

Hu, X., Neupane, B., Echaiz, L. F., Sibal, P., & Rivera Lam, M. (2019). *Steering AI and advanced ICTs for knowledge societies: A Rights, Openness, Access, and Multi-stakeholder Perspective.* UNESCO Publishing. https://unesdoc.unesco.org/ark:/48223/pf0000372132

IEEE. (2019). *Ethically Aligned Design: A Vision for Prioritizing Human Well-being with Autonomous and Intelligent Systems* (1st Ed.). The IEEE Global Initiative on Ethics of Autonomous and Intelligent Systems. https://standards.ieee.org/content/ieeestandards/en/industry-connections/ec/autonomous-systems.html

Kasneci, E., Sessler, K., Kuchemann, S., Bannert, M., Dementieva, D., Fishcher, F., ... & Kasneci, G. (2023). *ChatGPT for Good? On Opportunities and Challenges of Large Language Models for Education.* edArXiv preprint. https://doi.org/10.35542/osf.io/5er8f

Kitzinger, J. (1995) Qualitative Research: Introducing focus groups. *British Medical Journal, 311,* 299-302. https://doi.org/10.1136/bmj.311.7000.299

Morgan, D. L. (1997). *Focus Groups as Qualitative Research* (2nd ed.). SAGE Publications. https://doi.org/10.4135/9781412984287

OECD. (2022). *Recommendation of the Council on Artificial Intelligence.* OECD/LEGAL/0449. https://legalinstruments.oecd.org/en/instruments/OECD-LEGAL-0449

Prabhakaran, V., Mitchell, M., Gebru, T., & Gabriel, I. (2022). *A human rights-based approach to responsible AI.* arXiv preprint. https://doi.org/10.48550/arXiv.2210.02667

Perelman, L. (2020). The BABEL generator and e-Rater: 21st Century writing constructs and automated essay scoring (AES). *Journal of Writing Assessment, 13.* https://escholarship.org/uc/item/263565cq

Porayska-Pomsta, K., & Rajendran, G. (2019). Accountability in human and artificial intelligence decision-making as the basis for diversity and educational inclusion. In J. Knox, Y. Wang, & M. Gallagher (Eds.), *Artificial Intelligence and Inclusive Education. Perspectives on Rethinking and Reforming Education.* Springer. https://doi.org/10.1007/978-981-13-8161-4_3

Rudolph, J., Tan, S., & Tan, S. (2023). ChatGPT: Bullshit spewer or the end of traditional assessments in higher education?. *Journal of Applied Learning and Teaching, 6.* https://doi.org/10.37074/jalt.2023.6.1.9

Skitka, L. J., Mosier, K., & Burdick, M. D. (2000). Accountability and automation bias. *International Journal of Human-Computer Studies, 52,* 701-717. https://doi.org/10.1006/ijhc.1999.0349

Tolich, M. (2009). The principle of caveat emptor: Confidentiality and informed consent as endemic ethical dilemmas in focus group research. *Journal of Bioethical Inquiry, 6,* 99-108. https://doi.org/10.1007/s11673-008-9124-3

Tuomi, I. (2018). *The impact of artificial intelligence on learning, teaching, and education.* European Commission, Joint Research Centre. https://doi.org/10.2760/12297

UNESCO. (2021). *Recommendation on the ethics of artificial intelligence.* United Nations Educational, Scientific and Cultural Organization. https://unesdoc.unesco.org/ark:/48223/pf0000381137

Zawacki-Richter, O., Marín, V. I., Bond, M., & Gouverneur, F. (2019). Systematic review of research on artificial intelligence applications in higher education–where are the educators? *International Journal of Educational Technology in Higher Education, 16,* 1-27. https://doi.org/10.1186/s41239-019-0171-0

YES WE CAN (BUT MAYBE NOT YET): THE IMPACT OF DATA POVERTY ON REALISING THE POTENTIAL OF LEARNING ANALYTICS

Paul Prinsloo, University of South Africa, South Africa

Sharon Slade, Independent Researcher, United Kingdom

Mohammad Khalil, University of Bergen, Norway

***Correspondence**: Sharon Slade: sharon.slade@outlook.com*

Abstract

Learning analytics (LA), as research and practice, has been committed to contributing to understanding students' learning and the contexts in which their learning occurs since its emergence in 2011. Core to learning analytics is the measurement, collection, analysis and use of student data. As higher education becomes increasingly digitised and datafied, institutions have access to not only more data, but also a variety, velocity and granularity of data. However, there is also increasing evidence of data poverty - referring not only to students' unable to afford data, but also institutions without, inter alia, the data infrastructure and analytical skills to realise the potential of LA. In both cases, the fiduciary duty of higher education institutions to provide enabling and supportive learning environments are severely compromised. In this conceptual paper, we provide an introduction to the notion of data poverty as it relates to both students and institutions before mapping key dimensions of student data poverty and their implications for LA. We also discuss institutional data poverty before concluding with a number of pointers to move from 'not yet' to 'yes we can' in providing evidence-led teaching and student support.

Keywords:

Data poverty; Higher education; Learning analytics; student success.

Introduction

Learning analytics (LA) as research focus and practice has promised to impact positively on the quality of teaching and learning. This impact depends on access to students' digital data (amount and quality), by how student learning is understood, and the quality of any subsequent analysis and interpretation (Prinsloo, Slade & Khalil, 2021; Tsai et al. 2020).

What is often less considered are disparities in students' access to sustainable and affordable connectivity, and the impact of this on both the quality and scope of data provided and subsequently on data analyses and institutional responses. Students may become 'invisible' and be disenfranchised, excluded from resource allocation and pedagogical strategies.

In this conceptual paper, we first consider the notion of student 'data poverty' and its impact on effective, appropriate and ethical LA and more generally, on student support and success. In the second half of the paper we consider institutional data poverty and its impact on LA implementation.

Background

To speak of data poverty amid claims of a data revolution (Kitchin, 2014), of how data "is colonising human life" (Couldry & Mejias, 2019), in which "surveillance capitalism" (Zuboff, 2019) celebrates the commercial value of data abundance, and where we all have become our data (Cheney-Lippold, 2017), seems out of place. Despite an apparent abundance of data, some authors point to digital inequalities and a 'big data divide', referring to "those who have access and ownership to large-scale distributed datasets and those that do not" (McCarthy (2016, p. 1132). As such, the data divide raises concerns about students whose right to autonomy and self-realisation is affected due to user profiles created as a result of criteria and data over which they have no control. (Also see Cheney-Lippold, 2017).

Notions of 'data poor' and 'data poverty' (the sociomaterial effects of being data poor) are more often associated with educational contexts in the Global South (Heeks, 2022; McCarthy, 2016). However, the recent pandemic illustrated that data poverty is a global problem (Budnitz & Tranos, 2022). Many individuals, social groups and communities live off the digital grid, as a result of geographic location, low income or other factors (Graham, 2002). Such individuals may be unable "to get a data contract" (Lucas, Robinson & Treacy, 2020), seriously hampering their access to the affordances of connected services and opportunities in a networked society (Palmer, 2020). In such circumstances, they may also become invisible (Also see Hayes, 2021; Hayes, Connor, Johnson & Jopling, 2022; Palmer, 2016). Such invisibility "affects vulnerable populations within a variety of geopolitical and socio-political contexts, whereby data poverty constitutes a dangerous form of invisibility which perpetuates various forms of inequality" (Milan & Treré, 2020, p. 2).

As well as this, there is evidence that many educational institutions, particularly in (but not limited to) the Global South (Prinsloo & Kaliisa, 2022), do not have the digital infrastructure or capacity to measure, collect and analyse student data. Whilst higher education is increasingly digitised and datafied (Selwyn & Gasevic, 2020), much student and institutional operational data remains in analogue form and is not readily available for analysis. The notion of institutional data poverty can also include institutions who are data rich but are information or analysis poor (Spiker, 2014; Stichter, 2021).

(Student) Data poverty

The importance of access to student digital data for learning analytics is clear. The geopolitical and institutional contexts in which learning analytics have largely been implemented (e.g.,the United States, Europe and Australia) are broadly known for almost universal internet coverage, though coverage does not necessarily equate to access.

For Lucas et al. (2020) data poverty refers to "those individuals, households or communities who cannot afford sufficient, private and secure mobile or broadband data to meet their essential needs" (p. 16). They also state that "Going online is more costly for those who lack digital literacy" (Lucas et al. 2020, p. 9) and "the greater someone's need for data, the greater the impact reduced access has on their life" (p. 14).

Of particular interest here are Lucas et al's (2020) seven dimensions of data poverty, namely affordability; choice; infrastructure; privacy and security; quantity; skills; and usability (Table 1 below).

Table 1. Dimensions of data poverty (adopted from Lucas et al., 2020)

Dimension	Attributes
Affordability	Cannot afford to buy data without cutting spending on basic needs such as accommodation, food, etc.
Choice	Lack of access to open market of data services (e.g., barriers to preferential rates offered via contracts)
Infrastructure	Lack of coverage by sufficiently reliable and fast broadband or mobile infrastructure at an affordable price
Privacy and security	Lack of private internet access – it is accessible only via a shared device or public connection.
Quantity	Lack of access to an appropriate amount of data to meet an individual's essential needs for information (e.g., health, financial, safety, democratic), services (e.g. education), support (e.g., welfare benefits) and social needs (e.g. connection with family, friends and community)
Skills	Lack of digital skills sufficient to access affordable data or understand their data needs.
Usability	Presence of additional usability needs (including language and communication needs, disabilities, and long-term conditions) which demand greater bandwidth and online support.

It is easy to see how these dimensions of data poverty can be applied to students. While affordability of data and its impact on student learning is well-documented (e.g. Mirata, Hirt, Bergamin & van der Westhuizen, 2020), skills

(Ben Youssef, Dhamani & Ragni, 2022); privacy and security concerns (e.g. Prinsloo, Slade & Khalil, 2022); and issues pertaining to choice, infrastructure, quantity and usability are less-researched.

Lucas et al.'s (2020) data poverty dimensions intersect with issues around gender; race; (dis)ability; culture; and socio-economic, political, legal, and technological forces. As a result, students' data poverty which leads to (relative) invisibility may exacerbate inequalities.

Institutional data poverty

Along parallel lines, 'data rich' or 'data poor' institutions are those entities with access to more or less data than others. Companies such as Amazon or Google demonstrate that "Data is more powerful in the presence of other data" (Palmer, 2016, para 3). Palmer (2016) grounded this concept of data richness around time and resources spent "creating centers of excellence around data governance" (para.5) where data governance relates to, e.g., data availability, accessibility, and usability and analytics (Hussain et al., 2018).

Within higher education institutions (HEIs), although student data is plentiful, it is often distributed across departments and in a variety of formats, e.g., data from learning management systems, admission and library systems, creating significant challenges for data collection. Access to student data has also been brought into sharp focus by legislation such as the GDPR, resulting in data access on a need to know basis, as well as many other issues relating to privacy and data security.

To date, few HEIs have the necessary infrastructure to initiate effective data warehouses and to facilitate initiatives in learning analytics (Ferguson et al., 2016; Cechinel et al., 2020), posing barriers to both processing and analysing data at a larger scale. According to Macfadyen et al (2014), HEIs may lack a data-driven mindset, and this lack of available data impacts on LA implementation. As a result, they state that "It may not be surprising, then, that globally, education lags behind all other sectors in harnessing the power of analytics" Macfadyen et al, 2014, p.22).

Student data and institutional capacity can make a difference

Although LA research has been flourishing since 2011, implementation has lagged. In their review of LA in 84 higher education educations in Europe, Tsai et al. (2020), note that implementation is "primarily at small scales and few institutions had a dedicated strategy, policy, or evaluation framework". This echoes the findings of Khalil et al. (2022) who found that implementation remains relatively low and that evidence of impact is also often lacking.

Having said that, there are a number of examples of embedded implementation. The Open University (OU) in the UK has considerable experience in both research and in the application of learning analytics. In 2014, it introduced the world's first policy for the use of student data in learning analytics (Slade and Boroowa, 2014). Since then the OU has moved from small-scale experimentation to large-scale adoption of LA throughout all of its modules and qualifications. In their recent chapter, Boroowa & Herodotou (2022) describe some of the LA work of the OU, including the use of LA to inform the learning design of online courses and predictive learning analytics to identify students at risk. Other institutions, such as Monash University in Australia, have considerable practical expertise built on focused research. For example, its Centre for Learning Analytics has demonstrated capability in LA applications in feedback and assessment; text analytics; multimodal analytics and learning analytics adoption.

In descriptions of what has been needed for successful implementation of learning analytics, a number of recurring themes are identified:

- It is crucial to understand the *purpose* of the use of LA - what specifically is the institution trying to achieve and why? In support of this, having a policy or or adopting a framework such as SHEILA (Tsai et al., 2018) is extremely helpful. Macfadyen et al. (2014) argue that successful institutional adoption of LA requires comprehensive policies that recognise the institution as a complex adaptive system;
- Institutional leadership and management support is vital. Institutions can adopt small scale implementations, but rolling out a wholesale programme of learning analytics needs both support and sufficient human and technological capacity;

- A clear understanding of purpose should lead to clear identification of the data required. Data collection requires planning and integrated systems, as well as robust data protection policies;
- In addition, buy-in from other key stakeholders (students, faculty, support staff, etc) will make a considerable difference to the success of LA implementation. For example Prieto, Rodríguez-Triana, Martínez-Maldonado, Dimitriadis, and Gašević (2019) stress the need to reach a common understanding among stakeholders. Similarly, based on their experiences at the OU, Herodotou, Rienties, Verdin, and Boroowa (2019) recommend providing evidence (of benefits), promoting cross-stakeholder communication, allocating managerial time, and complementing teaching practice.

.In each of these cases, there is a clear message. Successful implementation takes time - LA implementation should be grounded on a clear purpose, have institutional and stakeholder support, and be able to demonstrate its effectiveness in order to become widely accepted. Fundamentally, when institutions have accessible, reliable and complete student data, they are better prepared to realise the benefits of learning analytics.

Conclusion: Moving from 'not yet' to 'yes we can'

Since 2011, LA has promised to deepen our understanding of students' learning and of the contexts in which their learning occurs. Realising this promise depends on a range of variables such as, but not limited to infrastructure, analytic expertise, and integrated and responsive systems, processes and procedures. Data - both access to it, and also its quality and formats - is obviously at the heart of effective learning analytics.

As explored in this paper, student and institutional data poverty is a reality in the context of higher education, and an important factor in realising LA's potential. Student data poverty may result, on the one hand, in invisibility and exclusion from resource allocation and support; and on the other hand, an absence from discussion forums, for example, may result in students being wrongly targeted as at-risk.

Institutions often use data proxies for student learning (e.g., online engagement, logins, and submission of assignments). There is growing awareness that such proxies should be based on research, and be useful and relevant. Whitman (2020) highlights concerns around proxies and 'data doubles', stating that "By making something called behavior and making it legible through data proxies that minimize gaps between data and what they purport to measure, the institution can track students and monitor them" (p.9) but also "The translation of data into predictions is not solely algorithmic; it is also wrapped up in structural inequalities and notions about what society is and ought to be" (p.3). As such, data poverty, in all of its dimensions, flows from, and often deepens existing structural inequalities, or creates new forms of pathogenic vulnerability.

Whilst some HEIs may remain unable to access good quality data internally, there are a number of open source datasets to train models. For example, the OU's learning analytics dataset (OULAD) includes both student demographic data and VLE interaction data (Kuzilek, Hosta & Zdenek, 2017). RapidMiner and Microsoft's Open Education Analytics are other examples of fully open-sourced data integration and analytics frameworks which can be used within the education sector. They include datasets provided by a variety of organisations and educational institutions around the world. Other approaches to obtaining a richer set of data include partnerships with similar educational institutions (see, for example, Krumm, Everson & Neisler (2022)).

As well as data sharing partnerships, educational institutions might consider pairing with other institutions. For example, the not-for-profit Consilience Education Foundation (2023) offers a Learning Analytics Collaborative for schools, forming partnerships between educational researchers, data scientists, and over 100 schools around the world, many in the Global South. In Europe, the Society for Learning Analytics Research (SoLAR) has an established Learning Analytics Community Europe group (LACE) which seeks to "serve as a meeting point for researchers working on LA in Europe, and help identify new opportunities and partnerships for further collaboration and funding" (SoLAR, 2023). It would be a positive move to see active examples of institution-to-institution mentoring to build further capacity and understanding.

Although partnerships can offer a welcome route into access to data, tools and approaches, care must be taken to ensure that shared approaches are contextually appropriate. For example, Krumm et al (2022) cite challenges arising from "misalignments between a partnership's goals and the purposes for which the data were originally collected" (p.26). In the UK, the Centre for Transforming Access and Student Outcomes in Higher Education

(TASO), an educational charity funded by the UK Government, is partnering with Nottingham Trent and Sheffield Hallam universities to evaluate the effectiveness of learning analytics interventions and any dependencies on context and design choices.

In the absence of key resources, educational institutions may opt to outsource their analytics practice. There are clearly advantages in doing this: access to skills, time savings, etc, but these should be balanced with the potential downsides of data security, loss of skills and insight etc.

Learning analytics is a maturing field, and one which thrives best in data rich environments. In realising better futures we should account for how data poverty - whether referring to students or institutions - impacts on the full potential of evidence-led teaching and student support. Evidence suggests that yes, we can - but maybe not yet.

References

Ben Youssef, A., Dahmani, M., & Ragni, L. (2022). ICT use, digital skills and students' academic performance: Exploring the digital divide. *Information*, 13(3), 129. https://doi.org/10.3390/info13030129

Boroowa, A., & Herodotou, C. (2022). Learning Analytics in Open and Distance Higher Education: The Case of the Open University UK. In *Learning Analytics in Open and Distributed Learning: Potential and Challenges*, eds: Prinsloo, P., Slade, S. & Khalil, M.,47-62. Singapore: Springer Nature.

Budnitz, H., & Tranos, E. (2022). Working from home and digital divides: resilience during the pandemic. *Annals of the American Association of Geographers*, 112(4), 893-913.

Cechinel, C., Ochoa, X., Lemos dos Santos, H., Carvalho Nunes, J. B., Rodés, V., & Marques Queiroga, E. (2020). Mapping learning analytics initiatives in Latin America. *British Journal of Educational Technology*, 51(4), 892-914.

Cheney-Lippold, J. (2017). *We are data. Algorithms and the making of our digital selves.* New York, NY: New York University Press.

Consilience Education Foundation (2023). Retrieved from https://www.consiliencelearning.org/

Couldry, N., & Mejias, U.A. (2019). *The cost of connection. How data is colonising human life and appropriating it for capitalism.* Stanford, CA: Stanford University Press.

Ferguson, R., Brasher, A., Clow, D., Cooper, A., Hillaire, G., Mittelmeier, J., & Vuorikari, R. (2016). *Research evidence on the use of learning analytics: Implications for education policy.* Joint Research Centre, Seville, Spain.

Graham, S. (2002). Bridging urban digital divides? Urban polarisation and information and communications technologies (ICTs). *Urban studies*, 39(1), 33-56.

Hayes, S. (2021). *Postdigital positionality. Developing powerful inclusive narratives for learning, teaching, research and policy in higher education.* Brill Publishing.

Hayes, S., Connor, S., Johnson, M., & Jopling, M. (2022). Connecting cross-sector community voices: Data, disadvantage, and postdigital inclusion. *Postdigital Science and Education*, 4(2), 237-246.

Herodotou, C., Rienties, B., Verdin, B., & Boroowa, A. (2019). Predictive learning analytics 'at scale': Towards guidelines to successful implementation in higher education based on the case of the Open University UK. *Journal of Learning Analytics*, 6(1), 85–95.

Heeks, R. (2022). Digital inequality beyond the digital divide: conceptualizing adverse digital incorporation in the global South. *Information Technology for Development*, 28(4), 688-704.

Hussain, S., Akif, C., Tamayo, J. D., & Safdar, A. (2018). Big data and learning analytics model. *International Journal of Computer Sciences and Engineering*, 6(7), 654-663.

Khalil, M., Prinsloo, P., & Slade, S. (2022). *A Comparison of Learning Analytics Frameworks: a Systematic Review.* Paper presented at LAK22: 12th International Learning Analytics and Knowledge Conference (pp. 152-163).

Kitchin, R. (2014). *The data revolution.* London, UK: Sage.

Krumm, A., Everson, H., & Neisler, J. (2022). A Partnership-Based Approach to Operationalizing Learning Behaviours Using Event Data. *Journal of Learning Analytics*, 9(2), 24-37. https://doi.org/10.18608/jla.2022.6751

Kuzilek, J., Hosta, M. & Zdenek, Z. (2017) Open University Learning Analytics dataset. *Scientific Data 4:170171*, Springer Nature. doi: 10.1038/sdata.2017.171.

Lucas, P.J., Robinson, R., & Treacy, L. (2020). What is data poverty? NESTA. Retrieved from https://www.nesta.org.uk/report/what-data-poverty/

Macfadyen, L. P., Dawson, S., Pardo, A., & Gaševic, D. (2014). Embracing big data in complex educational systems: The learning analytics imperative and the policy challenge. *Research & Practice in Assessment*, 9, 17–28.

McCarthy, M. (2016). The big data divide and its consequences. *Sociology Compass*, 10, 1131-1140. DOI 10.1111/soc4.12436

McCarthy, M. (2022). The big data divide and its consequences. In Carta, S. (ed), *Machine Learning and the City: Applications in Architecture and Urban Design* (pp. 547-559). London, UK: Wiley-Blackwell. DOI:10.1002/9781119815075

Milan, S., & Treré, E. (2020). <? covid19?> The Rise of the Data Poor: The COVID-19 Pandemic Seen From the Margins. *Social Media+ Society*, 6(3), 2056305120948233.

Mirata, V., Hirt, F., Bergamin, P., & van der Westhuizen, C. (2020). Challenges and contexts in establishing adaptive learning in higher education: findings from a Delphi study. *International Journal of Educational Technology in Higher Education*, 17, 1-25

Palmer, S. (2016, May 1). Rich Data, Poor Data: What the Data Rich Do – That the Data Poor and the Data Middle Class Do Not! Retrieved from https://www.shellypalmer.com/2016/05/rich-data-poor-data-data-rich-data-poor-data-middle-class-not/

Palmer, S. (2020, March 11). Can the data poor survive? Straight Talk. Retrieved from https://straighttalk.hcltech.com/blogs/can-the-data-poor-survive

Prieto, L. P., Rodríguez-Triana, M. J., Martínez-Maldonado, R., Dimitriadis, Y., & Gašević, D. (2019). Orchestrating learning analytics (OrLA): Supporting inter-stakeholder communication about adoption of learning analytics at the classroom level. *Australasian Journal of Educational Technology*, 35(4), 14–33.

Prinsloo, P., & Kaliisa, R. (2022). Learning Analytics on the African Continent: An Emerging Research Focus and Practice. *Journal of Learning Analytics*, 1-18

Prinsloo, P., Slade, S., & Khalil, M. (2021). Learning Analytics: A Primer. Commonwealth of Learning. Retrieved from http://hdl.handle.net/11599/3883

Prinsloo, P., Slade, S., & Khalil, M. (2022). The answer is (not only) technological: Considering student data privacy in learning analytics. *British Journal of Educational Technology*, 53(4), 876-893.

Selwyn, N., & Gašević, D. (2020). The datafication of higher education: Discussing the promises and problems. *Teaching in Higher Education*, 25(4), 527-540.

Slade, S., & Boroowa, A. (2014) Policy on Ethical use of Student Data for Learning Analytics. Retrieved from https://help.open.ac.uk/documents/policies/ethical-use-of-student-data/files/22/ethical-use-of-student-data-policy.pdf

SoLAR (2023) Introducing LACE. Retrieved from https://www.solaresearch.org/community/sigs/lace-sig/.

Spiker, S. (2014, November 24). Data rich, analysis poor. Retrieved from https://www.govloop.com/community/blog/data-rich-analysis-poor/

Stichter, A. (2021, June 16). Data rich and information poor. IoT World. Retrieved from https://iiot-world.com/industrial-iot/connected-industry/data-rich-and-information-poor/

Tsai, Y.-S., Moreno-Marcos, P. M., Jivet, I., Scheffel, M., Tammets, K., Kollom, K., & Gaševic, D. (2018). The SHEILA framework: Informing institutional strategies and policy processes of learning analytics. *Journal of Learning Analytics*, 5(3), 5–20.

Tsai, Y., Rates, D., Moreno-Marcos, P.M.,Muñoz-Merino, P.J., Jivet, I., Scheffel, M., Drachsler, H., Delgado Kloos, C., Gašević, D. (2020). Learning analytics in European higher education—Trends and barriers, *Computers & Education*, 155, https://doi.org/10.1016/j.compedu.2020.103933.

Whitman, M. (2020). "We called that a behavior": The making of institutional data. *Big Data & Society*, 7(1). https://doi.org/10.1177/2053951720932200

Zuboff, S. (2019). *The age of surveillance capitalism. The fight for a human future at the new frontier of power*. New York, NY: Public Affairs.

UNIVERSITIES AND THE CHALLENGE OF EMPLOYABILITY: LEVERAGING LABOR MARKET DATA FOR RELEVANT LIFELONG EDUCATION

Àngels Fitó, Universitat Oberta de Catalunya (UOC), Spain

Carmen Pagés, Universitat Oberta de Catalunya (UOC), Spain

Correspondence: Àngels Fitó:afitob@uoc.edu

Abstract

The economy and society are experiencing significant transformations fueled by the emergence of new technological advancements. These changes are affecting not just the job market, but also social norms and interactions. In light of this, universities cannot confine themselves to the mere creation and dissemination of knowledge, as education alone does not assure employment prospects. Rather, universities must strive to enhance the transformative impact of education on both individuals' employability and organizations' competitiveness. To accomplish this objective, it is essential to leverage labor market insights and artificial intelligence technology.

The Universitat Oberta de Catalunya (UOC) is an online university that serves almost 90,000 students and has over 100,000 alumni. Its primary mission is to provide lifelong learning opportunities to people. However, due to the rapidly changing job market and evolving skill requirements, the UOC is currently implementing a university-wide strategy to prioritize employability. This strategy involves three main components. Firstly, the UOC is establishing a scheme to collect, store, generate, analyze, and present labor market data in a user-friendly manner that supports informed decision-making. This scheme will also connect educational programs to learning outcomes that can be linked to labor market information. Secondly, new organizational roles are being created to ensure that labor market information is integrated into the design of course offerings and career guidance services. Lastly, an interface is being designed for students to independently evaluate their position in the labor market and make better career decisions. This strategy builds on existing employability services and creates a foundation for relevant lifelong learning.

The purpose of describing the UOC experience is to elucidate the strategy that universities should implement to enhance employability by capitalizing on the potential of artificial intelligence and big data.

Keywords:

Employability, reskilling, lifelong learning, labor market data, career advice.

Introduction

The term "employability" refers to the knowledge, skills, and abilities that graduates must possess to effectively practice the professions for which their degrees qualify them. This definition emphasizes the responsibility of universities as the providers of this skill profile in ensuring its attainment. However, job placement - which encompasses the securing, maintaining, and advancement of quality jobs by students or graduates throughout their careers - is contingent not only on employability but also on various personal, environmental, and institutional factors, including the universities they attended. Hence, while universities bear direct responsibility for promoting employability, the realization of this potential in the form of quality job placement is subject to external factors beyond their control, such as the economic climate, local economic specialization, labor market structures, or systemic issues in the education system as a whole.

The economy and society are experiencing significant changes, driven largely by new waves of technology, that are impacting not just the labor market but also social behavior and relations. The magnitude and rapid pace of these changes are contributing to the complexity and significance of employability, both in terms of supply (new training profiles) and demand (new occupations). Despite the increased demand for jobs that require a university degree, even during periods of economic downturn, the number of graduates has outstripped this demand, diminishing their chances of securing quality employment[1]. This trend is particularly pronounced in Spain, where a greater supply of skilled labor relative to demand and a productive specialization in low knowledge-intensive industries have resulted in a problem of overqualification.

Universities cannot simply limit themselves to creating and disseminating knowledge in today's social and economic landscape, which demands competent professionals. While education is undoubtedly crucial, it alone cannot guarantee employment. In the past, higher education institutions typically focused on training undergraduate students and catered to a relatively stable employment landscape. They also provided individual counseling for first employment, although scaling such personalized guidance is challenging. However, in the present work environment, characterized by multiple training stages and jobs across various industries, it is essential to equip individuals with the necessary tools to design their training and work paths and make timely decisions. As universities now train individuals beyond their first degrees and there is growing need for upskilling and reskilling, it is crucial to develop mechanisms for identifying reskilling opportunities by recognizing and creating adjacent skills.

Therefore, **higher education institutions must ensure that their graduates are prepared to manage their careers by providing: 1) relevant lifelong learning and 2) career self-management.** Accomplishing these goals, requires an updated and segmented understanding of the labor market, which can only be achieved through leveraging advanced technologies to gather and analyze big data on the labor market.

The aim of the paper is to describe the UOC strategy as an example of innovative models that universities can adopt to enhance employability. The organization of the document is as follows: Section 2 outlines conventional university approaches for enhancing employability. Section 3 presents the UOC's approach of complementing traditional approaches with an intense use of labour market data, the creation of new institutional roles, and the development of virtual professional guidance tools. Section 4 emphasizes the key takeaways, and the bibliography is provided at the end.

1. University strategies to promote employability

In addition to the intrinsic characteristics of the training offered (type of degree, specialization, learning outcomes, teaching staff, etc.), universities have developed their own particular strategies to promote greater and better employment prospects for their graduates. In this regard, career counseling centers, that used to support students and alumni in their career planning and job searches, have become dynamic networking centers. The transactional approach to career services has evolved into a 'connected communities' concept offering professionalized career development before, during and after the period of study.[2] This shift signifies an evolution towards a more proactive approach to career services.

Thus, what was once known as "career services" have become an integral educational resource that supports students during their entire training period, rather than a mere tool that students turn to when they are about to graduate or thereafter. The scope of these services and satisfaction with them is an increasingly important factor when it comes to attracting students. Consequently, these services have gone from occupying a peripheral place in strategic plans to holding a central position in many institutions.

[1] According to data from the Spanish National Statistics Institute (INE) (2017), the employment rate of university graduates is sensitive to the economic cycle, although to a lesser extent than that of those with a lower level of education. Still, according to data from the 2017 EPA (economically active population) survey, the difference in unemployment between those with the highest and lowest levels of education in Spain is 28 percentage points (for OECD countries as a whole, the difference is 7 percentage points).

[2] Dey, F., & Cruzvergara, C. Y. (2014). Evolution of career services in higher education. New directions for student services, 2014(148), 5-18.

Various studies[3] have documented the experiences and strategies employed by universities – aside from those aspects related to programme design – to promote the employability of their students and graduates. These studies highlight activities such as career coaching, mentoring programmes, awards, industry-specific programmes, complementary training, career libraries, employment observers, employer engagement activities, career fairs, simulators, and many others. When well-integrated and connected, these services can certainly impact student satisfaction and recruitment, as well as the institution's final employment outcomes.

A study from the Valencian Institute of Economic Research (IVIE) analyzes universities' actions to increase graduate employability. The study includes the analysis of 63 universities (including the UOC) that were also part of the last edition of the U-Ranking (2017). By analyzing the information available on their websites, the study calculates a synthetic index of their employability services, made up of 10 indicators:

IND1	Pre-university guidance services	Information sessions, academic orientation events, vocational training course tours, etc.
IND2	Awareness-raising	Welcome days, career service information sessions, expert talks, employability skills sessions, etc.
IND3	Information	Career opportunity web portals, newsletters, talks, etc.
IND4	Training	Competencies for professional practice, job searches, etc.
IND5	Career and vocational guidance	Coaching, mentoring, etc., services
IND6	Internships	Internships and mobility programmes
IND7	Employment	Job boards, job fairs, public employment services, recruiting, etc.
IND8	Entrepreneurship	Business incubators, self-employment advice services
IND9	Observers	Labour observers, employment studies
IND10	Career service quality certifications	ISO and EFQM quality seals

The results indicate a significant correlation between the overall indicator of employability with the U-Ranking performance indicators.

1.1. Students Perceptions

The UOC is a digital native university that operates online, with a mission to provide lifelong learning opportunities to a global audience. With over 105,000 alumni and 87,000 students, UOC students are around 30 years old and have prior education and professional experience. They often have family responsibilities and aim to balance their studies with their careers. Seeking to enhance their skills and achieve professional and personal goals, they highly value UOC's flexible schedule and self-paced modality of learning.

According to reports evaluating the UOC enrollment process, over two-thirds of students indicate that they join to increase their job opportunities, whether it be through self-employment or as employees. Among master's degree students, a recent survey conducted during the 2020/21 academic year shows that 76.5% of respondents

3 Mitchell, et al. (2015). Case studies to enhance graduate employability: Careers services. *Australian Government Office for Learning and Teaching, Sydney, Australia.*

identified employability as their primary motivation for enrolling. In the 2020/21 graduate survey, 75.5% of students stated that the UOC's training had enhanced their job skills. Additionally, a report on the UOC's reputation and brand awareness from the Marketing Area (2019) commissioned from IPSOS found that improving employability is the second most important factor for prospective students, following fees, when selecting a university. Other factors considered include faculty prestige, pedagogical model, flexibility and personalization, learning resources, research capacity, and community.

While student expectations are similar to those of other distance universities, such as UNED, UNIR, and UDIMA, the UOC's employability orientation was judged as weak in comparison to private face-to-face universities and business schools. Based on the 2019 study on alumni perceptions of the value of services offered, it can be inferred that career services are highly valued by younger students. However, the study also revealed that services related to employment (such as career guidance and job search assistance) received lower ratings compared to other services. This suggests that expectations for these services are high, but not always met.

1.2. The employability opportunity

The analysis of the current situation, factors that determine it, and the expectations of both graduates in general and UOC graduates in particular, leads to several opportunities that should be considered:

- The UOC's mission statement emphasizes employability as it aims to provide lifelong learning opportunities to individuals and advance society. Given the current context, there are increasing societal expectations for universities to contribute to their students' employability.
- The fact that the majority of UOC graduates are employed does not mean that the university can rest on its laurels, as this employment may not necessarily be of high quality (i.e. fast, well-suited, stable, and well-paid) or sustainable over the long term.
- Given the challenge of providing both lifelong learning and career self-management training, the UOC has implemented initiatives that can enhance its potential to promote employability if effectively aligned with the demands of the job market.
- The UOC has a clear professionalizing focus in its portfolio, but it requires effective tools to connect its offerings with the current labor market demands. To address this, the university needs: Surveys that are better oriented towards assessing the employability potential of its degree programs; Systematic information about the status and evolution of the labor market; A guidance service that is responsible for career counseling; and A smart and customizable career guidance system.
- Expanding and enhancing the visibility of a career service that covers students' academic and professional life can potentially serve as a marketing tool to attract new audiences. This is particularly relevant for those individuals who are concerned about the risk of losing their current job or those who aspire to improve or redirect their career path amidst the ongoing trend of professional profile replacement.
- To establish effective career services, it is essential to establish stronger ties with the industry, thereby accumulating valuable relational capital with the UOC's graduates, their employers, and other relevant companies.

2. Connecting higher education to the labour market

In response to the continuously changing job market and skill needs, as well as to the 2019 alumni study, UOC implemented a comprehensive university-wide employability strategy. This initiative includes three pivotal components: firstly, the establishment of a system for collecting, storing, producing, analyzing, and visualizing labour market data. Secondly, the creation of new organizational roles dedicated to producing labour market insights for course design and career guidance services. And thirdly, the development of a virtual platform that enables students to independently assess their position in the job market and make well informed career decisions. When fully deployed, these three components work in tandem with the existing employability services, such as career counseling, job fairs, and an online job board, to improve the overall employability services.

2.1. The data opportunity

Given the uncertain, complex, and constantly evolving labor market, universities must adopt a comprehensive approach to employability if they want education to be a means of personal and professional advancement. An updated and targeted approach is particularly crucial for lifelong learning, as learners typically have existing qualifications and work experience. Therefore, the university must identify which skills are still relevant for employment and which ones need further development to provide value.

To address this, the university must equip itself with more rigorous measurement tools capable of monitoring, locating, and segmenting new labor requirements. Additionally, the university is committed to reskilling and upskilling people, and as such, these information systems must facilitate the identification of complementary competencies that can boost employment and competitiveness. With this timely and tailored data, highly efficient and personalized lifelong learning plans can be created by combining short-term, high quality programs that integrate existing skills and develop new ones while workers are still employed. These programs, that complement traditional long degrees ones, must be certifiable through recognizable, stackable, and portable digital micro-credentials.

We contend that the establishment of a system of these characteristics relies on data. The availability of large, structured databases on the competency requirements of the labour demand, coupled with technology that enables the personalized processing of these data, opens the possibility of integrating the labour market's requirements into program portfolio structures and student and alumni employability support services.

There are a number of potential data sources that provide insights about the skills required in the labour market. One notable source is the ESCO project led by the EU, which offers a comprehensive list of the knowledge, skills and competencies that are required to perform an occupation. This list is curated by committees of occupational experts. A second source comes from market data gathered from millions of vacancies posted in online job portals. Another potential source arises from performing interviews, or surveys to individual companies and workers. Different types of data have their strengths and weaknesses. ESCO skills data is very comprehensive regarding specific skills, but relies on the input of a relatively small group of experts; market data relies on the actual skill requirements aggregated from a large number of vacancies, albeit with a focus on transversal skills, as many specific, technical skills may be implicitly embedded into educational requirements. Finally, interviews and surveys provide valuable first-hand information, but their execution can be costly for higher education institutions given limited access to companies and workers. Combining different sources of information can be a way of enhancing their relative strengths and minimizing their costs. Therefore, the first part of the strategy involves defining processes to gather, store, process, analyze, visualize and share this information with different stakeholders within the institution.

2.2. The organizational integration of employment data within UOC

In order to effectively fulfill its mission, the university must bridge the gap between the employment reality and the various processes and services that influence the employability of its future graduates. This involves designing relevant program portfolios, providing counseling to students on their initial choice of program, deciding on individualized training paths, offering guidance on teaching activities with a professional impact (such as internships and final projects), and identifying the need for complementary training for certain professional profiles, among other things. A comprehensive understanding of the employment reality is essential to accomplish these objectives.

To meet the need for labor market information and guidance on a large scale, the UOC has established a set of figures and roles at the organizational level. These figures and roles ensure that the evolution of the labor market is taken into account in course and program design and when providing career support for students and alumni.

This structure is presented in Figure 1

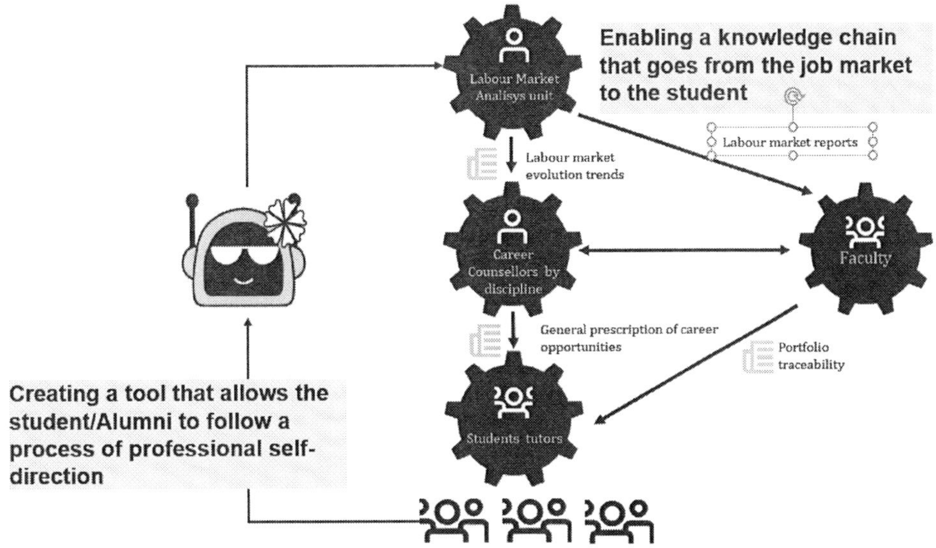

Figure 1: New university structure for employability

This framework involves augmenting the university staff with the following human resources: a newly formed unit for Labor Market Prospecting and Analysis, a new team of professional career orientation personnel, and a bolstered team of tutors. Their respective mandates are as follows:

The **Labour Market Prospecting and Analysis** unit´s mandate is to generate scientific knowledge about the labour market and the demand for skills and return this knowledge to the UOC community (students, faculty, administration staff and society) in ways that support better decision-making.

The **Career Counselors' team** converts the insights generated by the analysis unit into tailored information for the students. The information is disseminated to the student and alumni body through recommendations, courses, workshops, infographics, and other channels. Additionally, the professional counselors cater to the personalized needs of students and alumni who seek specific guidance.

On its part, **tutors**, each one of whom has a group of students assigned, are responsible for the dynamization of the information and activities developed by the Career Counselors' team. Their role is to ensure that all the effort invested by the previous links in the chain achieves the intended purpose for which they were established.

The Labour Market Prospecting and Analysis Unit

As previously stated, the Labour Market Prospecting and Analysis Unit (LMPAU)´s role is to gather, produce, analyse, visualize and share timely labour market information to different audiences, in a format that is conducive to better decision making by part of students, faculty and university staff. Data is gathered and analyzed through a combination of qualitative and quantitative research methods. The main objective is to attain a better understanding of people's needs, motivations and preferences regarding lifelong learning, as well as of employers' skills needs. As mentioned before, the availability of big data sets originated from job postings on online search portals allows the identification, almost in real-time, of in-demand occupations and skills, with a great degree of granularity. This information is complemented with ESCO data, and information coming from surveys, in-depth interviews, and focus groups with employers and sectoral experts. Similarly, on the learners' side, data on their motivations to engage in lifelong learning and their preferences regarding the best formats to do so, are also collected through surveys, focus groups and in-depth questionnaires. As it is the case with other research groups at a university, it is expected that this knowledge is shared at conferences and through peer-reviewed publications.

A key piece in the university's labor data strategy is establishing a link between labor market and program offerings data. Higher education institutions in Spain record information on programs´ learning outcomes in text-based documents. Moreover, existing program data tends to be organized around supply-side variables, such as teaching modality (online or face-to-face), number of credits/hours, assessment criteria, or the department responsible for provision. Instead, labor market data gathers information on knowledge, skills and competencies, and is organized by occupations and industries. This makes it difficult to relate each program to its labor market or to create personalized educational pathways that complete a person's existing set of knowledge, skills and competencies. The cross-walk of the two data sets requires recording learning outcomes and program prerequisites in the same language used in the labor market data: that is the language of knowledge, skills and competencies. This has been highly unusual in the context of higher education institutions, although recent regulatory developments are beginning to facilitate it.

Labor market Information is organized in a data model and analyzed and fed to different audiences through different channels:

Labour Market information for program directors, faculty and administration staff.

Each School or Faculty within the university receives an interactive dashboard-style report that presents information on labour market trends and skill needs taylored to that particular School. These reports equip program directors with specific information relative to their particular programs. This includes an analysis of the vacancies that specifically requested professionals with the skills imparted by a particular program. The report also includes Information on labour market trends and skill needs at the occupation level and at the level of individual skills. This allows for an assessment of the occupations, industries and locations that demand a particular skill, or bundle of skills. These reports serve to revise and update existing programs and to create new ones that align with labor market needs.

Labour market Information for tutors and career orientation staff.

Improving the employability and career development of students also requires strengthening professional orientation iniciatives. The objective is to shift from a focus on solely assisting on first job placement, to empowering students to recognize who they are, what knowledge, skills and competencies they already have, where they want to take their careers, and what knowledge, skills and competences they need to get there, throughout their professional lives. While career counselors are skilled at supporting learners to identify their interests, strengths, values and career goals, they may lack the up-to-date knowledge on the skill needs that are required to thrive in different roles across economic sectors, in a constantly evolving labour market. This is where labour market data can be a valuable tool to enhance career guidance. By providing up-to-date information to individuals on in-demand roles and occupations, skill needs, local labour market opportunities or earnings potential, they may be inspired to consider different roles or occupations, pursue upskill or reskilling or relocate to other areas to unlock new opportunities.

Labour market information is provided to career orientation staff in the form of an interactive style dashboard-style report, similar to the one provided to program directors. While the underlying data is the same as for the faculty reports, the information is presented and visualized in a way that supports and augments one-to-one, virtual, synchronous career orientation conversations between a professional career coach and a learner.

2.3 A virtual career orientation service

While it would be ideal to offer face-to-face or online synchronous career orientation to every student, providing personal orientation for 90,000 students and more than 100,000 alumni may prove to be unrealistic. However, leveraging data and technology provides the opportunity to offer high-quality, virtual autonomous career orientation services at scale. To that end, the university is currently developing a virtual orientation tool with the objective of providing labour market information to students and alumni via web and phone-based interfaces. These tools are designed to simulate online personal coaching, facilitating self-reflection about the learner´s needs and wants, and providing the required information to help them to identify the skills they already possess and the ones they need to achieve their goals. Additionally, the tool will provide recommendations for learning pathways based on the assessed skill gap, utilizing the data infrastructure described earlier.

Conclusions

The rapid changes in technology and the economy are not only affecting the labour market, but impacting social behavior and relations. As a result, universities like the open university of Catalunya, need to move beyond just creating and transmitting knowledge to ensure their student's employability. To support this goal, UOC is employing a three-pronged strategy to bring employability to its core, including gathering and analyzing labour market information, creating new roles at the organizational level that can provide and use this information, and designing an interface for students to analyze their position in the labour market. At the core of this strategy is the use of large databases on the competency requirements of the labour market to integrate labour market evolution into portfolio offerings and student and alumni employability support services. The ultimate goal is to provide learners with relevant lifelong learning education and services that help them achieve their life and career goals.

MINECRAFT: A REMOTE LABORATORY FOR GAME-BASED DISTANCE LEARNING

Andrea Nardi, Indire, Italy

Andrea Benassi, Indire, Italy

Elisabetta M. Cigognini, Indire, Italy

Correspondence: *Andrea Nardi:a.nardi@indire.it*

Abstract

Immersive learning environments are some of the technological and cognitive artifacts that can support active teaching approaches, in which product and process evaluation can sustain significant learning even in remote contexts, if well designed and calibrated for the students in training. The paper delves into the experience of remote laboratory teaching conducted within the MineClass project between 2018 and 2021, during which the pandemic school saw a reduction at a national level of active and collaborative laboratory activities due to social distancing, both in-person and remotely. The study integrates results from case studies, qualitative and quantitative surveys, and semi-structured interviews directed at participants in the experimentation. Within the larger primary sample, a follow-up questionnaire was administered in 2022 with the aim of exploring the didactic use of the video game during the pandemic years; most respondents reported continuing laboratory teaching activities with Minecraft even to support distance learning after the conclusion of the MineClass project. The results show the positive impact of the experimentation in terms of perceived added value by teachers for the development of cross-cutting competences, increased motivation, involvement, and autonomy of their students.

Keywords:

Laboratory-based Teaching, Immersive Learning, Distance Learning, Minecraft.

Laboratory teaching during the pandemic

The years of the pandemic represented a period of deep crisis for Italian schools: the health emergency caused a situation of strong uncertainty and schools found themselves operating in a context of unprecedented and constantly evolving challenges. With the suspension of in-person teaching activities and the introduction of distance learning, new difficulties but also precious opportunities emerged for a general rethinking and renewal of teaching and organizational practices (Carretero Gomez et al., 2021; CENSIS, 2020; Sun, 2020).

The restrictive measures forced experimentation with new approaches, tools, and learning environments, and this became particularly necessary for those subjects and disciplines that 'prefer' laboratory activities. The closure of institutions, the interruption of in-person teaching, and the inability to access school laboratories have had a greater impact on collaborative learning processes and on those teaching activities based on doing, physical manipulation, and peer interaction.

Internationally, a considerable number of schools and universities, to ensure the continuation of distance laboratory teaching, have adopted mixed and/or online modes of laboratory delivery (Gamage et al., 2020). Unfortunately, in our country, teachers prepared for distance learning were a "small minority" and this may have exacerbated that "destabilizing uncertainty" (Perla & Riva, 2016) produced by the interruption of traditional teaching methods and the need to necessarily reorient their actions (Mezirow, 2016). At the same time, the unprecedented situation in which they found themselves operating has certainly renewed reflection on the meaning, purposes, and methods of their teaching practice (Tramma, 2018). But in Italy this rethinking has not always translated into concrete actions and practices of renewal.

From surveys conducted during the lockdown period (INDIRE, 2020a; 2020b; 2021; SIRD, 2020), it emerges that teachers have rarely modified their methodological and didactic approaches and that a particularly high proportion has used, even during distance learning, frontal teaching and a traditional/transmissive style, rarely exploiting the potential offered by active methodologies (Ianes & Bellacicco, 2020). In the majority of cases, the typical practices of in-person teaching were transposed to distance learning (SIRD, 2021; INDIRE, 2020a; 2020b; 2021), leaving little room for that crucial passage towards the development of competencies and learning objectives, required even in the National Guidelines (MIUR, 2012) and for laboratory teaching that ensures that knowledge, skills and competencies are consciously put into action (Cigognini & Di Stasio, 2022).

While frontal lessons have essentially been transformed into live synchronous video conferences and asynchronous streaming, the problem has arisen for those courses characterized by practice-oriented activities that require teacher-student interaction and significant use of laboratory tools. The online approach, e-learning tools, and distance learning methods work very well for knowledge construction through content delivery and process supervision but have limitations in the development of practical laboratory skills. Research shows, however, that student learning outcomes in remote labs are equal and sometimes better than traditional labs (Byukusenge et al., 2022; Fadda & Vivanet, 2021; Rubim et al., 2019; Post et al., 2019), because they provide a more collaborative learning environment thanks to the higher level of interaction between students and teachers compared to in-person labs (Gamage et al., 2020).

Minecraft in Education

Minecraft is a 3D first-person sandbox videogame. In English, the term "sandbox" refers to the typical sandbox enclosure intended for children's games. Sandbox-type video games provide the player with a (digital) place to move freely and digital tools to modify it. In a sandbox videogame, the perimeter of the enclosure is much larger than physical sandboxes, and both the materials available and the tools for working with them change; one can think of it as a kind of digital LEGO® evolution. The substantial differences are that in Minecraft: you find yourself building inside a 3D world generated by the computer, with seas and mountains, trees, and animals; you are mediated by an avatar, a graphical representation of the player who acts in the game world at their command and signals to any other players (who are also mediated by an avatar) their presence and position in the game. The player sees the game world through their avatar's eyes.

To date, Minecraft is the most popular game in the world, with over 280,000,000 licenses sold, and for some years, examples of its use in school education have been seen. According to Cipollone et al. (2014), Minecraft offers students a unique opportunity to show their creativity and promote the understanding of concepts in ways that are more feasible than experiential learning in the real world. The use of Minecraft runs through the curriculum from STEM (Lane et al., 2017) to the Arts (Cayatte, 2013) and is also used in informal contexts, such as the development of socio-emotional skills (Ringland et al., 2016). With the increasing attention from schools, there has also been an increase in the production of texts that guide teachers in adopting Minecraft in their classroom teaching (Gallagher, 2014; Dikkers, 2015).

The MineClass Course

MineClass was an online training and experimentation course organized by The National Institute For Documentation, Innovation And Educational Research (INDIRE) in collaboration with Microsoft intended for primary and secondary school teachers, with the aim of training them in the didactic use of Minecraft. The first edition of MineClass started in December 2018 and ended in June 2019. Given the interest shown by teachers, the course was subsequently replicated in two additional editions, in the 2019/20 and 2020/21 school years. In total, the MineClass course trained more than 300 teachers over the three editions. The MineClass training, rather than on the functioning of the software, focused on the acquisition, by teachers, of a specific didactic methodology, developed by the reserchers together with a group of teachers and strongly inspired by the principles of Design Thinking (Brown, 2008). This methodology provides that:

- the activity of building in Minecraft by students is always preceded by paper planning, so that the action (building) always depends on a declared plan on paper, and that problems are addressed first in the definition, ideation, and planning stages, even before implementation;

- students are left with a good degree of autonomy in their activity. One of Minecraft's strengths is that it allows students to unleash their creativity and initiative. Classroom teaching activities should therefore tend towards a balance between constraints (necessary to guide students and prevent the activity from getting out of control) and degrees of freedom (which allow them to be creative and autonomous in their decisions);

- students work in teams (small groups of 3, 4, at most 5 students). Within the team, each student has a different role/responsibility.

Based on these and other indications, each participating teacher in the MineClass course was asked to design their own teaching activity based on their teaching discipline, incorporating it into the curriculum, and then experiment with it in class with their students during the training period. INDIRE conducted a study on the MineClass course to verify the conditions necessary for the teacher to implement effective and sustainable teaching activities that integrate the use of Minecraft in classroom teaching, such as training, support, materials, prior experiences, and the didactic-organizational context (Benassi et al., 2021).

Minecraft from Remote

Of the three editions of the MineClass course, the last two were strongly influenced by the pandemic.

In the 2019/20 edition, the lockdown occurred halfway through the course, when the participating teachers had already designed their teaching activity and were about to experiment with it in class. With schools closed, most of the teachers in that edition were unable to carry out the experimentation. However, some of them tried to redesign the activity so that it could be done by students (and the teacher) from home, using the potential of Minecraft as an online multiplayer platform. Minecraft, in fact, in its Education Edition version, allows the teacher to launch a game world on their computer and open it to other users connected remotely (Benassi et al., 2021 p. 112). In this way, students can access the game world made available by the teacher and work together under their supervision.

In the 2020/2021 final edition, the schools had been reopened in a strong situation of regional discontinuity throughout Italy, but the rules on social distancing and the continuous threat that, with the worsening of the pandemic situation, schools could be closed again, made it difficult to repeat the MineClass course as it had been conceived before the pandemic, without the necessary corrections. It was therefore decided to limit the registrations to those teachers who declared that they could manage and conduct the experimentation of the activities even in case of school closure, i.e. in "DaD" (Distance Teaching and Learning). As a result, the research applied to the MineClass course also expanded and adapted to be an observatory to accompany teachers and students in their learning paths related to the distance use of Minecraft and to investigate the methods involved.

Research Methodology

This study integrates results from case studies, quanti-qualitative surveys, and semi-structured interviews with participants in the MineClass project, using a mixed-method approach with the integration of quanti-qualitative tools for data collection (Mortari & Ghirotto, 2019; Trinchero & Robasto, 2019). Here the focus is on the results of the last year of the pandemic and the final follow-up.

The research protocol provided a set of quanti-qualitative investigation tools aimed at different subjects in various training phases: teachers were involved through an initial and final questionnaire while students' opinions were collected through a final questionnaire. The measurement tool's validity was construct-validated based on the dimensions of the European DigCompOrg framework, and a pilot study was conducted with a group of experienced teachers to evaluate the consistency of the questions and administration time.

Out of 320 initial enrollees, the 2019/2020 edition had a sample of 169 subjects who completed the classroom experiment, of whom 122 completed all investigation tools (initial and final questionnaires, project analysis, blog/forum interactions). The 2020/2021 edition saw the participation of 59 teachers who completed training and experimentation on the use of Minecraft for distance teaching during the pandemic. The teachers were involved in an initial and final questionnaire, as well as qualitative analysis of the works produced and the documentation of training activities in the diary blogs.

At the end of the project, a follow-up questionnaire was administered in 2022 to the larger main sample with the aim of deepening the didactic use of the videogame during the pandemic years. 150 out of 237 teachers completed the questionnaire, and most respondents stated that they continued to use Minecraft for distance teaching even after the conclusion of the MineClass project.

The research questions underlying the experimental activities concerned the sustainability and enabling conditions of using Minecraft in their curricular teaching, and how and if the immersive teaching thus prepared could enhance the development of transversal skills of the P21 framework (Mishra & Kereluik, 2021). Specifically, attention is directed towards autonomy, teamwork, and socialization skills.

The diachronic research activities for the three-year period of 2019-2021 have been restructured based on the evolution of the pandemic situation. The forced shift to distance learning has drastically reduced the sample size due to constraints related to connectivity and access to homogeneous distance laboratory teaching for the entire class. The research group has adapted to this situation by implementing a monitoring and observation approach, which includes dedicated meetings, semi-structured online interviews, textual analysis of the projects and blog diaries. Due to school closures, final questionnaires were not administered to teachers and students, as they were already being surveyed by the Indire Distant Teaching and Learning Observatory (Indire 2020a, 2020b).

The statistical analysis carried out focused on the description of all variables using simple and double frequency tables, with data presented and discussed as frequencies and percentages. Data analysis utilized statistical methodologies of univariate and bivariate analysis (Pearson's chi-squared test) for structured questionnaires, and posterior categorization by three independent judges for textual analysis of interviews, focus groups, online forums, blogs, and teachers' works. Below are the results related to the perspective of teachers who have implemented immersive distance teaching.

Results

The results show the positive impact of the experimentation in terms of perceived added value for teachers in the development of transversal skills, increased motivation, involvement and autonomy of their students. These data are particularly comforting and significant in relation to the unprecedented conditions posed by the pandemic and the forced closure of schools. Above all, Minecraft is perceived by the teachers involved in the follow-up, who have also used it remotely, as a strong element of cohesion for socialization and the reduction of social distancing, despite the initial technological gap that saw a reduction in the classes that could participate in the experimentation, due to technological access conditions. For those who have moved Minecraft to a distance setting, in the distributed and dislocated laboratory in the afternoon, there has been an increase in social well-being aspects in contrast to the pandemic school.

Some questions of the 2020/2021 teacher questionnaire specifically concern the activities conducted in distance learning: out of 59 teachers, 56% of respondents report that their students were able to work from home on Minecraft activities, compared to 44% of teachers for whom distance activities for their students were not possible. Why? What were the obstacles to the use of Minecraft at a distance? Firstly, connectivity (36.2%), then inadequate devices (32.2%) or completely absent (22.6%).

At the end of the school year (June 2022), a follow-up survey of the just-concluded experience was administered to the 237 teachers involved in the three-year experimentation, to which 150 subjects responded. Figure 1 shows the percentage distribution of teachers who continued to use Minecraft in their classroom teaching: over 41% of the subjects continued to use Minecraft as an immersive teaching environment, almost 29% used it for a period but not at the time of completing the questionnaire, and 30% of respondents ended the experience without further using Minecraft in school with their students.

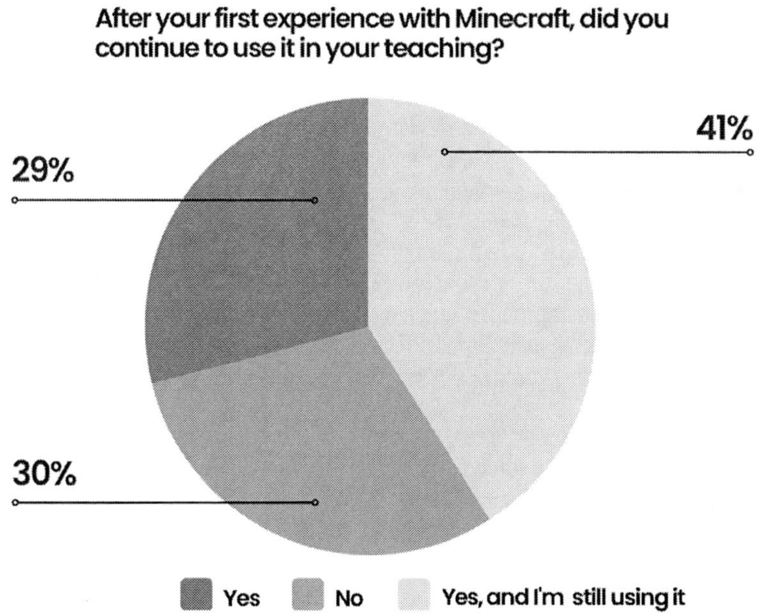

Figure 1. Percentage distribution of teachers who continued to use Minecraft in their teaching (database: 150 teachers out of 237).

The following graph delves into the characteristics of immersive teaching implemented. Immersive teaching has been practiced "at least once" for almost 55% of the subjects, "three to five times" for 24%, and for more than five activities for 21% of the respondents (see Figure 2).

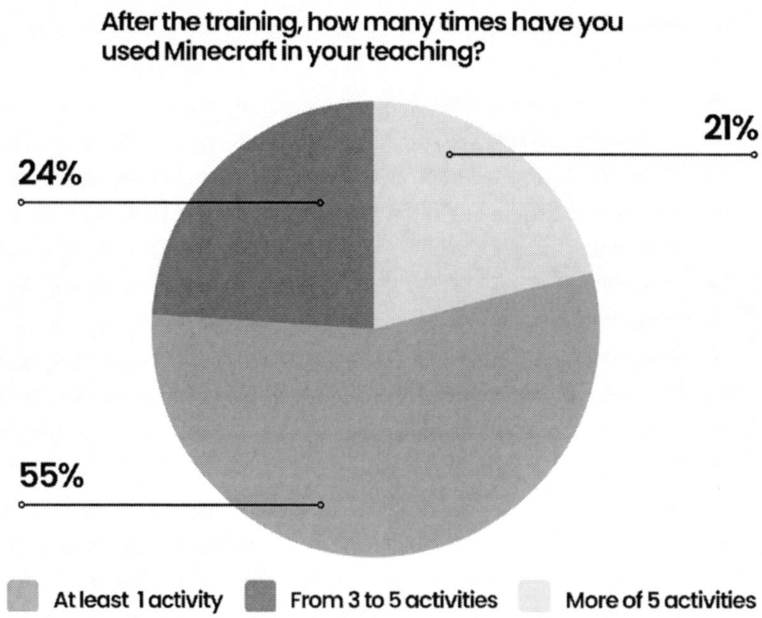

Fig. 2. Percentage distribution of teachers based on the number of times they used Minecraft in their teaching after the initial experimentation.

Minecraft has accompanied teachers' practice even in remote teaching for 63% of teachers, while 37% have not experimented with Minecraft remotely. This portion of teachers who have engaged in forced immersive distance teaching has highlighted some elements of using Minecraft in remote teaching as added value: the development of disciplinary skills (2.5% of respondents), socialization (5% of teachers), and above all motivation and engagement (for 43.6% of teachers), development of cross-cutting skills (23%) and autonomy of the students (20.5%); 5% of responding teachers do not find any added value. The data are summarized in Figure 3.

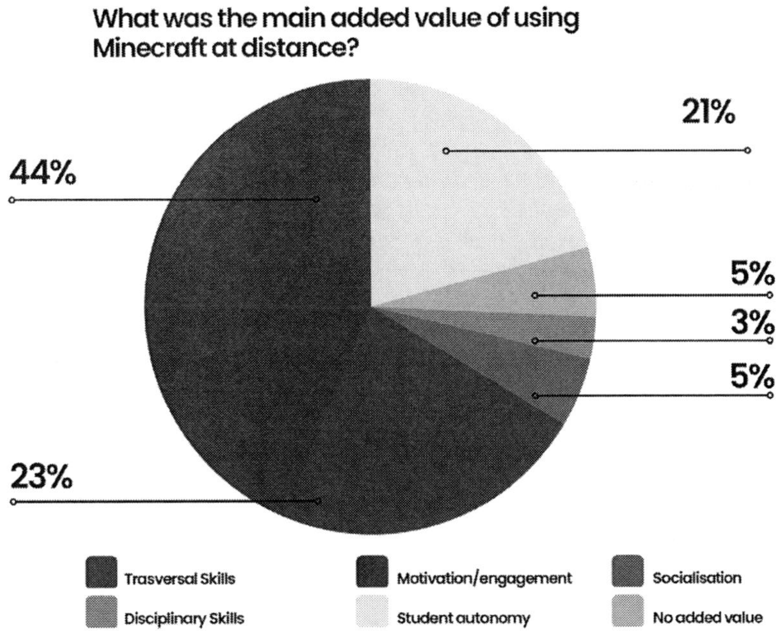

Fig. 3. Percentage distribution of teachers based on the added value observed in the use of Minecraft for distance learning.

In April 2020, in the midst of lockdown, semi-structured interviews were conducted with teachers who were carrying out activities in remote teaching with Minecraft, always within the MineClass project.

First and foremost, the importance of working together, albeit remotely, for the construction of a digital artifact emerges: collaboration among students is a skill that must be exercised from the earliest years of school, and the opportunity to experience it during the pandemic through a Minecraft game world was welcomed by teachers as a positive factor. A primary school teacher (Comprehensive Institute in northern Italy), who involved a first-grade class, responded:

> *First and foremost, the importance of working together, albeit remotely, for the construction of a digital artifact emerges: collaboration among students is a skill that must be exercised from the earliest years of school, and the opportunity to experience it during the pandemic through a Minecraft game world was welcomed by teachers as a positive factor.*

A primary school teacher (Comprehensive Institute in northern Italy), who involved a first-grade class, responded:

> *If there was a critical aspect, it was their collaboration: they are small, the collaborative competence has just started. For example, the girl who chooses a cube of a color that the boy doesn't like. But I wanted them to try to work together.*

We report in Figure 4, as an example, an exchange in chat between two girls in the teacher's class:

GIULIA: OK INTENT LET'S START WITH THE HOUSE, WHAT ABOUT MAKING THE SECOND FLOOR THE SMALL TERRACE AND THE THIRD FLOOR A BIG WIDE ONE?

WHAT FLOOR DO YOU WANT IN THE HOUSE: DO YOU WANT COLORED CARPETS? WHAT COLOR?
WHAT FLOOR DO YOU WANT ON THE TERRACE? SLABS OF WOOD? OF BETULE?
WHITE DOORS? WHAT COLOR WINDOW GLASS DO YOU WANT?
DILETTA: HELLO GIULIA, IT'S OKAY FOR THE COLORED CARPETS AND WHITE DOORS, NOW I WILL
INSERT THE BLOCKS. YOU BUILD. CAN YOU CHANGE THE COLOR PLEASE?
I HAVE A HARD TIME READING. OK THE TWO TERRACES AND MAKE A BIG CARPET, LET'S PUT MANY
COLORS

Figure 4. Communication between two girls in a first-grade class at a Comprehensive Institute in northern Italy while working on a collaborative building project in Minecraft.

A second recurring aspect in the interviews concerns how distance has influenced students' methods of documenting activities. A high school teacher explains:

> *I opened a Padlet in which individual student groups can put the material they are viewing for the design of their building in Minecraft. This mode was necessary to share the projects of individual buildings and the phases of work between groups, thus creating the advantage of documenting each phase of the work.*

From these words, it can be seen how the remote mode, combined with the need to coordinate in carrying out a shared construction, has pushed - almost forced - students to pay more attention to the quality of documentation.

Conclusions

Despite some obvious difficulties in conducting distance learning laboratory activities during the pandemic months (Gamage et al., 2020), the experience conducted and presented in this contribution confirms the benefits found in previous research on the use of remote laboratories (Fadda & Vivanet, 2021), the implementation of online game-based learning paths (Wardoyo et al., 2020; Yang et al., 2022), and immersive distance learning conducted with Minecraft (Rader et al., 2021; Sena & Jordão, 2021). The greatest benefits can be traced to students' ability to socialize, work in groups (even at a distance) and independently, showing greater motivation and engagement compared to more traditional educational and learning activities. A good portion of the teachers included in the study continued to take advantage of the potential of Minecraft-based education even during school closures, demonstrating the validity of the experimentation conducted in the years prior to the pandemic.

The level of use of this methodology compared to the overall educational offer of teachers is also significant. The results related to the development of socialization skills, teamwork, autonomy and distance problem solving are further experienced and deepened. With the increasing diffusion of laboratory education in secondary schools, product and process evaluation that supports competency-based learning processes has entered disciplinary learning spaces, and laboratory teaching activities focused on technological artifacts such as Mineclass seem to have supported the development of critical thinking among students, meta-reflection and co-construction of learning processes. Some 'side effects' of distance learning have widely favoured the use of online documentation (in these examples with a padlet) to follow step-by-step phases of group activities, and constitute some feedback on the development of students' metacognition and reflection on cognitive processes, implemented within the disciplinary aspects that make the school of doing increasingly practicable also in high school. The same national surveys on distance laboratory education underline this passage, for which distance laboratory work goes beyond the "synchronous hour" and spills over into afternoon group activities in secondary school (Indire, 2022). The results also show the emergence of a widespread mode of laboratory teaching, where the classic laboratory is displaced and exits the classroom: it opens up to a time of school at home for laboratory work and collaborative activities, and peer-to-peer laboratory work can also take place in the afternoon, be managed in small groups and deepen activities in a cross-cutting way. Without claiming to be exhaustive, the reflection is on how these aspects can constitute further enabling elements for deepening immersive teaching in high school as a laboratory mode, even in the context of a new normality school.

References

Benassi, A., Baldini, R., Bartolini, R., Cigognini M.E., De Maurissens, I., Mosa, E., Nencioni, P., Pedani, V., Pettenati, M. C., Zanoccoli, C. (2022). Impatto della Pandemia sulle Pratiche Didattiche e Organizzative delle Scuole

Italiane nell'Anno Scolastico 2020/21: Report Integrativo. INDIRE, Firenze. Retrieved from https://bit.ly/3lJmYYX (ver. 24.03.2023).

Benassi, A. (Eds.) (2021). A scuola con Minecraft. Progettare un mondo a cubetti. Giunti.

Brown, T. (2008). Design thinking, Harvard business review, 6, pp. 84.

Byukusenge, C., Nsanganwimana, F., Paulo Tarmo, A. (2022). Effectiveness of Virtual Laboratories in Teaching and Learning Biology: A Review of Literature, International Journal of Learning, Teaching and Educational Research, 6, 1-17.

Cayatte, R. (2014). Where game, play and art collide, in N. Garrelts (ed.), Understanding Minecraft: Essays on play, community and possibilities, McFarland and Company: Jefferson, NC, pp. 203-2013.

Carretero Gomez, S., Napierala, J., Bessios, A., Mägi, E., Pugacewicz, A., Ranieri, M., Triquet, K., Lombaerts, K., Robledo Bottcher, N., Montanari, M., Gonzalez Vazquez, I. (2021). What did we learn from schooling practices during the COVID-19 lockdown. Publications Office of the European Union: Luxembourg.

CENSIS (2020). Italia sotto sforzo. Diario della transizione 2020. La scuola e i suoi esclusi. AGI-Agenzia Italia: Roman. Retrieved from https://bit.ly/39XPveG (ver. 24.03.2023).

Cipollone, M., Schifter, C. C., Moffat, R. A. (2014). Minecraft as a creative tool: A case study. International Journal of Game-Based Learning (IJGBL), 2, 1-14.

Dikkers, S. (2015). Teachercraft. How teachers learn to use Minecraft in their classrooms. ETC Press: Pittsburgh.

Fadda, D. & Vivanet, G. (2021). Online laboratories for science education: a summary of evidence. Italian Journal of Educational Research, 26, 105-117.

Felszeghy, S., Pasonen-Seppänen, S., Koskela, A., Nieminen, P., Härkönen, K., Paldanius, K.M., Mahonen, A. (2019). Using online game-based platforms to improve student performance and engagement in histology teaching. BMC Med. Educ, 1, 1-11.

Gallagher, C. (214). An Educator's Guide to Using Minecraft®in the Classroom: Ideas, inspiration, and student projects for teachers. Peachpit Press: San Francisco, CA.

Gamage, K.A.A., Wijesuriya, D.I., Ekanayake, S.Y., Rennie, A.E.W., Lambert, C.G., Gunawardhana, N. (2020). Online Delivery of Teaching and Laboratory Practices: Continuity of University Programmes during COVID-19 Pandemic. Educ. Sci, 10, p. 291.

Ianes, D. & Bellacicco, R. (2020). Didattica a distanza durante il lockdown. L'impatto percepito dagli insegnanti sull'inclusione degli studenti con disabilità. L'integrazione scolastica e sociali, 3, 25-47.

INDIRE (2020a). Indagine tra i docenti italiani: pratiche didattiche durante il lockdown. Report Preliminare. Retrieved from https://bit.ly/3xPANy4 (ver. 24.03.2023).

INDIRE (2020b). Indagine tra i docenti italiani: pratiche didattiche durante il lockdown. Report Integrativo. Retrieved from https://bit.ly/3nl5438 (ver. 24.03.2023).

INDIRE (2021). Impatto della Pandemia sulle Pratiche Didattiche e Organizzative delle Scuole Italiane nell'Anno Scolastico 2020/21. Report preliminare-Dicembre 2021. Retrieved from https://bit.ly/3nkldog (ver. 24.03.2023).

Lane, H.C., Yi, S., Guerrero, B., Comins, N. (2017). Minecraft as a Sandbox for STEM Interest Development: Preliminary Results, in Hayashi, Y., et al. (eds.), Workshop Proceedings of the 25th International Conference on Computers in Education, New Zealand: Asia-Pacific Society for Computers in Education, pp. 387-397.

Mishra, P. & Kereluik, K. (2011). What 21st Century Learning? A review and a synthesis. In M. Koehler & P. Mishra (Eds.), Proceedings of SITE 2011--Society for Information Technology & Teacher Education International Conference (pp. 3301-3312). Nashville, Tennessee, USA: Association for the Advancement of Computing in Education (AACE). Retrieved from https://www.learntechlib.org/primary/p/36828/ (ver. 24.03.2023).

Mezirow, J. (2016). La teoria dell'apprendimento trasformativo. Imparare a pensare come un adulto. Raffaello Cortina: Milano.

MIUR, Ministero dell'Istruzione dell'Università e della Ricerca. Indicazioni nazionali per il curricolo della scuola dell'infanzia e del primo ciclo di istruzione, 2012.

Mortari, L. & Ghirotto, L. (2019). Metodi per la ricerca educativa. Carocci: Roma.

Perla, L. & Riva, M.G. (2016). L'agire educativo: manuale per educatori e operatori socio-assistenziali. Editrice La Scuola: Brescia.

Post, L.S., Guo P., Saab, N., Admiraal, W. (2019). Effects of remote labs on cognitive, behavioral, and afective learning outcomes in higher education, Computers & Education, 140, 2-9.

Rader, E., Love, R., Reano, D., Dousay, T. A., Wingerter, N. (2021). Pandemic Minecrafting: an analysis of the perceptions of and lessons learned from a gamified virtual geology field camp. Geosci. Commun, 4, 475-492.

Ringland, K.E., Wolf, C.T., Faucett, H., Dombrowski, L., Hayes, G.R. (2016). Will I always be not social? Re-Conceptualizing Sociality in the Context of a Minecraft Community for Autism. In Proceedings of the 2016 CHI conference on human factors in computing systems. ACM: New York, pp. 1256-1269.

Rubim, J.P., Mota, V.P., Garcia, L.G., Brito, G.L.R., Santos, G.F. (2019). The use of remote experimentation as a teaching tool: A literature review, International Journal of Information and Education Technology, 11, pp. 826-830.

Sena, C. C.R.G. D. & Jordão, B.G.F. (2012). Challenges in the teaching of Cartography during the COVID-19 pandemic: use of Minecraft in the remote classroom setting, Proc. Int. Cartogr. Assoc., 4, 1-7.

SIRD (2021). Ricerca nazionale SIRD. Per un confronto sulle modalità di didattica a distanza adottate nelle scuole italiane nel periodo di emergenza COVID-19 Retrieved from https://bit.ly/3A4vgqn (ver. 24.03.2023).

SIRD (2021). La DaD in emergenza: vissuti e valutazioni degli insegnanti italiani. Scelte metodologiche e primi risultati nazionali. PensaMultimedia: Lecce. Retrieved from https://bit.ly/3TfysWV (ver. 24.03.2023).

Sun, L., Tang, Y., Zuo, W. (2020). Coronavirus pushes education online. Nat. Mater, 19, pp. 687.

Tramma, S. (2018). L'educatore imperfetto. Senso e complessità del lavoro educativo. Carocci: Roma.

Trinchero, R. & Robasto, D. (201). I Mixed Methods nella ricerca educativa. Mondadori Università: Milano.

Wardoyo, C., DwiSatrio, Y., Ma'ruf, D. (2020). Effectiveness of game-based learning–learning in modern education. In G. Agustin (ed.), 3rd International Research Conference on Economics and Business, KnE Social Sciences, 2020, pp. 81-87. https://doi.org/10.18502/kss.v4i7.6844

Yang, J.C., Chung, C.J., Chen, M.S. (2021). Effects of performance goal orientations on learning performance and in game performance in digital game based learning, J. Comput. Assist. Learn, 2, 422-439.

CAN WE MAKE OUR STUDENTS PEDAGOGICAL DESIGN PARTNERS?

Meital Amzalag, Holon Institute of Technology, Israel

Sharon Hardof-Jaffe, Levinsky Wingate Academic College, Israel

***Correspondence**: Sharon Hardof-Jaffe: sharon.hardof@l-w.ac.il*

Abstract

In recent years, the Internet has become an integral part of our lives, which includes a wide variety of platforms and activities, different purposes, different uses, and different characteristics. Technology is present in all areas of life, but there are differences in the scope and type of activities young people do in their free time compared to the scope and type of activities during school hours. The purpose of this research is to make the young people's voices heard about their digital lives, to hear their suggestions for integrating technology in the school, and to make them partners in building curricula.

The methodological approach in this research is a mixed method. 129 students aged 13-18 and 17 teachers who teach these students participated in the study. The research tools are two online questionnaires, one for students and one for teachers, both with closed and open questions. The findings reveal the students' leisure activities (digital and non-digital), the richness of their digital activities and their attitudes towards integrating technology into learning. In addition, the study presents what their teachers think about their student's leisure time activities and highlights the gap between them. Our findings are presenting the importance of hearing the students' voices for teachers and curriculum designers.

Keywords:

Student voice, Digital life, SNS, Search activities, Computer Games

Introduction

Digital platforms are an integral part of modern life. They have a profound impact on the way we communicate, learn, shop, and entertain ourselves (Jackman et al., 2021; Malak, et al., 2017). Indeed, young people's lives are immersed in technology. Recent study found that the vast majority of teenagers use internet on a daily basis (97%)' they have access to smartphone (95%), personal computer (PC) (90%), and game console (80%)(Anderson et al., 2022). Youth have positive attitudes towards social network sites (SNS) (Anderson et al., 2022), and they use mostly YouTube (95%), after that TikTok (67%). Facebook, which was very popular among teenagers in 2014 (71%) dropped in 2022 (32%) (Vogels et al., 2022).

In spite of the fact that youth also use digital platforms for learning purposes, studies indicate that many teachers find it difficult to integrate technology in a way that is adapted to the students' world, and the advancement of innovative pedagogies as well (Evans, 2019; Putri et al., 2020). In other words, they are having difficulty integrating content knowledge, pedagogical knowledge, and technological knowledge (TPACK) (Mishra and Koehler 2006; Voithofer, et al., 2019). Therefore, as educators we must get to know technologies that take place in our students' life. We need to understand in depth the uses and activities of our students' digital activities. and to realize the importance and the essential impact of the student voice (Cook-Sather 2020; Holquist 2019; Lubicz-Nawrocka, 2018; Machisi, 2023). Previous studies reveal that students have interests and abilities to express critic and voluble ideas regarding: teaching practices, wide range of pedagogy asepcts, assessment design of curriculum, policy and decision making (Holquist 2019; Lubicz-Nawrocka, 2018; Machisi, 2023). Therefore, the purpose of this research is to answer the following questions:

1. What are the digital activities of youth? (Leisure time, social networks, gaming, information search)?

2. What do their teachers know about their digital activities?
3. What are youth attitudes and recommendations towards integrating digital activities in learning?

Methodology

The methodological approach in this research is a mixed methods approach that enables a more comprehensive understanding of complex educational phenomena and the learning environments in which they occur and facilitates new knowledge for educators and policy makers (Anderson & Shattuck, 2012; Kennedy-Clark, 2013). The use of a mixed approach makes it possible to create a solid basis for results, to understand them in depth and to discover new perspectives (Creswell, 2013; Dunning et al., 2008; Patton, 2002).

Therefore, combining qualitative and quantitative research allows us to gain a deeper understanding of students' digital lives and attitudes.

Research Participants

This study was conducted in a boys' school located in the center of Israel. The study included 146 participants: 129 students (69 in the seventh to ninth grade and 60 in the tenth to twelfth grade), and 17 teachers (6-35 years of teaching experience) who teach these students.

Research tools

The study was based on two self-reports and online questionnaires, one for students and one for their teachers.

The questionnaire covers the following topics: Digital activities: leisure time activities (hobbies, social networks, gaming types), search activities (information types and platforms), and attitudes toward digital integration in school. It also includes an open question: "If you were invited to a meeting of teachers and asked to consult with you on the proven ways teachers should use technology in lessons, what do you think you would advise them?"

The teacher's questionnaire includes questions about their assumptions concerning students' digital activities.

Ethics

An institutional ethics committee and the Chief Scientist of the Israeli Ministry of Education approved the study. All participants and their parents agreed to participate in the study.

Findings

RQ1: What are the digital activities of youth? (Leisure time, social networks, gaming, information search)?

Leisure time activities

The findings reveal that the students engage in the following activities, in descending order: meeting friends in person, playing mobile games, doing sports, watching TV series, searching the information on the internet, using social networks, and playing computer games. The activities that they are less engaged in are creating presentations, uploading pictures, internet shopping, creating videos, uploading videos and creating music. These findings indicate that most of the students' digital activities are characterized by interaction and consumption and not by creation.

Table 1: Students' leisure time activities

Activity	Average	Sd
Meeting friends (Ftf) *	3.88	1.02

Mobile games	3.67	1.13
Sport (outdoor) *	3.45	0.91
Watching TV	3.43	1.00
Information search	3.43	0.90
Social networks	3.38	0.90
Computer games	3.00	1.13
Reading *	2.71	1.17
Non digital games *	2.51	1.02
Homework (Digital platforms)	2.16	1.31
Hobbies activities and afternoon class	2.04	1.17
Volunteering *	2.04	1.00
SNS commenting	3.38	0.90
Internet shopping (with parents)	1.66	1.32
Creating presentations	1.50	1.31
Uploading pictures	1.32	1.59
Internet shopping (with out parents)	1.30	1.32
Creating videos	1.26	1.43
Uploading videos	1.22	0.95
Creating music	1.16	1.43

Note. *Non digital activity; The scale: 1 = does not do at all, 6 = every day, more than five hours a day).

Social Networks

It has been found that WhatsApp is the most popular social network among students. YouTube is also very popular among students. The use of Instagram and TikTok, however, is low, and Twitter, Pinterest, Facebook, and Snapchat are rarely used.

Table 2: Students' SNS uses

Social network	Average	Sd
WhatsApp	4.43	0.609
YouTube	3.75	0.848
Instagram	2.84	1.553
TikTok	2.45	1.686

Twitter	1.58	0.982
Pinterest	1.40	0.815
Facebook	1.34	0.702
Snapchat	1.29	0.640

Note. Scale: 1= not at all, 5= very much user

Digital Games

Computer games are played by students on a moderately frequent basis. The most popular computer games are strategy games, followed by sports, thinking, war, adventure, and construction games (in descending order).

Table 3: Students' digital games use

Digital games	Average	Sd
Strategy	2.90	1.249
Sport	2.78	1.474
Thinking	2.67	1.207
War	2.65	1.350
Adventure	2.28	1.334
Construction	2.12	1.225
Puzzle	2.03	1.096
Sudoku	1.64	0.967
Dress Up	1.39	0.921

Note. Scale: 1= not at all, 5= very much user

Information search

According to the findings, students search for a wide variety of information. The information that students look for most is about topics that they are interested in. After that, students search for information about music, translations from foreign languages, explanations of unfamiliar words, and information about people who interest them (in descending order).

Table 4: Students' information search

Information search	Average	Sd
Interest	3.78	0.960
Music	3.65	1.216
Translation	3.47	1.008
Definitions	3.34	1.057
People I'm interested in	3.02	1.176
School materials	2.81	0.969
Prices	2.72	1.159
Entertainment	2.51	1.133

Note. Scale: 1= not at all, 5= very much user

RQ2: What do their teachers know about their digital activities?

In the findings, gaps were revealed between the students' reported digital activities and what their educators assumed about them. Teachers were asked about three types of activities: social networking, computer games, and information searches.

Regarding the students SNS uses, The majority (52.9%) of teachers assumed that Tiktok was the most popular social networking site among their students (after WhatsApp). According to 29.4% of teachers, Instagram was the most popular SNS among their students, while only 17.6% recognized YouTube as the most common SNS.

However, as shown in table 2, YouTube is the most popular social networking site among students (after WhatsApp). Instagram and TikTok are not so popular among them.

It was also noted that there was a gap in students' use of computer games. The majority of teachers (76.5%) believe that their students spend a significant amount of time playing computer games, but only 17.6% believe that they play moderately.

In fact, the students report that they play about a couple of times a week on average (table 3). They play even the most popular game, strategy games, only occasionally (table 3).

According to our findings regarding search activity, teachers are aware that their students are searching for school materials at a medium level (teacher mean 2.47 std 0.800; students mean 2.81 std 0.969). However, 88.2% of teachers believed that their students searched extensively for videos (mean 4.35 std 0.861) and for games (mean 4.65 std 0.702).

RQ3: What are youth attitudes and recommendations towards integrating digital activities in learning?

As can be seen in table 5, students have a positive attitude toward the integration of technology in learning. As for challenges (table 6), we found that students do not believe that integrating technology into the classroom causes messy classrooms, distractions, wasted time or boredom.

Table 5: Students' attitudes towards technology integration

Items	Average	Sd
Promotes creativity and creative thinking	3.97	1.045
Promotes independent learning	3.88	1.005
Enhance the use of various teaching methods	3.78	1.053
Increase the students' interest in the lesson	3.74	1.227
Illustrate visually	3.54	0.944
Help to impart the learning material	3.50	1.112
Promotes active learning	3.43	1.164
Assist in practicing the learning material	3.42	1.041
Help to understand the learning material	3.42	1.021
Creating content in technological environments should be taught at school	3.40	1.234
Enable meaningful learning	3.39	1.120
Contributes to improving performance and outcomes	3.33	1.092
Assisting students with difficulties	3.22	1.111
Promotes text analysis skills (comparison, comparison, etc.)	3.22	1.062

Table 6: Attitudes towards technology integration challenges

Items	Average	Sd
In the classroom, technology creates a mess	2.72	1.125
Technology causes students' unnecessary distractions	2.89	1.062
The use of technology is causing a waste of time.	1.98	1.104
The use of technology is causing boredom and lack of interest in class	1.90	0.917

When we asked: if you were invited to a teachers' meeting and they were consulting with you about ways to use technology in school, what would be your suggestion? 54% of students choose to share their ideas. The analysis of this question raises three main themes: expend the use of technology. technology as an enhance for learning. students advocate for techno-pedagogy.

Expend the use of technology

In the analysis raise many expressions about the students wish to expand the use of technology in learning. They want more online activities and more presence of devices:

"Expending the use", "More technologies" "more online assignments" "use more computers."

Technology as an enhance for learning experience

The students' suggestions also expressed their need to improve the learning experience by using technology: "With technology, you can learn the material in a fascinating way instead of the dry way we do it now". Additionally, they recommend enhancing understanding through the use of a variety of technologies: There are many tools on the Internet that can help impart learning materials through digital visual means. For example, the Desmos website for graphs. This will both make it easier for the teacher and also give the students the opportunity to experiment and understand more.

Students advocate for techno-pedagogy

Interestingly, students also have creative suggestions on how to integrate technology into the classroom. They expressed techno-pedagogy understanding: "To make more presentations, so that the topics are divided among students, and they present them to the class", "to use more information search by digital means and not only using books", "At the end of each lesson, make a Kahoot on the material studied", "use presentations with questions and games", "I'd recommend three quarters of a regular learning lesson and one quarter of a technology lesson." And "watching videos on the Internet because they use visualization and help you learn". Table 7 reveals the students understanding the linkages between pedagogy and technology integration aspects in class.

Table 7: Students' attitudes towards the linkage between pedagogy and technology

Items	Average	Sd
Technology integration depends on the teacher	3.74	1.050
Integration of technology depends on the subject matter.	3.34	1.128

Discussion

Young people life in our days are immersed in digital platforms, during their leisure time activities (Jackman et al., 2021; Malak, et al., 2017). However, in schools, teacher are still challenge in integrating technologies in to their pedagogy (Evans, 2019; Putri et al., 2020). This study provides educators and policy makers with insights into students' digital lives in order to involve them in the development of new curricula and pedagogical approaches.

The findings reveal that students have a wide leisure activity, and they use diverse digital environments, for social interaction, content consumption and gaming. In line with the latest findings (Vogels et al., 2022), the students in our study mainly use WhatsApp and YouTube.

According to the study, there are three important pedagogical implications: First, students' digital activities are characterized by a high level of digital consumption and a low level of digital creation. Based on these findings, educators need to enhance digital creation activities in their pedagogical practices, since it is one of the new skills that are required in the digital age (Van Laar et al., 2017). Second, the students play in a wide range of computer games on a moderate basis. This can be used to improve pedagogical practices since computer games (for formal learning or leisure purposes) are found to enhance cognitive abilities, encourage motivation, raise engagement and promote knowledge construction, as well as digital learning games (Blumberg et al., 2019; Granic et al., 2014; Pan et al., 2022). Third, the students actively participating in non-formal information searching activities. During their free time, they search for information about their interests, music, world translation, and terms definitions. It should be noted, however, that they are not looking for a great deal of school materials.

Not surprisingly, the attitude of students towards the use of technology in the classroom is highly positive. Moreover, when we directly asked them about the challenges that technology integration brings into classrooms, they disagreed. Particularly noteworthy is their recommendation to teachers on how to use technology in the classroom. In light of these findings, it appears that students are capable of becoming partners and contributing to the process of TPACK assimilation. (Voithofer, et al., 2019).

Teacher-student partnerships are crucial, especially in light of the gap between students' digital lives and their teachers' knowledge of them. In order to enhance TPACK assimilation in relevant context in classes, we must make more efforts to listen to our students and integrate nonformal learning with formal learning.

References

Anderson, M, Vogels, E.A, Perrin, A. and Rainie, L. (2022). Connection, Creativity, and Drama: Teen Life on Social Media. *Pew Research Center*, November 16, 2022. https://www.pewresearch.org/internet/2022/11/16/connection-creativity-and-drama-teen-life-on-socialmedia-in-2022

Anderson, T., & Shattuck, J. (2012). Design-based research: A decade of progress in education research? *Educational researcher, 41*(1), 16-25

Blumberg, F. C., Deater-Deckard, K., Calvert, S. L., Flynn, R. M., Green, C. S., Arnold, D., & Brooks, P. J. (2019). Digital games as a context for children's cognitive development: Research recommendations and policy considerations. *Social Policy Report, 32*(1), 1-33.

Cook-Sather, A. (2020). Student voice across contexts: Fostering student agency in today's schools. *Theory into practice*, *59*(2), 182-191.

Creswell, J. W. (2013). *Research design: Qualitative, quantitative, and mixed methods approaches.* Sage publications

Dunning, H., Williams, A., Abonyi, S., & Crooks, V. (2008). A mixed method approach to quality of life research: A case study approach. Social Indicators Research, 85(1), 145-158Eshet, Y. (2012). Thinking in the digital era: A revised model for digital literacy. *Issues in informing science and information technology*, *9*(2), 267-276.

Evans, J. A., & Project Tomorrow. (2019). *Digital learning: Peril or promise for our K-12 students.* https://tomorrow.org/Speakup/speakup2018-19- Digital-Learning-Peril-or-Promise-october2019.html

Granic, I., Lobel, A., & Engels, R. C. (2014). The benefits of playing video games. *American psychologist*, *69*(1), 66.

Holquist, S. E. (2019). *Student Voice in Education Policy: Understanding student participation in state-level K-12 education policy making* (Doctoral dissertation, University of Minnesota).

Jackman, J. A., Gentile, D. A., Cho, N. J., & Park, Y. (2021). Addressing the digital skills gap for future education. *Nature Human Behaviour*, 5(5), 542-545.

Kennedy-Clark, S. (2013). Research by design: Design-based research and the higher degree research student. *Journal of Learning Design*, 6(2), 26-32

Lubicz-Nawrocka, T. (2018). From partnership to self-authorship: The benefits of co-creation of the curriculum. *International Journal for Students as Partners*, 2(1), 47-63.

Machisi, E. (2023). Secondary school mathematics teaching evaluations by students: A report card for the mathematics teacher. *Eurasia Journal of Mathematics, Science and Technology Education*, *19*(1), em2211.

Malak, M. Z., Khalifeh, A. H., & Shuhaiber, A. H. (2017). Prevalence of Internet Addiction and associated risk factors in Jordanian school students. *Computers in Human Behavior*, *70*, 556-563.

Pan, Y., Ke, F., & Xu, X. (2022). A systematic review of the role of learning games in fostering mathematics education in K-12 settings. *Educational Research Review*, 100448.

Patton, M. Q. (2002). *Qualitative research & evaluation methods*. (3rd ed.). Thousand Oaks: Sage Publications, inc

Putri, A. R. A., Hidayat, T., & Purwianingsih, W. (2020). Analysis of technological pedagogical content knowledge (TPACK) of biology teachers in classification of living things learning. In *Journal of Physics: Conference Series* (Vol. 1521, p. 042033).

Reynaldo, C., Christian, R., Hosea, H., & Gunawan, A. A. (2021). Using video games to improve capabilities in decision making and cognitive skill: a literature review. *Procedia Computer Science*, 179, 211-221.

Van Laar, E., Van Deursen, A. J., Van Dijk, J. A., & De Haan, J. (2017). The relation between 21st-century skills and digital skills: A systematic literature review. *Computers in human behavior*, *72*, 577-588.

Vogels, E. A., Gelles-Watnick, R., & Massarat, N. (2022). Teens, social media and technology. *Pew Research Center*, August 10, 2022. https://www.pewresearch.org/internet/2022/08/10/teens-social-media-and-technology-2022

Voithofer, R., Nelson, M. J., Han, G., & Caines, A. (2019). Factors that influence TPACK adoption by teacher educators in the US. *Educational Technology Research and Development*, *67*, 1427-1453.

Evaluation of 10 popular very YOUNG LEARNER VIDEOS on youtube

Aysegul Liman-Kaban, Bahcesehir University, Turkey

***Correspondence**: Aysegul Liman-Kaban: aysegul.liman@es.bau.edu.tr*

Abstract

This study aimed to evaluate the effectiveness of 10 popular very young learner (VYL) videos on YouTube. The purpose of the study was to investigate the suitability of these videos for children aged 2-6 years in terms of their educational content, visual and auditory quality, and engagement value. Content analysis was used to analyze the videos. A total of 2 raters were conducted content analysis for the study. They were asked to rate each video on a rubric. The study concludes that careful consideration must be given when selecting videos for VYLs, as their effectiveness depends on several factors, such as age appropriateness, educational content, and visual and auditory quality. The results show that most YouTuber videos used multimedia learning principles effectively in their videos, with varying degrees of success.

Keywords:

instructional videos, multimedia, design principles, multimedia learning, very young learners

Introduction

In recent years, YouTube has become a popular platform for content creators to share their knowledge, skills, and experiences with their audience (Anderson & Jiang, 2018). Design features of educational videos have been found to promote children's engagement and support early literacy skills. For instance, in Sesame Street's "Learning about letters" episode, learning objectives are explicitly stated at the beginning of the episode, and the phoneme-grapheme correspondence is reinforced by showing the written representation of the letter or word that corresponds to the sounds presented. Additionally, words in the storyline or songs are accompanied by images and their written form. Another Sesame Street episode about the moon integrates these techniques with songs related to the topic, animations presenting factual information about the moon, and counting backwards as part of a rocket launch sequence (Wright et al., 1990). While screen media has been shown to enhance children's vocabulary, it is unclear whether it can facilitate the acquisition of more advanced language skills such as grammar (Naigles & Mayeux, 2001). Linebarger and Walker (2005) conducted a longitudinal study spanning from 6 to 30 months of age, and found that certain television programs such as Dora the Explorer, Blue's Clues, and Dragon Tales were associated with greater vocabulary and expressive language development, while programs like Teletubbies were related to fewer vocabulary words and lower language expression. The study revealed that Sesame Street was only associated with smaller expressive language scores, while Barney was linked to fewer vocabulary words and more expressive language. These findings may be attributed to the interactive nature of shows like Dora the Explorer and Blue's Clues, which encourage children to talk to the screen, as opposed to Sesame Street, which does not. Barney and Friends, on the other hand, are designed to promote imaginative play, with simple language that may explain the differences in vocabulary acquisition. These results held even after controlling for factors such as parent education, home environment, and child cognitive ability. Television programs that facilitate language development through clear labelling, encouraging repetition, and interactions with on-screen characters have been shown to foster positive learning outcomes (Moussiades et al., 2019). In addition, the effectiveness of video screen media is dependent on specific content and design characteristics, including the inclusion of questioning, opportunities for child play, problem-solving, language and literacy learning through on-screen text, and the stimulation of curiosity (Moussiades et al., 2019). These features ought to be considered when designing YouTube video content that aims to facilitate early learning and development.

Screen Time and Child

Screen time refers to the duration individuals spend engaging with screens, encompassing television, computers, gaming consoles, and portable devices such as smartphones and tablets. Children's development is strongly influenced by the relationships they form within their environment (Williams, Biscaro, Clinton, 2019). In today's world, these relationships increasingly involve screens. The initial encounters that young children have with screens are particularly influential because they establish patterns of exposure and usage (Kostyrka-Allchorne, Cooper, Simpson, 2017; Hamilton, Spinks, White, Kavanagh, Walsh, 2016), which tend to persist into later stages of life (Hamilton et al., 2016; Sigman, 2019). Since parents largely control children's access to screens during this early period, it is easier to modify their exposure compared to later stages (Hamilton et al., 2016; Tang, Darlington, Ma, Haines, 2018). Implementing limits is crucial because infants and toddlers engage with screens in ways that can affect their language acquisition, cognitive development, and socio-emotional well-being (Kostyrka-Allchorne, Cooper, Simpson, 2017; Simonato, Janosz, Archambault, Pagani, 2018). According to Ofcom (2023), the majority of homes with children aged 0-18 (97%) had access to the internet in 2022, significantly higher than the average for all households (93%). Most children aged 3-17 went online (at home or elsewhere) via mobile phones (69%) and tablets (64%), although the types of devices used vary by age of child. Among 3-17-year-olds, YouTube emerged as the preferred online platform, with 88% of them using it. WhatsApp followed closely at 55%, while TikTok and Snapchat garnered usage rates of 53% and 46% respectively. Notably, the utilization of WhatsApp, TikTok, and Snapchat witnessed an upswing compared to 2021, with their percentages rising to 55%, 53%, and 46% respectively. According to the recent study of Gaudreau, Hirsh-Pasek,and Golinkoff (2022), children posed a lower number of questions in the cell phone compared to the control condition. Shah et al. (2021) observed a positive relationship between heightened curiosity levels in kindergarten children and a higher occurrence of parental conversation during shared television viewing. This association exhibited a more pronounced effect within low socioeconomic status (SES) families. Kirkorian et al. (2015) conducted a research in the context of the video condition, search performance in children was specifically predicted by visual attention directed towards the target location. However, in the case of in-person hiding events, children exhibited high success rates even when their visual attention towards the correct location was relatively low. These findings align with the hypothesis that toddlers demonstrate faster processing of information in the case of in-person events compared to video-based events. This accelerated processing enables them to achieve comparable or even superior learning outcomes, despite exhibiting relatively low levels of selective attention. Hence, the video deficit phenomenon may be attributed to both deficient encoding and memory retrieval processes, as suggested by Kirkorian et al. (2015). Although the study did not encompass assessments of television program content, digital media usage, and non-screen time conversation, our findings underscore the significance of parental conversation in fostering early childhood curiosity, particularly among children facing socioeconomic disadvantages. The findings of Moser et al., (2015) study reveal the existence of a persistent bidirectional transfer deficit that extends up to three years of age. Younger children exhibit a more pronounced transfer deficit, even in situations involving high perceptual similarities and social engagement. These results support the memory flexibility account of the transfer deficit, indicating that children tend to learn less in transfer tasks. The implications of these findings are discussed in relation to the use of screen media, such as video and tablets, in early education.

The video deficit effect, as described by Anderson and Pempek (2005), pertains to the limited ability of infants to transfer learning from television and static 2D images to real-life situations, particularly when compared to their ability to transfer learning from face-to-face interactions. This effect becomes noticeable around 15 months of age, reaches its peak, and persists until at least 36 months of age, varying slightly depending on the complexity of the task involved (Barr et al., 2007a; Barr et al., 2007b; Flynn & Whiten, 2008; Hayne, et al., 2003; Nielsen, et al., 2008; Sheffield & Hudson, 2006; Simcock & DeLoache, 2006; Simcock & Dooley, 2007). The non-apparent nature of the video deficit effect at 6 months of age is also worth noting. Several factors can be used to predict the potential for learning and improvement of the video deficit effect. These factors include the repetition of content (Barr et al., 2007a, 2007b), the unique auditory and visual cues found in media (Barr et al., 2009), social contingency cues (or their absence; Nielsen et al., 2008; Troseth et al., 2006), the demands on working memory (Krcmar, Grela, & Lin, 2007; Suddendorf, 2003), and the perceptual demands of the specific task used to examine the transfer of learning (Barr & Hayne, 1999; Schmitt & Anderson, 2002; Suddendorf et al., 2007). When the cognitive load exceeds the processing abilities of young children, there is a rapid decline in the transfer of learning. With over 2 billion monthly active users, YouTube has become an integral part of our daily lives. However, to create engaging and instructional content, content creators must have an understanding of the cognitive theory of multimedia learning. The cognitive theory of multimedia learning (CTML) is a theoretical framework that explains how individuals learn from multimedia content (Mayer, 2009). This theory suggests that learning occurs through cognitive processing and knowledge construction, where learners actively engage with the presented information (Mayer & Moreno, 2003). CTML emphasizes the importance of designing multimedia content in a way that optimizes cognitive processing, attention, and retention of information.

This study aims to analyse 10 popular YouTube video for very young learners with YouTube Evaluation Rubric. The analysis focus on how the content creators design and present their content to optimize the learning process for their audience. By analysing the content creators' strategies, this study hopes to provide insights into effective methods for designing multimedia content that maximizes learning outcomes.

Cognitive Theory of Multimedia Learning

The cognitive theory of multimedia learning (CTML) is a theoretical framework that explains how individuals learn from multimedia content by emphasizing the importance of optimizing cognitive processing, attention, and retention of information (Mayer, 2009). The CTML framework suggests that the use of multimedia elements, such as audio, video, and text, can enhance the learning process by providing multiple channels of information for the learner to process (Clark & Mayer, 2016). The cognitive load theory (CLT) is another theoretical framework that has been applied to multimedia learning. CLT suggests that learning can be impaired if the cognitive load of multimedia content is too high, leading to cognitive overload (Paas, Renkl, & Sweller, 2003). Studies have explored the effects of multimedia design on learning outcomes in various contexts. For instance, Mayer and Moreno (2003) found that presenting words as spoken text and images together led to better learning outcomes than presenting words as spoken text and images separately. Similarly, Mayer (2009) argued that the use of diagrams in multimedia presentations can lead to better learning outcomes than text-based presentations. These findings suggest that effective multimedia design can improve learning outcomes. The popularity of YouTube has led to an increasing number of content creators on the platform. These content creators use a variety of multimedia elements to engage and educate their audience. However, it is unclear how these content creators use multimedia design principles to optimize learning outcomes for their audience. Therefore, the present study aims to analyse 10 popular YouTube content creator accounts with respect to CTML and identify effective strategies for designing multimedia content that maximizes learning outcomes. In conclusion, the literature suggests that the use of multimedia elements can enhance the learning process. CTML and CLT are theoretical frameworks that emphasize the importance of optimizing the multimedia design to maximize learning outcomes. The present study aims to contribute to this literature by analysing 10 popular YouTube content creator accounts and identifying effective strategies for multimedia design.

Multimedia Design Principles

Richard Mayer, a prominent researcher in the field of multimedia learning, has developed a set of principles for designing effective multimedia learning materials. These principles are based on the cognitive theory of multimedia learning (CTML) and emphasize the importance of optimizing cognitive processing, attention, and retention of information (Mayer, 2009). The purpose of this literature review is to explore the concepts related to Mayer's multimedia principles and their impact on learning outcomes. Mayer's multimedia principles include coherence, redundancy, signalling, spatial contiguity, temporal contiguity, and modality. Coherence refers to the principle of ensuring that the words, images, and audio in a multimedia presentation are presented in a clear and organized manner that allows the learner to easily integrate the information. Redundancy refers to the principle of presenting information in multiple forms to support learning, while avoiding overloading cognitive resources. Signalling refers to the use of visual or auditory cues to draw attention to important information. Spatial contiguity refers to the principle of presenting text and images in close proximity to each other to facilitate integration. Temporal contiguity refers to the principle of synchronizing audio and visual information to enhance learning. Modality refers to the principle of presenting information in multiple modalities, such as audio and visual, to support learning (Mayer, 2009). Research has provided evidence for the effectiveness of Mayer's multimedia principles in improving learning outcomes. For instance, studies have found that coherence, redundancy, and signalling can enhance learning when used appropriately (Mayer & Moreno, 2003; Sweller, van Merriënboer, & Paas, 1998). The spatial contiguity principle has also been found to improve learning outcomes by reducing the cognitive load (Mayer & Sims, 1994). Temporal contiguity has been found to enhance learning by improving the integration of audio and visual information (Mayer & Anderson, 1991). Finally, the modality principle has been found to improve learning outcomes by providing multiple channels of information (Mayer & Moreno, 2003).

This discussion on the importance of video design features for facilitating learning encompasses Mayer's (2008) principles of multimedia design, which offer valuable guidelines in this domain. The principles can be summarized as follows: Coherence, where extraneous or irrelevant material should be minimized in relation to the learning objective; Signalling, which involves highlighting essential information or significant elements; Redundancy, suggesting the use of narrated animations without accompanying on-screen text; Spatial contiguity, advocating for the placement of printed words adjacent to relevant graphics; Temporal contiguity, emphasizing the simultaneous presentation of narration and animation; Segmenting, recommending the presentation of animations in learner-paced segments; Pretraining, involving the provision of preliminary instruction on key components; Modality, suggesting the presentation of words as spoken text rather than printed text; Multimedia, promoting the integration of words and pictures rather than relying solely on textual information; and Personalization, encouraging a conversational style and avoiding formal language by incorporating pronouns like 'your' instead of 'the.' These ten principles offer valuable insights into the design and delivery of videos to effectively support instructional practices in educational settings.

To sum up, Richard Mayer, a prominent researcher in the field of multimedia learning, has developed a set of principles for designing effective multimedia learning materials. These principles, based on the cognitive theory of multimedia learning, focus on optimizing cognitive processing, attention, and information retention. Mayer's principles include coherence, redundancy, signalling, personalization, spatial contiguity, temporal contiguity, and modality. Additionally, Mayer's work highlights the benefits of personalization in multimedia learning materials, suggesting that a conversational style and the inclusion of personal pronouns can enhance learner engagement and performance.

Methodology

The YouTube Evaluation Rubric was adapted from Neumann and Herodotou (2020). This rubric was designed by them to assess the educational quality of YouTube videos based on four main criteria: Age appropriateness, Content quality, Design features, and Learning objectives. To achieve this, the main criteria were further divided into 17 sub-criteria (questions). A 3-point scoring system was employed to assess each question, with a score of 0 for "No evidence," 1 for "Partial evidence," and 2 for "Ample evidence." The total numeric assessment per video was obtained by summing the scores of all sub-criteria (max score = 18 × 2 = 36). The overall quality rating classification of a video was determined by its total score, where videos scoring below 17 were considered "Not Recommended," and those scoring between 17 and 34 were "Recommended" for viewing by children aged 0–8 years old. To validate the proposed evaluation rubric, one popular YouTube videos for very young children was piloted. These videos were selected based on their level of popularity, which was determined by the number of YouTube channel subscribers and most popular categories. All the chosen videos were in Turkish. The most popular categories included songs and nursery rhymes, unboxing, fun toys, and play, and create and explore. The proposed evaluation rubric provides a comprehensive tool that can be used by parents, caregivers, and educators to assess the educational quality of YouTube videos targeting young children.

Interrater Reliability

To establish the interrater reliability of the rubric and scoring criteria, two people co-scored a test video and refined the rubric and scoring criteria. Next, each of the ten videos listed in Table 3 was independently scored by the two people, resulting in a total of 180 items scored (10 videos × 18 items). The level of interrater reliability was assessed using Cohen's Kappa, which was calculated to be 0.89, indicating substantial agreement between the two scorers. The disagreements were then reviewed and discussed by the two authors, who ultimately agreed on the 14 disputed items. Specifically, author one agreed with six of author two's scores, while author two agreed with nine of author one's scores. As a result, the final agreed-upon scores were used and presented in Table 3.

A. General Features of the YouTube Videos

Length in minute:

View:

Likes:

Dislikes:

Comments:

Channel Subscription:

B. YouTube Evaluation Rubric (Adapted from Neumann & Herodotou, 2020)

Age appropriateness	1. Can the child imitate the content presented (e.g. repeat song, make body movements or gestures)?
	2. Does the content share similarities with the child (e.g., age, gender, interests)?
	3. Is the behaviour on-screen positive (e.g., ethical, fair, caring, moral, non-violent, non-scary, healthy)?
	4. Does the on-screen behaviour receive appropriate reinforcement (e.g., positive behaviour is praised or encouraged, and negative behaviour is discouraged)?
Content quality	5. Are social relationships accurately represented (e.g., gender and cultural stereotypes, power relationships)?
	6. Does the video encourage children to perform creative tasks, solve problems or provide alternative ideas or ways of doing things?
	7. Does the video encourage children to repeat content?
	8. Are the images, audio, sounds and language used appropriately for children (i.e. the child can understand the content)?
	9. Is each scene clear, logical, and easy to follow?
Design features	10. Is some content repeated during the video (e.g., to reinforce learning in positive ways)?
	11. Is there low and gradual pace with infrequent scene and character changes?
	12. Are pictures/graphics/animations presented alongside words/narration?
	13. Is conversational style (personalization) used in wording (oral and written)?
	14. Is there irrelevant elements used in the video?
	15. Are learning elements highlighted in the video?
Learning objectives	16. Does the video support cognitive(e.g.,language, literacy, math,science knowledge)
	17. Does the video support physical development (e.g., gross and fine motor skills)?

18. Does the video support socio-emotional development (e.g., fosters positive relationships, communication skills, moral attitudes, resilience, self-regulation, self-confidence)?

General Features of Videos

Table 1 presents the distribution, mean, standard deviation, minimum, and maximum values for the general characteristics of the chosen videos, including their length, duration online, views, likes, dislikes, VPI, and channel subscription data.

Table 1 General Features of Videos

	Video 1 A Journey into Your Body	Video 2 Rotten Ali and Germ Necati	Video 3 Toy nursery: exclusive sections. Fun and educational videos!	Video 4 Educational cartoon - Smart cars - Vegetables – English	Video 5 Wash Your Hands and More educational cartoons	Video 6 Watch cartoons - Utility Cars - We are picking fruits! Educational series for babies)	Video 7 Blippi Learns 5 Senses | Blippi Turkish - Educational videos for kids | Turkish Dubbed	Video 8 Planets	Video 9 Learning Shapes | Cartoons for the little ones with Tino	Video 10 Eymen and Grass | robot brotherhoo d
Lenght (in minutes)	8.36	12.32	1:04:49	6.17	1:00:27	21:14	17.32	3.26	4.30	11.45
View	54.546.553	130.341.69 8	122.529.29 5	59.009.088	12.600.000	1.603.040	11.363.652	335.061.96 0	141.289.59 0	35.763.651
Likes	40.000	55.000	34.000	19.000	1.300	3000	2	882.000	466.000	69.000
Dislikes	-	-	-	-	-	-	-	-	-	-
Comments	1672	Comments are closed.	Comments are closed.	Comments are closed.	Comments are closed.	Comments are closed.	Comments are closed.	Comments are closed.	Comments are closed.	Comments are closed.
Channel Subscriptio n	3.55 million	554.000	1.33 million	3.21 million	259.000	3.21 million	292.000	1,06 million	496.000	6.2 million

Table 2 YouTube Evaluation Rubric (Adapted from Neumann & Herodotou, 2020)

Sub-criteria:	1 1	2	3	4	5	6	7	8	9	10	11	12	13	14	15	16	17	18	
Video 1 A Journey into Your Body	0	2	2	2	2	2	0	1	1	0	0	2	2	0	0	2	0	0	18
Video 2 Rotten Ali and Germ Necati	0	0	0	0	0	0	0	2	2	0	0	0	2	0	0	0	0	0	6
Video 3 Toy nursery: exclusive sections. Fun and educational videos!	0	2	2	2	2	2	0	2	2	0	0	0	2	0	2	0	0	2	20
Video 4 Educational cartoon - Smart cars - Vegetables – English	0	0	2	2	2	0	0	2	2	0	2	0	0	2	2	0	0	0	16
Video 5 Wash Your Hands and More educational cartoons	2	2	2	2	2	0	2	2	2	2	2	0	2	2	2	2	0	2	30
Video 6 Watch cartoons - Smart Cars - We are picking fruits! Educational series for babies)	2	2	2	2	2	0	0	2	2	2	2	2	2	2	2	2	2	2	32
Video 7 Blippi Learns 5 Senses | Blippi Turkish - Educational videos for kids | Turkish Dubbed	2	2	2	2	2	2	2	2	2	2	2	2	2	2	2	2	2	2	36
Video 8 Planets	0	2	2	2	2	2	2	2	2	2	2	2	2	2	2	2	2	2	34
Video 9 Learning Shapes | Cartoons for the little ones with Tino	0	2	2	2	2	0	2	2	2	2	2	2	2	2	2	0	2	2	30
Video 10 Eymen and Grass | robot brotherhood	0	2	2	2	2	0	0	2	2	2	2	2	2	0	0	0	0	2	22

*(See Table 2 for the 18 sub-criteria questions. Score 0 = No; Score 1 = Partial Evidence; Score 2 = Yes)

**(0 to <18 = Not recommended; 18 to 36 = Recommended)

It is interesting to note that video length varies greatly among the videos, ranging from just over 3 minutes to over an hour. This is likely due to differences in content and audience. For example, videos targeted towards young children tend to be shorter in length to match their attention span, while more in-depth educational videos for adults may require a longer run time.

Figure 1 Smart Cars - We are picking fruits! Educational series for babies

Figure 2 Rotten Ali and Germ Necati

Figure 3 Toy nursery: exclusive sections. Fun and educational videos!

The videos analysed according to learning objectives and some of the videos had wrong information was processed. The analysis of the videos based on their learning objectives revealed a concerning trend: several videos contained inaccuracies or incorrect information. In one particular video, a tomato was erroneously identified as a vegetable, while in fact, it is a fruit. This highlights a lack of accuracy and factual knowledge in the content presented. Another video titled "Rotten Ali and Germ Necati" raised concerns as the main characters emphasized the benefits of consuming sweet treats before going to bed. This message contradicts established health guidelines that discourage the consumption of sugary foods close to bedtime. Such misinformation could mislead young viewers and potentially have negative impacts on their health habits. In yet another video titled "Toy nursery: exclusive sections. Fun and educational videos!" an issue with spelling was observed. Specifically, the letters of the alphabet were misspelled. This undermines the educational aspect of the video, as the incorrect spelling could confuse or misinform young viewers who are in the process of learning their ABCs. Overall, these instances of wrong information and inaccuracies in the analyzed videos highlight the importance of ensuring that educational content for children is thoroughly reviewed and fact-checked. It is crucial to provide accurate information and promote healthy habits to support children's learning and development.

Figure 4 Blippi Learns 5 Senses | Blippi Turkish - Educational videos for kids | Turkish Dubbed

Bilippi is undeniably a renowned YouTube channel with a vast viewership among children worldwide. However, a critical analysis of one of their videos, titled "Blippi Learns 5 Senses | Blippi Turkish - Educational videos for kids | Turkish Dubbed," revealed some shortcomings in the video's content structure. Despite being titled "5 senses," the Blippi character's approach in the video seemed disjointed and lacked proper organization. Instead of focusing on the intended learning objective of the five senses, the video initially diverted attention towards colors and numbers. This departure from the primary topic could confuse young viewers and hinder their comprehension of the designated subject matter. It is crucial for educational content to maintain a coherent and logical flow to maximize its effectiveness. Furthermore, when the Blippi character eventually transitioned to discussing vehicles, there was an oversight in reinforcing the previously covered learning objective. Rather than incorporating the color aspect, such as mentioning a "yellow cement truck," the character merely mentioned "cement truck." This missed opportunity to connect the learning objectives and reinforce knowledge limits the video's educational impact.

Figure 5 Rotten Ali and Germ Necati

In addition to analyzing the videos based on their learning objectives and content accuracy, it is equally important to assess their on-screen behavior in terms of being positive, ethical, fair, caring, moral, non-violent, non-scary, and promoting a healthy environment. Unfortunately, during the analysis, it was observed that the main characters in the video "Rotten Ali and Germ Necati" exhibited behavior that could be considered scary for very young learners. For young children, a safe and non-threatening environment is crucial for their emotional well-being and healthy development. When the main characters in a video intended for educational purposes portray scary or intimidating behavior, it can create fear or discomfort among young viewers. This can have a negative impact on their learning experience and may even deter them from engaging with educational content in the future. To ensure that educational videos cater to the needs of young learners, content creators should be mindful of the on-screen behavior of their characters. It is important to prioritize creating a positive, caring, and non-threatening environment that fosters a sense of emotional security for children. By doing so, educational videos can effectively engage young learners and contribute to their overall positive development.

To ensure optimal learning experiences, educational content creators should strive to maintain a well-structured approach and provide consistent reinforcement of learning objectives. By doing so, they can enhance comprehension and retention among young viewers, making the educational content more effective and valuable. Overall, the table provides a snapshot of the diverse range of content available on video-sharing platforms and the popularity of different topics among viewers. The popularity of educational content and children's videos highlights the potential for online media to serve as a valuable learning tool for people of all ages.

Discussion and Conclusion

This paper presents a comprehensive review of studies that describe how specific design features of screen media may support very young children's learning. The authors have adapted the YouTube evaluation criteria from Neumann & Herodotou (2020), which are grounded in key theoretical frameworks such as sociocultural theory (Vygotsky, 1978), social-cognitive theory (Bandura et al., 1961), multimedia learning (Mayer, 1994) that can be used to guide the selection of YouTube videos for children. The present study is particularly relevant given the rising popularity of YouTube videos targeting very young children and the increasing amount of time children are spending on YouTube (Rideout & Robb, 2019). Although YouTube has been relatively underexplored compared to other screen media such as television (Khan, 2017), a few studies have investigated the design of educational videos and their relationship with behavior and engagement (Neumann & Herodotou, 2020; Shoufan, 2019). Informed by insights from a similar medium (TV), the present study provides a comprehensive set of evaluation criteria that teachers, parents, and caregivers can use to assess the learning quality of YouTube videos and make informed decisions about which videos their children should watch to maximize learning opportunities.

This research highlights the impact of screen time on children's development, particularly in the early stages of exposure. It emphasizes the role of parents in controlling children's screen time during this critical period, as it is easier to modify their exposure at this stage compared to later stages. The study emphasizes the importance of implementing limits on screen time due to its potential effects on language acquisition, cognitive development, and socio-emotional well-being. The study also provides insights into the prevalence of internet access and device usage among households with children. It reports that most homes with children have internet access, with mobile phones and tablets being the primary devices used by children. It also highlights the popularity of online platforms such as YouTube, WhatsApp, TikTok, and Snapchat among children, with increased usage compared to previous years. Additionally, the research refers to the video deficit effect, which pertains to the limited ability of infants to transfer learning from screens to real-life situations compared to face-to-face interactions. This effect becomes noticeable around 15 months of age and persists until at least 36 months of age. Several factors, such as content repetition, auditory and visual cues, social contingency cues, working memory demands, and perceptual demands, can influence the potential for learning and the extent of the video deficit effect. Finally, the study highlights the importance of understanding the cognitive theory of multimedia learning for content creators on platforms like YouTube.

The cognitive theory of multimedia learning emphasizes the active engagement of learners with multimedia content for effective learning, emphasizing the optimization of cognitive processing, attention, and retention of information in content design. To facilitate the development of crucial life skills such as language acquisition, self-regulation, and creative thinking in children below the age of 5, it is essential for them to engage in active play and spend quality time with their families. Parents play a significant role in shaping healthy screen habits for their young children. This can be achieved through the following practices:

Limiting personal screen usage in the presence of young children, particularly during meal times, play activities, and other significant opportunities for social learning.

Prioritizing interactions with children through meaningful conversations, play engagements, and fostering healthy and active routines.

Making informed decisions regarding media usage, engaging with media together with children, and ensuring screens are turned off when not in use.

Ensuring that any media consumed in the presence of children is devoid of stereotyping, advertising, or other potentially problematic content.

Children younger than 2 years: It is not advisable to expose them to screen time, except for video-chatting with caring adults. There is insufficient evidence to support the introduction of technology at an early age.

Children aged 2 to 5 years: Limit routine or sedentary screen time to approximately 1 hour or less per day.

Children younger than 5 years in child care: Avoid incorporating sedentary screen time as a regular part of their daily routine.

Establish daily periods free from screen usage, particularly during important family activities such as meals and book-sharing.

This study evaluated the quality of ten popular YouTube videos for very young children using a set of four criteria: Age Appropriateness, Content Quality, Design Features, and Learning Objectives. The videos 5, 6, 7 and 8 received the highest scores, indicating an acceptable level of quality with the potential to foster positive behavior and learning. However, it should be noted that further research is required to establish the actual learning benefits of watching these videos. On the other hand, the 2 and 4 received the lowest scores, indicating limited quality and the need for careful consideration when using them for educational purposes.

The use of conversational and guided interactions is an effective approach to supporting early learning when using YouTube videos in educational settings and at home (Davidson et al., 2014). Such interactions can include the use of question-answer strategies and embodied actions, such as nodding during co-viewing, which can enhance children's meaning-making processes. Additionally, research suggests that parental scaffolding, which is consistent with Vygotsky's (1978) Zone of Proximal Development, is critical for promoting positive learning outcomes in young children (Pempek et al., 2011). For instance, positive parental interactions, such as physical and verbal involvement and maintaining a positive tone, are linked to positive child outcomes.

Adults should engage in co-viewing, discussion, and reflection with children on the content of YouTube videos to identify and discourage negative messages, such as cyberbullying, violence, and stereotypes, while promoting and reinforcing positive behaviors, such as caring and sharing. These interactions can foster children's ethical and critical engagement in their online community by imparting them with the knowledge and skills necessary to participate thoughtfully. It is important to note that the findings of this pilot study should not be overgeneralized, nor should clear recommendations be made, given the limited number of videos assessed. Nevertheless, an inter-rater agreement check conducted between the two raters indicated a substantial level of agreement on the criteria items.

References

Anderson, D. R., & Pempek, T. A. (2005). Television and very young children. American Behavioral Scientist, 48(5), 505-522.

Anderson, M., & Jiang, J. (2018). Teens, social media & technology 2018. Pew Research Center.

Barr, R., Garcia, A., Muentener, P. (2007a). Age-related changes in deferred imitation from television by 6- to 18-month-olds. Developmental Science. 10:910–921.

Barr, R., Hayne, H. (1999). Developmental changes in imitation from television during infancy. Child Development. 70:1067–1081.

Barr, R., Lauricella, A., Zack, E., Calvert, S.L. (2010). The relation between infant exposure to television and executive functioning, cognitive skills, and school readiness at age four. Merrill Palmer Quarterly. 56:21–48.

Barr, R., Muentener, P., Garcia, A., Fujimoto, M., Chavez, V. (2007b). The effect of repetition on imitation from television during infancy. Developmental Psychobiology. 49:196–207.

Clark, R. C., & Mayer, R. E. (2016). E-learning and the science of instruction: Proven guidelines for consumers and designers of multimedia learning. John Wiley & Sons.

Flynn, E., Whiten, A. (2008). Imitation of hierarchical structure versus component details of complex actions by 3- and 5-year-olds. Journal of Experimental Child Psychology. 101:228–240.

Gaudreau, C., Hirsh-Pasek,K., & Golinkoff, R. M. (2022). What's in a distraction? The effect of parental cell phone use on parents' and children's question-asking. Developmental Psychology, 58(1), 55–68. https://doi.org/10.1037/dev0001268

Hamilton, K., Spinks, T., White, K.M., Kavanagh, D.J., Walsh, A.M. (2016). A psychosocial analysis of parents' decisions for limiting their young child's screen time: An examination of attitudes, social norms and roles, and control perceptions. British Journal of Health Psychology, 21(2):285–301.

Hayne, H., Barr, R., Herbert J. (2003). The effect of prior practice on memory reactivation and generalization. Child Development. 74:1615–1627.

Hirsh-Pasek, K., Golinkoff, R.M. (2008). Brains in a box: Do new age toys deliver on the promise? In: Harwood R, editor. Child development in a changing society. Hoboken, NJ: Wiley Press.

Kirkorian, H. L., Lavigne, H. J., Hanson, K. G., Troseth, G. L., Demers, L. B., & Anderson, D. R. (2015). Video deficit in Toddlers' object retrieval: What eye movements reveal about online cognition. Infancy, 21(1), 37–64. doi:10.1111/infa.12102

Krcmar, M., Grela, B., Lin, K. (2007). Can toddlers learn vocabulary from television? An experimental approach. Media Psychology. 10:41–63.

Kostyrka-Allchorne, K., Cooper, N.R., Simpson, A. (2017). The relationship between television exposure and children's cognition and behaviour: A systematic review. Develop Rev., 44:19–58.

Livingstone, S., & Helsper, E. J. (2007). Gradations in digital inclusion: Children, young people and the digital divide. New Media & Society, 9(4), 671-696.

Mayer, R. E. (2005). Cognitive theory of multimedia learning. In R. E. Mayer (Ed.), The Cambridge handbook of multimedia learning (pp. 31-48). Cambridge University Press.

Mayer, R. E. (2014). Cognitive theory of multimedia learning. In The Cambridge Handbook of Multimedia Learning (pp. 43-71). Cambridge University Press.

Mayer, R. E., & Anderson, R. B. (1991). Animations need narrations: An experimental test of a dual-coding hypothesis. Journal of Educational Psychology, 83(4), 484-490.

Mayer, R. E. (2008). Applying the science of learning: Evidence-based principles for the design of multimedia instruction. The American Psychologist, 63(8), 760–769. https://doi.org/10.1037/0003-066X.63.8.760.

Mayer, R. E., & Sims, V. K. (1994). For whom is a picture worth a thousand words? Extensions of a dual-coding theory of multimedia learning. Journal of Educational Psychology, 86(3), 389-401.

Mayer, R. E., & Wittrock, M. C. (2006). Problem-solving transfer. In P. A. Alexander & P. H. Winne (Eds.), Handbook of educational psychology (2nd ed., pp. 465-482). Lawrence Erlbaum Associates Publishers.

Moser, A., Zimmermann, L., Dickerson, K., Grenell, A., Barr, R., & Gerhardstein, P. (2015). They can interact, but can they learn? toddlers' transfer learning from touchscreens and television. Journal of Experimental Child Psychology, 137, 137–155. doi:10.1016/j.jecp.2015.04.002

Moussiades, L., Kazanidis, I., & Iliopoulou, A. (2019). A framework for the development of educational video: An empirical approach. Innovations in Education and Teaching International, 56(2), 217-228. https://doi.org/10.1080/14703297.2017.1399809

Neumann, M.M., & Herodotou, C. (2020). Evaluating YouTube videos for young children. Education and Information Technologies, 25, 4459-4475.

Nielsen, M., Simcock, G., Jenkins, L. (2008). The effect of social engagement on 24-month-olds' imitation from live and televised models. Developmental Science.11:722–731.

Ofcom, Children and parents: media use and attitudes report (2023). [online] Available at: Children and parents: media use and attitudes report 2023 [Accessed on 2 February 2023]

Paas, F., Renkl, A., & Sweller, J. (2003). Cognitive load theory and instructional design: Recent developments. Educational Psychologist, 39(1), 1-4.

Paivio, A. (1971). Imagery and verbal processes. Holt, Rinehart, and Winston.

Schmitt, K., Anderson, D.R. (2002). Television and reality: Toddlers' use of visual information from video to guide behavior. Media Psychology. 4:51–76.

Sheffield, E.G., Hudson, J.A. (2006). You must remember this: Effects of video and photograph reminders on 18-month-olds' event memory. Journal of Cognition and Development. 7:73–93.

Shah, P.E., Hirsh-Pasek, K., Kashdan, T.B., Harrison, K., Rosenblum, K., Weeks, H.M., Singh, P., Kaciroti, N. (2021). Daily television exposure, parent conversation during shared television viewing and socioeconomic status: Associations with curiosity at kindergarten. PLoS ONE 16(10): e0258572. https://doi.org/10.1371/journal.pone.0258572

Simcock, G., DeLoache, J. (2008). The effect of repetition on infants' imitation from picture books varying in iconicity. Infancy. 13:687–697.

Simcock, G., Dooley, M. (2007). Generalization of learning from picture books to novel test conditions by 18 and 24-month-old children. Developmental Psychology. 43:1568–1578.

Sigman, A. (2019). A Movement for Movement: Screen time, physical activity and sleep; a new integrated approach for children. Uttoxeter, UK: Association of Play Industries, 2019: https://www.api-play.org/wp-content/uploads/sites/4/2019/01/API-Report-A-Movementfor-Movement-A4FINAL WEB.pdf (Accessed June 10, 2023).

Simonato, I., Janosz, M., Archambault, M., Pagani, L.S. (2018). Prospective associations between toddler televiewing and subsequent lifestyle habits in adolescence. Prev Med.,110:24–30.

Suddendorf T. (2003). Early representational insight: twenty-four-month-olds can use a photo to find an object in the world. Child Development. 74:896–904.

Sweller, J. (1988). Cognitive load during problem-solving: Effects on learning. Cognitive Science, 12(2), 257-285.

Sweller, J., van Merriënboer, J. J. G., & Paas, F. G. W. C. (1998). Cognitive architecture and instructional design. Educational Psychology Review, 10(3), 251-296.Mayer, R. E., & Moreno, R. (2003). Nine ways to reduce cognitive load in multimedia learning. Educational Psychologist, 38(1), 43-52.

Tang, L., Darlington, G., Ma, D.W.L., Haines, J. (2018). Guelph Family Health Study. Mothers' and fathers' media parenting practices associated with young children's screen-time: A cross-sectional study. BMC Obesity, 5:37.

Van Merriënboer, J. J. G., & Sweller, J. (2005). Cognitive load theory and complex learning: Recent developments and future directions. Educational Psychology Review, 17(2), 147-177.

Williams, R.C., Biscaro, A., Clinton, J. (2019). Canadian Paediatric Society, Early Years Task Force. Relationships matter: How clinicians can support positive parenting in the early years. Paediatr Child Health ;24(5):340–57

YouTube. (n.d.). YouTube Press. Retrieved February 17, 2023, from https://www.youtube.com/about/press/

TOWARDS BEST PRACTICE IN DESIGNING SUSTAINABLE ONLINE PEER MENTORING AT SCALE – WHAT'S IN IT FOR THE MENTORS?

Julie Robson and Christopher Hutton, The Open University, UK

Correspondence: *Christopher Hutton: christopher.hutton@open.ac.uk*

Abstract

The benefits of peer mentoring for students studying in Higher Education are well established and have been demonstrated in online, blended and hybrid settings. Best practice in establishing financially sustainable schemes in online settings at a large scale is under researched. Motivations and barriers for peer mentors working effectively as volunteers are poorly established. Findings of a longitudinal study on undergraduate Earth and Environmental Science modules at The Open University, UK are presented. Peer mentors (who had already passed the module) were surveyed before and after completing a 9-month period supporting students asynchronously with non-academic support via a forum. Questionnaires established the challenges and benefits for the mentors, and were followed up by focus groups. Most mentors remained active and committed throughout, identifying few barriers; their expectations before starting were similar to their actual experience. More students volunteer for mentoring than are needed, with many completing more than one round of duty. It is therefore concluded that the mentoring scheme is financially sustainable and transferable to different modules and disciplines. While mentors valued their skills development, further work is required to help them appreciate their employability skills development and potential impact.

Keywords:

Volunteer peer mentor; distance education; online education; employability; skills; focus group; STEM.

Introduction

There is little literature available to assess the benefits of online peer mentoring, or online peer assisted learning, apart from the review by Tibingana-Ahimbisibwe et al., (2022, and references therein) and Marshall et al., (2021), but the consensus is that such mentoring can benefit online distance learning students in many ways. The present study aimed to assess the benefits and challenges of volunteering in an online peer mentoring programme for the mentors, as some authors (Dawson et al., 2014; Rockinson-Szapkiw and Wendt, 2020) recognise that mentors also benefit in: developing new employability skills; reinforcing their own learning; and, particularly for black women in STEM, strengthening their career aspirations. Marshall et al. (2021) noted that undergraduate mentors at two universities recorded benefits in knowledge, self-awareness and career development. This is supported by Carvalho and Santos (2022), who showed that peer mentoring developed mentors' collaborative and metacognitive skills in an online constructivist learning environment.

In contrast, the challenges for online peer mentors identified by Pollard and Kumar (2021) include setting mentee expectations, online communication, and the need for training and support. Furthermore, Marshall et al. (2021) noted challenges relating to mentors learning the role, engaging with and relating to students (e.g. final year undergraduates mentoring entry level students in face-to-face settings). Many challenges appear to cross discipline, academic level, faculties and affect all types of online peer mentoring, whether 1:1 or 1:many. However, these challenges can be largely overcome by using good strategies to manage expectations and the provision of mentor training (Pollard and Kumar, 2021). It is likely that the challenges are more programme specific than the benefits, as perceived by mentors.

Leidenfrost et al. (2011) identified three distinct peer mentoring styles; motivating, informative, and negative or minimalist, which may have a greater impact on how mentors themselves perceive the benefits and challenges of online mentoring. These can also provide guidance for training to improve the sustainability of a peer mentoring programme, as mentors who perceive more benefits than challenges are more likely to continue in the role.

In their systematic literature review of e-mentoring programmes, Tinoco-Giraldo, Sanchez and García-Peñalvo (2020) identified several criteria for effective mentoring programmes, including: a good programme management structure; initial training for mentors; ongoing support for mentors; and periodic reviews of the programme to ensure quality is maintained and improved.

The current "Student Buddies" online peer-mentoring programme in Earth and Environmental Sciences at The Open University started with a year-2 pilot, 60-credit module in 2017 and has now expanded throughout the curriculum (Table 1).

Table 1: Summary of the mentors in the "Student Buddies Programme" 2022-23

	Number of peer mentors	Number of registered students
Year 1 (1 module) 60 credits	10	1795
Year 2 (2 modules) 60 credits	9	1062
Year 3 (2 modules) 60 credits	5	915
Year 3 (capstone project module) 30 credits	12	1046
Total	36	4818

The programme conforms to the recommendations outlined above in the literature and is designed to be generically applicable as its focus is on non-academic student support. Run entirely online via asynchronous forums on the Virtual Learning Environment, the average ratio of student mentors to students is 1:134. The programme has expanded into four other Schools in the STEM Faculty, and two other Faculties.

Volunteers are recruited from the most recent cohort of students who have passed the module. This means mentors are only 1-2 modules ahead of the mentees, so are often mentoring students at a similar stage in their degree. Some mentors (on the capstone project module) are returning graduates. Diversity and inclusion is embedded in the recruitment process, and is a strength of the programme. In particular, students with a range of pass grades are welcomed, as are students with varied backgrounds and characteristics (e.g. age, gender, neurodiversity, declared disability, varying personal commitments). Students who are selected as peer mentors are provided with synchronous online training; resources (a handbook, template forum posts, and IT guidance); and an Associate Lecturer to support their team. The mentoring forum is kept as a student space (with Associate Lecturer support) and advertised to all students studying the module.

A sustainable online peer-mentoring programme is dependent on a continuous inflow of new volunteer mentors, and while some mentors have carried on for 3 or 4 years across different modules on their student journey, to ensure sustainability we wanted to find out:

1. Are online, distance, peer mentoring schemes involving volunteer students sustainable?
2. What are the benefits and challenges of being a mentor?
3. Can mentoring contribute to students' employability skills?

Methods

Following the University's approval processes for student research projects, participating mentors were recruited after giving their explicit, informed consent. Data collection used a mixed methods approach to provide a robust, detailed investigation of the research questions (Creswell and Creswell, 2018). Participants completed either one or two anonymous questionnaires, the findings of which were enriched and triangulated through two identical focus groups (attended by 4 and 2 students respectively).

Online questionnaires [JISC Online Surveys, www.onlinesurveys.ac.uk] gathered information prior to mentoring for the first time (Questionnaire 1), and post completion of their first year (Questionnaire 2) to capture changes in mentors' perceptions and expectations.

Questionnaire 1 was sent to 44 new volunteers on modules starting between October 2019 and February 2021. Mentors were asked about:

- their availability, and expected time commitment
- why they volunteered
- which skills and attributes they thought would be useful
- their concerns and thoughts prior to starting
- comments on their induction, and training.

Questionnaire 2 was sent to 46 mentors from the same modules as Questionnaire 1, asking about:

- their time commitment and activity as mentors throughout the module
- if they would volunteer again, and why
- how well their team worked / communicated, and associated challenges
- skills that had been useful, or developed through mentoring
- strengths of, and improvements for the programme.

Questionnaire responses were used to derive open questions for two, 1-hour focus groups (FGs). Each FG was held online in Microsoft Teams [Microsoft Corporation, www.microsoft.com] in July 2022. Mentors were asked about:

- advice they'd give to new prospective mentors
- how well the practical aspects of mentoring online worked
- what were the main rewards and challenges involved
- how did mentoring contribute to personal/professional development.

Open questions facilitated more in-depth exploration of the research questions and as for the questionnaires, responses were analysed anonymously from transcripts by inductive thematic analysis in NVivo [QSR International Pty. Ltd., www.qsrinternational.com]. Closed questions from the questionnaires were analysed quantitatively using graphical techniques.

Results

Questionnaire 1

Thirty-five responses (79%) were received and 94.3% of respondents had >2 years of university study prior to volunteering. Most students (62.9%) had 2-4 hours available per week for mentoring. The most important self-selected personal attributes for mentoring were knowledge of the module, ability to help others, and interpersonal skills (Figure 1).

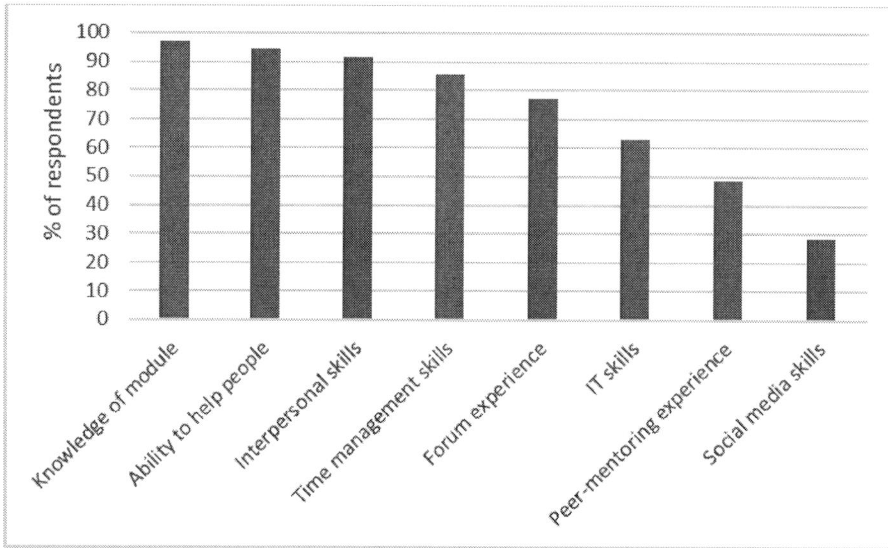

Figure 1. Number of respondents (%) agreeing to importance of personal attributes for buddying.

When students were asked about further attributes (not included in Figure 1), specific interpersonal skills, such as patience, positivity, teamwork, friendliness and tact were mentioned. The importance of any relevant prior experience (e.g. in education and training) was also identified, along with the need for reliability.

91.4% found the resources and training provided were helpful, and 94.3% engaged with pre-start online training.

Results from three open questions about motivation, concerns and thoughts before starting were analysed by thematic analysis (Table 2).

Table 2: Most common themes from free text questions in Questionnaire 1.

Question	Themes
Motivations for volunteering	1. Provide help 2. Personal development 3. Flexible role
Concerns before starting	1. No concerns 2. Ability to help effectively 3. Time commitment
Thoughts about starting	1. Eager and excited 2. Confident 3. Supported

Questionnaire 2

Twenty-two responses were received (47%); 86.4% of respondents had remained active for the duration of the module and 77.3% would consider volunteering again. Most (81.8%) respondents found the time commitment to be the same or less than what they had expected, at about 1 – 2 hours per week. 63.6% of students did not find the role impacted negatively on their current studies, while a further 22.7% were not studying at the time of volunteering.

Respondents repeated their skills selection as in Questionnaire 1 (Figure 2) and identified skills they felt they had developed while mentoring (Figure 3).

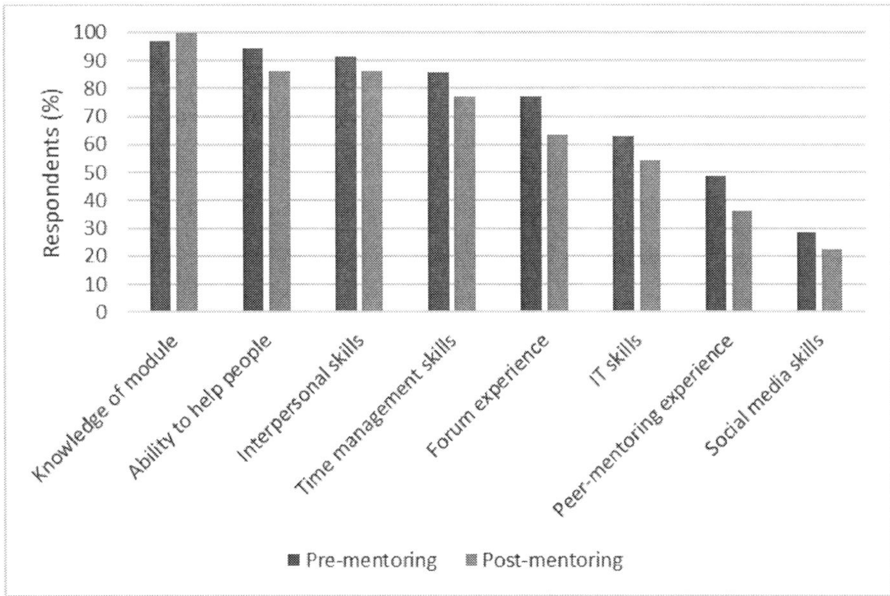

Figure 2. Comparison of personal attributes' importance pre- and post-mentoring experience.

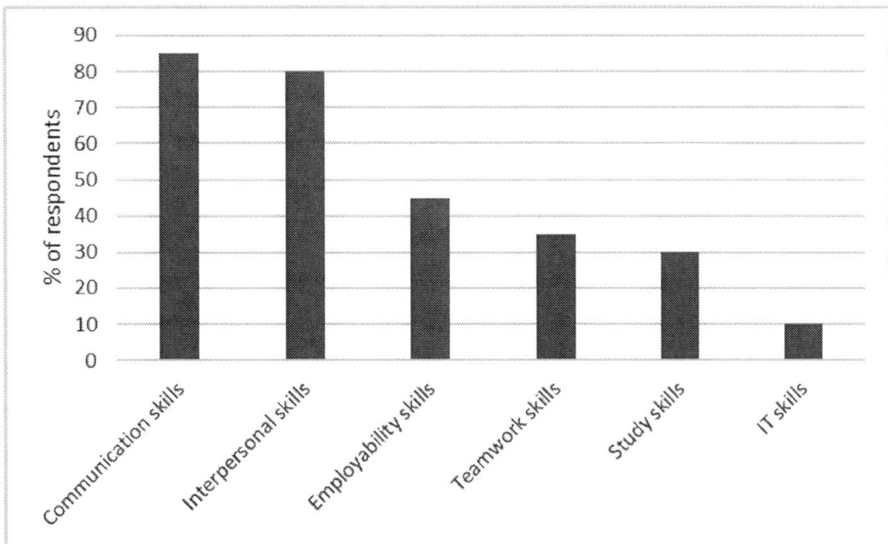

Figure 3. Skills identified as having developed during mentoring

Knowledge of the module they were working on was the only attribute that students said was more important than they initially thought, while prior experience in forums and peer-mentoring was much less important than they originally believed (Fig.2). Unsurprisingly, reflection indicated the most important skills to have improved were communication and interpersonal skills, singling out communication as the most important interpersonal skill of all. These, together with teamworking are all sound employability skills, though students see them separately.

Regarding team functionality, 90.9% felt it worked satisfactorily or better, and 72.7% felt part of the team. The majority (81.8%) reported communicating with fellow mentors, mostly via their own forum (88.9%) as important. Thematic analysis of open text questions revealed minor problems with team function including one buddy dominating the forums, and poor communication. However, a much greater number of positive themes emerged, the most common of which were effective teamwork, and a sense of inclusion during a respectful, supportive experience.

Open questions which invited identification of challenges and improvements elicited few responses. The main challenges were infrequent communication between mentors, personal time management, and students' expectations of what the mentoring role was. Suggested improvements were more frequent communication within the mentor team, and to provide opportunities for informal discussion between mentors across different modules.

Asked to identify the best thing about mentoring, a variety of responses were forthcoming, but the dominant theme was helping others. Feeling part of a team, giving back, being thanked, general satisfaction, and sharing knowledge and experience were also mentioned.

Focus Groups

The dominant themes, mapped against each focus group question, are presented in Table 3.

Table 3: Main themes from Focus Groups.

Question	Dominant themes
Advice offered to someone thinking of volunteering.	• Draw on own knowledge and experience • Need to be confident, flexible and patient • It is not time consuming • Rewarding to help others
How the practical aspects worked.	• Training was helpful • Include more training on dealing with difficult situations • Access to forums was mostly good • Support available if needed • No need for similar responses to same question • Good to work together in a team • Care needed to avoid academic input
Main rewards and challenges	• Networking / professional development • Helping others is rewarding • Improved learning having studied module before • Reassures of own worth: more confident • Better communication skills • Time management was challenging

Discussion and Conclusions

The peer mentoring scheme appears to be sustainable, being now in its 7th year with student mentors repeatedly volunteering year on year. Contributing factors to this include mentors identifying the same pattern and order of beneficial attributes after their mentoring experience as beforehand – i.e. their expectations were not far from the reality of their experience (Figure 2). The nature of the programme and flexibility of the non-academic support facilitates mentors moving between cognate modules and also renders the model transferable to unrelated modules outside the faculty. Neither IT skills nor time management have been barriers to participation in the scheme in its current form. Furthermore, recruiting volunteers from those who have already studied and passed the module satisfies the pre-requisite attribute of "knowledge of the module" which almost all respondents identified as important (Figure 2). The small proportion of mentors who do not remain active for the duration of a module usually withdraw for personal reasons not linked to difficulties with the programme.

The study shows that mentors value the benefits to their skills development and recognise these to a certain degree. However, they do not seem to clearly recognise the development of employability skills. For example, interpersonal and communication skills – which are employability skills - were developed by at least 80% of respondents while "employability skills" were developed by only 45% (Figure 3). Further work is needed to determine whether this is students' perceptions of employability or maybe an artefact of the methodology in the range of questions asked.

Before the scheme reached its present size, an attempt to establish a mentoring community between modules failed with too few student contributions to generate discussion. However, with 35-36 mentors per year, the programme has now grown sufficiently to again trial building a mentoring community to facilitate the exchange of experience and views between cognate modules, and perhaps more widely across the Faculty and University.

The lack of challenges to mentoring, or recommendations for improvements to the programme could reflect a lack of confidence on the part of mentors to raise such things, or again could be a limitation of the study (e.g. the small sample and question format). It is unlikely that the programme is flawless though the mentors do feel that the training and support were adequate and beneficial. Student mentors have increased responsibility as they have to moderate their forums (albeit supported by an Associate Lecturer): this was not a barrier, but there is a need for additional training to help mentors deal with difficult situations that do (though rarely) occur, e.g. students breaking module assessment rules or posting inappropriate content which breaches expected conduct. Another area for improvement lies around educating the mentors with regard to the value of their role in developing recognisable employability skills, though one mentor did secure a job based on their mentoring role after recording their experience in their Curriculum Vitae.

Overall, we conclude that the programme is sustainable, with several benefits and few challenges for the majority of mentors. The principal future improvement for the scheme needs to be helping students recognise their employability skills development, and the potential value this adds to their experience.

References

Carvalho, A. R. and Santos, C. (2022) Developing peer mentors' collaborative and metacognitive skill technology-enhanced peer learning program. *Computers and Education Open, 3.* Retrieved from: https://www.sciencedirect.com/science/article/pii/S2666557321000410?via%3Dihub

Creswell, J.W., & Creswell, J.D. (2018). *Research Design (5th edition).* SAGE Publications Ltd.

Dawson, P. van Der Meer, J. Skalicky, J. & Cowley, K. (2014) On the effectiveness of Supplemental Instruction: A Systematic Review of Supplemental Instruction and Peer-Assisted Study Sessions Literature Between 2001 and 2010. *Review of Educational Research,* 84(4), 609-639 Retrieved from: https://www.jstor.org/stable/24434251

Leidenfrost, B. Strassnig, B. Schabmann, A. Spiel, C. & Carbon, C-C. (2011) Peer Mentoring Styles and Their Contribution to Academic Success Among Mentees: A Person-Oriented Study in Higher Education. *Mentoring & Tutoring: Partnership in Learning,* 19(3), 347-364. Retrieved from: https://www.tandfonline.com/doi/abs/10.1080/13611267.2011.597122

Marshall, M. Dobbs-Oates, J. Kunberger, T. & Greene J (2021) The peer mentor experience: benefits and challenges in undergraduate Programs. *Mentoring & Tutoring: Partnership in Learning,* 29(1), 89-109. : 10.1080/13611267.2021.1899587

Pollard, R. and Kumar, S. (2021) Mentoring Graduate Students Online: Strategies and Challenges. *International Review of Research in Open and Distributed Learning,* 22(2). Available from: https://web-p-ebscohost-com.libezproxy.open.ac.uk/ehost/pdfviewer/pdfviewer?vid=0&sid=5347069f-3787-4cb1-8148-aa9afa876ea7%40redis

Rockinson-Szapkiw , A. & Wendt, J.L. (2020) The Benefits and challenges of a blended peer mentoring program for women peer mentors in science, technology, engineering and mathematics (STEM). *International Journal of Mentoring and Coaching in Education,* 10(1), 1-16. Retrieved from: https://www-emerald-com.libezproxy.open.ac.uk/insight/content/doi/10.1108/IJMCE-03-2020-0011/full/html

Tibingana-Ahimbisibwe, B.Willis, S. Catherall, S. Butler, F. & Harrison, R. (2022) A systematic review of peer-assisted learning in fully online higher education distance learning programmes. *Open Learning: The Journal of Open Distance and e-Learning,* 33(3), 251-272. Retrieved from: https://www.tandfonline.com/doi/full/10.1080/02680513.2020.1758651

Tinoco-Giraldo, H. Sanchez, E.M.T. and García-Peñalvo, F.J. (2020) E-Mentoring in Higher Education: A Structured Literature Review and Implications for Future Research. *Sustainability,* 12(11). Retrieved from: https://www.mdpi.com/2071-1050/12/11/4344

EMPOWERING AI: RECONTEXTUALIZING OUR PEDAGOGICAL IMPACT THROUGH SUPPORTIVE USES OF MACHINE LEARNING

Angela Gunder, Online Learning Consortium, United States
Vincent Del Casino, Jr., San Jose State University, United States
Melissa Vito, The University of Texas at San Antonio, United States
Reed Dickson, Pima Community College, United States

Correspondence: *Angela Gunder: angela.gunder@onlinelearning-c.org*

Abstract

Over time, the use of digital technologies has transformed the landscape of higher education, and the recent advancements in artificial intelligence (AI) are no exception. At the same time, there is a need to move from a binary of use versus eradication of AI systems in higher education toward critical examination and curation of the plurality of examples of how AI may lead to the empowerment of educators and students. This paper explores the potential benefits and challenges of incorporating AI into higher education while also discussing the implications for educators and students, as well as the ethical concerns surrounding the use of AI in education. The paper examines the benefits of using AI in higher education, including personalized learning, adaptive assessments, and predictive analytics, as well as emerging challenges, such as data privacy and algorithmic bias. The paper proposes a set of guiding ethical principles for the empowering use of AI in education, including transparency, collaboration, creativity, and accountability. Each author offers a call to action for educators who are required to reevaluate their relationship with technology broadly and the seismic shifts in interaction and communicative modes within a landscape forever changed by machine learning.

Keywords:

Artificial intelligence, digital learning, digital strategy, Chat GPT, assisted intelligence, augmented intelligence, automated intelligence, autonomous intelligence

Introduction

While the historical application of artificial intelligence (AI) within education spans decades (Bozkurt et al., 2021), recent advancements in the functionality and accessibility of machine learning tools like ChatGPT, Bing, and DALL-E have resulted in myriad educators categorizing the usage of these tools along a volatile spectrum running from cataclysmic disruption to limitless opportunities for innovation and advancement (Dhawan & Batra, 2021). Even in examining the plurality of definitions of the initialism "AI," including artificial intelligence, assisted intelligence, augmented intelligence, automated intelligence, and autonomous intelligence (Rao & Verweij, 2017), one can make inferences about how the interactions between humans and machines are positioned in terms of their ethicality, value, and impact (Lynch and Del Casino 2020). Usage of AI in education has included a variety of cases and stakeholder groups and has been inclusive of the instructional design and curriculum development processes, student support services such as adaptive learning and personalized tutoring, as well as administrative tools like data reporting and analytics (Ouyang & Jiao, 2021). The benefits of incorporating AI into education have focused on creating new efficiencies within the teaching and learning process promoting accessibility and retention of learning content for students, rethinking assessment practices, and personalize course content and teaching to better align the educational experience to the specific needs and goals of individual learners (Chaudhry & Kazim, 2022; Chen et al., 2020). As discussions continue to surface regarding the positioning of AI within our ecosystem of teaching and learning practices, these lines of discourse have also raised new questions about the purpose, nature, and impact of interactions between humans and machines within education (United States Department of Education, 2022a; United States Department of Education, 2022b).

Moving from a harmful binary of use versus eradication, a need emerges for scholars and practitioners to critically examine and curate a plurality of examples of AI in education across a spectrum of empowerment. This paper explores the role of empowering AI in education across a series of cases, looking reflexively at both how AI enhances and supports educational experiences, as well as how we enable and advance the abilities of AI in education through our roles as designers, developers, evaluators, researchers, and leaders. Ultimately, this paper provides a shared perspective for reframing this critical moment in the rapidly evolving history of AI as a point of reflection, criticality, and strategy for defining our learning futures through the lens of empowering uses of technology.

Case Study: Negotiating a World of Machine Learning and AI in Higher Education

Where some see a dramatic shift, as provost at San José State University, I have seen a slow but ongoing set of changes that have shifted how higher education, as an industry, intersects with a world of technological change. It was not too long ago, in historical terms, that academics lamented the changes wrought by radio and television, concerned that distributed education would "cheapen" higher education (House-Peters, Del Casino, and Brooks 2019). Online education was seen as the next great "onslaught" against the hegemony of a higher education regime that valued the professor as an independent operator filled with knowledge that few (if no) others possessed (ibid.). And, yet, this moment does feel different in that the human-centered notion of education is being challenged by automated practices and machine learning algorithms that can be as, if not more, responsive to student learning needs, albeit in still quite idiosyncratic ways. This has further decentered the "sage-on-the-stage" and disrupted the notion that the core values of a liberal arts education, which stretches back centuries, based on the Socratic Method are now suspect. The so-called revolution in artificial intelligence also enters the milieu of higher education at a time when the fragility of the industry has been heightened by COVID-19 and dramatic changes in patterns of enrollment.

And yet, the world of human-nonhuman relations, automated life, and technological interventions in our teaching and learning environments are here to stay. In that way, we are trying to build a curriculum that more effectively engages the robotic worlds in which we now inhabit and build the critical skills to assess what it means to live in a world where machines can take on many of the mundane tasks that were reserved for the most educated. In practical terms, we are working toward a new suite of pedagogical practices that educate students in digital and creative literacy, that give them the tools to operate in, and better yet, navigate an automated world. ChatGPT is but a first step into a much wider world. So, why not teach with it instead of assuming that we can regulate it? Can we also educate students on its limitations - after all, AI and machine learning algorithms remain based on the world in which we live and are also always based on human constructs of that world. Put another way, there are more than enough examples of how such AI systems reflect back the deeply imperfect, if not at times outright sexist, racist, and ableist, practices of a world that remains deeply tense and fraught. On the flip side, such AI practices can help students take a step forward in ways that could help them build confidence in their own intellectual capacities. Embedding, for example, the criticality that comes with investigating how AI engines co-produce our worlds is not only a valuable intellectual exercise but a practical skill that helps students earn degrees and jobs in the future.

At San José State University, an institution located in the "heart of the tech best," so to speak, we are beginning conversations on how to not just regulate the spaces of automated academic life but how to build the creative capacities of our students so that they are better equipped to step into a world that is governed by the reality that all of us work alongside and with robots and robotic technologies. This means that we are investing in pedagogical strategies that not only take on the complexity introduced by automatic learning systems but also provide new ways for students to express their authentic selves and find opportunities to invest themselves in their education. One material example of this work is a recent project on counter-storytelling led by my colleague, Dr. Jonathan Gomez from Chicana and Chicano Studies, as part of a broader suite of HSI Initiatives at our institution (see Gomez 2023). This project teaches faculty to engage students in their own stories and find stories that help them reflect not only on their own learning experience but also on course content. A particular example is a project that helps students create a sense of self through a project that asks them to trace the history of women in STEM fields. Another asks students to examine how their own stories can trace their classroom learning in new ways. Presenting through a digital format provides an opportunity for students to work beyond the space of automated knowledge production - the rote response that often comes from stale prompts that ask students to all answer the question in a similar way - and find a way to express their own experience while demonstrating their subject-matter competency. The ideas that undergird this approach are not necessarily new ones, but the evaluation of AI in the spaces of higher education have forced academics to pivot more quickly to alternative teaching, learning, and assessment strategies. Such counter-storytelling strategies that re-center human creativity within the learning environment and challenge the AI engines that offer to provide students with rote answers to rote questions.

Generative AI in Faculty Development and Student Learning

The case outlined below describes the approach taken at the University of Texas San Antonio (UTSA) in addressing the academic use of generative AI, with a focus on the specific tool, ChatGPT. The Academic Innovation team at UTSA began planning in early December 2022 to be ready to roll out programs and resources as faculty returned to campus in mid-January. With input from the provost and academic deans, the UTSA Academic Innovation team quickly developed a plan to focus on education, while regularly seeking feedback to understand faculty and student behavior, interest, concerns, and opportunities. Our goal was to support faculty in experimenting with ChatGPT and exploring its usage in the classroom. By mid-January, UTSA unveiled a proactive faculty development plan. Central to this plan was the establishment of an extensive, constantly evolving repository of research and resources. This trove of information was made readily available to the faculty via diverse channels such as the university website, Teams site, and other media. While efforts were made to enhance education for faculty members, there were no new policies introduced that would limit or prohibit the use of ChatGPT. A unique aspect of this initiative was the gathering of a diverse cohort of 35 faculty members from fields as varied as business, physics and astronomy, writing, communication, and math. All of these faculty members were active users of ChatGPT, collaborating regularly to provide instantaneous feedback, share ideas, and contribute to the development of best practices. The Academic Innovation Center, newly inaugurated at UTSA, served as the central hub for this initiative, fostering a communal space for faculty to discuss ChatGPT, whether virtually or in person. The center not only encouraged experimentation and the formation of learning communities but also facilitated connections with teaching and learning consultants and instructional designers. Furthermore, it provided specific resources tailored to aid the testing of innovative ideas. Included in the development plan were regular educational sessions that leveraged the knowledge of local and national experts on the application of ChatGPT in education. There was also utilization of the nationally recognized model of Faculty Champions, department-specific faculty members acting as peer experts, to distribute resources for ChatGPT within their own departments. Finally, a critical component of this progressive plan was the active involvement of both faculty and student governance, which ensured a constant flow of communication and an ongoing, real-time pulse-checking mechanism. The incorporation of concise surveys was a key part of this feedback mechanism.

Examples of Usage at UTSA

ChatCPT is currently being integrated into the UTSA Writing Program within six different courses involving eight faculty and over 400 students. Students respond to an assignment without using ChatGPT, then run the same assignment through ChatGPT, and compare the two examples for style, accuracy, and engagement.

In addition to the Writing Program, an interdisciplinary community of practice has convened and is engaging in multiple pedagogical strategies for incorporating ChatGPT into the curriculum. Math faculty at UTSA challenge students to determine the accuracy of the information they receive using ChatGPT to help them think critically and expand their information literacy skills. Communications students use ChatGPT to brainstorm approaches to assignments, using the tool for support with thematic analyses and organizing ideas. One of our Business faculty has flipped his classroom and employs active learning in conjunction with the usage of ChatGPT. A faculty member in the Physics department is exploring combining gamification of learning and the usage of ChatGPT to create new activities and assessments.

The reflections and efforts of these faculty have helped us identify key questions and early opportunities:

- What types of assignments are best handled through ChatGPT?
- What are the best types of prompts and questions to deploy to increase the accuracy of ChatGPT?
- What types of communications are best handled by ChatGPT?
- What skills and knowledge in this area will students need to prepare them for the workforce?
- What benefits exist for students in writing courses for whom English is not their first language? How

might ChatGPT support them in checking their grammar, sentence construction, and spelling? And how might this process help them with increased confidence and knowledge?

- How might we encourage our students to think of ChatGPT as a potential tutor or 24/7 virtual assistant?
- What are the best assessments and strategies to measure the impact on student learning?

The dynamic nature of this topic means that our knowledge and resources will continue to evolve in the coming months and years, but by working through this values-centered approach, we are confident in the innovations and efficiencies that will emerge from the holistic support of generative AI within our academic contexts.

AI and Critical Digital Literacies

While my role as the chief academic officer for the Online Learning Consortium, a global non-profit supporting digital learning, has brought me into the raging debates on the usage of AI in education, I have been most profoundly impacted by machine learning tools within my course design and facilitation work as a lecturer for The University of Arizona. For almost a decade, I've taught fully-online classes for the university at both the undergraduate and graduate levels on topics of instructional design, web design, and digital media, serving in the roles of instructional designer, curriculum developer, facilitator, and quality assurance specialist. In that my strategy and policy development work within my CAO role is informed by my work as an educator, I was keen to explore the ways in which augmented intelligence, or the process of using systems to "augment human decision making and continuously learning from their interactions with humans and the environment" (Rao & Verweij, 2017, p. 2), might support my teaching. Furthermore, I was interested in better understanding the voiced struggles and difficulties of educators who were engaging with the difficult process of renegotiating their own teaching experiences through the lens of AI.

Using ChatGPT and content from a course on the sociocultural significance of the evolution of digital media, I used the machine learning tool to generate elements of a course map (i.e. learning objectives, thematic unit descriptions), syllabus, and lecture content (i.e. lecture notes, presentation scripts). I also asked ChatGPT to generate summaries of content that I had created for the course as a way to assess which salient points it would glean from the curriculum. Both the challenges and benefits of ChatGPT as instructional design assistant stood out immediately. While the process of generating learning content was reduced from days to seconds, the content that was generated required a level of informed review before it could be incorporated into my course. Beyond the documented issues with ChatGPT producing incorrect or non-existent citations and references, there were also significant issues with the positioning of the content around the dominant sources that it was summarizing. For a course that focuses on international examples of digital media authorship, ChatGPT provided only Western, colonial examples from the global north, an example of AI carrying the biases and discriminatory views of its creators (Benjamin, 2019; Noble, 2018). This provoked immediate questions about the critical digital literacies required to use machine learning tools ethically and effectively within my classroom, both as teacher and student.

While these challenges could have immediately been codified as reasons for banning ChatGPT from the educational experience, they instead surfaced new opportunities to reimagine the usage of machine learning as a lever for quality and equity within the educational experience. Beyond validating my role as facilitator of the learning experience through its limitations in determining veracity and bias within the information generated, ChatGPT also presented me with new opportunities to engage my students in using machine learning tools to understand the importance of a plurality of digital literacies, cultural relevance, and discourse analysis within digital environments. My experience also highlighted a burgeoning perspective on machine learning as catalyst for reimagining assessment practices, opening up new questions on what we should be teaching (Siemens, 2023), as well as reflecting on where we are failing by "assessing process rather than outcome" (Gleason, 2022). These challenges to curriculum design, thankfully, sit squarely within the opportunity space for AI to be incorporated into the teaching and learning process as a catalyst for critical conversations around our roles and responsibilities as co-constructors of knowledge, with both educators and learners seated at the table.

Pedagogical Openings through AI-Connected Reflective Practice

Alongside every crisis in education, critical opportunities emerge for rethinking how we approach equitable teaching and learning. As Program Manager for Faculty Development at Pima Community College, I have seen countless tech-averse faculty suddenly pivot amidst the COVID outbreak toward daily workshops on multi-modal teaching, and toward the short courses we offer in educational technology, online pedagogy, and instructional design. Likewise, amidst daily headlines about Bing and ChatGPT, faculty are suddenly reaching out with an openness toward pausing and reflecting, existentially, on the hows and whys of teaching. As faculty begin to explore use cases for the latest large language models (LLMs), we again are witnessing what I call a "pedagogical opening." While it's hard to say how long this opening will last, it is clearly an opportunity to help faculty revisit their core beliefs about teaching and learning - and find new ways to sustain it.

As a designer of faculty development experience, I have been especially interested in examining emerging AI-connected practices that help faculty make space for parallel inquiry into reflective practice, tech-enhanced pedagogy, and equitable learning. Through my work with deans, department heads, and faculty across and within their disciplines—which involves one-to-one course walkthroughs, and departmental and college-wide workshops—I have observed pedagogical openings that appear to be less transient than what emerged with the COVID outbreak. In other words, amidst these new AI technologies, there appears to be a more sustainable path toward supporting critical reflective practice (Brookfield, 2017) in higher education through AI-connected reflective practice. This practice, in my analysis, emerges through collaborative AI learning experiences that center around applied inquiry around essential questions (Wiggins & McTighe, 2005) that we might call "evergreen" or recurring essential questions. What can teachers do that generative AI cannot? How can students advance, rather than bypass, substantive inquiry through AI? How can we expand equitable learning through AI? How do we communicate to students our expectations for the ethical, educative use of AI? How can we respond, educatively, to the perceived misuse of AI? These new kinds of AI-connected questions are also accompanied by a re-emergence of older, evergreen essential questions about pedagogy, albeit with a new AI spin. Faculty are suddenly open to imagining new practices that move beyond writing-as-assessment or banking models of teaching (Freire, 2017) toward promoting digital learning artifact creation, and the co-construction of knowledge. Perhaps faculty are revisiting these questions of practice simply due to the unmistakable recognition that students may already know more than faculty do about generative AI. Or perhaps it is simply because we are suddenly facing a technology so disruptive that it renders traditional teaching practices untenable. As educational development practitioners, many of us have been promoting pedagogy-driven tech, as opposed to tech-driven pedagogy. Amidst the latest generative AI, however, this case study demonstrates that the more urgent and sustainable educational development imperative resides in the work of promoting AI-connected, reflective practice.

References

Benjamin, R. (2019). *Race after technology: Abolitionist tools for the new jim code.* Polity Books.

Brookfield, S. (2017). *Becoming a critically reflective teacher*, 2nd ed. San Francisco: Jossey Bass.

Bozkurt, A., Karadeniz, A., Baneres, D., Guerrero-Roldán, A. E., & Rodríguez, M. E. (2021). Artificial intelligence and reflections from educational landscape: A review of ai studies in half a century. *Sustainability: Science Practice and Policy*, 13(2), 800.

Chaudhry, M. A., & Kazim, E. (2022). Artificial intelligence in education (AIEd): A high-level academic and industry note 2021. *AI and Ethics*, 2(1), 157–165.

Chen, L., Chen, P., & Lin, Z. (2020). Artificial intelligence in education: A review. *IEEE Access, 8*, 75264–75278.

Dhawan, S., & Batra, G. (2021). *Artificial intelligence in higher education: Promises, perils, and perspective.*

Freire, P. (2017). *Pedagogy of the oppressed.* Penguin Classics.

Gleason, N. (2022, December 9). *ChatGPT and the rise of AI writers: how should higher education respond?* Times Higher Education. https://www.timeshighereducation.com/campus/chatgpt-and-rise-ai-writers-how-should-higher-education-respond

House-Peters, L. A., Del Casino Jr, V. J., & Brooks, C. F. (2019). Dialogue, inquiry, and encounter: Critical geographies of online higher education. *Progress in Human Geography*, 43(1), 81-103.

Lynch, C. and V.J. Del Casino Jr. (2020) Smart spaces, information processing, and the question of intelligence. *Annals of the Association of American Geographers*, 110(2), 382-390, DOI: https://doi.org/10.1080/24694452.2019.1617103.

Noble, S. U. (2018). *Algorithms of oppression.* New York University Press.

Ouyang, F., & Jiao, P. (2021). Artificial intelligence in education: The three paradigms. *Computers and Education: Artificial Intelligence*, 2, 100020.

PimaOnline Faculty Guide (2023, March 10). *ChatGPT and AI for teaching.* PimaOnline, Pima Community College. https://onlinefaculty.pima.edu/chatgpt.

Rao, A. S., & Verweij, G. (2017). *Sizing the prize: What's the real value of AI for your business and how can you capitalise*. PwC.

Siemens, G. (2023, March 3). *Beingness: From epistemology to ontology.* Elearnspace. https://elearnspace.org/blog/beingness-from-epistemology-to-ontology/

Gomez, J. (2023) Digital Counter-Storytelling for Student Leaders as part of a presentation organized by SJSU Library, *Networked Connections: Digital Storytelling/Electronic Literature*, https://www.youtube.com/watch?v=gnqMXBFafcM (accessed March 10).

United States Department of Education. (2022a, April 1). *Artificial intelligence.* Office of Educational Technology. https://tech.ed.gov/ai/

United States Department of Education. (2022b, April 4). *AI and the future of teaching and learning: Defining artificial intelligence.* Medium. https://medium.com/ai-and-the-future-of-teaching-and-learning/ai-and-the-future-of-teaching-and-learning-defining-artificial-intelligence-f31d20628280

Wiggins, G., & McTighe, J. (2005). *Understanding by design.* ASCD.

IMMERSION AND IMPLOSION: ENABLING SOCIAL SPACES THROUGH THE DESIGN OF INTERACTIVITY AT SCALE

Peter Bryant, University of Sydney Business School, Australia

***Correspondence**: Peter Bryant: peter.j.bryant@sydney.edu.au*

Abstract

The didactic lecture is a well-established but contentious practice in higher education. It is an essentially mono-directional experience delivered in purposefully designed spaces that entrench modes of learning and expected behaviours by both staff and students. This paper will challenge the ongoing primacy of the didactic lecture in higher education and posit a dialogical alternative that supports students to interact and connect at scale through the creation of social spaces. A case study of a program at the University of Sydney Business School will interrogate the role of technology in simulating an immersive hyperreality for students in large-group teaching settings that blurs the boundaries of disciplinary knowledge and the abstractions and realties of their work, life, play and learning.

Keywords:

Immersion; Interactivity; Large Group Pedagogy; Higher Education; Learning Technology

Introduction

The use of didactic (or traditional) lectures in higher education is an extensively debated practice, despite their relatively ubiquitous status as the at-scale pedagogy *de rigueur* for most institutions (Gibbs, 1981; Nordmann et al., 2021). There is a persistent debate in both institutional and pedagogical contexts as to the primacy of the didactic lecture, supported in equal measure by passionate defences and disruptive rebuttals (see Black, 1993; Richardson, 2008). There have been several waves of technological innovation that have challenged the efficacy and future of the didactic lecture including flipped learning (Zainuddin et al., 2019), personal response systems (Sun, 2014) and the emergence of online polling platforms like Menti (Compton & Allen, 2018). In the face of these changes, the lecture continues to thrive as key component of the modern education experience. Lecturing in large theatres is one of the defining stereotypes of the university journey, reinforced in popular culture, and one where expectation does not always equal the reality of experience (Schei et al., 2018). The patterns of lecture attendance by students, the flexibility facilitated by lecture recording technologies (amplified by the growth of do-it-yourself media capabilities) and transactional models of engagement all bring into question, in both literature and through social media, the operational and pedagogical benefits of didactic lecturing (Nordmann et al., 2022).

Some scholars valorise the traditional lecture model arguing that it provides students with structure and necessary scaffolding of key concepts and skills at scale, and the shared oratorial experience can contribute a sense of identity and belonging (French & Kennedy, 2017; Fulford & Mahon, 2020). The rise of scale as a business model in higher education has further entrenched the lecture as both an economic and logistical necessity (Schlegelmilch, 2020). Scale offers productivity benefits to the institutional bottom line and leverages the finite resource of academic 'facetime'. The imperative to massify class or cohort sizes or expand the scope of programs and units of study has arisen from a confluence of several factors, including the increased reliance of university funding models on international students (Song & McCarthy, 2018), the financial affordances of economies of scale (Mahat & Goedegebuure, 2016), the leveraging of scarce space on campus (Fisher et al., 2021) and the possibilities of technology to magnify and recreate education with little or no decay to large audiences (Ryan et al., 2021). There are also pedagogical benefits created by students being in large cohorts that include leveraging the processing power and collective intelligence that is catalysed by immersing yourself in the noise and chaos of a large group (Allais, 2014) and the epistemic benefits from listening and reflecting in lectures (Abedin et al., 2009).

The detractors of the didactic lecture argue that they are ineffective for learning, do not develop transdisciplinary skills like critical thinking and through low attendance and monological communications leave students cognitively disengaged (Schmidt et al., 2015). Kalantzis et al (2020) argue that 'sitting in classes and listening to lectures is an absurdly sub-optimal cognitive load for today's students who on their personal devices have become habituated to designing their own information feeds then skipping through their messages.' The student has limited opportunities to exercise agency over their learning in didactic lectures, other than through attendance. They cannot influence the structure, pace, absorption, and connections of the information presented to them. The larger the lecture gets, the more difficult it becomes for the teacher to engage and interact directly with students and to support engagement and interaction between students, which Jerez et al (2021) argue is critical to ensure the pedagogical effectiveness of the lecture as a large group teaching activity. The student experience in didactic lectures can become receptive and passive. Interaction is one way, between the teacher as the performer and the students acting as the audience. Intra-audience interaction is thereby shunted to technology-mediated messaging apps and social media, acting as an unedited, unfiltered but efficacious backchannel which frequently offers positive support for learning but rarely involves the teacher (Kjærgaard & Hachmann, 2022).

The need to change the way we lecture

Max Muller in the *New Review* (1890) observed the controversy around lectures noting presciently that '...the system of imparting instruction by means of lectures, has for some time been subjected to an uncompromising criticism', arguing that they were too long and too large. Gibbs (1981) excoriates many of the myths and excuses that he claims define the defence of the lecture arguing that we continue to lecture out of fear and mistrust, asserting that 'we do not trust [students] to work alone or find out for themselves and we feel more secure when they are sitting in front of us doing exactly what we want them to. The security this brings may be much greater than the insecurity which comes with knowing that what we want them to be doing is not necessarily of much benefit to them'. Many writers argue that large-group teaching can be made more effective with the introduction of non-lecturing activities such as peer-to-peer interaction, problem sets and multimedia (Jerez et al., 2021; Kuepper-Tetzel, 2021; Robson et al., 2022). There have been various methodologies enacted to overcome the communicative and architectural limitations of lecture theatres and the didactic lecturing mode and encourage peer-to-peer interactivity, including personal response systems (Gauci et al., 2009), collaborative lecture theatre design (Swinnerton, 2021) and flipped learning pedagogies (Seery, 2015). Whilst each methodology has their advocates, none of the approaches have challenged the continued primacy of the one-to-many monologic of didactic lectures. Through the proliferation of digital learning tools, interaction has been shunted out of the lecture theatre and into polling platforms, asynchronous discussion forums on learning management systems and deferred commentary on lecture recordings (Ludvigsen et al., 2015).

The purposeful design of models of effective interactivity at scale to replace the didactic lecture poses epistemic, pedagogical, and technological challenges for educational developers, learning designers and academics. Interactivity must transcend the abstraction of some of the previous models of lecture mode transformation (such as flipped learning), which effectively replaced the lecture with another passive form of sociality. The passive reception of knowledge compromises the ability of students to actively solve problems, to reflect and apply learning in situ, to be immersed in a context or scenario or create experiences that feel like the reality in a *yet to be experienced* future. These higher-order transdisciplinary skills require active learning, the leveraging of resonant intra-cohort connections and the exposing of disciplinary and creative tensions between theoretical, practical, and personal positions. Designing for interactivity at scale must engage with the different spaces that teaching and learning inhabit to deliver an effective and sustainable inclusive pedagogical experience that achieves learning outcomes, builds a true and lasting sense of connection and collaboration within a cohort, whilst not compromising the embedded institutional benefit of offering at-scale learning. The lived experiences and the remembered perceptions of chaos and the calm that interactivity at scale can generate as a learning experience remain powerful antecedents to any redesign of the lecture to become more interactive.

Social space as a design principle for interactivity at scale

Henri Lefebvre in his seminal 1974 work 'The Production of Space' argues that spaces appropriated for and enabling social relations (social spaces) are complex constructs that defy analysis. He notes that 'from the point of view of knowing (connaissance), social space works...as a tool for the analysis of society. To accept this much is at once to eliminate the simplistic model of a one-to-one or 'punctual' correspondence between social actions and social locations, between spatial functions and spatial forms' (Lefebvre, 1991, p. 34). In Lefebrve's conceptualisation, the triad of social space (*conceived space*, as articulated by designers, *perceived space* as it exists in practice or in the day-to-day mundanity of use, and *lived space*, as space is experienced by those within it) fractures the structural limitations of power-informed 'correspondence' between a student and the teacher and exposes the cohort to the possibility of analysis of complexity, rather than the sharing of the functions of it, however abstract that might be. Didactic lectures and the spaces they are delivered in do not generally inhabit Lefebvre's notion of social spaces as they offer limited purposefully designed opportunities for sociality and collaboration. For the student they become dominated spaces that are 'transformed – and mediated – by technology, by practice" which is "usually closed, sterilized, emptied out' and experienced passively by the receiver (Lefebvre, 1991, pp. 164-165).

Audio-visual technology and architecturally designed lecture spaces privilege monological practices that elevate the academic as dominant in the space, further entrenching the dynamic of didacticism. The symbols and images associated with lecture spaces, such as the tiered seating, the large teaching desk, and the control of the technology to amplify sound and share vision determine how the experiences are lived, rather than supporting students to appropriate their space for their own learning experience. As opposed to being social spaces despite their intrinsic relationship to communication, didactic lectures are more closely aligned to the affordances of consumption space and the role of the 'consumer' within them. In urban studies, consumption spaces are retail areas, recreational facilities and other places purposefully designed for the consumer to enable consumption (in a consumerist sense) (Song, 2023). Most lecture theatres are designed to create a lived consumption experience for the majority of users as a in the same way a restaurant or music venue is designed to facilitate consumption over production and sociality (Gottdiener, 2000).

Social spaces designed or appropriated for the purposes of large-group teaching support a production of knowledge that transcends the singular interactions of an audience member interpreting and receiving the intentions of the lecturer. The creation of social spaces that trigger and facilitate interactivity at scale offer opportunities for knowledge production arising from the quantum and breadth of the interacting crowd, facilitated effectively in and through technology mediated platforms and spaces. Interactivity triggers deeper learning, more active engagement with lived and living experiences and more challenging, curious, and creative learners. The design of a social space to enable interactivity at scale is not independent of the architecture, or the technology or the relationships teachers and students have with the space but can transcend the affordances and limitations of the physical and representational structures. It is the interactivity itself that imprints onto the space. It challenges the expectations of embodied behaviour that defines the didactic lecture and its spaces.

Hyperreality and interactivity at scale

The University of Sydney Business School (USBS) has 15,000 students, primarily in pre-experience undergraduate and postgraduate commerce programs. It is part of the larger research-intensive institution University of Sydney (Australia). In 2020, the School designed a program of leadership education called *Leading in a Post-Crisis World* (LPC). The LPC program had the ambition to support student's capabilities to acquire and then apply transdisciplinary knowledge to understand the liminality of crisis and to both navigate and lead others through the rites of passage it triggers. LPC was built engaged students with different perspectives and transdisciplinary capabilities critical to being a leader through and past crisis. The program was designed with a deliberate sense of exposing students to connected experiences, drawing on the principles of social spaces to encourage students to explore, discover, play, take risks, feel a little unsafe and uncertain and through those experiences, enable the opportunity to develop their identity as a leader for good.

Replacing the primacy of the didactic lecture, content was reimagined as chunked asynchronous multimedia delivered through the digital stories of over 100 academics, leaders, community members and students. Using the flexibility of HTML5, students were able to create their own journey through the content, finding associations and representations of leadership that resonated or challenged them, and that were invariably different to any other student in the cohort. The personal lived and living experiences of students were brought together in four purposefully designed large group interactive sessions that were structured to enhance the smaller-group workshops in the unit and initiate the transitional experiences critical to developing the leadership skills of students. The design moved past the mediated structuralism of flipped interaction and enabled learning through the integration of epistemic and connected experiences within a constructed and accessible social space. These sessions were run in standard lecture theatres but with an ambition by the designers and academics to break the dominator/dominated nexus. This was achieved by the design of immersive experiences informed by a sense of hyperreality.

Baudrillard (2001) positions hyperreality in a simulacrum of simulation and imitation that finds fulfilment, happiness, or joy (and I would add learning) in simulated rather than a real reality. The simulation in a hyperreality is grounded in the authenticity of the experiences of reality. Didactic lectures are abstracted from reality in part because of the consumerist stance that enable, either explicitly or tacitly a transactional mindset to higher education (Wong & Chiu, 2019). I am using the concept of hyperreality here in its Baudrillardian, postmodernist sense, where technology can be used to blur the boundaries between abstraction and reality, between disciplinary knowledges and between the teacher and the student, in what Baudrillard refers to as implosion. LPC used implosion and hyperreality to undermine the safety of knowledge acquisition and engage students with connected learning opportunities that simulated the pressures, fears, and possibilities of a leader in crisis. The hyperreality took the form of an immersive theatre performance, where live actors had their narrative directly controlled by the cohort using polling tools and collective discussions in the room that built to a scenario on ethical and responsible decision making. A second session was led by an AI bot personified as a human character on the screen who posed the questions to a panel and then the students. Once revealed to be artificial, the bot asked students to discuss what it would be like to find out that your line manager was in fact not human (Peterson et al., 2022). A third session was led by an indigenous community leader who, in the traditions of his people, told the story of a crisis he was involved in part to ensure the life of that story and then to engage students in an active debate as they took on the personification of roles within that crisis, with the elder offering a sense of both simulated and real realities, reacting to their discussions in real time through the lens of his lived experiences.

In all of these large group sessions, the space was transformed into a canvas where interactivity defined how students and staff represented their learning. For brief moments, people in the room forgot they were in a university lecture theatre and through the immersion in these constructed forms of hyperreality, were applying their knowledge in a board room of a land rights group or were faced with the real possibility of being led by an AI bot, or in a fourth session, were directly confronted with the issue student homelessness and how their ideas and input could help solve the problem. These moments of implosion were not sustained across the entire duration of the class as the realities of grades and the connection of learning content to student achievement is a kinetic force against hyperreality. They did, however, succeed in creating an immersive hyperreality that allowed students the opportunity to apply their skills, knowledge and lived experiences to a simulation of the *yet to be experienced* future.

Conclusion

The evaluation of the learning gain effectiveness of creating and leveraging social spaces through interactivity at scale at USBS is ongoing as the project is still in its infancy. Further research is critical to ascertain whether some of the impediments to learning that didactic lectures have been accused of (low attendance, distraction, consumerism, and replacement with recordings) are ameliorated by the purposeful design and deployment of immersive interactivity at scale. The current set of projects whilst located within the transdisciplinary context of leadership has only been deployed in business education programs.

The displacement of monological interaction with dialogical using a modification of Baudrillard's hyperreality has provided a medium for mediated, technology-enabled interactivity by creating an immersive environment that simulates reality and enables students to learn and apply skills and knowledge to a reality that is not real but replicates the constructs, emotions, and pressures of a *yet to be experienced* crisis. The role of technology in the design and delivery of a hyperreality informed social space cannot be underestimated but requires of designers and academics to acquire and apply highly developed senses of creativity, communication, empathy with students and the imagination to develop highly engaging narrative storytelling approaches and technology to trigger longer periods of immersion that satiate the learned desire to mirror content to achieve outcomes.

References

Abedin, M. M., Majlish, S. H. K., & Akter, S. (2009). Listening skill at tertiary level: A reflection. *Dhaka University Journal of Linguistics, 2*(3), 69-90.

Allais, S. (2014). A critical perspective on large class teaching: the political economy of massification and the sociology of knowledge. *Higher Education, 67*, 721-734.

Baudrillard, J. (2001). *Jean Baudrillard: selected writings*. Stanford University Press.

Black, K. A. (1993). What to do when you stop lecturing: Become a guide and a resource. *Journal of Chemical Education, 70*(2), 140.

Compton, M., & Allen, J. (2018). Student Response Systems: a rationale for their use and a comparison of some cloud based tools. *Compass: Journal of Learning and Teaching, 11*(1).

Fisher, R., Perényi, A., & Birdthistle, N. (2021). The positive relationship between flipped and blended learning and student engagement, performance and satisfaction. *Active Learning in Higher Education, 22*(2), 97-113.

French, S., & Kennedy, G. (2017). Reassessing the value of university lectures. *Teaching in Higher Education, 22*(6), 639-654.

Fulford, A., & Mahon, Á. (2020). A philosophical defence of the university lecture. *Oxford Review of Education, 46*(3), 363-374.

Gauci, S. A., Dantas, A. M., Williams, D. A., & Kemm, R. E. (2009). Promoting student-centered active learning in lectures with a personal response system. *Advances in physiology education, 33*(1), 60-71.

Gibbs, G. (1981). *Twenty terrible reasons for lecturing*. SCED Occasional Paper No. 8.

Gottdiener, M. (Ed.). (2000). *The consumption of space and the spaces of consumption*. Rowman and Littlefield.

Jerez, O., Orsini, C., Ortiz, C., & Hasbun, B. (2021). Which conditions facilitate the effectiveness of large-group learning activities? A systematic review of research in higher education. *Learning: Research and Practice, 7*(2), 147-164.

Kalantzis, M., & Cope, W. (2020, 10/22). After the COVID-19 crisis: Why higher education may (and perhaps should) never be the same. *ACCESS: Contemporary Issues in Education, 40.*

Kjærgaard, T., & Hachmann, R. (2022, 27-28 October). Backchannels: Covert Digital Backchannels in the Overt Classroom. European Conference on e-Learning, Brighton, UK.

Kuepper-Tetzel, C. E., & Nordmann, E. . (2021). Watch Party Lectures: Synchronous Delivery of Asynchronous Material. *Preprint*.

Lefebvre, H. (1991). *The Production of Space*. Blackwell.

Ludvigsen, K., Krumsvik, R., & Furnes, B. (2015). Creating formative feedback spaces in large lectures. *Computers & education, 88*, 48-63.

Mahat, M., & Goedegebuure, L. (2016). Strategic positioning in higher education: reshaping perspectives. In J. Huisman & M. Tight (Eds.), *Theory and Method in Higher Education Research*. Emerald Group Publishing Limited.

Nordmann, E., Clark, A., Spaeth, E., & MacKay, J. R. (2021). Lights, camera, active! appreciation of active learning predicts positive attitudes towards lecture capture. *Higher Education*, 1-22.

Nordmann, E., Hutchison, J., & MacKay, J. R. D. (2022). Lecture rapture: the place and case for lectures in the new normal. *Teaching in Higher Education, 27*(5), 709-716.

Peterson, S., Brock, A., & Huber, E. (2022, 23rd February 2023). At-scale Immersive Events. *Transforming Business Education and the Student Experience*. https://cdrg.blog

Richardson, D. (2008). Don't dump the didactic lecture; fix it. *Advances in physiology education, 32*(1), 23-24.

Robson, L., Gardner, B., & Dommett, E. J. (2022). The post-pandemic lecture: views from academic staff across the UK. *Education sciences, 12*(2), 123.

Ryan, T., French, S., & Kennedy, G. (2021, 2021/07/03). Beyond the Iron Triangle: improving the quality of teaching and learning at scale. *Studies in higher education, 46*(7), 1383-1394.

Schei, E., Johnsrud, R. E., Mildestvedt, T., Pedersen, R., & Hjörleifsson, S. (2018, Dec). Trustingly bewildered. How first-year medical students make sense of their learning experience in a traditional, preclinical curriculum. *Med Educ Online, 23*(1), 1500344.

Schlegelmilch, B. B. (2020). Why business schools need radical innovations: Drivers and development trajectories. *Journal of Marketing Education, 42*(2), 93-107.

Schmidt, H. G., Wagener, S. L., Smeets, G. A., Keemink, L. M., & van Der Molen, H. T. (2015). On the use and misuse of lectures in higher education. *Health Professions Education, 1*(1), 12-18.

Seery, M. K. (2015). Flipped learning in higher education chemistry: emerging trends and potential directions. *Chemistry Education Research and Practice, 16*(4), 758-768.

Song, X., & McCarthy, G. (2018, 2018/05/27). Governing Asian international students: the policy and practice of essentialising 'critical thinking'. *Globalisation, Societies and Education, 16*(3), 353-365.

Song, Y. (2023). "I'll be there for you": affective production of a "hyper-real" cultural-consumption space. *Multilingua*.

Sun, J. C.-Y. (2014). Influence of polling technologies on student engagement: An analysis of student motivation, academic performance, and brainwave data. *Computers & education, 72*, 80-89.

Swinnerton, B. (2021). Collaborative lecture theatres: Does redesign of teaching space impact on pedagogy? *Journal of Learning Spaces, 10*(3).

Wong, B., & Chiu, Y.-L. T. (2019). Let me entertain you: The ambivalent role of university lecturers as educators and performers. *Educational Review, 71*(2), 218-233.

Zainuddin, Z., Haruna, H., Li, X., Zhang, Y., & Chu, S. K. W. (2019). A systematic review of flipped classroom empirical evidence from different fields: what are the gaps and future trends? *On the Horizon, 27*(2), 72-86.

TEACHING ON ZOOM IN THE EYES OF THE LECTURER: AN EYE TRACKING STUDY

Hayley Weigelt, Oren Ben-Aharon, Faculty of Instructional Technologies, Holon Institute of Technology, Israel

***Correspondence**: Oren Ben-Aharon: orenba@hit.ac.il*

Abstract

The shift to "Zoom" online learning in higher education, has aroused questions regarding the professional vision of lecturers- which is the core of this study. Since teaching on "Zoom" is screen based, it was possible to use an eye-tracking device to study lecturers' vision gazes during teaching. The study describes ten lecturers vision behaviours by fixations and lecturer's personal perception of vision. Main results revealed that sidelong variability between lecturers' eye gazes, lecturers mainly focused on their presentations. They felt high vision interaction with participated students yet, more than fixations revealed. These results and more discussed in the study, emphasis the importance of understanding lecturers' professional vision on "Zoom", for improving the quality of teaching on this rather new method of teaching.

Keywords:

Eye tracking, professional vision, online learning

Introduction

The awakening of technologies in the current decade enabled pedagogical staffs to overcome barriers such as the need to teach only by attending physically the traditional classroom. In fact, since the Covid-19 pandemic and its aftermath, many higher educational institutions around the world, including Holon Institute of Technology in Israel, have shifted many of their studies to online synchronous classes. Using the "Zoom" videoconference software, both lecturers and students participate in virtual classes together, utilizing features such as screen sharing of visual content (e.g. presentations), open web cameras and microphones for communication. Conducting classes via the "Zoom" with open cameras "face to face" indeed amplify opportunities for interaction between the lecturer and students. However, these interactions are different in nature, to those in the traditional classes. First, using the "Zoom" software does not demand opening cameras or microphones of all participants. This means that the lecturer does not necessarily see face-to face all the students attending, but rather sees closed camera screens. Never the less, the lecturer cannot control opening students' cameras (for obvious legal and privacy reasons). Second, the limited visual range offered by web cameras can often make it challenging to observe participants' body gestures and eye gaze, affecting the interpersonal interactions. Additionally, teaching on "Zoom" cannot reveal all participants cameras at once, and therefore the lecturer can only look towards a specific group of students, rather than the full class. And last, the self-awareness generated by observing oneself through the camera display on the "Zoom", also known as 'mirror observation' (Bailenson, 2021), may shift the lecturer's focus and impact their teaching.

The effect of opening cameras while participating in an online video conference was presented during the beginning of this century. Several studies discussed the interaction effect of opening cameras on self-awareness in different interpersonal communication situations (non-academic), such as during a conversation in an introductory meeting or a discussion of several participants. There findings were not conclusive however, they emphasize that opening web cameras and being watched, increased participants attention and self-awareness, resulting in a positive impact on overall behaviour during meetings (Joinson, 2001; Miller, Dechant & Mandryk, 2021; Miller, Mandryk, Birk, Depping & Patel, 2017; Nielsen, 2017). Other studies of that time, dealt with the use of video conferencing interfaces for distance learning purposes, focusing on the effectiveness and/or students' degree of satisfaction learning with such an interface (Candarli & Yuksel, 2012; Knipe & Lee, 2002). Beside presenting difficulties, advantages and disadvantages of general distance learning, they emphasized the importance of opening the web camera during online classes for enhancing communication and establishing stronger relationships with the lecturer and classmates, as well as promoting student engagement and commitment to learning (Yamada & Akahori, 2009).

A significant increase in studies regarding online learning interfaces occurred during the Covid-19. Yet, at that period of "Ad-Hock" actions, they focused either on the technological aspects of using video conference tools (Dias, Lopes & Teles, 2020; Orhan, & Beyhan, 2020); or students' feelings and perspective using online learning (Aguilera-Hermida, 2020; Atmojo, Muhtarom, & Lukitoaji, 2020; Serhan, 2020). They mostly overlooked the lecturer or methodlogical aspects regarding teaching with online tools leaving these matters unattended.

Studies regarding the lecturers behaviour on "Zoom" underlined, once more, the degree of confidence in the tool as a pedagogical key factor (for example, Joia & Lorenzo ,2021). Yet, Bailenson (2021) suggests that the utilization of web cameras in lecturers resulted in an increased cognitive load (due to the various stimuli present), which differ from those encountered in traditional classroom settings. He assumed that lecturers may endure similar negative emotions as those reported by students in similar web-based learning environments (Castelli & Sarvary, 2020; Gherheș, Simon & Para, 2021), both at the level of internal effects (such as: anxiety, preoccupation with self-awareness) and at the level of external effects (such as: awareness of the lecturer environment). Following these assumptions, it is possible to assume that lecturers' degree of online teaching experience, using web cameras, influences their teaching and lecturer-student interactions, as shown in studies regarding "Teachers' Professional Vision".

"Teachers' Professional Vision"

The term "Teacher Professional Vision-TPV" (Goodwin, 1994), defines teachers' ability to perceive and interpret relevant classroom situations during teaching. It is considered a main component of teaching, alongside components of knowledge and belief, and its goal is to improve professional teaching and teacher-student interactions (Muhonen, Pakarinen, & Lerkkanen, 2020; Meschede, Fiebranz, Möller, & Steffensky, 2017). The working model of TPV uses observations (mostly video recordings) of teachers while teaching in a classroom (Kleinknecht & Schneider 2013; Van Es & Sherin, 2008). The model includes two layers of analyse: (a) noticing significant events and situations that occurred during a lesson, (b) knowledge-based interpretation, explanation and reasoning of those situations by the teachers (Grub, Biermann, & Brünken, 2020).

Using this model enables studying teachers' attention allocation and interactions in their ecological environment- the classroom (as opposed to a lab setting). It is mainly used as a pedagogical tool. Yet, it has also been included in recent academic studies (Grub, Biermann, & Brünken, 2020), such as studies using eye-tracking method (Beach, & McConnel,2019).

Eye- Tracking studies

Eye tracking studies are based upon data collection and analyse of participants' eye position and eye movements while conducting a study (Carter & Luke, 2020). Eye tracking technologies (e.g., "Tobii Pro-Lab", see physical setting of device Fig.1) are non-invasive, and consist of a hardware (e.g., immobile or mobile device) and a software. Eye tracking is used for human behaviour studies in various fields such as: psychology, education, human-computer interaction, educational technology, design, advertising, and in various fields of medical sciences. Its main purpose is to collect voluntary and involuntary participant eye positions and movements in the visual field due to the study stimuli. The information collected enables the understanding of visual gaze positions and visual patterns of gaze for better understanding of the human behaviour.

Following this, there are two main output measurements collected in the eye-tracking device: "fixations"- representing when the eyes "stops" (for milliseconds) at a certain point in the visual space, at which the brain receives the visual information; and "saccades"- representing the eye movements, between the starting point and the next target point gaze focus. These measures can be presented as raw data (for statistical analyses), and as visualization outputs such as "gaze plots" (presenting the order of fixations and saccade patterns, see Fig 3-4). Collecting this data enables knowing where a participant looked at, for how long, towards where the eye continued? etc.

Eye- tracking has been used in TPV studies to better understanding authentic teachers' actions during class. For example, using eye- tracking glasses, it was found that experience teachers tend to turn their gaze more towards struggling students and/or distractions during lessons and refer to them. On the contrary, less experienced teachers tend to turn their gaze mainly to the material being taught (Cortina, Miller, McKenzie, & Epstein, 2015; Jarodzka, Skuballa, & Gruber, 2021; Wyss, Rosenberger, & Bührer, 2021). These findings are obviously important in the pedagogical aspects of teaching. To the best of our knowledge, there are no published studies regarding lecturer's eye gaze during online teaching and/or video conference teaching in higher education.

In light of this, using an eye-tracking device, the purpose of the current study was to examine lecturer eye gaze on the "Zoom" while teaching students in higher education. To reveal where do the lecturers mostly look at while teaching, and where do they look at when a lecturer-student interaction occurs?
The presented study is considered a pioneering study. It has both a theoretical and an applied contribution. At the theoretical level, its findings will shade new light in the field of "professional vision" which up to today focused on teaching in a classroom rather also on the web platforms. At the applied level, findings regarding lecturer's eye gaze patterns and preferences, most possible, will refine recommendations for teaching on "Zoom".

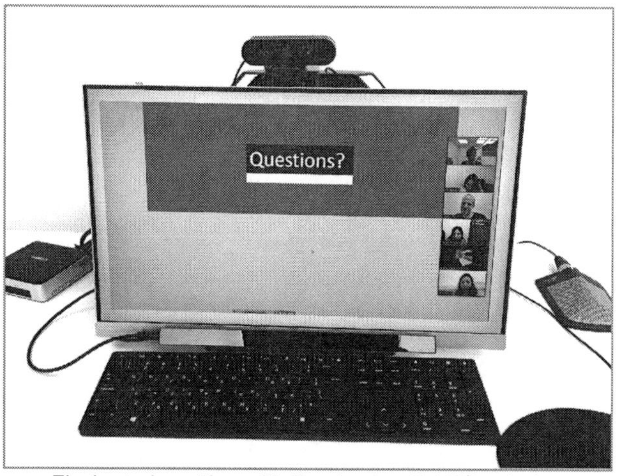

Fig 1. study setting with Eye tracker Tobii Pro-Lab.

Method

Participants and procedure

Using the "Tobii Pro-Lab 1200hz", ten participants (five females, five males), lectured on the "Zoom" at the "User Experience Lab", at HIT. Various subjects were taught as a "Pitch" (Komulainen, Siivonen, Kasanen, & Räty, 2020), using open cameras by lecturers. All lecturers had experienced previous "Pitch" lectures. The students attending these "Pitchs" were paid viewers. Each student had a specific role and opened the camera upon prior request (not known to the lecturer). Each "Pitch" was accompanied by a Power Point presentation (PPT), which included five fixed template slides: an opening slide, personal introduction (about me-the lecturer), main subject presentation slide, questions slide (for a more specific lecturer- student interaction) and an ending thank you slide. See Fig 1 as an example of the setting while teaching the "Pitch". Following each "Pitch", a short semi-structure interview (5-6 questions) was conducted with each lecturer to understand their perspective of the "Pitch" (for example: What did you feel during teaching? what did you mostly look at during the "Pitch"? etc).

Data analysis

This is a descriptive study, using raw data collected by the eye-tracker and narrative information collected via 5-6 questions in a semi- structure interview.
Lecturers' eye tracking gaze were measured by fixations. Each lecturers "Pitch" was divided into five "Time Of Interest" (TIO) frames in according with the five PPT slides accompanying each "Pitch". Each TIO was than divided in to five "Areas of interest" (AOI) of the "Zoom" screen: The PPT presentation page AOI, the lecturers' open camera AOI (mirror of himself), and three student AOIs, according to their role in the study (the listening and participating students AOI, the non-listening students AOI with open cameras, and students with closed cameras).

Due to differences in "Pitch" durations (Mean= 7.38 minutes, SD=2.06) and differences in AOI sizes (e.g., AOI of page size bigger than AOI "Zoom" participants camera boxes), number of fixations in each AOI were converted to percentage of fixations per AOI and slide. Data analysis included averages and standard deviations of fixations.

Results

<u>Overall lecturers gaze</u>

Data examination of lecturers' overall percentage of fixations for each AOI during the "Pitch", revealed variability between subjects and each lecturer divided his gaze differently in his lecture (see Fig 2, 3-4). Additionally, there were no gender differences between gaze patterns. Despite this, the highest observation fixation percentage for most lecturers was towards the PPT pages accompanied their lecture (AOI Mean= 52, SD=20). After which, most lecturers' fixations focused on the students that were listening and participating (AOI Mean=29, SD=12), also seen in Fig 2. High lecture gaze variability was found within the AOI of the students which were not listening, but had their cameras open (AOI Mean= 9, SD= 7), and within the AOI of the lecturer's camera (AOI Mean= 7, SD= 13). The AOI of students closed cameras had received little gaze, if at all (AOI Mean=3, SD=3).

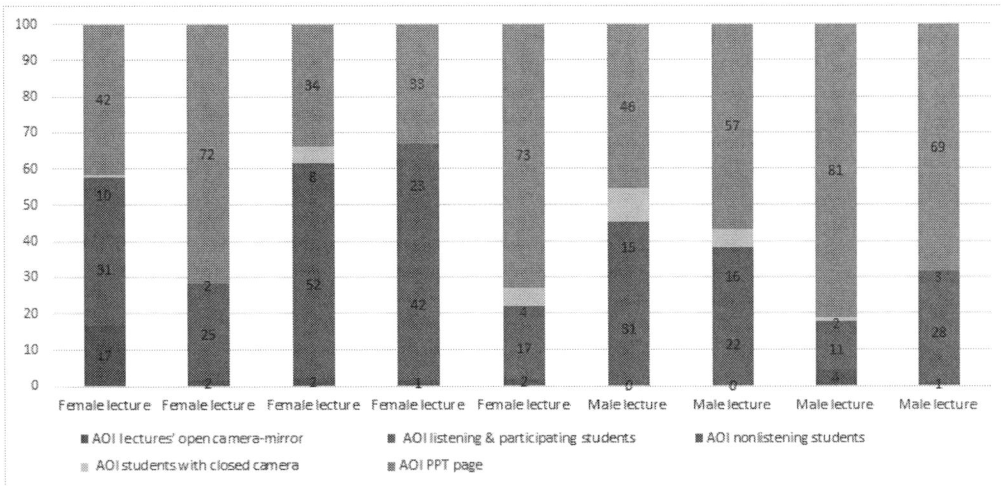

Fig 2. Percent of lecturer fixations by AOI.

Fig 3-4. Examples of results of two lecturers' "Gaze Plot" on "Zoom". Circles represent fixations, number indicates their order of appearance.

Lecturers gaze during lecturer-student interactions

The "questions" slide of each "Pitch" represented a lecturer-student interaction, in which a student asked a question regarding the "Pitch's" subject and received an answer by lecturer. As seen in Fig 5, not all of the lecturer- interaction time was allocated to looking at the student. On average, only 54% of fixations of all 10 lecturers were divided to looking at the students that asked the questions. The other 46% of eye attention of the lecturers while answering, focused mainly on the PPT page (although the slide had no information on it, only the word "Questions?"). The rest of lecturers' fixations were divided between looking at the non-listening students, mirror looking and/or looking at closed cameras.

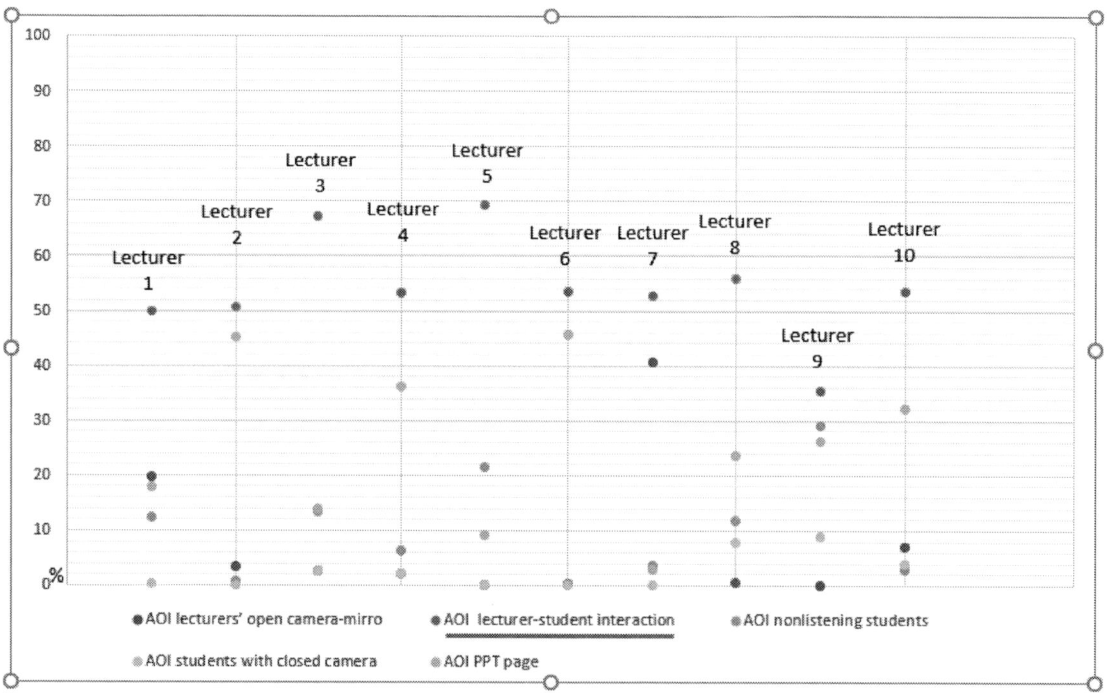

Fig 5. lecturers' gaze references (percent of fixations) while answering students' question.

Lecturers main interview reports

Lecturers narratives were divided to three themes:

1.Lecturers' self-confidence during the "Pitch". All participants described high levels of stress at the first moments of their lecture, mainly due to the notion that they were teaching within an eye- tracking study. Yet, all described that this feeling passed quickly and changed to feelings of relaxation and confidence.

2. Noticing visual attention. Lecturers reported mainly looking at the PPT and alternately at listening and participating students. They emphasised looking at the student whom had asked a question while answering it, although understanding that he cannot see that.

3. Reasoning-All lecturers explained they had the mental need to look at their presentation pages either to "catch" main terms or "lay" their eyes while thinking. Three (one female and two male), were aware of their open camera. One deliberately noted he made sure not to look at himself, the others mentioned that it was important to mirror look in order to verify that they were seen properly on the "Zoom". All lecturers noticed that there were closed cameras, and chose not to refer to them.

Conclusions and Discussion

The purpose of this study was to examine lecturer eye gaze on the "Zoom" while teaching students in higher education. All though fixation results revealed variability between lecturers' gaze, most lecturers' fixations focused on their presentation slide and only then at their students. Within the later, lecturers mainly looked at participating students, neglecting those which had open cameras but did not participate or closed cameras. Lecturers interviews revealed they were aware of their gaze behaviours, yet in a much wider feeling than noted by the eye-tracker. A strong emphasize to this was noted during lecturers' gaze while answering a student's question- which showed rather low fixations on the student cube (only 54% average gaze), and rather a broader gaze towards other various componence on the screen. This can be explained by the lecturers reports of being aware that the students cannot see they are looking directly at him. Surprisingly, they were less mirror looking by the lecturers than expected, perhaps due to high confidence of the lecturers using the "Zoom".

The "Zoom" platform for teaching is based on verbal, vision and upper body communication. Our findings focused on one of these main components. Findings reflect a rather narrow vision behaviour of lecturers on the "Zoom", leaving many other vision variables neglected. Additionally, it appears that it is not enough to use a professional presentation, and/or feel confident during teaching on "Zoom" to communicate with students. Instead, a set of recommendations are needed to increase lecturer's visual communication. Even if students do not see precisely towards where a lecturer is looking, he is in control of his lesson also in the vision field and this must be emphasized. For example, lecturers' vision referring to non-listening students, may invite action to change these students' behaviours during lessons, rather than the lecturer deliberately ignoring them by eye sight. Nevertheless, to do so, there is a need to continue studying this matter, as being done currently at our lab.

References

Aguilera-Hermida, A. P. (2020). College students' use and acceptance of emergency online learning due to Covid-19. *International Journal of Educational Research Open, 1*, 10001.

Atmojo, S., Muhtarom, T., & Lukitoaji, B. (2020). The Level of Self-Regulated Learning and Self-Awareness in Science Learning in the Covid-19 Pandemic Era. *Journal Pendidikan IPA Indonesia, 9*(4), 512-520.

Bailenson, J. N. (2021). Nonverbal Overload: A Theoretical Argument for the Causes of Zoom Fatigue. *Technology, Mind, and Behavior, 2(*1).

Beach, P., & McConnel, J. (2019). Eye tracking methodology for studying teacher learning: A review of the research. *International Journal of Research & Method in Education, 42*(5), 485-501.

Candarli, D. & Yuksel, H.G. (2012). Students' perception of video-confrencing in the classrooms in higer education. *Procedia-Social and Behavioural Science, 47*, 357-361.

Carter, B. T., & Luke, S. G. (2020). Best practices in eye tracking research. International Journal of Psychophysiology, 155, 49-62.

Castelli, F. R., & Sarvary, M. A. (2021). Why students do not turn on their video cameras during online classes and an equitable and inclusive plan to encourage them to do so. *Ecology and Evolution, 11(*8), 3565-3576.

Clifford, C. W., & Palmer, C. J. (2018). Adaptation to the direction of others' gaze: A review. *Frontiers in psychology, 9*, 2165.

Cortina, K. S., Miller, K. F., McKenzie, R., & Epstein, A. (2015). Where low and high inference data converge: Validation of CLASS assessment of mathematics instruction using mobile eye tracking with expert and novice teachers. *International Journal of Science and Mathematics Education, 13*, 389-403.

Crook, C., & Schofield, L. (2017). The video lecture. The Internet and Higher Education, 34, 56-64.

de Oliveira Dias, M., Lopes, R. D. O. A., & Teles, A. C. (2020). Will virtual replace classroom teaching? Lessons from virtual classes via zoom in the times of COVID-19. *Journal of Advances in Education and Philosophy, 4*(5), 208-213.

Gherheș, V., Șimon, S., & Para, I. (2021). Analysing Students' Reasons for Keeping Their Webcams on or off during Online Classes. *Sustainability, 13*(6), 1-13.

Goodwin, C. (1994). Professional Vision. American Anthropologist, 96(3), 606–633.

Grub, A. S., Biermann, A., & Brünken, R. (2020). Process-based measurement of professional vision of (prospective) teachers in the field of classroom management. A systematic review. *Journal for educational research online, 12*(3), 75-102.

Halszka, J., Holmqvist, K., & Gruber, H. (2017). Eye tracking in Educational Science: Theoretical frameworks and research agendas. *Journal of eye movement research, 10*(1):3,1-18.

Hietanen, J. O., & Hietanen, J. K. (2017). Genuine eye contact elicits self-referential processing. *Consciousness and Cognition, 51,* 100-115.

Jarodzka, H., Skuballa, I., & Gruber, H. (2021). Eye-tracking in educational practice Investigating visual perception underlying teaching and learning in the classroom. *Educational Psychology Review, 33*(1), 1-10.

Joinson, A. N. (2001). Self-disclosure in computer-mediated communication: The role of self-awareness and visual anonymity. *European journal of social psychology, 31*(2), 177-192.

Joia, L. A., & Lorenzo, M. (2021). Zoom in, zoom out: The impact of the COVID-19 pandemic in the classroom. *Sustainability, 13*(5), 2531.

Kaakinen, J. K. (2021). What can eye movements tell us about visual perception processes in classroom contexts? Commentary on a special issue. *Educational Psychology Review, 33*(1), 169-179.

Kleinknecht, M., & Schneider, J. (2013). What do teachers think and feel when analyzing videos of themselves and other teachers teaching? *Teaching and Teacher Education, 33,* 13–23.

Knipe, D. & lee, M. (2002). The quality of teaching and learning via videoconferencing. *British Journal of Educational Technology, 33*(3), 301-311.

Komulainen, K., Siivonen, P., Kasanen, K., & Räty, H. (2020). "How to Give a Killer Pitch?" Performances of Entrepreneurial Narratives as Identity Models in Higher Education. *Entrepreneurship Education and Pedagogy, 3*(3), 214-235.

Lai, M. L., Tsai, M. J., Yang, F. Y., Hsu, C. Y., Liu, T. C., Lee, S. W. Y., Lee M., H., Chiou, G.L., G.L., Jyh-Chong, L.B. & Tsai, C. C. (2013). A review of using eye-tracking technology in exploring learning from 2000 to 2012. *Educational research review, 10,* 90-115.

Meschede, N., Fiebranz, A., Möller, K., & Steffensky, M. (2017). Teachers' professional vision, pedagogical content knowledge and beliefs: On its relation and differences between pre-service and in-service teachers. *Teaching and teacher education, 66,* 158-170.

Miller, M.K., Johannes Dechant, M., & L. Mandryk, R. (2021, May). Meeting You, Seeing Me: The Role of Social Anxiety, Visual Feedback, and Interface Layout in a Get-to-Know-You Task via Video Chat. *In Proceedings of the 2021 CHI Conference on Human Factors in Computing Systems* (pp. 1-14).

Miller, M. K., Mandryk, R. L., Birk, M. V., Depping, A. E., & Patel, T. (2017, May). Through the looking glass: The effects of feedback on self-awareness and conversational behaviour during video chat. *In Proceedings of the 2017 CHI conference on human factors in computing systems* (pp. 5271-5283).

Muhonen, H., Pakarinen, E., & Lerkkanen, M. K. (2021). Do teachers' professional vision and teaching experience always go hand in hand? Examining knowledge-based reasoning of Finnish Grade 1 teachers. *Teaching and Teacher Education, 106*, 103458.

Nielsen, M. I. S. (2017). Computer-mediated communication and self-awareness–A selective review. Computers in Human Behavior, 76, 554-560.

Orhan, G., & Beyhan, Ö. (2020). Teachers percpetions and teaching experience on distance education through synchronous video conferencing during Covid19 pandemic. *Social Sciences and Education Research Review, 7*(1), 8-44.

Serhan, D. (2020). Transitioning from Face-to-Face to Remote Learning: Students' Attitudes and Perceptions of Using Zoom during COVID-19 Pandemic. *International Journal of Technology in Education and Science, 4*(4), 335-342.

Van Es, E. A., & Sherin, M. G. (2008). Mathematics teachers' "learning to notice" in the context of a video club. *Teaching and Teacher Education, 24*(2), 244–276.

Yamada, M., & Akahori, K. (2009). Awareness and performance through self-and partner's image in videoconferencing. *Calico Journal, 27*(1), 1-25.

Wang, X., Lin, L., Han, M., & Spector, J. M. (2020). Impacts of cues on learning: Using eye-tracking technologies to examine the functions and designs of added cues in short instructional videos. *Computers in Human Behavior, 107*, 106279.

Wyss, C., Rosenberger, K., & Bührer, W. (2021). Student Teachers' and Teacher Educators' Professional Vision: Findings from an Eye Tracking Study. *Educational Psychology Review, 33*(1).

Integrating SOCIAL Robot in a Jigsaw cooperative Activity: Insights From an international workshop with students from universities in Germany and Israel

Dan Kohen-Vacs, Holon Institute of Technology (HIT), Israel

Gila Kurtz, Holon Institute of Technology (HIT), Israel

Ilona Buchem, Berliner Hochschule für Technik (BHT), Germany

***Correspondence**: Dan Kohen-Vacs: mrkohen@hit.ac.il*

Abstract

A Jigsaw activity represents an educational approach providing students opportunities to exercise collaborative learning targeting topics from across domains and levels including those addressing innovative technologies. This paper presents our efforts targeting a Jigsaw workshop addressing educational activities enhanced by Social Robots (SR). SR includes AI-enabled features becoming accessible through software affording to develop motivating and engaging cooperative learning processes. In light of these trends, we present a Jigsaw learning activity we conducted and supported by a Social Robot (SR). We conducted the activity as part of a mutual effort exercised by the authors of this paper in the framework of an Erasmus+ project in Social Robotics involving German and Israeli higher education Institutions. We examined this activity while focusing on various aspects corresponding to its interrelated phases and the educational interactions exercised by students. Results reveal a high potential for applying Jigsaw learning activities in groups of international students. The positive effects seem to be enhanced by choosing to focus the collaboration on an innovative learning environment such as social robots, designing the activity to maximize creativity, autonomy, and ownership, and addressing authentic application contexts to enhance the quality of the educational experience.

Keywords:

Active learning, cooperative learning, collaborative learning, Jigsaw activity, group of specialists, social robot

Introduction

In recent decades, researchers and practitioners seek to implement effective, innovative, engaging, and appealing education that addresses the realistic context and settings required by students in the world of the 21st century (Dominguez et al., 2019; Papert, 1980). Nowadays, practitioners constantly aim to implement approaches combining inclusiveness and cooperation exercised by students taking responsibility for their educational process (Papert, 1980). In many cases, practitioners aspire to implement educational approaches that foster students' activeness along a process exercised by students individually as well as in groupwork (Jeng, 2019).

In this sense, cooperative learning reflects a pedagogical approach in which students actively work together in small groups toward completing a task or a problem (Aronson, 1972). Such an educational approach is well known and exercised by practitioners seeking to exploit its various advantages including its potential to foster critical thinking toward problem-solving among students (Edrogan, 2019; Johnson & Johnson, 1987). In our efforts, we combine aspects of cooperative learning with collaborative learning. Collaborative learning relies on the concept of knowledge constructed through social interactions among team members working together (Johnson & Johnson, 1987). As implied, both learning approaches have mutual aspects including the nature of the activity in a workgroup, in which students share responsibility and accountability for achieving common goals in an ongoing process in which they receive feedback and refine artifacts they are working on (Aronson, 1972; Johnson & Johnson, 2005; Slavin,2005).

The activity approach known as Jigsaw is considered to involve aspects from both mentioned approaches. There, students work in groups to develop an educational outcome. Each of them is assigned the role of specialist addressing the aspired outcome. Each student is responsible to master and contribute to the development of their unique role as a specialist (Aronson, 1972; Johnson & Johnson, 1987, Johnson & Johnson, 2005). During this activity, students may be required to consult with their peer specialists assigned to other groups. As implied, Jigsaw activities require educators to enroll students in groups as well as to assign them to the roles of specialists. Occasionally, a Jigsaw activity may require task groups to deal with challenges concerning the design of innovative ideas later developed into modern forms of technological implementations reflecting the spirit of the 21st century (Gorlewicz & Jayaram, 2020). Kohn & Chia (2018) exercised their research as they focused on the exploration enactment of a Jigsaw activity supported by innovative technologies in the forms of Social Robotics (SR) exploited for educational purposes.

The applicability of SRs in a Jigsaw activity offers students the potential to exercise learning about an emerging field that is striving to deploy technological devices that resemble and mimic human movements, gestures, and behaviors (Kurtz & Kohen-Vacs, 2022). Occasionally in these activities, the design and development of scenarios for social robots aim at enhancing the learning or training experience (Kurtz & Kohen-Vacs, 2022). There, students may benefit from all advantages of a Jigsaw activity as they practice various skills associated with SR such as design thinking as well as computational thinking. Furthermore, students exercise tasks related to technological development that are also exploitable to benefit educational strategies (Koh & Chia, 2018; Kurtz & Kohen-Vacs, 2022; Voon et al., 2022).

In this paper, we present an enactment of a Jigsaw activity conducted as part of a mutual research effort among the authors of this paper conducted in the framework of an Erasmus+ project focused on Social Robotics involving a German and an Israeli Institution. We conducted this activity as part of our mutual efforts to explore techno-pedagogical aspects concerning the affordances of social robots for enhancing learning and training scenarios. As part of our aims, we examined this activity while focusing on its various aspects including the series of steps needed for deploying the outcomes of such efforts as part of a Jigsaw activity. Hence, we emphasize an activity requiring students to coordinate their efforts and work with their peers in task groups while designing, developing, and deploying the outcomes of their efforts. Specifically, we aim to examine the design and development of SR scenarios usable for enhancing learning and training. Additionally, we include in our exploration aims other educational aspects potentially beneficial to the learning process including students' ability to take responsibility for their tasks as individuals as well as members in groups working together in a group. We also examine the socio-educational dynamics occurring during this process. Last but not least, we do so as we believe that the aspects of the activity we design reflect the realistic settings students are expected to encounter following their study period.

Workshop Planning

The activity we present in this paper was conducted as part of an Erasmus+ visit made by the Israeli delegation to the German University that took place in May 2022. The Israeli team included two instructors and six students while the German team included one instructor and six students. There were altogether three lecturers and twelve students. The Israeli students were attending a master's program on Instructional technologies while the German students studied in a bachelor program on Humanoid Robotics. We conducted our planning efforts for the mentioned activity including a design of a workshop targeting the topic of social robots for enhancing learning and training. The activity was conducted in a form of a workshop that took place at a University in Germany. There, we used the research and development facilities available on the campus. During the workshop, German and Israeli students were required to participate in practical sessions enabling them to develop a scenario enhanced by social robots.

The Jigsaw activity including its planning addressed 7 main phases conducted chronologically according to its enumeration and description presented in Table 1.

Table 1: Overview of the activity phases and their goals conducted along the workshop

Number of Phases	Name	Day Number in Workshop	Aim
1	Introduction	1	Students are divided into heterogenous groups consisting of participants from both institutions capacitated with different skills: team leaders, designers, and developers. Teams are briefed about the phases they are about to experience during the workshop
2	Discussions of ideas for the selection of the theme	1	Each group brainstorms and selects an educational theme used for designing and developing an educational scenario enhanced by SR
4	Initial design	1	Team members work together on their concepts later designed as educational scenarios enhanced by SRs
4	Brain Storm in the group of specialists	2	Team members roam to new groups of specialists for brainstorming purposes in a manner creating homogeneous groups of specialists
5	Maturing the initial design	2	Specialists roam back to their original groups and share the insight they brought from the groups of specialists as they aim to mature their designs from phase 4
6	Development	3	Groups exercise actual development of educational scenarios enhanced by SRs according to
7	Presentations and summary of activity	4	Groups present their design and development outcomes to er groups and peers

Activity Proceeding and Outcomes

The students participating in this workshop were divided into 4 groups, each group selected a different theme for the educational scenario it would pursue along its conceptualization, design, and development efforts. The teams were briefed that their efforts should aspire to achieve the level of a Proof of Concept (PoC). All groups needed to submit a detailed report to the teachers at the end of each phase of the Jigsaw activity. As groups concluded their initial briefing of the activity they selected various themes for each group and reported them to the team of lecturers for their approval.

Participants in the 1st team choose to design and develop an experience enabling students to acquire new vocabulary in the English language through singing. There, the robot was designed and programmed to lead the signing encompassed with sub-titles shown on the display attached to the chest of a Pepper[1] robot manufactured by SoftBank robotics. To encourage students, singing was designed and developed to be encompassed by the body gestures of the robot. Participants in the second team choose to design and develop an educational scenario focused on improving students' cognitive skills aimed at the population of seniors while using a Nao[2] robot that is also manufactured by Softbank robotics. There, they exploited the robot's capability to patiently teach while repeating messages as necessary. Participants in the third group aimed on designing concepts for a

[1] https://www.softbankrobotics.com/emea/en/pepper

[2] https://www.softbankrobotics.com/emea/en/nao

robotic scenario capable to facilitate meditation. This group used various abilities of the robot including its capability to play relaxing music while providing instructions for meditation encompassed by appropriate body gestures. In this case, participants completed a concept and matured design applicable across different types of humanoid robots. Lastly, participants in the fourth group addressed a learning scenario focused on teaching students to play chess. They aimed their design and development to be enacted on a Nao robot capable to walk and imitate steps on a chess board during a game of chess. Figure 1 illustrates the work of all four groups during the workshop.

Figure 1. Illustration of work in all four groups working on scenarios with social robots (from upper-left in a clockwise direction): (1) teaching new vocabulary through singing, (2) improvement of cognitive skills, (3) meditation, (4) playing chess.

The outcomes achieved in groups 1, 2, and 4 resulted in a working Proof of Concepts (PoC) while the outcome of group 3 demonstrated a plausible design applicable across various types of humanoid robots.

Figure 2 is a picture taken during the final phase in which all group members were provided with the opportunity to present their outcomes and receive feedback on their work during the activity.

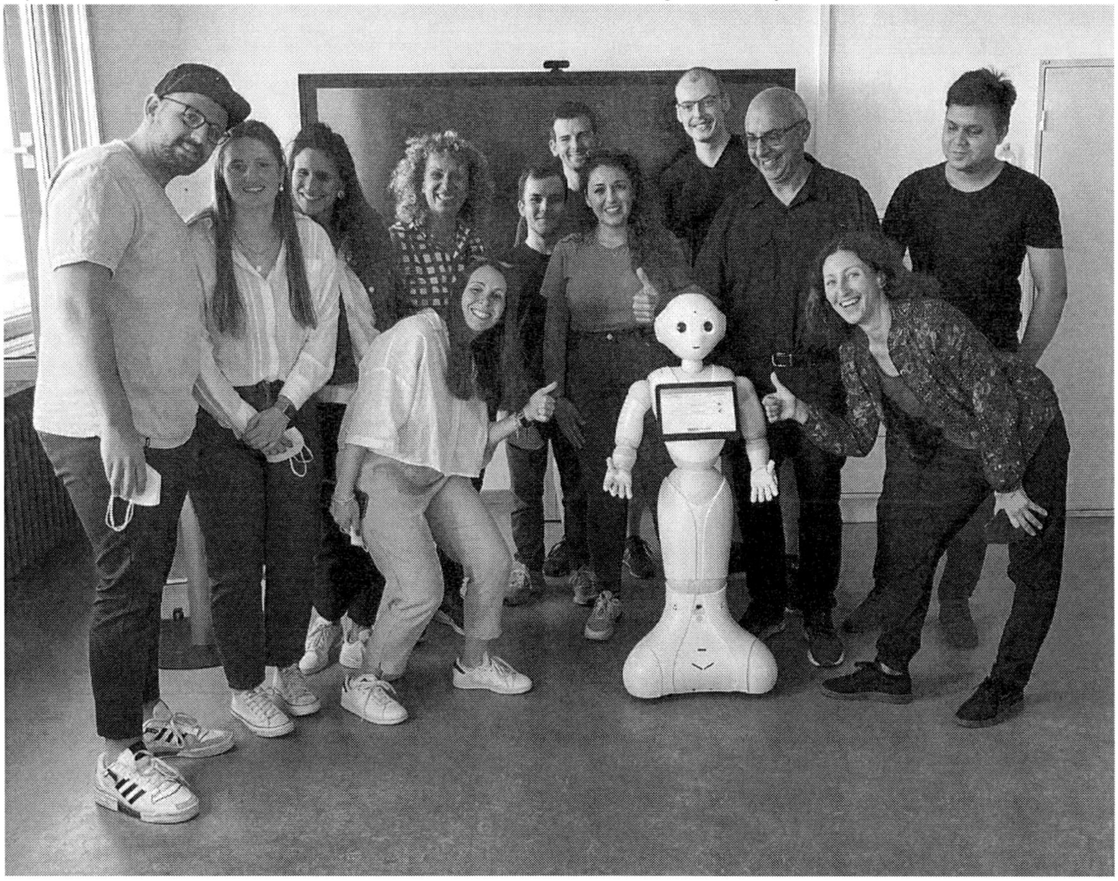

Figure 2. Captured moment from activity presenting teachers, some of the students, and the Pepper robot.

In the final phase of the activity, students shared their insights and reported that they were concerned about conducting their efforts in groups consisting of participants from another university from a foreign culture. They mentioned their appreciation for the opportunity to learn from their peers as they work on a role or task they were unfamiliar with. Additionally, students valued the opportunity to work with peers from different institutions.

Students who participated in the workshop included six members from Israel and six from Germany, 50% female, and 50% male. All of them answered a questionnaire at the end of the activity. The results revealed that 75% of respondents rated the learning experience in international groups with the highest value on the scale from "1 = not at all" to "5 = very much", and 25% gave a rating of 3 to 4. The next item in the questionnaire required students to rate the skills and attitudes they learned through participation in joint sessions in international groups on a scale from "1 = I have not been learning this at all" to "5 = I have been learning this very intensely". The skills and attitudes with the highest rank were the ones in the area of creativity and innovation, life and career skills, openness towards people from other cultures, as well as social, emotional, and communication skills in ethnically, culturally, and linguistically diverse contexts. Finally, the majority of participants expressed the opinion that the joint workshops provided them with valuable experience of collaborating in international teams and that the diversity of students contributed to creative and innovative solutions which emerged during joint sessions.

Discussion and Future Work

International students assessed the Jigsaw-based activity related to designing human-robot interaction (HRI) as a valuable learning experience, which allowed them to create and innovate together, express and experience openness towards students from different cultures, and use their communication skills in an ethnically, culturally, and linguistically diverse context. Moreover, the students felt that the experience of the Jigsaw activity in international teams was helpful for their life and career skills. As noted by Costouros (2020), cooperative learning during a Jigsaw activity allows students to take ownership of their learning as well as responsibility for teaching one another in groups of experts. This feeling of ownership is very likely to enhance the experience of autonomy, empowerment, and control. This is in line with emancipatory approaches, such as Personal Learning Environments (PLE), which emphasize the shift of control and ownership from the educator or the designer to the learner (Buchem, Tur & Hölterhof, 2013). This shift is characterized by allowing learners to take a decision and make choices concerning the content of learning, the sequence of the learning steps, and the selection of the tools (Buchem, Tur & Hölterhof, 2013). These characteristics are found in the Jigsaw activity as shown in the example presented in this paper, in which students could choose the topic for their cooperation in teams, co-define the steps of collaboration and select the tools for collaboration such as the software to design and present prototypes. The Jigsaw activity affords learner control at different levels including those related to the task and its progress. Additionally, it enables control addressing the social interaction, its included level of cooperation, and exploitation of tools based on own competencies and preferences (Buchem, Attwell & Torres, 2011). As opposed to deterministic approaches, this empowering pedagogical approach resulted in a high level of engagement and motivation of participants as observed by the teachers taking place in the activity and reported by their students. One of the key observations of the teachers during the activity was the high energy in the classroom, demonstrated by lively discussions and at the same time by a strong focus on the task at hand. As indicated by Buchem, Tur & Hölterhof (2013), control and ownership of learning may be looked at from a cross-cultural perspective and specific elements of control may be valued differently by learners from different national and academic cultures. The study presented in this paper did not explore such possible differences in detail, hence our recommendation for future research is to explore possible cross-cultural differences in assigning value to different elements of control, ownership, and autonomy in cooperative learning in intercultural student teams, using the Jigsaw activity as an example. Furthermore, our results show that the implementation of the focus of the Jigsaw activity on applying social robots for learning additionally ignited students' engagement. This may be contributed to the perception of both social robots and an activity targeted toward designing a novel solution with social robots as a possible innovation field. At the same time, the Jigsaw activity brought together students with different knowledge and backgrounds to work together on designing prototypes with social robots. These combined factors, i.e. the pedagogical approach of the Jigsaw activity, the topic of the cooperation with a focus on the application of social robots, and the diversity of students in terms of their cultural and academic backgrounds may be increased engagement and motivation for innovation. As pointed out by Osterloh & Frey (2000) intrinsic motivation for innovation may be affected by tasks that afford creativity and the transfer of tacit knowledge. These two aspects (call for creativity and knowledge transfer in teams) were applied in the example of the Jigsaw activity presented in this paper. Further studies could explore these aspects in more detail focusing on factors that may impact motivation for innovation in international student teams. Future studies could also explore other aspects affecting learning during a Jigsaw activity in more detail, such as social relatedness and connectedness among students, quality of experience of confidence, autonomy, and competency. Finally, the limitations of the study presented in this paper must be mentioned. The key limitation is the small sample size and the limited number of research instruments used in the follow-up evaluation. Future studies could include larger sample sizes and apply a more diversified set of research instruments, going beyond self-reported evaluations by study participants. Also, following the argument by Costouros (2020), another limitation is the comparability of topics, tools, and materials used in the Jigsaw activity presented in this paper. Future studies could explore how variations in topics, tools, and materials may impact the perceptions of participants in Jigsaw activities. In summary, the results of this study reveal a high potential for applying Jigsaw collaborative learning activities in groups of international students. The positive effects seem to be enhanced by choosing to focus the collaboration on innovative topics such as social robots, designing the activity to maximize creativity, autonomy, and ownership addressing authentic application contexts to enhance the quality of the educational experience.

References

Aronson, E. (1972). The Theory of Cooperative Learning. Holt, Rinehart, & Winston.

Buchem, I., Attwell, G., & Torres, R. (2011). Understanding personal learning environments: Literature review and synthesis through the activity theory lens. Proceedings of the The PLE Conference 2011, 10th - 12th July 2011, Southampton, UK. Retrieved 1 March 2014 from: http://journal.webscience.org/658

Buchem, I., Tur, G., & Hölterhof, T. (2013). The Role of Ownership and Control in Personal Learning Environments: A Cross-Cultural Study. In the Proceedings of the 4th International PLE Conference 2013, Berlin/Melbourne. URL http://www.literacyandtechnology.org/uploads/1/3/6/8/136889/ib.pdf

Costouros, T. (2020). Jigsaw Cooperative Learning versus Traditional Lectures: Impact on Student Grades and Learning Experience. Teaching & Learning Inquiry, 8(1), 154-172.

Dominguez, A., Alarcon, H., & García-Peñalvo, F. J. (2019). Active learning experiences in Engineering Education. Innovations in Education and Teaching International, 56(2), 230-240. https://doi.org/10.1080/14703297.2018.1546155

Erdogan, F. (2019). Effect of cooperative learning supported by reflective thinking activities on students' critical thinking skills. Eurasian Journal of Educational Research, 19(80), 89-112. https://doi.org/10.14689/ejer.2019.80.5

Gorlewicz, J. L., & Jayaram, S. (2020). Instilling curiosity, connections, and creating value in entrepreneurial minded engineering: Concepts for a course sequence in dynamics and controls. Entrepreneurship Education and Pedagogy, 3(1), 60-85. https://doi.org/10.1177/2515127419885034

Jeng, Y., Chen, W., & Chen, S. (2022). Developing and Evaluating an Active Learning Environment in the K-12 Classroom. Journal of Educational Technology Development and Exchange, 15(1), 1-18.

Johnson, D. W., & Johnson, R. T. (1987). The Socialization of Cooperative Learning. American Journal of Education, 96(2), 187-205. https://doi.org/10.1086/443900

Johnson, D. W., & Johnson, R. T. (2005). New developments in social interdependence theory. Genetic, Social, and General Psychology Monographs, 131(4), 285-358.

Johnson, D. W., & Johnson, R. T. (2009). An educational psychology success story: Social interdependence theory and cooperative learning. Educational Researcher, 38(5), 365-379.

Koh, C. H., & Chia, L. (2018). Jigsaw Activities in Social Robotics Education: Promoting Student Engagement and Learning Outcomes. Journal of Educational Technology Development and Exchange, 11(1), 1-17.

Kurtz, G., & Kohen-Vacs, D. (2022). Humanoid robot as a tutor in a team-based training activity. Interactive Learning Environments, 1-15. doi: 10.1080/10494820.2022.2086577

McInnerney, J. M., & Roberts, T. S. (2009). Collaborative and cooperative Learning. In Encyclopedia of Distance Learning, Second Edition (pp. 319-326). IGI Global.

Osterloh M, Frey B (2000). Motivation, Knowledge Transfer and Organizational Forms. Organizational Science, 11, pp. 538-550.

Papert, S. W. (1980). Children, computers, and powerful ideas. New York: BasicBooks.

Slavin, R. E. (1995). Cooperative Learning: Theory, Research, and Practice. Boston, MA: Allyn & Bacon.

SoftBank Robotics. (2021). Pepper. Retrieved from https://www.softbankrobotics.com/emea/en/pepper

SoftBank Robotics. (2021). NAO. Retrieved from https://www.softbankrobotics.com/emea/en/nao

Tran, V. D. (2019). Does Cooperative Learning Increase Students' Motivation in Learning?. International Journal of Higher Education, 8(5), 12-20. doi: 10.5430/ijhe.v8n5p12

Voon, X. P., Wong, S. L., Wong, L. H., Khambari, M. N. M., & Abdullah, S. I. S. S. (2022). Developing computational thinking competencies through constructivist argumentation learning: A problem-solving perspective. International Journal of Information and Education Technology, 12(2), 53-59. doi: 10.18178/ijiet.2022.12.2.1866

EASYCOMVI: A TOOL FOR THE INTERACTIVE LEARNING OF COMPUTER VISION IN DISTANCE EDUCATION

Blanca Quintana, National University of Distance Education, UNED, Spain

Clara Pérez, National University of Distance Education, UNED, Spain

Sergio Martín, National University of Distance Education, UNED, Spain

Manuel Castro, National University of Distance Education, UNED, Spain

Elio San Cristóbal, National University of Distance Education, UNED, Spain

***Correspondence**: Blanca Quintana: bquintana@ieec.uned.es*

Abstract

This article presents the EasyComVi Tool, an interactive application developed to facilitate the study of Computer Vision for students enrolled in an Engineering Master degree with a Distance Learning methodology. The main objective of this tool is to enable students in subjects related to Computer Vision with a distance learning methodology, to acquire a better understanding of different concepts about the subject studied in a theoretical way, through its interactive visual illustration, in an autonomous way. This tool offers the students the possibility to visualize the results of applying different image processing operations to various example images selecting the value of a set of input parameters. The usefulness and applicability of the tool has been evaluated by means of a questionnaire disseminated among the students of a subject on Computer Vision in a Master's degree in Industrial Engineering. This paper presents the preliminary results obtained in the study carried out, which are very promising and encourage further research in this work.

Keywords:

Computer Vision; Image Processing; Distance learning; Interactive Tool; Assisted learning.

Introduction

For the development of applications capable of applying computer vision algorithms to solve problems of diverse nature, it is necessary to have a solid theoretical knowledge of the subject. Therefore, the theoretical study of the basic concepts of computer vision is essential to be able to tackle these problems successfully in practice. However, over time it has been observed that students enrolled in subjects related to Image Processing and Computer Vision encounter problems in translating the knowledge acquired through theoretical study of computer vision into practice.

On the one hand, although the students understand the concepts studied theoretically, they encounter problems when it comes to understanding the results obtained by applying these algorithms in practice. On the other hand, some students have difficulties when it comes to programming, which prevents them from being able to easily use the existing programming tools to check in a practical way what the result of the theoretical application of these concepts is. Therefore, there is a gap between the theoretical knowledge acquired and its understanding in practice.

The importance of Computer Vision Education was already highlighted several years ago (Bebis et al., 2003). In recent times, the education community has made efforts to make contributions to the improvement of computer vision education (Geronimo et al., 2013; Lámer et al., 2013; Reimer et al., 2011; Sigut et al., 2020; Vital et al., 2019). (Geronimo et al., 2013) presented a graduate course project on computer vision, whose aim was to detect and recognize traffic signs in video sequences. In (Lámer et al., 2013), a step by step system to teach object recognition and tracking in computer vision systems is presented, for students without any knowledge about mathematical principles for computer based object detection. (Reimer et al., 2011) present Raydiance, a tangible interface for teaching computer vision controlled by the spatial arrangement of physical tokens. A methodology to learn computer vision using an humanoid robot is presented in (Vital et al., 2019). Some authors have worked in the development of applications to support the teaching of computer vision concepts (Sigut et al., 2020). The aim of the mobile application developed in this work is to provide support for the teaching of Computer Vision concepts to complement the theoretical lectures.

The main purpose of this work is to bridge the gap between the theoretical basis and the practical application in the learning of computer vision related concepts, overcoming the problem that the lack of a minimum programming knowledge can cause in the first instance, in a distance learning context. In order to achieve this objective, the interactive tool EasyComVi has been designed and developed, whose aim is to assist students in the autonomous study of concepts related to Computer Vision and Image Processing, learnt in a theoretical way.

The paper is divided as follows. Section 2 presents the analysis and design of the interactive tool. The development of the tool is presented in Section 3. The questionnaire developed for the evaluation is presented in Section 4, whereas Section 5 and 6 present the dissemination plan and the preliminary results obtained. Finally, conclusions are presented in Section 7.

Analysis and design of the interactive tool EasyComVi

At this first stage, the first objective has been to carry out an analysis of the basic theoretical material studied in the subject and the selection of those concepts whose learning through the study of written material is considered to be more complicated, and which we want to make easier for the students. The selected topics around which the application will be designed are two: morphological operations and basic operations between pixels.

Based on the analysis carried out, the second step was the design of the application and the establishment of the criteria that must be met in order to facilitate the learning of these concepts to the students. These criteria are detailed below:

- The application must be intuitive and easy to use.
- The application must have a separate module for each of the topics, so that it can offer personalised options depending on the topic addressed.
- The application must display on screen both, the original image and the image resulting from applying an operation.
- The application must allow the user to choose between several test images, so that he/she can observe how the result varies by applying the same operation, depending on the type of input image.
- The application must allow the user to select different operations and vary the parameters of these, observing in real time how the result varies depending on the options selected.
- In order for the student not only to better understand the concepts and operations, but also to be able to reproduce them through programming, the application must show the user how the operation he/she is currently performing could be carried out using a programming language.

Development of the EasyComVi Tool

Based on the analysis carried out and the established criteria presented in the previous section, the EasyComVi tool has been developed. This tool has been developed in Matlab (MathWorks, n.d.).

The tool is composed of two main tabs: Morphological Operations and Basic Operations between Pixels.

Figure 1 a) shows an example of how the Morphological Operations between Pixels tab looks like. In this tab, the user can choose from a drop-down menu between 5 different possible binary images. The operations that the user can execute are: dilation, erosion, opening, closing, denoising, edge extraction, hole filling and thinning (see

Figure 1 b)). In the operations that allow it, the user can choose the type of structuring element to be used to perform the operation, as well as its size (see Figure 1 c)). Finally, the tool displays the code that should be written in Matlab in order to implement the selected operation (see Figure 1 d)).

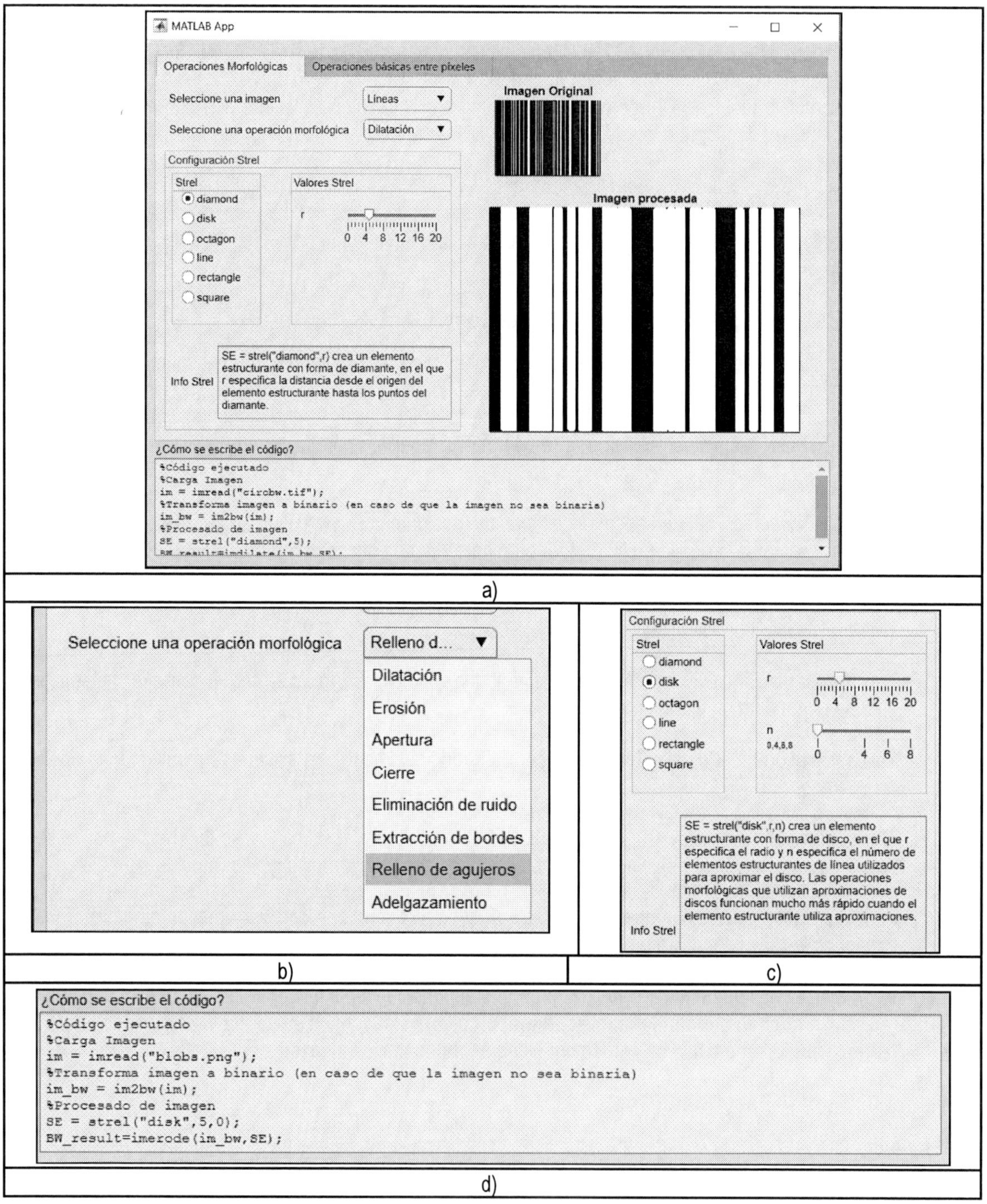

Figure 1. Morphological Operations tab in the EasyComVi application. a) Appearance of the application. b) Drop-down menu with the possible operations that can be performed. c) Example of possible configuration options that can be selected by the student. d) Example of proposed code to be implemented in Matlab automatically generated by the application.

An example of the appearance of the Basic Operations between Pixels tab is shown in Figure 2 a). In this tab, the student must select two example images, which will be used in order to carry out different basic operations. It is possible to choose among 7 different images, being possible to select the same image in both cases if desired (Figure 2 b)). The basic operations between pixels that the user can select are: A and B, A or B, not A, not B, A or (not B) and A and (not B) (Figure 2 c)). Finally, as in the Morphological Operations tab, an example of the code in Matlab that could be used in order to implement the selected operation is shown (see Figure 2 d)).

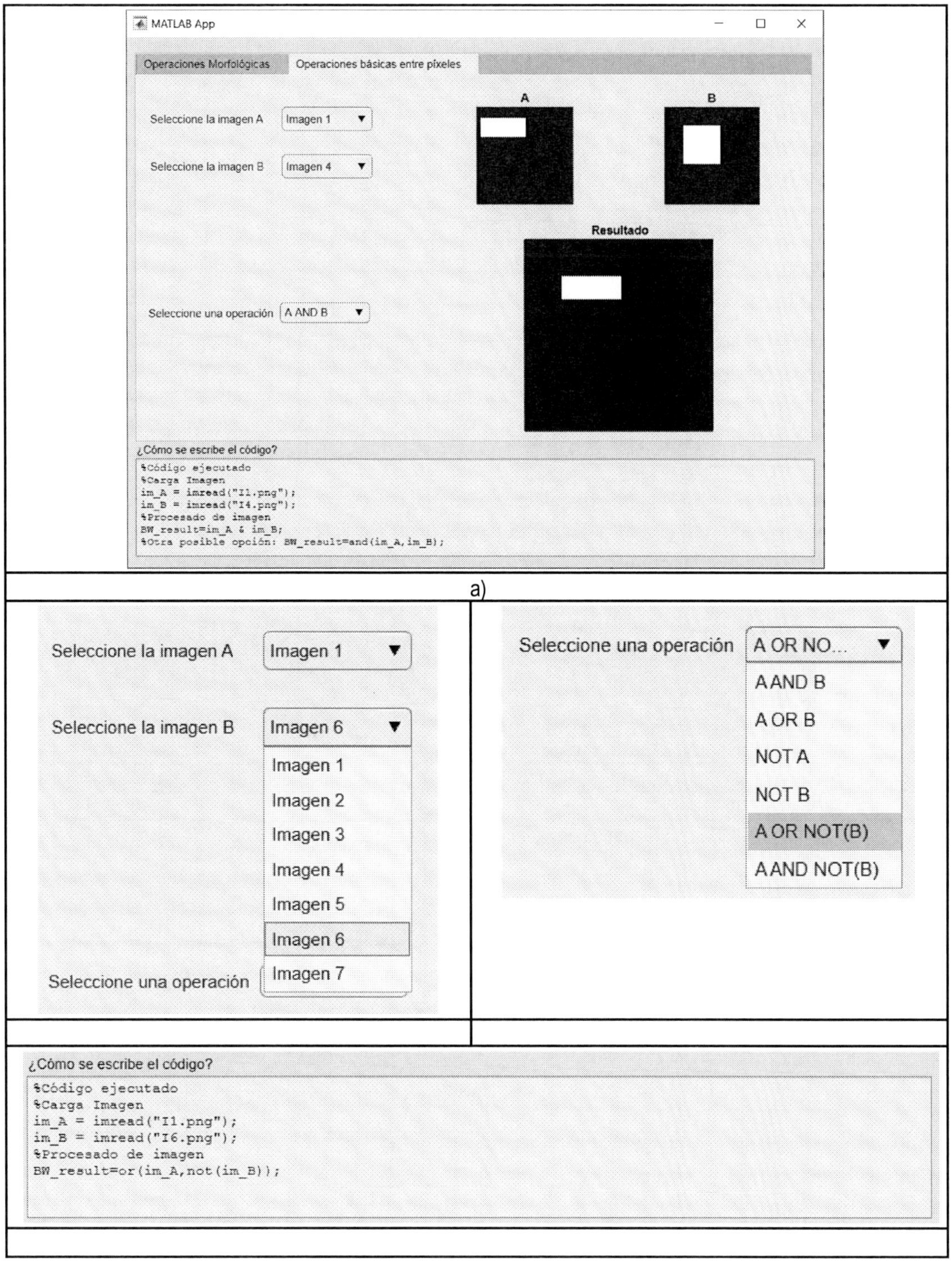

Figure 2. Basic Operations between Pixels tab in the EasyComVi application. a) Appearance of the application. b) Drop-down menu with the possible example images that can be selected. c) Drop-down menu with the different operations that can be carried out. d) Example of proposed code to be implemented in Matlab automatically generated by the application.

Design of the evaluation questionnaire

The EasyComVi tool has been evaluated in the context of a Computer Vision subject in an Industrial Engineering Master's degree. For the evaluation of the tool, a questionnaire has been designed to find out the opinion of the students who have used it. This questionnaire is shown in Tables 1-4. For the assessment, students have been asked to answer the questions by choosing a value between 1 and 5 that indicates their level, or how much they agree or disagree with the issues presented, depending on the type of question.

For a better assessment of the results, the questionnaire has been divided into three main stages:

- A pre-assessment, which seeks to find out the level of the students regarding several areas related to Computer Vision before starting the course.
- An intermediate evaluation, which seeks to know the student's opinion in an intermediate phase, in which the student has already studied part of the theoretical material of the subject but has not yet used the application.
- A final evaluation, which aims to find out the learner's opinion after having used the tool for study.

With this evaluation by stages, the aim is to find out how the student has evolved and the possible usefulness of using the application developed in this article to help during the study, as opposed to studying only the theoretical material.

Finally, a fourth part has been included in the questionnaire, the aim of which is to obtain an overall assessment of the application itself. This last part includes a free space question, which allows the student to express any additional information he/she wants about the application, the process of learning, possible improvements, etc.

Table 1. Evaluation questionnaire. Part 1

Questionnaire: Part 1	NP	1	2	3	4	5
Pre-assessment: What was your level before you started the course? *Choose a value between 1 and 5, where 1-None and 5-Very high.*						
My level of knowledge of computer vision and image processing.						
My level of knowledge about programming.						
My level of knowledge about Matlab.						
My level of motivation with regard to learning computer vision and image processing.						

Table 2. Evaluation questionnaire. Part 2

Questionnaire: Part 2	2NP	1	2	3	4	5
Intermediate assessment. After studying the written material in the basic bibliography on image processing, and before using the application, how much do you agree or disagree with the following statements? *Choose a value between 1 and 5, where 1-Not at all agree and 5-Strongly agree.*						
The study of the written material has allowed me to easily understand the basic relationships between pixels.						
The study of the written material has allowed me to easily understand basic morphological operations.						
I am able to visualise approximately what the result of applying basic relations between pixels is when viewing images, without the need to use Matlab or another tool to see the result.						

I am able to visualise approximately what is the result of applying basic morphological operations when viewing images, without the need to use Matlab or another tool to see the result.						
I can easily understand the Matlab examples on computer vision and image processing provided in the course.						
The study of the Matlab examples has allowed me to easily understand the basic relationships between pixels.						
The study of Matlab examples has allowed me to easily understand basic morphological operations.						
I am able to write my own Matlab scripts for the implementation of basic pixel relations examples.						
I am able to write my own scripts in Matlab for the implementation of examples on basic morphological operations.						

Tabla 3. Evaluation questionnaire. Part 3

Questionnaire: Part 3	NP	1	2	3	4	5
Final evaluation. After having used the EasyComVi application to study the subject, how much do you agree or disagree with the following statements? *Choose a value between 1 and 5, where 1-Not at all agree and 5-Strongly agree.*						
Using the tool has allowed me to understand more easily the basic relationships between pixels.						
Using the tool has allowed me to understand basic morphological operations more easily.						
After having used the tool, I am able to visualise approximately what the result of applying basic relations between pixels is when viewing images, without the need to use Matlab or another tool to see the result.						
After having used the tool, I am able to visualise approximately what the result of the application of basic morphological operations is when viewing the images, without the need to use Matlab or another tool to see the result.						
The use of the tool has allowed me to understand more easily the Matlab examples on computer vision and image processing provided in the course.						
Using the tool has allowed me to understand more easily the basic relationships between pixels.						
After having used the tool, it is easier for me to write my own scripts in Matlab for the implementation of examples on basic pixel relationships.						
After having used the tool, I find it easier to write my own scripts in Matlab for the implementation of examples on basic morphological operations.						

Tabla 4. Evaluation questionnaire. Part 4

Questionnaire: Part 4	NP	1	2	3	4	5
Overall rating of the EasyComVi application *Please choose a value between 1 and 5, where 1-Not at all agree and 5-Strongly agree.*						
The tool is easy to use.						
I think that the tool is useful to better understand the concepts explained in a theoretical way without the need to have programming knowledge.						
The application has helped me to better understand some of the contents of the subject in an autonomous way.						
My interest in this field has increased after using the application.						
The use of this tool has increased my motivation with the subject.						
I think that the use of the tool can mean an improvement in my performance throughout the course.						

The autonomous learning of the contents of the subject is favoured by the use of this type of applications.						
I think it would be useful to extend this tool to other contents of the subject.						
I think it would be interesting to introduce similar tools to this one in other subjects of the degree.						
Please indicate below any comments you would like to make regarding the tool that have not been reflected in previous questions.						
(Write in this space whatever you want. E.g.: any outstanding positive aspect, any outstanding negative aspect, etc.)						

Dissemination

The EasyComVi tool has been disseminated on 3 occasions.

The first time, it was done approximately 2 months after the beginning of the course, so that the students could have had a first approach to the subject using only the theoretical resources and practical programming examples available. In this way, it is possible to evaluate, by means of the questionnaire designed, the students' learning of the contents through the use of only the theoretical-practical material, and through the use of the application developed. This makes it possible to obtain more reliable results in terms of its possible usefulness and the students' satisfaction with it. In this first dissemination, only the tool was offered to the students together with a set of instructions for its use.

The second and third disseminations were made in the middle and at the end of the teaching period by sending the evaluation questionnaire presented in the previous section to the students. The data collection of the evaluation form was carried out by means of a form elaborated in Microsoft Forms, which allows an anonymous data collection, while verified by means of a corporate email account, which on the one hand allows the students to express their opinion in an honest way, and on the other hand, the same person cannot fill in the same questionnaire more than once.

Preliminary results and analysis

In this paper we present the preliminary results obtained in the academic year 2022/2023, carrying out the evaluation in a subject of a Master's degree in Industrial Engineering. Of the 10 students enrolled in the subject, only 3 completed the survey. The results obtained are shown in Figure 3.

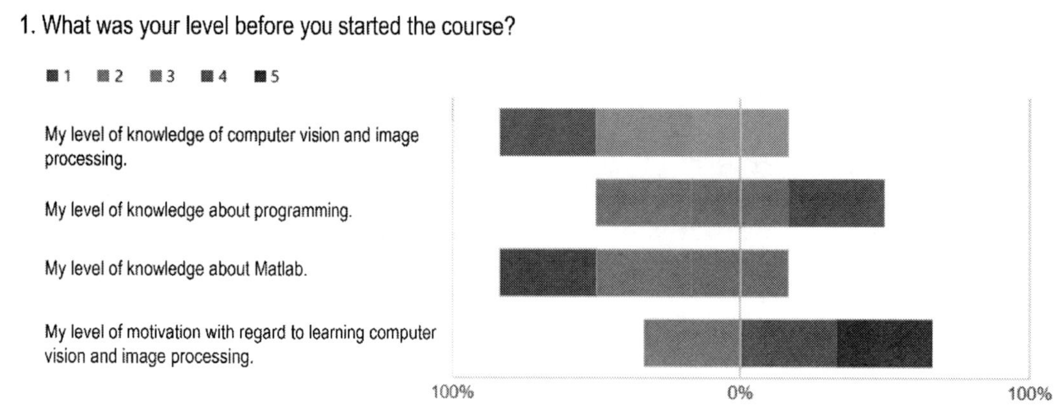

a)

2. After studying the written material in the basic bibliography on image processing, and before using the application, how much do you agree or disagree with the following statements?

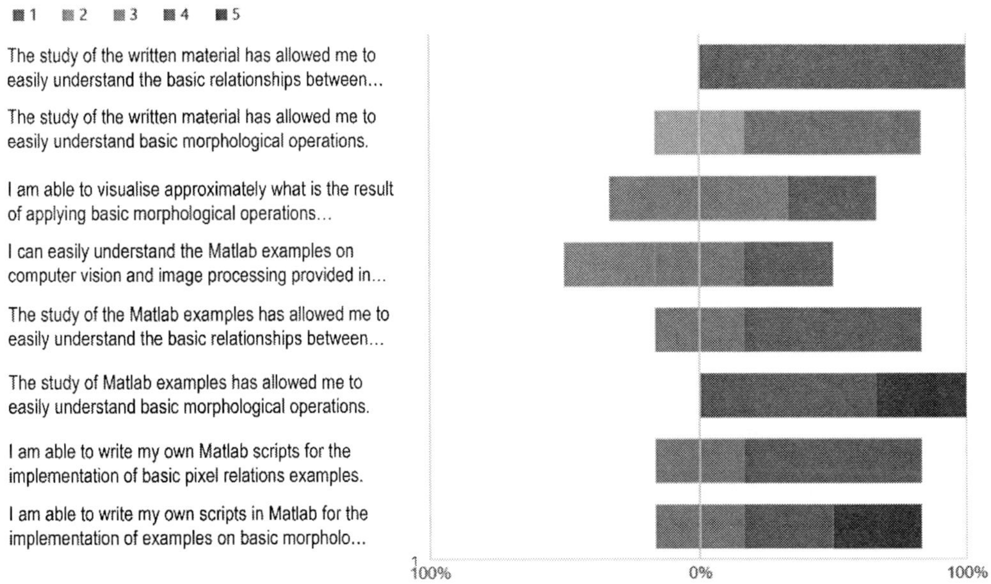

b)

3. After having used the EasyComVi application to study the subject, how much do you agree or disagree with the following statements?

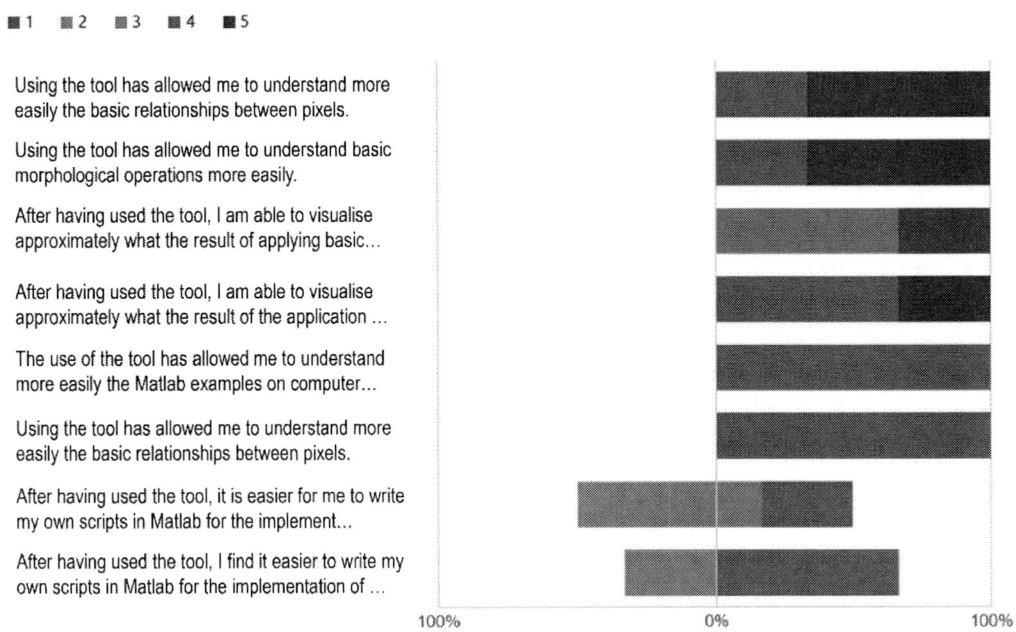

c)

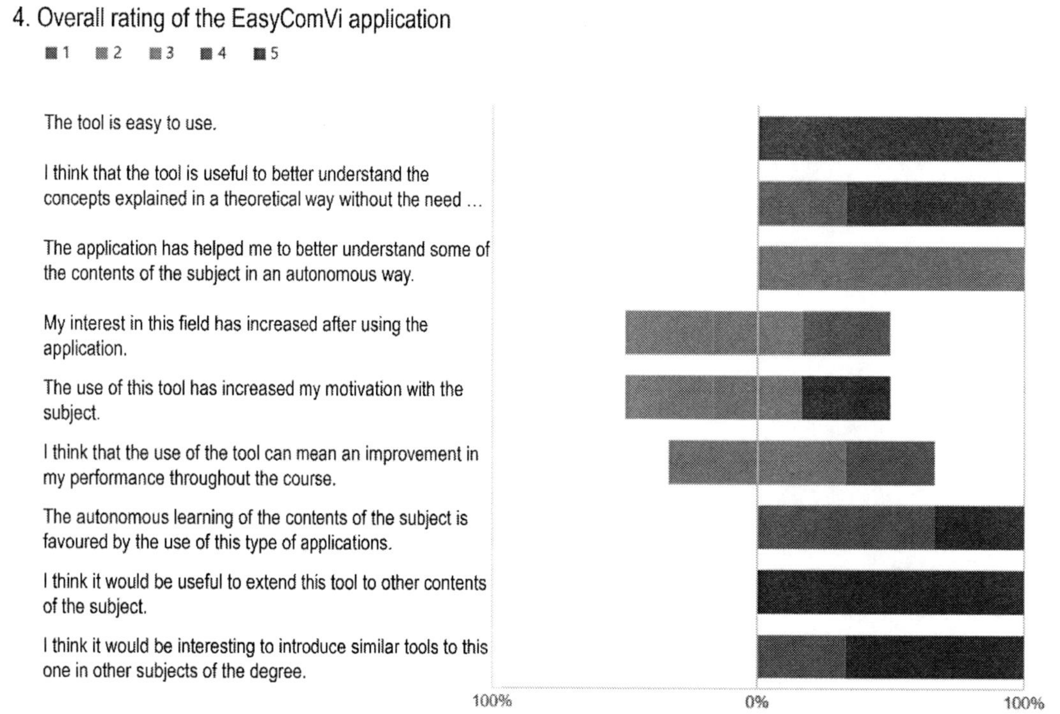

d)

Figure 3. Preliminary results obtained through the evaluation questionnaire. a) Part 1, b) Part 2, c) Part 3 and d) Part 4.

As can be observed in the data presented in Figure 3 a), before starting the course, student's level of knowledge about Computer Vision and image processing and Matlab was among none or medium.

Comparing data in Figure 3 b) (before using EasyComVi Tool) and data in Figure 3 c) (after using EasyComVi Tool), it can be observed that the students can understand more easily concepts about image processing and better visualize the results of applying certain image processing operations after having used the tool developed in the frame of this work.

Finally, if we observe graph in Figure 3 d), we can note that students think that EasyComVi tool is easy to use and is useful to understand better concepts about computer vision studied by means of theory without the need to have programming knowledge. In addition, all students agree that the application has helped them to better understand some of the contents of the subject in an autonomous way. The questions concerning their motivation about the subject and the improvement in their performance along the course were the questions that received lowest values (between 2 and 3). However, the students highly agreed that the use of this type of applications could favoured the autonomous learning of the contents of this subject and that it would be useful to extend the tool to other contents of the subject. Furthermore, students would be interested in the introduction of similar tools to EasyComVi in other subjects of the degree.

Finally, one of the students left an additional comment in the comment box, stating the following: "The effort to develop tools of this style is much appreciated". This, once again, highlights the usefulness of this tool valued by the students.

Conclusions

The study of Computer Vision concepts in distance learning degrees is often a great challenge for students, especially when the main material consists mainly of textbooks, therefore an advantageous educational tool capable of making easier and expanding knowledge can contribute to a better understanding of theoretical concepts.

In this work, EasyComVi, a tool for assisting students in the study of computer vision concepts in distance learning subjects has been described. The tool has been made available to students of a subject on Computer Vision belonging to a Master's degree. The tool has been evaluated by means of a questionnaire. The results obtained are preliminary, but the feedback of the students for this new educational tool is extremely positive. The analysis of the evaluation questionnaires reflects the students' interest in this kind of tool and its usefulness in the study of this type of subject, as well as their interest in extending the tool to other contents of the subject, and even to other subjects.

In the future, the aim is to extend the scope of this innovative educational tool to reach new contents, as well as to improve its design, so that it could provide a better support to students.

Acknowledgements

Authors would like to thank UNED the support provided to this work through the UNED PID 2022-2023 call, with the project titled “Desarrollo de una herramienta interactiva para el aprendizaje de Visión por Computador”, the Higher Technical School of Industrial Engineering, project 2022-ETSII-UNED-11, and the Teaching Innovation Group of the UNED GID2016-17, G-TEIC. This publication is part of the In4Labs project with reference TED2021-131535B-I00 funded by MCIN/AEI/10.13039/501100011033 and by European Union “NextGenerationEU”/PRTR. It has also been co-funded by the Madrid Regional Government, through the project e-Madrid-CM (P2018/TCS-4307), co-financed by the Structural Funds (FSE and FEDER).

References

Bebis, G., Egbert, D., & Shah, M. (2003). Review of computer vision education. *IEEE Transactions on Education*, *46*(1), 2–21. https://doi.org/10.1109/TE.2002.808280

Geronimo, D., Serrat, J., Lopez, A. M., & Baldrich, R. (2013). Traffic sign recognition for computer vision project-based learning. *IEEE Transactions on Education*, *56*(3), 364–371. https://doi.org/10.1109/TE.2013.2239997

Lámer, J., Cymbalak, D., & Jakab, F. (2013). Computer vision based object recognition principles in education. *ICETA 2013 - 11th IEEE International Conference on Emerging ELearning Technologies and Applications, Proceedings*, 253–257. https://doi.org/10.1109/iceta.2013.6674439

MathWorks. (n.d.). *MathWorks - MATLAB & Simulink*. MatLab Central. Retrieved March 7, 2023, from https://es.mathworks.com/

Reimer, P., Branzan Albu, A., & Tzanetakis, G. (2011). Raydiance: A tangible interface for teaching computer vision. *Lecture Notes in Computer Science (Including Subseries Lecture Notes in Artificial Intelligence and Lecture Notes in Bioinformatics)*, *6939 LNCS*(PART 2), 259–269. https://doi.org/10.1007/978-3-642-24031-7_26

Sigut, J., Castro, M., Arnay, R., & Sigut, M. (2020). OpenCV Basics: A Mobile Application to Support the Teaching of Computer Vision Concepts. *IEEE Transactions on Education*, *63*(4), 328–335. https://doi.org/10.1109/TE.2020.2993013

Vital, J. P. M., Fonseca Ferreira, N. M., Valente, A., Filipe, V., & Soares, S. F. S. P. (2019). Learning computer vision using a humanoid robot. *IEEE Global Engineering Education Conference, EDUCON, April-2019*, 639–645. https://doi.org/10.1109/EDUCON.2019.8725196

H5P and Canvas - the best pair since salt and pepper?

Lauren Maher, Munster Technological University, Ireland

***Correspondence**: Lauren Maher: lauren.maher@cit.ie*

Abstract

The demand from lecturing staff that desire to improve the engagement levels of their students is continuously increasing. Learning Management System integrations such as H5P are a simple and effective way to improve student engagement and learning within modules. This paper explores the benefits of staff adopting the H5P integration in Canvas for developing engaging and interactive content in the context of higher education. It examines a pilot initiative developed by Munster Technological University's Department of Technology Enhanced Learning that investigated the needs of individual staff members and how they could make small changes to their teaching content to help improve student engagement. The results of this pilot indicated that participating staff had improved knowledge surrounding the development of interactive content through the use of H5P following one-to-one sessions carried out as part of the initiative and revealed that staff intends to apply the H5P approach to their everyday teaching activities to encourage student motivation and engagement in modules. This paper discusses further plans for the use of H5P within the Learning Management System at Munster Technological University and how it will be facilitated by the Department of Technology Enhanced Learning.

Introduction

This paper explores the benefits of using the H5P integration in Canvas for developing engaging and interactive content in the context of higher education, as the H5P integration continues to become more platform-agnostic. This paper focuses primarily on Canvas, as this is where Munster Technological University's (MTU) institutional focus is, and looks at the various ways MTU staff are interested in H5P within Canvas, reflected through the piloting and evaluation of a one-to-one training initiative set up by MTU's department of Technology Enhanced Learning (TEL). This paper also discusses the future prospects of continuing to use H5P within the context of Munster Technological University and how the department of Technology Enhanced Learning can further improve related resources for staff.

Enabling Engagement through the LMS

Canvas is the Learning Management System (LMS) implemented within MTU. One of the many integrated tools available within Canvas is H5P. H5P is a simple way to improve student engagement and learning in any Canvas module. Reports show that including Online Interactive Activities as part of module delivery increased student engagement, and improved grades (MacKenzie, & Ballard, 2015). Some additional benefits of using H5P include ease of access, the ability to create various content types, and ease of use.

H5P allows instructors to chunk content into manageable pieces and enables students to apply knowledge easily and come better prepared for class (Singleton, R., & Charlton, A., 2020). It also allows instructors to develop a more diverse range of content for students to interact with before, during, or after lessons, all of which can be viewed at https://h5P.org/. This can be done by incorporating content as pre-learning material, to increase student motivation and participation, and as assessment tools or knowledge checks. H5P can also be used, for example, to increase student motivation and participation in class through the use of Quizzes, Interactive Videos/ Presentations, and creating gamified content types (Chen, S. 2022).

Current literature shows that institutions are inclined to use plugins such as H5P for an array of reasons, a popular justification for developing content using H5P among higher education professionals is for Open and Distance Learning (ODL) and for the creation of "Open Educational Resources" (OER). Open and Distance Learning is an education system where students do not attend live classes on campus. The learning process instead typically takes place at a distance and without the need to physically meet up with an instructor. Instead, a variety of alternative asynchronous methods are facilitated such as online classes, recordings of classes, online class discussions via course discussion boards, and individual or group projects (Moore, Dickson-Deane,

& Galyen, 2011). OERs within the context of open education - are most often commonly understood by a 2019 UNESCO definition: "Open Educational Resources (OER): Open Educational Resources (OER) are learning, teaching and research materials in any format and medium that reside in the public domain or are under copyright that have been released under an open license, that permit no-cost access, re-use, repurpose, adaptation and redistribution by others." (UNESCO, 2019).

The H5P integration works well with Canvas in a variety of ways, for example, it is mobile-friendly, which allows students to interact with content types from their smart devices in an environment that suits their circumstances. Having mobile-friendly integrations are important for online learning for convenience, portability, and overall ease of use as it facilitates the ability to 'learn anytime and anywhere' and for learning content to be widely available and accessible for those that do not have easy access to computers. Several studies yielded positive results on the efficacy of mobile learning (Luo et al., 2015). These studies confirmed that mobile devices worked well in learning vocabulary, and writing skills (Dolgunsöz, Yıldırım 2021). The way in which devices are used for course-related activities varies, with reasons for use including note-taking, reading course materials, downloading those materials, communicating, and socialising (Kukulska-Hulme, 2002). According to a recent report, more than 95% of people in developed countries now use a mobile device, while desktop PC usage is about 77% (Pew Research Center, 2021).

A recent study by Mohan et al. (2020) which looked at the impact of the COVID-19 pandemic on second-level education in Ireland finds that half of the schools surveyed reported issues with a lack of access to high-speed broadband and/or a lack of access to appropriate digital devices for their students. This figure increases to approximately 58% for disadvantaged schools characterised by lower-than-median household incomes (Mohan et al., 2020). Therefore the kind of mobile-friendly flexibility offered by H5P to MTU students is crucial to student success in a context where connectivity is often done through phone data plans rather than wifi/broadband at home.

Below are the usage statistics from Moodle.org that highlight the number of Moodle sites currently using the H5P plugin (https://moodle.org/plugins/mod_hvp/stats). The number currently sits at 26630, which has more than doubled since the beginning of the COVID-19 pandemic, and the corresponding demand for remote learning content to be made available within Higher Education.

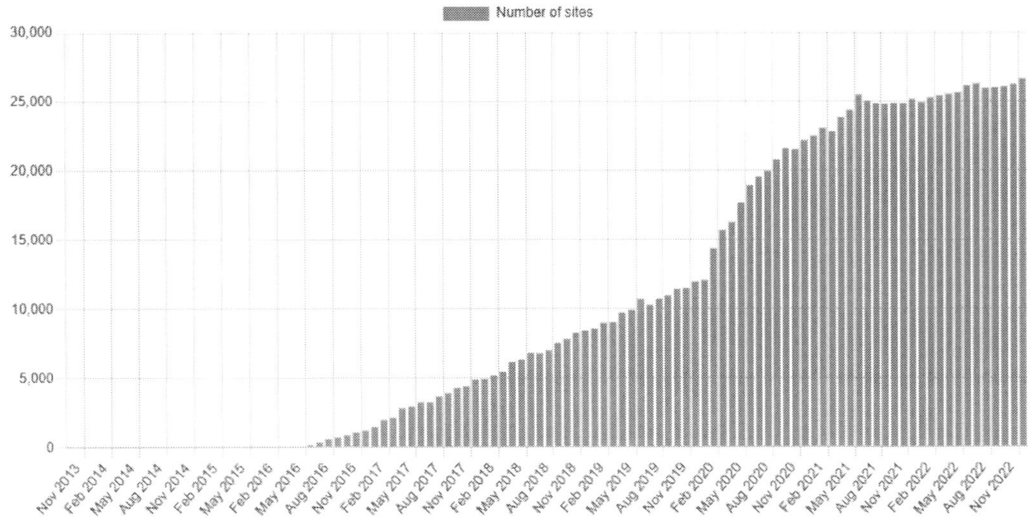

Figure 1. Usage stats - Number of sites using H5P plugin: 26630

The H5P integration within Canvas is currently used by lecturers within MTU to develop a variety of content types including Course Presentations, Interactive Videos, and Multiple Choice Questions. There is an interest and demand among the teaching staff at MTU to develop new and engaging content for students. This statement is reflected in the views of one of the recent H5P training videos offered by the department of TEL, which has 5,484 views on the department's YouTube Channel. The recording of the training session introduced staff to H5P and gave them an overview of the integration within Canvas and how to access it from inside of a module. The session also covered how to develop a variety of H5P content types such as Course Presentations, the Documentation Tool, and Interactive Videos/ Images. The training session gave staff insight into how they can implement these types of content into their Canvas modules and existing content to increase student engagement. The training session also covered the reporting features (Drill Down Reports) inside of H5P, which allows for tracking of student access to these resources and keeps a record of student interactions, scores of students, and answers given by students.

Promoting Small but Mighty Changes in Digital Practices

The interest and demand among teaching staff to develop new and engaging content for students were also reflected through a series of 1-1 training sessions conducted by MTU's department of Technology Enhanced Learning throughout the first semester of this academic year (2022/ 2023). MTU developed and piloted a new initiative named 'TEL Me More!' with teaching staff over the first three weeks of Semester 1. This initiative encouraged staff to sign up for one-to-one sessions with members of the Technology Enhanced Learning Department, designed to assist lecturers in finding out how their Canvas module can do more for them and their students using a range of tips and tricks designed to reduce manual effort and/or support engagement. Although group staff training sessions were provided by the department of Technology Enhanced Learning throughout the year, these sessions did not necessarily lead to 'on-the-ground' change. Training sessions are typically broad and one-to-many, and although useful, these sessions do not really address the specific needs of individual users/ circumstances. Feedback from these training sessions indicated that many staff felt they couldn't ask specific questions during the group training sessions. Therefore, the department of Technology Enhanced Learning launched the one-to-one initiative to create an individual experience for staff. The one-to-one initiative was designed based on The Prosci ADKAR (Awareness, Desire, Knowledge, Ability, Reinforcement) Model (Hiatt, 2006), and the Student outcome-led design model by UCEM (University College of Estate Management).

Throughout this pilot, the largest number of queries from staff indicated they would like to develop more engaging and interactive content for their learners. Some of the participants of this initiative expressed their interest in making classes more engaging and interactive through the use of activities. Staff that teaches primarily online, had queries revolving around how to increase student engagement within a module. The department of Technology Enhanced Learning offered a variety of resources, tips, and tricks to assist lecturers with these queries. Some of the tips centred around making content more engaging through the use of Canvas features such as Scheduled Announcements, Grade Messaging, Video Messages, and using the H5P integration to update or enhance existing content.

Throughout these sessions, the department of TEL looked at H5P content types that staff needed and how they would be beneficial for staff and students. Discussions included 'when and where to use H5P in Canvas', with examples being demonstrated in Canvas Pages, Announcements, Assignments, Discussions, etc. Throughout these sessions, the department of TEL also looked at what H5P items staff wished to use, and their benefits. The department of TEL identified three content types that the staff were most interested in during these sessions. Participants were shown how to develop the content types, given examples of them in use, and shown how to use content types such as Branching Scenarios and an Interactive Book to link various content types and activities together for the students. The following is a short overview of the content types recommended to staff during the one-to-one sessions. These content types were recommended as they are some of the most effective digital teaching approaches.

1. Video - This content type is perfect for when staff already have a video clip (e.g. as an MP4 or a YouTube video), that they want to enrich with interactive elements, as outlined by Noetel et al (2021), Video presents many benefits for learning, including allowing learners more control, which can improve student motivation and regulate their cognitive load. The department of TEL suggested that lecturers facilitate differentiated learning by adding in-depth information such as pictures, tables, text, and links that the learner can interact with during video playback. There is a variety of interactive elements that can be included in the videos such as puzzles for the learners to solve at any given time in the video. These puzzles can be included by adding Multiple Choice Questions, Fill in the Blanks, Drag and Drop questions, and Summaries. The interactive content types typically consist of three steps: Upload/ embed video, Add interactions, and Summary task. These three steps represent a natural workflow for creating

interactive content. Figure 2 shows a video training session on 'Remote Teaching' developed by the department of TEL, which has interactive elements included. These elements are broken up by Bookmarks indicated by the white circles throughout the video where the interactions have been placed. In this example, the interactions include a Multiple Choice Question, a Fill in the Blanks activity, and a Drag and Drop activity.

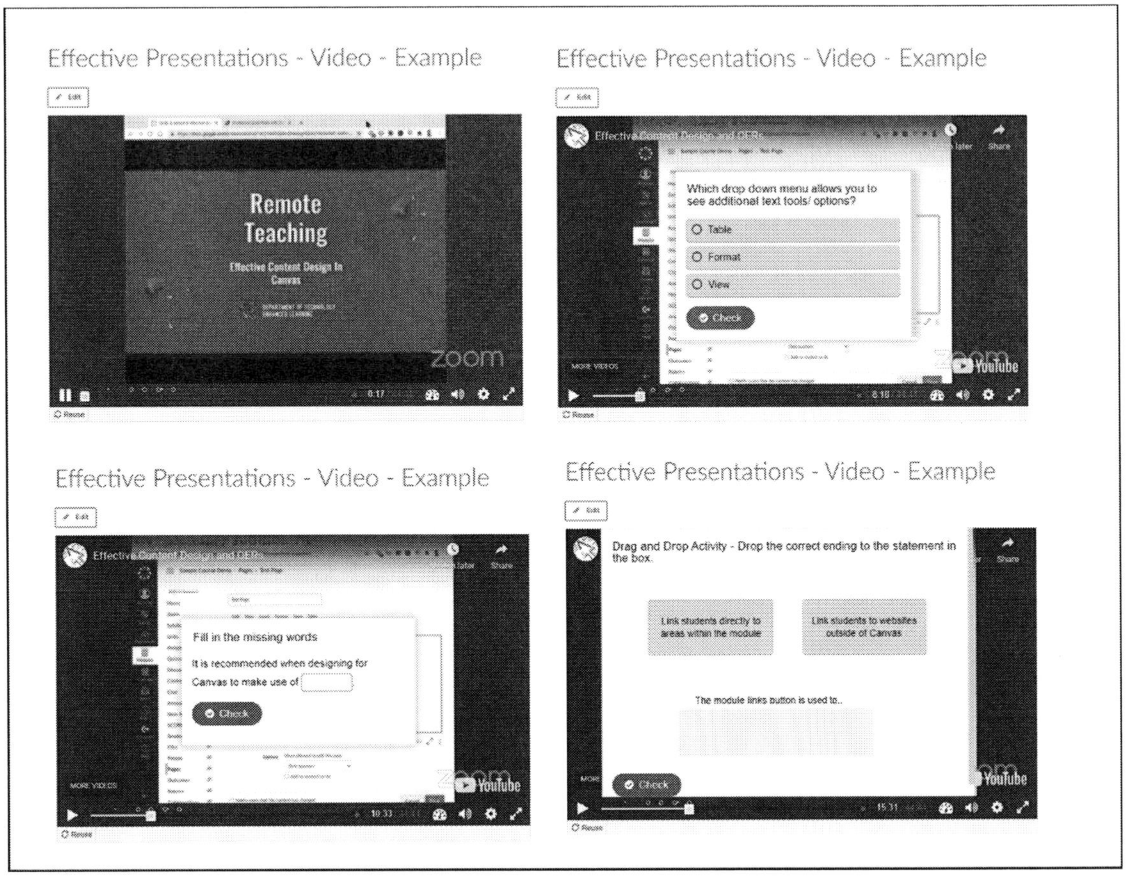

Figure 2. Interactive Video Example

2. Image - This content type is great for staff that has images that are important for student learning, this activity facilitates turning static images interactive, as noted by Sinnayah et al (2021), image-based activities may be "peppered throughout the course to actively engage and stimulate students with an asynchronous teacher presence". The department of TEL suggested using interactive images as both a way for students to access relevant useful information and/ or as a formative assessment activity. Examples of H5P content types were suggested to staff, which included turning a static image such as a diagram relevant to the module into an Image Hotspot using H5P. Hotspot images are interactive images where students can click on specific areas to access additional information, links, etc. When designing the content, staff choose a background image and have the ability to place hotspot markers around the image to make it more interactive by adding text, links, images, etc to the hotspot areas. Below is an example of an interactive image (Figure 3) created to assist students with learning about referencing software. Students can click on the purple plus icons and pop-ups will show additional text relevant to the part of the image.

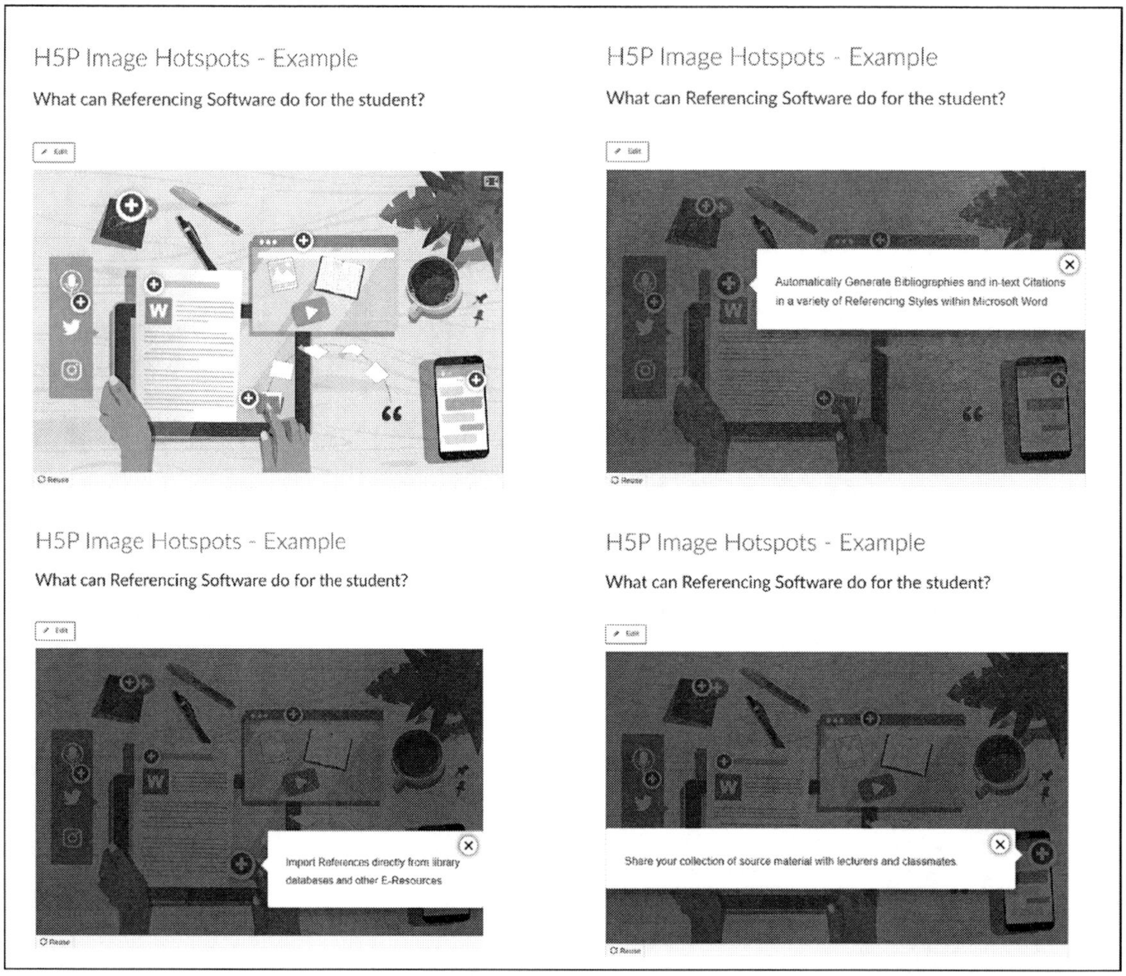

Figure 3. Image Hotspot Example

3. PowerPoint Presentation - This activity type is one that the department of TEL recommended to many staff that had a PowerPoint Presentation which they used regularly and wanted to develop into more interactive/ engaging content for students. Course Presentations contain slides where you can add various multimedia and interactive elements to engage the learner. This activity type allows the creator to add elements on top of their existing PowerPoint including additional Text, Links, Videos, Images, Quiz pop-ups, Drag and Drop exercises to make the presentation more engaging and interactive for students. Below (Figure 4) is some examples of slides from a Course Presentation on 'Edtech for staff' put together as part of a staff training session to help them visualise some of the elements they could create using H5P. Course Presentations are used by staff who want to package a piece of learning content in a structured and interactive format. Learners can swipe through the slides to experience the learning material while solving various quizzes, completing activities, or watching videos along the way. Course Presentations were recommended to staff as an alternative to presenting their learning content as PowerPoint Presentations, PDFs, or text-based web pages. Course Presentations are very flexible to use, as they are simple to create, publish and edit. Presentations can also be built into other features such as Interactive Books and Branching Scenarios. These two content types allow for a mixture of various content types all in one place.

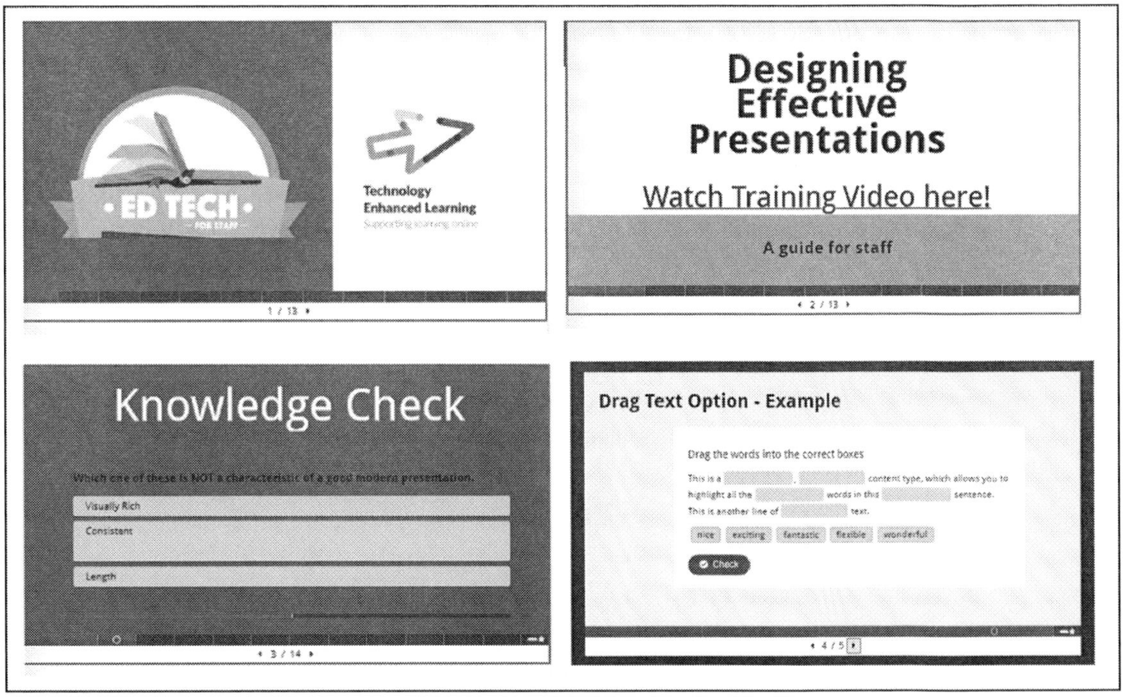

Figure 4. Interactive Course Presentation Example

4. Branching Scenario - A Branching Scenario content type is used for creating interactive content through developing decision-based paths. The department of TEL recommended to staff that they make use of this content type to develop learning materials that branch to different paths based on the student's answers and to incorporate a variety of content types into one activity. One of the features of the Branching Scenario is to branch out questions that will determine the branching logic. The staff has the ability to create a question by dragging a "Branching Question" and dropping it on available drop zones. Staff can add as many alternatives as needed for their lesson, and each alternative will send the user down a different path determined when developing the content. Staff also have the ability to specify what should happen if an alternative is chosen, and feedback can be provided to the student if using 'correct' and 'incorrect' answers, or custom feedback can be given to the student using the designated input fields.

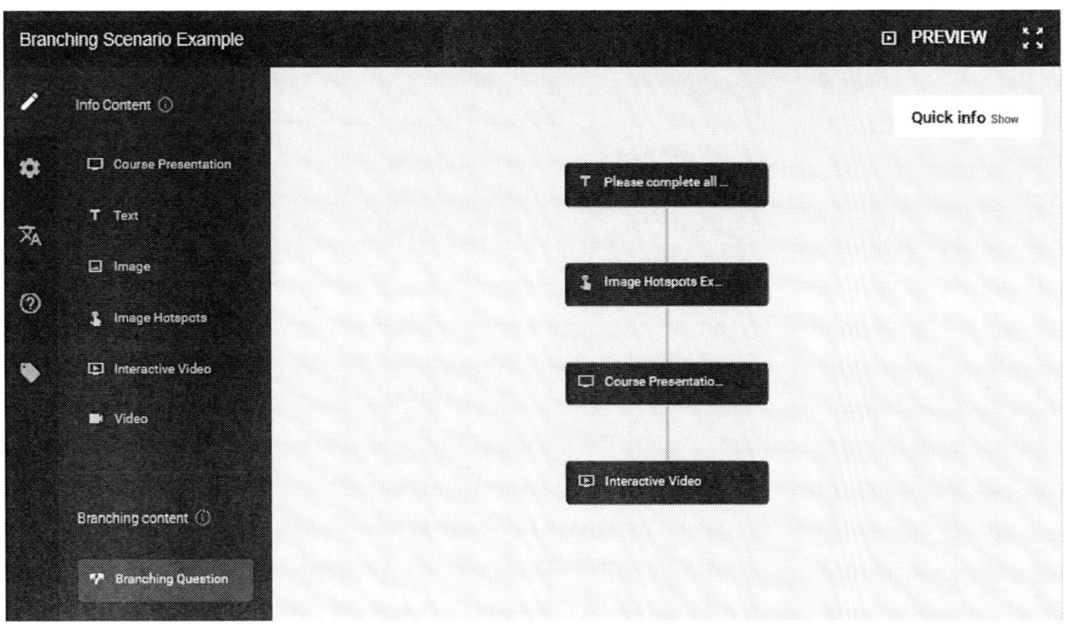

Figure 5. Branching Scenario Example

Conclusions and Outlook

Following the pilot of this initiative, a total of 28 participants took part in the one-one sessions over a three-week period. All participants are part of the lecturing staff at MTU, teaching a variety of courses. Some of these courses include Biological Sciences, Process Energy and Transport Engineering, and Tourism and Hospitality (Figure 6). After each session, the participants were sent additional resources to facilitate them in developing more engaging content and to assist them with the implementation of what they have learned throughout the sessions into their classes. Staff were also sent an evaluation survey after each session. The evaluation survey was sent to all 28 participants, 16 participants responded to the survey with their feedback and evaluation of the initiative. Resources provided to participants included a recording of the session, guides on topics discussed, and interactive resources such as the department of TEL's 'Learn H5P Module' on Canvas. The results of the survey showed that 94.1% of respondents marked the usefulness of the initiative 5/5 and 5.9% marked it 4/5. Results also showed that all participants who responded to the survey felt they have the potential to apply what was learned in the sessions to their everyday teaching activities and that staff has improved knowledge of the topics covered in the sessions (Figures 7 and 8).

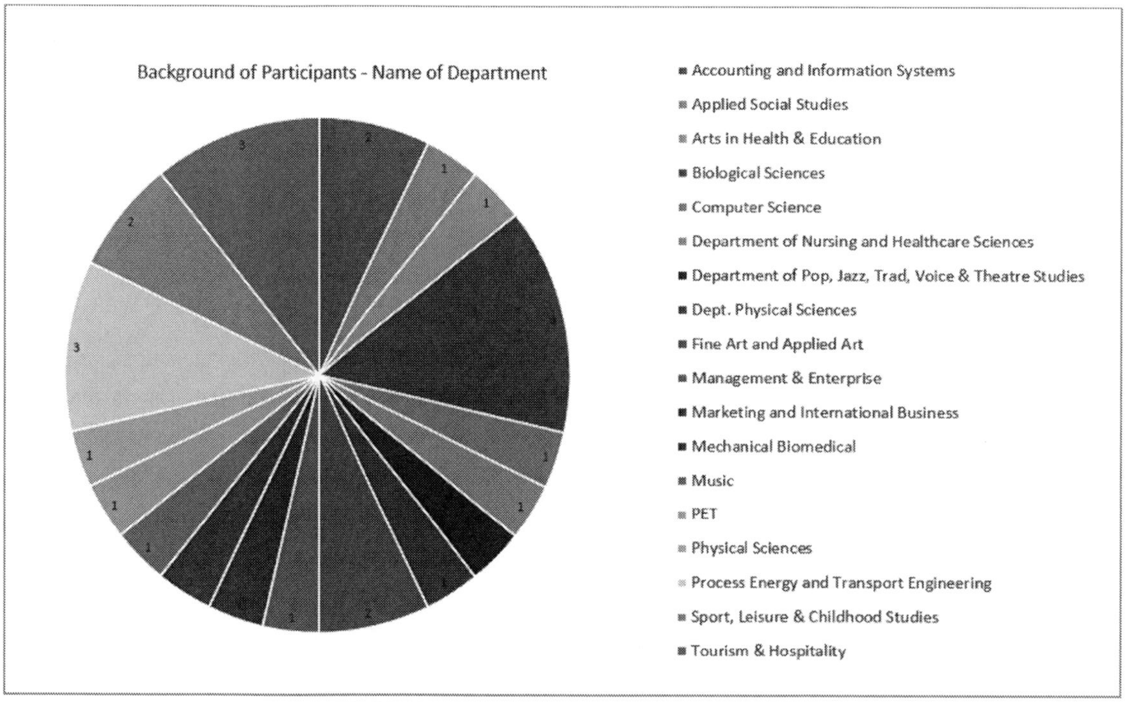

Figure 6. Background of Participants – Name of Department

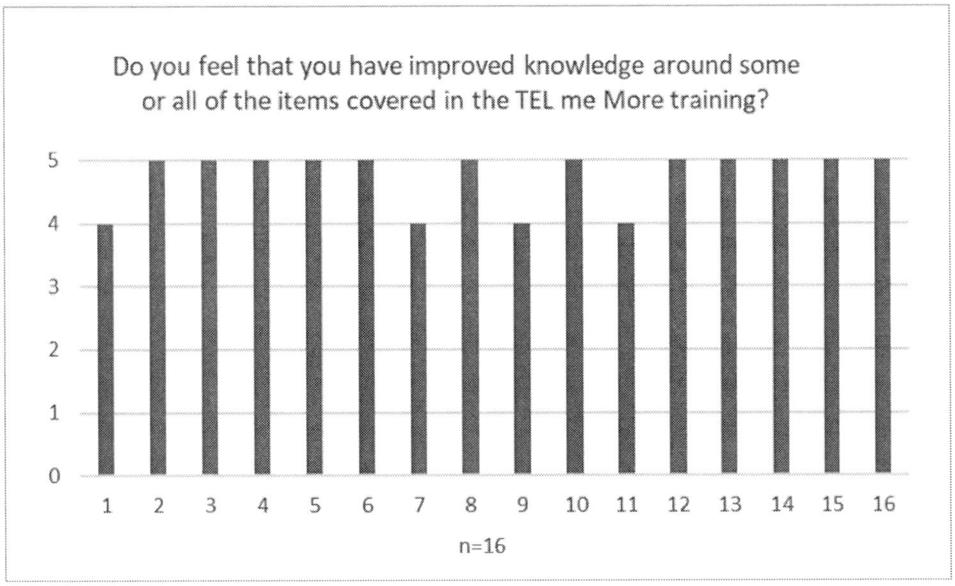

Figure 7. Survey question regarding improved knowledge around training topics.

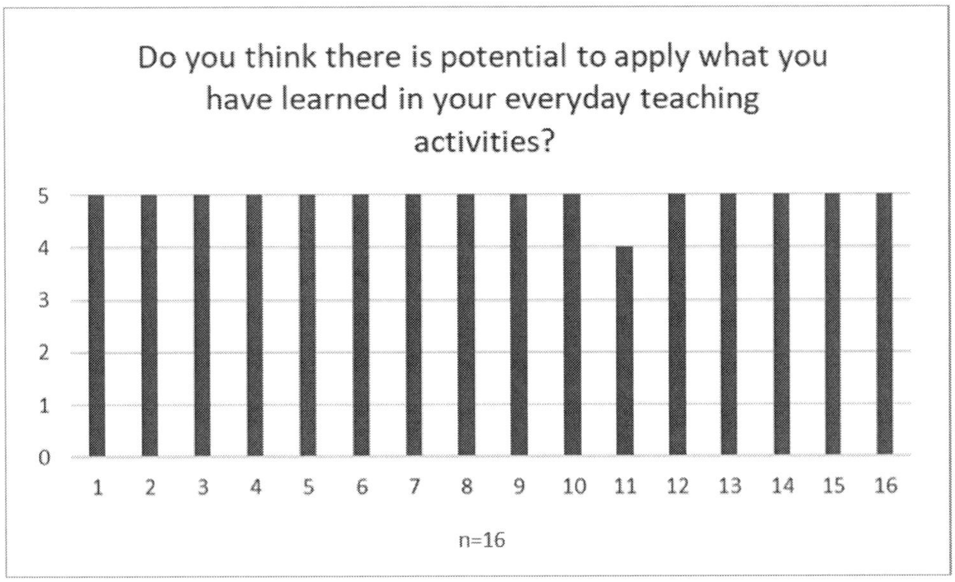

Figure 8. Survey question regarding applying knowledge to everyday teaching activities.

Overall, the department of Technology Enhanced Learning was pleased with the engagement, interest, and feedback of staff throughout the pilot of the one-to-one initiative. Future plans for the department of TEL regarding H5P are to continue to engage with staff to further increase their knowledge of developing interactive content types using H5P in Canvas and improve engagement levels in their modules. This will be facilitated with a range of resources developed by the department of Technology Enhanced Learning such as group training sessions, recordings on the department's YouTube Channel, a self-paced 'Learn H5P module,' the 'TEL knowledge base' filled with 'how to' guides and continued 1-1 sessions with teaching staff. These resources have been developed and maintained by the department of TEL to increase accessibility for staff looking to learn more about H5P and Canvas.

References

Chen, S. (2022) 'Collaborating with Students: Reflections on UCC Library Co-Creating Learning Experiences', CONUL Teaching & Learning Committee Annual Seminar 2022, Dublin, Ireland, 17 Nov.

Cullinan, J., Flannery, D., Harold, J., Lyons, S., & Palcic, D. (2021). The disconnected: COVID-19 and disparities in access to quality broadband for higher education students. International Journal of Educational Technology in Higher Education, 18(1), 26. https://doi.org/10.1186/s41239-021-00262-1

Dolgunsöz, E., & Yıldırım, G. (2021). The role of mobile devices on online EFL skill courses during Covid-19 emergency remote education. Acuity: Journal of English Language Pedagogy, Literature and Culture, 6(2), 118–131. https://doi.org/10.35974/acuity.v6i2.2486

Hiatt J. M. (2006). Adkar : a model for change in business government and our community (1. ed.). Prosci Learning Center.

Kukulska-Hulme, A. (2002). Cognitive, Ergonomic and Affective Aspects of PDA Use for Learning. In European Workshop on Mobile and Contextual Learning. Open.ac.uk. Retrieved March 9, 2023, from http://oro.open.ac.uk/49020/2/kukulska-hulme%20-%20mlearn2002.pdf

Luo, B.R., Lin, Y.L., Chen, N.S., Fang, W.C. (2015). Using mobile device to facilitate English communication and willingness to communicate in a communicate language teaching classroom. Proceedings of the 15th International conference on Advanced Learning Technologies (pp. 320–322). IEEE.

MacKenzie, L., & Ballard, K. (2015). Can using individual online interactive activities enhance exam results. Journal of Online Learning and Teaching, 11(2), 262-266.

Miao, F., Mishra, S., Orr, D., & Janssen, B. (2019). Guidelines on the development of open educational resources policies. UNESCO Publishing.

Mohan, G., McCoy, S., Carroll, E., Mihut, G., Lyons, S., & Mac Domhnaill, C. (2020). Learning for All? Second-level Education in Ireland During COVID-19. ESRI Survey and Statistical Report Series No. 92. Dublin: Economic and Social Research Institute.

Moore, J. L., Dickson-Deane, C., & Galyen, K. (2011). e-Learning, online learning, and distance learning environments: Are they the same? The Internet and Higher Education, 129-135.

Noetel, M., Griffith, S., Delaney, O., Sanders, T., Parker, P., del Pozo Cruz, B., & Lonsdale, C. (2021). Video improves learning in higher education: A systematic review. Review of educational research, 91(2), 204-236.

Mobile fact sheet. (2021, April 7). Pew Research Center: Internet, Science & Tech. http://www.pewinternet.org/factsheet/mobile/

Singleton, R., & Charlton, A. (2020). Creating H5P content for active learning. Pacific Journal of Technology Enhanced Learning, 2(1).

Sinnayah, P., Salcedo, A., & Rekhari, S. (2021). Reimagining physiology education with interactive content developed in H5P. Advances in Physiology Education, 45(1), 71-76.

Lindsay, K. (2019). Designing modules: our educational framework. University College of Estate Management Ucem.ac.uk. Retrieved March 9, 2023, from https://blog.ucem.ac.uk/onlineeducation/posts/937

UNESCO recommendation on open educational resources (OER). (2022, April 21). Unesco.org. https://www.unesco.org/en/articles/unesco-recommendation-open-educational-resources-oer

Gap in pagination due to unavailable paper.

Pages 203-209

STORY AS PEDAGOGY: LEVERAGING NARRATIVE DIGITAL LEARNING PRACTICES IN THE INSTRUCTIONAL DESIGN PROCESS

Angela Gunder, Online Learning Consortium, United States
Melody Buckner, The University of Arizona, United States

***Correspondence**: Angela Gunder: angela.gunder@onlinelearning-c.org*

Abstract

This paper examines the pedagogical value of using narrative digital learning practices (NDLP) in instructional design. Through a thematic review of the literature, the authors illustrate that NDLP, which are the intentional use of storytelling techniques to inform and enhance the student experience within digital learning environments, can increase student engagement and help them meet the outcomes and goals for instruction. It discusses the different ways in which NDLP can be used to support such practices as course mapping, digital storytelling, adaptive and/or differentiated learning, scenario-based and case-based learning, gameful learning, and the application of universal design for learning principles. Additionally, the authors present backward design as a way to ensure that narrative structures used in courses are supportive of learning objectives. The future of learning is discussed, including the role of NDLP in facilitating more personalized and immersive learning experiences. The paper concludes by noting that NDLP is a valuable tool for instructional designers and educators and has the potential to transform teaching and learning through the unique affordances of narrative structure and digital tools.

Keywords:

Narrative digital learning practices, digital learning, digital storytelling, narrative structures, narrative practices, online learning, instructional design, course mapping

Introduction

Across a multitude of teaching and learning contexts, educators continue to prioritize engagement, relevance, belongingness, and community as essential components of effective course design and facilitation. As a field, we constantly look for innovative practices for designing instruction that will capture the minds and hearts of our learners, particularly those historically marginalized students who may otherwise feel alienated or divorced from the learning experience. In reflecting on these barriers to encouraging students' connection to the learning process, designers and educators can hinge the educational experience around metaphors, such as building a modular course that is experienced as a book that you simply cannot put down (Gunder et al., 2019), or resituating learners as heroes within an epic journey where their trials are the assessments of the course (Gunder, 2016). This employment of metaphor within the educational process is an example of a narrative practice, which is the use of elements of storytelling within a specific context or use case (Bal & van Boheemenm 2009; Bruner, 1991; Bruner, 2004; Fisher, 1984; Herman, 2004; Hewett, 2021; Newman, 1851; Ricoeur, 1990). Employing narrative practices within teaching and learning contexts has a multitude of benefits, including achieving the goal of education to create an authentic and engaging experience for students by honoring their unique goals, needs, and lived experiences (Adams et al., 2021), as well as helping learners to encode and retain knowledge more deeply (Mayer, 2020; Weinschenk, 2011) to be applied within real-world environments. Narrative practices within education harken back to the traditions of storytelling within teaching and learning, particularly in their sociocultural roots for engendering a plurality of literacies and discourse modes within oral, written, and aesthetic contexts (Collins & Blot, 2003; Gee, 1999; Jewitt, 2009; Street, 1984; Street et al., 2009).

Building upon this rich and storied tradition of storytelling within education, digital learning environments have been established as uniquely situated to supporting the use of narrative practices for creating authentic points of relevance and engagement for students (Buckner, 2018; Robin, 2008). Authentically and powerfully incorporating narrative practices in digital learning environments entails leveraging the unique affordances of digital learning environments to impart knowledge in deeper ways than simply presenting information transactionally or as a static didactic. These affordances include the ability to present content access multiple communicative modes, engage students in multimodal practices, and connect learners within a constructivist and experiential community of inquiry (Abrahamson, 2005; Hull & Nelson, 2005; Landrum et al., 2019; Vasudevan et al., 2010).

Using an ethnographically-informed approach, this paper illuminates the connection between narrative practices and digital learning as defined as narrative digital learning practices, which are the intentional use of storytelling techniques to inform and enhance the student experience in digital learning environments. Through a series of autoethnographic portraits celebrating the opportunities for educators to advance efficacy and impact through narrative digital learning practices, we offer 1) a brief, sociocultural contextualization of narrative digital practices within higher education, 2) a discussion of the diverse benefits of narrative digital learning practices with a focus on applications in higher education, and 3) a collection of applicable narrative digital learning practices that can be utilized within the instructional design process.

Narrative Digital Learning Practices (NDLP)

The origins of narrative digital learning practices take their roots in one of the oldest traditions for organizing and presenting information as a meaningful sequence of events. Newman's definition of the four rhetorical modes—narration, description, exposition, and argumentation—positions narrative as a tool for building engagement and connection with audiences through a logical organizational structure (Hewett, 2021; Newman, 1851). Scholars and educators have written about the sequencing process as a way to guide audiences in meaning-making within an educational process (Bal & van Boheemenm 2009; Bruner, 1991; Bruner, 2004; Fisher, 1984; Herman, 2004; Ricoeur, 1990). Narrative has also served as a core practice within the field of ethnography, allowing for the creation of stories rich with detail and description (Geertz, 1973), representative of sociocultural practices and perspectives of a specific context, environment, or time (Behar, 2022; Clifford, 1986). Across disciplines, narrative can be positioned as both a product (the creation of a story) and a process (the act of storytelling) (Hall, 2018), and the process of engaging in narrative practices can be employed within individual contexts, as well as group settings as collaborative, goal-oriented work (Gunder & Shellgren, 2022).

In the past few decades, educators have documented and reflected upon the impact of the narrative practice of storytelling as utilized within diverse teaching and learning contexts (Wu & Chen, 2020; Rodriguéz et al., 2021). Digital learning, defined as the "use of technology and teaching practices enabled by digital tools to enhance learning" (Fox et al., 2021, p. 7), provides a limitless ethea for incorporating narrative practices, both in the design of instruction for online, blended, and digital environments, as well as student usage within activities, assessments, and collaborations with their peers. When digital learning and narrative are intentionally married within the educational experience, narrative digital learning practices (NDLP) emerge as the intentional uses of storytelling techniques to inform and enhance the student experience within digital learning environments. NDLP represent a wide variety of practices and methods, and are becoming increasingly ubiquitous within learning content, assessments, and community engagement activities in digital learning environments. The essential characteristics of NDLP include (but are not limited to) the following:

- **Outcomes Driven**: Engaging with NDLP helps educators align objectives to activities and assessments
- **Assessment Aligned**: NDLP within assessments help learners build critical-thinking, problem-solving, and collaboration skills
- **Humanized**: NDLP celebrate learner identity, providing them with opportunities to share experiences, perspectives, and goals
- **Socioculturally-Situated**: NDLP offer insights on the cultural contexts of sharing stories across different communities
- **Multimodal**: NDLP leverage the unique affordances of combining text, visuals, audio, and other semiotic modes as a means of imparting meaning
- **Constructivist**: NDLP support hands-on, experiential learning that centers on engaging in the active process of building knowledge

Benefits of Narrative Digital Learning Practices for Teaching and Learning

In that storytelling and narrative have long served as pedagogy in the creation of curriculum, the benefits of NDLP are actualized through the reimagining of course content through the lens of narrative structures. Narrative structures are the sequences of events within a story and involve the combination of story elements such as characters, plot, setting, and actions to help (Shaw, 2017; Weischenk, 2011; Weinschenk, 2012). By designing courses to include an intentional and thoughtful flow of information, educators can draw learners in and help them follow along with the salient content (Shaw, 2017). The schema used to organize course content into narrative structures can take many forms, including linear and non-linear sequences, as well as formats that allow for interactivity and choice (Prosser, 2014; Shaw, 2017). From lectures and presentations to assessments and activities, educators can use metaphorical and/or literal elements such as characters, setting, plot, and action to increase cognition and retention of knowledge (Weinschenk, 2011). Narrative elements can also be employed within digital environments to evoke specific emotions that build connections between learners, the course content, and their peers. This can include leveraging drama and suspense to maintain attention throughout instruction or sharing personal experiences to create empathy and connection within the class community. These connections to the content are supported by cognitive psychology—Mayer's cognitive theory of multimedia learning describes the combination of narrative and digital media as a way to help students connect with prior knowledge, build mental maps of learning content, and create extensions from the content to their lived experiences (Mayer, 2020).

The usage of NDLP also support the development of a plurality of digital literacies, including cultural, creative, and critical literacies (Belshaw, 2016). From the use of multimodal tools and communicative modes within the expression of creative literacies to the interrogation of identity and meaning within narratives that employ critical literacies in their construction, NDLP are situated within specific sociocultural contexts, helping learners to not only understand their presence and engagement within digital learning spaces but also their growth in capabilities along a spectrum of learning (Goldstein & Driver, 2014). Within this model of growth, students also sit at a point of reflection in examining their role in conjunction with the role of their teacher. NDLP support character development within the classroom, allowing for the locus of control to be shifted from teacher to learner, engaging students in the metaphorical and literal creation of stories as part of the educational process (Gunder, 2016). Furthermore, storytelling within digital learning environments extends the accessibility and reach of the content, allowing online spaces to be inclusive across modalities. Lastly, and most importantly, NDLP honor the unique identities of students by creating space for enculturating belongingness and cultural representation. With the inclusive act of inviting learners to share their stories, we create environments for deeper understanding, connection, and collaborative growth, extending the benefits of the curriculum into the world.

Leveraging Narrative Digital Learning Practices for Instructional Design

Course Mapping

The use of NDLP in the design of instruction can be an indispensable tool for instructional designers and faculty, particularly when applied to the course mapping process. Thinking about the sequence of events within a course as a narrative arc of rising and falling actions can help to build engagement while also ensuring that students understand and meet the learning outcomes for the course. Course developers can also consider the relationship between objectives, assessment, and learning content plotted across a narrative structure by utilizing backward design. Backward design is a process that starts with the end goal in mind, and works backward to develop instructional strategies and assessments that support the attainment of the desired outcomes (Wiggins & McTighe, 2005). This process can be applied to the incorporation of narrative structures in a course, to ensure that the narrative arc supports the articulated learning objectives. Lastly, designers can utilize metaphors commonly employed within popular narrative structures, like character development and plot structure, to organize instruction around a compelling and engaging story format. The Monomyth Online Framework remixes Joseph Campbell's monomyth and "the hero's journey" into a course mapping tool that can be used to assign the parts of the course to different aspects of an epic narrative (Gunder, n.d.). The framework can also serve as a reflective tool for assessing and redesigning a course around learner agency, differentiation, and scaffolding content to help students build their skills throughout the course.

Digital Storytelling

Digital storytelling is the expansion of traditional storytelling techniques through the combination of media such as photos, audio, and videos into digital stories (Buckner, 2018). Digital storytelling engages individuals in creatively and skillfully leveraging NDLP to convey resonant meaning with the target audience (Mclellan, 2007), coming alive when the NDLP are utilized as an assessment practice within courses (Buckner, 2018). When utilized as an authentic assessment practice, digital storytelling requires learners to apply creativity, problem-solving skills, and effective communication (Buckner, 2018). Digital storytelling also serves as a bridge between curricular and co-curricular activities, giving learners the opportunity to bring the cultural traditions and community wisdom they carry into the educational experience. These digital stories open up a dialogue about who can be an author, how can stories preserve and protect the wisdom passed down through communities, and how authentic stories can be used to build connection (Shuman, 2006).

Gameful Learning

NDLP have been increasingly used to create gameful learning environments that motivate learners and promote engagement. Gameful learning is a pedagogical approach that leverages game design to enhance student motivation, participation, and learning outcomes (Aguilar et al., 2018). The use of NDLP in gameful learning can offer learners an immersive experience that simulates real-life scenarios and promotes active participation. Furthermore, engaging with educational games and game-based narratives can be used to teach complex topics, and encourage students to utilize creative problem-solving to progress through the game (Schrier, 2016). One example of a tool that leverages NDLP in gameful learning is Gradecraft, a gamified LMS designed to enhance student motivation and engagement (Holman et al., 2013). Gradecraft uses a non-linear narrative structure with branched learning paths that enable students to navigate the learning environment according to their learning pace and interests (Holman et al., 2013).

Personalized and Adaptive Learning

NDLP also serve to create a highly-personalized learning experience through the use of adaptive and differentiated learning and provide a new perspective on how to uniquely address the needs of our students. One approach to using NDLP for adaptive learning is to incorporate branching storylines into digital learning materials. These storylines can offer students choices and alternate paths, allowing them to navigate content in a way that meets their individualized learning needs and goals. For example, a student who excels in a particular subject area might be directed down a more challenging storyline, while a student who struggles in that same area might be given more foundational material to work through.

In addition, the principles of universal design for learning (UDL) can be leveraged in conjunction with NDLP to make learning more accessible in a proactive and intentional way (Rose, 2000). UDL principles emphasize flexibility and provide multiple means of engagement, representation, and expression, allowing educators to create learning experiences that are accessible to all learners by design. By incorporating humanizing and inclusive narrative practices that emphasize diverse perspectives and learning preferences, educators can help ensure that all students are engaged and able to connect with material in ways that work best for them (Hall et al., 2014).

Scenario- and Case-Based Learning

Scenario-based learning and case-based learning both involve presenting learners with a realistic scenario that requires them to apply their knowledge and skills to solve a problem (Seren Smith et al., 2018). The use of case studies or scenarios in a course can provide students with an opportunity to analyze real-world situations and apply the knowledge learned in the course to solve problems, particularly when they are constructed through engaging and thought-provoking NDLP. Incorporating narrative structures into scenario-based or case-based learning can make the experience more engaging and memorable for learners. For example, a narrative arc can be used to create a storyline that is compelling and helps learners to relate to the scenario or case. This can be achieved by using tools such as Joseph Campbell's monomyth, which outlines the stages of a hero's journey and can be applied to create characters, setting, and plot for a course that unfolds like an epic journey where the learner is the hero (Gunder, 2016). Using digital tools such as interactive videos, animations, and simulations can also help to create a more immersive and interactive learning experience. By allowing learners to interact with the scenario or case, they can make decisions and see the consequences of their actions, which can help to reinforce learning.

Conclusion

In conclusion, the use of NDLP in the instructional design process can be a valuable tool for engaging students and helping them to meet the outcomes and goals for instruction. NDLP creates a more interactive and personalized learning environment that caters to the diverse needs of students. By incorporating storytelling techniques, students can relate to the material and understand it on a deeper level. As we move towards the future of learning, NDLP will play a crucial role in creating innovative and effective learning experiences. As technology continues to evolve, the use of NDLP will become more prevalent in education, redefining the ways in which we provide students with an impactful and equitable learning experience.

References

Adams, S., Bali, M., Eder, Z., Fladd, L., Garrett, K., Garth-McCullough, R., Gibson, A. M., Gunder, A., Iuzzini, J., Knott, J. L., Rafferty, J., & Weber, N. L. (2021). *Caring for students playbook: Six Recommendations for caring for students*. Every Learner Everywhere. http://files.eric.ed.gov/fulltext/ED613431.pdf

Aguilar, S. J., Holman, C., & Fishman, B. J. (2018). Game-inspired design: Empirical evidence in support of gameful learning environments. *Games and Culture*, *13*(1), 44–70.

Bal, M., & van Boheemen, C. (2009). *Narratology: Introduction to the theory of narrative*. University of Toronto Press.

Behar, R. (2022). *The Vulnerable Observer: Anthropology That Breaks Your Heart*. Beacon Press.

Bruner, J. (1991). The Narrative Construction of Reality. *Critical Inquiry*, *18*(1), 1–21.

Bruner, J. (2004). Life as Narrative. *Social Research: An International Quarterly*, *71*(3), 691–710.

Buckner, M. J. (2018). "Let Me Show You": An Application of Digital Storytelling for Reflective Assessment in Study Abroad Programs. In *Handbook of Research on Human Development in the Digital Age* (pp. 43–65). IGI Global.

Clifford, J. (1986). Introduction: Partial Truths. In *Writing Culture* (pp. 1–26). https://doi.org/10.1525/9780520946286-003

Collins, J., & Blot, R. (2003). *Literacy and Literacies: Texts, Power, and Identity*. Cambridge University Press.

Fisher, W. R. (1984). Narration as a human communication paradigm: The case of public moral argument. *Communication Monographs*, *51*(1), 1–22.

Gee, J. (1999). *The New Literacy Studies and the "Social Turn."* http://files.eric.ed.gov/fulltext/ED442118.pdf

Geertz, C. (1973). *The Interpretation of Cultures*. Basic Books.

Goldstein, B., & Driver, P. (2014). *Language Learning with Digital Video*. Cambridge University Press.

Gunder, A. (n.d.). *Monomyth Online - Framework*. Monomyth Online. http://monomythonline.com/framework/

Gunder, A. (2016, April 22). *The Hero's Journey - Leveraging Narrative in Online Course Design*. Monomyth Online. http://monomythonline.com/the-heros-journey-leveraging-narrative-in-online-course-design/

Gunder, A., Buckner, M., Romanoski, M., & Carríon, L. Incubators of Innovation: Building Creativity, Diversity and Engagement into the Online Learning Environment. https://wcol2019.ie, 401.

Hall, T., Strangman, N., & Meyer, A. (2014). Differentiated instruction and implications for UDL implementation. *Wakefield, MA: National Center on Accessing the General Curriculum.*

Hall, T. (2018). *Education, Narrative Technologies and Digital Learning*. Palgrave Macmillan UK.

Herman, D. (2004). *Story Logic: Problems and Possibilities of Narrative*. U of Nebraska Press.

Hewett, B. (2021). *A Scholarly Edition of Samuel P. Newman's a Practical System of Rhetoric*. Brill.

Holman, C., Aguilar, S., & Fishman, B. (2013). GradeCraft: what can we learn from a game-inspired learning management system? *Proceedings of the Third International Conference on Learning Analytics and Knowledge*, 260–264.

Hull, G. A., & Nelson, M. E. (2005). Locating the Semiotic Power of Multimodality. *Written Communication*, *22*(2), 224–261.

Jewitt, C. (2009). An introduction to multimodality. In *The Routledge Handbook of Multimodal Analysis* (pp. 14–27).

Mayer, R. E. (2020). *Multimedia Learning*. Cambridge University Press.

McLean, S. F. (2016). Case-Based Learning and its Application in Medical and Health-Care Fields: A Review of Worldwide Literature. *Journal of Medical Education and Curricular Development, 3.* https://doi.org/10.4137/JMECD.S20377

Mclellan, H. (2007). Digital storytelling in higher education. *Journal of Computing in Higher Education; Dordrecht, 19*(1), 65–79.

Newman, S. P. (1851). *A Practical System of Rhetoric*. M.H. Newman & Company.

Prosser, A. (2014). *Getting off the straight and narrow: Exploiting non-linear, interactive narrative structures in digital stories for language teaching* (S. Jager, L. Bradley, E. J. Meima, & S. Thouësny (eds.); pp. 318–323).

Ricoeur, P. (1990). *Time and Narrative, Volume 1*. University of Chicago Press.

Robin, B. R. (2008). Digital Storytelling: A Powerful Technology Tool for the 21st Century Classroom. *Theory into Practice*, *47*(3), 220–228.

Rose, D. (2000). Universal Design for Learning. *Journal of Special Education Technology*, *15*(4), 47–51.

Schrier, K. (2016). *Knowledge Games: How Playing Games Can Solve Problems, Create Insight, and Make Change*. JHU Press.

Seren Smith, M., Warnes, S., & Vanhoestenberghe, A. (2018). Scenario-based learning. In J. P. Davies & N. Pachler (Eds.), *Teaching and Learning in Higher Education: Perspectives from UCL* (pp. 144–156). UCL IOE Press.

Shaw, A. (2017, February 3). *The Use of Narrative Structure in Course Design*. Center for Teaching and Learning | Wiley Education Services. https://ctl.wiley.com/the-use-of-narrative-structure-in-course-design/

Gunder, A., & Shellgren, M. (2022). Advancing Universal Access to Quality Digital Learning through Global Coalitions and Narrative Practices. An Open Knowledge Product for the 3rd UNESCO World Higher Education Conference (WHEC 2022). *Online Learning Consortium*. http://files.eric.ed.gov/fulltext/ED622501.pdf

Shuman, A. (2006). *Storytelling Rights: The Uses of Oral and Written Texts by Urban Adolescents*. Cambridge University Press.

Street, B. V. (1984). *Literacy in Theory and Practice*. Cambridge University Press.

Street, B., Pahl, K., & Rowsell, J. (2009). Multimodality and New Literacy Studies. *The Routledge Handbook of Multimodal Analysis*, 191–200.

Vasudevan, L., Schultz, K., & Bateman, J. (2010). Rethinking Composing in a Digital Age: Authoring Literate Identities Through Multimodal Storytelling. *Written Communication*, *27*(4), 442–468.

Weinschenk, S. (2011). *100 Things Every Designer Needs to Know About People*. New Riders.

Weinschenk, S. (2012). *100 Things Every Presenter Needs to Know About People*. New Riders.

Wiggins, G., & McTighe, J. (2005). *Understanding by Design*. ASCD.

LESSONS FROM A 2-HUB LIFE-SCIENCE TRAINING COURSE: FROM HEIDELBERG TO BANGALORE AND BEYOND

Irena Provazníková, Nathalie Sneider, Swetlana Krez, Maria M. Bacadare G., Juergen Deka and Elisabeth M. Zielonka, EMBL Heidelberg, Germany

Correspondence: *Elisabeth M. Zielonka: elisabeth.zielonka@embl.de*

Abstract

Technologies are rapidly evolving in the life sciences and other STEM areas. Advanced hands-on practical courses are key for life-science researchers to stay ahead of the game. Although the Covid-19 pandemic propelled/accelerated the transformation in remote training opportunities, it is clear that training in molecular biology methodologies requires and greatly benefits from hands-on face-to-face courses. Here we present a novel 2-hub course format, with teaching of cutting-edge technologies simultaneously in Germany (EMBL Heidelberg) and India (BLiSC in Bangalore). The format combines active-based learning on a scientific case study with collaborative exercises and networking that foster scientific exchange. We describe the digital technologies utilised in course design and delivery, and the multi-layered planning phase. Analysis of the participant and trainer feedback questionnaires demonstrates the benefits and challenges of the 2-hub format and illustrates the success of the course. The concept allows us to broaden our reach, while reducing overall CO_2 emission in comparison to a 1-hub course. We show that thanks to digital tools and collaboration of dedicated organisers, we can provide conceptual design and create sophisticated active-learner training opportunities with world-wide reach.

Keywords: 2-hub course, innovation, STEM, life-long learning, EMBL, technology-enhanced learning, advanced life-science training

Introduction

The European Molecular Biology Laboratory (EMBL) is an intergovernmental life science organisation, located at six sites in Europe. We conduct world-class life science research, provide training for students and scientists, and state-of-the-art research infrastructures for a wide range of scientific and experimental services. EICAT, EMBL's International Centre for Advanced Training, located at EMBL Heidelberg, Germany, provides advanced training for researchers in state-of-the-art technologies and fosters scientific exchange. During pre-pandemic times, EMBL was offering more than 60 onsite courses per year. Half of them happened in the EMBL Advanced Training Centre (ATC) in Heidelberg covering whole scientific technology workflows of experimental and computational methods. All EMBL Heidelberg designed courses apply learner centred approaches in combination with engaging activities to enhance discussions and networking. The course organisers, trainers and speakers are leading scientists in their research fields, from EMBL and world-wide.

At the beginning of the Covid-19 pandemic in 2020, we were forced to stop our onsite course programme. We managed to convert our events from onsite to virtual and successfully delivered 26 virtual courses from 2020 to 2022. These virtual courses contained theoretical and practical sessions paired with networking activities. With our innovative course design, we were not only able to provide live hands-on computational sessions but also successfully delivered training in experimental laboratory methodologies. At the beginning of the pandemic, we implemented a Moodle-based learning management system (LMS) called EMBLeCampus (https://ecampus.embl.de), which has played an essential role in delivering virtual courses as well as the post-pandemic onsite courses (Zielonka et al. 2021). This LMS allowed us to utilise even more blended learning approaches during our virtual courses and since 2022 also in our face-to-face courses.

There were many benefits of the virtual courses, including time zone management by the LMS, Zoom as a virtual classroom and virtual machine-based IT set-ups for computational practicals. Since hands-on laboratory methodology is essential (Hofstein A. & Lunetta V.N. 2004) and cannot be replaced but rather complemented virtual training offerings we further improved our blended learning conceptual designs (Stoytcheva 2017). Paired with the possibility to allow increased impact and reach, for example to less wealthy laboratories (Parncutt et al. 2021), these developments led to the idea of a life science based 2-hub course including experimental laboratory and computational practical sessions. Here we describe the development of the EMBO Practical Course: Metabolite and species dynamics in microbial communities held 16-21 October 2022 at 2-hubs; in the ATC at EMBL Heidelberg in Germany and on the Bangalore Life Sciences Cluster campus in Bangalore (BLiSC), India. The central learning objective was that all participants will be able to apply the concepts and methodologies in their own research. Further we aimed at enabling networking among participants, speakers and trainers to further foster scientific exchange (source: https://www.embl.org/about/info/course-and-conference-office/events/mcd22-01/). The course received funding from the European Molecular Biology Organisation (EMBO) and was organised by the scientific organisers and the EMBL External Training team.

Criteria and recruitment of second course hub

In line with EMBL´s scientific programme and high demand for training in cutting-edge microbiology technologies, we focused this 2-hub course on the characterisation of microbial communities. The case study for this course was based on the publication Blasche *et al.* (2021) studying dynamics of microorganisms in Kefir over time.

In addition to the first course hub, the scientific training laboratory in the EMBL ATC, a second course hub was required. Scientifically, this second hub would require a molecular biology lab and instrument availability for DNA sequencing, microorganisms culturing and mass-spectrometry. This second hub needed to fulfil the following criteria and requirements:

a) Distance - it should be far enough to benefit from the CO_2 reduction based on shorter travel distances by the participants. At the same time the time zone difference should still allow for synchronised course sessions.

b) Commitment of co-organisers and trainers is key for a successful planning and course conduction.

c) Technological infrastructure requirements (machines, laboratory space, computational facility) - an equal set of technologies at the hub in order to conduct the same experiments.

d) The course topics overlap with the research interests of scientific institutes in the host and neighbouring countries.

The hub that fulfilled all criteria was the BLiSC in Bangalore, India. Both locations (Germany and India) reach a broad geographical distribution of audience, and allow reduced pandemic-related risks of long-distance travel. Additionally, the 2-hub concept had a positive impact on CO_2 reduction caused by air travel as the majority of participants travelled to the nearest hub.

Technologies in the 2-hub course

Technology enhanced learning has been evolving for many years. The Covid-19 pandemic has boosted further technological developments (Sen & Leong, 2020). While the isolation measures have been lifted now in most countries, the benefits of these technologies remain and provide opportunities for new training designs. The following technologies allowed us to hold the first international focused 2-hub course containing hands-on laboratory experiments and computational analysis sessions.

Our LMS (EMBLeCampus) was used for content (protocols, literature etc) exchange and communication. The system offered the opportunity to manage a complex programme at the 2-hubs. DTEN screens (at the Heidelberg hub) for lectures, group and round-table discussions, and laptops during networking breaks were used to bring speakers, trainers and participants from both hubs together and to foster the cross-continent interaction. The Bangalore hub used a combination of beamer and laptops. In addition to the onsite lectures, we welcomed 3 international experts remotely to share their newest research. The computational practical sessions were implemented with the support of the EMBL-IT department on virtual machines from EMBL Heidelberg. This ensured equal access to the same software tools and packages from both sites. Prior to the course, there was a test run of all equipment and software to ensure everything would run smoothly during the course.

Conceptual 2-hub course design

This 2-hub course was designed to allow the participants access to cutting-edge technologies at two different locations. Both hubs needed to offer the same high-level access to methodologies, trainers and scientific lectures, as well as various scientific exchange and networking opportunities across both sites in order to achieve the long-term gains of the scientific content (Stryer et al. 2018). To accomplish this, the course programme was carefully planned to combine cross-site synchronised and unsynchronised sessions bridging the time-zone difference of 3.5 hours. Course content was shared via EMBLeCampus. Two weeks prior to the actual face-to-face course, the course started with a purely virtual on-boarding event for all participants including the organisers. A detailed outlook of the course programme was shared with the participants and access to the course content was granted (incl. protocols and literature). A first virtual ice-breaker activity on EMBLeCampus initialised communication and scientific exchange prior to the course.

The 6-day long course programme was mainly focused on hands-on experimental and computational practical sessions which were accompanied by theoretical lectures and networking opportunities within each hub but also cross-hub. The computational practical sessions, lectures including Q&A and various networking opportunities were synchronised via a virtual classroom to enhance the engagement. All scientific lectures were streamed to both hubs and were followed by a Q&A session moderated by a chair at each hub. The number of speakers as well as the number of questions asked by participants at both hubs was balanced to ensure equal chances for everyone and stimulated discussions.

Due to operational practicalities the laboratory experiments were conducted in an unsynchronised approach at the two respective sites. Precise timing of all course elements was crucial for this course to avoid gaps and discrepancies in the agenda, delayed talks and networking sessions at both hubs. However, participants had opportunities to discuss the protocols and results during the cross-site networking breaks. Computational practical sessions were carried out simultaneously at both hubs. Participants had remote access to pre-installed virtual machines provided by the EMBL-IT department.

All experiments were designed and adjusted to fit the schedule and were tested and timed by the trainers before the course to ensure precise timing for the live sessions and generation of back-up samples and datasets. Each hub also planned individual social activities.

Experimental case study

The kefir microbial community was chosen as a model system to profile its species and metabolite dynamics during fermentation. Experiments and data analyses were based on work of Blasche *et al.* (2021). Participants followed a complete experimental workflow from set-up of kefir culture, time point sampling, genomic DNA extraction to 16S rDNA library preparation and sequencing using Oxford Nanopore Technologies (ONT), metabolomics analysis by mass spectrometry, and interaction mapping plating experiments. Furthermore, during computational practical sessions, obtained datasets were analysed with the emphasis on data management, reproducible data analysis and the FAIR principles. All experiments carried out during the course were in compliance with the laboratory biosafety level 1 (S1). Regular synchronised sessions were used to update the respective other hub about the experiments and its pitfalls, potential challenges and problems, and tips and tricks. This increased the cross-site interactions and was appreciated by the course participants.

Laboratory and experimental equipment and support

Having high quality video conferencing equipment with Zoom setup on both sites was crucial for successful delivery of cross-site theoretical lectures, computational practical sessions, discussions and networking sessions. Moreover, using the EPI2ME data analysis platform from the Genomics Core Facility at EMBL Heidelberg, we were able to live-stream to participants at both sites the start of the Nanopore sequencing run and the real-time identification of sequenced species and their phylogenetic relationships. This setup stimulated participants' interest in the technique and enhanced their curiosity and motivation.

International course audience

The main target audience for this course was PhD students and post-doctoral researchers who would apply the methods and knowledge that they learnt during the course in their home institutes. From a total of 101 applicants, 20 participants (10 for each hub) were selected by the scientific organisers based on their application and motivation letter summarising their current research and their need for the methods addressed in this course and promoting diversity, equality, and inclusion (DEI). We received 23 applications for the Bangalore hub and 78 applications for the Heidelberg hub. Notably, the Heidelberg hub received more applications from female than male scientists (45 female, 32 male, 1 did not want to disclose) than the Bangalore hub (10 female, 13 male). 96% of the scientists who applied to attend the course at the Bangalore hub were affiliated with a scientific institution in Asia. 66% of the applications for the Heidelberg hub were submitted from European host institutes. The Heidelberg hub still received 14 applications from Asia, although we promoted them to apply to the closest hub location in order to reduce the overall CO_2 emissions of the event [Figure 1] as airborne travel has significantly negative impact on climate change (Lee et al., 2021) and can represent great portion of carbon emissions in academia (e.g. Wynes and Donner 2018, Ahonen et al. 2021).

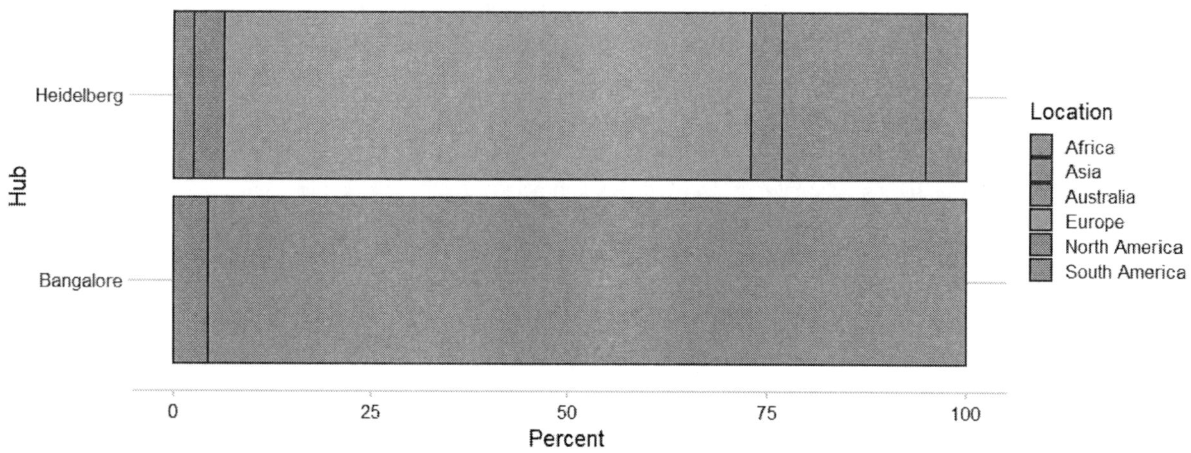

Figure 1: Course applications received for the Bangalore and Heidelberg hub. The graph illustrates the respective continent representation [%] in combination with the actual application numbers from the respective continent.

Fostering exchange and networking

The EMBLeCampus platform (Zielonka et al. 2021) was essential for communication, networking and providing learning material to everyone involved in the course. Participants had a chance to contact each other as well as the trainers, organisers and speakers before, during and after the course. Participants were encouraged to network during cross-site coffee breaks which were part of the programme. Participants were divided into several smaller cross-site teams for scientific exchange and networking Zoom meetings using course laptops. To further foster networking and team-spirit, we designed a "treasure hunt" team activity for the participants. Participants had the majority of the course to work on their challenges and results were submitted on the last evening and evaluated by the course organisation team. Results were presented on the last day of the course. All participants were rewarded with a small present to recognise their efforts.

Feedback questionnaires

To collect feedback about the course design and content, participants received a questionnaire after the course. A similar questionnaire was also sent to the scientific organisers, speakers and trainers to collect feedback from the trainer perspective. The feedback from participants and also speakers/trainers was very positive and illustrated the success of this new practical course format for life-science methodologies [Figure 2]. The course logistics at both hubs were mainly rated excellent or good e.g. the venue, EMBLeCampus, technical support [Figure 2].

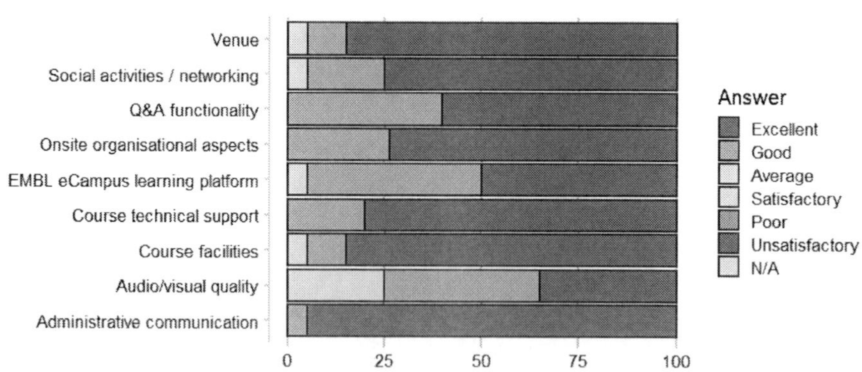

Figure 2: Participants' evaluation of various aspects and logistics elements of the 2-hub course.

The audio/visual quality rating received 25% average and 75% excellent or good. 17 of 20 participants stated that the balance of theoretical and practical content in this 2-hub course was about right. Most participants used the networking sessions to interact with remote speakers or speakers at the respective other hub instead of the forum or chat function in EMBLeCampus. 100% of the participants recommended the course according to the feedback survey. In addition, 100% stated that the topic was adequately covered and that this 2-hub course provided them with new information in their field.

We also analysed evaluation of key factors for the 2-hub course from the two groups, participants, and trainers and speakers, from the feedback questionnaires [Figure 3]. Results indicate that audio-visual quality (and internet connection) was mostly good, however, could be improved. Occasional technical issues such as internet connectivity disruptions and problems with audio were noticeable and addressed. Also, Q&A and discussions during computational practical sessions, have potential to be improved to provide better instant feedback to the trainers and overall flow of the session. The EMBLeCampus platform and the social and networking activities were very well received by both groups.

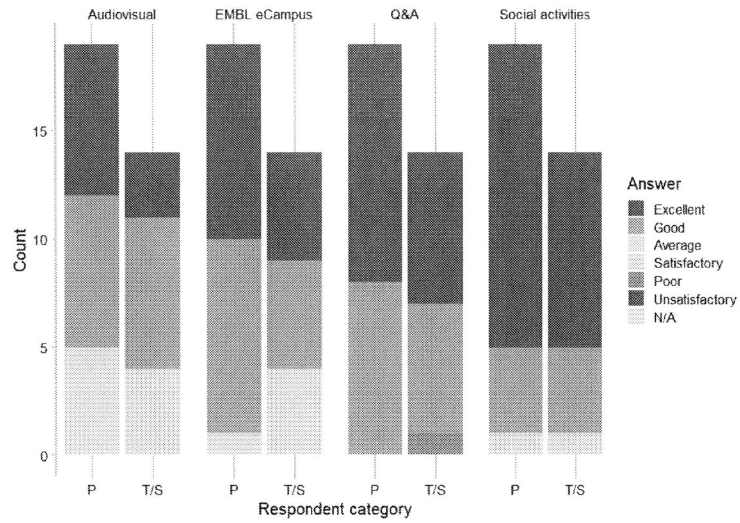

Figure 3: Questionnaire respondents' evaluation of key elements of the 2-hub course. Graph shows satisfaction of participants (P), and trainer and speakers (T/S) with an audio-visual setup (Audiovisual), usage of EMBLeCampus platform (EMBLeCampus), Q&A sessions (Q&A) and networking opportunities (Social activities). Count = number of received answers.

To assess the desired course learning outcome of enabling methodology application and collaboration we utilized a 6 months post-course survey. More than 70% of the participants indicated that they have successfully applied the course methodologies in their own research projects and have already or will in the close future publish their result. 85% stated that new collaborations were established during the 2 -hub course.

Conclusions and lessons learned

The first ever EMBO 2-hub practical course with experimental and computational practical sessions entitled "EMBO practical course: Metabolite and species dynamics in microbial communities" took place from 16 to 21

October 2022. 10 participants were located in the Bangalore hub and 10 in Heidelberg. Most of the sessions, consisting of computational practicals, lectures and networking, were held synchronously with the use of Zoom and other digital tools. Experimental laboratory practical sessions were unsynchronised and undertaken independently in each hub.

The 2-location set-up, with EMBL Heidelberg (Germany) as the European hub and BLiSC Bangalore (India) as the Asian hub, offered a concept that allowed cutting-edge technology training and access to world class speakers from two continents while limiting the necessity of inter-continental flights. The 2-hub concept saved 6.9 tonnes CO_2 in terms of speaker and trainer travel in comparison with a course based only in Heidelberg. The second hub provided a unique and empowering training opportunity for participants from Asia, many of whom would not have been able to join this course if it had taken place only in Heidelberg. Our data show that the two-hub concept is beneficial, sustainable and inclusive which is in an agreement with previous findings (Parncutt et al., 2021).

During the planning phase it was highly valuable to have regular update meetings with both hubs as well as carry out test sessions for the experimental workflow and the technologies for the general course delivery (lecture rooms, networking area, etc). Even though everything was tested before the course, there were unexpected challenges: i) Internet connection problems in Heidelberg that interfered with the speaker streaming to the Heidelberg hub, ii) the audio-visual system in Bangalore encountered problems due to heavy rain. Both challenges will need solutions in order to ensure the smooth delivery for a potential repeat of the course. The work involved in planning and preparing for this 2-hub format was more time consuming (appr. 40% increase) than a course hosted in the EMBL training facilities in Heidelberg only. This was a first-time event and a repeat of this 2-hub course would benefit from procedures and lessons learned and therefore require less time.

In 2020 the pandemic forced us to digitalise our hands-on practical course programme on advanced scientific technologies and methods. The investment into a Moodle-based learning management system and innovative virtual course delivery formats enabled us to develop new courses that further increased the international reach and impact of EMBL´s external scientific courses. We were able to empower international young scientists with training on the newest developments in the field of microbial communities. The 2-hub format allowed to reduce the overall CO_2 footprint of the course. Taken together, we presented a successful example of a novel hands-on scientific course model that has the potential to further increase our training reach.

Acknowledgement

We highly acknowledge the scientific organisers and instructors of this course: The merit of the success of this course goes to Sonja Blasche, University of Cambridge, United Kingdom; Sunil Laxman, inStem, India; Sandeep Krishna, NCBS, India; Kiran Patil, University of Cambridge, United Kingdom; Maria Zimmerman-Kogadeeva, EMBL Heidelberg, Germany; We would like to thank and acknowledge EMBO for their financial support of this course (event ID: pc22/02), ONT and Qiagen for sponsoring respective reagents and consumables. We would like to thank the course organisers, speakers, trainers, IT department, Photolab and Core facility staff for their help before and during the course. We also thank Jan Provazník for help with data visualisation and Brendan Rouse for carbon footprint calculation.

Literature

Ahonen, V., Siljander, M., Pellikka, P., Johansson, T., and Rask, M. (2021). The Sustainability of Academic Air Mobility in Finnish Universities. *Sustainability 13*, 2948. doi:10.3390/su13052948

Blasche, S., Kim, Y., Mars, R. A. T. *et al.* (2021). Metabolic cooperation and spatiotemporal niche partitioning in a kefir microbial community. *Nature Microbiology 6*, 196–208. doi: 10.1038/s41564-020-00816-5

Hofstein, A., & Lunetta, V. N. (2004). The Laboratory science education: foundations for the twenty-first century. *Science Education, 88*(1), 28-54. doi: 10.1002/sce.10106

Lee, D. S., Fahey, D. W., Skowron, A., Allen, M. R., Burkhardt, U., Chen, Q., et al. (2021). The Contribution of Global Aviation to Anthropogenic Climate Forcing for 2000 to 2018. *Atmospheric Environment 244*, 117834. doi: 10.1016/j.atmosenv.2020.117834

Parncutt, R., Lindborg, P. M., Meyer-Kahlen, N., and Timmers, R. (2021) The Multi-hub Academic Conference: Global, Inclusive, Culturally Diverse, Creative, Sustainable. *Frontiers in Research Metrics and Analytics, 6*. 699782. doi: 10.3389/frma.2021.699782

Sen, A., & Leong, C. K. C. (2020). Technology-enhanced learning. In: Tatnall, A. (eds) Encyclopedia of education and information technologies. *Springer,* Cham. doi: 10.1007/978-3-319-60013-0_72-1

Stoytcheva, M. (2017). Collaborative distance learning: Developing an online learning community. *AIP Conference Proceedings. 1910*, 060009. doi: 10.1063/1.5014003.

Styers, M. S., Van Zandt, P-A. , Hayden, K. L. (2018). Active learning in flipped life science courses promotes development of critical thinking skills. *CBE-Life Science Education*, *17*(3), ar39, 1-13. doi: 10.1187/cbe.16-11-0332

Wynes, S., and Donner, S. D. (2018). Addressing Greenhouse Gas Emissions from Business-Related Air Travel at Public Institutions: A Case Study of the University of British Columbia. Victoria, BC: Pacific Institute for Climate Solutions.

Zielonka, E. M., Yeboah A. Y., Provazníková, I. and Deka, J. (2021). From bench to monitor – turning advanced life science courses into virtual. *EDEN Proceedings,* ISSN 2707-2819. doi: 10.38069/edenconf-2021-ac0046.

INNOVATIVE TOOL FOR RURAL SCHOOLS - VIRTUAL CLASSROOM

Genutė Gedvilienė, Monika Dievaitytė, Ugnė Supranavičienė
Vytautas Magnus University, Lithuania

Correspondence: *Genutė Gedvilienė: genute.gedviliene@vdu.lt*

Abstract

The article presents the application of a virtual classroom in a rural school in collaboration with other institutions. The Erasmus+ Strategic Partnerships project to develop a virtual classroom in a rural school aims to create a virtual collaborative space where rural schools can support each other and immediately fill their gaps in terms of teachers, content and activities. The idea involves not only the technological environment, but also the surrounding community, which is primarily made up of rural schools and other organisations active in the field of education and rural development.

Keywords: Education, classroom, innovative, rural, virtual.

Introduction

Education processes plays a significant role in maximizing individual's potentials (I. Amosa, M. James, and C. Olubode, 2013). It is important to highlight that virtual schooling brought a different perspective to the teaching and learning experiences for rural classrooms. Furthermore, virtual schooling reminds that technology integration is a social, not technical problem, largely hindered by how technologies reify or disrupt existing power and organizational arrangements. What is missing from virtual classrooms is less particular technologies but educational practices with the same technologies (Squire, K. D., 2021).

The design of virtual learning is based on the conceptual frameworks of dialogue, structure and autonomy. Dialogue, based on a humanistic approach, where the implication of humanistic approach in education is how to educators encourage students to think critically and act according to the values of humanity (Firdaus, F. A., & Mariyat, A., 2017), is linked to student communication and student engagement in educational activities, because only through active participation in dialogue is successful learning possible, and students' reasoning, debating, and critical thinking skills develop. The principle of structure involves detailed planning, systematic organisation and development of virtual meetings, calendaring, time-keeping, control, i.e. the responsibility of the students to participate. The principle of autonomy allows the learner to act creatively in the virtual learning environment, with independent tasks and decision-making (Gedvilienė G., Vaičiūnienė V, 2016).

Indeed, during virtual teaching/learning, there should be mutual interaction between teacher and student (Simonson et al., 2015). Virtual teaching is making a breakthrough in pedagogy and is effective in that it focuses on the role of the self-learning student (Coombe P. (2017).

Motivating students to participate, engage socially and discover themselves in a virtual learning environment is essential. It is also important to build positive relationships and develop supportive classroom communities (Greenan K.A., 2021).

EU rural virtual classroom

The systematic development of technologies, the abundance of various sources and forms of information and the technological skills acquired during the covid 19 pandemic influence the need for virtual learning not only in general education schools, but also in remote rural schools.

The EU Rural Virtual Classroom project - number 2021-1-ES01-KA220-SCH-000023731 is strongly anchored in ICT, has an innovative approach to face educational deficiencies in rural areas: a collaborative virtual space in real time where rural schools can support each other, filling their deficiencies in teachers' shortage, content, and activities immediately.
Project aim to focus on education in rural areas, where 28% of the EU population lives. In these areas the early dropout rate is higher than in urban areas (12% as opposed to 9% in urban settings). Rural areas also face other challenges such as insulation of centres, less students, insecure facilities, or fewer materials which reinforces the need to target rural education.

Rural schools, as well as their students and teachers and the educational community, are the direct beneficiaries of the project and will benefit by improving connectivity and educational resources. Likewise, public and private entities will benefit from the project indirectly.

Project partners: Vytautas Magnus University, Associaco d'Initiatives Rurals de Catalunya, Universidad de la Inglesia de Deusto Entidad Religiosa, Roscommon Integrated Development Co. Ltd t/a Roscommon Leader Partnership, Instituto Omnicompresivo di Bobbio Capoluogo.

Methodology

Within the framework of the Rural Virtual Classroom (RVC) Erasmus+ project an inventory of best practices in education has been developed for rural classrooms. This inventory corresponds to Work Package 2 (WP-2), Best practices Study and includes methodology. It shows the process of identification, selection and analysis of best practises.

The search for best practises started with selection of information. It was focused mainly on scientific articles published in indexed journals of impact in education. In addition, reports and documents from international organizations (e.g. European Commission, Unesco, Unicef, etc.) that provide relevant information for the proposed objective were selected and reviewed. To simplify the research for information, certain keywords facilitated the identification of relevant publications. To enhance the search Spanish words were also included in the keywords.

Keywords	
Target / Population	**Intervention / Context**
Rural education, Primary school, Rural school, Rural community, Family, Student Teacher, Community.	School activities, ICT, Educational resources Educational deficits, Collaborative learning, Education project, Active learning, Training project, Virtual classroom, Good practices Best practises, Impact, Evidences.

Fig. 1 Keywords for the search

In the Figure number 1 it is seen that while searching for the information, two categories of keywords were used for the search – words describing target or population and words about context/intervention. Keyword were kept simple, consisting of 1-2 words only, to not overcomplicate the search, narrow it also to be as clear as possible to get the best results.

The bibliographic sources chosen for the search were:
Scientific databases, such as Scopus, Web of Science (WoS) and Education Recources Information Center (Eric); Erasmus+ projects; Toolkits; European projects; Other education-related organizations.
Based on analysis of scientific literature it was considered that a best educational practice can be defined as an exemplary education intervention, that guides the teaching process supported by actions already carried out and with satisfactory results. For the identification of the best educational practices, only those that met the following requirements have been considered in elaboration of this repository:

- o It produced conclusive results when implemented.

- Evidence of social impact has been identified, meaning that there are scientifically endorsed evidence.
- The social impact required from these practises had to reflect the improvement in academic success, individual and school well-being, motivation, social cohesion of the community and families also promotes equity and inclusion.
- A best practice must be sustainable, whose social, economic and environmental requirements must be maintained over time and produce long- lasting effects (Unesco, 2021).
- Finally, a best practice should be replicable, i.e. to serve as a model for developing educational policies, initiatives and actions in other places and contexts (Includ-ed Consortium, 2015).

To summarize, the methodology for researching the best practises that would be used in Rural Virtual Classroom (RVC) Erasmus+ project was clearly defined. Specific keywords were used in the search to narrow it down and get the best results possible. These keywords were utilized in scientific bibliographic sources to find relevant scientific literature for the project and to create a database of best practises. However, not all scientific articles describing best practises have been considered as a reasonable example. A definition of best practices term was established and examples of best practises needed to met certain requirements to be considered applicable in this project, therefore that means that only the best of good practises will be applied at rural schools during the implementation of this project.

Structure, content and delivery of virtual learning in rural schools Implementation

Activities are planned to achieve the desired results in EU_VRC project are organized into work packages (WP) co-managed by all partners. The WP are executed according to the planned schedule of 24 months in an orderly manner, generating specific results needed to reach final products.
WP1 - Project Management: Signing of contracts, design and implementation of project management and monitoring manuals, preparation of interim and final reports. Project monitoring, preparation of interim and final reports. Design of dissemination and exploitation plans, , IPR agreement, monitoring and evaluation tools. Result: Management tools and Project management. Month 1 - Month 24. Leader: Estela Cantabria.
WP.2- Good Practice Inventory: Systematic search in scientific literature, research and training projects of European Commission, as well as other international databases. Input Collection of form partners as well as from existing rural education networks in Europe and internationally. Purpose of the study: source of information for development of project´s platform. Collection of information/resources for professional development rural teachers. Result: Publication of report, list of resources to be uploaded in teachers' area. Month 2 - Month 4 Leader: Deus to.
WP 3- Platform Design: Logical and functional design of Collaborative Rural Learning Space with 4 areas. Area of collaborative exchange for joint educational projects, area of online multigrade classes/workshops, area of professional development and resources for rural teachers, community area. Design assessment and validation process with teacher's experts group (associated partners). Outcome: Final design of the Product. Assessment by the expert group. Month 5 -8. Leader: Estela Cantabra.
WP.4 - Technical development: IT, technological and functional development of the product, internal testing, testing of programmable routines, incorporation and testing EU languages, partners training on platform operation. Result: Collaborative Rural Virtual Learning Space Collaborative (in the 4 languages of the partners). Multi-grade classroom delivery area (in all EU languages), Training of partners in the use of the platform. Months 9 -14 Leader: Estela Cantabria.
WP.5- Pilot testing. To pilot an educational project among the participating schools, for primary schools' pupils (multigrade) to learn English language. Participation of observers (expert teachers, parents and researchers). Outcome: Implementation of the pilot test, Evaluation Questionnaire to participants, collection of evaluation data. Months 9 -14 Leader: RLP and Institute di Bobbio.
WP.6- Dissemination and Exploitation: Design and Implementation of Dissemination Plan and Intermediate and Final Dissemination Report, Project information leaflet, Project presentation card, 4 newsletters at key points of the project. Design and Implementation of Exploitation Plan: parallel actions of dissemination (national database with key contacts to exploit the results), signing of intellectual property agreement, coordination of exploitation events (half-day events, at least 15 participants where the project and its results will be presented) Results: Dissemination and Exploitation Plan, Intellectual Property Agreement, 5 Multiplier Events, Final Exploitation and Dissemination Report, 1 key database for each partner. Virtual Classroom Community: Launching of the virtual community around the collaborative Rural Virtual Classroom, inclusion of information about the project in the

Estela Cántabra (Spain)	Associació d'Iniciatives Rurals de Catalunya (Spain)	Istituto Omnicomprensivo di Bobbio (Italy)	Universidad De Deusto (Italy)	Roscommon LEADER Partnership (Ireland)	Vytautas Magnus university (Lithuania)
VET Communities	Educational communities	Public National institutions	Public Regional Institutions	Public Regional Institution	Public National Institutions
Government bodies	Rural schools	Rural schools	Regional education communities	Universities	Educational centres
Policy makers	Public Regional Institutions		National Education Related Asociation	Rural schools	Rural schools
VET centres			Rural schools		Universities
Communities					Research centers

e-twinning and school education gateway platforms. Leader Associació d'Iniciatives Rurals de Catalunya Month 1 – 24

WP 7- Quality management: design and implementation of the Quality Control Plan and tools. Results: Quality Plan, control questionnaires. 5 Intermediate Reports and 1 Final Report. Leader: VMU Month 1 – 24.

Exploitation database

EU Rural Virtual Classroom project's consortium is composed of six partners from four European Union countries: Spain, Italy, Ireland and Lithuania. All the partners have a long experience in EU-funded projects and that is one of indicators, that this project will be successful and sustainable. The overall sustainability of the project will be ensured with project's exploitation within each partner.

The main goal of project's exploitation is to ensure that the virtual platform will be used after the project is over. Each partner of the project had to establish a database which will promote the widespread use of the product inside each country and be a foundation for effective exploitation.

Fig. 2. Exploitation database

By looking at the exploitation database it is visible, that each partner chose different target groups where the project could be applied. By analysis of the database it is clear that the project's partners from Spain chose two strategies, how to exploit created platform's use. Estela Cantabra will exploit project more wider with government institutions – government bodies, policy makers, VET centres and communities. The Associació d'Iniciatives Rurals de Catalunya on the other hand concentrated more on regional public bodies – rural schools, educational communities and public regional institutions. In this way it will be ensured that exploitation will be more expanded and ensure that wider network of institutions would be reached and benefit from this project implementation.

According to the information seen in the Figure nr. 2, partners from Italy will take more regional approach to exploitation. Istituto Omnicomprensivo di Bobbio will concentrate only on public national institutions and rural schools, because it is organization based on rural schools in Italy. As a university Universidad De Deusto have a lot more connections with various public regional institutions linked with education that is why it chose to exploit project to rural schools, regional education communities, education related associations. Although these two organizations are different, they will exploit project according to their organization's background and will include various regional institutions from Italy that will benefit from this project.

Project partner from Ireland - Roscommon Leader Partnership is an organisation that brings together key development projects including rural enterprise, development and social inclusion that is why it chose to exploit project to various public regional institutions, universities and rural schools. It chose only regional institutions, because this organization concentrates only working in one regions in Ireland – county Roscommon.

Similarly to university in Italy, Vytautas Magnus university from Lithuania will also exploit project to organizations mainly related to education – educational and research centres, other universities and schools. The exploitation by university will also reach public national institutions linked with education and through them it is believed that project would reach even more schools located in various areas in Lithuania.

To summarize, in order to ensure successful and sustainable exploitation of EU Rural Virtual Classroom project's results all the partners will take steps and exploit project to various organizations. The exploitation database analysis shows that project's partners focus not only on rural schools, that already cooperates with partners, but also on other national, regional and public organizations that would spread project result more wider geographically to other schools that could benefit from this project. It is also seen that partners choose involve organizations to database according to what type of organization the partner are – public organization like Roscommon Leader Partnership and Estela Cantabra, chose to exploit project to governmental institutions while universities chose organizations linked with education and development. Nonetheless analysis of the database shows, that exploitation will involve many institutions, that would ensure effective process of exploitation and sustainable project existence after its implementation.

Project's results

A virtual European rural collaborative learning space for rural schools (initially aimed at primary education) will be created that will consist of:
a) Area of exchanging offers and demands of collaborative educational projects
b) Teaching area of workshops / classes in real time structured for multigrade classrooms
c) Area of professional development and resources for rural teachers
The project will also start a community around the space created with an initial adhesion of 100 members (schools, entities and professionals / entities from the educational field and relevant rural development).

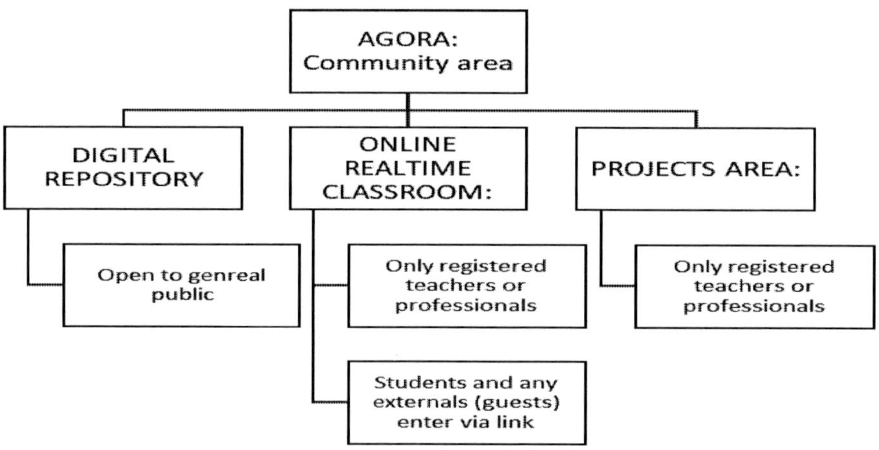

Fig. 3. Platform structure

The space will be multilingual, schools will be able to freely agree on the language in which they will carry out their educational projects. All virtual area will be protected by EU data protection legal regulations (3 fig.).

Conclusions

- With the rapid development of technology and the proliferation of information sources and their forms of delivery, the significance of distance learning is undeniable, as it impacts on the quality of learning, changes the culture of university studies and is often a major contributor to the shaping of this culture. Since the information consumer is involved in the communication process with a specific intention, his behaviour and values require a deep and consistent analysis.
- Virtual learning, as a contemporary phenomenon, is closely linked to the new information technologies, which are radically changing the quality of life and having a major impact on education in schools. Virtual learning is an

effective tool for promoting learning. It is therefore essential to apply it to the technological development of rural schools.

- The latest technology and the opportunities it bring with it allow students to learn remotely, to interact with each other and with teachers.

The use of virtual learning can facilitate the solving of learning problems of students in rural schools and can form the basis for innovative learning in this area.

References

Coombe P. (2017). Online Learning in a Rural School Setting. Dissertation, Georgia State University, 2017. doi: https://doi.org/10.57709/10134621. Online Learning in a Rural School Setting (gsu.edu)

Firdaus, F. A., & Mariyat, A. (2017). Humanistic Approach In Education According To Paulo Freire. *At-Ta'dib, 12*(2), 25. https://doi.org/10.21111/at-tadib.v12i2.1264.

Gedvilienė G., Vaičiūnienė V. (2016). Distance learning at university from a lifelong learning perspective // European scientific journal. Macedonia : European scientific institute.

Greenan K. A. (2021). The Influence of Virtual Education on Classroom Culture. *Front. Commun.* 6:641214. doi: 10.3389/fcomm.2021.641214. https://www.frontiersin.org/articles/10.3389/fcomm.2021.641214/full

Erasmus+ Strategic Partnership Project "EU Rural Virtual Classroom" https://erasmus-plus.ec.europa.eu/projects/search/details/2021-1-ES01-KA220-SCH-000023731

I. Amosa, M. James, and C. Olubode, "Effectiveness of video-based cooperative learning strategy on high, medium and low academic achievers," *The African Symposium, An Online Journal of the African Educational Research Network*, vol. 13, no. 2, pp. 77–85, 2013.

"Virtual Learning Rural Space" project "EU Rural virtual classroom" https://ruralvirtualclassroom.eu/#about

Simonson, M., Smaldino, S. & Zvacek, S. (2015). Teaching and learning at a distance: Foundations of distance education (6th ed.), Charlotte, NC: IAP

Squire, K. D. (2021). From virtual to participatory learning with technology during COVID-19. *E-Learning and Digital Media, 19*(1), 204275302110229. https://doi.org/10.1177/20427530211022926

UNESCO (2021). *UNESCO education strategy 2014-2021*. Retrieved from:

https://unesdoc.unesco.org/ark:/48223/pf0000231288.spa

INCLUDE-ED Consortium (2015) *Successful Educational Actions for Inclusion and Social Cohesion in Europe*. Springer international Publishing.

AICOMP - FUTURE SKILLS IN A WORLD INCREASINGLY SHAPED BY AI

Ulf-Daniel Ehlers, Baden-Wurttemberg Cooperative State University, Germany

Martin Lindner, DHBW, Germany

Stephanie Sommer, DHBW, Germany

Emily Rauch, DHBW, Germany

***Correspondence**: Ulf-Daniel Ehlers: ulf.ehlers@gmail.com*

Abstract

Globalisation and modernisation are creating an increasingly diverse and interconnected world. To make sense of and function well in this world, individuals need, for example, to master changing technologies and to make sense of large amounts of available information. They also face collective challenges as societies - such as balancing economic growth with environmental sustainability, and prosperity with social equity. In these contexts, the competences that individuals need to meet their goals have become more complex, requiring more than the mastery of certain narrowly defined skills.

Keywords:

Artificial Intelligence, Future Skills, AI-Competence

1. Introduction

The development of artificial intelligence (AI) is already having a massive impact on the world of work and daily life. The automation of processes and the optimisation of systems through the use of AI technologies are leading to constant change and new demands on people. Already today, certain competences are particularly in demand in order to be able to act successfully in a world shaped by artificial intelligence. These include, for example, the ability to collaborate with AI systems (distributed cognition) in creative problem solving or the ability to analyse and interpret large amounts of data.

The question of which competences are needed in a living and working world that is influenced by artificial intelligence to be able to act in both private and professional contexts is one of the most important questions in various fields of science. In order to answer this question we have conducted several research steps and have now constructed an initial competence framework which we call "AIComp" (Acronym: Artificial Intelligence Competences).

The aim of this study is to process the currently available scientific work on AI-related competences, create a synopsis of competence requirements and bundle them in form of AI-related "Future Skills-Profiles", which serve as larger and overarching competence fields. They each contain knowledge-, skills- and value-related requirements that are important for successful actions in a world permeated by AI.

This paper follows a four step flow: In the first part (section 2), the State of the art research literature on AI literacy and competence is analysed and classified. In the next part (section 3), a methodology for qualitative meta-studies is described. A six-step research-, analysis- and design process is described step-by-step, leading into the design of the AIComp model in section four. This is presented in overview and fully presented in the appendix online.

2. Which competences for AI?

We base our work on the consideration that AI needs to serve individuals and society to freely and actively develop in a changing world. Our ambition is to cover competences for both economic and social purposes. This is rooted in an understanding of human capital in a wide sense including social-, educational- and economic capital (Bourdieu 1983). We strive to identify competences of behavioural nature that follow the underlying concept of "action competence" (Ehlers 2020) which we call "Future Skills" and which support individuals to act

successfully in AI-related contexts in their professional and private lives. Thus, we strive to identify AI-related Future Skills which are important for a broad range of individuals, instead of focussing those competences that are of use only in a specific trade, occupation or walk of life.
In the international literature, the so-called "KSAVE model" has become established for the operationalisation of action competences (Binkley et al. 2012). It provides that action competences are constituted by the three dimensions already mentioned above: Knowledge - Skills - Attitudes/Values/Ethics (see fig. 1).

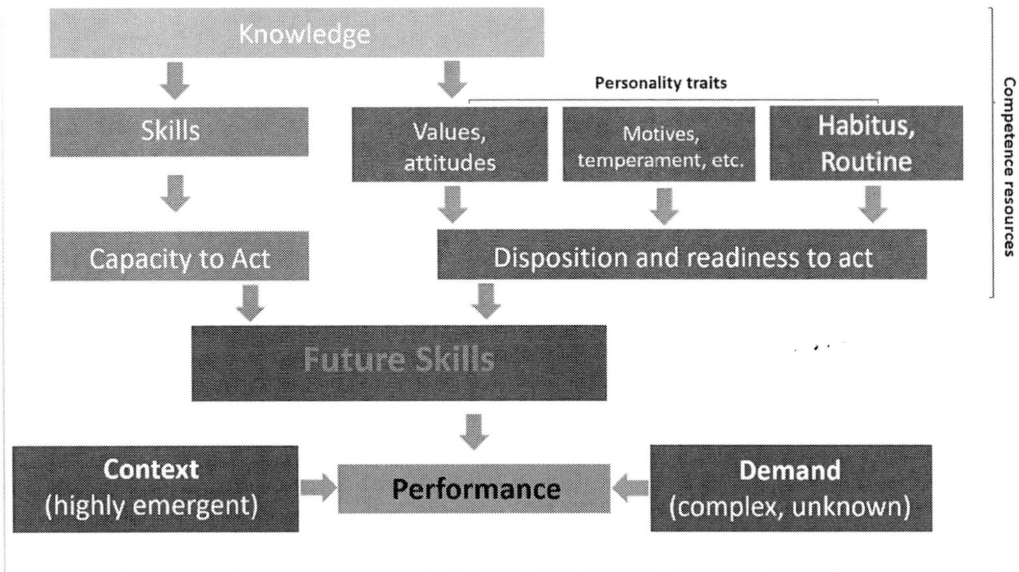

Fig. 1: Competence structure model for Future Skills (Ehlers 2020)

For the competence model "AIComp", we also chose this three-part competence structure for each AI-related Future Skill-Profiles. In addition we formulated larger clusters in which we group Future Skills profiles which are called "areas of action". Overall, this results in the following structure:

- Areas of action, which contain
- AI-related Future Skills Profiles, which include
- Knowledge (K) + Skills (S) + Attitudes(A)

Interim conclusion: Requirements for an AI skills framework

In conclusion, it appears that AI-related competence as an action competence model is not yet sufficiently elaborated and represents a research gap. With the present research overview, we intend to take a first step, based on the existing literature, to establish an action competence-oriented framework. As a first definition of AI-related competences we propose: Future Skills for a lifeworld that is increasingly shaped by AI is the ability to successfully act in emergent and complex situations. The framework concept should fulfil the following functions in particular:

1. systematise already empirically based and/or analytically derived competences and competence requirements and relate them into a model based on KSAVE components and action competence,

2. make visible competence requirements that are placed on certain groups.

3. AI-Related Competences: A Qualitative Meta-analysis

In this chapter we give an overview of the step-by-step process we used to analyse existing AI-related competence frameworks. We are then going to present our aggregated new AI-related competence framework.

3.1 On the Methodology of Qualitative Meta-analysis

A qualitative meta-analysis is a systematic summary of empirical studies using the instrument of qualitative content analysis (Timulak 2009). It serves to find (meaning) structures, concepts and constructs in the present study on the topic of AI competences. We proceed in the following steps:

Research and analysis stage

1. Research: Keyword-based search in search engines on the topic of AI-related competence approaches as well as lists of skills and descriptions.
2. AIComp I: Create a unified list of skills and competences and their descriptions.
3. AIComp II: Cleaning the data by expanding multidimensional formulations into one-dimensional ones as well as paraphrasing and deleting duplicate mentions.
4. AIComp III: Synthesis and grouping based on four content dimensions: Knowledge Assets, Application Skills, Creative Skills and Innovation, and Critical Analysis, Reflection and Ethics. Further paraphrasing to increase concept clarity. Finally, mapping of K-S-A where possible.

Design stage

5. AIComp IV: Mapping of the individual skills to the Future Skills-Profiles. The result is competence descriptions for individual competence profiles, which are operationalised by K-S-A in each case.
6. AIComp qualitative final: Recontextualisation of the competence descriptions into a final qualitative model of AIComp.

3.2 Research and Analysis Stage

In the following section, we describe the meta-analysis and the research steps carried out for this purpose.

Step 1: Research

The research phase pursued the goal of collecting international research papers in German or English on the topic of AI-related competences from the period of the years 2019 to 2023. The following keywords were used for the search:

- Artificial intelligence, or AI for short
- AI competence and AI competence framework
- AI Skills, AI Abilities
- AI Learning, AI Education, AI Training
- KI Learning objectives

The focus of the search was on elaborated competence frameworks and lists of competence elements for non-technical learners. Furthermore, publications that explicitly deal with the concepts of AI literacy or AI competence but do not contain lists or frameworks themselves were classified as relevant. (see Table 1).

Table 1: Competence/Literacy approaches for AI-related competences

No.	Title	Author	Year	Education sector
1	A.I. and Digital Transformation. Competencies for Civil Servants	UNESCO Broadband Commission	2022	VET
2	What is AI Literacy? Competencies and Design Consideration	Long, Magerko	2020	not specified
3	EU DigComp 2.2: The Digital Competence Framework for Citizens	Vuorikari, Kluzer, Punie (EU)	2022	Life-long learning
4a	Competences for AI. Changes, needs, options for action	André et al.	2022	VET
4b	AI competence development in material and production work. Micro study (project report)	André et al.	2022	VET
5a	AI Literacy: Competence dimensions and influencing factors in the context of work	Wienrich, Carolus et al.	2022	VET

5b	MAILS - Meta AI Literacy Scale: Development and Testing of an AI Literacy. Questionnaire Based on Well-Founded Competency Models and Psychological Change- and Meta-Competencies	Carolus et al.	2022	VET
6	Delphi study for the development and preliminary validation of an item set for the assessment of non-experts' AI literacy	Laupichler et al.	2023	not specified
7	AI Literacy: Definition, Teaching, Evaluation and Ethical Issues	Ng, Leung et al.	2021	not specified
8	AI Skills. A Preliminary Assessment of the Skills Needed for the Deployment, Management and Regulation of Artificial Intelligence. 2022	National Skills Council (Ireland)	2022	not specified
9	Artificial Intelligence Competency Framework. A success pipeline from college to university and beyond.	Blok, Trudeau, Cassidy	2021	higher education
10	Necessary competences for administrative staff in dealing with AI - Practice-related competence grid	Catakli/Punt Shoe	(2023, in progress)	VET
11	Artificial intelligence and AI-related skills. A research overview.	Sūna/Hoffmann (currently in preparation)	2021 (in progress)	not specified

Step 2: Creating a unified list of skills and competences and their descriptions

In an inventory, all formulations of competence inventory items related to AI were then listed. In this way, a total of 167 competence items of different types, lengths and complexity could be listed in an inventory.

Step 3: Data cleaning, expanding multidimensional formulations, paraphrasing and deleting duplicate items

A further version was then created using qualitative content analysis procedures. For this purpose, all formulations of competence inventory items that were included twice were removed (115 mentions). Then the formulations were checked for their dimensionality. In this process, those formulations that contained several aspects or dimensions in one item were broken down into their parts and checked to see whether these were already contained in other formulations. New aspects were included as paraphrased formulations. In a further step, all formulations were paraphrased and adapted to a common linguistic style, while retaining the content-related aspects. The result was 34 individual formulations of competence inventory items.

Step 4: Synthesis and grouping based on four content dimensions

The competence was now analysed and allocated to a literacy model for media literacy in order to check to what extent they contained balanced dimensions according to the model (see Baacke 1997). These dimensions included: knowledge assets (13), application skills (5), creative skills and innovation (6) and ability for critical analysis, reflection and ethics (10).
Marginal wording changes were made to sharpen the clarity of the concept.

In addition, all these collected competence inventory items were roughly assigned to the competence dimensions: Knowledge (19) - Skills (18) - Attitudes (26).

3.3 Design Stage: Design of the AIComp Model

The design of the initial AIComp model into a Future Skills-structure for AI took two further steps. A three-level structure was used as guiding concept. At the level one, this consists of items from the competence inventory that describe knowledge, skill descriptions or attitudes. At level two these are summarised into AI-related Future Skills-profiles. At level three, the Future Skills-profiles are divided into three areas of action:

- those that relate more to personal competences,
- those that relate to competences that enable creative use of AI technologies, applications or concepts,

- those that contain the necessary competences to master the changes in organisations, communication and cooperation structures resulting from AI.

Step 5: AIComp - Mapping the individual skills to the Future Skills-profiles. The result is competence descriptions for individual competence profiles, each of which is operationalised by K-S-A.

First of all, 13 AI-related Future Skills-profiles were developed from the Future Skills-profiles of the NextSkills-study and on the basis of the inventory of 167 AI-related skills determined qualitatively in the state of research. These include those competences that are required when the corresponding Future Skills-profile is related to AI-infused living and working environments. The qualitative inventory items assigned to each of these competences answer the question of which knowledge, which skills and which attitudes are considered necessary in order to be able to act successfully within this framework.

Step 6: AIComp qualitative final recontextualisation of the competence descriptions into a final qualitative model of AIComp

In the last step of the process, the formulations of the Future Skills-profiles are made more precise on the basis of the existing inventory items. As a result, the qualitative inventory currently contains 67 AI-related items that are grouped into 13 Future Skills-profiles.

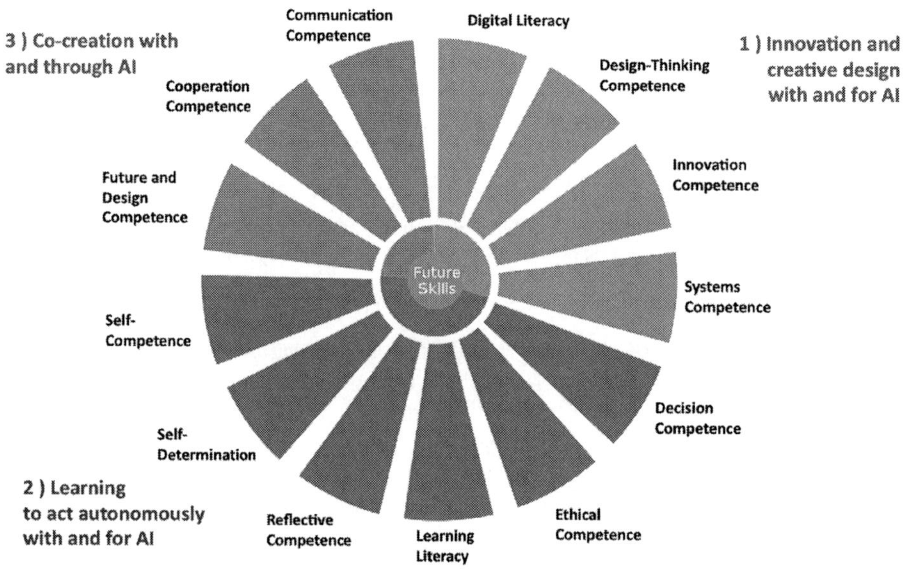

Fig. 2: AI-related Competences (Ehlers, Lindner, Sommer, Rauch 2023)

Table 2: Description of AI-related competences

Area 1: Innovation and creative design with and for AI Competences to use AI technologies and applications as an object and/or method, to develop them further or to develop solutions and concepts in connection with AI for concrete tasks and for organisationally or individually significant contexts of action.	
I – Digital competence	Being able to utilise AI tools and apps, to develop them in a productive way, to leverage them for one's own purposes; and to reflectively, critically and analytically comprehend their technical modes of action in relation to the individual and society as a whole, including knowledge of the potentials and limits of AI and its modes of action.
I.1	Being able to thoroughly evaluate and analyse the implications of the technological inner logic of AI systems based on their impact on organisations or society.
I.2	Being able to evaluate, analyse and make sense of AI technologies and applications regarding their functions and the benefits of their application.

I.3	Being able to assess and analyse the influence of AI technologies on the handling of data.
II. Design thinking competence	Being able to employ concrete methods and techniques for realising creative development processes dealing with problems and issues related to AI in a wayin way that is open ended and involving all stakeholders in a collaborative process for problem-solving and solution design.
III. Innovation competence	Being willing to advance AI innovation within organisations as a subject andans theme as well as in processes, and to incorporate AI into organisational innovation ecosystems.
IV. System competence	Being able to comprehend AI tools and AI concepts as embedded within complex personal-psychological, social and technical systems, as well as identifying and grasping their mutual effects, and being able to design and/or accompany coordinated planning and implementation processes for new projects within a given system.
IV.1	Being able to perceive and analyse AI systems from the perspective of integrating them in a larger social system (of an organisation, of society).
IV.2	Being able to consider AI technologies and applications from the perspective of system architecture and system design, and to derive appropriate actions based on this.
Area 2: Learning to act autonomously with and for AI Competences necessary to act as an individual in a sovereign and responsible manner in an AI-permeated world and to use AI concepts and tools for one's own objectives in a responsible, productive and reflective way.	
I. Decision-making competence	Being able to recognise the need for decisions in AI-related situations and to evaluate alternative choices to make a decision and take responsibility for it.
II. Ethical competence	Being able to perceive AI-related issues as ethically relevant (perception), to formulate and test premises in relation to AI-relevant issues (evaluation) as well as the ability to test the application conditions of AI-related conceptions and their alternatives (judgement).
III. Learning competence	Being open, able and willing to learn about AI issues and through the use of AI tools and applications.
IV. Reflection competence	Being able and willing to recognise the underlying behaviours, thought systems and value systems related to topics connected with AI, and to holistically assess how they inform actions and decisions.
V. Self-determination	Being able to act productively in the tension between external determination and self-determination brought about by data and AI algorithms, and to create self-determined spaces for one's own needs-oriented development.
VI. Self-competence	Being able to use AI tools to support one's own personal and professional development, and to deal with self-organisation, time management as well as cognitive load management with a high degree of personal responsibility when using AI tools.

Area 3: Co-creation with and through AI Competences that support the ability to act in relation to AI-issues affecting the social, organisational and institutional environment. These include, for example, the ability to design alternative "AI futures", to help shapingshape the social impact of AI in a critical and reflective manner, to work and cooperate with others, and to communicate, criticise and reach consensus in manners appropriate to a specific situation, also in intercultural contexts.	
I. Future and design competence	Being open, courageous and creative to embrace the new; being willing to change and to look forward in order to further develop and transform existing AI-related concepts in the direction of new, unprecedented visions of the future.
II. Cooperation competence	Being able to work in interdisciplinary and interorganisational teams on projects and plans relating to AI, also across cultures, to overcome existing differences and find common ground.
III. Commu-nication competence	Having discourse, dialogue and strategic communication skills, in order to being able to communicate successfully relating to AI subjects in different contexts, in a situationally appropriate manner.

Conclusions

This paper summarises the interim results of a work in progress that aims at systematically developing a Future Skills framework, suited for helping individuals, organisations and educational institutions to build the action-oriented competences needed for a future world that will be permeated by AI on all levels, in all fields of private and working life.

Six different lists of all in all 160 granular competence inventory items, representing elements of holistic competences, were identified, analysed, evaluated and set in relation. From this pool relevant elements were selected and included in a set of Future Skills-Profiles, thus creating a context in which the separate, more granular concepts of "skills", "competences" and "literacies" of workers, students, citizens and consumers become recognizable as part of one big picture.

References

AgenturQ (2021). *Future Skills: Which skills are critical for success in Baden-Württemberg today and in the future.* https://www.bw.igm.de/downloads/artikel/attachments/ARTID_101055_CAJemF?name=studie.pdf.

André, E. & Bauer W. et al. (eds.). (2021). *Competence Development for Artificial Intelligence - Changes, Needs and Options for Action.* Whitepaper from the Learning Systems Platform, Munich. DOI: https://doi.org/10.48669/pls_2021-2.

Ashoka Germany, McKinsey & Company (2018). *The Skilling Challenge.* https://www.ashoka.org/de/files/2018theskillingchallengeashokamckinseypdf.

Binkley, M. et al. (2012). *Defining Twenty-First Century Skills.* In Griffin, P. & Care, E. (eds.): Assessment and teaching of 21st century skills. Methods and approach. Dordrecht, pp. 17-66.

Blok, S., Trudeau, J. & Cassidy, R. (eds.). (2021). *Artificial Intelligence Competency Framework. A success pipeline from college to university and beyond.* Concordia Continuing Education (CCE), Concordia University and Dawson College, Montreal. https://www.dawsoncollege.qc.ca/ai/wp-content/uploads/sites/180/Corrected-FINAL_PIA_ConcordiaDawson_AICompetencyFramework.pdf.

Booth, A., Sutton, A. & Papaioannou, A. (2016). *Systematic approaches to a successful literature review.* Second Edition. Sage, Thousand Oaks, CA. https://www.researchgate.net/profile/Andrew-Booth-2/publication/235930866_Systematic_Approaches_to_a_Successful_Literature_Review/links/5da06c7f45851553ff8705fa/Systematic-Approaches-to-a-Successful-Literature-Review.pdf.

Bourdieu, P. (1983). *Economic capital, cultural capital, social capital.* In Kreckel, R. (ed.), Social Inequalities (Social World Special Volume 2), Göttingen. pp. 183-198.

Carolus, A. & Koch et al. (2023). *MAILS - Meta AI Literacy Scale: Development and Testing of an AI Literacy.* Questionnaire Based on Well-Founded Competency Models and Psychological Change- and Meta-Competencies. https://arxiv.org/abs/2302.09319.

Catakli, D. (2021). *Administration in the digital age. The role of digital competences in the acquisition of personnel in the higher civil service.* Springer, Berlin. https://link.springer.com/book/10.1007/978-3-658-38958-1.

Davies, H. (2017). *Competence-Based Curricula in the Context of Bologna and EU Higher Education Policy.* In Pharmacy 5(2):17. DOI 10.3390/pharmacy5020017.

Digital Germany (2020). *Digital Germany. Framework concept.* https://digid.jff.de/wp-content/uploads/2021/06/Rahmenkonzept_DigitalesDeutschland_Vollversion.pdf.

Ehlers, U-D. (2020). *Future Skills: Learning of the Future - University of the Future.* Wiesbaden, Springer VS.

Ehlers, U-D. (2022). *Future Skills in Comparison. On the Construction of a General Framework Model for Future Skills in Academic Education.* Karlsruhe. https://next-education.org/downloads/2022-01-Future-Skills-Bildungsforschung_final_Vs_3.pdf.

Erpenbeck, J. (2012). *What "are" competences?* In Faix, W.G. (ed.). Competence. Festschrift Prof. Dr. John Erpenbeck zum 70. Geburtstag. Vol. 4. Steinbeis-Edition, Stuttgart.

Expert Group on Future Skills Needs (2022). *AI Skills. A Preliminary Assessment of the Skills Needed for the Deployment, Management and Regulation of Artificial Intelligence.* National Skills Council (ed.). Ireland. https://www.skillsireland.ie/all-publications/2022/ai-skills-report.html.

Faix, W. G. (ed.) (2012). *Competence.* Festschrift. Prof. Dr. John Erpenbeck. On the occasion of his 70th birthday. Vol. 4. Steinbeis-Edition, Stuttgart. https://www.google.com/url?q=https://www.steinbeis-edition.de/shop/out/pictures/media/9783943356076.pdf&sa=D&source=docs&ust=1680161181709540&usg=AOvVaw2sqcPaQdMXk4Qn3twx-iUK.

Faulstich-Christ, K., Lersch, R. & Moegling, K. (2010). *By way of introduction: competence orientation - a pedagogical paradigm shift?* In Faulstich-Christ, K., Lersch, R. & Moegling, K. (eds.). Kompetenzorientierung in Theorie, Forschung und Praxis. Sekundarstufe I und II, Immenhausen.

Finfgeld-Connett, D. (2018). *A guide to qualitative meta-synthesis.* Routledge. https://www.routledge.com/A-Guide-to-Qualitative-Meta-synthesis/Finfgeld-Connett/p/book/9780815380627.

Fricke, R. & Treinies, G. (1985). *Introduction to meta-analysis.* Huber, Bern; Stuttgart.

Huber, L. (2016). *"Studium Generale" or "Key Qualifications"? An attempt at orientation in the field of higher education.* In Konnertz, U. & Mühleisen, S. (eds.), Education and Key Qualifications. On the role of key qualifications at universities. pp. 101-122. Peter Lang.

Huber, L. (2019). *"Education through science" as a quality of study.* The Higher Education System (67).

Kim, S. W. & Lee, Y. (2022). *The Artificial Intelligence Literacy Scale for Middle School Students.* In Journal of the Korea Society of Computer and Information 27, 3 (2022), pp. 225-238. https://doi.org/10.9708/jksci.2022.27.03.225.

Kirchherr, J., Klier, J., Lehmann-Brauns, C. & Winde, M. (2018). *Future Skills: What skills are missing in Germany.* Discussion paper. Stifterverband & McKinsey. https://www.stifterverband.org/medien/future-skills-welche-kompetenzen-in-deutschland-fehlen

Klieme, E. & Leutner, D. (2006). *Competence models for recording individual learning outcomes and for balancing educational processes.* Description of a newly established priority programme of the DFG. In Zeitschrift für Pädagogik 52 (2006) 6, pp. 876-903

Laupichler, M., Aster, A. & Raupach, T. (2023). *Delphi study for the development and preliminary validation of an item set for the assessment of non-experts' AI literacy.* In Computers and Education: Artificial Intelligence 4 (2023), 100126. DOI: https://doi.org/10.1016/j.caeai.2023.100126.

Laupichler, M., Aster, A., Schirch, J. & Raupach, T. (2022). *Artificial intelligence literacy in higher and adult education: A scoping literature review.* In Computers and Education: Artificial Intelligence, 3 (2022), 100101. DOI: https://doi.org/10.1016/j.caeai.2022.100101.

Long, D. & Magerko, B. (2020). *What is AI Literacy? Competencies and Design Considerations.* In Conference on Human Factors in Computing Systems - Proceedings. ACM, Honolulu, Hawaii, pp. 1-16. DOI: https://doi.org/10.1145/3313831.3376727.

McClelland, D. C. (1973). *Testing for competence rather than for "intelligence."* In American Psychologist, 28(1), pp. 1-14. https://doi.org/10.1037/h0034092

McKinsey Global Institute (2017). *Jobs lost, jobs gained: Workforce transitions in a time of automation.* https://www.mckinsey.com/featured-insights/future-of-work/jobs-lost-jobs-gained-what-the-futureof-work-will-mean-for-jobs-skills-and-wages.

Miao, F. & Holmes, W. et al. (2021). *AI and education. Guidance for policy-makers.* In UNESCO (ed.) Education 2030. https://unesdoc.unesco.org/ark:/48223/pf0000376709.

Ng, D., Leung, J., Chu, S. & Qiao, M. (2021). *AI literacy: definition, teaching, evaluation and ethical issues.* In Proceedings of the association for information science and technology 58/1. pp. 504-509. DOI: https://doi.org/10.1002/pra2.487.

Ng, D., Leung, J., Chu, S. & Qiao, M. (2021). *Conceptualizing AI literacy: An exploratory review.* In Computers and Education: Artificial Intelligence 2. https://www.sciencedirect.com/science/article/pii/S2666920X21000357.

Ng, D., Leung, J. & Chu, S. et al. (2023). *Teachers' AI digital competencies and twenty-first century skills in the post-pandemic world.* In Educational technology research and development. https://doi.org/10.1007/s11423-023-10203-6.

OECD (2016), *"What does low proficiency in literacy really mean?".* Adult Skills in Focus, No. 2, OECD Publishing. Paris. https://doi.org/10.1787/5jm0v427jl9p-en.

OECD (2018). *The Future of Education and Skills: Education 2030.* https://www.oecd.org/education/2030/E2030%20Position%20Paper%20.

Pilgrim, J. & Martinez, E.E. (2013). *Defining Literacy in the 21st Century: A Guide to Terminology and Skills.* In Texas Journal of Literacy Education. Vol. 1(1). pp. 60-69. https://www.researchgate.net/publication/288246131_Defining_literacy_in_the_21st_century_A_guide_to_terminology_and_skills.

Pinski, M. & Benlian, A. (2023). *AI Literacy - Towards Measuring Human Competency in Artificial Intelligence.* In Proceedings of the 56th Hawaii International Conference on System Sciences. IEEE Computer Society Press, Maui, USA, pp. 165-174. https://scholarspace.manoa.hawaii.edu/bitstreams/06fa6203-9d34-4c05-89c5-d00eebaca1e8/download

Polanco-Levicán, K. & Salvo-Garrido, S. (2022). *Understanding Social Media Literacy: A Systematic Review of the Concept and Its Competences.* In International journal of environmental research and public health 19, 14. pp. 1-16. https://doi.org/10.3390/ijerph19148807.

Schaper, N., Schlömer, T. & Paechter, M. (eds.) (2012). *Competences, competence orientation and employability in higher education.* In Zeitschrift für Hochschulentwicklung Jg.7/Nr.4. Graz. https://zfhe.at/index.php/zfhe/article/view/506.

Schlaeger, J. & Tenorth, H.-E. (2020). *Education through science.* Berliner Wissenschafts-Verlag. Berlin.

Stepstone/Kienbaum (2021). *Future Skills - Future Learning.* Study 2021. https://media.kienbaum.com/wp-content/uploads/sites/13/2021/06/Kienbaum-StepStone-Studie_2021_WEB.pdf.

Suessenbach, F., Winde, M., Klier, J. & Kirchherr, J. (2021). *FUTURE SKILLS 2021. 21 competencies for a changing world.* Discussion paper 3. Stifterverband & McKinsey (eds.). https://www.stifterverband.org/medien/future-skills-2021.

Sūna, L. & Hoffmann, D. (2021). *Artificial intelligence and AI-related competencies.* A research overview. In Digital Germany (project website). https://digid.jff.de/auswertung-ki-kompetenzen/.

Timulak, L. (2009). *Meta-analysis of qualitative studies: A tool for reviewing qualitative research findings in psychotherapy.* In Psychotherapy Research, Vol. 19 (2019). pp. 591-600. https://www.tandfonline.com/doi/abs/10.1080/10503300802477989?journalCode=tpsr20

Timulak, L. & Creaner, M. (2013). *Experiences of conducting qualitative meta-analysis.* In Counseling Psychology Review, 28(4). pp.94-104. https://psycnet.apa.org/record/2014-07362-008

UNESCO Broadband Commission (2022). *Artificial Intelligence and Digital Transformation - Competencies for Civil Servants.* Working Group Report on AI Capacity Building. https://broadbandcommission.org/publication/artificial-intelligence-and-digital-transformation/

Vuorikari, R., Kluzer, S. & Punie, Y. (2022). *DigComp 2.2. The Digital Competence Framework for Citizens - With new examples of knowledge, skills and attitudes.* Publications Office of the European Union, Luxembourg. https://publications.jrc.ec.europa.eu/repository/handle/JRC128415.

Wang, B., Rau, P. L. P. & Yuan, T. (2022). *Measuring user competence in using artificial intelligence: validity and reliability of artificial intelligence literacy scale.* In Behaviour & Information Technology. pp. 1-14. https://doi.org/10.1080/0144929X.2022.2072768.

Weinert, F. E. (ed.). (2001). *Performance measurement in schools.* Beltz. Weinheim, Basel. pp. 27f. https://www.pedocs.de/volltexte/2021/20038/pdf/EWR_2001_1_Schwippert_Rezension_Weinert_Leistungsmessungen_in_Schulen.pdf.

Wienrich, C. & Carolus, A. et al. (2022). *AI Literacy: Competence dimensions and influencing factors in the context of work.* Denkfabrik Digitale Arbeitsgesellschaft (ed.). https://www.denkfabrik-bmas.de/fileadmin/Downloads/Publikationen/AI_Literacy_Kompetenzdimensionen_und_Einflussfaktoren_im_Kontext_von_Arbeit.pdf.

Wild, S., Deuer, E. & Pohlenz, P. (2018). *Study success perceptions of full-time teaching staff in the business studies department of the Baden-Württemberg Cooperative State University (DHBW) - An attempt at typification.* Journal of Evaluation - ZfEv, 17(2).

World Economic Forum (ed.). (2020). *The Future of Jobs Report 2020.* http://www3.weforum.org/docs/WEF_Future_of_Jobs_2020.pdf.

DIGITAL TEACHER EDUCATION FOR A BETTER FUTURE: RECOMMENDATIONS FOR TEACHER PREPARATION FOR AN ONLINE ENVIRONMENT

Michael Barbour, Touro University California, United States

Charles Hodges, Georgia Southern University, United States

***Correspondence**: Michael Barbour: mkbarbour@gmail.com*

Abstract

In light of current or future pandemics, natural disasters, war, or personal preferences, remote or online learning is becoming increasingly common. This reality means that teachers need to be equipped with the skills necessary to effectively teach online. In this paper the authors highlight the importance of preparing teachers with effective online teaching skills and knowledge, and suggest two areas for improvement: (1) research support for scholars to build a knowledge base to better understand effective online teaching, and (2) changes to teacher preparation programs to better equip teachers for this changing reality. Before presenting these recommendations, a brief discussion of the state of K-12 online learning globally, as well as the limitations of existing teacher education, prior to the COVID-19 pandemic is provided.

Keywords:

K-12 online learning, K-12 distance education, virtual schooling, cyber schooling, online learning, online teaching, teacher education, teacher preparation, pre-service teachers, in-service teachers, pandemic, remote learning, emergency preparedness.

Introduction

As noted in *Reimagining our Futures Together: A New Social Contract for Education*, "in the era of COVID-19 we have seen that digital technologies are essential for public health and public education: an indispensable tool for distance education, for contact and vaccine tracing, for reliable information about the virus and more" (International Commission on the Futures of Education, 2021, p. 37). Globally, teachers need to know how to teach online because of the need for students to engage in remote or online learning with increasing frequency due to factors such as the COVID-19 pandemic, natural disasters, war, or personal preference, etc.. In this paper we outline the necessity of equipping teachers with the skills to effectively teach in an online environment and provide recommendations for improved teacher preparation for online learning, which consist of two general areas: (1) research directions and supports for scholars, and (2) changes to teacher preparation programs. These recommendations rely on the needed digital infrastructure to support online learning, but a discussion of that infrastructure is beyond the scope of the present paper. Before providing the goals and recommendations, we begin with a discussion of the state of K-12 online learning prior to the pandemic.

State of K-12 Online Learning Prior to 2020

Prior to the pandemic, K-12 distance and online learning had a long history in certain jurisdictions. For example, correspondence education has been used in the K-12 environment in places like Australia, Canada, New Zealand, and the United States for over a century (Barbour, 2014; Clark, 2003; Rumble, 1989; Stevens, 1994). Educational radio has been used since the 1940s (Moore & Kearsley, 1996; Stacey & Visser, 2005), while telematics have been common since the 1980s (Brown et al., 2000; Oliver & Reeves, 1994). Throughout the 1990s and early 2000s, nations on just about every continent began to experiment with K-12 online learning (Barbour, 2018), but the level of K-12 online learning activity varied from nation to nation. There were a small number of jurisdictions, such as South Korea (Cho, 2009; Jang, 2006), where K-12 online learning was prevalent. In countries where K-12 online learning was common, it often only touched 5% to 10% of the overall K-12 student population (Barbour et al., 2020; Digital Learning Collaborative, 2020). Finally, in most cases K-12 online learning only accounted for a very small portion of the overall K-12 education system (Bacsich et al., 2012a, 2012b; Barbour et al., 2011).

While distance education may have a long history in the K-12 system, the use of K-12 online learning was still quite uncommon in most jurisdictions prior to the pandemic. Even in locations where it was more common, few teachers had direct experience with teaching online, and even fewer had been provided specific training as a part of their teacher preparation. Kennedy and Archambault (2012) found only 1.3% of U.S. teacher education programs were preparing pre-service teachers for K-12 online learning by providing field experiences in virtual settings. More recently, Archambault et al. (2016) reported an increase to 4.1% of teacher education programs who prepared pre-service teachers for online learning. Further, Archibald et al. (2020) indicated similar findings when they found 32% of Canadian teacher education programs offered field experiences in K–12 online program settings to pre-service or in-service teachers. This problem was compounded by the fact that researchers behind the "Going Virtual" studies into K-12 online teacher professional development found that less than 40% of all K–12 online teachers reported receiving professional development prior to beginning to teach online (Dawley et al., 2010; Rice and Dawley, 2007; Rice et al., 2008). Similar findings have been reported in India (Nautiyal & Sinha, 2015), the United Kingdom (Kidd & Murray, 2020), and elsewhere (Bacsich et al., 2012a, 2012b). For example, Coyle et al. (2010) found that Spanish teachers were unprepared to engage in digital teaching techniques in their own instruction. Simply put, prior to the pandemic even teachers involved in K-12 online learning were often underprepared to teach online.

An Historical Gap in Teachers' Preparation to Use Technology to Teach

Shulman (1986) proposed the concept that there was a type of knowledge that went "beyond knowledge of subject matter per se to the dimension of subject matter knowledge for teaching" (p. 9). Today pedagogical content knowledge is embedded in most teacher education programs. Yet more than 15 years after it was first introduced, Mishra and Koehler (2006) proposed expansion of this framework to include technological pedagogical knowledge has not gained similar acceptance within the broader teacher education community. However, the recent sudden and dramatic shift to technology-mediated forms of learning - such as K-12 online learning - have exposed a long known reality. While some pedagogical skills from a standard teacher education program still apply, many of the necessary online teaching competencies are completely new to even recently licensed teachers (An et al, 2021; Davis & Niederhauser, 2005; Davis & Roblyer, 2005).

This is not to suggest that teacher education programs are solely to blame for the lack of preparation witnessed over the past three years, or even that the problem began with the dramatic shift to remote learning that was caused by the pandemic. For example, Bond et al. (2019) wrote that "issues of educator professional development with technology has been a particularly recurring theme across the past five decades, with institutions at all levels struggling to find the resources to release educators, or to implement sufficient preservice teacher education with technology" (pp. 39–40). More recently, Lahr and Welch (2023) indicated that while "teacher preparation [had] grown to accommodate and consider virtual teaching practices, to a degree, but integration into pre- and in-service teaching preparation [was] nowhere near universal, and the curriculum of teacher preparation for online teaching [was] murky at best" (p. 162). The reality is that even if teacher education programs had sought to include this knowledge the research in the field is so fragmented "that teacher preparation programs cannot even determine what future teachers who may be working in an online or blended environment should be exposed to" (Molnar et al., 2021, p. 69).

Recommendations for Teacher Preparation

To address this lack of research, Hodges et al. (2022) argued that "a validated set of standards would provide accrediting bodies a guide to effective online teaching practices that could be used to hold teacher education programs accountable" (p. 206). The International Commission on the Futures of Education (2021) echoed this point, suggesting that one of the main limitations of teacher education programs in general was the "lack of standards of practice or of standards for teacher preparation institutions" (pp. 22-23). Hodges et al. (2022) also argued that "metrics and instruments must be created or refined to further assess and support growth of [teacher's] knowledge, skills, and attitudes of teaching in K-12 online and blended learning" (p. 205). However, in order to achieve specific goals of research-based standards and validated assessment metrics and instruments, scholars need funded efforts to develop promising practices and frameworks that teacher education programs can use and be evaluated against. Leaving school technologies to the demands of the free market and commercial interests has been observed to have serious problems (Barbour, 2017; International Commission on the Futures of Education, 2021; Krutka et al., 2021). The need for funded research is an area where national and local authorities can play a role to provide encouragement, direction, and - most importantly - resources to ensure the public interest is at the forefront of this scholarship.

Even without this research-based framework, scholars have started to provide recommendations for teacher education programs in response to issues observed during the COVID-19 pandemic to better prepare teachers for teaching online. Trust and Whalen (2020) recommended to "provide teachers with the opportunity to develop K-12 online and blended teaching competencies so that they are prepared to teach in different formats, settings, and situations" (p. 193). Lahr and Welch (2023) were more specific with their recommendation, stating that pre-service teachers should have experience through an online teaching practicum. Hodges et al. (2022) offered a more detailed list of objectives to improve global teacher preparation for online and blended teaching. The most important of these, at least with respect to the preparation of teachers to be able to teach online, was to ensure that accrediting bodies and state agencies require that all teacher education programs have meaningful and useful preparation to deliver online and blended learning.

According to the American Association of Colleges for Teacher Education (2022), "the importance of accreditation, particularly its role in assuring that the preparation of professional educators ultimately serves the interests and learning of PK-12 students" (para. 2). While this is an American organization and example, the same would be true of the national and professional accrediting bodies of any European nation. As Hodges et al. (2022) noted that one of the main reasons why teacher education programs have "not normalized the preparation of all teachers to teach effectively with technology, including in different modalities such as online and blended learning" is because they haven't been required to do so (p. 207). In fact, often the stated requirements for teacher education are so expansive and onerous that they account for most, if not all of the allocated focus within the teacher preparation program.

Hodges et al. (2022) also recommended that there must be sufficient course work in teacher preparation programs to give teachers access to knowledge, skills, and attitudes related to K-12 online and blended learning. How to provide that coursework is a matter of debate. Starkey (2020), in a systematic literature review of teacher preparation for the use of digital technologies, found that from 2008-2018 "perspectives ranged from having standalone courses with no link to in school practice to teach generic digital competencies, to a view that programmes should have digital competencies infused across courses" (p. 52). That observed range, from standalone courses to infusion across the teacher preparation curriculum, has been reported by several other scholars (Brush et al., 2001; Foulger et al., 2019; Mehlinger & Powers, 2002), many of whom have noted apparent problems with how the technology infusion approach is often implemented (Clausen, 2022; Wetzel et al., 2014). Regardless, it has been recommended by some that teacher education programs should stop the pendulum-like swing between a course and infusion in the middle by including specific coursework and infusion throughout the teacher education program (Mellon, 1999; Wang & Chen, 2006).

Further, Hodges et al. (2022) recommended that teacher candidates should have experiences as online learners. It has been long accepted that online teachers should experience online learning as a student. As Zucker and Kozma (2003) indicated, in order to fully appreciate the challenges that students may face, teachers need to first have the experience of being an online student themselves. In fact, one of the first virtual schools in the US built this into its initial teacher induction program. In order to design an online course or teach an online class, you had to first complete an online course in either effective online course design or effective online teaching (Pape et al., 2005). This model is based on the belief that "teachers teach the way they were taught" (Davis & Rose, 2009, p. 7) – and in order to be able to teach online one must experience being taught online themselves. The authors also suggested it was "important for all online course designers and instructors to have professional development that uses the online media they will be teaching through" (p. 7). Similarly, Cavanaugh (2009) also believed online teachers needed to have experience as students in an online learning setting. Essentially, by having the experience of being an online learner, it would provide e teachers with a sense of empathy for the struggles that their own online students might face – which should enhance student learning (Bouton, 2016; Meyers et al., 2019). Additionally, Akcaoglu and Akcaoglu (2022) wrote that having teachers experience effective online learning would increase their own self-efficacy about teaching online, which according to Correy and Stella (2018) would also lead to greater student success.

Finally, recommendations have been made for quite some time that pre-service teachers need to be prepared to teach online. For example, Duncan and Barnett (2009) concluded that "future teachers must have the skills and knowledge to teach effectively in online as well as in traditional environments" (p. 373), while König et al. (2020) found there was a need to foster teacher expertise in online teaching and learning both in initial teacher preparation and on-going teacher professional development. Yet despite calls like these, most teacher preparation programs are not addressing this need (Kennedy & Archambault, 2012; Archambault et al., 2016; Archibald et al., 2020). The COVID-19 pandemic exposed the critical need for all teachers to be prepared to teach online. An important component of this preparation appears to be a field or practicum experience in online teaching. Luo et al. (2017) observed that pre-service teachers being exposed to an online teaching field experience had many benefits, including positive attitudes toward online learning, the possibility of positive relationships between teachers and students online, and their ability to create interactive learning online. More recently, Mohebi and Meda (2021) found that a "virtual field experience was a milestone of achievement for trainee teachers" (p. 1196). These findings should be no surprise as teacher education has routinely included field experiences for in-person teaching for decades (Cruickshank & Armaline, 1986). Thus, teacher education programs should also include field experiences in online learning (Hodges et al., 2020).

A New Social Contract for Teacher Education

As the International Commission on the Futures of Education (2021) indicated, "key responsibilities fall to governments whose capacity for the public financing and regulation of education should be strengthened" (p. 4). This sentiment is true not just of the provision of public education, but also in the preparation of the teachers who work in the public education system. As the commission succinctly summarized:

> *"The continued development of digital technologies in education in directions guided by sustainability, justice, and inclusion will require action from governments, support from civil society, and a broad public commitment to treating education not as an arena for profiteering, but as a space for public investment in sustainable, just, and peaceful futures." (p. 10)*

There must be a public investment into research that develops promising practices and frameworks that teacher education programs can use and be evaluated against. Then teacher education programs need to use that research to provide teachers with experience in designing, delivering, and facilitating instruction, as well as the opportunity to learn online themselves.

Widespread readiness for remote online learning prior to COVID-19 was limited by various factors such as funding, infrastructure, and technical capacity. There were, however, warnings that were either unseen or not addressed. For example, the U.S. Department of Education recommended that schools develop continuity of learning plans in response to possible pandemic flu as early as 2006 (U.S. Department of Education, 2006), and as early as 2010 the U.S. Department of Education (2010) had observed that:

> *"As online learning becomes an increasingly important part of our education system at all levels, this creates both the need and opportunity for educators who are skilled in online instruction and the demand for greater knowledge of the most effective practices." (p. 47)*

These warnings were not exclusive to the United States. Other countries have been prepared for alternate delivery of instruction for some time. For example, Singapore has prepared to respond to a pandemic or natural disaster through annual drills for online learning (Barbour et al., 2020). Historically, in 1948 New Zealand employed correspondence education and educational radio during a polio epidemic (Germain, 2020). More recently, Hong Kong learned valuable lessons from SARS and H1N1 that were useful during this most recent pandemic (Alpert, 2011; Latchem & Jung, 2009), as did Boliva (Barbour et al., 2011).

The world does not need to be caught off guard again with respect to the need to deliver quality education in the time of disaster. Our vision is that a new social contract for teacher education includes preparation of all teachers to be able to deliver quality instruction online if needed. Additionally, as Darling-Hammond and Hyler (2020) remind us, this recommendation is not exclusive to students' academic needs. The lack of preparation of teachers to fully engage students in online environments also had impacts on students' social emotional needs, creating greater expectations for teacher education programs to be able to equip teachers for equity-focused teaching and learning - even in online settings. To achieve this vision governments must provide funding for scholars to develop and disseminate the necessary tools for effective practice and evaluation of online teaching, and teacher education programs must reform to incorporate preparation for online teaching, not as a novelty, but as part of the standard course of teacher preparation. As König et al. (2020) concluded, "preparing teachers for the digitalisation in schools can [and should] be regarded as a chance that teacher education should not miss" (p. 12).

Conclusions

It is often said that you campaign in poetry, but you govern in prose. In *Disrupting Class: How Disruptive Innovation Will Change the Way the World Learns*, Christensen et al. (2008) predicted that by the end of the next decade that half of all learning in the United States would be done online. The prediction was based on their premise that schools had adapted well to the demands of society and had changed dramatically over time - with the authors citing examples such as (1) the transition from one room schools to larger, industrial-size schools, (2) the desegregation of schools following Brown v. Board of Education, (3) the focus upon mathematics and sciences after the Soviet launch of Sputnik, (4) the broadening of the curriculum (such as Advanced Placement or International Baccalaureate), (5) the expansive testing regimes put in place under the No Child Left Behind legislation, among others. While all of these examples represent change in the education system, do any of them represent a fundamental change in the nature of schooling?

Would any of these changes have made a difference in what someone would see if they walked into a classroom in the year 2008, as compared to walking into a segregated classroom in the American south in the 1950s? Or into a one-room school in rural Australia in the early 1900s? How about as compared to walking into the University of Bologna, the University of Paris, or the University of Oxford in the 1200s? Or even if that individual were walking the streets of Athens listening to Socrates himself? The fact is that the actual act of teaching and learning that occurs within the classroom hasn't changed all that much since the first "schools" were created (Barbour, 2009). The pandemic-induced worldwide closure of schools and the provision of learning through technology-based remote education **was** a fundamental change in the nature of schooling. This sudden pivot to remote learning, along with the subsequent calls for fundamental changes to both how we provide formal education and how we prepare those who facilitate that education, invite us to be poets.

The poetry that we wish to write is based on a vision of equipping teachers with the skills to effectively teach in both face-to-face and online learning environments - to allow an education system where the quality of learning is not based on the medium in which that learning occurs. In order to achieve that vision, we propose the following goals for teacher education. (1) While there is an abundance of research to guide teacher education on how to prepare educators for the face-to-face classroom, there needs to be funded efforts to develop promising practices and frameworks that teacher education programs can use to prepare educators to be effective in the distance and online learning environment. In order to achieve this first goal, we need (a) validated, research-based standards must be developed and (b) metrics and instruments must be created or refined to assess and support growth of teacher's knowledge, skills, and attitudes for teaching in the distance and online learning environment. (2) While content related to teaching with technology is often included in teacher preparation, teacher education programs must fundamentally change their focus to include teaching in distance and online environments in the same pervasive manner as teaching in the face-to-face classroom. In order to achieve this second goal, we need (a) accrediting bodies and state agencies to require teacher education to prepare educators to deliver online learning, (b) sufficient course work to give educators the necessary knowledge, skills, and attitudes related to distance and online learning, (c) educators to have experiences as online learners themselves, and (d) the opportunity - even requirement - for educators to undertake field experiences in distance and online learning settings..

References

Akcaoglu, M., & Akcaoglu, M.O. (2022). Understanding the relationship among self-efficacy, utility value, and the community of inquiry framework in preservice teacher education. *International Review of Research in Open and Distributed Learning, 23*(2), 86–106. https://doi.org/10.19173/irrodl.v23i1.5717

Alpert (2011). Online education in Hong Kong. In M. K. Barbour, L. Hasler Waters, & J. Hunt (Eds.), *Online and blended learning: Case studies from K-12 schools around the world* (pp. 37-59). International Association for K-12 Online Learning.

An, Y., Kaplan-Rakowski, R., Yang, J., Conan, J., Kinard, W., & Daughrity, L. (2021). Examining K-12 teachers' feelings, experiences, and perspectives regarding online teaching during the early stage of the COVID-19 pandemic. *Educational Technology Research and Development, 69*(5), 2589-2613. https://doi.org/10.1007/s11423-021-10008-5

Archambault, L., Kennedy, K., Shelton, C., Dalal, M., McAllister, L., & Huyett, S. (2016). Incremental progress: Re-examining field experiences in K-12 online learning contexts in the United States. *Journal of Online Learning Research, 2*(3), 303–326. https://www.learntechlib.org/primary/p/174116/

Archibald, D., Barbour, M. K., Leary, H., Wilson, E. V., & Ostashewski, N. (2020). *Teacher education and K-12 online learning*. Canadian eLearning Network. https://k12sotn.ca/wpcontent/uploads/2020/07/k12ol-teacher-ed.pdf

American Association of Colleges for Teacher Education. (2022). *High-quality educator preparation*. https://aacte.org/resources/high-quality-educatorpreparation/

Bacsich, P. Bristow, S. F., Camilleri, A., de Beeck, I. O., Pepler, G., & Phillips, B. (2012). *VISCED handbook – Volume 2 – Virtual schools and colleges – Providing alternatives for successful learning*. ATiT bvba. http://www.virtualschoolsandcolleges.archive.atit.be/sites/default/files/VISCED_Handbook-Volume-2/index.pdf

Bacsich, P., Pepler, G., Phillips, B., Öström, M., & Reynolds, S. (2012). *VISCED handbook – Volume 1 – Virtual schools and colleges – Providing alternatives for successful learning*. ATiT bvba. http://www.virtualschoolsandcolleges.archive.atit.be/sites/default/files/VISCED_Handbook-Volume-1/index.pdf

Barbour, M. K. (2009). Book review of Disrupting class: How disruptive innovation will change the way the world learns. *Education Canada, 49*(5). https://www.edcan.ca/wp-content/uploads/edcan-2009-v49-n5-barbour.pdf

Barbour, M. K. (2012). Training teachers for a virtual school system: A call to action. In D. Polly, C. Mims, & K. Persichitte (Eds)., *Creating technology rich teacher education programs: Key issues* (pp. 499–517). IGI Global.

Barbour, M. K. (2014). A history of international K-12 online and blended instruction. In R. Ferdig & K. Kennedy (Eds)., *Handbook of Research on K-12 Online and Blended Learning* (pp. 25-50). Entertainment Technology Center Press, Carnegie Mellon University. https://press.etc.cmu.edu/books/handbook-research-k-12-online-and-blended-learning

Barbour, M. K. (2017). K-12 online learning and school choice : Growth and expansion in the absence of evidence. In R. A. Fox & N. K. Buchanan (Eds.), *School Choice: A Handbook for Researchers, Practitioners, Policy-Makers and Journalists* (pp. 421-440). John Wiley & Sons Ltd..

Barbour, M. K. (2018). A history of K-12 distance, online, and blended learning worldwide. In K. Kennedy & R.E. Ferdig (Eds.), *Handbook of research on K-12 online and blended learning* (2nd ed., pp. 21-40). Entertainment Technology Center Press, Carnegie Mellon University. https://press.etc.cmu.edu/books/handbook-research-k-12-online-and-blended-learning-second-edition

Barbour, M. K., Brown, R., Hasler Waters, L., Hoey, R., Hunt, J., Kennedy, K., Ounsworth, C., Powell, A., & Trimm, T. (2011). *Online and blended learning: A survey of policy and practice from K-12 schools around the world*. International Association for K-12 Online Learning. https://aurora-institute.org/resource/online-and-blended-learning-a-survey-of-policy-and-practice-from-k-12-schools-around-the-world/

Barbour, M. K., LaBonte, R., Kelly, K., Hodges, C., Moore, S., Lockee, B., Trust, T., Bond, A., & Hill, P. (2020). *Understanding pandemic pedagogy: Differences between emergency remote, remote, and online teaching*. Canadian eLearning Network. https://k12sotn.ca/wp-content/uploads/2020/12/understanding-pandemic-pedagogy.pdf

Barbour, M. K., LaBonte, R., & Nagle, J. (2020). *State of the nation study: K-12 e-learning in Canada*. Canadian eLearning Network. https://k12sotn.ca/wp-content/uploads/2021/09/StateNation20.pdf

Bond, M., Zawacki-Richter, O., & Nichols, M. (2019). Revisiting five decades of educational technology research: A content and authorship analysis of the "British Journal of Educational Technology". *British Journal of Educational Technology, 50*(1), 12–63. https://doi.org/10.1111/bjet.12730

Bouton, B. (2016). Empathy research and teacher preparation: Benefits and obstacles. *SRATE Journal, 25*(2), 16–25. https://eric.ed.gov/?id=EJ1113829

Brown, J., Sheppard, B. & Stevens, K. (2000). *Effective schooling in a tele-learning environment.* Centre for TeleLearning and Rural Education, Faculty of Education. https://web.archive.org/web/20050105204359/http://www.tellearn.mun.ca/es_report/index.html

Brush, T., Igoe, A., Brinkerhoff, J., Glazewski, K., Heng-Yu, K., & Colette Smith, T. (2001). Lessons from the field: Integrating technology into preservice teacher education. *Journal of Computing in Teacher Education, 17*(4), 16-20.

Cavanaugh, C. (2009) *Getting more learning time online: Distance education in support of expanded learning time in K-12 schools.* Center for American Progress. https://www.americanprogress.org/article/getting-students-more-learning-time-online/

Cho, Y-S. (2009). *Cyber Home Learning System improves quality of public education.* Advanced Distributed Learning.

Christensen, C. M., Horn, M. B., & Johnson, C. W. (2008). *Disrupting class: How disruptive innovation will change the way the world learns.* McGraw Hill.

Clark, T. (2003). Virtual and distance education in American schools. In M. G. Moore & W. G. Anderson (Ed.), *Handbook of distance education* (pp. 673-699). Lawrence Erlbaum Associates, Inc.

Clausen, J.M. (2022). Learning to fly: Development and design of a micro-credentialing system for an educator preparation program in the absence of a required educational technology course. *TechTrends 66*(2), 276–286. https://doi.org/10.1007/s11528-021-00673-x

Corry, M., & Stella, J. (2018). Teacher self-efficacy in online education: A review of the literature. *Research in Learning Technology, 26.* http://dx.doi.org/10.25304/rlt.v26.2047

Coyle, Y., Yanez, L., & Verdu, M. (2010). The impact of the interactive whiteboard on the teacher and children's language use in an ESL immersion classroom. *System, 38*(4), 614-625. https://doi.org/10.1016/j.system.2010.10.002

Cruickshank, D. R., & Armaline, W. D. (1986). Field experiences in teacher education: Considerations and recommendations. *Journal of Teacher Education, 37*(3), 34-40. https://doi.org/10.1177/002248718603700307

Darling-Hammond, L., & Hyler, M. E. (2020). Preparing educators for the time of COVID… and beyond. *European Journal of Teacher Education, 43*(4), 457-465. https://doi.org/10.1080/02619768.2020.1816961

Davis, N., & Niederhauser, D. S. (2005). Socio-cultural analysis of two cases of distance learning in secondary education. *Education and Information Technologies, 10*(3), 249-262. https://doi.org/10.1007/s10639-005-3006-7

Davis, N. E., & Roblyer, M. D. (2005). Preparing teachers for the "schools that technology built": Evaluation of a program to train teachers for virtual schooling. *Journal of Research on Technology in Education, 37*(4), 399-409. https://doi.org/10.1080/15391523.2005.10782445

Davis, N., & Rose, R. (2007). *Research committee issues brief: Professional development for virtual schooling and online learning.* North American Council for Online Learning. https://aurora-institute.org/resource/professional-development-for-virtual-schooling-and-online-learning/

Dawley, L., Rice, K., & Hinck, G. (2010). *Going virtual! 2010: The status of professional development and unique needs of K-12 online teachers.* Boise State University.

Digital Learning Collaborative. (2020). *Snapshot 2020: A review of K–12 online, blended, and digital learning.* https://static1.squarespace.com/static/5a98496696d4556b01f86662/t/5e61341d879e630db4481a01/1583428708513/DLC-KP-Snapshot2020.pdf/

Duncan, H. E., & Barnett, J. (2009). Learning to teach online: What works for pre-service teachers. *Journal of Educational Computing Research, 40*(3), 357-376. https://doi.org/10.2190/EC.40.3.f

Ferdig, R.E. & Pytash, K.E. (Eds). (2021). *What teacher educators should have learned from 2020.* Association for the Advancement of Computing in Education. https://www.learntechlib.org/p/219088/

Foulger, T. S., Wetzel, K., & Buss, R. R. (2019). Moving toward a technology infusion approach: Considerations for teacher preparation programs. *Journal of Digital Learning in Teacher Education, 35*(2), 79-91. https://doi.org/10.1080/21532974.2019.1568325

Hodges, C.B., and Barbour, M.K., & Ferdig, R.E. (2022). A 2025 vision for building access to k-12 online and blended learning in pre-service teacher education. *Journal of Technology and Teacher Education, 30*(2), 201-216. https://www.learntechlib.org/primary/p/221153/

International Commission on the Futures of Education. (2021). *Reimagining our futures together: A new social contract for education.* United Nations Educational, Scientific and Cultural Organization. https://unesdoc.unesco.org/ark:/48223/pf0000379707.locale=en

Jang, S-H. (2006). *Analysis on the effectiveness of Cyber Home Learning System.* South Korea Ministry of Education, Science and Technology.

Kennedy, K., & Archambault, L. (2012). Offering preservice teachers field experiences in K-12 online learning: A national survey of teacher education programs. *Journal of Teacher Education, 63*(3), 185–200. https://doi.org/10.1177/0022487111433651

König, J., Jäger-Biela, D. J., & Glutsch, N. (2020). Adapting to online teaching during COVID-19 school closure: teacher education and teacher competence effects among early career teachers in Germany. *European Journal of Teacher Education, 43*(4), 608-622. https://doi.org/10.1080/02619768.2020.1809650

Lahr, E. & Welch, S. (2023). Calling for changes in pre-service teacher education to prepare for more than face-to-face teaching: Learning from the covid-19 pandemic. In A.S. Zimmerman (Ed.), *Research, Practice, and Innovations in Teacher Education During a Virtual Age* (pp. 158-174). IGI Global.

Latchem, C., & Jung, I. (2009). *Distance and blended learning in Asia.* Routledge.

Luo, T., Hibbard, L., Franklin, T., & Moore, D. R. (2017). Preparing teacher candidates for virtual field placements via an exposure to K-12 online teaching. *Journal of Information Technology Education: Research, 16*, 1-14. http://www.jite.org/documents/Vol16/JITEv16ResearchP001-014Luo3094.pdf

Mehlinger, H. D., & Powers, S. M. (2002). *Technology and teacher education: A guide for educators and policymakers.* Houghton Mifflin Co.

Mellon, C. A. (1999). Technology and the great pendulum of education. *Journal of Research on Computing in Education, 32*(1), 28–35. https://doi.org/10.1080/08886504.1999.10782267

Meyers, S., Rowell, K., Wells, M., & Smith, B. C. (2019). Teacher empathy: A model of empathy for teaching for student success. *College Teaching, 67*(3), 160–168. https://doi.org/10.1080/87567555.2019.1579699

Mishra, P., & Koehler, M. J. (2006). Technological pedagogical content knowledge: A framework for teacher knowledge. *Teachers College Record, 108*(6), 1017-1054. https://doi.org/10.1111/j.1467-9620.2006.00684.x

Mohebi, L., & Meda, L. (2021). Trainee teachers' perceptions of online teaching during field experience with young children. *Early Childhood Education Journal, 49*(6), 1189-1198. https://doi.org/10.1007/s10643-021-01235-9

Molnar, A. (Ed.), Miron, G., Barbour, M.K., Huerta, L., Shafer, S.R., Rice, J.K., Glover, A., Browning, N., Hagle, S., & Boninger, F. (2021). *Virtual schools in the U.S. 2021.* National Education Policy Center. http://nepc.colorado.edu/publication/virtual-schools-annual-2021

Moore, M. G. & Kearsley, G. (1996). Distance education: A systems view. Belmont, CA: Wadsworth.

Oliver, R., & Reeves, T. C. (1994). *Telematics in rural education: An investigation of the use of telematics for the delivery of specialist programmes for students in rural schools.* InTech Innovations.

Pape, L., Adams, R., & Ribeiro, C. (2005). The virtual high school: Collaboration and online professional development . In Berge, Z. L., & Clark, T. (Eds.), *Virtual schools: Planning for success* (pp. 118–132). Teachers College Press.

Pape, L, Leavey, S., Michalowski, A., Ribeiro, C., & Worrell, C. (2011). Lessons learner: The VHS Collaborative teacher mentoring model. In K. Kennedy, & L. Archambault (Eds.), *Lessons learned in teacher mentoring: Supporting educators in K-12 online learning environments* (pp. 3-16). International Association for K-12 Online Learning. https://aurora-institute.org/resource/lessons-learned-in-teacher-mentoring-supporting-educators-in-k-12-online-learning-environments/

Rice, K., & Dawley, L. (2007). *Going virtual! The status of professional development for K-12 online teachers.* Boise State University.

Rice, K., Dawley, L., Gasell, C., & Florez, C. (2008). *Going virtual! Unique needs and challenges of K-12 online teachers*. Boise State University.

Rumble, G. (1989). The role of distance education in national and international development: An overview. *Distance Education, 10*(1), 83-107. https://doi.org/10.1080/0158791890100107

Shulman, L. S. (1986). Those who understand: Knowledge growth in teaching. *Educational Researcher, 15*(2), 4-14. https://doi.org/10.3102/0013189X015002004

Stacey, E., & Visser, L. (2005). The history of distance education in Australia. *Quarterly Review of Distance Education, 6*(3), 253-259.

Starkey, L. (2020). A review of research exploring teacher preparation for the digital age. *Cambridge Journal of Education, 50*(1), 37-56. https://doi.org/10.1080/0305764X.2019.1625867

Stevens, K. (1994). Australian developments in distance education and their implications for rural schools. *Journal of Research and Rural Education, 10*(1), 78-83. https://jrre.psu.edu/sites/default/files/2019-08/10-1_6.pdf

Trust, T., & Whalen, J. (2020). Should teachers be trained in emergency remote teaching? Lessons learned from the COVID-19 pandemic. *Journal of Technology and Teacher Education, 28*(2), 189-199. https://www.learntechlib.org/primary/p/215995/

Van der Spoel, I., Noroozi, O., Schuurink, E., & van Ginkel, S. (2020). Teachers' online teaching expectations and experiences during the Covid19-pandemic in the Netherlands. *European journal of teacher education, 43*(4), 623-638. https://doi.org/10.1080/02619768.2020.1821185

Wang, Y. M., & Chen, V. D. T. (2006). Untangling the confounding perceptions regarding the stand-alone IT course. *Journal of Educational Technology Systems, 35*(2), 133–150. https://doi.org/10.2190/V16T-8612-6758-8K31

Wetzel, K., Buss, R., Foulger, T.S., & Lindsey, L. (2014) Infusing educational technology in teaching methods courses: Successes and dilemmas. *Journal of Digital Learning in Teacher Education, 30*(3), 89-103. https://doi.org/10.1080/21532974.2014.891877

Zucker, A., & Kozma, R. (2003). *The virtual high school: Teaching generation V*. Teachers College Press.

BUILDING LIFELONG LEARNING PARTICIPATION WITH THE HIGHER EDUCATION 4.0 PROJECT AT THE ATLANTIC TECHNOLOGICAL UNIVERSITY IN IRELAND: RECOGNISING PRIOR LEARNING (RPL) AND PROVIDING CAREER AND LEARNING PATHWAYS WITH MYCAREERPATH.IE

Carina Ginty, Bridie Killoran and Gavin Clinch, Atlantic Technological University (ATU), Ireland

Correspondence: *Carina Ginty: carina.ginty@atu.ie*

Abstract

Higher Education 4.0 (HE 4.0) is an ambitious, innovative, and collaborative project from the Atlantic Technological University (ATU), Ireland. A €12.3 million project supported by the Higher Education Authority (HEA) in Ireland under the HCI, Human Capital Initiative. It is a vision for future agility in higher education and provides for opportunities into and through higher education.

The Careers and RPL Learning Pathways platform under HE 4.0 incorporates a regional service from the ATU for the assessment of Recognised Prior Learning (RPL) and the development of personalised career and learning pathways. This new university service is delivered through an online platform at www.mycareerpath.ie and an RPL information site for the ATU at www.myexperience.ie

The online MyCareerPath.ie platform involves engagement with employers and potential students to the Atlantic Technological University. The service involves advising candidates on the learning pathways available and appropriate to them, and how to achieve their career objectives or improve their employability.

This paper will explore the ATU Career and RPL learning pathways project development journey to date and how the findings emerging from the research and evaluation activities, are informing the establishment of a regional careers and RPL service, supporting lifelong learning participation and upskilling in the workforce. In addition, the process is informing enhancements to the university's RPL assessment process, policy development and access to higher education initiatives. To conclude, industry pilot case exemplars will be discussed and their engagement with MyCareerPath.ie assessment services, an RPL assessment portfolio and a variety of micro-courses supporting the transition to higher education.

Keywords: Learning Pathways, Recognised Prior Learning (RPL), RPL Assessment, Career Guidance, Digital Education, Online Learning.

Introduction to ATU

Atlantic Technological University (ATU) is one of the largest multi-campus universities in Ireland, serving a diverse group of learners, staff, communities and organisations from the west and north-west region and further afield. ATU includes eight campuses in the west and north-west of Ireland with 22,000+ students including 40+ nationalities. The university offers a rich combination of academic and research excellence, quality of life and opportunity – all of which can be experienced in the most beautiful part of Ireland.

ATU (www.atu.ie) has the critical mass and academic depth to attract, educate, nurture and retain talent in the west, north-west and cross-border region. The university collaborative approach ensures that ATU deliver practice-orientated study, and research that seeks to address the major challenges facing society and the world. ATU are dedicated to enabling sustainable economic, social and cultural development; connected to the region and with a mindset that reaches far beyond it.

The term RPL Explained

Recognition of Prior Learning (RPL) is the generic term for learning assessment mechanisms and is used within Higher Education Institutions to describe the awarding of credit/exemptions to applicants on the basis of demonstrated learning that has occurred prior to admission.

RPL is defined as a process whereby prior learning is given a value and this provides opportunities for advanced entry to a further or higher education programme and/or awarding credits for elements within programmes and in some cases RPL can result in a full award from a higher education institute. Furthermore, the European Inventory on validation of non-formal and informal learning, country report Ireland 2014, explains "RPL incorporates prior, formal, informal and non-formal learning and that which is validated within the context of a specified destination award from level one to ten on the national framework of qualifications" (European Commission, CEDEFOP, ICF International; 2014 p. 3).

The National Strategy for Higher Education (2011, p.55) states that "RPL is particularly important as flexible and workplace learning opportunities expand. A national framework for RPL must be developed, based on the expertise and experience already built up in the higher education institutions. Progress in this regard will help to shift the emphasis from educational inputs towards learning outcomes. This student-centred philosophy lies at the heart of the National Framework of Qualifications (NFQ)".

Recognition of Prior Learning (RPL) is therefore a key foundation for lifelong learning policies, and it is critical to the development of an accessible, further and higher education system. RPL encourages people of all ages to participate in learning and attributes value to all their work and life experiences.

Background to the My Experience RPL Project

In 2012 the My Experience project was initiated to inform, support and facilitate Irish or international applicants in applying for RPL to gain entry onto a programme or seek exemptions from parts of a programme at ATU. The project outputs to date include: the development of an information website at www.myexperience.ie; a RPL online ePortfolio assessment tool at www.rplportfolio.ie; the development of an open online educational course for staff working in higher education available to access at www.cpdlearnonline.ie; and in 2016 and 2017 a My Experience RPL roadshow and a series of webinars took place, delivered by ATU staff to other universities across the country.

About the My Experience RPL Toolkit

A dedicated information website at www.myexperience.ie was created to provide relevant information on RPL through short videos and text. The website defines the different mechanism of RPL assessment, provides details on the process and links to the RPL ePortfolio assessment tool. The ePortfolio application tool was created in Moodle as this provided for assessment of learning. It can be accessed directly at www.rplportfolio.ie. As a paperless tool, it provides an electronic submission of evidence and allows the learner to submit their portfolio in a sequence of stages resulting in the creation of a professional RPL portfolio. The ePortfolio of evidence includes certified learning; experiential learning; references; work experience outputs and motivational statements. The

RPL ePortfolio tool has been used successfully at the ATU with over 300 applicants to date (see Figure 1, outlining the process candidates experience at ATU).

In addition, an accredited RPL module for higher education staff (Level 9, worth 10 ECTS) was developed. This module provides participants with a deep understanding of the policies and procedures associated with the process of RPL. It provides participants with an appreciation of the complexities associated with the management of RPL at a Higher Education Institution. This module, which is practically based and interactive, is aimed at developing mentors and assessors with the knowledge and competencies to enable them to become effective assessors of RPL candidates.

Figure 1: RPL candidate experience at ATU

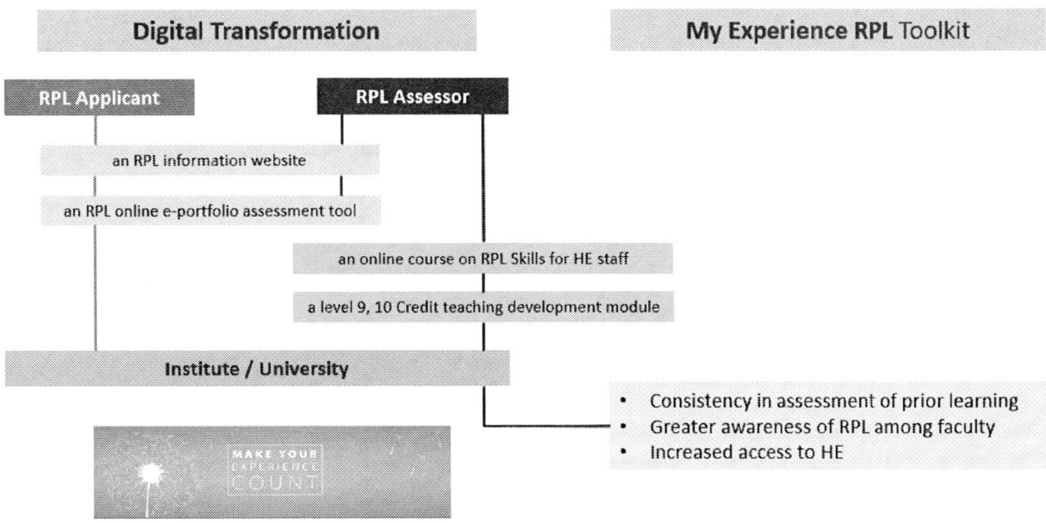

Student Experience of the RPL Toolkit

Since the introduction of the RPL My Experience Toolkit, several RPL candidates have shared their experiences of their RPL journey. Alan Lowe (Engineering graduate) said "while I did not meet the standard entry criteria for an online programme at ATU, I was made aware of the www.myexperience.ie website and experiential learning could form part of a successful application. I reflected on my membership of numerous professional and trade association committees and regular attendance at conferences and seminars, and I realised I had developed knowledge and skills associated with a Level 8 Civil Engineering degree. This enabled me to gain advanced entry to the Level 9, Certificate in Road Maintenance Engineering and Network Management programme at ATU." Another former student, Lucy Bracken, shared "I read about the Certificate in Food Innovation and Entrepreneurship course available at ATU and made inquiries, knowing it would be something that may help me embark on my business idea. My only concern was that although I had a vast amount of relevant experience, I had no formal third level qualification and I felt I would not be eligible to apply for the Level 9 certificate. On meeting with the RPL mentors and assessors in ATU, it was confirmed that I did not meet the formal entry requirements, but that RPL was an access route, and my 25 years of relevant experiential learning would be recognised when making my application. Using the myexperience.ie website, I submitted my RPL ePortfolio including all supporting evidence required for the application. I found the tool very user friendly and felt that I gained a lot from creating the ePortfolio realising the importance of my experience and skillset, I sometimes took for granted".

Background and Growth of Online Learning at ATU

ATU delivered its first online programme, BSc (Hons) in Quality Management, in 2002 to 5 students. By 2011 the number of online learners had grown to 850 and the University established the Centre for Online Learning with the remit to develop online learning, grow student numbers and support both staff and students. Since 2011 online development has grown to over 140 online programmes across all disciplines, at levels 6, 7, 8 and 9 on the Irish National framework of Qualifications (NFQ) (see https://www.qqi.ie/what-we-do/the-qualifications-system/national-framework-of-qualifications) with 5000+ online students enrolled for 2019/2020 academic year. Over the years ATU has won several awards for online education and digital education design and development services.

Online learning from ATU has been very successful with high examination marks and good feedback from students. Many of ATU's online programmes are bespoke and have been created specifically for large multinational and SME companies such as: Intel, Coca-Cola, Boston Scientific, Abbott, Masonite, Eli Lilly, Janssen Biologics, Pfizer, Stiefel, GSK and Merck, Sharp and Dohme (MSD). The University also collaborates with NIBRT (National Institute for Bioprocessing Research and Training) in the delivery of biopharma programmes. Another collaborative programme is the B.Eng. in Data Centres Facilities Engineering which was developed in partnership with industry providers including Google, Facebook and Microsoft in order to meet the growing need for upskilling of service personnel in the industry. This course has been structured in order to serve the pan-European Data Centre services community.

Development Journey of MyCareerPath.ie

In 2022, Atlantic Technological University (ATU) and Higher Education 4.0 MyCareerPath.ie project established an online career and learning pathways service for people in the workplace wishing to upskill, re-skill or retrain as well as incorporating the assessment of Recognised Prior Learning (RPL). This new innovative mentored online service and platform assists learners to look at their skills, strengths, abilities, and overall self-confidence and acknowledges their significant experiential learning using the Recognition of Prior Learning (RPL), in order to improve their employability, career prospects and engagement in Higher Education.

The overall aim of the project is to enhance employee satisfaction in the workplace, encourage the development of career progression pathways, increased engagement in Higher Education and improved regional output (see Figure 2).

Figure 2: Student Pathways with MyCareerPath.ie

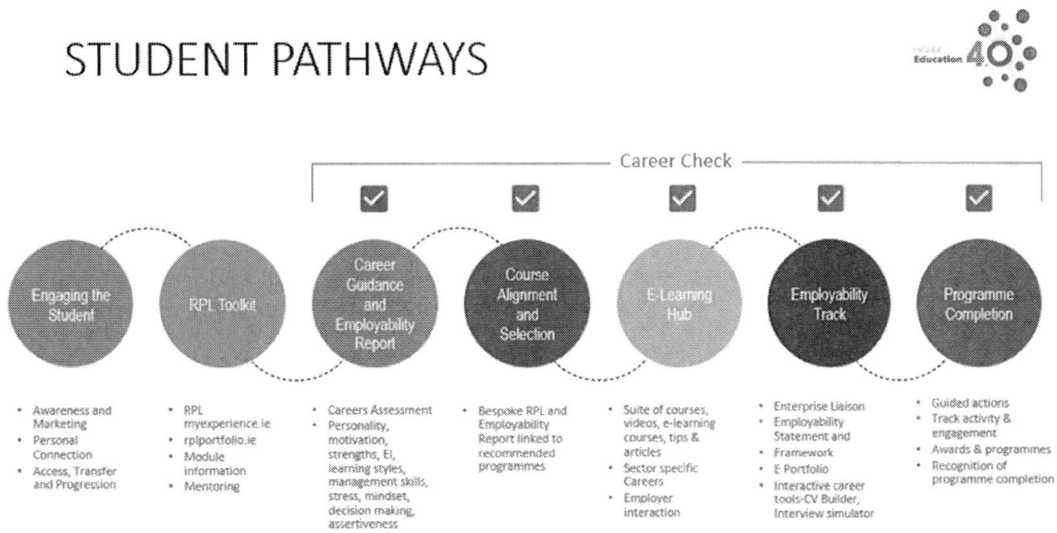

The new ATU career and RPL assessment platform is designed to cater for five student personas, each with their own learning pathway. These student profiles and pathways are:

- Pathway 1: New Beginnings (youth)
- Pathway 2: Career Accelerator (early-career)
- Pathway 3: Mastery Programme (mid-career)
- Pathway 4: Dream Builder (fulfilment)
- Pathway 5: Entrepreneur (innovator)

Online and customised resources have been carefully coordinated and tailored to address the needs of employees at different career stages (see Figure 3).

Figure 3: Customising the needs of employees at each stage of career development

	Who I am?	What I bring?	What I need?	Mycareerpath.ie supports
New Beginnings	Beginner/career starter/first job/first course/returning to education/workplace	Excitement, enthusiasm, energy. Also, confusion and insecurity	Support in understanding myself and my career needs. Confidence and assurance in my career decisions	Personalised career advice. Self-exploration tools. Information and advice on courses, Recognition of Prior Learning (RPL), CVs, applications, work-based learning
Career Accelerator	Graduate (recent or completed degree some time ago), employee with significant experience (needs qualification to progress).	Experience, knowledge and skills. Sense of fulfilment and achievement. Confident, energised and engaged in career activities.	Support in gaining employment or promotion, exploring career directions, finding a postgraduate course.	Personalised career advice. Self-exploration tools. Information and advice on courses, Recognition of Prior Learning (RPL), CVs, applications, work-based learning.
Career Mastery	Seeking promotion or career advancement, job changer, looking for a new challenge	Substantial experience, knowledge and skills. Looking forward to a new challenge.	Specialised training and development, support in gaining promotion or changing job, redefine career direction. Consolidate experience, knowledge and skills.	Personalised career advice. Self-exploration tools. Information and advice on courses, Recognition of Prior Learning (RPL), CVs, applications, work-based learning.
Dream Builder	Considerable achievements in my life and/or career. Now looking to pursue my passions.	Significant experience, knowledge and skills. Self-understanding and self-efficacy, passion for subject knowledge.	Acknowledge achievements, strengths and passions. Redefine personal and career needs. Change of scene. Consolidate experience, knowledge and skills.	Personalised career advice. Self-exploration tools. Information and advice on courses, Recognition of Prior Learning (RPL), CVs, applications, work-based learning.
Entrepreneur	An ideas person, innovator, dynamic, creative, interested in business, problem-solver.	Passionate, energetic, visionary, risk -taker, creative and innovative.	Understand self-employment and business needs. Access to information on training and development requirements, relevant networks and supports	Personalised career advice. Self-exploration tools. Information and advice on courses, Recognition of Prior Learning (RPL), CVs, applications, work-based learning.

We measure the learners' employability both at the beginning and at the end of their learning pathway and incorporate actions on how to enhance the 5 key areas of employability. The employability model that underpins the MyCareerPath.ie AI (artificial intelligence) assessment is based on the CareerEDGE model, developed by Darce, Pool and Sewell (2007) from the University of Central Lancashire. They believe that learners in possession of heightened self-confidence, self-efficacy and self-esteem are more likely to adopt active and independent learning strategies, to be confident in their career and life decision making and to develop skills and attributes that employers seek. Five critical elements are identified (see Figure 4) that need to be addressed for employees to be both satisfied and successful in their occupations.

- Career Development Learning (Self-awareness, decision-making)
- Experience (Work and Life)
- Degree Subject Knowledge, Understanding & Skills
- Generic Skills
- Emotional and Cultural Intelligence (Self-Confidence, Self-Esteem)

Each component in the model is essential and if one is missing this greatly reduces the learner's employability. The model of development for a learner's employability skills has a long-standing impact on people's careers as it ensures lifelong and sustainable employability. The learners engaging with MyCareerPath.ie platform have support in reflecting on and evaluating their development in the five key areas, which leads to enhanced self-efficacy, self-esteem and self-confidence and greater prospects for employability.

Figure 4: Employability Model from Darce, Pool & Sewell (2007)

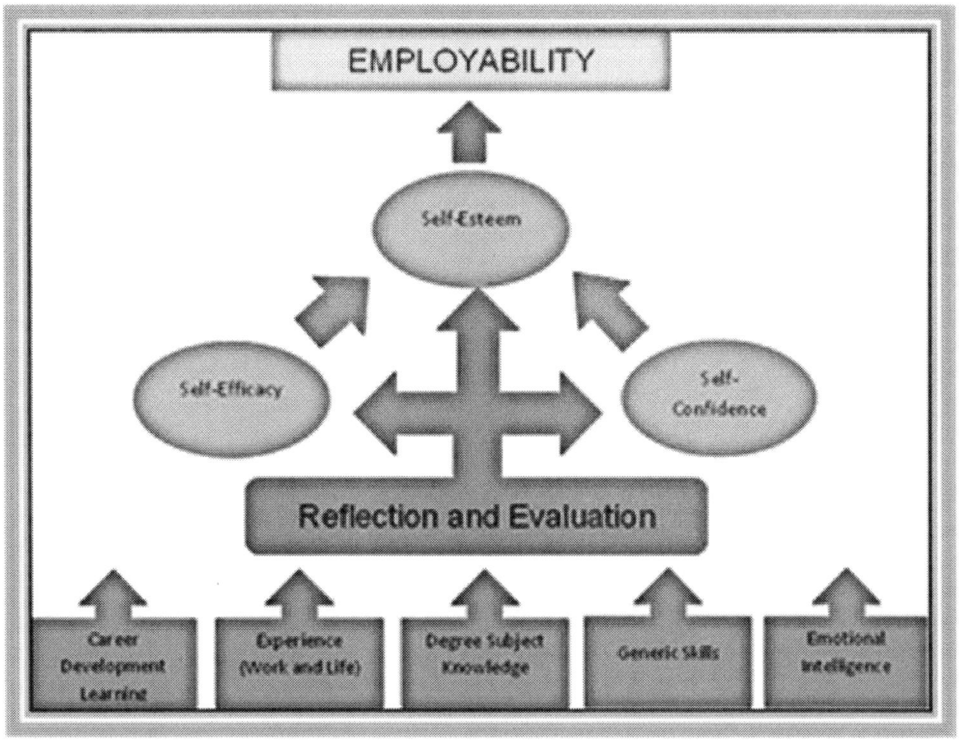

All Learners are brought through a 4-stage developmental programme with the help of the most up to-date e-learning tools and assessments as well as support from Careers and Learning Pathways Advisers (CLPAs) and RPL Co-Ordinators (see Figure 5). Each Learning Pathway incorporates a process of self-discovery leading to the development of successful career plans as learners reflect and focus on their career goals as they proceed through the programmes

The materials provided offer access to an innovative platform with customised eLearning content, psychometric assessment tools, a relevant structure and support for navigation of the current RPL process which will help in the identification of suitable courses. An RPL portfolio of evidence pathway was developed by the CLPA's and RPL Co-Ordinators using the AI online tools on the platform, including a skills extractor feature, which looks at matching skills from the workplace to the curriculum learning outcome.

Figure 5: Careers and Learning Pathways 4 Stage Developmental Programme

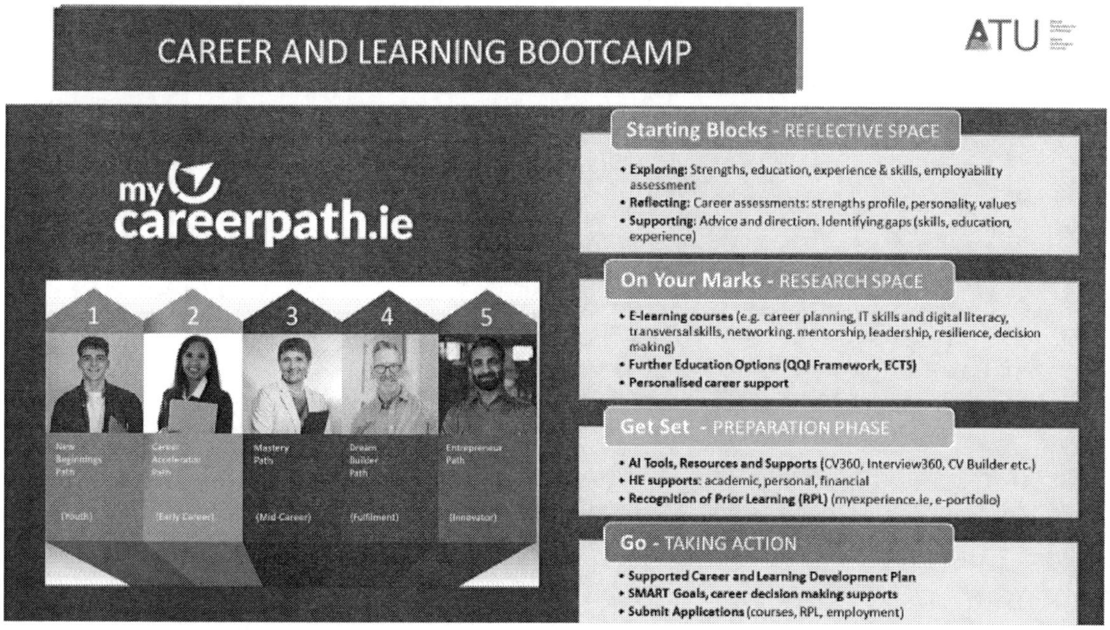

Developing Recognition of Prior Learning in Ireland

A national RPL project is underway in collaboration with THEA (Technological University Higher Education Association in Ireland) and the IUA (Irish Universities Association), also funded by the HEA in Ireland under HCI funding and this project is developing in parallel to the HE 4.0 My Career and Learning Pathway and RPL Assessment Portfolio Tool. Outputs from the RPL national project are feeding into the ATU RPL and career and learning pathway plans. This includes an ATU RPL experience survey, focus groups and an RPL action plan that involves consultations with all stakeholders across the university.

This project strategically aligns at regional, national, and international levels where career and learning pathways development and RPL are important elements of EU policy for widening access to further and higher education and supporting lifelong learning. Results from the European Union (EU) labour force survey (Eurostat, 2021) show that since 2010, the participation rate of adults in lifelong learning rose gradually until 2019, from 7.8 % to 10.8 %. However, in 2020, it dropped by 1.6 percentage point reaching 9.2 % (Eurostat, 2021). Latest EU reports indicate it is on the rise again.

Challenges with RPL and Life-Long Learning Participation

There are several challenges associated with the development of recognition of prior learning practices in the higher education sector. To begin, historically there is an emphasis on the school leaver (high school) cohort pathway to higher education through the traditional leaving certificate state exam. There is a lack of awareness among the general population on RPL pathways and opportunities. In addition, some universities in Ireland are not as active in promoting RPL pathways and there can be little knowledge among educators on how to manage and assess RPL candidates. As a result, there is a fear factor around assessing experiential learning. On the learner challenges, many are unsure how to build a portfolio and structure evidence of recognised learning. Most of all, RPL candidates need guidance on mapping experiential learning experiences to learning outcomes on the national qualifications award standards.

The adult participation in learning was one of the benchmarks of the strategic framework for European cooperation in education and training up to 2020, called "Education and Training 2020" (ET 2020). This benchmark aimed to attain an average of at least 15% of adults participating in lifelong learning in the EU. The participation rates in nearly all Member States increased steadily between 2010 and 2019. This trend reversed between 2019 and 2020 as only three Member States showed a small increase in this period: Spain (+0.4 percentage point), Greece and Lithuania (+0.2 percentage point for both). In Ireland, lifelong learning participation currently lags behind the European average with a participation rate of approximately 6% to 7%. The EU set a target of 15% of adults in Lifelong Learning by 2020. Ireland plans to reach 15% by 2025 (Aontas, 2019).

This HCI funded project output MyCareerPath.ie learning pathway and RPL assessment platform, aims to address the RPL challenges in the sector and to increase participation in lifelong learning in the west and north-west region of Ireland. Through engagement with the MyCareerPath.ie learning pathways, staff training digital badges on Understanding RPL and Assessing RPL, learner RPL portfolio training, and a competency based RPL assessment framework that is aligned with the NFQ in Ireland, will help address the challenges in the sector.

MyCareerPath.ie Impact Case-Study: MEDTRONIC

In 2022 Medtronic in Galway engaged with a pilot programme with ATU MyCareerPath.ie team. The pilot involved mapping a suite of Learning Pathways including Career Guidance & Recognition of Prior Learning (RPL) with Medtronic employees in Galway. This following section of this paper (see Figure 6) will present a summary of the pilot process and the impact on the pilot participants.

Case Study Keywords: Upskilling, Assessment, Career Learning Pathways, eLearning Hub, RPL Toolkit, Career Guidance, Employability, ATU Courses, Career Learning Development Plan, CPD, Skills Development, Mentoring.

Figure 6: Medtronic Pilot Experience (what we did and the output from the process)

WHAT WE DID

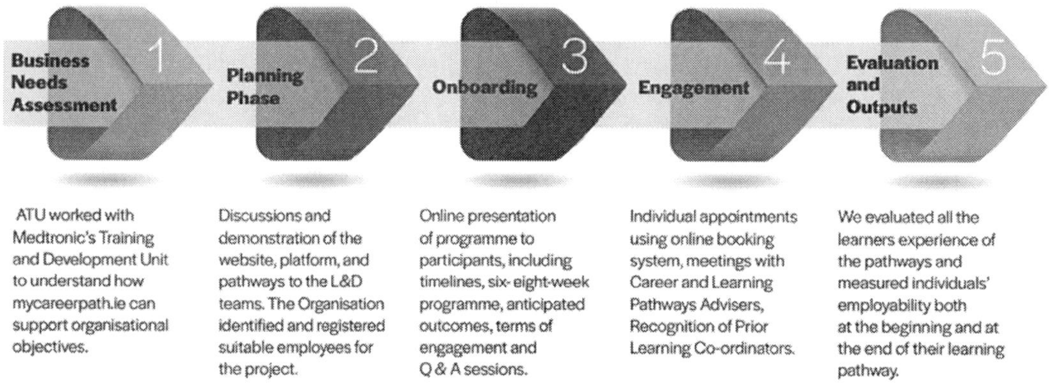

OUTPUT FROM THE PROCESS

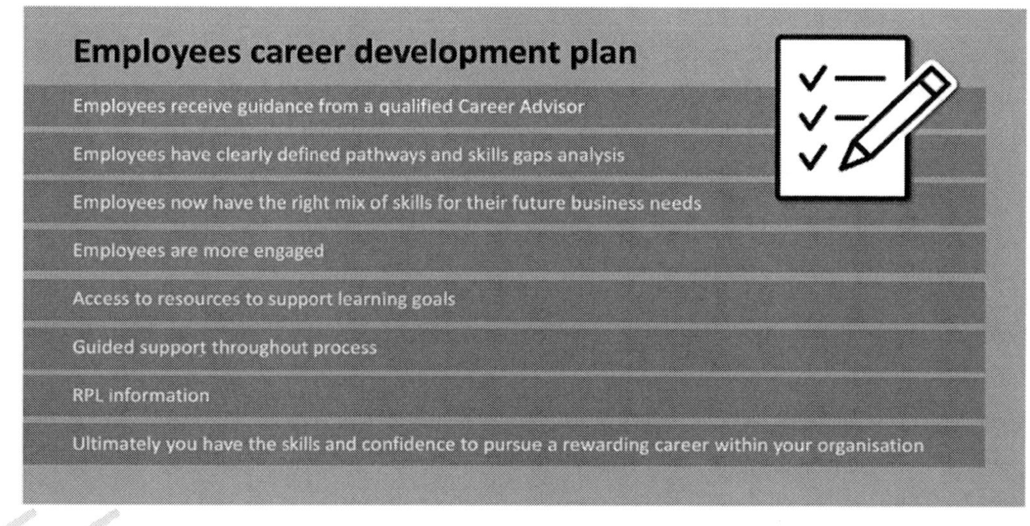

Conclusion, why RPL needs multiple voices

Working in collaboration with higher education partners in Ireland and internationally has enabled change and transformation in how we manage RPL (see Figure 7). Change agent partners in Ireland including ATU and SETU (South-East Technological University), in the US the State University of New York (SUNY) and CAEL, and in Canada Thomson Rivers University (TRU), have delivered multiple opportunities and benefits to all involved. In addition, national higher education development organisations such as THEA and the IUA and the RPL national funded project (see www.priorlearning.ie) is influencing policy development in RPL, a shared RPL framework and a need to create accessible pathways into higher education.

Since establishing the MyExperience.ie RPL project back in 2012, change and enhancements have been driven through partnership, collaboration and the need to involve multiple voices in building access opportunities into Higher Education through RPL. In particular, ATU has learned from SUNY and TRU, on how the assessment process can be structured and made inclusive to all learners. Through examining the value of competency based assessment rubrics and competency based portfolios of evidence, this is challenging ATU to develop new modes of assessing RPL and ensuring alignment with the National Framework of Qualifications award standards in Ireland.

Furthermore, there is a need to expand the range of learning and training resources to support RPL candidates. In response to this, ATU launched the MyCareerPath.ie platform in April 2022, and more than 254 industry learners have completed their career and learning pathway on www.mycareerpath.ie (as at November 2022). From May to November 2022, the learners have logged in to the learning platform a total of 5,335 times and have completed 26,368 activities as part of their career and learning pathway. A further, five specific industries, ranging from MedTech, ICT, Business and Tourism within the region, are also engaging with the new ATU platform.

Overall, the feedback from RPL candidates engaging with the platform has been very positive with learners expressing that it has given them the confidence to take the next step in their career and they have learnt a lot about themselves during this process. What's striking is how learners have all mentioned how much the pathways have helped their self-confidence and how they are now considering educational opportunities they would never have considered before. In addition, the process and case studies are informing enhancements to the ATU's RPL assessment process, policies and access to higher education initiatives.

Figure 7: ATU & Partners Driving Enhancement in RPL Experiences

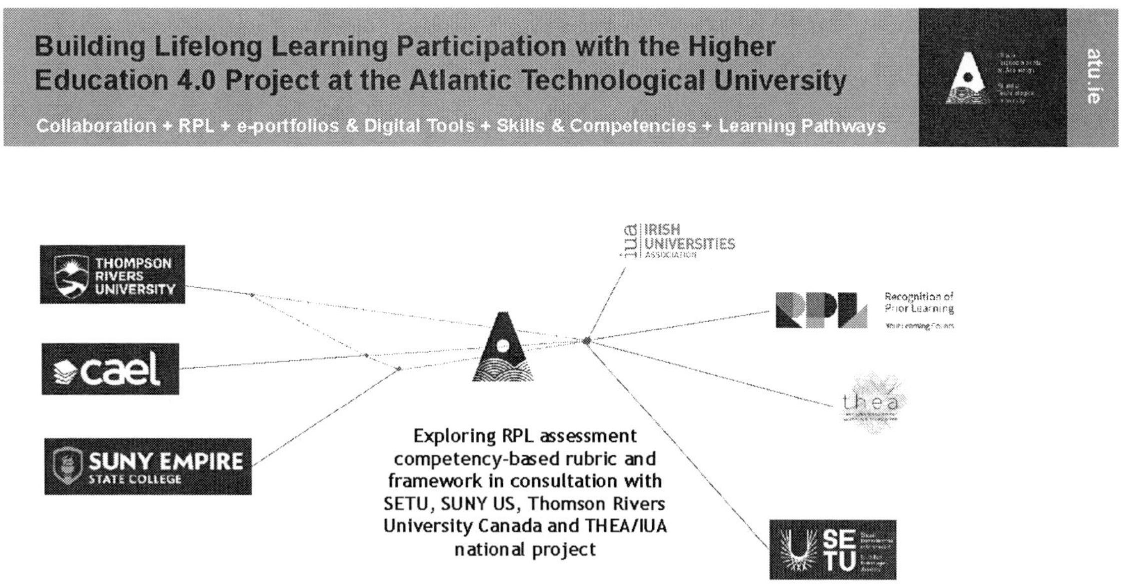

References

Cedefop (2015). European guidelines for validating non-formal and informal learning. Access at http://www.cedefop.europa.eu/en/publications-and-resources/publications/3073

Dacre, Pool, L., & Sewell, P. (2007). The key to employability: developing a practical model of graduate employability. Education and Training, 49(4), 227-289 http://clok.uclan.ac.uk/8347/1/Dacre_Pool__Sewell_2007_CareerEDGE_Article.pdf

Dept. Education and Skills (2011). National Strategy for Higher Education 2030. Available to access at https://hea.ie/assets/uploads/2017/06/National-Strategy-for-Higher-Education-2030.pdf

European Commission; Cedefop; ICF International (2014). European inventory on validation of non-formal and informal learning 2014. Final synthesis report available at http://libserver.cedefop.europa.eu/vetelib/2014/87244.pdf

National Forum (2015). A Current Overview of Recognition of Prior Learning (RPL) in Irish Higher Education. Full report available at A Current Overview of Recognition of Prior Learning (RPL) in Irish Higher Education – National Resource Hub (teachingandlearning.ie)

Useful links

https://atu.ie
https://www.myexperience.ie/
https://MyCareerPath.ie
Glossary:Lifelong learning (LLL) - Statistics Explained (europa.eu) and
https://ec.europa.eu/eurostat/statistics-explained/index.php?title=Glossary:Lifelong_learning_(LLL)
https://www.tru.ca/distance/plar-ol/plar-sample/plar-sample-1.html
https://www.cael.org/what-we-do/credit-predictor-pro

The MyCareerPath platform can be accessed at www.mycareerpath.ie
An ATU RPL information site can be accessed at www.myexperience.ie
Information on the HigherEd 4.0 HCI themes is available at www.highered4.ie

SUPPORTING THE MOVE TO POST-PANDEMIC BLENDED TEACHING: REFLECTIONS ON A PROFESSIONAL LEARNING SHORT COURSE

Greig Krull, University of the Witwatersrand, South Africa

Fiona MacAlister, University of the Witwatersrand, South Africa

Correspondence: *Greig Krull: greig.krull@wits.ac.za*

Abstract

Emerging from the COVID-19 pandemic meant that universities had to reconsider ways of teaching. However, academics and students in South African higher education are still dealing with lingering challenges from the pandemic and are largely unfamiliar with good practices in blended learning and teaching. As learning and teaching support professionals working with academics in a specific faculty, our challenge was to consider how to best support academics to (re)design their courses, aligned to an institutional shift. The purpose of this case study is to critically reflect on the design and offering of a professional learning short course, within a specific faculty, to assist academics in adapting to blended teaching. The research objective is to determine how the professional learning course could support the needs of academics in moving to post-pandemic blended teaching. The paper makes use of a qualitative reflective approach, consisting of the reflections of two faculty learning and teaching support staff and evaluation data from academic staff participants. The paper argues that i) a contextualized and responsive approach to academic professional learning is required to better support academics in embedding different forms of learning and teaching; and ii) that academics require dedicated time and space for course (re)design.

Keywords:

blended learning, academic development, micro-course, curriculum development.

Introduction

The COVID-19 pandemic had a major impact on higher education, including how learning and teaching support is provided to academics. However, prior to the pandemic, not many academics in South African universities had integrated technologies into their learning and teaching. Moving beyond the pandemic, the challenge facing learning and teaching support professionals is which professional learning approaches to adopt to best support academics in moving to blended teaching. Adopting a reflective and reflexive approach, this study considers the perspectives of two support staff in designing and offering a blended mode short course for academics in a specific faculty and the feedback from staff who have completed the course. The paper first contextualises the research, then sets out the research aim and questions. This is followed by a brief review of relevant literature and a discussion of the research design. We then provide the research findings and conclusion.

Background and Contextualisation

The two researchers in this study work in the Faculty of Commerce, Law and Management's Teaching and Learning Unit at a contact university in South Africa. The university, like many others, had to transition to Emergency Remote Learning and Teaching (ERTL) (Hodges et al., 2020) in 2020. Even before the pandemic, the University's five-year teaching strategy (2020-2024) emphasised the need for a blended learning and teaching approach, characterised by increased flexibility. This strategy also emphasises the need to enhance academics as university teachers, strengthen the institutional capacity for curriculum development and renewal, and diversify assessment methods (Wits University, 2019). Furthermore, the 2022 operational plan for this strategy called for the implementation of blended approaches as a new default mode for learning and teaching going forward (Wits University, 2021). Yet, this is an area that is still unfamiliar to many academic staff and students, with many being unaware of good practices. Therefore, professional learning approaches are required that support academics to design or redesign their courses for a blended mode.

The "Introduction to Blended Course Design" short course for academics was designed in 2021 and offered in January 2022, February 2022, March 2022 and July 2022. The facilitators aim to offer the course before the start of each semester. The course is a part-time course that consists of 30 notional study hours and takes place over three weeks. Each cohort consists of 10-20 participants, with two co-facilitators. Key resources that influenced the design of the course were from Bates (2019), Cleveland-Innes and Wilton (2018) and Joosten et al. (2021).

Research Aim and Objective

The purpose of this case study is to critically reflect on the design and offering of a professional learning course to assist academics in adapting to blended learning and teaching. This is part of the authors' role of within faculty teaching and learning unit that offers support services to academics through short courses, webinars, workshops and consultative support around learning, teaching and assessment. The research objective is to determine how the professional learning course could support the needs of academics in moving to post-pandemic blended teaching.

Literature Review

This section provides a review of the literature related to curriculum development in higher education, course planning for academic professional learning, and the move to blended learning and teaching. These aspects informed the design and facilitation of the short course.

Curriculum Development and Change

Emphasising the importance of context, Cornbleth (1988) states that "[c]ontext situates and shapes curriculum; thus, changing a curriculum involves changing its context" (p. 91). Lindén et al. (2017) point out the fundamental purpose of curriculum should be to consider "what is learned and how it is learned" (p. 138). While considering the contextual transition to blended learning and teaching, the initial curriculum focus may be on the "how?" in making decisions about what it taught face-to-face and what is taught online. However, this may raise broader questions for academics about what they teach in specific courses. Bens et al. (2021) characterise the role of academic developers as supporting academics in higher education as facilitators and change agents for curriculum development. The design and offering of a blended course for academics not only requires decisions around and how to teach for the course itself, and the alignment to contextual needs, but also requires considerations of how it may affect the decisions of academics in changing their own curricula. This implies awareness of the sociocultural influences (Cornbleth, 1988) enabling and constraining academic agency.

Academic Professional Learning

Academic developers focus on providing holistic support to academics around learning and teaching matters in a joint enterprise (Sutherland, 2018). The COVID-19 pandemic had a major impact on higher education, including how those in academic professional learning (academic development) provided support to academics (Kuntz et al., 2022; Stanton & Young, 2022). Professional learning support interventions had to be available to academics in a timely and responsive virtual mode (Kuntz et al., 2022). In the researchers' institution, this mainly took the form of synchronous webinars, supplemented with resources on a faculty support course site (Krull & MacAlister, 2022) aligned to centralised support services. However, not all academics participated across the different webinars and going into depth about theories, pedagogies and technologies is constrained in a webinar format.

Stanton & Young (2022) propose that academic developers must act with care and promote self-reflection and empathy to be responsive and facilitative. Considerations need to be made about which professional learning approaches to adopt to best support academics in moving to blended teaching. Bens et al. (2021) advise on the importance of academic development being dialogic and flexible and adapting to emerging conditions, while Evans et al. (2020) promote providing appropriate support and "hands-on" modelling. Curriculum decisions have to be made around offering face-to-face, online or blended options as well as interventions of differing lengths (seminars, workshops or short courses). A course could promote deeper understanding and more opportunities for the sharing of good practices when compared to shorter forms of academic development, such as workshops and webinars. A course may also provide more opportunities for academics as participants to share good practices and insights across disciplines (Kuntz et al., 2022). However, for academics dealing with multiple identities and pressures (Sutherland, 2018), some may not be willing to participate in a course or have the time to dedicate to a course.

Moving to Blended Learning and Teaching

Alammary et al. (2014, p. 443) define a blended course as a course that "[t]houghtfully integrates different instructional methods and contains both F2F and computer-mediated components". Joosten et al. (2021) advocate for blended learning to be thoughtfully and strategically designed "to create meaningful connectedness across distance through active learning pedagogies" (p. 5) that results in "high-quality blended learning experiences for students" (p. 8). Bates (2019) argues that educational institutions can support the development of the knowledge and skills required to teach in a digital age by ensuring there is adequate training and support for academics and there is an institutional strategy that guides these approaches. Academics need to review their current courses and make curriculum decisions around choices of modes, learning and teaching strategies and assessments, as well as consider the experiences of their students. However, moving to blended teaching requires considered use of various learning technologies (CHE, 2014) and can result in academics being overwhelmed by the options and choices. Additionally, academics also need to consider the different theories of learning and different teaching methods and pedagogies (Bates, 2019; Evans et al., 2020). Previous research has shown the effectiveness of providing professional learning around becoming an online teacher in a blended mode (Evans et al., 2020).

Research Design

A case study is suited to understanding unique programmes or offerings in specific settings to establish what happened (Yin, 2009). A case study approach was used to consider what happened (the experiences of facilitators and participants) during each offering of the course to determine whether support needs were perceived to have been met (Yin, 2009). Olsson & Roxa (2012) discuss how observations of learning and teaching, together with reflecting on these, could reveal new possibilities. This case study made use of reflective methods. Olsson & Roxa (2012) highlight Schon's different types of reflection which were used to guide the reflections in this study: reflection-in-action, reflection-on-action, and reflection-for action. Reflection-in-action takes place in the midst of teaching practice, while reflection-on-action takes place during observations and draws upon theoretical knowledge. Reflection-for-action is linked to planning pedagogical practice.

Ethical permission for the study was obtained from the University's Human Research Ethics Committee (Non-Medical). All data collected was treated confidentially and all information collected is securely stored, and only accessible by the researchers. Qualitative data was collected from the course designers/facilitators and participants. The two co-facilitators met to discuss their experiences of designing the course, demonstrating reflection-for-action. Participant reflections were collected via an anonymous online evaluation form while the facilitators held a reflective meeting at the end of each cohort. This demonstrated reflection-in-action and reflection-on-action, with the aim of continuous improvement. Participants provided evaluations at the end of each cohort: 10 evaluations from 15 participants (Cohort 1), six evaluations from 15 participants (Cohort 2), three evaluations from 11 participants (Cohort 3) and three evaluations from nine participants (Cohort 4). The reflective data was analysed using inductive thematic analysis. Thematic analysis involves considering the perspectives and interpretations of the reflections through "sets of techniques used to analyse textual data and elucidate themes" (Vaismoradi et al., 2016, p. 100). Data was coded and grouped under potential categories or themes to enable comparisons (Vaismoradi et al., 2016).

Findings and Discussion

This section discusses the themes that emerged from the designer/facilitator reflections and the participant evaluation feedback. Five key themes emerged. The first two themes relate to the principles that affected the design and offering of the course, while the next three themes focused on the facilitation and ongoing redesign of the course.

Adopting a Responsive and Reflective Approach

An important principle for the course design was to model blended teaching and course design practices to participants. A framework underpinning the unit's work with academics is an ethic of care (Noddings, 1988). Table 1 provides an overview of the structure of the course. Due to COVID-19 restrictions, the initial cohorts were offered fully online, but Cohort 4 was offered in a blended mode (with weekly face-to-face synchronous sessions) to model good blended learning and teaching practices. Several participants commented on the value of changing how they could approach synchronous sessions with their students. For example, "I found the synchronous sessions the most valuable as this allowed for a more interactive space" (Participant 02-Cohort3).

Table 1: Overview of the Course Structure

Unit	Overview
Introduction to Blended Learning	(i) Different modes of delivery, (ii) Asynchronous vs synchronous learning, (iii) Benefits and challenges of blended learning, (iv) Blended teaching methods
Introduction to Blended Learning Models and Principles	(i) Blended learning frameworks (e.g., Community of Inquiry), (ii) Approaches to blended learning (e.g., flipped classroom), (iii) Design principles for blended learning
Introduction to Blended Course Design and Tools	(i) Tools for blended teaching, (ii) Supporting students, (iii) Using the ADDIE model, (iv) Design a blended course blueprint

Another key design principle was to take a responsive approach to the needs of academics (Noddings, 1988) through discussions of their needs during the course as well as through the course evaluation survey. Based on earlier discussions with academics, the designers felt a key outcome was to ensure a common basis for terminology around "blended" and the introduction of models, principles and tools that could be utilised in the course (re)design process. The reflective component was yet another design principle. This is emphasised in how learning does not take place unless there is reflection and action taken (Gibbs, 1988). A weekly reflection activity was the final learning activity for each unit. Several participants commented on the value of this approach. For example: "It allowed one to reflect and put your thoughts down in writing. It provided for conversation and learning" (Participant 03-Cohort3).

Adopting an Ungrading Approach

A further key principle adopted for this course was to focus on facilitators giving feedback and participants interacting with this feedback for future learning. The facilitators gave constructive feedback to the learning activities as they took place during a unit and participants could choose to redo any of the learning activities based on this feedback. A participant noted that the most useful aspect of the course was the "feedback provided on each one of my reflections. It [provided] me with good constructive feedback and some additional things to consider. I found this very useful as this is where my real learning took place" (Participant 05-Cohort1). Participants were also encouraged to share and give feedback to other participants, enabling the sharing of insights and ideas (Kuntz et al., 2022). Initially, a percentage grade and summary feedback were provided for each learning activity at the end of each unit, but from the third cohort, this was changed to competency-based learning (Bates, 2019) aligned to an ungrading approach to assessment (Stommel, 2018). This became an additional design principle that participants could look to adopt in their own teaching practices.

Promoting Continuous Improvement

Bens et al. (2021) call for an approach that enables continuous improvement in curriculum development and review. The facilitators met after each cohort to reflect on their own and participant feedback with a view to improvements needed. This led to small changes taking place each time the course is offered, such as increasing the variety of learning activities. One key aspect was the timing of the course. While the aim was to offer the course before a semester started, this was not always possible, leading to some participants struggling with their workload or not completing the course: "It was great for me that this course took place during the semester break, yet, it is hard to balance with work demands" (Participant 01-Cohort 4). The course has a 57% average completion rate, which is an area that needs improvement.

Importantly, relevance of the context in which learning and teaching takes place needs to remain a priority. The initial design of the course made use of several YouTube videos to illustrate various blended learning and teaching theories and practices. However, the aim is to slowly replace these with local examples from the university. Several interviews have taken place with academics about how they have adopted various blended teaching practices and these recordings have been embedded into the course.

Evaluating the Course Impacts

As noted earlier, participants are invited to complete an anonymous evaluation form at the end of each cohort and this feedback is utilised to ensure that the course remains fit-for-purpose. These evaluations have generally been very positive about the course. For example, one participant noted:

> *"The course exceeded my expectations. I learned so much during this course and the way it was structured and planned out was great. I enjoyed the fact that it required engagement and for me to spend time doing self-reflections and taking part in discussions." (Participant 01-Cohort 1)*

Another participant highlighted the need for sharing these learnings to facilitate broader change: "I will hold a roundtable discussion in my [department] to discuss how we can improve utilising [...] the various presences" (Participant 03-Cohort3). However, there is a need to still implement a mechanism to evaluate the longer-term impact of the course and the extent of any changes to learning and teaching practices and course (re)design approaches in the faculty. Future research could also look at the perspectives of students.

Future Support for Transitioning to Blended Teaching

Any professional learning initiative must consider the multiple identities, tensions, and commitments that academics must deal with and the need for a reflective lens and caring approach (Sutherland, 2018; Stanton & Young, 2022). Feedback received from academics indicated that the time to redesign their courses is minimal given their workload responsibilities, including teaching and supervision duties, research and administrative functions. A frequent complaint by academics is that there is insufficient time available to implement some of the ideal practices discussed in the course. Therefore, a course such as this one is only one aspect of a holistic support strategy needed for academics to successfully transition to blended learning and teaching. Another mechanism being piloted in the faculty as part of such a support strategy is the use of course design retreats for academics (similar to research writing retreats), where academics spend a few days focused on making changes to their courses.

Conclusion

Stanton and Young (2022) argue that the effectiveness of the work of academic developers is dependent on both the approaches or ways of working and the actions taken (the opportunities provided to academics). The purpose of this study was to critically reflect on the design and offering of a responsive professional learning course, within a specific faculty, to assist academics in adapting to post-pandemic blended learning and teaching. The research objective was to determine how a professional learning course could support the needs of academics in moving to blended teaching. Reflective data was collected from the course designers/facilitators and participant evaluations. The findings indicate that the course has broadly achieved the objective of supporting staff to transition to blended learning and teaching in a specific context, although longer term impacts still need to be considered. The focus of being responsive to participants' contextual needs, promoting reflection and taking an ungrading approach to assessment have supported this objective. Adopting a continuous improvement mindset means that redesign is always a focus. The conclusion is that i) a contextualized and responsive approach to academic professional learning is required to better support academics in embedding different forms of learning and teaching; and ii) that academics require time and space to dedicate to course (re)design.

References

Alammary, A., Sheard, J., & Carbone, A. (2014). Blended learning in higher education: Three different design approaches. *Australasian Journal of Educational Technology, 30*(4). https://doi.org/10.14742/ajet.693

Bates, A. W. (2019). *Teaching in a digital age: Guidelines for designing teaching and learning.* (2nd ed.). BCcampus.

Bens, S., Kolomitro, K., & Han, A. (2021). Curriculum development: enabling and limiting factors. *International Journal for Academic Development, 26*(4), 481-485.

Cleveland-Innes, M., & Wilton, D. (2018). *Guide to blended learning*. Commonwealth of Learning. http://oasis.col.org/bitstream/handle/11599/3095/2018_Cleveland-Innes-Wilton_Guide-to-Blended-Learning.pdf

Cornbleth, C. (1988). Curriculum in and out of context. *Journal of Curriculum and Supervision, 3*(2), 85-96.

Evans, J. C., Yip, H., Chan, K., Armatas, C., & Tse, A. (2020). Blended learning in higher education: Professional development in a Hong Kong university. *Higher Education Research & Development, 39*(4), 643-656.

Gibbs, G. (1988). *Learning by Doing: A Guide to Teaching and Learning Methods*. Further Education Unit.

Hodges, C., Moore, S., Lockee, B., Trust, T and Bond, A. (2020). The difference between emergency remote teaching and online learning. Educause Review. https://er.educause.edu/articles/2020/3/the-difference-between-emergency-remote-teaching-and-online-learning

Joosten, T., Weber, N., Baker, M., Schletzbaum, A., & McGuire, A. (2021). *Planning for a Blended Future: A Research-Driven Guide for Educators*. Every Learner Everywhere Network. https://www.everylearnereverywhere.org/resources/

Krull, G. & MacAlister, F. (2022). Rapidly orienting academic staff for emergency remote teaching: responsive approaches for academic professional learning. In U. Singh, C.S. Nair, C. Blewett, & T. Shea. (Eds.) *Academic Voices: A Conversation on New Approaches to Teaching and Learning in the post-COVID World*. (283-294): Elsevier.

Kuntz, A., Davis, S. & Fleming, E. (2022). 7 ways the pandemic changed faculty development. *Educause Review*. https://er.educause.edu/articles/2022/5/7-ways-the-pandemic-changed-faculty-development

Lindén, J., Annala, J. & Coate, K. (2017). The role of curriculum theory in contemporary higher education research and practice, in J. Huisman & M. Tight (eds.) *Theory and Method in Higher Education Research*. (Vol. 3, 137-154): Emerald.

Noddings, N. (1988). An ethic of caring and its implications for instructional arrangements. *American Journal of Education, 96*(2): 215-230.

Olsson, T., & Roxå, T. (2013). Pedagogical competence–a model promoting conceptual change in higher education. *Practice*, 7(8).

Stanton, K., & Young, S. (2022). Academic developers as flexible generalists: responding to COVID-19. *International Journal for Academic Development*, 1-4.

Stommel, J. (2018). How to ungrade. https://www.jessestommel.com/how-to-ungrade/

Sutherland, K. A. (2018). Holistic academic development: Is it time to think more broadly about the academic development project? *International Journal for Academic Development, 23*(4), 261–273.

Vaismoradi, M., Jones, J., Turunen, H., & Snelgrove, S. (2016). Theme development in qualitative content analysis and thematic analysis. *Journal of Nursing Education and Practice, 6*(5).

Wits University. (2019). Wits Learning and Teaching Plan 2020-2024. University of the Witwatersrand.

Wits University. (2021). Learning and Teaching at Wits in 2022. University of the Witwatersrand.

Yin, R. K. (2009). How to do better case studies, in L. Bickman & D. J. Rog (eds.). *The SAGE Handbook of Applied Social Research Methods* (2nd ed., 254–282): SAGE.

ADEQUATE DIGITAL COMPETENCE IN EARLY CHILDHOOD EDUCATION

Davoud Masoumi, University of Gävle, Sweden,

Maryam Bourbour, University of Gävle, Sweden

***Correspondence**: Davoud Masoumi: davoud.masoumi@hig.se*

Abstract

The key questions this study seeks to answer is what adequate digital competence is and how preschool teachers characterise young children's adequate digital competence. A variety of frameworks and models have been developed to exemplify and characterise teacher's digital competences. However, to date, there is hardly any study examining young children's digital competencies in early childhood education. The data were collected through semi-structured interviews with 13 preschool teachers at seven preschools in the centre of Sweden and analysed using qualitative content analysis. The findings of the study show that children's digital competence in early education is an increasingly complex notion which can be characterised by seven key aspects: *To get better understanding and be familiar with digital technologies, To use digital technologies, To have a critical approach toward digital technologies, To have ethical media competences, To have problem-solving skills, To be producers, not just consumers, of digital technologies, and* To *dare trying digital technologies.* This study, further, portrayed the digitally competent preschool teacher's qualifications in order to fulfil preschool teachers' complex task (i.e. educare) in children's learning and development.

Keywords:

Adequate digital competence, young children, early childhood education, preschool teachers, digital technologies

Introduction

The key questions this study seeks to answer is what constitute young children's adequate digital competence in early childhood education. The Swedish national curriculum for preschools addressing the importance of using digital technologies to support children's learning emphasizes that early childhood education should:

> *give children the opportunity to develop adequate digital skills by enabling them to develop an understanding of the digitalization they encounter in everyday life. Children should be given the opportunity to develop a critical, responsible attitude towards digital technology, so that eventually they can see opportunities and understand risks, and also be able to evaluate information (The Swedish National Agency for Education, 2018, p. 10).*

The preschools in Sweden are, accordingly, obliged to develop children's digital competences in an adequate level (The Swedish national curriculum for preschools, 2018). However, there are significant variations in defining what constitutes digital competence in early education. The notion of developing children's "digital competence" in a "adequate" level is rather vague (Olofsson, Fransson, & Lindberg, 2020). The teacher's professional digital competence and its many dimensions have been addressed in a large number of studies and frameworks (see for intance European, Joint Research, Redecker, & Punie, 2017; International Society for Technology in Education (ISTE), 2017; Koehler, Mishra, Akcaoglu, & Rosenberg, 2013; UNESCO, 2018). However, as far as we are aware, there is hardly any framework or study examining young children's digital competences in early childhood education.

Thus, developing children's digital competences mainly depends on preschool teachers' agency (Bourbour, 2020; Johnston, Hadley, & Waniganayake, 2020; Lund, Furberg, & Gudmundsdottir, 2019; Stephen & Plowman, 2008) and the ways they translate the curriculum's educational goals into practices including developing children's digital competences in adequate level, as indicated in Swedish national strategy for the digitalisation, (Government decision 1:1, 2017; Government decision, 2022).

In the same line of thoughts, UNICEF report shows that unskilled and unmotivated preschool teachers are the main barrier in developing children's digital competences (Nascimbeni & Vosloo, 2019). It may signify that the preschool teacher's digital competence and the way they understand and conceptualize the value of technologies in early education inform if and how the children's "adequate digital competence" can be developed. There have been increasing calls, as results, for developing preschool teachers' digital competences (Forsling, 2023; Vidal-Hall, Flewitt, & Wyse, 2020).

The ways preschool teachers integrate digital technologies in their educational practices to develop children's adequate digital competence, further, can be informed by different factors such as policy-makers, technology companies, content providers, and parents (Selwyn, 2011). These actors' diverse expectations and interpretation from digitalization in early childhood education and "adequate digital competence" can add to the complexity of characterising what adequate digital competence is in early education and then conceptualising how preschool teachers professional digital competences can be developed as part of a preschool's digitalisation process (Forsling, 2023). This study addressing a grand challenge in early childhood education, aims to explore how preschool teachers characterise young children's adequate digital competence in early childhood education.

Contextualisation: Adequate digital competence in Swedish early child education

The Swedish preschool is based on a model that internationally labelled as *educare* (education and care). In this model care and teaching are embedded with each other and childhood is not merely regarded as a time of preparation for adulthood but has value in itself (Masoumi, 2021). Informed by socio-cultural perspective, the preschool learning environment mostly structured to actively engage children in the learning activities, to construct and create their own knowledge through interaction with others in a social context (Bourbour, 2020).

The Swedish National Agency for Education (2020) addresses children's digital competence in four focus areas including a) understanding the impact of digitization on society; b) getting familiar and use of digital tools and media; c) having a critical and responsible approach; d) solve problems and turn ideas into action. These focus areas map a continuum of digital competences which can be seen as a part of the notion of digital *Bildung* in Nordics countries in term of "how knowledge, competencies, skills, and attitudes make it possible for us to function as citizens in an increasingly complex society" (Amdam, Kobberstad, & Tikkanen, 2022, p. 18).

Developing children's digital competences, accordingly, seen as ongoing process which goes beyond the children's seemingly use of digital tools (please see Government decision 1:1, 2017; Government decision, 2022). The expression of "adequate digital competence" is therefore used in these documents to highlight that, digital competence as a continuously changing capability that is shaped based on the societies needs and circumstances that children's is located in. This approach also contributes to an understanding of how policy is interpreted, transformed, and enacted (Olofsson et al., 2020).

Data-collection and analysis

A qualitative approach was adopted, and empirical data was collected through Semi-structured interviews with preschool teachers in Gavleborg County, Sweden. To locate preschool teachers, convenience sampling was employed where the participants were chosen because they were belonging to a group of preschool teachers working with digitalization issues in preschools and "known" for their advanced use of digital technology in preschool. The participants in the interviews were recruited by the preschool principles.

The interview guide consisted of 6 open ended questions designed to address what constitute young children's adequate digital competence, how it can be characterised in early education. The interviewed preschool teachers were encouraged providing concrete examples illustrate their answers to the questions. To ensure the credibility and dependability of the study, the developed interview questions were expert-piloted by four experienced teachers. The interviews were conducted by the authors, lasting approximately 45 minutes. Thirteen semi-structured interviews were conducted with preschool teachers. All interviews were recorded and transcribed verbatim.

The transcripts were then analysed through a grounded-theory methods to explore preschool teachers' tacit meanings. An iterative (constant comparative) method was used to identify themes in the interview data (Glaser & Strauss, 1999). In this iterative process, the collected data was analyzed. A thorough analysis of the transcribed interviews initially were conducted inductively and individually by the authors where all meaning units related to characterizing young children's digital competences practices in early childhood education. A brief description or keywords for each theme were created. The initial list of codes was reduced into a set of 13 overarching themes. Through constant comparison, the similar themes merged into categories according to the study's research question. The analysis was facilitated by ATLAS.ti 9 qualitative data analysis software, which helped to ensure a systematic scrutiny of all collected data. The ethical issues were carried out in accordance with Swedish ethical regulations for research (Quennerstedt, Harcourt, & Sargeant, 2014; Vetenskapsrådet, 2011).

Preliminary results

The preschool teachers considered the integration of digital technologies as an artifact that not only mediate their educational practices in preschool but as means to promote equality of educational opportunities among children. All preschool teachers underline the importance of developing children's digital competences as well as the role that using digital technologies can play in learning and developing young children.
A number of the preschool teachers addressing their confusion, put forward that the notion of adequate digital competences is vague. Some addressing the increasing advances in digital technologies, put forwards that "it is hard to define what adequate digital skills is". Such confusions, according to the preschool teachers, have led to discussions in working teams about how they should develop children's digital competence in an adequate level. One of the preschool teachers, addressing such challenges states that "Based on what adequate digital competence is today, we try to update our skills, and maybe what we have today won't be relevant tomorrow..." (Sofia).
Analysis of the collected empirical data reveals seven different facts that characterise young children's digital competences in early childhood education.

- To get better understandings and be familiar with digital technologies,
- To use digital technologies (to operate/use digital technologies in effective way)
- To have a critical approach toward digital technologies
- To have ethical media competences
- To have problem-solving skills
- To be producers, not just consumers, of digital technologies
- To dare trying digital technologies.

*To have a critical and responsible approach to DT (*preliminary results*)*

Developing children's critical understanding about the potential of digital technologies and how these technologies can be used in different means and for different purposes was one of the issues which underlined in the data collected as key part of adequate digital competence. One of the preschool teachers, Mona, put it as "we should develop children's critical and responsibility approach to the digital technologies". Preschool teachers state that children encounter a lot of information in their everyday lives, movies and fantasies. They, thus, underline developing children's skills to critically and responsibly evaluate and use provided information.

> *Children should be provided opportunities to develop understanding of the digitization they encounter in everyday life and where they can have critical and responsible approach to digital technologies (Mona)*

Having a critical approach in early childhood education may means to think about what is genuine and manipulated on the screen. One of the preschool teachers, Annika, addressing this notion notes that:

> *Children can't believe everything either...That's one of the hardest parts, I think...[for instance in a teaching situation] We manipulate pictures that couldn't be true. In a teaching situation I showed a picture showing I stood in the hand of my colleague. In realty, I sat behind her with a certain distance and then the picture is taken. We showed the picture to four years old children saying look how strong I am. It's hard for the children to understand that we miniplate the picture. ....*

As indicated in the excerpt the preschool teachers try to develop children's critical approach to digital technologies through, manipulating of pictures and letting children to explore that what they are seeing on the screen may not be true. By taking examples, the teacher notes that this abstract issue is hard for young children to understand, thus, they need to concretize and exemplify different objects, to create space for children to discover what is true and what is false.

To concretise this issue and to develop children's critical and responsible approach to digital technologies, a majority of the preschool teachers note that they use green screen where they can create and manipulate images and videos. A preschool teacher puts it this way:" ... the children can understand that one can't fly and jump high tower buildings like Superman in reality but they can create such pictures/movies using applications like green screen". Preschool teacher addressing the importance of developing children critical approach to technologies argues that they can discuss with older children about what is sensible or no-sensible on the internet, while with the younger children you need to concertize and exemplify how the pictures and movies can be manipulated.

Discussion (an outline)

The study explores how preschool teachers characterise adequate digital competence in early childhood education. Seven dimensions have been constructed that maps children's digital competence in early educations. Five of the identified dimensions including the "To get better understandings and be familiar with digital technologies, To use digital technologies, To have a critical approach toward digital technologies, To have ethical media competences, and To have problem-solving skills" are aligned with the addressed four areas of digital competence in the Swedish National Agency for Education (2020). The empirical findings, further, identifies three other dimensions including, To be producers, not just consumers of digital technologies, and To dare trying digital technologies.

Preschool teacher's characterisation of children's adequate digital competence shows that the notion of 'adequate' covers a wide spectrum from getting to know to have critical approach to digital technologies. The findings further reflect that children's digital competence is a dynamic and ongoing process which is informed by the socio-technological factors. This leads to variations in how adequate digital competence is interpreted and enacted in preschool pedagogical practices. Addressing children's digital competence as a dynamic and ongoing process has consequences for how to design and conduct educational practices in the early education (Lund et al., 2019; Olofsson et al., 2020).

In characterizing children's digital competence, the preschool teachers, further, highlighted the importance of integrating and combining analog and digital technologies. To develop children's digital competence in early education, thus, preschool teachers need more sophisticated skills where they can use both analog and digital technologies to create a lively learning space.

References

Amdam, S., Kobberstad, L. R., & Tikkanen, T. (2022). Professional digital competence in strategy and management: A case study of three teacher education programs in Norway. *Nordic Journal of Digital Literacy.*

Bourbour, M. (2020). *Digital technologies in preschool teaching: The Interactive Whiteboard interplay with teachers' teaching practices.* (PhD). Örebro university, Örebro.

European, C., Joint Research, C., Redecker, C., & Punie, Y. (2017). *European framework for the digital competence of educators : DigCompEdu*: Publications Office.

Forsling, K. (2023). Collegial Learning and Digital Literacy Education in a Swedish Preschool. *Early Childhood Education Journal, 51*(1), 139-148. doi:10.1007/s10643-021-01289-9

Glaser, B., & Strauss, A. (1999). *Discovery of grounded theory: Strategies for qualitative research.* New York: Routledge.

Government decision 1:1, S. t. G. D. (2017). *Nationell Digitaliseringsstrategi För Skolväsendet [in English: National Digitalisation Strategy for the School System].* Stockholm: The Swedish Ministry of Education

Government decision. (2022). *Förslag till nationell digitaliseringsstrategi för skolväsendet 2023–2027 [in English: National Digitalisation Strategy for the School System: A proposal].* Stockholm: The Swedish Ministry of Education

International Society for Technology in Education (ISTE). (2017). *ISTE Standards for Educators: A guide for teachers and other professionals.* Eugene, Oregon: International Society for Technology in Education.

Johnston, K., Hadley, F., & Waniganayake, M. (2020). Practitioner inquiry as a professional learning strategy to support technology integration in early learning centres: Building understanding through Rogoff's planes of analysis. *Professional Development in Education, 46*(1), 49-64. doi:10.1080/19415257.2019.1647871

Koehler, M. J., Mishra, P., Akcaoglu, M., & Rosenberg, J. (2013). The technological pedagogical content knowledge framework for teachers and teacher educators. In R. Thyagarajan (Ed.), *ICT integrated teacher education: A resource book* (Vol. Retrieved from: http://cemca.org.in/ckfinder/userfiles/files/ICT%20teacher%20education%20Module%201%20Final_May%2020.pdf). New Delhi, India: CEMCA.

Lund, A., Furberg, A., & Gudmundsdottir, G. B. (2019). Expanding and Embedding Digital Literacies: Transformative Agency in Education. *Media and Communication, 7*(2), 47-58. doi:https://doi.org/10.17645/mac.v7i2.1880

Masoumi, D. (2021). Situating ICT in early childhood teacher education. *Education and Information Technologies, 26*(3), 3009-3026. doi:10.1007/s10639-020-10399-7

Nascimbeni, F., & Vosloo, S. (2019). *Digital literacy for children: Exploring definitions.* Retrieved from New York: https://www.unicef.org/globalinsight/media/1271/file/%20UNICEF-Global-Insight-digital-literacy-scoping-paper-2020.pdf

Olofsson, A. D., Fransson, G., & Lindberg, J. O. (2020). A study of the use of digital technology and its conditions with a view to understanding what 'adequate digital competence' may mean in a national policy initiative. *Educational Studies, 46*(6), 727-743. doi:10.1080/03055698.2019.1651694

Quennerstedt, A., Harcourt, D., & Sargeant, J. (2014). Forskningsetik i forskning som involverar barn: Etik som riskhantering och etik som forskningspraktik. *Nordic Studies of Education, 33*(2), 77-93.

Selwyn, N. (2011). *Education and Technology - Key Issues ans Debates.* London: Continuum International Publishing Group.

Stephen, C., & Plowman, L. (2008). Enhancing learning with information and communication technologies in pre-school. *Early Child Development and Care, 178*(6), 637-654. Retrieved from http://dx.doi.org/10.1080/03004430600869571

The Swedish National Agency for Education. (2018). *Curriculum for the Preschool- Lpfö 18.* Stockholm: Swedish National Agency for Education.

UNESCO. (2018). *UNESCO ICT Competency Framework for Teachers.* Retrieved from Paris: https://www.oercommons.org/hubs/UNESCO

Vetenskapsrådet. (2011). *God Forskningssed.* Retrieved from Stockholm:

Vidal-Hall, C., Flewitt, R., & Wyse, D. (2020). Early childhood practitioner beliefs about digital media: integrating technology into a child-centred classroom environment. *European Early Childhood Education Research Journal, 28*(2), 167-181. doi:10.1080/1350293X.2020.1735727

FIVE PRACTICES FOR HIGHLY EFFECTIVE POSTGRADUATE ONLINE COURSE DESIGN

John P Egan, University of Auckland, Aotearoa New Zealand

Correspondence: *John P Egan: j.egan@auckland.ac.nz*

Abstract

In this paper I offer five practices for those making their first, self-directed foray into redesigning a postgraduate course for online delivery. Any of these individually will allow academic staff to create an online learning experience that works better than the COVID19 pivot: taking up all of these largely integrates many of the process elements of our course redesign short course. In lieu of any workshop or short course, bespoke support can be provided iteratively and individually.

Keywords: online learning, postgraduate, practices

As someone who has supported academic development in learning design, pedagogical praxis, and elearning for many years, the pace of change these last three years has been unprecedented. In 2020 many of the world's universities rapidly "pivoted" to remote delivery of teaching, as staff and students were required to isolate at home.

From a public health standpoint, this was the right decision: COVID19, as a novel respiratory virus, presented challenges for our immune systems (which tend to over-react to pathogens it cannot identify, leading to severe illness in many and risking death in those already vulnerable) and our health systems (in order to avoid potential inundation with severely, acutely ill patients). As our understanding of COVID19 rapidly evolved—and as more precise and effective treatments were identified, and vaccines developed and distributed—the need for remote learning has waned. In the regions of the world with high vaccination access and uptake, the combination of previously COVID19 exposure and vaccination means most persons' immune systems can now identify and effectively respond to this virus.

Not online

However, this pivot has erroneously been characterised by some as "online learning". With regards to the platforms and technologies used to deliver teaching and learning during COVID19, this is an accurate description of the *technologies* deployed in many contexts.

But within higher education—and specifically within contexts where courses and degrees have been wholly provisioned online for more than two decades, using particular and purpose learning designs, pedagogical methods and assessment practices—online learning is more relevant as a holistic description rather than a platform of delivery. Even among those of us who had previous experience designing and delivering online courses, what we did with our face-to-face courses in 2020 was still, for the most part, a switch to rapid remote delivery, since it was not feasible to create a comprehensive range of high quality digital collateral, or to redesign entire courses for online delivery in a matter of days.

Characteristics

Rapid remote delivery had several characteristics:

- Migration of existing learning design to online delivery: few or no changes are made to how a course is structured and delivered, in terms of scheduling, activity types, or timelines.
- Repurposing of educational collateral for online delivery: distribute lecture recordings from previous course iterations.
- As if: delivery of learning experiences like lectures, seminars, tutorials, laboratories, and competency-based pedagogies "as if" in person, synchronously.

- Assessment: few or no changes to assessment design, though administration of assessment was entirely digital.

As a just-in-time strategy in early 2020, remote learning was the best tack available to many. However, as the requirement to deliver online persisted into 2021 and 2022, students quickly began to expect more from us. In many instances 2021 commenced with academic staff de-emphasising extant collateral and developing more bespoke content, often multimedia in nature.

Unlearning

The pivot has also fomented a dynamic where staff with little or no exposure to purposively designed online learning—many of whom who were sceptical about online learning prior to COVID19—saw some positive elements of the pivot to remote learning. These well-intentioned colleagues endeavoured to integrate such elements into their post-COVID19 courses—and academic practice: some also expressed an interest in moving one or more of their courses permanently online. There was potential for an unintended curricular crisis: many individual course teams concurrently redesigning courses within a programme, with varying levels of expertise or support, and students receiving an inferior experience.

As an academic leader of a faculty-specific educational services unit at a large, research-intensive university, my team and I identified a need to provide staff development opportunities around course redesign. A significant aspect of this work has been facilitating an unlearning process, in particular ceasing with some of the 2020/2021 just-in-time practices.

In this paper I offer five practices for colleagues making their first, self-directed foray into redesigning a postgraduate course for online delivery. Any of these individually will allow academic staff to create an online learning experience that works better than the COVID19 pivot. Taking up all of these largely integrates many of the process elements of our extant course redesign short course. In lieu of any workshop or short course, bespoke support can be provided iteratively and individually.

Although many of these have applicability to undergraduate education, these recommendations are calibrated towards the sorts of specialist knowledge emphasised in the postgraduate space.

Read less; think, reflect and interact more

For many academic staff, teaching wholly online for the first time, the lack of any quantified "contact time" can be daunting: one does not realise how cognitively significant we view lecture or tutorial time until it is taken away from us. Unfortunately, some colleagues' instinct is either to try delivering the existing session synchronously, or to overcompensate by providing a plethora of content—usually reading materials, but also multimedia collateral.

The synchronous option can work for relatively short (60 or fewer minutes) sessions, but screen time can be exhausting for 180 minutes (a typical length of postgraduate seminar at our university). In general, a lecture can work well: facilitating collaborative learning can be more challenging.

In terms of a surfeit of reading material, rather than compensate for the loss of contact time this increases student anxieties related to workload. Many students will surface read, selectively read, or give up on reading at all.

Instead, we recommend having a well written lesson or unit, supported with one or two key readings. The lesson should include an interactive asynchronous discussion designed to unpack or apply key concepts.

Examples: Scenario-based learning, including case-base, problem-based, and inquiry-based learning, allows students to analyse and synthesise the course materials well. If this is an approach you want to use multiple times, scenarios' complexity and nuance can deepen over the length of the course. Academic staff posting a synthesis message at the end of each unit's discussion gives them an opportunity highlight the key takeaways and transition to the next lesson or unit.

Assess early, particularly academic writing.

One strong predictor of academic success for postgraduate students—regardless of discipline or programme—is the ability to write a compelling, articulate, and literature-informed argument. While it often makes good sense for major written assessments to be due from the course midpoint or thereafter (in order for students to benefit from the course itself), this leaves a relatively narrow window for remediation with students whose writing deficiencies present a substantive barrier to postgraduate study success.

Having a small-yet-substantive written assessment due by the end of the second or third week obviates many of these challenges. For students whose writing is problematic, offer to meet with them to discuss how they can improve their subsequent written work. Matters of grammar, usage, syntax, style, punctuation, or other aspects of writing quality can be identified and presented to them as a task list, ideally with five or fewer items.

If a student successfully works to remediate these in their subsequent assessments, they can be guaranteed an agreed minimum grade (often a B) if they meet the other requirements of each assessment. This approach can detoxify and make manageable the amelioration process of "bad writing" from the amorphous and into the concrete.

At the end of the course you can indicate if there are other writing issues for them to work on beyond those in the initial task list. As the student now has experience with writing development as a process, they should be ready to self-regulate their own writing competency development with the next task list you have given them. Subsequently they can conduct their own self-reflection (Schön, 1983) of their writing, including collation, enumeration, amelioration—and repetition, as their writing improves.

Examples: reflective flight path (course-specific goal identification), reading response, essay or project proposal.

Leverage structured, quasi-synchronous discussion forums

Many students (and staff) presume online learning is wholly asynchronous and flexible: in practice, it rarely can be. Interactivity in your course will not cohere if students are encouraged to work through an online course entirely at their own pace and sequencing. Rather than a course-based cohort of learners, it becomes a collective of wholly self-directed learners, which can be isolating for them.

Despite the integration of rich multimedia and the availability of synchronous virtual classroom and web conferencing software, learning management system discussion forums often remain the heart of online learning: it is important to scaffold and sequence them accordingly. In terms of course structure, have a set of thematic modules works well. Within a module there might be one, two or three weeks, each with its own unit or lesson. Give the students access to all the units in a module when the module opens: in a three week module this gives them 21 days to structure when they make their initial postings. That also gives them ample time to check in with others' contributions and to comment accordingly, with a great deal of flexibility. This is what is meant by quasi-synchronous.

Discussion forums need not require students to write mini essays, which can be labourious (to craft and to read) and crush interactivity through formality: students can do that sort of writing in their assessments. Instead, interactivity should be the focus. Encourage students to write "as if" in a seminar or tutorial discussion, using collegial, professional language to engage with the topic, rather than striving to quote from the literature verbatim. But their contributions still largely need to be substantive, rather than cursory.

A good strategy to ensure student engagement is to delineate clear participation frequency and quality expectations. Follow up early around students' initiation with discussion forums, making it clear that while there is some built-in flexibility there are expectations with respect to the temporality of participation. Chase any who lag early on, offering support and reminding them of your expectations—and then leave them to it. Even students who perhaps bristled at being chased in the first week will have seen the benefit of having minimal benchmarks for participation and interactivity—and will, in fact, exceed them—as the course progresses.

Example: My course units run Monday to Sunday. I require students to post an initial contribution to the discussion by the end of Wednesday, along with a day by which they need to respond to their peers' postings (usually midday Saturday). If your LMS offers it, only allowing students to see their peers once they make their own gives every student a clean slate—and precludes those "Aoife/Hone/everyone already said what I was thinking" posts.

Integrate team-based learning, early

For many students, studying wholly online can feel isolating. In addition to interesting discussion forums each week, it is often worth purposively integrating some team-based learning (Michaelson, Bauman Knight & Fink, 2004).

Purposive team-based learning is structured in ways that allow different students to bring their particular strengths to a shared task, while also learning from the contributions of others. We know that in terms of post-degree employability, the ability to work effectively in a team environment has great currency (Berquist, et al, 2019). Team-based learning is one excellent tack towards developing a range of collaborative or communicative competencies including:

- Project management, scoping and planning
- Written communication
- Presentation skills
- Team management

However, team-based learning only works well if it is done *authentically*. Students can ascertain quickly if a shared task is more about rationalising (staff) assessment workload than their own learning.

An initial team-based learning activity is largely a catalyst. In addition to its own value, subsequently encouraging your students to continue working collaboratively, including peer review of each others' assessments prior to submission, deepens the benefits of collaboration. In my courses, the students who avail themselves of this collaborative learning all do very well: the small number who struggle to pass are always among those who have eschewed team-based learning.

Examples: Ask student teams to create a just-in-time prototype of an object, template, or rubric in response to a scenario. Require them to share this with the wider class in a discussion forum. This forum will give each group exposure to a range of other scenarios, as well as how different teams approach the same task.

Model your assessment expectations in your scoping requirements

The instructions for an assessment cannot be longer than the word (or page) count for the assessment itself: if you cannot delineate a task's parametres within the same constraints required of your students, it is unrealistic to expect students to meet said requirements.

To be fair this usually happens via "creep", incrementally, over time:

1. Staff person introduces a new assessment, often one requiring brevity.
2. Students provide feedback that indicate more information would have supported their success, so staff person adds more information.
3. Subsequent cohorts of students pose further interesting and valid queries about the task, so responses to these are also integrated in the task information.
4. Students are vexed trying to meet all these expectations within a constrained word count.

We want our assessments to be cognitively challenging, in terms of the subject matter and the task. Our materials, regardless of any good intentions, should not create complexity in terms of understanding our expectations.

Example: structure your assessment instructions in the format you require students to use for the assessment. You are then confident of aligning your intentions and your practice.

Next steps

Our team will be building out two resources regarding this framework. The first will be a series of self-directed online modules, where staff can work through each of these with some exemplars and interactive, iterative engagement. The second will be a self-directed tool for staff to identify potential areas for them to explore in terms of their academic development. Our aim to begin piloting these later in 2023.

References

Anderson, T. (2008). Towards a Theory of Online Learning in (T. Anderson, Ed.) *The Theory and Practice of Online Learning,* (pp. 45- 74), Edmonton: Athabasca University Press. https://www.aupress.ca/app/uploads/120146_99Z_Anderson_2008-Theory_and_Practice_of_Online_Learning.pdf

Baker, M. G, Kvalsvig A. & Verrall, A.J. (2020). New Zealand's COVID-19 elimination strategy, Medical Journal of Australia. 213(5), 198-200, 2020. doi:10.5694/mja2.50735

Berquist, B., Hall, R., Morris-Lange, S., Shields, H., Stern, V., & Tran, L. T. (2019), 'Global perspectives on international student employability', International Education Association of Australia (IEAA).

Biggs, J. & Tang, C. (2007). Teaching for quality learning at university. Berkshire: McGraw-Hill, Society for Research Into Higher Education and Open University Press.

Chung, D. (2020). Coronavirus: PM Jacinda Ardern outlines NZ's new alert system, over-70s should stay at home," New Zealand Herald, 21 March 2020. https://www.nzherald.co.nz/nz/coronavirus-pm-jacinda-ardern-outlines-nzs-new-alert-system-over-70s-should-stay-at-home/

Michaelson, L.K., Bauman Knight, A. & Fink, L.D. (2004). Team-Based Learning: A Transformative Use of Small Groups in College Teaching. Sterling VA: Stylus Publishing.

Schön, D.A. (1983). The Reflective Practitioner: How Professionals Think In Action. New York, NY: Basic Books.

THE PREEDTECH PROJECT – PREPRIMARY SCHOOL TEACHING IN THE DIGITAL ERA

Stefan Colibaba, Al.I.Cuza University/EuroEd Foundation Iasi, Romania

Irina Gheorghiu, Albert-Ludwigs University Freiburg, Germany

Ramona Cirsmari, EuroEd School Iasi, Romania

Alexandra Hanu, EuroEd School Iasi, Romania

Ovidiu Ursa, University of Medicine and Pharmacy Cluj-Napoca, Romania

Correspondence: *Stefan Colibaba: stefan.colibaba1954@gmail.com*

Abstract

The article is a study of the PreEdTeh project (Erasmus + programme), developed within a partnership of kindergartens and education and ICT institutions from Romania, Greece, Italy, Lithuania and Turkey. The innovative project is deeply rooted in the partners' pandemic experience and aims at providing pre-primary teachers with the means of adapting their activities to the online environment. It promotes professional development by strengthening the profiles of educators, empowering and equipping them with digital and pedagogical skills, as well as providing them with essential and logically structured open educational resources (OER), necessary for the developmental needs of preschool children. The article introduces the project's objectives and outputs and gives insights into the development of the PreEdTech Guide, its online course, tutorials, lesson plans and curriculum. These provide teachers with all the elements and steps necessary for successful online activities with children as well as for a good collaboration with parents, which is the basis for teachers' performance and well-being. The paper also presents the feedback collected from teachers participating in the pilot.

Keywords:

pre-primary educators, pandemic, digital and pedagogical skills, open educational resources.

The European context

Due to the closure of schools and kindergartens brought on by the SARS-CoV-2 pandemic, teachers had to adapt to online teaching and keep students' interest and the relevance of their classes in the new context. One of the primary issues, however, was that children aged seven and up were the target audience for the educational process supported by the education authorities whereas the kindergarten children were left behind. Teachers of primary, secondary, and high school found a functional approach relatively quickly. Pre-primary teachers were limited on the one hand by the lack of online resources and clear explanations of procedures, on the other hand by their students' age-related communication and interaction issues. All this resulted in a constant cry for parents' help (Florian, B., & Toc, S., 2020; Hosszu, A., & Rughiniș, C., 2020). Furthermore, even though these children are digital natives and their parents frequently use the internet and mobile phones as "modern pacifiers," people still reinforced the assumption that using technology and the internet when very young is inappropriate.

Globally, educational institutions and authorities responded to the COVID19 pandemic differently, with few options open to all children, parents, and teachers, depending on the community resources available and the expertise or experience of the teachers. When everything abruptly moved online and the first lockdown occurred nobody was ready. Teachers worked together, established forums, shared material they discovered or found useful, assisted one another, and searched for solutions to problems they encountered. They eventually received invitations to enrol in several e-training programs to advance their knowledge of ICT, the usability of e-learning platforms, and online teaching techniques.

The problem arose when these training courses specifically addressed school students and primary and secondary teachers, but not kindergarten educators. Thus, teachers working with preschool children had to adapt the information and resources provided by webinars and courses aimed at the other age groups. The success of this adaptation process depended very much on each teacher, individually. Studies show that from March 2020 until the end of the school year 2020-2021, during the lockdown period, most kindergarten teachers focused on transferring information and worksheets to children through informal channels (e.g., WhatsApp, Facebook) rather than delivering synchronous online lessons. In Romania, the National Centre for Policy and Evaluation in Education conducted research which clearly showed that during the suspension of the face-to-face school courses, high school and middle school children were in the limelight while preschoolers were left in the background (Centrul național de politici și evaluare în educație, 2020). The digital platform for sharing academic research, Academia.edu., registered 18,524 research articles in the collection "Schools out but classes on" between April to Oct. 2020, a few of which superficially dealt with preschool education. Another study, "School of the online elements for the innovation of education (Report of the evaluative research)", conducted by a group of university professors of Iasi, Romania, highlighted a number of challenges identified by teachers when teaching at a distance: technical difficulties (lack of devices or devices that did not meet the requirements); lack of educational content (digital resources) in the field of their respective subject areas; teachers' lack of time allocated for understanding and using educational-digital tools and resources in an appropriate way; teachers' lack of training in designing attractive and interactive activities to stimulate the interest of all the children (Botnariuc, P. et al, 2020; European Commission, 2020; IRES, 2020; (Velicu, A.,2020; Cezar, M.et al, 2020). As a consequence, the past years widened the gaps and discrimination in accessing quality education in all countries.

The PreEdTech project

To cope with the sudden change brought about by online learning, teachers formed support communities and sought help to deal with the abrupt change to online learning. This is how the idea of this project was born, from the need to provide much-needed support to other kindergarten teachers. The project's idea is even more relevant as it is based on EuroED primary school's institutional approach to Covid preschool education from March 2020 – April 2021 and the lessons its teachers learned. The PreEdTech project aims to fulfil such teaching and parental needs and fill the gaps in teacher knowledge and training regarding online teaching methods and tools, by developing materials and other products derived from the experience of the EuroED primary school during 2020-2021. At EuroEd primary school, there was an early development effort aimed at transferring teaching materials and practices in the online environment and preparing the actors involved in the teaching-learning effort for a different procedure and set of tools. In this respect, teachers benefitted from technical explanatory materials and pedagogical training activities, parents were helped to understand the teaching process and their potential involvement in it, and children were provided with a high-quality set of materials and activities, designed and delivered via digital means. The end result was positive and very positive feedback on the quality of digital teaching from parents and from children. This was clearly shown in the results of a survey form filled in by the parents, who assessed, almost unanimously, that the quality of online teaching at EuroED primary school is very good, mainly due to the teachers' improved set of skills and clear explanations and guides provided to the parents throughout the distance learning period. This endeavour included classroom observation of didactic activities carried out by EuroEd preschool teachers in March 2021 and the feedback for these activities given by the Iasi school Inspectorate and Cuza University education specialists as part of the procedure of preschool and primary school didactic degrees.
The pandemic brought about the forced digitization of education, which will stay. This project is aimed specifically at kindergarten teachers in order to develop their digital and pedagogical skills and to provide them with the most appropriate resources to work with kindergarten students - aged 3-6 years.

The PreEdTech project's objectives

We came to the current project after considering the dynamics and unpredictability of the contemporary context, how the project's partner institutions adapted to online learning, and the difficulties they encountered during the epidemic. Given the current challenges of distance and digital teaching and learning, the project aims to strengthen the profiles of educators, empower and equip them with digital and pedagogical skills, as well as provide them with essential and logically structured open educational resources (OER), necessary for the developmental needs of preschool children. The project supports educators as they successfully adopt cutting-edge teaching strategies that are pertinent to the digital transformation of school culture.

The project's partnership

The issues tackled by the project needed addressing in a transnational manner. The most important benefit resulting from the transnational cooperation proposed by this project was the input and perspectives provided by the background experience and expertise of the partners. The partnership is composed of eight institutions sharing various experiences in the field, especially in the COVID-19 context, and which adapted immediately to remote learning. Thus, the project's consortium consists of four kindergartens, two from Romania – EuroEd and Sfantul Sava, one from Lithuania- Sviesa and one from Turkey- Anafartalar, three non-profit associations with a focus on educationb from Lithuania - EMundus, Spain - XANO, Italy- Pixel and one private tech company from Italy - Connectis. All the above-mentioned institutions have kindergartens as associated partners, interested in improving the quality of teaching by introducing educational technologies and modern resources to engage and motivate pupils.

Target groups

The project targets preschool educators, principals, parents, and children. The justification for choosing to target teachers at this level is that they are less fortunate than teachers at higher levels in terms of the accessibility of materials, tools, guidelines, and general resources online. Parents are frequently more than passive participants in an online class: they are crucial to the success of online education. They play a crucial role in engaging preschoolers in activities and reaching out to them. Lack of parental involvement, technical limitations, and unfavourable viewpoints (e.g., distance learning is less effective than traditional learning, young children's eyesight problems like myopia due to increased screen time, and restricted physical activity) can all have an impact on the learning process (Hosszu, A. & Rughiniș, C., 2020).

The PreEdTech project's Results

To create the project's results a mixed team of teachers, trainers and technicians within the project consortium identified the main topics and their subtopics to be approached when designing the structure of the guide. The project's guide was elaborated based on the institutional approach, the research, experience and lessons learned collected and gained by partners during the pandemic between March 2020 – April 2021. This endeavour included classroom observation of didactic activities carried out by EuroEd preschool teachers in March 2021 and the feedback for these activities given by the education specialists from the Iasi school Inspectorate and Cuza University as part of the procedure of preschool and primary school didactic degrees. The contents of the guide can serve, with the appropriate adjustments, as a starting point in online teaching for teachers involved in the next level of teaching and, with suitable amendments, to online secondary school or university teaching.

The Teaching in the Digital Era Guide

The *Teaching in the Digital Era* Guide is the main result. For educators and caregivers, the *Teaching in the Digital Era Guide* offers priceless insights into useful methods and resources for online teaching. There are three sections in the Guide. The first discusses the pedagogical strategy in full and offers the hints, ideas, and techniques required to support the online teaching procedure. This section seeks to address issues including online teaching principles, student motivation, online assessment, class management, lesson planning, and welfare, among other things. The technological elements of online instruction are the subject of the second section (skills and tips, account creation, online classroom administration, modifying settings, ensuring security, creating digital resources and using interactive platforms etc.). The third section examines topics related to online safety for children and parents.

The *Teaching in the Digital Era* Guide includes the following chapters:
Introduction
About the Guide
Chapter 1 - Pedagogical Competencies in online teaching (Sviesa + Emundus + Pixel)

1.1. The main principles of online teaching and activities to implement them
1.2. Stimulating children's motivation
1.3. Classroom management and online planning
1.4. Synchronous and asynchronous activities. Face-to-face, blended and hybrid lessons
1.5. Managing online wellbeing
1.6. Assessment in online teaching (Pixel)

Chapter 2 - Technical Competencies in online teaching (Xano, Pixel, Connectis + EuroEd)
2.1. Skills and tips for using Microsoft Office (Word, PowerPoint, Excel)
2.2. Asynchronous teaching. Creating an online workspace for children (Google accounts, Google classroom)
2.3. Synchronous teaching. How to use online platforms in teaching (Zoom, Webex, Teams)
2.4. How to create digital resources and use interactive platforms (Bookwidgets, World wall, Liveworksheets, Canva, Animaker, Kahoot)

Chapter 3 - Teacher-Student-Parent cooperation
(Sf.Sava + EuroEd + Anafartalar)
3.1. Online learning is not an enemy. Rules for online learning for small-age children
3.2. Digital Threats and Online safety skills
3.3. How to involve parents in the online learning process of their children
3.4. Useful approaches and tools to online teaching at home

The Teaching in the Online Era Course

The *Teaching in the Online Era Course* relies on the Guide. The main difference between the two project results is that the Guide includes a theoretical comprehensive approach to online teaching whereas the online course applies theory into practice and demonstrates how this theory can be applied to the main subjects taught in preschool: Mathematics, Environmental Education, Language and Communication in the children's mother tongue and English. The structure of the *Teaching in the Digital Era online Course* is divided into four units: Mathematics, Environmental Education, Language and Communication in children's mother tongue and English. Each unit has two chapters. Chapter one is a theoretical part meant to develop and improve educators' pedagogical, technical and teacher-student-parent cooperation competencies in online teaching. It comprises ppt presentations, in-depths pdf detailed contents and a final quiz. Chapter two is practical and consists of tutorials teaching educators how to produce digital resources for their discipline. Each unit is accompanied by an evaluation test.

Chapter One: Learn the use of these TOOLS (account creation, functionalities, opportunities and limits)

1. How to create a Gmail account
2. How to use Google Drive
3. How to use Google Docs, Google Drive, Google Forms
4. How to use BookWidgets
5. How to use Google Classroom
6. How to use Google Meet
7. How to use the Zoom platform
8. How to use WordWall
9. How to use Animaker
10. How to use Genially
11. How to use Storyboards

Chapter Two: Learn the use of these TOOLS applied for specific disciplines (Math, Environment, Language and Communication, English)

1. How to use Google Drive to archive teaching resources
2. Using Google Docs, Google Forms, Google Sheets, Google Presentations to create teaching resources
3. Using BookWidgets to create specific exercises for children
4. Example of Google Classroom used in a lesson with children
5. Example of Google Meet used in a lesson with children
6. How to use the Zoom platform for synchronous teaching

7. How to use WordWall to create digital exercise for Math
8. Using Animaker to use animated teaching resources for environmental education
9. Genially´s applicability in English lessons
10. Create Storyboards for the Language and Communication discipline

The Online Interactive Annual Plan Handbook

The goal of this project's output is to inspire preschool teachers to include cutting-edge technology and online learning materials in their lessons. It includes a ready-made collection of materials and online lesson plans for four academic subjects—mathematics, environmental education, language and communication—in both the student's mother tongue and English. The Handbook offers teachers four annual curricula for mathematics, environmental education, language and communication—mother tongue and English—as well as lesson plans for 30 weeks for each subject (a total of 120 lesson plans) and relevant digital resources. It aims at children aged 5 to 6 years old. Its purpose is to support teachers by providing all the tools they require in one pack, including lesson plans and the materials needed to implement a one-year preschool curriculum.

Teachers' feedback

The project's results were tested on 30 pre-primary teachers in each country in January-March 2023. The feedback shows that the project's results have impacted the participants in diverse ways so that they are better prepared for the current challenges kindergartens face. Thus, in their opinion, the project's results:

-have provided teachers and kindergartens with standardized online teaching principles to organize online learning/teaching processes. As the online teaching principles express the basic requirements for educational objectives, content, methods, assessment, they are essential in contributing to creating a safe and rigorous framework for learning/teaching processes (online/blended).

- have increased and diversified the way teachers implement learning activities with preschoolers. The guide and its course provide teachers with a wide range of materials, tips and hands-on activities to use with children.

- have provided teachers with better strategies/activities to teach those children who cannot attend face-to-face classes every day due to health issues.

-have raised teachers' awareness of best practices to adapt an offline content to an online course.

- have enabled teachers to connect and relate to parents so that parents have become more involved in their offspring's school development for the child's benefit

- have encouraged the development of a new type of teacher: focused on children and better prepared for challenges while coordinating technology, pedagogy and content effectively and creatively.

- have increased the prestige of the schools as well as parents' trust in teachers and schools.

All participants agreed that the project´s results provide teachers with all the elements and steps necessary for successful activities with children and good collaboration with parents, which is the basis for teachers' performance and well-being.

Conclusions

The epidemiological crisis has brought on issues which affect the entire world. In teaching, these issues are an increase in distance teaching and learning and in the use of digital resources. Hence, this project is specifically designed for kindergarten teachers to help them improve their digital and pedagogical skills and equip them with the tools they need to engage with kindergarten children of ages ranging from three to six. Given the current challenges of distance and digital teaching and learning, the project aims to strengthen the profiles of educators, empower and equip them with digital and pedagogical skills, as well as to provide them with essential and logically structured open educational resources (OER), necessary for the developmental needs of preschool children. The initiative enables educators to implement cutting-edge instructional approaches which are appropriate for the digital change in school culture.

The project meets the needs of both target groups and partners through the following outputs:

- a concrete guide on how to organize an online lesson with young children. The Guide in question addresses the problem of online learning from both technical and pedagogical perspectives, providing teachers with the complete picture and pursuing both the development of teachers' digital skills and the adaptation of pedagogical doctrines related to the use of new technologies.
- basic digital instructions for parents and caretakers to support children in the instructional-educational process.
- online courses for educators focusing on four basic subjects taught at the preschool level (science - mathematics, environmental knowledge, communication in mother tongue, and English).

References

Periodicals

Botnariuc, P., Cucos, C., Glava, C., Iancu, D, Ilie, M, Istrate, O., Labar, A., Pânișoară, O., Ștefănescu, D., Velea S. (2020). Scoala online - elemente pentru inovarea educatiei, *Ed Universitatii Bucuresti.*

Hosszu, A., & Rughiniș, C. (2020). The Digital divides in education. An analysis of the Romanian public discourse on distance and online education during the COVID-19 pandemic. *Sociologie Românească*, *18*(2), 11-39.

Websites and online resources

Cezar, M., Grama, C. and Pârvu, S. (2020). Școala virusată. Cum arată educația online în viziunea profesorilor din România Și Moldova. Expertforum.ro. https://expertforum.ro/raport-scoala-virusata/

Centrul național de politici și evaluare în educație - unitatea de cercetare în educație. (2020). Scoala la distanță în perioada pandemiei. https://www.ise.ro/wp-content/uploads/2020/08/Rezumat_ancheta_Scoala-la-distanta.pdf

European Commission. (2020). Education and Training Monitor în viziunea profesorilor din România Și Moldova. Expertforum.ro. https://expertforum.ro/raport-scoala-virusata/https://op.europa.eu/webpub/eac/education-and-training-monitor-2020/countries/romania.html

Florian, B., & Toc, S. (2020). Policy note: Educația în timpul pandemiei. Răspunsuri la criza nesfârșită a sistemului educațional românesc. https://bibliotecadesociologie.ro/en/download/florian-bogdan-toc-sebastian-2020-policy-note-educatia-in-timpul-pandemiei-raspunsuri-la-criza-nesfarsita-a-sistemului-educational-romanesc/

IRES. (2020). 32% dintre elevi nu au acces la echipament electronic. la criza nesfârșită a sistemului educațional românesc. *https://romania.europalibera.org/a/ires-jum%C4%83tate-dintre-elevi-nu-au-participat-la-%C8%99coala-online-32-nu-au-acces-la-echipament-electronic/30601273.html*

Velicu, A. (2021). The school year 2020-2021 in Romania during the pandemic. file:///C:/Users/user/Downloads/edu_covid_techical_report_romania_final_28.06_v2.pdf

EXPLORING THE USE OF IMMERSIVE TECHNOLOGIES TO ENHANCE THE STUDENT EXPERIENCE

Geraldine Mc Dermott, Assumpta Byrne, Rory McLaughlin, Noëlle O'Connor, Sandra Griselain,
Technological University of the Shannon, Ireland

***Correspondence**: Geraldine Mc Dermott: gmcdermott@ait.ie*

Abstract

This paper reports on the initial phase of a National Forum funded Learning Enhancement Project (LEP), under the Strategic Alignment of Teaching and Learning Enhancement (SATLE) funding stream. The purpose of the LEP is to explore the use of immersive technologies such as Augmented Reality, Virtual Reality and 360° Learning in three key domain areas within one higher education institution in Ireland. While significant research has been conducted into the use of these technologies in training and business contexts, the application and use in higher education is still scarce. Radianti et al. (2020) suggest that while the use of virtual reality in higher education is promising, it is still quite experimental and focuses more on performance and usability than learning-oriented applications. Augmented Reality has been used in areas such as teacher education (Sáez-López, 2020) and EFL (Arkhipova, 2022) but is also largely experimental. Together with Mixed Reality and 360-degree Learning, these technologies have the potential to offer students a more immersive learning experience. Three domain areas are involved in this project: Online Learning; the university library; and the academic discipline of Business Tourism. It is envisaged that based on their expertise and experience team members will trial at least two of the immersive technologies with their students during the academic year 2023-2024. Engaging the students in the research will foster a partnership approach and provide an understanding of how this new approach to learning benefits the students but will also reveal the challenges associated with introducing new technologies.

Keywords:

Virtual reality, augmented reality, immersive learning, 360-degree learning, higher education.

In line with the ambition of the theme of Digital Transformation in the Irish Tertiary Sector, promoted by the National Forum for the Enhancement of Teaching and Learning (2023), this project seeks to examine how immersive technologies can be used within a variety of contexts to enhance the student learning experience.

Significant research has been conducted into the use of immersive technologies in the domains of Engineering (Fracaro et al., 2022; Halabi, 2019) and Medecine (Dhar et al., 2021; Pottle, 2019; Tang et al, 2022) in particular. However, their wider application and use in HE is still evolving. According to Radianti et al. (2020), while the use of virtual reality in higher education is promising, it is still quite experimental and focuses more on performance and usability than learning-oriented applications. Augmented Reality has been used in areas such as teacher education (Sáez-López,2020) and EFL (Arkhipova, 2022) but is also largely experimental. Together with Mixed Reality and 360o Learning, these technologies have the potential to offer students a more immersive learning experience.

As far back as 1994 Milgram and Kishino presented a reality-virtuality continuum (Figure 1). Here the authors distinguish between the real environment and the virtual environment and attempt to provide a taxonomy of the main aspects of each class.

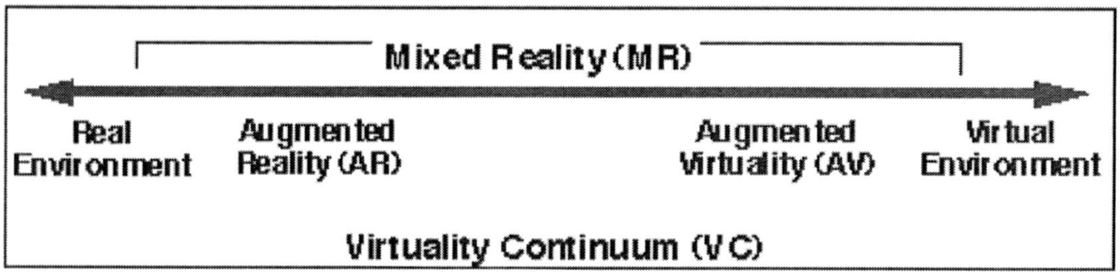

Figure 1: The Simplified representation of a "virtuality continuum" (Milgram & Kishino,1994, p.3)

This taxonomy provides a simple visualization of the relationship between the different environments. Virtual Reality allows users to enter a virtual world, removing them from their physical surroundings. Using a Head-Mounted Device (HMD), users immerse themselves in a different, computer-generated environment. The terms Mixed Reality and Augmented Reality are often used interchangeably, with both extending the physical world, augmenting reality with digital information. However, Milgram and Kishino (1994) consider the former as an overarching term to describe the 'grey area' in the centre of the continuum (p. 4). More recently 360o video is often listed alongside these immersive technologies. While 360-degree video differs from virtual reality in providing the learner with 360-degree videos stitched together from a series of two-dimensional images taken from different angles, it provides the user with a similarly interactive learning experience.

Immersive Learning

The potential of immersive virtual reality to enhance learning was explored by Coban et al. (2022) in a meta-analysis of 49 articles, where the authors conclude that "teaching based on VR technologies is more effective than other environments" (p.11). They determine that immersive VR facilitates "inquiry-based learning and a constructivist learning approach" (ibid), though they specify that this is more prevalent in K-12 education based on their research. In higher education the benefit of VR is particularly notable in simulation-based teaching and learning contexts, where students could use equipment in a virtual context before working with it in a laboratory environment.

Rogers (2019) describes VR as the learning aid of the 21st century, while Krokos et al. (2018) found that VR using HMDs showed an improvement in recall accuracy when compared to a similar desktop activity. 40 participants took part in the experiment which showed 42 faces in two scenes and were invited to familiarize themselves with the faces. The improvement in recall performance was 8.8% higher in the use of HMD compared to the desktop version and the authors concluded that memory recall could be enhanced through immersion in a virtual environment.

Marks & Thomas (2021) document the use of virtual reality for higher education (HE) teaching in a purpose-designed laboratory and conclude that there was a clear need for a pedagogical framework which would allow for "experiential and discovery learning, reflective observation, abstract conceptualization and active experimentation" (p.1302). They also advise that in-house content creation support is important, but with appropriate educational frameworks. The authors report that some students experienced discomfort using the VR technologies, citing motion sickness and difficulty navigating the content. However, most students surveyed in the study said they would like to use VR technology again.

A learning model which considers both Human-Computer Interaction and pedagogy was developed by Zhou et al. (2018) to explore how Bloom's Taxonomy, together with the Technology Acceptance Model (TAM) might be used to evaluate student learning with VR in skills training and operational learning. Following their survey of 32 students, they concluded that the learner experience was positive, with both flow and positive affect scoring highly, while tension, annoyance, challenge, and negative affect scored low. While it is acknowledged that this is a small-scale study, the combination of HCI and pedagogical models reflects the widely held opinion that an educational framework is needed to guide the implementation of immersive technologies within the curriculum to support learning.

The benefits of AR within the education setting have also been well-documented. Findings from research suggest that using AR improves students' motivation (Irwanto et al., 2022), engagement and student satisfaction (Saltan & Arslan, 2016), learning performance and learning experience (Akçayır & Akçayır, 2017). However, research conducted by Zumbach et al. (2022) compared AR-based learning environment with a paper-based learning environment for participants to learn about the human digestive system. They concluded that the positive effects of AR were limited to a higher experience of immersion. However, in terms of learning gains, the paper-based instruction showed significantly higher results. Buchner and Kerres (2022) argue that the research on AR has to date focused primarily on comparing AR to other technologies. In a meta-analysis of 92 primary studies, they note that many of the studies compare AR to traditional and established media focusing on a "technology-centred understanding of teaching and learning, while ignoring the theories of learning and instruction.

The current project aims to address this deficit to explore how AR/VR and 360-degree video might enhance the student experience, through the integration of immersive technologies into the curriculum. It also responds to the Next Steps Report from the National Forum (2021), which advocates a reimagining of our learning environments to support "diverse approaches to teaching, learning and assessment" (p.12).

Research Design

A qualitative approach to the research has been chosen to explore student and teacher experiences of immersive technologies within the curriculum. The key research question which guides this study is:

To what extent can immersive technologies such as AR/VR and 360-degree learning enhance teaching and learning in higher education?

While many of the studies cited above include quantitative approaches, the desire to understand in detail students' perception of AR/VR/MR provided a rationale for a qualitative research design. Three key student/teacher cohorts will be included in the research, as outlined below.

Business Tourism students on two academic programmes will be offered the opportunity to experience an immersive learning environment. The students involved will be given the opportunity to experience immersive technologies in a professional context. The project aims to encourage students to consider the application of immersive technologies in a professional context and will also demonstrate their knowledge of these relatively new technologies which are increasingly used in many professions such as Tourism (Londoño, 2022). However, to examine the potential of the immersive technology tool for teaching and learning, the lecturer-researcher will align the activity to at least one learning outcome within each academic programme. To guard against the novelty effect (Wells et al., 2010) and to encourage students to engage in a meaningful way with the immersive technologies, the selection of one learning outcome for each of the academic domains will provide a focus for the student participants. The resources chosen by the lecturer-researchers will be relevant to the selected learning outcomes and may be of benefit to students for the assessment of these learning outcomes.

Immersive pedagogy (Gauthereau et al., 2020) is a creative, active teaching and learning approach which puts the student at the centre of the learning experience, developing critical thinking and problem-solving skills. The approach adopted by teacher-researchers for this project will be informed by current research in immersive pedagogy.

This project will also focus on the potential to enhance the educational environment for students studying an online programme. The growth of online teaching has also been well-documented in academic research to the extent that Palvia et al. (2018) contend that online teaching will become mainstream by 2025. The growth in online enrolments cannot be separated from the development of technologies such as VR/AR which enhance what can be delivered, either via synchronous or asynchronous modes. Immersive technologies offer a variety of means of engagement between teachers (including HE lecturers) and students. This responds to the expectations on the part of students for the use of technology-enhanced learning and teaching methods has increased (Ashour, 2020). In this instance the teacher-researcher will evaluate the use of at least one approach with adult, part-time learners on an online business programme. The use of immersive technologies will be evaluated to consider the Quality of the User Experience (Keighery, 2020), as well as the potential Learning Gains (Evans et al., 2018). The Next Steps report also recognises the need to cater for our "increasingly diverse learner profiles" (p. 12). Immersive technologies offer a multimodal approach to learning, engaging all the senses in the learning experience and cultivating a more inclusive learning environment.

Additionally, collaboration with the university library will provide an opportunity to explore how immersive technologies might enhance student engagement with the library. According to Greene (2020), several libraries are now offering AR/VR services to their students, both in-library and as a service to academic faculties. The potential to design experiences through the creation of content (e.g., 360-degree video or AR-based library tours) will be explored as part of the research project.

Finally, this cross-campus collaboration builds on current work in immersive technologies already underway within the university. The development of a Community of Practice of researchers and practitioners in immersive technologies will encourage academic and professional staff to combine knowledge and expertise to create further opportunities for teaching and learning in this domain.

Conclusion

Outputs from this funded project will include a comprehensive literature review on the use of immersive technologies in higher education; a proposed pedagogical framework for using AR/VR/MR/360-degree learning within the curriculum, and an evaluation of the research project, with student and teacher-researcher input.

This project does not just focus on the use of immersive technologies. Its purpose is also to explore how immersive technologies can contribute to a more immersive, multimodal, inclusive educational experience. As these technologies become more affordable and more robust, they offer greater potential for our educational context. It is hoped that the learning from this project will inform further research in this area.

References

Akçayır, M. and Akçayır, G. (2017) 'Advantages and challenges associated with augmented reality for education: A systematic review of the literature', *Educational Research Review, 20,* pp. 1–11. Available at: https://doi.org/10.1016/j.edurev.2016.11.002.

Arkhipova, M. V., Zhulina, E. V., Zhernovaya, O. R., Dunaeva, N. I., Orlova, O. A., & Tolonkina, G. Y. (2022, November). Gamification in teaching EFL through computer games and augmented reality. In AIP Conference Proceedings (Vol. 2647, No. 1, p. 040080). AIP Publishing LLC.

Ashour, S. (2020) 'How technology has shaped university students' perceptions and expectations around higher education: an exploratory study of the United Arab Emirates', *Studies in Higher Education, 45*(12), pp. 2513–2525. Available at: https://doi.org/10.1080/03075079.2019.1617683.

Buchner, J., & Kerres, M. (2023). Media comparison studies dominate comparative research on augmented reality in education. *Computers and Education,* 195.

Coban, M., Islam Bolat, Y., & Goksu, I. (2022). The potential of immersive virtual reality to enhance learning: A meta-analysis | Elsevier Enhanced Reader. *Educational Research Review, 36*(10452).

Dhar, P., Rocks, T., Samarasinghe, R. M., Stephenson, G., & Smith, C. (2021). Augmented reality in medical education: students' experiences and learning outcomes. *Medical Education Online,* *26*(1). https://doi.org/10.1080/10872981.2021.1953953

Evans, C., Howson, C. K., & Forsythe, A. (2018). Making sense of learning gain in higher education. *Higher Education Pedagogies, 3*(1), 1–45.

Garcia Fracaro, S., Glassey, J., Bernaerts, K., & Wilk, M. (2022). Immersive technologies for the training of operators in the process industry: A Systematic Literature Review. *Computers and Chemical Engineering, 160,* 107691. https://doi.org/10.1016/j.compchemeng.2022.107691

Gauthereau, L., Linker, J., Slayton, E., & Wermer-Colan, A. (2020). Immersive Pedagogy: Developing a Decolonial and Collaborative Framework for Teaching and Learning in 3D/VR/AR. *The Journal of Interactive Technology and Pedagogy*. Available at: https://assetstore.unity.com/.

Greene, D., & Groenendyk, M. (2020). An environmental scan of virtual and augmented reality services in academic libraries. Library Hi Tech.

Halabi, O. (2020). Immersive virtual reality to enforce teaching in engineering education. *Multimedia Tools and Applications*, *79*(3–4), 2987–3004. https://doi.org/10.1007/s11042-019-08214-8

Irwanto, I., Dianawati, R. and Lukman, I.R. (2022) 'Trends of Augmented Reality Applications in Science Education', *International Journal of Emerging Technologies in Learning (iJET), 17*(13), pp. 157–175.

Keighrey, C. (2020). A Quality of Experience Evaluation of an Immersive Multimedia Speech & Language Application.

Krokos, E., Plaisant, C., & Varshney, A. (2019). Virtual memory palaces: immersion aids recall. *Virtual Reality, 23*(1), 1–15.

Londoño, J. (2022). The Potential of AR/VR Technology to Promote Tourism. Available at: https://itif.org/publications/2022/06/30/the-potential-of-ar-vr-technology-to-promote-tourism/

Marks, B., & Thomas, J. (2022). Adoption of virtual reality technology in higher education: An evaluation of five teaching semesters in a purpose-designed laboratory. *Education and Information Technologies, 27*(1), 1287–1305.

Milgram, P., & Kishino, F. (1994). A taxonomy of mixed reality visual displays. *IEICE Transactions on Information Systems, E77-D*(12). http://vered.rose.utoronto.ca/people/paul_dir/IEICE94/ieice.html

National Forum for the Enhancement of Teaching and Learning. (2021) Next steps for teaching and learning: moving forward together. Available at: https://hub.teachingandlearning.ie/resource/next-steps-for-teaching-and-learning-moving-forward-together/.

Palvia, S. et al. (2018) 'Online Education: Worldwide Status, Challenges, Trends, and Implications', *Journal of Global Information Technology Management, 21*(4), pp. 233–241.

Pottle, J. (2019). Virtual reality and the transformation of medical education. *Future Healthcare Journal*, *6*(3), 181–185. https://doi.org/10.1016/j.soin.2019.05.007

Radianti, J., Majchrzak, T. A., Fromm, J., & Wohlgenannt, I. (2020). A systematic review of immersive virtual reality applications for higher education: Design elements, lessons learned, and research agenda. *Computers & Education,* 147, 103778.

Sáez-López, J. M., Cózar-Gutiérrez, R., González-Calero, J. A., & Gómez Carrasco, C. J. (2020). Augmented reality in higher education: An evaluation program in initial teacher training. *Education Sciences, 10*(2), 26.

Saltan, F. and Arslan, Ö. (2016) 'The Use of Augmented Reality in Formal Education: A Scoping Review', *EURASIA Journal of Mathematics, Science and Technology Education, 13*(2). Available at: https://doi.org/10.12973/eurasia.2017.00628a.

Rogers, S. (2019). Virtual Reality: THE Learning Aid of the 21st Century. Available at: https://www.forbes.com/sites/solrogers/2019/03/15/virtual-reality-the-learning-aid-of-the-21st-century/

Tang, Y. M., Chau, K. Y., Kwok, A. P. K., Zhu, T., & Ma, X. (2022). A systematic review of immersive technology applications for medical practice and education - Trends, application areas, recipients, teaching contents, evaluation methods, and performance. Educational Research Review, 35(June 2021), 100429. https://doi.org/10.1016/j.edurev.2021.100429

Wells, John & Campbell, Damon & Valacich, Joseph & Featherman, Mauricio. (2010). The Effect of Perceived Novelty on the Adoption of Information Technology Innovations: A Risk/Reward Perspective. Decision Sciences. 41. 10.1111/j.1540-5915.2010.00292.x.

Zhou, Y., Ji, S., Xu, T., & Wang, Z. (2018). Promoting Knowledge Construction: A Model for Using Virtual Reality Interaction to Enhance Learning. *Procedia Computer Science*, 130, 239–246.

Zumbach, J., von Kotzebue, L., & Pirklbauer, C. (2022). Does Augmented Reality Also Augment Knowledge Acquisition? Augmented Reality Compared to Reading in Learning About the Human Digestive System? *Journal of Educational Computing Research, 60*(5), 1325–1346.

MAPPING DIFFICULTIES IN PROBLEM-SOLVING PROCESS DURING VIDEO-ASSISTED SELF-REGULATED LEARNING TRAINING FOR STUDENTS: INTRODUCING THE PS-SOS MAP

Guy Cohen, Anat Cohen, Tel Aviv University, Israel

Correspondence: *Guy Cohen: cohen.guy.mail@gmail.com*

Abstract

In the ever-changing landscape of the Information Age, the development of self-regulated learning (SRL) skills has become increasingly important. Problem-solving is a critical SRL skill, and teachers play a vital role in fostering these abilities among their students. However, learners and teachers face challenges during the problem-solving process and in evaluating its incorporated strategies. To address these issues, this study explored students' difficulties in problem-solving while implementing a video assisted SRL training program. This program was developed based on an integrative framework to facilitate a structured problem-solving process in disciplinary or generic contexts. The program aimed to activate additional SRL skills, such as time management, feedback, elaboration, and critical thinking, through a digital toolkit of learning support materials. This paper focuses on 241 students' difficulties identified and classified according to the problem-solving framework that reported by teachers in different disciplines and grades (6-11). The analysis revealed that the most significant difficulties arose during the problem identification, followed by time planning and management, problem exploration, solution development, and solution evaluation. Based on this study, a dedicated map was developed called PS-SOS MAP to identify difficulties in different steps and tasks throughout the problem-solving process. The utilization of this mapping can also aid in the creation of feedback systems based on technology, such as chatbots or virtual assistants, that can provide valuable assistance to students during problem-solving training, facilitating the process of overcoming difficulties.

Keywords:

Video-based training; Problem-solving; Problem-based learning; Self-regulated learning; K-12 education

Introduction

Self-regulated learning (SRL) is crucial as it empowers individuals to take control of their own learning process, enabling them to learn more effectively, adapt to new situations, and achieve their goals (Alderman & MacDonald, 2015; Efklides & Metallidou, 2020; OECD, 2021). Numerous studies have emphasized the importance of fostering SRL skills during the developmental stage of young adolescence, as it plays a vital role in their lifelong learning (Alderman & MacDonald, 2015; Hanewald, 2013; Schloemer & Brenan, 2006). Video-based technology has been recommended to facilitate SRL strategies and enhance the learning process (Wang, 2011; Dresel & Haugwitz, 2008; Jansen, 2020). Despite the growing use of video for various purposes, including video conferencing and subject knowledge delivery, its primary utilization for SRL training has been limited, especially among young adolescents (Arifin et al., 2020; Dresel & Haugwitz, 2008; Cohen et al.,2022; van Alten et al., 2020).

Within the context of SRL, problem-solving is a fundamental skill that involves a multifaceted cognitive process, requiring individuals to utilize a diverse range of skills and strategies to effectively navigate and overcome challenges (Csapó & Funke, 2017; Khoiriyah & Husamah, 2018; OECD, 2021). Teachers play a critical role in promoting these abilities among their students (De Smul et al., 2019; Sulisworo et al., 2020; Uka & Uka, 2021). In addition, feedback is essential to the learning process in general, and particularly in promoting SRL skills (Cohen et al., 2022; Nicolaidou, 2013; van Ginkel et al.,2019). Through targeted feedback, learners can monitor their progress, identify areas for improvement, and adjust their strategies accordingly. Therefore, it is essential that instructional practices incorporate feedback mechanisms, especially in SRL training (Araka et al., 2020; Panadero et al., 2016; Zheng, 2016). To provide feedback on problem-solving strategies, it is crucial to define, measure, and evaluate the difficulties that related to these strategies (Yavuz et al., 2017; Liu & Israel, 2022).

Literature often highlights two primary challenges: the difficulties learners encounter during the problem-solving process; and the challenges involved in measuring the use of strategies (Liu & Israel, 2022; Tissenbaum, 2020).

In response, this study aims to identify and map the challenges that students face during problem-solving while undergoing video based SRL training. The study intends to measure and identify specific steps and tasks within the problem-solving framework where students encounter difficulties, based on teachers' perspectives. The study's contribution lies in creating a comprehensive map that facilitates the identification of challenges during the problem-solving process. This map can aid in developing SRL training programs that offer supportive feedback, be it from a human or technology-based source, thereby addressing the identified difficulties.

The current research

Research objective and question

This study focused on analyzing the responses of teachers regarding the difficulties their students encountered while working on problem-solving within a video-based training program. The aim was to gain a better understanding of the specific challenges that learners face during the problem-solving process and to identify the gaps in their SRL skill development. The analysis of teacher responses provides valuable insights into the practical application of SRL training programs in the classroom; and highlighting areas where further support may be needed to promote effective problem-solving strategies among students. Therefore, the research question is what are the difficulties students encounter when engaging in the process of problem-solving during video assisted SRL training?

Research context and population

In this study, teacher and student training programs were established. The teacher training program consisted of 10 blended sessions, both face-to-face and online, and accompanied by a student intervention program. The students were exposed to a generic problem-solving framework called VAST (Video assisted SRL training) that incorporates specific SRL strategies such as time management, feedback, elaboration, and critical thinking. The VAST framework was developed based on existing literature (Davidson & Sternberg, 2003; Kim & Hannafin, 2011; Mourtos et al., 2004; Snyder, & Snyder, 2008) and presents a systematic approach to problem-solving, consisting of several distinct steps and tasks that are conveyed through a digital toolbox. The digital toolbox included interactive videos, checklists, and problem-solving tasks. The videos' content was created in alignment with the problem-solving framework's various steps and the specific tasks involved in each step. Table 1 outlines the steps and tasks of the framework.

Table 1:The developed VAST problem-solving framework.

Learning stages	Forethought		Performance	Reflection
SRL strategies related to time	**(S1) Time planning**		**(S4) Time management**	**(S7) Time management evaluation**
	(T1.1) Define deadline for final solution. (T1.2) Define steps deadlines. (T1.3) Assess schedule feasibility. (T1.4) Use an assistive tool to document the planned schedule.		(T4.1) Monitor planned schedule. (T4.2) Detect time deviations. (T4.3) Reschedule deadlines. (T4.4) Assess reschedule feasibility.	(T7.1) Detect time deviations. (T7.2) Define reasons for time deviations. (T7.3) Use time deviations reasoning to explore alternatives for future problems.
Problem-solving strategies integrating other SRL strategies (critical thinking, elaboration, and feedback)	**(S2) Problem identification**	**(S3) Problem exploration**	**(S5) Solution development**	**(S6) Solution evaluation**
	(T2.1) Define the problem in your own words to ensure under-standing. (T2.2) Determine the rules and constraints. (T2.3) Define criterion for judging solution. (T2.4) Break the problem down into smaller questions. (T2.5) Reflect on the activity in this step.	(T3.1) Identify related topics based on prior knowledge. (T3.2) Determine the given/known information that might assist in solving the problem. (T3.3) Identify and complete information gap necessary for moving forward with the solution. (T3.4) Pose operational questions concerning the problem. (T3.5) Reflect on the activity in this step.	(T5.1) Identify candidate solutions. (T5.2) Analyze candidate solutions - using constraints and criteria. (T5.3) Investigate needed information for each solution. (T5.4) Choose the best solution according to the criteria. (T5.5) Implement a detailed work plan. (T5.6) Reflect on the activity in this step.	(T6.1) Present and communicate the solution (when relevant) (T6.2) Justify/ defend/ Update the solution. (T6.3) Monitor the problem-solving process. (T6.4) Improve the problem-solving process. (T6.5) Reflect on the activity in this step.

(S#): Chronological step number; (T#): Chronological task number.

During the intervention program, students worked in groups to solve a problem using the framework's process, while their teachers provided feedback on the difficulties they faced. The study involved 11 teachers who represented a range of disciplines and implemented the video-based training program for a total of 269 students in grades 6-11. To gather data, teachers completed two questionnaires: one describing classroom situations where difficulties arose, and another outlining successful practices for addressing difficulties.

Research method and procedure

This paper presents primary findings on student difficulties reported by their teachers, using both qualitative and quantitative methods with a focus on the latter. The teachers' responses were initially analyzed qualitatively to identify difficulties faced by students in the classroom. The research team filtered these difficulties according to the problem-solving framework and categorized them based on the specific tasks where the difficulties arose.

This filtering process was independently conducted by two experts in the SRL field who developed the problem-solving framework. The filtered results were then consolidated and compared. The number of occurrences of each difficulty was calculated for each task within each step of the framework. Quartiles were calculated to compare the occurrences of difficulties across tasks, providing insight into which tasks posed more challenges. Data analysis was conducted using JASP 17.01 software.

Findings

A total of 40 responses were provided by teachers, yielding various difficulties (N=241) that were categorized according to the different steps and tasks within the problem-solving framework. Notably, certain difficulties pertaining to issues such as motivation, emotions, and technology, were not clearly associated with any specific task or steps and tasks in the framework. Thus, these difficulties were excluded from the analysis.

In order to compare the frequency of difficulties reported by teachers in different tasks at various steps, a quartile calculation was conducted. The aim was to identify the tasks where students encountered more difficulties. The results of the analysis are presented in Table 2.

Table 2: Quartile calculation of difficulties in 32 problem-solving tasks within the VAST framework

	Valid	Missing	Mean	Std. Deviation	Minimum	Maximum	25th percentile	50th percentile	75th percentile
Students' difficulties	32	0	7.531	4.501	1.000	17.000	4.000	7.000	9.000

According to the analysis, the highest number of difficulties was classified as part of the *problem identification* step: problem definition (n=17), constraints identification (n=17), solution criteria definition (n=17), questioning (n=17), as well as reflection (n=12). In addition, a high number of student difficulties were classified in the *time planning* (n=9) and *time management* (n=9) steps. For the *time management evaluation* step, only a limited number of difficulties were classified in each task (n=4). Moreover, a significant number of difficulties were classified in the reflection task of the *problem identification* (n=16), *problem exploration* (n=15), and *solution development* (n=14) steps, compared to other tasks within each step. Furthermore, in the *solution evaluation* step, the task of presenting and communicating solutions to peers was found to be particularly challenging for students compared to other tasks in this step (n=8).

The difficulties that students faced during problem-solving, as identified by their teachers, were compared across different tasks within the framework and visualized as the PS-SOS map using the previously mentioned calculation. This map provides an overview of the specific tasks and steps within the problem-solving framework where students encountered difficulties. Each quartile represents the difficulty level of a particular task, with the color scale representing the amount of difficulty levels associated with each task. Red represents a high number of difficulties, and green represents relatively few. The PS-SOS Map, which visualizes the difficulties reported by the teachers, is presented in Figure 1.

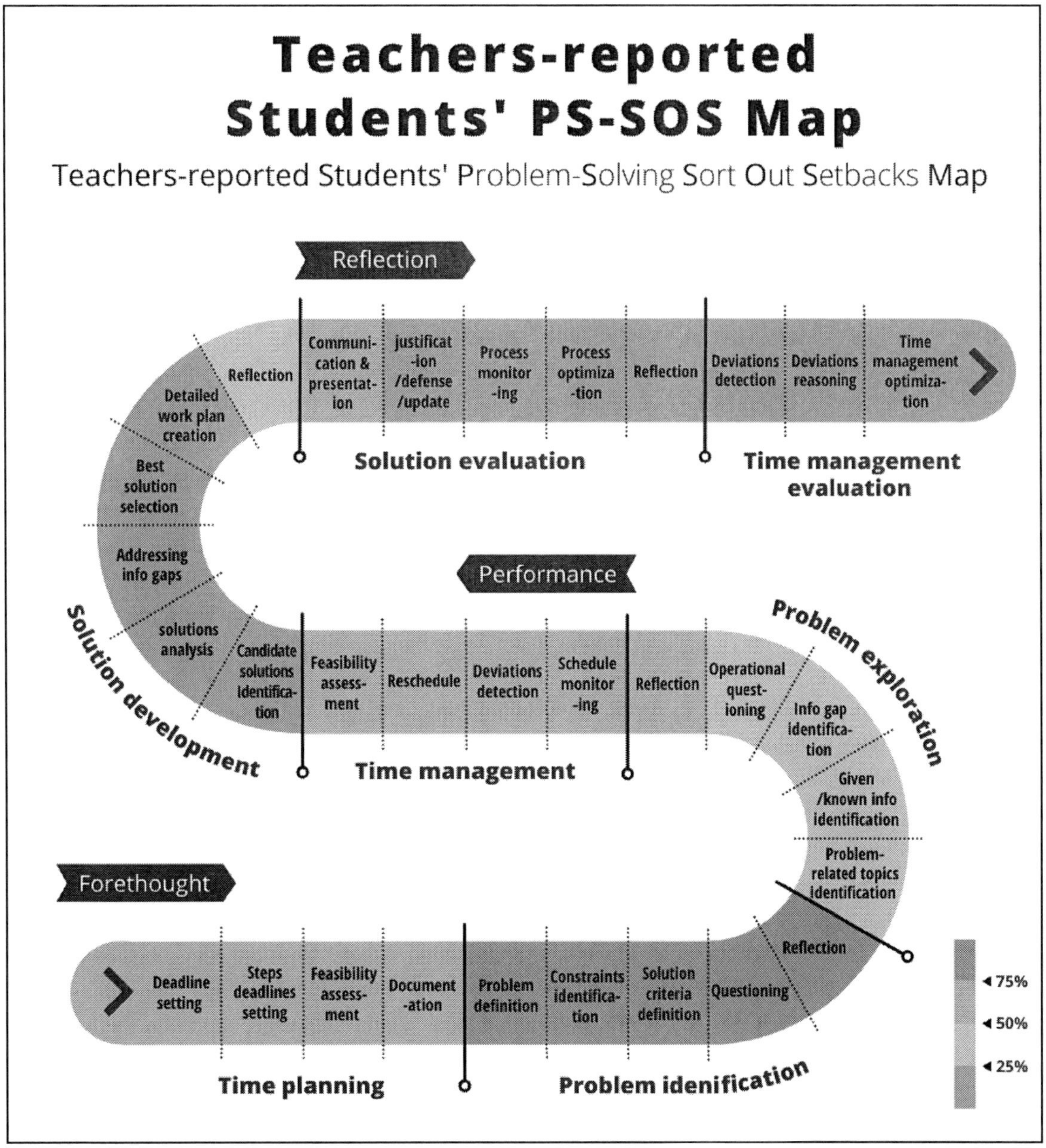

Figure 1. Teachers-reported Students' PS-SOS Map: The relative share of students' difficulties in each task of the problem-solving framework. For example, the number of difficulties in the task 'Deadline setting' (indicated by the orange color) is higher than 50% of the other tasks.

Discussion and conclusion

Measuring SRL strategies and identifying students' difficulties during problem-solving can be complex tasks (Liu & Israel, 2022; Tissenbaum, 2020). The present study addresses these research gaps by classifying the difficulties students experience during problem-solving based on the specific steps and tasks where they face relatively higher levels of difficulty compared to others. The resulting PS-SOS map can facilitate the creation of support mechanisms for students during their independent problem-solving process, providing accurate scaffolding in real-time.

Specifically, the study found that students struggled the most with problem identification, which may have had a cascading effect on their ability to evaluate solutions. Additionally, students encountered difficulties with planning and time management. These SRL skills are crucial for successful problem-solving (Davidson & Sternberg, 2003; Kim & Hannafin, 2011; Mourtos et al., 2004; Snyder, & Snyder, 2008). These findings emphasize the need for additional support in these areas during SRL training.

Feedback is essential for learning, as it provides students with evaluations of their knowledge and skills, as well as suggestions for improvement (Cohen et al., 2019). However, in this study, students encountered significant challenges when presenting solutions to their classmates for feedback during the solution evaluation step. The difficulties could stem from collaborative work issues, lack of confidence, and unfamiliarity with evaluation and reflection strategies. The high level of reported difficulties in the reflection task throughout the various steps supports this conclusion. These findings highlight the importance of providing students with support in developing effective communication skills related to feedback, particularly in group settings (Nicolaidou, 2013; van Ginkel et al.,2019).

It's worth noting that the problem-solving framework and video-based training were introduced to both teachers and students for the first time. This emphasizes the need for further implementation and investigation. In addition, difficulties related to motivation, emotions, and technology were difficult to link to specific steps or tasks. Hence, additional research is necessary to identify motivational and emotional strategies that could enhance the mapping framework and collect data on task-level difficulties. Furthermore, the data on student difficulties are based solely on teacher self-reports, which may not accurately capture individual differences among students. To address this issue, it's crucial to gather feedback from students during the process and use a more personalized approach in dealing with student difficulties.

In summary, addressing the difficulties that students face during problem-solving tasks is crucial for promoting effective learning and SRL skills. Teachers play a critical role in gaining valuable insights and using this information to train their students. The developed problem-solving framework and the PS-SOS map can aid in identifying problematic steps and tasks. To improve problem-solving skills, future training programs should prioritize addressing these difficulties. Additionally, research should explore the potential of difficulty-based feedback provided by teachers or technology, such as chatbots or virtual assistants, to facilitate the learning process for students.

Acknowledgement

This research is supported by the Chief Scientist of the Israeli Ministry of Education.

References

Alderman, M. K., & MacDonald, S. (2015). A self-regulatory approach to classroom management: Empowering students and teachers. *Kappa Delta Pi Record, 51*(2), 52-56. https://doi.org/10.1080/00228958.2015.1023145

Araka, E., Maina, E., Gitonga, R., & Oboko, R. (2020). Research trends in measurement and intervention tools for self-regulated learning for e-learning environments—systematic review (2008–2018). *Research and Practice in Technology Enhanced Learning, 15*, 1–21. https://doi.org/10.1186/S41039-020-00129-5

Arifin, S., Setyosari, P., Sa'dijah, C., & Kuswandi, D. (2020). The effect of problem-based learning by cognitive style on critical thinking skills and students" retention. *Journal of Technology and Science Education, 10*(2), 271–281. https://doi.org/10.3926/jotse.790

Cohen, G., Assi, A., Cohen, A., Bronshtein, A., Glick, D., Gabbay, H., & Ezra, O. (2022). Video-Assisted Self-Regulated Learning (SRL) Training: COVID-19 Edition. In: Hilliger, I., Muñoz-Merino, P.J., De Laet, T., Ortega-Arranz, A., Farrell, T. (eds) *Educating for a New Future: Making Sense of Technology-Enhanced Learning Adoption. EC-TEL 2022. Lecture Notes in Computer Science,* (p.p. 59-73). Springer, Cham. https://doi.org/10.1007/978-3-031-16290-9_5

Csapó, B., & Funke, J. (2017). *The nature of problem solving.* OECD. http://dx.doi.org/10.1787/9789264273955-en

Davidson, J. E., & Sternberg, R. J. (Eds.). (2003). *The psychology of problem solving.* Cambridge university press.

De Smul, M., Heirweg, S., Devos, G., & Van Keer, H. (2019). School and teacher determinants underlying teachers' implementation of self-regulated learning in primary education. *Research Papers in Education, 34*(6), 701–724. https://doi.org/10.1080/02671522.2018.1536888

Dresel, M., & Haugwitz, M. (2008). A computer-based approach to fostering motivation and self-regulated learning. *The Journal of Experimental Education, 77*(1), 3-20. https://doi.org/10.3200/JEXE.77.1.3-20

Efklides, A., & Metallidou, P. (2020). Applying metacognition and self-regulated learning in the classroom. In Oxford *Research Encyclopedia of Education*. https://doi.org/10.1093/acrefore/9780190264093.013.961

Hanewald, R. (2013). Transition between primary and secondary school: Why it is important and how it can be supported. *Australian Journal of Teacher Education, 38*(1), 62-74. https://doi.org/10.14221/ajte.2013v38n1.7

Jansen, R. S., van Leeuwen, A., Janssen, J., Conijn, R., & Kester, L. (2020). Supporting learners' self-regulated learning in Massive Open Online Courses. *Computers and Education, 146*, 1-17. https://doi.org/10.1016/j.compedu.2019.103771

Kim, M. C., & Hannafin, M. J. (2011). Scaffolding problem solving in technology-enhanced learning environments (TELEs): Bridging research and theory with practice. *Computers & Education, 56*(2), 403-417.

Khoiriyah, A. J., & Husamah, H. (2018). Problem-based learning: Creative thinking skills, problem-solving skills, and learning outcome of seventh grade students. *JPBI (Jurnal Pendidikan Biologi Indonesia), 4*(2), 151-160. https://doi.org/10.22219/jpbi.v4i2.5804

Liu, T., & Israel, M. (2022). Uncovering students' problem-solving processes in game-based learning environments. *Computers & Education, 182*, 1-14. https://doi.org/10.1016/j.compedu.2022.104462

Mourtos, N. J., Okamoto, N. D., & Rhee, J. (2004). Defining, teaching, and assessing problem solving skills. In *7th UICEE Annual Conference on Engineering Education* (pp. 1-5).

Nicolaidou, I. (2013). E-portfolios supporting primary students' writing performance and peer feedback. *Computers & Education, 68*, 404-415. https://doi.org/10.1016/j.compedu.2013.06.004

OECD. (2021). *OECD Skills Outlook 2021: Learning for Life.* OECD Publishing, Paris. https://doi.org/10.1787/0ae365b4-en

Panadero, E., Klug, J., & Järvelä, S. (2016). Third wave of measurement in the self-regulated learning field: When measurement and intervention come hand in hand. *Scandinavian Journal of Educational Research, 60*(6), 723–735. https://doi.org/10.1080/00313831.2015.1066436

Schloemer, P. & Brenan, K. (2006). From students to learners: Developing self-regulated learning. *Journal of Education for Business, 82*(2), 81-87. https://doi.org/10.3200/JOEB.82.2.81-87

Snyder, L. G., & Snyder, M. J. (2008). Teaching critical thinking and problem-solving skills. *The Journal of Research in Business Education, 50*(2), 90-99.

Sulisworo, D., Fatimah, N., & Sunaryati, S. S. (2020). A Quick Study on SRL Profiles of Online Learning Participants during the Anticipation of the Spread of COVID-19. *International Journal of Evaluation and Research in Education, 9*(3), 723-730. https://doi.org/10.11591/ijere.v9i3.20642

Tissenbaum, M. (2020). I see what you did there! Divergent collaboration and learner transitions from unproductive to productive states in open-ended inquiry. *Computers & Education, 145*, 1-15. https://doi.org/10.1016/j.compedu.2019.103739

Uka, A., & Uka, A. (2020). The effect of students' experience with the transition from primary to secondary school on self-regulated learning and motivation. *Sustainability, 12*(20), 2-16. https://doi.org/10.3390/su12208519

van Alten, D.C.D., Phielix, C., Janssen, J., & Kester, L. (2020). Self-regulated learning support in flipped learning videos enhances learning outcomes. *Computers & Education, 158*, 1-16. https://doi.org/10.1016/j.compedu.2020.104000

van Ginkel, S., Gulikers, J., Biemans, H., Noroozi, O., Roozen, M., Bos, T., van Tilborg, R., van Halteren, M., & Mulder, M. (2019). Fostering oral presentation competence through a virtual reality-based task for delivering feedback. *Computers & Education, 134*, 78-97. https://doi.org/10.1016/j.compedu.2019.02.006

Wang, T. H. (2011). Developing web-based assessment strategies for facilitating junior high school students to perform self-regulated learning in an e-learning environment, 7(2), 1-12. *Computers & Education.* https://doi.org/10.1016/j.compedu.2011.01.003

Yavuz, G., Yasemin, D., & Arslan, Ç. (2017). Elementary School Students Perception Levels of Problem-Solving Skills. *Universal Journal of Educational Research, 5*(11), 1896-1901. https://doi.org/10.13189/ujer.2017.051106

Zheng, L. (2016). The effectiveness of self-regulated learning scaffolds on academic performance in computer-based learning environments: a meta-analysis. *Asia Pacific Education Review, 17*(2), 187–202. https://doi.org/10.1007/s12564-016-9426-9

COMPETENCES FOR THE APPLICATION AND PROMOTION OF TECHNOLOGY IN VOCATIONAL PROFESSIONAL TEACHER EDUCATION: A CASE STUDY OF CHINA

Wang Bin, Vytautas Magnus University, Lithuania
Genutė Gedvilienė, Vytautas Magnus University, Lithuania

Correspondence: *Genutė Gedvilienė: genute.gedviliene@vdu.lt*

Abstract

The application of technology in vocational education teacher education is becoming more and more important, and it has become a trend that cannot be ignored, especially under the influence of the digital age and the epidemic, the process of technology application has been accelerated. Studies have shown that the use of technology-based teaching resources such as multimedia courseware, digital textbooks, and distance online courses can provide students with a rich and varied learning experience, thereby improving the quality of teaching. Technology can also increase the effectiveness of teacher training programs by providing teachers with flexible and convenient ways to acquire new knowledge and skills. This paper takes China as a case study on higher vocational education in different regions of the country, using methods such as investigation, interview and analysis, to explore the status quo, problems and reasons for the application of technology in the current vocational professional teacher education process. Finally, try to make some suggestions on how to use technology to improve the competence of vocational teachers in higher vocational colleges.

Keywords*:* Vocational education, professional teacher education, competencies and technology.

Introduction

In the world, many countries attach great importance to the cultivation of professional teachers' competencies: Yang Y. (2014) mentioned that Germany adopted the "dual system" VET model. Dual-system universities have strong practicality, and the integration of theory and practice is close. Full-time teachers in German dual-system universities must obtain a doctorate and should have more than five years of internship experience. Most teachers are part-time and come from all fields of society. These teachers have strong practical skills and a rich theoretical knowledge level. Zhao Y. (2004) mentions that teachers in vocational education in Denmark must receive theoretical and in-service training before entering the profession and that these teachers must have professional teaching experience and teaching ability, after which they are required to take the in-service teacher qualification examination. Only after they are all qualified can they take up their post.

Through the analysis of the practice of each country, it can be found that most developed countries have established the vocational teacher qualification access system and VET plan, and all attach great importance to the quality of vocational education teacher training and teacher continuing education. Although the improvement of professional teacher education in China's vocational colleges can learn from foreign training systems and methods, we need to further explore and practice the innovation of teacher education technology in a specific practice. Through the discussion of different techniques, the education competencies of professional teachers in vocational colleges is improved, and the improvement of teachers' personal competencies promotes the improvement of vocational education quality.

Methodology

This study analyzed sources and applied qualitative and quantitative research methods (questionnaires, interviews). Literature analysis is based on research by multiple authors. The empirical part of the paper presents the case of China. Four kinds of abilities of vocational teachers in higher vocational colleges are analyzed. Conduct a survey of teachers in higher vocational colleges across the country to explore the main characteristics and existing problems of technology and application in the process of vocational professional teacher education.

Interviews were conducted with vocational teachers from vocational schools in different regions and specialties in China. The research aimed to find out the role technology plays in the professional teacher education process. It also analyzes the actual situation of vocational teacher education in higher vocational colleges.

Definition of Higher Vocational Teachers' competence

Here are scholars' definitions of teacher competency from different perspectives. Wu Q. (2014) believes that vocational education teachers should not only have excellent professional theoretical foundation and professional technical competence related to career, but also master knowledge related to work process, technology and career development; In addition to being committed to imparting professional knowledge, we should also have the competence to integrate this knowledge into education and teaching from the perspective of pedagogy; In addition to the competence to find problems, it must also have the competence to formulate solutions and strategies to solve problems; In addition to being familiar with the working process knowledge in relevant professional fields, we must also have the competence to integrate it into Curriculum Development on the premise of following the teaching law of vocational education, and realize the goal of vocational competence training through action-oriented teaching. Lu J., Li P. Zhang H. (2016) summarized the abilities of vocational teachers as teaching cognitive competence, teaching design competence, teaching control competence, teaching scientific research competence, teaching practice competence, teaching technology competence, etc. Jiang J. (2016) believes that the competence of vocational teachers should be "rational and practical". "Integration of theory and practice" refers to the equal emphasis on theory and practice, and the integration between the two. Specifically, vocational education teachers should not only have rich professional theoretical knowledge and theoretical teaching competence but also have solid professional skills and practical guidance competence, which should be connected with each other. when establishing the competency model of higher vocational teachers, Zhou F. (2017) subdivided the summary of teachers' competency teaching competence into six aspects, including teaching competence literacy, scientific and technological competence literacy, practical competence literacy, work attitude, professional literacy and self-management literacy.

After analysis of Song W. (2017), he believes that the competency of higher vocational teachers includes ten contents: practical operation competence, competence to integrate theory with practice, teaching competence, learning and innovation competence, professional knowledge, compound knowledge, professional ethics, educational concept, enterprise work and training experience, character and characteristics. Jiang Y. (2021) roughly divided the teaching competence of higher vocational teachers into three types: first, classroom teaching competence, including the competence to understand the learning situation, design teaching contents and activities, organize teaching, teaching implementation and teaching reflection; Second, professional curriculum construction competence, including curriculum development, curriculum resource integration, curriculum teaching evaluation and so on; The third is the competence to support the expansion of teaching, including the competence of technical guidance and training, reform and innovation, scientific research and development and so on. Jiao X. (2021), after summarizing the relevant research at home and abroad, defined the professional competence of higher vocational teachers as the high-level competence of cognition, affection and skills that higher vocational teachers should have when engaged in teaching, mainly including their own education and teaching, application of educational technology, scientific construction, discipline construction, organization and management, professional practice and so on. Sun D. al. (2022) based on the "double high school plan", summarized the contents of Higher Vocational Teachers' abilities as follows: political competence, integration and innovation competence, scientific research and social service competence, digital application and transformation competence, national production and education resource integration and promotion competence, etc.

Based on the definition of teacher competence provided by relevant foreign institutions and the Chinese definition of teacher competence, the author believes that teacher competence can be summarised in four points: 1. Teachers' competence to lead by example, high moral character, knowledge of national policies and the ability to convey progressive vocational education ideas to students. 2. Competence in teaching and learning: competence in mastering the content of teaching (basic and complex material), competence in teaching students learning methods, competence in teaching students according to their abilities and in the flexible application of teaching methods, competence in instructional design, competence in scientifically organising and managing students' homework, competence in the organisation of teaching. 3. Assessment and management competencies: competence to guide pupils' practice, competence in the practical workplace, competence to understand and investigate pupils' psychological characteristics and level of knowledge, competence to stimulate pupils' interest in learning and to mobilise pupils' initiative and enthusiasm, competence to assess pupils' competences in a scientific and fair way. 4. Developing innovation competence: the use and encouragement of new technologies for learners (ICT, virtual learning, use of modern access to IT systems, etc.) competence in scientific and technological innovation and competence in research.

Technology and Application in Vocational Professional Teacher Education

According to relevant research, the application of modern technology has significantly promoted the training of vocational education teachers. According to Feng T. (2021) research, the professional development model of vocational education teachers is closely related to technical support. With the support of modern technology, teachers can conduct online teaching and interaction in different locations by using remote teaching techniques such as video conferencing and online classrooms. At the same time, interactive courseware production software can produce vivid and interesting teaching content, and improve learners' learning interest and participation. The application of virtual simulation laboratory can improve learning effect and practical ability. Artificial intelligence technology can analyze and evaluate the learning process of students, and provide personalized learning suggestions and feedback. Mobile learning applications can increase the convenience and flexibility of learning. Social media teaching can make teaching more interactive and interesting. Data analysis technology can conduct in-depth analysis of students' learning process and provide more accurate learning suggestions and assistance. Course management system can improve teaching efficiency and management effect.

In addition, Li T. and Li L. (2018) pointed out in their research that under the background of the mobile Internet, the vocational education teacher training model needs to be innovated. Through the use of modern technology, the constraints of time and space can be broken and educational resources can be better utilized. At the same time, under the background of networkization, Yan J. and Shen M. (2019) believe that the technical application of vocational education teacher training needs to focus on network construction, strengthen the construction of learning platforms, and improve training effects. Zheng Y. (2016) pointed out that the technological innovation and application of vocational education teacher training is a key issue, which can provide help for the improvement of education and training.

In summary,, the development of technology application in professional teacher education is of great significance to the improvement of teachers' competence.

Data analysis

This online questionnaire survey among teachers in higher vocational colleges in different regions of the country from February to May 2021.The questionnaire was conducted by distributing links to the teacher WeChat group. A total of 525 valid questionnaires were collected.

Table 1: *Descriptive statistical analysis*

	Minimum	Maximum	Mean	Std. Deviation	Skewness	Kurtosis
Exemplary competence	1.00	5.00	4.40	0.56	-1.29	3.22
Educational and teaching competence	2.00	5.00	4.28	0.50	-0.83	1.19
Evaluation and guidance competence	2.20	5.00	4.12	0.51	-0.60	0.27
Developing and innovative competence	2.00	5.00	4.12	0.54	-0.64	0.46

Descriptive statistical results show that the average values of Exemplary competence, Educational and teaching competence, Evaluation and guidance competence, developing and innovative competence are all above 4 points, indicating that teachers' evaluation of their own abilities is above average. The standard deviation of each competence development is about 0.5, indicating that different teachers have different scores of each competence. The results of skewness and kurtosis show that there is some skewness in each competence, but it is not serious.

Generally speaking, the competence of Chinese vocational professional teachers still need to be further improved.

This is a multiple-choice question to find out whether teachers like technology and applications. There are five levels of liking. Among the 525 samples, 77 people said they liked it very much, accounting for 14.74%. 180 students expressed their liking, accounting for 34.29% of the total number. 138 students, accounting for 26.28%, said they like it a little bit. 93 people (17.63%) said they didn't like it. 37 people, 7.05% said they dislike it very much. (See Figure 1)

Figure 1: *Favorability of technology and applications in teacher education*

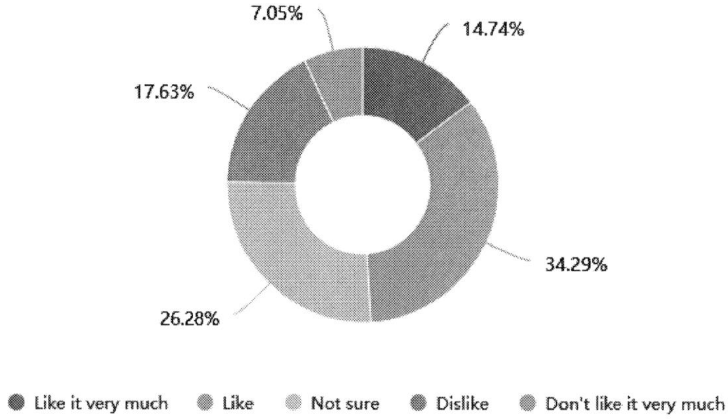

According to the survey results, 235 respondents chose "like" or above, accounting for 75.32% of the total. This partly reflects teachers' general acceptance and acceptance of technology and applications in education. Despite this, 24.67% of teachers still dislike the technology and applications for some reason, which reflects the lack of technology and application. The following issues will be studied in more detail.

This is a survey on the comparison between technology and application and traditional education. It is a matrix of multiple choice questions, with a total of 4 questions. (See Figure 2)

Figure 2: *Technology & Application vs. Traditional Learning Styles*

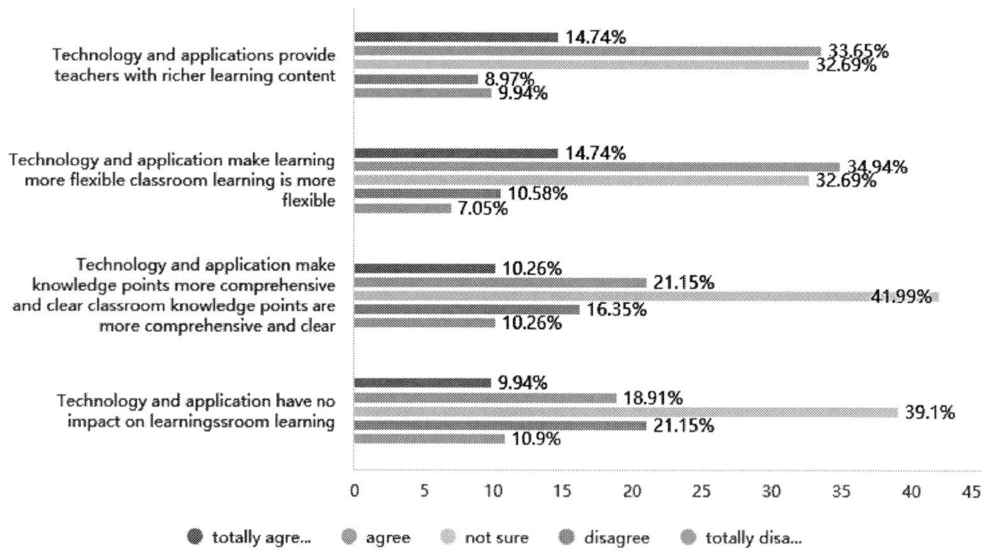

It can be seen from the survey data that technology and application have an advantage in terms of the provision of teaching content and the diversity of learning methods. In terms of knowledge point explanation and learning effect, the advantages of technology and application are slightly lower. In the process of teacher education in vocational education, technology and application are different from traditional teaching.

Advantages and disadvantages of application and technology in the improvement of professional teachers' competence

Through data analysis, we can find that some teachers hold negative attitudes towards technology and applications. In order to fully understand the impact of technology and application on professional teacher education, the author conducted interviews with professional teachers in vocational colleges,

Zhang B, a teacher at the School of Industrial Engineering of Ningxia Vocational and Technical College, often uses "micro-classes". In the interview, he believes that "micro-classes" are very helpful for vocational education. Generally, before learning, he will screen high-quality "micro-lessons" according to the learning content, and list the main knowledge points first. In class, if it involves some of the latest technical content, or knowledge that cannot be obtained in the classroom, he will also use the "micro class" platform. The content of the micro-lecture is precise, the time is short, and the key points are clear. With the help of network resources, it can be downloaded and watched by teachers or students who need it. Knowledge cognition becomes more convenient and effective. However, he also believes that current technology and applications still have certain limitations, such as network instability and equipment differences, which may affect teachers and students in the teaching process.

Lu X, a teacher at Lanzhou Resources and Environment Technology Vocational College in Gansu Province, mentioned in the interview that the school attaches great importance to the use of Internet + for blended teaching. On May 23, 2020, the school's School of Metallurgical Engineering and the Lanzhou Institute of Chemical Physics, Chinese Academy of Sciences cooperated to hold a themed online public science day. Teachers conduct online live broadcasts and open class learning during the event. There are also more ways for students to complete homework, from paper-based homework and on-site defines to email, learning forums, online APP homework submission, batch correction of homework, and online defence. Various resource platforms can also monitor the learning situation in real-time, quickly analyse and obtain intuitive data, answer questions online, etc., saving a lot of unnecessary time wastage. However, this learning method puts forward new requirements for teachers' competence. Because vocational education teachers are different in age, educational background, technical level and other factors, there are differences in their technology application. Some teachers may lack the competence and confidence in technology application.

Liu G, a teacher at Shaoxing Vocational and Technical College, said in an interview that Zhejiang Province has great advantages in virtual reality technology. Shaoxing Vocational and Technical College is currently the first designated teaching base for the national medical information technology training and examination project in Zhejiang Province, and the first "digital upgrade training base for small, medium and micro businesses" in the country. They have built a virtualized training base. In addition, the school also attaches great importance to students' practical operation, regularly holds skill competitions, and simulates the actual working environment on the Internet, so that teachers can actually apply the skills they have learned to future teaching. However, he said that although the application of modern technology can break through geographical restrictions, with the construction of more and more virtual training bases, some vocational education schools may face the problem of insufficient educational resources, such as insufficient network resources and equipment resources.

Through literature research and interviews with professional teachers we uncover the relationship between education, technology and competence, (See Figure 3)

Figure 3: *The relationship between competence, education and technology*

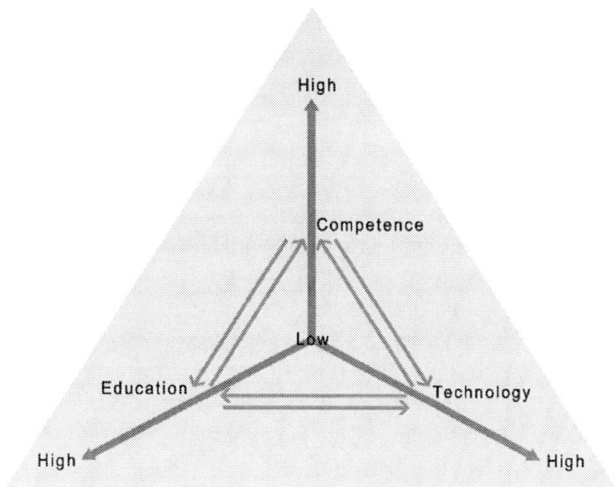

Education and technology are the basis of competence, and knowledge that is educated through technology and widely applied and transferred can be transformed into competence. competence not only includes the level of achievement that a person has reached now but also includes the potential that a person has. For example, a person who reads a lot may have rich knowledge, but his competence to solve practical problems is low, which means that his knowledge only stays in books and cannot be widely transferred, nor can it be used to solve practical problems.

Education, technology and competence are closely related. First, the formation and development of competence depend on the support of education and technology. With the accumulation of people's education and technology, people's competence will continue to improve. Secondly, the level of competence will affect the level of knowledge and technology mastered in the education process.

Conclusions

With the increase in social needs and the continuous advancement of industrialization, the demand for high-quality technical personnel is also increasing year by year. Higher vocational colleges shoulder the important task of cultivating and delivering high-quality technical talents. In this process, higher vocational colleges need to provide students with advanced teaching concepts, high-quality teaching services, and provide rich practical training opportunities. The development of technology and applications has provided very favourable conditions for vocational education, but at the same time several problems have emerged:

Limitation of technology application: The current technology application still has certain limitations, such as network instability, equipment differences, etc. These problems may cause teachers and students to be affected in the teaching process.

Teachers' technology application level is uneven: Vocational education teachers' age, educational background, technical level and other factors are different, resulting in differences in their technology application. Some teachers may lack the ability and confidence in technology application.

Insufficient educational resources: Although the application of modern technology can break geographical restrictions, some vocational education schools may face the problem of insufficient educational resources, such as insufficient network resources and equipment resources.

Teachers are unwilling to accept training: Some vocational education teachers have a negative attitude towards technical training. They believe that technology is not the focus of teaching, which also leads to poor application effect of technology application in vocational education teacher training.

Single training mode: In vocational education teacher training, a single training mode is often adopted, which has great limitations and cannot meet the needs of different teachers.

Faced with the above problems, schools should strengthen the maintenance and management of networks and equipment to ensure the stability and reliability of technology applications. At the same time, schools can regularly organize teachers to participate in technical training to improve teachers' technical application ability and confidence. In terms of the construction of educational resources, schools should strengthen the construction of educational resources, improve the adequacy and quality of educational resources, and ensure that teachers and students can make full use of modern technology for teaching and learning. For the problem that teachers are unwilling to accept training, it can be solved by guiding teachers to change their attitudes. Luo M (2020) proposed that by setting up practical operation links, teachers' interest and learning motivation can be stimulated, and teachers can be made aware of the importance of technical skills for teaching so that they are willing to receive training. In order to meet the needs of different teachers, vocational education teacher training should promote diversified training models. Yang B (2021) suggested that online education, virtual simulation training, etc. can be used, and personalized training plans can be formulated according to the different needs of different teachers so that teachers can independently choose training methods and content to improve training effects.

In conclusion, the application of technology in vocational education teacher training needs to be continuously refined and improved to meet the ever-evolving educational needs.

References

Feng T. (2021). Research on Professional Development Model and Technical Support of Vocational Education Teachers [J]. *Vocational and Technical Education, 42(19)*, 44-50.

Jiang J. (2016). Focus and Enlightenment on the characteristics of pre-service training of vocational teachers in developed countries, *Education and occupation, (2),* 17.

Jiao X. (2021). Professional competence structure and promotion path of Higher Vocational Teachers -- an interview study based on 20 higher vocational professional teachers. *Higher vocational education, (08).*16.

Jiang Y. (2021). Connotation, challenge and path of improving teaching competence of higher vocational teachers. *Education and occupation, (10),* 78.

Lu J., & Li p, Zhang H. (2016). Continuing education of Vocational Education Teachers: Interpretation Based on teaching competence structure model. *CHINA ADULT EDUCATION, (21),* 32-36.

Luo M. (2020). Research on the Current Situation and Improvement Strategies of Vocational Education Teachers' Informatization Skills [J]. *Science and Technology Wind, (09),* 52-53.

Li T,, & Li L. (2018). Research on the Innovation of Vocational Education Teacher Training Model under the Background of Mobile Internet [J]. *Chinese Vocational and Technical Education, (8),* 37-41.

Sun D.,& Lin Y, Lei Y. (2022). Problems and Countermeasures of Higher Vocational Teachers' competence construction under the "double high plan". *Education and occupation, (1),*98-103.

Song W. (2017). Application of competency model in higher vocational teacher training. *Modern economic information, (3),* 34-37.

Wu Q. (2014) interpretation of the connotation and competence structure of Vocational Education [double qualified] teachers. *Chinese Vocational and Technical Education, (21),*63-70.

Yang B. (2021). Discussion on the Training Mode of Vocational Education Teachers under the Background of Networking [J]. *Science and Technology Wind, (03),* 51-52.

Yan J.,& Shen M. (2019). Technical Application of Vocational Education Teacher Training under the Background of Networking [J]. *Electronic Education Research, 35(1),* 20-26.

Yang Y. (2014). The Study on Double Qualified Teachers Construction Paths of Multi-dimensional Perspective [D]. *Hubei: Hubei University of Technology,(6),* 17-21

Zhou F. (2017). Competency model and application value analysis of higher vocational teachers. *Higher vocational education, (6),* 17-21.

Zheng Y. (2016). Technological Innovation and Application of Vocational Education Teacher Training [J]. *Educational Technology Forum, 10,* 152-153.

Zhao Y. (2004) Comparative Analysis on the Construction of Teaching Staff in Foreign Higher Vocational Education. *Journal of Jilin Provincial College of Economic Management Cadres, 18,* 58-59.

TRANSFORMING THE CULTURE AND INNOVATING THE PRACTICES OF DIGITAL ASSESSMENT: HOW MOOCS CAN SCALE UP THE IMPACT

António Moreira Teixeira, Laboratório de Educação a Distância e eLearning, Universidade Aberta, Portugal; Lúcia Amante, Laboratório de Educação a Distância e eLearning, Universidade Aberta, Portugal; Elizabeth Souza, Laboratório de Educação a Distância e eLearning, Portugal; Maria do Carmo Teixeira Pinto, Laboratório de Educação a Distância e eLearning, Universidade Aberta, Portugal; João Paz, Laboratório de Educação a Distância e eLearning, Universidade Aberta, Portugal

Correspondence: *António Moreira Teixeira: antonio.moreira.teixeira.pt@gmail.com*

Abstract

The emerging new learning scenarios made possible by the rapid dissemination of adaptive digital technologies are deeply changing higher education processes. They provide educators and learners with new opportunities for transforming their educational practices. encouraging learning innovation and challenging traditional teaching methods. This transformation is particularly significant in how learning achievement is measured, assessed, and certified. The use of learning analytics and adaptive digital technologies not only contribute to consolidate an assessment for learning approach as call for it. In the face of this challenge, educators must speedily adapt their practices to ensure that they are effectively using digital tools to support this new assessment culture. In the framework of the Erasmus+ project PROF-XXI, a Massive Open Online Course (MOOC) entitled "The 21st Century Teacher: Learning to Teach with Digital Technologies" was designed and delivered to facilitate teachers' access to good practices in this field. The MOOC included four modules covering various aspects of digital education and was designed taking as a reference the competences defined in the DigCompEdu framework. It was delivered on an Open edX instance. A total of 5,660 participants, mainly from Latin America, took this course in two cohorts, with 681 participants completing it. In this paper we describe the experience of designing a learning module specifically dedicated to digital assessment innovation for this MOOC, The aim was to inspire educational change and promote a more sustainable approach to assessment for learning based on the PrACT framework. The main results of this experience are presented and discussed, as well as lessons learnt.

Keywords:

Open Education; MOOC, Digital Learning; Digital Alternative Assessment; Assessment for Learning; Latin America.

Introduction

Traditional classroom teaching falls short of providing an immediate learning environment, engaging and personalised, flexible enough to accommodate the increasing diversity of learners, their needs, and expectations (Haleem et al., 2022). As digital technologies rapidly disseminate across educational institutions, its impact is immediately felt, leading to the transformation of teaching and learning. This creates a need for teachers and educators in general, as well as students and non-formal learners, to develop digital competencies. The Erasmus+ PROF-XXI Project (http://www.profxxi.org/) focuses on enhancing the capacity of Teaching and Learning Centers (TLCs) in Latin American Higher Education Institutions (HEIs) to fulfil the requirements of the twenty-first century (Delgado Kloos et al., 2021; Pérez-Sanagustín et al, 2022).

Digital competence involves the confident, critical and responsible use of, and engagement with, digital technologies for learning, at work, and for participation in society. It includes information and data literacy, communication and collaboration, media literacy, digital content creation (including programming), safety (including digital well-being and competences related to cybersecurity), intellectual property related questions, problem solving and critical thinking (Vuorikari et al., 2022). The European Framework for the Digital Competence of Educators (DigCompEdu) characterizes it more specifically: "As professionals dedicated to teaching, they need, in addition to the general digital competences for life and work, educator-specific digital competences to be able to effectively use digital technologies [...] to foster efficient, inclusive and innovative teaching and learning strategies" (Redecker, 2017, 15-16). Developing these competences is therefore critical to ensure that educators can use digital tools effectively and provide innovative teaching methods. This transformation is particularly significant in how learning achievement is measured, assessed, and certified. The implementation of learning analytics and adaptive digital technologies have been contributing to consolidate a new approach to assessment. However, teachers must have the necessary competences to integrate digital tools into their teaching practices. As demonstrated in the context of the higher education system to the Covid-19 pandemic, this difficulty is aggravated by the fact that digital transformation in education refers to the incorporation of digital technologies into teaching and learning practices to improve educational outcomes, which not only involves the adoption of new technologies, but also the development of new teaching methodologies, strategies, and pedagogies (Abad-Segura et al., 2020). To address this massive challenge, the PROF-XXI partnership developed a Massive Open Online Course (MOOC) entitled "The 21st Century Teacher: Learning to Teach with Digital Technologies." One of the modules of this MOOC was specifically dedicated to digital assessment. The option for an open education format was based on its suitability to deliver a highly scalable, flexible, inclusive and speedy teacher training experience. In fact, MOOCs provide a space for problematizing and analyzing practices in an open and collaborative working environment (Teixeira et al., 2018). The outcomes and insights learned from designing and delivering this course and specifically the course unit on digital assessment are detailed in the following sections.

A MOOC on the 21st century teacher: learning to teach with digital technologies

The MOOC developed by the PROF-XXI partnership was aligned with the DigCompEdu framework and it targeted higher education teachers and other educators from Latin American countries. It provided participants with a significant learning experience in which they had access to research-validated concepts, methodologies, strategies, and good practices on technology-enhanced teaching and learning. The purpose of the MOOC was to contribute to the development of teachers' and other educators' digital competencies.

The open course was deployed on the Campus MOOC-Maker platform (http://campus.moocmaker.org) which resulted from the Erasmus+ project MOOC-Maker (Alario-Hoyos, 2018). This decision reflected the fact that most PROF-XXI partners had been also part of the MOOC-Maker consortium. Therefore, it added to the sustainability of the initiative taken.

MOOC participants learned on how effectively leveraging digital technologies to enhance their teaching practices. It encouraged them to promote active learning and to create more engaging and effective learning environments for their students.

The MOOC was implemented in two cohorts, the first one from 8th November to 13th December 2022 and the second cohort took place from 26th February to 10th April 2023. In total, 5,660 participants registered in this MOOC, with 681 of them obtaining a certificate of completion (see table 1). It should be noted that 55.44% of the participants were female, while 43.99% were male, which represents a proportionate gender representation. Of the other participants, 10 of them declared to be non-binary and 22 did not provide information.

Table 1: MOOC Cohort comparison (participants)

	First cohort	Second cohort	Total
Registered participants	3,734	1,926	5,660
Active participants	792	426	1.218
Certified participants	426	255	681
Completion rate	11.4%	13.2%	12%

Source: Alario Hoyos, C.; Delgado Kloos, C. & Morales, M. (2022, 2023).

The MOOC was developed collaboratively by an international multidisciplinary team of experts from Spain, Guatemala, Portugal and France. To ensure a coherent learning design, a common strategy adjusted to the features of the Open edX platform was devised and shared among the partners. However, each one acted autonomous in the way it implemented those general principles to the production of the different modules. Each module covered a distinct digital competence, as follows: active teaching methodologies; instructional design for active and hybrid learning; digital assessment of learning, and evidence-based continuous improvement. They included multiple educational resources, as videos, exercises, formative activities, forums, a podcast, and a final exam.

Each module started with an introduction video lecture which presented the key concepts, explained them and gave concrete examples to facilitate comprehension. Videos had closed captions for easy understanding and accessibility. Participants were given access to a list of complementary references on each module. They were also required to answer a series of questions at the end of each module to receive feedback on what they had learned. The non-scored formative activities were a useful tool for students to apply the module's concepts and deepen their understanding of the topics. Forums were interactive spaces where students could share their experiences and perspectives on the module's topics.

The MOOC also included a course presentation module with a welcome video, a course syllabus, a learning path, faculty information, a section on frequently asked questions, the initial survey, and the welcome forum. The participants were required to spend a minimum of 4 hours and a maximum of 16 hours per week in this course.

Promoting a new digital assessment culture

The traditional perspective of "measuring" learning at given points in the learning process, with a special focus on the use of written tests, has long been inadequate and insufficient. Especially so when dealing with the assessment of complex and diversified knowledge resulting from the new work dynamics demanded by the challenges of the contemporary world (Pereira et al.2021).

Assessment is still generally linked to tasks of little relevance, disconnected from reality, driven by the purpose of obtaining a qualification and not as meaningful evidence of how competences acquired may be applied to respond to real problems and challenges. As a result of very transmissive teaching methods, traditionally assessment was centred on content. It appeared as something almost exclusively linked with the role of classification and certification, highlighting therefore the concern with "measuring" learning.

The need to transpose curricula based on mere content to competence-based curricula making it possible to face current challenges associated with pedagogical proposals that go beyond the transmission of knowledge, determined the evolution of conceptions of assessment and its various roles. As a result, the final assessment role associated with giving a mark (summative role) has been giving way to a greater importance of the formative function of assessment, i.e. to the processes of regulating learning. Considering this perspective, a new understanding of assessment has been emerging, giving rise to the so-called 'Culture of Assessment' (Pereira et al.,2015; Birenbaum, 1996).

From this perspective, it is worth highlighting some key ideas or concepts, such as the concept of competence. This concept refers to the ability to respond successfully to a personal/social demand or to perform a task or activity that requires the convergence of knowledge (implicit and/or explicit), skills, abilities, capacities, skills, attitudes, emotions and values (Pereira et al.2021). It is developed through action and interaction both in educational contexts (formal, non-formal or informal) and in professional contexts, and requires the mobilisation of knowledge rather than just its reproduction.

The assessment of competences therefore requires a new approach, integrating knowledge, skills and attitudes. As such, it implies the use of a variety of assessment strategies and modes of assessment that go beyond the traditional written test. This new approach requires assessing performance in authentic tasks, close to real contexts, which provide the application of the competences to be developed.

Another key concept refers to the 'digital alternative assessment' strategy. The expansion of the use of electronic tools in assessment, from multiple-choice tests to questionnaires, blogs and e-portfolios, among others, calls for the need to clarify the understanding of e-assessment. In this regard, a concept is proposed that incorporates the technological dimension, but is specifically aimed at competence assessment. The concept of digital alternative assessment strategy (Amante et al., 2017) refers to a set of alternative assessment proposals, where design, implementation and feedback are mediated by technologies. The design involves the definition of the competences to be assessed, the indications about the activity to be carried out by the student and the use of electronic devices for its implementation.

In this perspective, the traditional idea of assessment of learning gives way to the concept of assessment for learning. In assessment of learning, the data collected are used to make judgments about the level of performance of learners. The data collected are used to make judgements about the level of achievement of learners. The information collected by the assessment process is basically summative and, when translated into a numerical or qualitative rating, certifies the learning achieved. This type of assessment may also indicate learning that has not been achieved, but it is not intended to be remedial and occurs on an ad hoc basis, usually

at the end of the learning process. Error is understood as failure. Assessment for learning focuses on certification.
By contrast, in assessment for learning, the formative and empowering role of assessment is emphasised in contrast with the measurement role. Teachers use the information from the assessment process, including errors, to change their teaching practice, with the aim of helping the learner to improve his or her performance. Rather than being seen as something that happens at the end of the learning process, assessment is now considered as an integral part of the learning process. Consequently, similarly, to learning it is a process of social interaction in which all stakeholders should be involved (Pinto, 2016).
In the networked society a new culture of learning is emerging and, with it, necessarily also a new culture of evaluation (Birenbaum, 1996). One that is characterised by:
- Emphasis on the interconnection of assessment with teaching and learning.
- Student participation in the elaboration of their own assessment in dialogue with the teacher.
- Evaluation of process and product.
- Assumption of a diversity of forms of assessment, associated and interconnected with teaching practices.
- Use of assessment tasks close to real-life situations.
- Cognitively challenging activities.
- Continuous and ongoing process.
- Use of feedback that reinforces students' reflection on their learning.
- Valuing qualitative assessment over simple grading.

The MOOC module on "Digital Assessment for Learning"

The course module on "Digital Assessment for Learning" was developed by a multidisciplinary team from the Laboratory of Distance and eLearning of Universidade Aberta, Portugal. It involved 6 researchers and 4 technicians. The team had a large experience in designing MOOCs for teacher training. As such, it applied some of the general principles of its own pedagogical model for massive open online education, the iMOOC (Teixeira & Mota, 2015), to an Open edX environment.
The MOOC module had the following learning objectives:

- Characterise the new assessment culture, differentiating it from the traditional one.
- Identify the main dimensions and parameters of the PrACT framework for digital assessment.
- To reflect on the use of self and peer assessment in Higher Education
- Distinguish digital assessment tools, instruments and media.
- To design an assessment plan

The course module included five (5) topics, as follows:

- A new culture of assessment.
- The PrACT framework for digital assessment.
- Self-assessment and peer assessment in higher education.
- Digital tools, instruments and means of assessment.
- Planning digital assessment and feedback.

The first topic of the course module focused on the new culture of assessment, as analysed in the previous section of the paper. The second topic related to the PrACT framework for digital assessment. The PrACT model corresponds to a conceptual matrix designed to support an alternative model of digital assessment, based on four main dimensions: authenticity, consistency, transparency and practicality. The idea behind it is to tackle the emerging challenges of the digital society in what refers to competence development, particularly in higher education (Pereira et al., 2015).
These dimensions make it possible to characterise the determining features of the digital assessment strategies to be developed and are also essential for the quality of assessment in the educational process, each of them being characterised by a set of parameters. It is important to mention that these dimensions are articulated, representing different degrees of reciprocal influence, and the alteration of a parameter in one of them can affect another or others: practicability, for example, often neglected, can decisively influence the level of implementation of the remaining dimensions.
The third topic related to self and peer Assessment in Higher Education. The aim was to build teachers' awareness of the importance of giving learners co-responsibility for their own learning pathways, which requires engaging their participation in the assessment process. Beyond the concept of hetero assessment, i.e. the evaluation carried out by the teacher, teachers are trained and stimulated to introduce practices of

self-assessment and peer assessment, in order to apply a co-assessment approach (Souza & Amante, 2021; Relvas et al., 2020; Amante & Oliveira, 2019).

As for the fourth topic, teachers were familiarised with a wide range of technological resources and tools which characterise the new learning contexts, online, hybrid and even face-to-face. These resources favour the rethinking of assessment practices, making them closer to authentic situations in which learners will have to know how to act and intervene, thus replacing the traditional idea of test/examination.

Finally, the fifth topic was an activity dedicated to allowing participants to train assessment and feedback planning. The new assessment strategies aim to focus on the competences required in real-life/professional practice, ensuring that the ways of assessing them enable the knowledge, skills and attitudes that need to be mobilised in these contexts. They also aim to consider clear and transparent assessment criteria, as well as to promote a communication of results that favours the regulation of learning (Panadero et al., 2019; Panadero, Jonsson & Strijbos, 2016). This perspective raises the need to design an assessment plan that responds to these new concerns, as follows:

- what do we want to assess?
- how to evaluate?
- who assesses?
- by what standards is it evaluated?
- how are the results communicated?

Impact of the massive open learning experience

At the end of each cohort, all participants who completed the MOOC were invited to fill in an online satisfaction survey conformed of Likert Scale and open-ended questions. The survey intended to collect relevant information on the demographic characteristics, levels of satisfaction, perceived utility of the course content, and overall learning experience of the participants. The survey was electronically disseminated via the MOOC platform.

The data collected and participant feedback (Alario Hoyos et al. 2022, 2023) allow us to conclude that most of the participants (70,25%) considered the course to be moderately difficult to follow and complete. They have found a good balance in the course design between providing meaningful challenges and facilitating comprehension. There was also a minor percentage of participants (12,33%) who have found the course to be extremely simple. This may result from prior knowledge or their familiarity with the topic. A similarly small number of participants (13,11%) identified difficulties in understanding some concepts and mastering the course materials.

In total, 97,3 % of participants strongly agree (73,97%) or agree (24,46%) with the statement that the course helped them to develop their competences to understand how to teach with digital technologies. Almost all the participants strongly agree (80%) or agree (19,96%) with the statement that the course helped them to develop their competencies to recognize the importance of active learning in the teaching-learning process.

In what regards the learning materials and learning activities, most participants found them very useful and aligned with their perception of the learning goals (78%). These results demonstrate the effectiveness of the course in fostering substantial student learning and the success in providing valuable educational content and engaging teaching strategies. The positive perception of learning outcomes indicates that the course met its educational objectives and provided participants with meaningful knowledge and skills.

Conclusions

Teaching and learning methodologies are rapidly changing as a result of the dissemination of new digital technologies. Accelerated by the dramatic context of the Covid-19 pandemic and also by new educational policy, technology-enhanced learning has become mainstream in Higher Education. Assessment of learning outcomes is one of the areas in which the impact of new digital technologies, such as learning analytics and artificial intelligence, is leading to a major reengineering of educational processes and a deep transformation of concepts, methods and tools. A new culture based on a assessment for learning is emerging However, as educators worldwide embrace digital education, they face a major challenge: how to speedily develop new competences, update teaching methodologies and innovate educational practices. The speed and scope required by such massive effort of training teaching staff can only be meet in a sustainable and successful way by fully exploring the affordances of open education.

In this paper we describe an experience of designing a course module on digital assessment in the framework of a MOOC produced and delivered to support the development of digital education competences of Latin American educators. The aim was to inspire educational change and the innovation of teaching practices, promoting a new more sustainable approach to assessment for learning based on the PrACT framework.

The evidence collected from the two iterations of the MOOC seem to demonstrate a significant impact of this open education format for enabling innovation transfer in teaching training contexts. The high number and diversity of participants show a wider outreach than could be expected from using traditional in presence formats. Additionally, the learner's achievement measured by the completion rates is in line with standards for this course format. Naturally, this will need to be corroborated by the actual transformation that may occur in the field of educational practice as a result of this training experience. Nevertheless, the very positive feedback received from participants evidence the perceived high quality of the topics, notably the ones related to the innovation of learning assessment. This is in line with the results of previous research conducted in Europe (Teixeira et al, 2018) and it seems to suggest that the MOOC module may have succeeded in inspiring Latin American teachers to transform their learning assessment culture and practices. The success of this initiative has led the PROF-XXI partners to plan the relaunch of the MOOC in the edX platform which should increase even further the outreach of the course.

Acknowledgement

The authors acknowledge PROF XXI, an Erasmus+ project funded by the European Commission (609767-EPP-1-2019-1- ES-EPPKA2-CBHE-JP). This publication reflects the views only of the authors.

References

Abad-Segura, E., González-Zamar, M.-D., Infante-Moro, J. C., & Ruipérez García, G. (2020). Sustainable Management of Digital Transformation in Higher Education: Global Research Trends. *Sustainability*, *12*(5), 2107. MDPI AG. http://dx.doi.org/10.3390/su12052107

Alario Hoyos, C.; Delgado Kloos, C. & Morales, M (2023). Material de Apoyo para Formación de Docentes: Resultados cohorte número 2 (D2.5b.). http://www.profxxi.org/?page_id=958&lang=pt

Alario Hoyos, C.; Delgado Kloos, C. & Morales, M. (2022). Material de Apoyo para Formación de Docentes (D2.5). http://www.profxxi.org/?page_id=958&lang=pt

Alario-Hoyos, C., Pérez-Sanagustín; Morales, M., Delgado Kloos, C., Hernández-Rizzardini, R., Román, M., Ramírez-González, G., Luna, T., Teresa, Jerez, O., Gütl, C., Teixeira, A. M., Maldonado-Mahauad, J., Amado-Salvatierra, H. R., Meléndez, A. & Solarte, M. (2018, October 11-12). MOOC-Maker: Tres Años Construyendo Capacidades de Gestión de MOOCs en Latinoamérica [Paper presentation]. *II Internacional Conferencia MOOC-Maker.* Medellín, Colombia. https://www.researchgate.net/publication/328049125_MOOC-Maker_Tres_Anos_Construyendo_Capacidades_de_Gestion_de_MOOCs_en_Latinoamerica

Amante, L. & Oliveira, I. (2019). *Avaliação e Feedback. Desafios Atuais*. Universidade Aberta. http://abre.ai/akkr.

Amante, L., Oliveira, I. & Pereira, A. (2017). Cultura da avaliação e contextos digitais de aprendizagem: o Modelo PrACT. *Revista Docência e Cibercultura*, 1(1), 135-150. https://repositorioaberto.uab.pt/handle/10400.2/7266

Birenbaum, M. (1996). Assessment 2000: Towards a Pluralistic Approach to Assessment. In: Birenbaum, M., Dochy, F.J.R.C. (eds) Alternatives in Assessment of Achievements, Learning Processes and Prior Knowledge. Evaluation in Education and Human Services, vol 42. Springer, Dordrecht. https://doi.org/10.1007/978-94-011-0657-3_1

Delgado Kloos, C., Alario-Hoyos, C., Morales, M., Hernández Rizzardini, R., Jerez, Ó., Pérez-Sanagustín, M., Kotorov; I, Recinos Fernández; S. A., Oliva-Córdova, L. M., Solarte, M., Jaramillo, D., Teixeira, A. M., & González López, A.H. (2021, November 15-18). *PROF-XXI: Teaching and Learning Centers to Support the 21st Century Professor* [Paper presentation].2021 World Engineering Education Forum/Global Engineering Deans Council (WEEF/GEDC), Madrid, Spain. https://doi.org/10.1109/WEEF/GEDC53299.2021.9657301

Haleem, A., Javaid, M., Qadri, M. A. & Suman, R. (2022). Understanding the role of digital technologies in education: A review, *Sustainable Operations and Computers*, 3, 275-285. https://doi.org/10.1016/j.susoc.2022.05.004.

Panadero, E., Broadbent, J., Boud, D. & Lodge, J. (2019) Using formative assessment to influence self- and co-regulated learning: The role of evaluative judgement. *European Journal of Psychology of Education, 34*(3), 535–557. https://doi.org/10.1007/s10212-018-0407-8. [also available at https://eprints.mdx.ac.uk/id/eprint/25814]

Panadero, E., Jonsson, A., & Strijbos, J. W. (2016). Scaffolding self-regulated learning through self-assessment and peer assessment: Guidelines for classroom implementation. In D. Laveault & L. Allal (Eds.), *Assessment for Learning: Meeting the challenge of implementation* (pp. 311-326). Springer. https://www.researchgate.net/publication/305365530_Scaffolding_Self-Regulated_Learning_Through_Self-Assessment_and_Peer_Assessment_Guidelines_for_Classroom_Implementation

Pereira, A., Amante, L., Oliveira, I., Pinto, M. C., Monteiro, V., Paz, J., Oliveira, R., Santos, J. & Alexandre, F. (2021). Evaluación Digital de Competencias. Recurso Pedagógico Abierto REP@ https://doi.org/10.13140/RG.2.2.27513.13923

Pereira, A., Oliveira, I., Tinoca, L., Pinto, M.C. & Amante, L. (2015). *Desafios da avaliação digital no Ensino Superior.* Universidade Aberta. https://repositorioaberto.uab.pt/handle/10400.2/5774

Pérez-Sanagustín, M., Kotorov, I., Teixeira, A., Mansilla, F., Broisin, J., Alario-Hoyos, C., Jerez, O., Pinto, M.C.,García, B., Delgado Kloss, C., Morales, M., Solarte, M., Oliva-Córdova, L. M., & Gonzalez Lopez, A. H. (2022). A Competency Framework for Teaching and Learning Innovation Centers for the 21st Century: Anticipating the Post-COVID-19 Age. *Electronics, 11*(3), 413. https://doi.org/10.3390/electronics11030413

Pinto, J. (2016) A avaliação em educação: Da linearidade dos usos à complexidade das práticas. In L. Amante & I. Oliveira (Coord.), *Avaliação das Aprendizagens: Perspetivas, contextos e práticas* (pp. 3-40). Universidade Aberta https://goo.gl/IWwZc8

Redecker; C (2017). *European Framework for the Digital Competence of Educators DigCompEdu*. Publications Office of the European Union. https://publications.jrc.ec.europa.eu/repository/handle/JRC107466

Relvas M.J., Pinto, M.C., Oliveira, I. & Pereira, A. (2020, October 21-23). Online Peer Assessment in a First Cycle University Degree – Which Challenges? [Paper presentation]. *EDEN 2020 Research Workshop. Enhancing the Human Experience of Learning with Technology: New Challenges for Research in Digital, Open, Distance & Networked Education.* http://hdl.handle.net/10400.2/10549

Souza, E. & Amante L. (2021) A autoavaliação e a avaliação entre pares: Estudo piloto numa Unidade Curricular do 2º Ciclo do ensino superior em Portugal. *RE@D - Revista de Educação a Distância e Elearning*, *4*(2), 97-115. https://revistas.rcaap.pt/lead_read/article/view/25358

Teixeira, A., Miranda, B., Oliveira, I., & Pinto, M. C. (2018). MOOC "Competências digitais para professores": uma prática formativa inovadora. *RIED. Revista Iberoamericana de Educación a Distancia, 21*(2), pp. 243-261. http://dx.doi.org/10.5944/ried.21.2.19784.

Teixeira, A. M. & Mota, J. (2015). A Proposal for the Methodological Design of Collaborative Language MOOCs. In Martín-Monje, E. & Bárcena, E. (Ed.), *Language MOOCs: Providing Learning, Transcending Boundaries* (pp. 33-47). Berlin: De Gruyter Open. https://doi.org/10.2478/9783110420067.3

Vuorikari, R., Kluzer, S. & Punie, Y. (2022). *DigComp 2.2: The Digital Competence Framework for Citizens - With new examples of knowledge, skills and attitudes*, Publications Office of the European Union. https://doi:10.2760/115376, JRC128415.

CREATING EDUCATIONAL DIGITAL ARTIFCATS COLLABORATIVELY IN A VIRTUAL REALITY ENVIRONMENT

Vlad Mihaescu, Politehnica University Timisoara, Romania

Diana Andone, Politehnica University Timisoara, Romania

***Correspondence**: Vlad Mihaescu: vlad.mihaescu@upt.ro*

Abstract

This paper discusses the use of virtual reality (VR) technologies in education and the collaborative creation of educational digital artifacts in a virtual reality environment. The paper presents a case study of students who collaborated creating digital artifacts in a VR environment. The artifacts were designed with the purpose of presenting the history of a local community. The study analyzed the interactions between learners, the effectiveness of the VR environment in facilitating collaboration, and the impact of the VR environment on learning outcomes. The study concludes that creating educational digital artifacts collaboratively in a virtual reality environment can lead to improved student engagement, motivation, and learning outcomes.

Keywords:

collaborative learning, digital skills, digital artifacts, virtual reality, open education.

Introduction

Virtual reality (VR) technologies are being used in education to create engaging and memorable learning experiences for students.

The collaborative creation of educational digital artifacts in a virtual reality environment has become a popular research topic in recent years. Researchers and teachers have explored the potential benefits of using virtual reality environments for collaborative learning and creation of digital artifacts. For instance, one study (H. Huang et al., 2021) investigated the effectiveness of using a virtual reality platform for creating a new model of learner's design collaboration. They found that students who participated in the virtual reality-based collaborative project had a higher level of engagement, motivation, and creativity compared to those who used traditional methods.

The use of virtual reality has been explored in multiple higher university settings, such as a collaboration between Queensland University of Technology Library and ProQuest in an attempt to provide high quality VR content and resources to the staff and students (Howard et al., 2018) or a research project between the departments of Law and Computer Science of Westminster University which developed a new framework in which law students can explore real case scenarios in a criminal law course using VR technology (Mentzelopoulos et al., 2016).

Virtual reality, which can be used on any type of computer, has followed this trend. In its broad bibliography, which includes papers and publications and dates from 1991 to 2009, Pantelidis (1991-2009) identifies about 800 written resources about virtual reality in education and training (Pantelidis, 2010).

In 2014, a meta-analysis study provided evidence that Virtual Reality can enhance learning outcomes (Merchant et al., 2014). The paper analyses studies in virtual reality-based instruction, in K-12 or higher education settings, on games, simulations and virtual worlds, until 2011. Games showed higher learning gains than the other two categories, a fact which is not surprising. From a constructivist point of view, a Virtual Reality educational environment can provide the students with an active role in their learning; can provide experiential and case based learning, but also social interaction (H.-M. Huang et al., 2010).

CoSpaces is a virtual reality platform that has gained increasing attention in recent years due to its potential for use in education. As educators seek to incorporate more technology into their teaching, the ability to create immersive, interactive experiences through CoSpaces has become an attractive option for many.

Since 2017, the TalkTech international project matches students at universities in the United States and Romania, to work as members of international teams as a virtual mobility, mainly to devloep Virtual Reality applications using CoSpacesEdu software (Frydenberg & Andone, 2019). The project, initiated in 2008, indicates that the use of VR, but in a context that encourages enquiries in a project based learning setting have improved their digital competences, communication skills, their motivation to STEM education and also it sparks students' interest in possible future business applications of VR (Whewell et al., 2022).

Overall, the literature suggests that creating educational digital artifacts collaboratively in a virtual reality environment can lead to improved student engagement, motivation, and learning outcomes. Virtual reality environments offer a unique and immersive experience that can facilitate collaborative learning and creation of digital artifacts. These findings have important implications for educators and researchers interested in leveraging technology to enhance student learning experiences.

Assignment

In the 2021-2022 academic year, we proposed to the students the following activity part of their exam – to create an OER as a digital educational artifact collaboratively in the CoSpaces virtual reality environment.

They had to make teams of 3-4 students in order to carry out an OER activity, as per the description offered in the Moodle LCMS platform of our university. The students had a "choice" option from where to choose the OER topic that suited them the most. Each OER subject was limited to a maximum of 3-4 students, depending on the quantity of information. All topics were related to our university's project *Patrimoniul sub reflectoare/Spotlight Heritage*[1], part of Timișoara 2023 European Capital of Culture.

Spotlight Heritage Timisoara is a digital cultural initiative of the Politehnica University of Timisoara, through the eLearning Centre and the Multimedia Center, realized in partnership with the National Museum of Banat, part of the Timisoara European Capital of Culture program. Spotlight Heritage Timisoara reveals, by digital storytelling, the city of Timisoara through stories of cultural and historical heritage, technical development, communities, and neighborhoods, interwoven with the personal stories of the inhabitants of yesterday and today.

The OER product was to be made in English or Romanian and was supposed to contain an original digital artifact that presents the station differently than what is found on the website, more specifically a story or experience of the students related to one of the "stations" of the project. If they didn't have a memory/story they were supposed to go and create one until the exam. All stations must have been presented through one or more scenes, like a virtual tour, with information, images, pictures, video, link to additional information from the website, etc. For each station the students had access to several 360 photos which they could include in their scenes.

The OER artifact should have been CC licensed and the students were told that the best OERs will be integrated into courses of the university, or in the Spotlight Heritage application, keeping the authors' information. The students were supposed also to answer an online questionnaire.

Results

There were 48 students who participated in the Web 2.0 Technologies course, 4th year of the Bachelor program in Electronics, Telecommunications and Information Technology of the Politehnica University of Timisoara. 30 were male and 18 were female, most of them around 22-23 years old. 16 projects were elected in total, each of them being comprised of 2-8 "stations" from the Spotlight Heritage Timisoara project. A "station" in this context refers to a point of interest, namely a point of historic relevance from Timisoara. Most of the students received good grades, with a 9.4 average out of a maximum of 10, and from the point of view of the teachers who evaluated, created good digital artefacts.

In Figure 1 and 2 you can see as an example one of the projects created by students. Each project was created with a script in mind, and contained multimedia elements integrated in the scene, characters created and dialogues for the visitors to read, everything with an educational and instructive component in mind.

[1] https://spotlight-timisoara.eu/

The students were supposed to complete an anonymous questionnaire after they finished the projects. We are going to present the results of some of the questions, which the authors have considered to be most relevant for this paper.

Figure 1. The „Corneliu Mikloși" Public Transport Museum artifact created by students in CoSpaces – outdoor.

Figure 2. The „Corneliu Mikloși" Public Transport Museum artifact created by students in CoSpaces – indoor.

We asked the students to rate from 1 (very poor) to 10 (very good) the experience and way of working in Co-spaces, from the point of view of the Co-Spaces application. The results are presented in Table 1 and show that 49% of students rated the experience extremely high (9-10) and other 34% rated it as high (7-8), which brings the positive result to a total of 83%.

Table 1: Results of rating of the Co-Spaces application

Rate level – 1 (very poor) to 10 (very good)	Percentage of responses
3	2%
4	2%
5	8%
7	16%
8	18%
9	14%
10	35%

Next, we asked the students to rate how the following aspects of working in Co-Spaces have enabled them to be creative? (strongly disagree -1, strongly agree - 5): information on the Spotlight Heritage website, the 360 image on the Spotlight Heritage website, the background adaptation for Co-Spaces, creating animations in Co-Spaces, and discussing with colleagues about the model for creating the virtual tour in Co-Spaces. The results are presented in Figure 3. What this shows is that all the options provided were considered by respondents as creative enablers. However, the most positive effect was given by the collaboration with colleagues and the creation of animations.

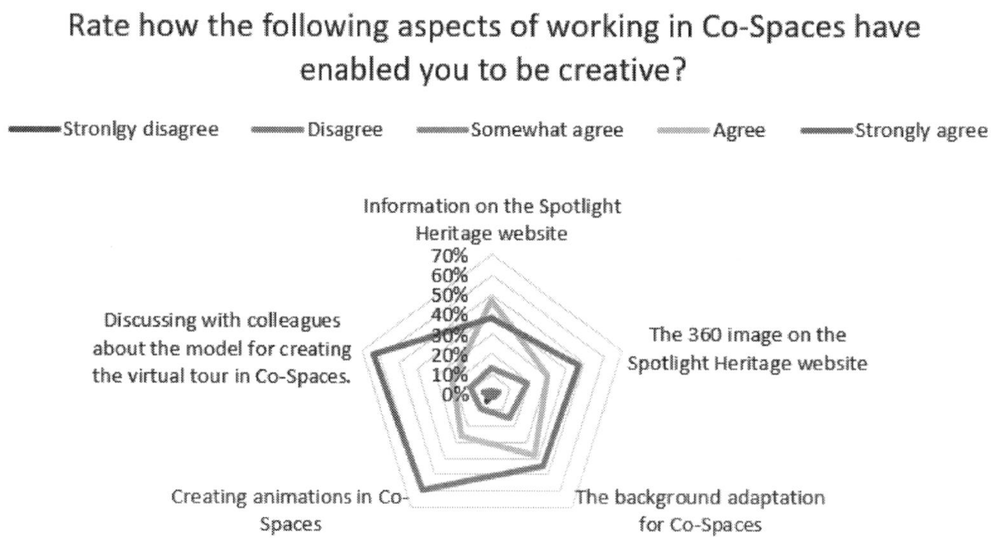

Figure 3. Results of the question "rate how the following aspects of working in Co-Spaces have enabled you to be creative".

The following question was for the students to write two of the most important things they learned in creating the virtual tour in Co-Spaces, in terms of the VR technology used, without offering a list of words to choose from. The most used words were Programming/modelling (8), Images (7 times), Animations (7), Vision (6), Imagination (6), Orientation/Placement (6), Creativity (4), Information (3), Interactivity (3), Design (2), VR (2), Usefulness (2), Punctuality, Easy, Action, Sound, Innovation, Future, Possibilities, Videos, Collaboration, Integration, Experience,

Diversity, Script. 2 students said there was nothing important and one said that everything was important. From this we can conclude that this activity helped the students to learn programming, multimedia manipulation, orientation in creating digital scenes the most.

Next, we asked students to write two of the most difficult situations encountered in creating virtual tour in Co-Spaces and how they overcame them. 17% of respondents stated that there weren't any difficulties to mention. The problems mentioned were the perspective in space (17%), coding/programming (15%), integrating animations (13%), finding information (11%), integrating characters (11%), the application layout (11%), Image quality and lack of images (9%), Image positioning (6%), object manipulation (6%), lack of imagination (4%). Other things mentioned were lack of time, lack of motivation, user interaction, video integration and certain limitations. The solutions mentioned to overcome all these difficult situations were tutorials, learning by doing and discussing with the tutors.

The final question was for them to describe the experience of taking a virtual tour in Co-Spaces from the perspective of using cultural and heritage information in a VR application. We generated a word cloud from the answers of the students, which can be seen in Figure 4.

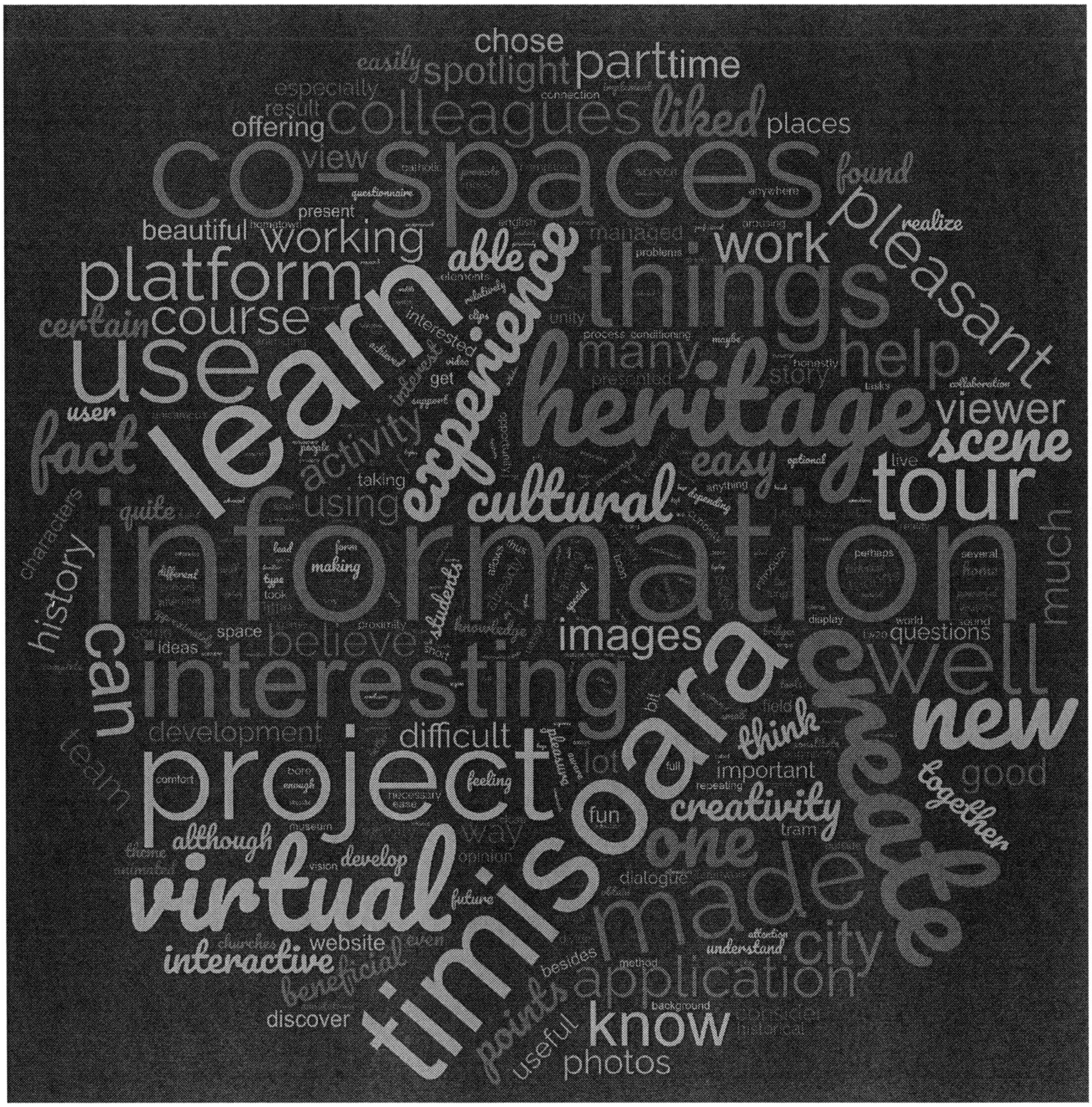

Figure 4. Word cloud generated from reports of students describing the experience of taking a virtual tour in Co-Spaces from the perspective of using cultural and heritage information in a VR application.

The world cloud was tailored for the purpose of this research. The text was cleaned and pre-processed, removing any irrelevant or redundant information. Plurals and variations of the same word were considered as one word, for emphasis. Analysing the world cloud, we can see a total of 393 words. The words appearing the most are, in order, information (32 times), experience (28), learn (27), co-spaces (25), create (25), Timisoara (25), project (23), heritage (22), things (21), use (21), virtual (20), interesting (19), made (19) and new (19).

Here are a couple of examples of responses from the students:

"It was an interesting experience, which made me realize the heritage we have that we are not aware of. Many cultural information that I learned and that will be useful to me another time were part of the process. Thus, through VR we can learn new things about anything in a very short time and from anywhere."

"It was a new experience. I think it's a good method to present the main ideas of a project, in a more friendly way, that takes you into a story that doesn't bore you and that keeps you attentive throughout the presentation, by creating a scene with a lot of action, dynamism, images and videos that keep you constantly focused. From my point of view, it is suitable for any type of audience, regardless of the weight of the topic discussed."

Conclusions

After conducting this activity with the students and analysing the results we can conclude that collaboratively creating educational digital artifacts in virtual reality environments can be an effective way to enhance student engagement, motivation, and learning outcomes.

The use of virtual reality technology can create an immersive and interactive learning experience that is more engaging than traditional classroom settings. This can lead to increased motivation and interest in the subject matter.

The Co-Spaces platform provides a user-friendly and accessible platform for creating educational digital artifacts collaboratively. The platform allows for real-time collaboration, which can facilitate group work and promote peer learning. This has encouraged students to express freely their creativity and to 'play' by creating memorable stories.

The OER activity proposed to the students was a successful way to incorporate virtual reality technology into the curriculum and to encourage collaborative learning and creation of digital artifacts, helping the students to learn about local history and heritage. As some of the students have shared openly their artifacts, will encourage future generations in looking into creating VR artifacts.

The collaborative creation process also promotes the development of important skills such as teamwork, communication, and problem-solving. These skills are transferable and can be applied to various real-world scenarios.

We also acknowledge the conclusions of one of our previous studies, where we found that students confirmed that the education process could be improved if the VR technologies would be used more in the practical sessions of classes. The immersiveness that VR technologies add to a virtual world cannot be achieved in a simple 3D application/simulation, this being the main reason students prefer a VR application over a classic one (Tataru et al., 2022).

While the use of virtual reality technology is still relatively new in education, the results of this study suggest that it has great potential for improving learning outcomes. Further research is needed to fully explore the possibilities of virtual reality technology in education and to identify best practices for its implementation.

Overall, the results of this study suggest that incorporating virtual reality technology and collaborative digital artifact creation into the curriculum can be an effective way to enhance student learning outcomes and engagement. The use of platforms like CoSpaces can provide a unique and immersive experience for students, and the creation of OERs can contribute to the open educational resources available to educators and learners worldwide, but also to encourage students to share openly their work, to gain a sense of fulfilment through the public display of their work, and to encourage future students' generations to experiment with digital creation.

References

Frydenberg, M., & Andone, D. (2019). Does Creating Shared Projects in Virtual Reality Capture Students' Interest in Technology? An International Project in STEM Education. *2019 IEEE Integrated STEM Education Conference (ISEC)*, 311–315. https://doi.org/10.1109/ISECon.2019.8882080

Howard, S. K., Serpanchy, K., & Lewin, K. (2018). *Virtual reality content for higher education curriculum.*

Huang, H., Lin, C., & Cai, D. (2021). Enhancing the learning effect of virtual reality 3D modeling: A new model of learner's design collaboration and a comparison of its field system usability. *Universal Access in the Information Society*, *20*, 429–440.

Huang, H.-M., Rauch, U., & Liaw, S.-S. (2010). Investigating learners' attitudes toward virtual reality learning environments: Based on a constructivist approach. *Computers & Education*, *55*(3), 1171–1182. https://doi.org/10.1016/j.compedu.2010.05.014

Mentzelopoulos, M., Parrish, J., Kathrani, P., & Economou, D. (2016). REVRLaw: An Immersive Way for Teaching Criminal Law Using Virtual Reality. In C. Allison, L. Morgado, J. Pirker, D. Beck, J. Richter, & C. Gütl (Eds.), *Immersive Learning Research Network* (pp. 73–84). Springer International Publishing.

Merchant, Z., Goetz, E. T., Cifuentes, L., Keeney-Kennicutt, W., & Davis, T. J. (2014). Effectiveness of virtual reality-based instruction on students' learning outcomes in K-12 and higher education: A meta-analysis. *Computers & Education*, *70*, 29–40. https://doi.org/10.1016/j.compedu.2013.07.033

Pantelidis, V. S. (2010). Reasons to use virtual reality in education and training courses and a model to determine when to use virtual reality. *Themes in Science and Technology Education*, *2*(1–2), 59–70.

Tataru, M., Berzescu, S., Vert, S., Mihaescu, V., Stamatoiu, R., & Vasiu, R. (2022). Designing Applications for Collaborative Learning in Virtual Reality. *2022 International Symposium on Electronics and Telecommunications (ISETC)*, 1–4.

Whewell, E., Caldwell, H., Frydenberg, M., & Andone, D. (2022). Changemakers as digital makers: Connecting and co-creating. *Education and Information Technologies*. https://doi.org/10.1007/s10639-022-10892-1

PRE-VISIONS – FIRST RESULTS OF THE EDEN FELLOWS SURVEY ON THE FUTURES OF LEARNING

António Moreira Teixeira, Laboratório de Educação a Distância e eLearning, Universidade Aberta, Portugal; Deborah Arnold, Universitat Oberta de Catalunya, Spain; Diana Andone, Politehnica University Timișoara, Romania

Correspondence: *António Moreira Teixeira: antonio.moreira.teixeira.pt@gmail.com*

Abstract

Technology is pervasive and intertwined in many aspects of modern life and society. The digital revolution that is sweeping the world has shown its potential in education during the Covid-19 pandemic. It is rapidly transforming the way students learn, and as a result, technology is expected to improve the face of education by making it more inclusive and accessible. In the framework of the EDEN Pre-Visions project, the EDEN fellows conducted a prospective study on the future trends of open and digital education in Europe in the next decade. 40 EDEN Fellows took part in an online survey launched in January 2023. In this paper, we present and analyse the first results of this exercise, describing the views of the experts on six dimensions: the European context evolution and socio-economic dynamics; EdTech research and development; EdTech practices; institutional digital transformation; societal impacts and implications; policies and regulations.

Keywords:

Open Education; Digital Education; EdTech; Educational policies and strategies; Future trends; EDEN Fellows.

Introduction

The context in which education institutions operate is complex, influenced by global megatrends such as war, pandemics, climate and energy crises as well as technological evolutions (Olcott et al., 2023). With respect to the Covid-19 pandemic in particular, the education sector was faced with the major challenge of rapidly pivoting to online education, with varying degrees of success (Bozkurt et al. (2020). This has also significantly impacted established open and distance education institutions which had to reposition, reengineer processes, innovate practices and speed up organisational transformation (Teixeira & Mota, 2020). Yet the challenges and trends stretch way beyond that of the pandemic, however immediate its impact. We thus need to take into consideration larger European and global social, economic, technological, cultural, environmental and political trends, as well as research and practice in educational technology (EdTech).

Methodology

This research was conducted between January and March 2023 in the form of a survey distributed to EDEN Fellows. The EDEN Fellows form a body of over 100 individuals who have received recognition for their contribution to EDEN and the field of distance, online and open education since 2007, in the form of EDEN Fellows and Senior Fellows Awards[1]. This community is thus among the best placed to identify such trends and challenges and formed the population for the current study. Forty (40) Fellows and Senior Fellows responded to the survey, representing a response rate of almost 35%. The survey was viewed 1155 times, which indicates to us that it was consulted and analysed several times before completion and the answers are very well distributed among Europe, North and South America, with between one and three answers per country [exceptions Romania (4), Spain (4), UK (4)].

The survey consisted of 20 questions organised into 7 sections: European context evolution and socio-economic dynamics; EdTech Research and Development; EdTech practices; Institutional digital transformation; Societal impacts and implications; Policies and regulations; Leading actors and inspiring persons. The majority of sections consisted of a 5-point Likert scale (5 being the highest score) with optional text responses for further comments.

[1] https://eden-europe.eu/team/department/fellows-council/

The survey was designed, tested and validated by members of the EDEN Fellows Council Board, and consent obtained from all respondents.

Different methodologies were mobilised to analyse the data. In this paper the authors present basic statistical descriptions combined with selected data snapshots to provide initial insights into the main trends identified by the respondents. The data presented in the tables correspond to the number of respondents in the dataset for the respective item. The number in brackets after each data snapshot corresponds to the line number in the dataset The more detailed qualitative and quantitative analyses will be reported in subsequent publications.

European context evolution and socio-economic dynamics

Education is always shaped by context. In the Pre-Visions survey, EDEN Fellows were invited to rate the importance of a number of social, economic, technological, cultural, environmental and political trends that may affect the future development of teaching and learning in the next decade.

Table 1: Social trends

Trend/Score	**1**	**2**	**3**	**4**	**5**
Well-being and health	3	0	12	15	10
Demographic changes	4	0	6	13	17
Equity, accessibility and inclusion	3	2	5	10	20

Fellows clearly identified two social trends as potentially affecting more significantly the field. These are *equity, accessibility and inclusion* and *demographic changes*. Regarding the first one, a Fellow stated: "It is very important to ensure that all students have access to high-quality education, regardless of their socio-economic status, geographic location, or other factors. That is essential for promoting social mobility and supporting the development of a skilled workforce" (33). However, Fellows also warned that the in many countries there is an emerging trend towards a more elitist view of higher education which may lead to a depreciation of these issues. As for the second, a Fellow stated: "Demographic changes will certainly have a big impact but may not be fully recognised and addressed by institutions and government" (39). Surprisingly, due to the impact of the Covid-19 pandemic, *well-being and health* was not as highly rated. Even so, one of the Fellows expressed its critical importance "for deep learning and engagement, as well as effective support to learning" (33). Yes, Fellows also see digital learning as a positive force for social change: "Digital learning can improve well-being and health by enabling learning to take place in situ, rather than requiring expensive relocation and attendance in a new social milieu" (38).

Table 2: Economic trends

Trend/Score	**1**	**2**	**3**	**4**	**5**
Shift to remote work	1	2	3	17	17
Future work and new skills	2	1	2	10	25
Shift to remote teaching and learning	2	2	8	10	18

As for economic trends, which the Fellows seem to take as the most impactful for the future of open and digital learning, *future work and new skills* was paramount for them. "[It] is high on the agenda in Europe" (39), as one respondent stated. Another Fellow noted: "Remote work and the need for new skills will require asynchronous, readily available solutions" (38). Overall, Fellows acknowledged all these three trends to be potentially impactful as well as interdependent. However, Fellows also noted an existing backlash in the trends towards remote work and education following the dramatic impact of the Covid-19 pandemic. As one respondent stated: "Similar to remote work, there is a concerning pushback against remote teaching and learning, which the field needs to address" (39).

Table 3: Technological trends

Trend/Score	**1**	**2**	**3**	**4**	**5**
Artificial intelligence	1	4	8	5	22
Next-generation digital learning environment	2	3	12	14	9
Analytics and data privacy	3	1	14	12	10

Regarding technological trends, most of the Fellows indicated *Artificial Intelligence (AI)* to be the most promising development. This is coherent with their views on EdTech trends. Interestingly, they seem to award almost the same level of importance to both the *next-generation digital learning environment* and *analytics and data privacy.*

Table 4: Cultural trends

Trend/Score	1	2	3	4	5
Ethical governance	1	3	18	7	11
Expansion of digital citizenship / digital literacies	2	2	5	12	19
Disinformation in social media and the internet	3	3	7	12	15

Concerning emerging cultural trends, the majority of Fellows elected the *expansion of digital citizenship/digital literacies* as the most important development. In second place came *disinformation in social media and the internet*, awarded slightly less importance. Differently, Fellows evaluated *ethical governance* as not such a significant factor.

Table 5: Environmental trends

Trend/Score	1	2	3	4	5
Focus on sustainability	1	2	13	9	15
Implications of climate change	3	7	10	9	11
Decrease of carbon footprint	3	7	11	8	11

As to environmental trends, which impact Fellows feel less important to the future of open and digital learning, the *focus on sustainability* was the most rated. Less concern was given to the *implications of climate change* and the *decrease of carbon footprint.* Only 47,5% of the respondents rated this as important or very important.

Table 6: Political trends

Trend/Score	1	2	3	4	5
Decrease in public funding in education	1	0	7	16	16
Authoritarian surveillance	2	5	16	8	9
Deteriorating international relations	3	2	15	10	10

Finally, regarding political trends, the overwhelming concern is the *decrease in public funding in education.* As many as 80% of the Fellows rated highly. The second major concern of the Fellows is with the *deteriorating international relations*, while fewer respondents indicated a concern with *authoritarian surveillance.*

EdTech R&D

Research is a major driver for innovation and quality of educational practices. In this section we describe the results of the Fellows evaluation of the current trends in educational research which may inform future teaching and learning practices in Europe in the next decade.

Table 7: Trends in online pedagogy and learning experience design

Trend/Score	1	2	3	4	5
Open Educational Resources and Practices (including MOOCs)	1	4	9	9	17
Authentic learning experiences	1	2	9	17	11
Redesigning learning spaces	2	4	10	9	15
Hybrid learning designs (e.g., blended learning, flipped classroom)	1	3	7	8	21
Growing focus on measuring learning	1	5	10	14	10
Modularized and disaggregated degrees	1	3	8	14	14
Microcredentialing	1	4	4	13	18
Participatory learning experiences (incl. peer learning and assessment)	1	4	12	10	13

Regarding the online pedagogy and learning experience, the most rated trend was *hybrid learning designs.* More than half of the respondents rated this trend as very important. A clear majority also highlighted *microcredentialing.* As one Fellow noted: "the digitalisation of (micro-)credentials, combined with the use of standards and digital signatures can help citizens have their knowledge and skills certified, verifiable and portable in EU/global education settings and on the labour market" (17). Another Fellow also stated that "students will increasingly opt for part-time study and micro-credentials and short-term credentials aimed at employment. They will come back to earn their formal degrees at their discretion, not ours" (7). Coherently, Fellows also awarded a very high rating to *modularized and disaggregated degrees* and to *authentic learning experiences*. Two thirds of them rated both as important or very important. *Open Educational Resources and Practices (OER/OEP)* were also considered very important by the Fellows. As pointed out by one of them: "OERs and OEPs continue to be the most powerful and influential transformation in digital learning. This is due to the flexibility they provide to learners and teachers and to the interoperability between non formal and formal learning" (11). These emerging trends seem to show an increased focus on changing how learning is organised, assessed and certified and also the disaggregation of the degree system. Interestingly, Fellows didn't rate as highly the *growing focus on measuring learning*. The less rated trend was *participatory learning experiences*, even if one third of the respondents rated this trend as very important.

As for other powerful trends, one of the Fellows suggested *skills and competence-based learning*, which they considered to have a major impact on ODL. Additional new features may become even more important in the future, as another Fellow reminded: "Expectations of learners may change in the future. There will be necessary further differentiation between what may be fancy and what may be really accepted and used" (26).

Table 8: Emerging Technologies

Trend/Score	1	2	3	4	5
Adaptive learning technologies	2	3	5	18	12
AI/Machine learning education applications	2	2	9	5	22
Learning analytics	2	3	10	14	11
BYOD	3	6	12	14	5
Games and gamification	3	4	9	14	10
XR (AR/VR/MR/Haptic) technologies	4	4	9	11	12
The Internet of Things	3	8	8	13	8
Robotics	3	8	12	9	8

Concerning emerging technologies, Fellows were more divided. Most of the respondents elected *adaptive learning technologies* as a relevant trend. 75% of them considered it as important or very important. However, if we look only at the trends rated as very important, the majority of Fellows chose *AI/Machine learning*. Significantly, about one third of the respondents rated *XR (AR/VR/MR/Haptic) technologies* as very important, although overall it appears only as the fourth most voted trend. *Learning analytics* was not so highly rated. The same applies to the *Internet of Things*, although over half of the Fellows still rated it as important or very important. Finally, there are two technologies which were not much valued: *robotics* and *BYOD*. As one Fellow stated, it is important to note though that "technology is not always synonymous with progress" (7) and it's important not to destroy the humanistic foundations of education.

EdTech practices

In terms of EdTech practices, respondents were invited to identify these for different sectors: child education and K12; Higher Education; further and adult education; non-formal learning. In Child education and K-12, Fellows mentioned practices such as flipped classrooms, problem-based learning, gamification and simulations, as well as broader approaches such as personalised learning and teaching and co-creation. It would be interesting to explore further the relationship between these two approaches. Accessibility concerns were mentioned, as was the fact that the technology used must be free and/or easily available. One respondent preferred to put the emphasis on mastery of writing skills at this level, as a prerequisite for later education and life.

In Higher Education, microcredentials and e-portfolios were mentioned in relation to competency-based education and employability. The technologies highlighted by respondents as good practice included the use of Virtual and Augmented Reality (VR/AR) for safety training and interactive video. Other responses focused on pedagogical approaches, with co-design of the curriculum, flipped classrooms and service learning, on the design of learning spaces, and on the use of learning analytics to support both learning and decision-making. Flexibility, equity and the need to keep the 'open' in open and distance learning were also mentioned.

Turning now to further and adult education, microcredentials were again mentioned in relation to employability, as were competency-based approaches, flexibility and the mobilisation of appropriate learning and teaching approaches such as heutagogy and andragogy. For non-formal learning, interestingly several respondents recommended formalising the outcomes in terms of microcredentials to facilitate the recognition of this learning 'outside the system'. Digital and media literacy were considered important, as well as second-chance education and open learning provision. Methods related to experiential learning were cited, including project-based learning and design thinking. Finally, a focus on self-directed learning and self-assessment combined with peer and mentor guidance or coaching featured among the approaches considered to be good practice in this area.

Institutional digital transformation

EDEN fellows support the idea that the digital transformation of educational institutions has been highly accelerated by the pandemic. As this process requires that a number of conditions be met, and resources be available in order to be successful, the study explored how these processes are developing and how they are changing the education sector. 47% of the fellows declared that they believe that digital citizenship and digital literacy have expanded tremendously in the last years. At the same time, only some consider that next generation digital learning environments will be further developed, as 30% consider that these will not change the fundamental characteristics of educational institutions.

The EDEN fellows also identified key issues regarding transitions across the educational institutional landscape and the resources needed. A leader from one university indicated how the university has moved from planning the digitalisation of resources and technical development to strategically thinking and planning a digital transformation that looks more at the full eco-system, the transformation of learning and changing academic culture. Indeed, another respondent pointed out that "digital transformation [is] about leadership and creating sustainable business models and not about technology" (7), a view reflected by several others. The majority pointed to the need for a holistic approach, for digital leadership combined with a vision, a true understanding of "the transformative process which is, in effect, about transforming people not technologies" (7) and deep organisational changes for a full digital transformation.

Societal impacts and implications

Fellows seem divided in how they address this topic. On the one hand, the impact of the Covid-19 pandemic in accelerating change in education is still controversial. For some respondents the negative aspects of emergency remote teaching - ERT (Hodges et al., 2020) and other online learning practices not grounded in research have produced a pushback against digital education. This may delay any significant positive transformation for some years. Others, although recognizing the poor teaching quality and lack of leadership, training and support services, draw a positive lesson from the experience. They expressed belief on educators having realised that they need to return to human basic values such as empathy and compassion. This should inspire governments, but also companies, to invest in building up the digital infrastructure. For others, the shift to online education is irreversible. In the words of one respondent: "the pandemic has shown that most work and study can be done from home offering greater flexibility for those with limited mobility, family ties and work" (35) adding: "We have shown that online education can be effective, engaging, social and rewarding if planned carefully and with suitably trained teachers. There is (...) enormous demand for higher education in remote areas, reskilling, professional development, promoting local development, in-company training (...) [which] will be mostly online or in partnership with local institutions and companies" (35).

On the other hand, there are also contrasting perspectives regarding the benefits and risks of the digital transformation of educational institutions and processes. It's important to note that Fellows do not share a single scenario. In fact, many understand this movement not towards a fully online learning environment, but an increasingly hybrid one. Others view it differently. In fact, some of the Fellows expressed clear concern with, and even criticism of, the whole process. The major risks identified relate to, as one respondent put it: "the lack of capacity of formal education systems and lifelong learning supply to sustain social inclusion and limit inequalities" (5). The risk of continual growth of the digital divide and exclusion, due to the insufficient digital competences and proper infrastructure was also mentioned by several Fellows. One other respondent mentioned the risk of "an unhealthy increase in the surveillance of learners and the learning process" (14). This also relates to the increased need for an ethical governance of data and its use, as pointed out by another Fellow. But there are also several positive approaches to digital transformation. Some Fellows highlight its cultural implications, for instance the change in the perception of value. Others mention the dissemination of a more collaborative and less individualistic culture of learning, as well as increased diversification and personalisation of learning experiences and learner participation in the design and assessment processes.

Policies and regulation

At the transnational level, Fellows understandably highlighted the contribution and impact of European policies. Respondents mentioned the European universities alliances and the strong input of the EC on digital education. There were references to the long-tail Effect of the "Bologna Process' and accompanying regulatory framework in HE, as well as the ECVET and lifelong learning initiatives, and the ESCO system. Most attention was given to the impact of the Digital Europe Programme[2] and particularly the Digital Education Action Plan 2021-27 (DEAP)[3], considered by many to be the main driver. In the words of a respondent, it is: "a good example how EU policies and initiatives can be implemented on the national level" (24). Another Fellow stated: "We can no longer talk about a national and international level. Whether a country is a member of the EU or not, each country has to work together again in the creation of international digital ethics, culture, technology use and new laws" (34). Having pointed out the high number of ongoing initiatives supported by the EC leading to the establishment of competency frameworks, one Fellow expressed the wish for these frameworks to become mandatory in the EU.

Nevertheless, Fellows recognise that major differences persist between national legislations, which hinders the internationalisation of educational provision. It was noted some disbelief towards the DEAP. One respondent characterised it as a weak EU response given its "very poor achievements, except for actions by wealthy countries" (28). This is taken by others as clear ground for future improvement of DEAP: "the coming years will be crucial for contributing to shaping its successor" (39). This expectation regarding a more active European policy and cooperation was perfectly expressed by one Fellow: "The Europeans underestimate the power of the collaborative spirit in education and practice. It is remarkable and an invaluable asset for the future" (7).

In addition, the Fellows identified some emerging policy issues which need to be addressed. These were: cross-border/cross-sector micro-credential articulation, the combination of formal and non-formal credentials, Ethical issues related to A.I., and the clarification of the EU-UK regulatory issues created by Brexit. There was also a suggestion to improve the connection between professional associations and institutions with peer organisations in other geographic regions of the World, such as North and South America, Africa, and Asia.

On a national level, Fellows expressed more differentiated perspectives. Some did not provide information as they operate in global scenarios. As one respondent stated: "Digital technologies have created a common culture in all countries of the world. Regional and local conversions will not be enough. Change and transformation must be done according to global rules" (9). But many others defended an alternative view: "I believe in the local initiatives! on a local scale (city level) Cooperation between schools and the local community will result in understanding of the situation and in sustainable cooperation" (8). In this line of reasoning, some Fellows indicated national initiatives which should be reported for their significance. This was the case, for Portugal, of the recent Distance Education Regulation for Higher Education and the Distance Education Regulation for the Portuguese School System were highlighted. Regarding Spain, reference was made to the Digital Programme *Educa en digital* and the Digital Education Plan of Catalonia. Finally, in the case of Sweden, it was mentioned the publication of a national report on open education commissioned by the Government and carried out by the National Library of Sweden.

Conclusions

The results detailed above provide valuable insights into future trends in the field of open and digital education, as seen by respondents possessing significant knowledge and experience in both research and practice. From the preliminary analysis of the data, we can identify the following as the most impactful factors for the field:

- Future work and new skills
- Equity, accessibility, and inclusion

---

[2] https://digital-strategy.ec.europa.eu/en/activities/digital-programme

[3] https://education.ec.europa.eu/focus-topics/digital-education/action-plan

- Digital citizenship and digital literacies

Regarding the most promising areas emerging in open and digital education, Fellows appear to select the following:

- Artificial Intelligence and machine learning applications in education
- Hybrid learning environments
- Microcredentials and new forms of certifying learning outcomes
- Open educational resources and practices, including MOOCs

These are all topics which have already been addressed by research in the field, including other prospective studies, such as the Horizon Reports (Pelletier et al., 2023) and the Open University UK Innovating Pedagogy series (Kukulska-Hulme et al., 2022) but which would benefit from being connected more explicitly. For example, the use of Artificial Intelligence and other technologies in education should not be studied (and even less so applied) without a consideration for ethical implications, linking these to digital literacies and citizenship, to sustainability in terms of the human and environmental impact (Selwyn, 2023) and to the inclusion of learners in the design of their learning.

The authors recognise the limitations of this research in the relatively small population surveyed, however the high level of knowledge and expertise of this well-defined group largely compensates in terms of the quality and relevance of the results. Furthermore, the response rate of almost 35% is a positive sign that the EDEN Fellows are engaged with the field and motivated to share their perspectives to drive forward both research and practice. Further analysis of the dataset is planned, combined with follow-up consultations, in order to generate a finer understanding of the trends that need to be addressed, while taking a critical view of technological evolutions to ensure that we embrace their potential while preserving the humanistic foundations of education.

Acknowledgement

The authors acknowledge the EDEN Fellows who kindly responded to the online survey on which this paper is based and the ID / IFR and e-Learning Center (CeL) of the Politehnica University Timisoara who assured the technical infrastructure for the implementation of the online survey. This publication reflects the views only of the authors.

References

Bozkurt, A., Jung, I., Xiao, J., Vladimirschi, V., Schuwer, R., Egorov, G., Lambert, S. R., Al Freih, M., Pete, J., Olcott, Jr, D., Rodes, V., Aranciaga, I., Bali, M., Alvarez, Jr, A. V., Roberts, J., Pazurek, A., Raffaghelli, J. E., Panagiotou, N., de Coëtlogon, P., Shahadu, S., Brown, M., Asino, T. I., Tumwesige, J., Ramírez Reyes, T., Barrios Ipenza, E., Ossiannilsson, E., Bond, M., Belhamel, K., Irvine, V., Sharma, R. C., Adam, T., Janssen, B., Sklyarova, T., Olcott, N., Ambrosino, A., Lazou, C., Mocquet, B., Mano, M., & Paskevicius, M. (2020). A global outlook to the interruption of education due to COVID-19 pandemic: Navigating in a time of uncertainty and crisis. *Asian Journal of Distance Education, 15*(1), 1–126. https://doi.org/10.5281/zenodo.3878572

Kukulska-Hulme, A., Bossu, C., Charitonos, K., Coughlan, T., Maina, M., Ferguson, R., FitzGerald, E., Gaved, M., Guitert, M., Herodotou, C., Prieto-Blázquez, J., Rienties, B., Sangrà, A., Sargent, J., Scanlon, E., Whitelock, D. (2022). *Innovating Pedagogy 2022: Open University Innovation Report 10.* Milton Keynes: The Open University. https://www.open.ac.uk/blogs/innovating/?p=774

Hodges, C., Moore, S., Lockee, B., Trust, T., & Bond, A. (2020). The Difference Between Emergency Remote Teaching and Online Learning. *EDUCAUSE Review*, 27. https://er.educause.edu/articles/2020/3/the-difference-between-emergency-remote-teaching-and-online-learning.

Olcott, D. Jr., Arnold, D. & Blaschke, L. (2023). Leadership 2030: Renewed visions and empowered choices for European university leaders. *European Journal of Open, Distance and E-Learning, 25*(1) 74-92. https://doi.org/10.2478/eurodl-2023-0006

Pelletier, K., Robert, J., Muscanell, N., McCormack, M., Reeves, J., Reeves, J., Arbino, N., Grajek, S., Birdwell, w.T., Liu, D., Mandernach, J., Moore, A., Porcaro, A., Rutledge, R. & Zimmern, J. (2023). *2023 EDUCAUSE Horizon Report Teaching and Learning Edition.* Boulder, CO: EDUCAUSE23. https://library.educause.edu/-/media/files/library/2023/4/2023hrteachinglearning.pdf?

Selwyn, N. (2023). Digital degrowth: Toward radically sustainable education technology. *Learning, Media and Technology*, 1–14. https://doi.org/10.1080/17439884.2022.2159978

Teixeira, A. M. & Mota, J. (2020). The Importance of Being Open: How European open universities can reposition in the post-pandemic higher education landscape. In Kucina Softic, S., Teixeira, A. & Szucs, A. (Eds.) (2020). *Enhancing the Human Experience of Learning with Technology: New challenges for research into digital, open, distance & networked education. Short Paper Book of the European Distance and E-Learning Network (EDEN) 2020 Research Workshop*. 178-188. doi: 10.38069/edenconf-2020-rw0020

MEDIA USAGE PATTERNS OF AFRICAN HIGHER EDUCATION STUDENTS: A GHANAIAN PERSPECTIVE

Frank Senyo Loglo, Center for Open Education Research (COER), Carl von Ossietzky University Oldenburg, Germany

Correspondence: *Frank Senyo Loglo: frank.senyo.loglo@uni-oldenburg.de*

Abstract

The study examined the media usage patterns of 598 university students in Ghana to understand their demands for digital teaching and learning, as well as their patterns of media use for learning, with the goal of informing the media selection process. Overall, the study found that the universities fell short of meeting students' expressed need for digital learning formats. The gap represents both a challenge and an opportunity for the expansion of digital teaching and learning formats in Ghanaian universities. Furthermore, the media usage patterns reveal significant leisure-seeking and recreational uses of media by students, emphasizing the pervasiveness and embeddedness of smartphones in academic contexts. The emphasis on entertainment usage and the prevalent use of media for hedonistic purposes may suggest a deficit in digital skills regarding the use of media for learning. The study found no significant differences in user profiles between traditional and non-traditional students. The implications for instructional design activities and strategies for a mobile-saturated context are discussed.

Keywords:

Media Usage Patterns, Digital Media, Higher Education, Digital Education

Introduction

The use of digital technologies in the teaching and learning processes within higher education has become commonplace all over the world. Ross et al. (2010) acknowledged three key roles of technology in education, namely: (i) technology as a tutor, (ii) technology as a teaching aid, and (iii) technology as a learning tool. They contend that understanding these clear roles helps to explain implementation differences across educational contexts. Technology is increasingly influencing not only what is taught, but also how it is taught (Daniel, 2015; Watters, 2014). Therefore, to fully benefit from digital education, the digital learning environment must be thoughtfully designed. This includes an examination of the teaching and learning environment, as well as learner characteristics, to gain a better understanding of their needs, experiences, and motivation, as well as to inform the media selection process. Thus, understanding students' media usage behaviour aids in determining the most effective media to use in a given instructional situation (Bates, 2015; Morrison et al., 2011).

Brandzaeg (2010) defines a user typology as "the categorisation of users into distinct user types that describes the various ways in which individuals use different media, reflecting a varying amount of activity/content preferences, frequency of use and variety of use" (pg. 941). He argued that typologies allow for the classification of media users based on their actual usage patterns rather than on demographic or contextual factors. While there is pervasive use of digital media by higher education students, there is little evidence about their pattern of use for learning. In the meta-analysis of 22 studies on media usage typologies conducted by Brandtzaeg (2010), only Johnson and Kulpa (2007) focused on higher education students. Since then, there have been a number of studies on media usage typologies conducted in various country contexts, notably Germany (Dolch et al., 2021; Dolch & Zawacki-Richter, 2018; Zawacki-Richter et al., 2015), Spain (Gonzalez et al., 2019), and Turkey (Özlü & Kalyoncuoglu, 2017).

Despite the valuable contribution these studies have made to our understanding of higher education students' media usage patterns, they have primarily been conducted in contexts that are digitally advanced, as defined by advancements in learning technologies, high internet connectivity and speed, early adoption of technologies, and high skill levels in the use of digital media (Gierdowski et al., 2020; Higher Education Academy, 2014; Zawacki-Richter, 2020). For example, in a JISC Report that surveyed 20,575 students across 28 universities in the United Kingdom, only 3% rated their institution's digital provision as poor, while 77% gave a positive rating of the quality of digital teaching and learning on their courses (Killen & Langer-Crame, 2020). In comparison, developing-countries are confronted with challenges of inconsistent power supply, low technology infrastructure, lower internet penetration, and low digital skills (Agba, 2020; Gama et al., 2022; Guri-Rosenblit, 2014; Pete & Soko, 2020).

Given that structural and sociocultural factors influence how people use media (Barnes et al., 2007; Balakrishnan et al., 2016; Dutton & Blank, 2015), media users cannot be viewed as a globally homogeneous group. Culture plays an important role in online learning and should therefore be considered during the instructional design process (Bhagat & Chang, 2018; Milheim, 2014; Nguyen, 2015), especially in resource-constrained settings that face enormous technological challenges. The apparent digital divide warrants additional research in order to arrive at a nuanced description of the media usage characteristics of students in a developing country context, which appear to have been overlooked in the literature regarding media-user typologies. Consequently, this study seeks to generate a clearer understanding of the media usage behaviour of students in the Ghanaian higher education context. More specifically, the study addresses the following research questions:

1. What kind of digital devices do the students in Ghana's higher education have access to?

2. What is the difference between the supply and demand of digital teaching and learning practices that higher education institutions in Ghana offer?

3. What kinds of different media usage types can be identified among higher education students in Ghana?

Methodology

Sample and Instrument

This study deployed an online survey, which was conducted between April and October 2020. The questionnaire was distributed via an e-mail list of contact persons within the participating higher education institutions (HEIs). Participation was voluntary and self-recruited. In total, 598 students from 26 Ghanaian HEIs, comprising 16 public universities and 10 private universities, participated in the study. Participants had a mean age of 25 years (*SD* = 5.72), with a range of 18 to 49 years, and had studied for an average of four semesters (*SD* = 2.23) at the university. Majority were Business Sciences and Economics students (30.83%), followed by students in the STEM subject areas (27.67%). Table 1 shows the distribution of study subjects.

Table 1: Study subjects of survey participants

Rank	Study Area	n	Valid %
1	Business Sciences & Economics	78	30.8
2	Science, Technology, Engineering, and Mathematics (STEM)	70	27.7
3	Arts & Humanities	37	14.6
4	Education & Social Sciences	35	13.8
5	Medical & Health Sciences	20	7.9
6	Natural and Agricultural Sciences	13	5.2
	Valid Total	**253**	**100**

The study utilized a questionnaire adapted from previous studies (Zawacki-Richter et al., 2015; Dolch and Zawacki-Richter, 2018). Participants were asked to rate the importance of 10 digital teaching and learning formats (5 = very important to 1 = not important at all), as well as their frequency of use of these formats (5 = very often to 1 = not at all) at their respective universities. The answers "I'm not familiar with that" or "I don't know" were defined as missing values. Additionally, Zawacki-Richter et al.'s (2015) computation of the supply and demand of digital teaching and learning formats was adopted to index the difference between the mean values of students demand and the current provisions supplied by the institutions (i.e., $\Delta MV = MV_{Demand} - MV_{Supply}$; see also Dolch et al., 2021; Dolch & Zawacki-Richter, 2018).

Results and discussions

Access to digital media and internet

Table 2 shows extensive access to digital devices by students, particularly Smartphones (96.2%) and Notebooks/Laptops (85.3%). Netbooks and MP-3 players recorded low access rates of 23.1% and 33.1%, respectively. Furthermore, access to mobile internet connections (71.9 %) was much higher than fixed broadband internet connections (32.5). Participants reported spending an average of 7 hours a day on the internet. This confirms a high degree of preference for mobility, which permits location-independent study.

Table 2: Access rate of digital devices

Device	Access Rate (%)
Smartphone with internet access	96.2
Notebook/Laptop	85.3
Mobile Internet	71.9
Desktop-PC	61
Cellphone without internet access	59.1
Tablet-PC	49.8
Printer	49.3
Scanner	42.2
Wearable devices	40.4
E-Book-Reader	39.1
MP3-Player	33.1
Internet @ home (Fixed Broadband)	32.5
Netbook	23.1

Demand and supply of digital teaching and learning formats

Students were required to indicate the availability of use (supply), and the importance they placed on the use (demand) of ten digital teaching and learning formats in their universities. The availability indicates the current provision made by the university while the importance signals a need for the use of such formats. The difference between the supply and demand of digital teaching and learning practices provides an indication for expandability prospects for digital teaching and the learning formats. From Table 3, the difference in mean values (ΔMV) suggest that audience response systems and lectures via podcasts/vodcasts jointly have the highest disparity between supply and demand ($\Delta MV = 0.74$). This means that while the students consider these tools as very important for their studies, their availability for use is relatively low. The low difference between the desired and actual values for course material in the university's learning management system and the deployment of online assessments suggest that student needs for these media are being met to a large extent.

Table 3: Demand and supply of digital teaching and learning formats

Digital Teaching and Learning Format	Desired			Actual			
	N	MV	SD	N	MV	SD	ΔMV
Audience Response Systems	239	3.68	1.163	250	2.94	1.355	0.74
Lectures via podcast/vodcast	238	3.3	1.118	255	2.56	1.358	0.74

Virtual practical courses and labs	241	3.34	1.177	254	2.62	1.351	0.72
Virtual seminars and tutorials with tele-cooperation	245	3.4	1.168	256	2.69	1.294	0.71
Interactive multimedia-based study materials	254	3.5	1.117	260	2.92	1.265	0.58
E-portfolios	227	3.16	1.11	234	2.59	1.209	0.57
Collaborative online tools	252	3.27	1.223	263	2.83	1.318	0.44
Web-based trainings / study course on the intranet or internet	250	3.29	1.191	263	2.87	1.323	0.42
Material accompanying courses in LMS	260	3.55	1.119	270	3.15	1.256	0.40
Online tests and assessments	257	3.38	1.146	264	2.98	1.348	0.40

Table 4: Differences in the demand for digital teaching and learning formats between traditional students (TS) and non traditional students (NTS).

Digital Teaching and Learning Format	**Student type**	**N**	**M**	**SD**	**T**	**df**	**p(2- tailed)**
Audience Response Systems	TS	131	3.53	1.21	-2.801	221	.006*
	NTS	92	3.97	1.08			
Material accompanying the courses LMS	TS	142	3.5	1.16	-0.659	239	.510
	NTS	99	3.6	1.04			
Interactive multimedia-based study materials	TS	136	3.54	1.15	1.000	233	.319
	NTS	99	3.39	1.12			
Virtual seminars and tutorials with tele-cooperation	TS	135	3.45	1.20	0.835	227	.405
	NTS	94	3.32	1.16			
Lectures via podcasts/vodcast	TS	128	3.38	1.08	1.181	219	.239
	NTS	93	3.19	1.19			
Virtual practical courses and labs	TS	132	3.42	1.17	1.072	221	.285
	NTS	91	3.24	1.24			
Online tests and assessments / E-Assessment	TS	139	3.45	1.15	1.127	233	.261
	NTS	96	3.28	1.15			
Web-based trainings / study course on the intranet or internet	TS	138	3.3	1.20	0.287	229	.774
	NTS	93	3.26	1.21			
E-portfolios	TS	125	3.11	1.12	-0.922	209	.357
	NTS	86	3.26	1.10			
Collaborative online tools	TS	139	3.25	1.25	0.061	228	.951
	NTS	91	3.24	1.16			

An independent t-test was run to determine any possible differences between traditional students and non-traditional students in terms of their demand for each of the 10 digital teaching and learning formats as shown in Table 4. Only audience response systems showed a significant difference between the two student types. The fact that non-traditional students had a higher demand for the use audience response system may not entirely be surprising given the media's inherent ability to promote high classroom engagement.

Use of mobile phones for academic purposes

Students were asked to rate how frequently (1=not at all - 5=very often) they utilized their moile phones for various university-related academic tasks. Results show it was mainly for sending instant messaging/chats to other students. Additional noteworthy uses of smartphones include information-seeking on the internet outside classes, research for assignments, and browsing social networks. The top 10 activities students frequently undertook with smartphones in the university are shown in Figure 1.

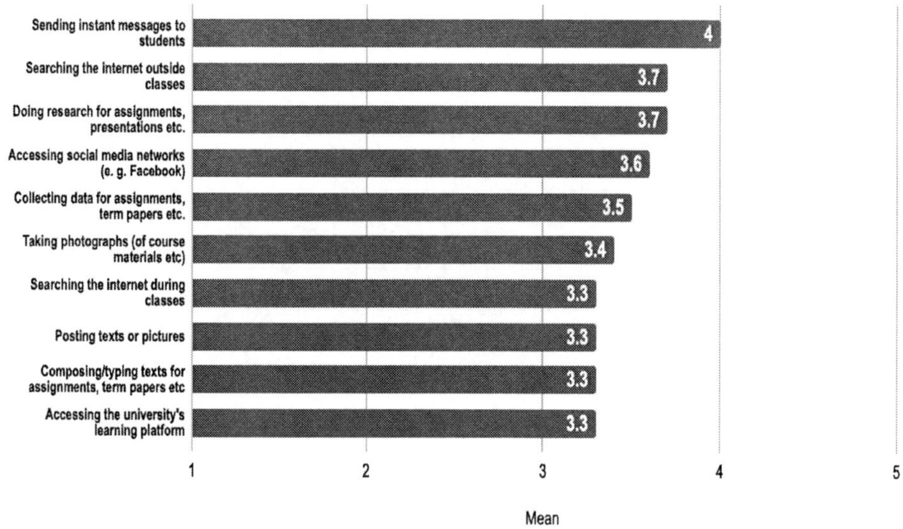

Figure 1. The use of smartphones by university students

Media usage profiles types identified among higher education students in Ghana

In a longitudinal study of German higher education students, Zawacki-Richter et al. (2015) established a typology of media users with four profiles, namely: *entertainment users*, *peripheral users*, *advanced users*, and *instrumental users*. This study adopted the same scales used for the latent class analysis (LCA) in the Zawacki-Richter et al. (2015) study to identify user types among Ghanaian higher education students. The percentages of identified profiles are shown in Figure 2. More than half (53.1%) of the students were identified as entertainment users, defined by a high propensity for intense use of the internet for leisure activities including being active on social networks. Advanced users constituted 40.4% of the students whose profile include the characteristics of entertainment users but, in addition, possess a high preference and use of e-learning, productivity and creativity tools for learning. Peripheral users formed 5.7% of the sample and were defined by the tendency for low acceptance of all media tools and services. Lastly, instrumental users accounted for only 0.8% of the sample and were defined as users likely to accept and use productivity tools including office software but rarely use media for leisure and recreational activities. They tend to use media for only specific ativities when needed. No significant differences were observed between the user profiles of traditional students versus non-traditional students ($\chi^2 = 4.8$, $df = 4$, $p > .05$; Cramer's $V = .45$).

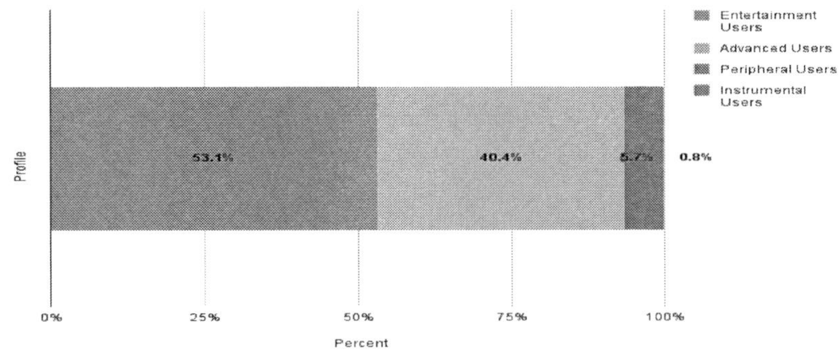

Figure 2. Distribution of media usage types of higher education students in Ghana

Conclusion and Further Perspectives

The study highlights how mobile devices are embedded in the academic activities of students in Ghanaian universities, underscoring a preference for mobility which promotes location-independent studies. Students used smartphones mainly to achieve communication and information searching tasks, which confirms the highly transmissive nature of learning in digital environments in African higher education (Loglo & Zawacki-Richter, 2023). The high access rate and use of smartphones among students represents an opportunity for the implementation of mobile learning strategies, which have been a subject of interest in recent studies (Adzifome & Agyei, 2023; Edumadze et al., 2019). However, given that the pedagogical opportunities for mobile technologies are still under-exploited in developing countries (Kaliisa et al., 2019), the necessary capacity and professional development efforts for teachers and instructional designers in the design of appropriate instructional materials, and to the support for students to use mobile technologies must be intensified.

The study demonstrates a clear demand for the use of digital teaching and learning formats, with no significant differences generally observed between traditional and non-traditional students. While fixed broadband internet connectivity offers educational advantages such as higher speed and consistent performance compared to mobile internet connections, the poor internet infrastructure in Ghana makes mobile internet connections the most viable option for digital learning. Grothaus et al.'s (2021) study of media usage in a Thai university mirrors this same phenomenon in Ghana. Therefore, it is highly recommended that the government siezes the opportunity to provide incentive schemes for mobile network operators, encouraging investments and partnerships with institutions of higher learning, similar to successful examples in Kenya[1] and South Africa[2].

The media usage types identified reveal high leisure-seeking and recreational usage of media among higher education students in Ghana. The substantial numbers of entertainment users compared to advanced users perhaps suggest that a deficit in digital skills of Ghanaian students could contribute to the use of media for hedonistic purposes within learning contexts. Similar findings were made regarding the typology of users in the German higher education (Dolch et al., 2021) who may necessarily not have the same digital skills defiencies. However, the identified typologies provide pointers for instructional designers and teachers in utilizing social networks, videos, and messaging applications to achieve educational outcomes in a digitally challenging context. The long term goal is to optimize the use of context-appropriate technologies, and ultimately cause a shift towards increased numbers within the advanced user group.

In conclusion, this study only lays the foundation for understanding the characteristics of the learner and context which informs the media selection stage in the instructional design process. Further studies are required to compare data from a developed country and developing country perspective regarding media usage of students to identify key patterns. Additionally, it would be useful to assess the digital education efforts in Ghana from a macro, meso, and micro perspective (Zawacki-Richter et al., 2009) to derive a comprehensive understanding of

---

1 https://news.mku.ac.ke/mku-partners-with-telkom-kenya-to-boost-odel-programmes/

2 https://www.universityworldnews.com/post.php?story=20200408201225155

the digital transformation efforts within the context. Beyond that, the need for major investments in the technical and technological infrastructure cannot be overemphasized.

Note: This Conference paper presents only the preliminary results of a doctoral project.

References

Adzifome, N. S., & Agyei, D. D. (2023). Learning with mobile devices—Insights from a university setting in Ghana. *Education and Information Technologies, 28*(3), 3381–3399. https://doi.org/10.1007/s10639-022-11300-4

Agba, P. C. (2020). Media Technology and The Enlarging World of Distance Education in Nigeria. University of Nigeria *Interdisciplinary Journal of Communication Studies,* 2(1). https://journal.ijcunn.com/index.php/IJC/article/view/87

Balakrishnan, V., Teoh, K.-K., Pourshafie, T., & Liew, T. K. (2016). Social Media and Their Use in Learning: A Comparative Analysis between Australia and Malaysia from the Learners' Perspectives. *Australasian Journal of Educational Technology, 33*, 81–97.

Bhagat, K. K., & Chang, C.-Y. (2018). A Cross-cultural Comparison on Students' Perceptions towards Online Learning. *Eurasia Journal of Mathematics, Science and Technology Education, 14*(3), 987-995. https://doi.org/10.12973/ejmste/81151

Barnes, S. J., Bauer, H., Neumann, M. & Huber, F. (2007). Segmenting cyberspace: A customer typology for the Internet. *European Journal of Marketing, 41*(1), 71–93.

Bates, A., W. (2015). Teaching in a digital age. Tony Bates Associate Ltd. P. 201.

Brandtzaeg, P. (2010). Towards a unified media-user typology (MUT): A meta-analysis and review of the research literature on media-user typologies. *Computers in Human Behaviour, 26*(5), 940–956. doi:Article

Conole, G. (2014). The use of technology in distance education. In O. Zawacki-Richter and T. Anderson (Eds.), Online distance education: Towards a research agenda. AU Press, 217-236

Daniel, B. (2015). "Big Data and Analytics in Higher Education: Opportunities and Challenges." *British Journal of Educational Technology 46* (5): 904–920.

Dolch, C., Zawacki-Richter, O., Bond, M., & Marín, V. I. (2021). Higher education students' media usage: A longitudinal analysis. *Asian Journal of Distance Education,16* (1), 31-53.

Dolch, C., & Zawacki-Richter, O. (2018). Are students getting used to learning technology? Changing media usage patterns of traditional and non-traditional students in higher education. *Research in Learning Technology, 26.* https://doi.org/10.25304/rlt.v26.2038

Dutton, W. H., & Blank, G. (2015). Cultural Stratification on the Internet: Five Clusters of Values and Beliefs among Users in Britain.

Edumadze, J. K., & Kuadey, N. A. (2019). Students' perception of Mobile Learning at University of Cape Coast, Ghana. *The Online Journal of Distance Education and E-Learning, 7*(3).

Gama, L. C., Chipeta, G. T., & Chawinga, W. D. (2022). Electronic learning benefits and challenges in Malawi's higher education: A literature review. *Education and Information Technologies, 27*(8), 11201–11218. https://doi.org/10.1007/s10639-022-11060-1

Gierdowski, D. C., Brooks, C., & Galanek, J. (2020). EDUCAUSE 2020 Student Technology Report: Supporting the Whole Student. EDUCAUSE. https://www.educause.edu/ecar/research-publications/student-technology-report-supporting-the-whole-student/2020/technology-use-and-environmental-preferences

Gonzalez, R., Gasco, J., & Llopis, J. (2019). University students and online social networks: Effects and typology. *Journal of Business Research, 101*, 707–714. https://doi.org/10.1016/j.jbusres.2019.01.011

Grothaus, C., Dolch, C., & Zawacki-Richter, O. (2021). Use of Digital Media in Higher Education across Country Contexts: A Comparison between Germany and Thailand. *International Journal of Emerging Technologies in Learning (IJET), 16*(20), 64–83.

Guri-Rosenblit, S. (2014). Distance education systems and institutions in the online era: An identity crisis. In O. Zawacki-Richter & T. Anderson (Eds.), Online distance education: Towards a research agenda (pp. 109–130). Athabasca University Press.

Higher Education Academy (2014). Flexible Pedagogies: technology-enhanced learning. Retrieved from: https://www.heacademy.ac.uk/system/files/resources/tel_report_0.pdf

Johnson, G. M. & Kulpa, A. (2007). Dimensions of online behavior: toward a user typology. *CyberPsychology & Behavior, 10*(6), 773–779

Kaliisa, R., Palmer, E., & Miller, J. (2019). Mobile learning in higher education: A comparative analysis of developed and developing country contexts. *British Journal of Educational Technology, 50*(2), 546–561. https://doi.org/10.1111/bjet.12583

Killen, C., & Langer-Crame, M. (2020). Student digital experience insights survey 2020: UK higher education findings. Jisc. https://www.jisc.ac.uk/reports/student-digital-experience-insights- survey-2020-uk-higher-education

Loglo, F. S., & Zawacki-Richter, O. (2023). Learning with Digital Media: A Systematic Review of Students' Use in African Higher Education . *Journal of Learning for Development, 10*(1), 1–23. https://doi.org/10.56059/jl4d.v10i1.857

Milheim, K. L. (2014). Cultural inclusivity in online learning Student-Teacher Interaction in Online Learning Environments (pp. 76-88).

Morrison, G. R., Ross, S. M., Kalman, H. K., & Kemp, J. E. (2011). Designing effective instruction (6th ed.). Wiley.

Nguyen, T. Q. T. (2015). The influence of traditional beliefs on Vietnamese college lecturers' perceptions of face. *Journal of Education for Teaching, 41*(2), 203–214. https://doi.org/10.1080/02607476.2015.1031542

Ozlü, M., & Kalyoncuoglu, S. (2017). Grouping University Students According to Their Social Media Usage Behaviours. *Journal of Internet Applications and Management, 8*(2), 5–29. https://doi.org/10.5505/iuyd.2017.97269

Pete, J, & Soko, J, J. (2020). Preparedness for online learning in the context of Covid-19 in selected Sub-Saharan African countries. *Asian Journal of Distance Education, 15*(2). https://doi.org/10.5281/zenodo.4292688

Ross, S. M., Morrison, G. R., & Lowther, D. L. (2010). Educational Technology Research Past and Present: Balancing Rigor and Relevance to Impact School Learning. *Contemporary Educational Technology, 1*(1), 17-35. https://doi.org/10.30935/cedtech/5959

Selwyn, N., Gorard, S., & Furlong, J. (2005). Adult learning in a digital age. London: Routledge/Falmer.

Watters, A. 2014. The monsters of education technology. Seattle, WA: Amazon.

Zawacki-Richter, O., Bäcker, E. M., & Vogt, S. (2009). Review of distance education research (2000 to 2008): Analysis of research areas, methods, and authorship patterns. *The International Review of Research in Open and Distributed Learning, 10*(6), 21. https://doi.org/10.19173/irrodl.v10i6.741

Zawacki-Richter, O. (2020). The current state and impact of Covid-19 on digital higher education in Germany. Human *Behavior and Emerging Technologies, 3.* https://doi.org/10.1002/hbe2.238

Zawacki-Richter, O., Müskens, W., Krause, U., Alturki, U., & Aldraiweesh, A. (2015). Student media usage patterns and non-traditional learning in higher education. *International Review of Research in Open and Distributed Learning, 16*(2), 136–170. https://doi.org/10.19173/irrodl.v16i2.1979

PROTECTING CHILDREN ONLINE: STRATEGIES FOR A SAFER FUTURE

Kirra Pendergast, Safe on Social Media Pty Ltd, Australia

***Correspondence**: Kirra Pendergast: kirra@safeonsocial.com*

Abstract

The internet has provided immense benefits to society, but it has also posed significant risks, particularly for children. Child exploitation and privacy risks associated with digital technology have become a growing concern, as predators have found ways to exploit the anonymity of the internet to target vulnerable children. This paper presents an overview of the challenges and strategies for taking a proactive approach to child safety online, with a focus on online child exploitation and the risks associated with day-care and school journaling apps, online gaming, social media and messaging apps.

Keywords:

Cyber Safety, Child safety, Child Safety Online, Child Exploitation, Online Gaming, social media, Proactive, education.

Protecting Children Online:

While the internet provides immense benefits, it also poses significant risks, particularly for children. Child exploitation and privacy risks associated with digital technology have become a growing concern, as predators have found ways to exploit the anonymity of the internet to target children. As such, it is crucial to take a proactive approach to child safety online to protect children and create a safer and brighter future for all.

Online child exploitation has become a significant concern, with predators using online gaming platforms and social media to engage in inappropriate behaviour with children. For example, on Roblox, an online gaming platform, predators can offer children money (usually in-game currency) for sexual acts, engage in role-play games that involve sexual activity, and move conversations to other platforms such as TikTok, where children can be groomed, sextorted, and threatened.

It is essential to invest in up-to-date education in training for educators, staff and parents enable them to understand risky online activity, particularly on social media and messaging apps, where predators often move their activities. Law enforcement must also have the necessary resources and expertise to identify and apprehend predators, including working closely with companies operating online platforms to identify and report suspected abuse.

Local community social media groups frequently feature callouts from parents asking for recommendations for the best childcare centre, or sometimes advice on which ones to avoid. Many centres and schools are recommended based on the use of their centre App, and how engaged the service is, with the App keeping you up to date on everything your child is doing during the day.

The App, you will be told, makes life so much easier. You'll be sold on how much information is put into it. General newsletters, the weekly menu, photos of your child, observations, and reflections, you'll know just how much they slept and ate and all about their toilet habits. App and software developers have seen the benefit of creating childcare (and school) Apps. The industry is lucrative and seemingly has an infinite future supply of user accounts.

When we as adults download an App, we consent to the Terms and Conditions, whether we read them or not, and honestly, how many people really read the fine print? By simply downloading and ticking that little 'I agree' box, we are consenting for our own data to be used by the App as well as consenting to permissions such as accessing our photos, comments, phone contacts, and sometimes even our location. We understand that we are adding to our own digital footprint, and for the most part, that's fine, we're adults, and we get to make that decision. But what happens to the rights of our children? What data are the apps collecting, and who can see it? How will the data these apps collect affect them in the future?

These are the questions we raise regarding the Apps that most childcare centres enforce for communication purposes when a child first attends their centre or when the Centre chooses to introduce one.

The General Data Protection Regulation (GDPR) is a set of privacy and data protection rules enforced by the European Union (EU) to protect the personal data and privacy of individuals within the EU. The GDPR changes the way data processors deal with data for residents in the European Union. GDPR is one of the first regulations that exports the marketplace principle which means that even companies outside the EU that process personal data of EU citizens are subject to GDPR and must adhere to the same privacy and data protection standards as companies within the EU. It is applicable for every European whose data is processed on digital platforms no matter where it is used. GDPR sets guidelines for the collection, processing, and storage of personal data and outlines the rights of individuals regarding their personal data.

In the case of childcare applications, data about the child is indirectly processed, so should be stated in the privacy policies. Parents should be made aware that their children's data is processed, and training should be provided on what they are signing up for and how to use these apps. This will help the parents make informed choices and it will also help to protect the centre or school using the apps, so they have evidence that formal training was provided to parents and documented.

The use of Apps in a childcare and school settings is very commonplace but what many don't realise, is that when we as parents and/or carers agree to these Apps on behalf of our children, we are aiding in the creation and building of their digital footprint, a footprint that they have no control over, and this footprint can be very sensitive. Arguably, your childcare service provider does not have control over this footprint either. Nor do their staff completely understand the crossover with Cyber Security and Cyber Safety and the issues caused for a child's future and safety.

When a childcare service provider or school enters into an agreement with an App provider, the contract of service is between the service provider and the App provider. The parent or guardian is merely a user, not a party to the contract. In basic legal terms, if you are not a party to a contract, you cannot enforce it or seek a remedy for any breach or damage.

When a parent submits the completed enrolment forms, the service provider enters the personal details of parents/guardians in the administrators' side of the App. A child's data is also entered into the App, including sensitive medical information, insurance, any medical providers, and medical reports.

The provider then uses the App to upload daily routines, toileting data, sleep data, feeding data, photos, observations, stories, and incident reports, including behavioural notes and other tailored reports. Likely a parent/guardian can comment on the entries made. Sometimes other children will be included in these entries. And yes, mistakes can be made with a simple click on the wrong child or parent, seeing your child's photo, sensitive information, being shared with other families. The enormous amount of information shared on every child every day is also a distraction for the Teacher or Childcare staff member taking away from their actual job of educating a child and keeping children safe while onsite at the service provider.

Many Apps allow 'family' to view a child's journal, which also includes other children if they are featured in a child's account (which is highly likely). There is no vetting of who can get these invitations; it's on the user to invite others. This could be an aunt, an uncle, the grandparents, or even the man who lives next door, 'just in case.' This means that someone else is seeing a child, someone a parent hasn't consented to. You do not get to approve additional users who are added or given access by other parents, only those you choose to provide access to yourself.

Additionally, there is rarely two-factor authentication in these Apps to protect login details and to track that people are who they say they are. Let's not forget it's common to practise to share login details with family than have them set up their profiles, so commentary, viewership, and communications can be from someone who is not the intended user.

Mandating the use of Apps is becoming standard for the convenience of childcare providers. Recently, we have been made aware of more and more After School Care services mandating the use of Apps. In some cases, even including that, the service provider can only be notified of absences in the app. Otherwise, an 'administration fee' will apply. This is also applicable to many primary and secondary schools.

What's the problem with using a childcare App if, seemingly, every other industry has one? Very little research has been conducted into the childcare App market. It doesn't even raise eyebrows as these Apps are seen as convenient and a timesaver for the provider and a key engagement driver for parents. And the Apps aren't silly; some are designed with the whole mummy/daddy guilt in mind, played on by the developers, so parents feel that they can't sign up without suffering from major FOMO and a massive case of the guilts.

A Privacy and Security Analysis of Mobile Child Care Apps is a study that was released in March 2022. The study looked at 42 Apps and found a direct threat to privacy by tracking mechanisms embedded in the applications. Another risk it noted was information leakage.

We forget that children cannot consent to their data being stored. That in itself raises privacy issues. As the authors of this study state, it is the job of the parents and educators to act with caution. Always remember that we are the product if something is free to use. If a child's daycare centre or school is using a free App to keep parents up to date with what a child is doing, that means that they could be paying with external access to all the data stored within it.

Serious questions need to be considered about the mandatory use of these Apps when considering anti-discrimination laws and the privacy rights of a child. There appears to be a giant black hole, and these two do not meet. On a cursory glance, forcing an individual or family to use an App for convenience appears to be nothing short of indirect discrimination against those exercising their rights to keep their lives offline.

The Human Rights Commission defines indirect discrimination as:
"Where an unreasonable rule or policy that is the same for everyone but has an unfair effect on people who share a particular attribute."

Yet, for many, they will not satisfy the protected attributes required under our discrimination laws, such as gender, disability, or race (amongst others). Some will, however, for example, the vision impaired who may not be able to utilise these apps or perhaps families who are not from an English-speaking background. Those of us who have, for want of a better expression, a 'conscientious objection' to putting our children's data online have no protection.

Interestingly, the Convention of the Rights of the Child states that:

" 1. No child shall be subjected to arbitrary or unlawful interference with his or her privacy, family, home or correspondence, nor to unlawful attacks on his or her honour or reputation, and
2. The child has the right to the protection of the law against such interference or attacks"

These Apps that have been designed for convenience do not seem to consider either of these aspects, and there is a gaping hole. How can we protect our children from storage and usage of their data?

The concerns with this are many, including that most services do not consult or are not consulting with parents/guardians about using an App, moving to an App, or in the case of new families to a service, even providing them with an option to use the App or to inform them that one is being used.

Some families have no choice due to vacancy rates for centres in specific geographical locations. At best, you'll be presented with a Privacy Policy or referred to the Centre's Privacy Policy on their website that concerns the Centre itself and how it handles your and your child's personal information. In one instance that has been observed, the Centre's Privacy Policy is very vague, stating "... realises the importance of privacy to families/guardians and as such does not release any information of records stored to a third party for their use without the account holders' authority unless required by law".

Arguably, the transmission of personal information is not being 'used' by the third party. Still, this Privacy Policy makes no mention that the service utilises an App and that, as part of the Terms of Use of the service, personal details will be disclosed. You also need to agree to the Apps' Terms and Conditions and their Privacy Policy.

One service provider state in their Terms and Conditions that whilst they take care to provide services and ensure that the App and website is free of any virus or malware, they are not responsible for damage caused, and that you indemnify the developer from all liabilities, costs and expenses. In relation to privacy, it states that whilst it aims to take due care, they do not warrant and cannot ensure the security of any information which is provided, and information is transmitted solely at your risk.

The first generation of social media users are now parents, and they are the target market for these Apps. This generation had little or no guidance about the risks of what they were using when they were in school in the early 2000s, and now they are becoming parents; many don't know the questions that they should be asking because it all just feels like 'the way it is'.

However, the problem with some of these apps, especially for those who are not tech savvy, is that you may not know what questions to ask regarding what vulnerabilities these Apps may have, what trackers are in place for analytics, or how they are used. We also don't know how our data is used to 'better the product,' how secure the cloud storage is, and what country it is in (many Apps state that data is 'stored in an external data storage facility.'

And what happens to photographs and videos uploaded of our children? Who can download them, and who is taking screenshots? Who are the other parents, grandparents, siblings, aunties, or uncles who now have access to photos of your children through the App? For parents with no choice as to providers, their children's data, along with their own, is being held for ransom because the use of the App is mandated by using the service.

On top of all this, we have no idea what this data will look like for our children in the future. Already, some life insurers are using the reason a person has accessed mental health services, including youth mental health services, even without a formal diagnosis of a mental health condition, to decline or heavily restrict offering insurance coverage to an individual. This has been identified in various complaints to State Anti-Discrimination Tribunals and highlighted in a 2021 report by the Australian Public Interest Advisory Centre.

Whilst there is clear discrimination here, some insurers are finding their way around the Anti-Discrimination laws. Often, consumers do not know or understand their rights to challenge the decisions made. In addition to these reports, Safe on Social has been informed of cases where individuals are being declined insurance coverage for having had episodes of anxiety, including young adults.

What about the possible impact of this data being released or otherwise located by our children's potential employers down the track? How will the possible disclosure of this information impact their job-seeking? Already we know that employers are searching for prospective employees, with many scrutinising their social media presence, and the perceived reality of a candidate is an influencing factor for some employers. Adding an extra layer of sensitive information could be devastatingly adverse for some individuals.

There is no suggestion that these Apps or the data collected is being misused at present, but any data collection is open to exploitation. Data such as sleep patterns, toileting, and what our children eat during the day is essential for some parents, but does it need to be collected and stored, especially when we don't know who the App developers may share the data with? or sell it to?

Photographs of our children are lovely, but do they need to be stored in a third-party Application that cannot guarantee our children's privacy? Who monitors or vets who are allowed to use the App, and what invitations can be sent to what family members or friends?

Other issues are more subtle but of equal importance. For starters, forcing a parent to utilise an App may disadvantage some members of our society (the vision impaired or other language speakers), potentially resulting in some form of indirect discrimination. It may even go further to discriminate against parents with family responsibilities who feel they have no choice but to remove their children from services because of a desire to protect their privacy. Those parents are forced to choose between work or placing their child in the care of a service provider who mandates storing their child's data and who has no control over disclosing that data.

We all sign Permission to Publish forms for our children, and there used to be a choice. If you opted out, you would be emailed the photo or given a printed copy. But lately, Safe on Social has been contacted more and more by parents that feel discriminated against. For example, a parent contacted us who was very upset that she had to pull her child from an early childhood after-school activity because she didn't agree to photos of her child being published online. She had escaped domestic violence and did not want photos of her child online. She was told that her child could not participate if they could not be photographed and published on the business's social media pages.

Newer parents are learning from older parents and are indeed becoming wiser. New parents are making conscious choices to keep their children's data offline; they're not posting photos and are thankfully starting to be more cyber-street smart. But are they thinking about the Apps they use to keep track of their children's activities during the day in childcare or just not sharing them on the major social media platforms?

We teach our children about being safe online, and generally, we are now becoming more cautious about when we allow them online and what we allow them to do. These Applications and mandating their use of them take that control away from parents who cannot make informed decisions about what or how their data and their children's is being used. Isn't it time we had a conversation about how best to manage the delicate balance between convenience and our children's privacy?

Kirra is a renowned cyber safety expert, with over 30 years of experience in the fields of cyber security, IT Business consulting, and Cyber Safety. She is also passionate about working with children and has dedicated the last 15 years of her career to educating and training people on cyber safety ranging in age from 5yrs - 75+. In 2021 she spoke to more than 106,000 young people in Schools across Australia.

As the Founder of Safe on Social, Kirra splits her time between the Asia Pacific Headquarters in Byron Bay, Australia, Safe on Social's UK, and European Headquarters in London, England, and Florence, Italy. Her experience of enduring online bullying and abuse inspired her to create Safe on Social, which has now become the largest and most trusted cyber safety education and training group of companies globally.

Kirra is a global thought leader in cyber safety, providing organisations of all sizes with cyber safety and social media risk management awareness training on an international scale. She is a dynamic and engaging public speaker and media commentator, having written for numerous media organisations and appeared on major international news channels. She is also a regular guest on podcasts across the world.

Kirra's straightforward, no-nonsense approach empowers people with knowledge, giving them the skills to consume technology positively rather than have their lives consumed by technology. Her extensive experience advising governments and organisations of all sizes for 18 years before founding Safe on Social has powered the training programs provided by the company.

In 2020, Kirra appointed a first-of-its-kind advisory committee of young people to help guide Safe on Social's work. She is known for her dedication to the cyber safety cause and expertise in every aspect of the sector, making her a highly sought-after speaker and commentator.

More information about Kirra and the Safe on Social team can be found on their website www.safeonsocial.com

References

United Nations Convention on the rights of the child.

https://www.ohchr.org/en/instruments-mechanisms/instruments/convention-rights-child

A privacy and security analysis of Mobile Child Care Applications

https://www.researchgate.net/publication/358904572_We_may_share_the_number_of_diaper_changes_A_Privacy_and_Security_Analysis_of_Mobile_Child_Care_Applications

WAYS OF FORMING STUDENTS' DIGITAL COMPETENCE IN COMPUTER SCIENCE CLASSES

Natalia Grushko, Zalishchyky State Gymnasia Zalishchyky, Ternopil Region, Ukraine

Roman Hrushko, Department of Informatics and Its Teaching Methods, Ternopil National Pedagogical University Named After V. Hnatyuk

Correspondence: *Natalia Grushko: grushko.nat@gmail.com*

Abstract

The most important condition that the modern information society puts forward for the school is the competitiveness of the graduate, his acquisition of such qualities as independent, critical and creative thinking; the ability to competently work with because today this is one of the most important factors of a young person's success. Therefore, general educational institutions should form in students the ability to learn, find information, critically evaluate it and creatively use it, that is, form digital competence in students, which in the future will provide them with the opportunity to study successfully throughout their lives; prepare for the chosen professional activity and constantly improve one's professional qualifications; to live and work in the information society, in the conditions of the technological economy. Digital competence is a vital skill in today's digital era, where technology is an integral part of our lives. The importance of digital competence has increased even further in the current global pandemic situation, where digital literacy has become essential for continuing education and working remotely. Therefore, computer science classes play a crucial role in fostering students' digital competence. In this article, we will explore different ways of forming students' digital competence in computer science classes.

Keywords: competence, digital competence, digital literacy, information technologies, computer science lesson

Introduction

Digital competence refers to the ability to use digital technologies effectively and responsibly to achieve personal, social, and professional goals. Computer science classes provide an excellent opportunity for students to learn and develop digital competence. However, it is not enough to teach students just how to use digital tools; they also need to learn how to use them responsibly and safely.

The European Commission has defined eight key digital competencies that are considered essential for individuals to participate fully in a digital society. These competencies are often referred to as the "DigComp" framework. Information and data literacy: This competence includes the ability to search for, locate, and evaluate information using digital tools. It also involves the ability to use data effectively and ethically. Communication and collaboration: This competence involves using digital tools to communicate and collaborate with others. It includes skills such as online etiquette, digital communication, and teamwork. Digital content creation: This competence involves the ability to create and edit digital content using a range of tools and formats. It includes skills such as multimedia production, graphic design, and coding. Safety: This competence involves being aware of the risks and threats associated with digital technology, and knowing how to protect oneself and others from them. It includes skills such as online privacy, cyber security, and safe browsing. Problem-solving: This competence involves using digital tools to solve problems and make decisions. It includes skills such as critical thinking, analytical reasoning, and creativity. Career-related: This competence includes the ability to use digital tools to find, apply for, and manage jobs. It also involves knowing how to use digital tools to develop one's career and professional skills. Learning: This competence involves using digital tools to support learning and personal development. It includes skills such as e-learning, online courses, and digital self-assessment. Active citizenship: This competence involves using digital tools to participate in social and civic activities. It includes skills such as digital activism, online voting, and digital volunteering. (Dubov, 2010, p.64)

These eight digital competences are designed to provide a comprehensive framework for individuals to develop their digital skills and knowledge. They are also used by educational institutions and employers to design digital literacy programs and job training courses.

Ways of forming students' digital competence in computer science classes

Let's consider some recommendations that will help to form the digital competence of students.

Digital citizenship involves teaching students about their rights and responsibilities when using digital technologies. Computer science classes should focus on imparting these skills, such as understanding online privacy, creating and maintaining a positive digital footprint, and avoiding cyber bullying. Teachers can use case studies and real-life examples to teach students about the consequences of irresponsible digital behavior. It is also important to teach students about online security and safety. Teachers can provide tips and guidelines for students to follow, such as using strong passwords, avoiding phishing scams, and keeping their personal information private. Students should also be taught about the dangers of sharing personal information online and how to identify and report online abuse. (Genseruk, 2019, p.8-16)

Encouraging students to be creative with digital technologies can help develop their digital competence. Computer science classes should incorporate activities that challenge students to use digital tools in innovative ways, such as creating websites, animations, or games. Teachers can provide opportunities for students to explore different digital tools and experiment with their features. In addition to creativity, it is important to teach students about digital design principles. Students should learn about user interface design, visual design, and typography. These skills will help students to create digital products that are easy to use and visually appealing.

Collaborative learning helps students to develop communication and teamwork skills, which are crucial in the digital age. Computer science classes should encourage group projects that require students to work together on digital projects and communicate effectively. Teachers can use group projects to teach students about project management, task delegation, and conflict resolution. Collaborative learning also provides students with an opportunity to learn from each other. Students can share their knowledge and expertise, and learn from the different perspectives and approaches of their peers. (Litvynova, 2016, p.354)

Introducing coding at an early age can help students develop computational thinking, problem-solving skills, and logical reasoning abilities. Computer science classes should include coding exercises to teach students how to think logically and solve problems using technology. Teachers can use visual programming languages such as Scratch or Code.org to teach students the basics of coding. In addition to coding, students should also learn about algorithms, data structures, and programming concepts. These skills will help students to understand how technology works and how to create their own digital products.

Practice is essential for developing digital competence. Computer science classes should provide opportunities for students to practice using digital tools and receive feedback to improve their skills continually. Teachers can provide formative assessments and constructive feedback to help students understand their strengths and weaknesses. It is also essential to provide students with opportunities to apply their digital skills outside of the classroom. Teachers can encourage students to participate in coding competitions, hackathons, and other digital events.(Golovan, 2008, p.23-30)

By focusing on digital citizenship, encouraging creativity, promoting collaborative learning, introducing coding, and providing practice and feedback, teachers can help students develop the skills they need to navigate the digital world safely and effectively. These skills will prepare students for a future where digital technologies will play an increasingly important role in every aspect of their lives.

Integrating digital competences into subject teaching can enhance students' learning experiences and equip them with essential skills for the digital age. Here are some digital competences that subject teachers may develop when integrating subjects.

Digital literacy involves the ability to use digital tools and technologies to find, evaluate, and communicate information effectively. Teachers who integrate digital technologies into their teaching can help students develop digital literacy skills, such as using search engines, social media, and digital libraries to access information related to the subject matter.

Digital communication involves the ability to use digital technologies to communicate effectively with others. Teachers can use various digital tools, such as online discussion forums, chat rooms, and video conferencing, to facilitate communication among students and between students and teachers. This can help students develop digital communication skills, such as how to express themselves clearly and appropriately in various digital contexts. (Hrytsenchuk, 2019, p.129-134)

Data literacy involves the ability to use digital tools and technologies to collect, analyze, and interpret data. Teachers can integrate data analysis tools and technologies into their teaching, such as spreadsheets and data visualization software, to help students develop data literacy skills. This can help students understand how to collect and analyze data related to the subject matter and draw meaningful conclusions.

Collaboration and teamwork involve the ability to work effectively with others to achieve common goals. Teachers who integrate digital tools and technologies into their teaching can provide opportunities for students to work collaboratively on digital projects. This can help students develop collaboration and teamwork skills, such as how to communicate and work effectively with others in online environments.

Digital creativity involves the ability to use digital tools and technologies to create and produce new content. Teachers who integrate digital tools and technologies into their teaching can provide opportunities for students to create digital content related to the subject matter. This can help students develop digital creativity skills, such as how to use digital tools and technologies to design and produce creative content. (Galatyuk, 2011, p.21-26; Lytvinova, 2016, p.354)

Overall, integrating digital competences into subject teaching can help students develop essential skills for the digital age and enhance their learning experiences.

In order to successfully develop digital competence in students, it is advisable to pay attention to our recommendations. Introduce students to programming languages: Teach students programming languages like Python, Java, C++, or HTML/CSS, as these are foundational skills that are essential in the digital world. Offer hands-on opportunities for students to experiment with digital tools and platforms, such as creating websites, designing mobile apps, or building games. Encourage students to work together in groups or pairs, and provide opportunities for them to share their knowledge and expertise with one another. This fosters a collaborative learning environment that is conducive to the development of digital competence. Use game-based learning techniques to teach coding concepts, algorithms, and programming logic. This can make learning more engaging and interactive for students. Assign projects that require students to use digital tools and technologies to solve real-world problems or create practical applications. (Bykov, 2011, p.8-13) This approach helps students see the relevance and applicability of digital competence in their daily lives. Incorporate multimedia resources such as videos, interactive tutorials, and simulations to help students understand complex digital concepts. Educate students about the importance of online safety and privacy, and how to protect themselves from cyber threats, including phishing, hacking, and identity theft. Help students develop digital literacy skills such as information literacy, media literacy, and digital citizenship, which are important for navigating the digital world. Encourage students to use digital tools to express their creativity, such as creating digital art, music, or videos. This helps them develop their digital skills while also fostering their creativity. Provide ongoing support and resources to help students continue developing their digital competence, even after the class has ended. This may include access to online tutorials, digital tools, and networking opportunities. (Kosharuk, 2016)

Digital skills are becoming increasingly important in today's world, and Ukraine is no exception. Computer science classes can play a significant role in developing these skills among students. In recent years, Ukraine has made significant efforts to promote digital skills in its education system. The Ministry of Education and Science of Ukraine has included digital literacy as one of the key competencies that students must develop. This includes proficiency in using digital devices and software, as well as understanding the ethical, legal, and social issues related to the use of technology.

Computer science classes in Ukraine are designed to provide students with a strong foundation in computer programming, algorithm development, and problem-solving skills. These classes can help students develop digital skills by teaching them how to use programming languages, software development tools, and other digital technologies. Furthermore, the government of Ukraine has launched several initiatives to promote digital skills among students. For example, the "New Ukrainian School" project, which aims to modernize the education system in Ukraine, includes a focus on developing digital skills. This project includes the creation of new computer science curricula, the development of digital resources and tools for teachers and students, and the provision of training programs for teachers to help them incorporate digital skills into their classes. Additionally, the Ukrainian government has launched various programs and initiatives to support the development of digital skills. For example, the "Digital Skills for Ukraine" program aims to provide training and support to individuals, businesses, and the government to help them improve their digital skills. The program offers a range of courses and workshops, including coding, data analysis, and cybersecurity. Another initiative is the "Code Club Ukraine" program, which aims to teach coding skills to children aged 9-13. The program is run by volunteers and offers free coding classes in schools and community centers across Ukraine. (Koneshchynska, 2018; Vlasii, 2017, p.117-122)

In addition to these initiatives, Ukraine has a vibrant tech industry, which provides students with opportunities to gain practical experience and develop their digital skills. Many tech companies offer internships and apprenticeships to students, providing them with hands-on experience working with digital technologies.

In Ukraine, the ways of forming students' digital competence in computer science classes typically involve a combination of theoretical and practical approaches. The Ukrainian curriculum for computer science classes is designed to teach students the fundamentals of computing, programming, and digital literacy. The curriculum is designed to be age-appropriate and is updated regularly to reflect the latest trends and developments in the field. Students are often given practical assignments to work on, which require them to use their digital skills to solve problems. (Kartashova, 2020) This approach helps students to develop their critical thinking and problem-solving abilities. Computer science classes in Ukraine often use interactive learning tools such as multimedia presentations, videos, and animations to engage students and make learning more fun and interactive. Ukrainian computer science classes often make use of online resources such as educational websites, online forums, and virtual learning environments to supplement their teaching materials and help students stay up-to-date with the latest developments in the field. To encourage students to take an active interest in computer science, schools and universities in Ukraine often organize coding contests and hackathons. (Lyashenko, 2015, p.173-177). These events allow students to showcase their skills, learn from their peers, and gain valuable experience working on real-world problems. Overall, the focus of computer science classes in Ukraine is on developing students' digital literacy and problem-solving skills, as well as their ability to work collaboratively and think creatively. Computer science classes in Ukraine are playing an important role in the development of digital skills among students. The government's efforts to promote digital literacy and the country's growing tech industry provide students with a range of opportunities to gain practical experience and develop their digital skills. (Ovcharuk, 2004, p.112)

Conclusions

Integrating technology into the curriculum can improve students' digital competence. This includes using digital tools to enhance learning and allowing students to use technology to create their own projects. Creating a collaborative and supportive environment can help students feel comfortable using technology and allow them to learn from each other. Providing students with opportunities to engage in hands-on learning activities, such as coding projects, can help develop their digital competence. Encouraging students to take ownership of their learning and explore technology independently can lead to greater development of digital competence. Providing teachers with professional development opportunities can help them stay up-to-date with the latest technology and teaching methods, which can in turn benefit their students' digital competence. Ensuring that all students have access to technology, regardless of their background or socioeconomic status, is crucial for developing digital competence. Schools should work to provide equal access to technology for all students. Overall, the research suggests that developing students' digital competence requires a combination of technology integration, a supportive classroom environment, hands-on experience, self-directed learning, teacher professional development, and equal access to technology.

References

Bykov, V. Ju. (2011). Cloud computing technologies, ICT outsourcing and new functions of ICT subdivisions of educational institutions and research institutions. Informacijni tekhnologhiji v osviti: Zb. nauk. pracj., (10), 8-23

Competency approach in modern education: collective monograph / under general editorship. O. V. Ovcharuk. - K.: "K.I.S.", 2004. - 112 p.

Digital competence of the modern teacher of the new Ukrainian school: coll. theses add. All-Ukrainian science and practice seminar, Kyiv, February 28, 2018. ed. O. E. Konevshchynska, O. V. Ovcharuk. Kyiv: IITZN National Academy of Sciences of Ukraine, 2018.

Dubov D. V. Information society in Ukraine: global challenges and national opportunities: analyst. add. / D. V. Dubov, M. A. Ozhevan, S. L. Hnatiuk. - K.: NISD. - 2010. - 64 p.

Galatyuk M. Model of educational and cognitive competence in the context of studying natural sciences / M. Galatyuk // Scientific notes. - Issue 98. – Series: Pedagogical sciences. – Kirovohrad: KDPU named after V. Vinnichenko, 2011. – pp. 21–26.

Genseruk G. R., "Digital competence as one of the professionally significant competences of future teachers", Open educational e-environment of modern University, No. 6, p. 8-16, 2019.

Gis I. Cloud technologies as a means of forming an innovative educational environment: methodical recommendations. Lutsk, 2016. 56 p.

Golovan M. S. Competence and competence: experience of theory, theory of experience / M. S. Golovan // Higher education of Ukraine. – 2008. – No. 3. – P. 23–30.

Hrytsenchuk O. O., Ovcharuk O. V. Model of information and education environment for the development of teacher's civic competence based on the approaches of the Council of Europe. Proceedings. Series: Pedagogical sciences/ Tsentralnoukr. state ped. University named after Volodymyr Vinnichenko. Vinnytsia, 2019. Vol. 183. P. 129–134.

Kartashova L.A. The digital agenda of education development: focus on the formation of digital competences / L. A. Kartashova, I. V. Plish / Scientific Bulletin of the Mukachevo State University. Series "Pedagogy and Psychology", Vol. 1 (11). - 2020

Kosharuk, O.O. (2016). Competency approach in computer science classes. Computer science at school, 12 (96).

Litvynova S. G. Designing a cloud-oriented learning environment of a general educational institution: monograph. Kyiv: CPU "Comprint", 2016. 354 p.

Lyashenko K. I. Peculiarities of the formation of informational competences of younger schoolchildren / K. I. Lyashenko // Actual problems and prospects for the development of modern pedagogical education: Scientific and methodological collection of materials Days of Science. – Stakhanov-Lysychansk, April 2015. – Lysychansk, 2015. – P. 173-177.

Lytvynova, S. Gh. (2016). Designing a cloud-based learning environment for a general education institution. Kyiv: CP «Komprynt», 354 p.

Vlasii, O.O., Dudka, O.M., & Kuljchycjka N.V. (2017). The Role of Cloud Based Technologies in Realization of Blended Learning. Naukovyj chasopys NPU imeni M. P. Draghomanova. Serija #2. Komp'juterno-orijentovani systemy navchannja: Zb. nauk. Pracj. Redrada. K.: NPU imeni M.P. Draghomanova, 19 (26). 117-122.

CENTERING EQUITY AND QUALITY IN ONLINE, BLENDED, AND DIGITAL LEARNING

Angela Gunder, Online Learning Consortium, United States
Kristen Gay, Online Learning Consortium, United States

Correspondence: *Angela Gunder: angela.gunder@onlinelearning-c.org*

Abstract

This case study evaluates the Online Learning Consortium's (OLC's) five pillars of Quality Online Education – learning effectiveness, scale, access, faculty satisfaction, and student satisfaction – against equity criteria. The authors argue that the pillars could more effectively mobilize equity and quality for a range of stakeholders in the field of online, blended, and digital learning. The study addresses two primary questions: how the OLC pillars surface the relationship between quality and equity in online, blended, and digital learning, and how these pillars can be situated within the field's current practices of designing, facilitating, and evaluating equitable and sustainable education in digital learning environments. The review process followed a case study approach informed by autoethnographic principles and involved reflecting on the pillars' role in the current context of online learning. The findings highlight the need to differentiate between disparate definitions of online, blended, and digital learning to embrace both quality and equity, provide a set of guiding principles to support the variety of contexts within which instructors and learners pursue sustainable and equitable educational experiences, and focus on learning effectiveness that prioritizes learners meeting articulated outcomes and gaining relevant knowledge, skills, and abilities.

Keywords:

Digital learning; online learning; blended learning; equity; quality; instructional design; digital strategy; institutional transformation

Introduction

The Online Learning Consortium's (OLC's) five pillars of Quality Online Education – learning effectiveness, scale, access, faculty satisfaction, and student satisfaction – have defined quality online learning and advanced its facilitation since their introduction in 1997. These interrelated pillars form a framework designed for educators and institutions seeking to design and assess online, blended, and digital learning experiences that center equity and quality. The pillars were also central to the development of the OLC's Quality Scorecard Suite (QSS), which provides a comprehensive set of benchmarking tools for institutions seeking to advance and assess quality program administration, blended learning programs, course design, quality course teaching, and instructional practice, digital courseware instructional practice, and online student support (Online Learning Consortium, n.d.).

Although these pillars remain foundational to online, blended, and digital educational excellence, online learning has changed drastically over the past 26 years, and so have the needs of educators and learners globally. As we proposed a book project that would explicate foundational principles and best practices for mobilizing the QSS, we were mindful of the need to assess our pillars to ensure that our definition of quality reflected the altered landscape of higher education. We were especially aware of a field-wide need to resituate our definition of quality online, blended, and digital learning within global conversations about educational equity. As we reviewed the pillars through an equity lens, we also sought to make the pillars themselves more actionable for educators, practitioners, researchers, decision-makers, and administrators.

This study details our process of evaluating the OLC pillars alongside equity criteria and reflecting on how the pillars of quality fit into the field's current work to make education more equitable through the unique affordances of online, blended, and digital learning. More specifically, we sought to answer two primary questions: (1) how do the OLC Pillars of Quality surface the relationship between quality and equity in online, blended, and digital learning? and (2) how might the OLC Pillars of Quality be situated within the field's current practices of designing, facilitating, and iteratively improving equitable and sustainable education in digital learning environments? To answer these questions, we engaged in a multi-stage, collaborative review of the pillars that involved reflecting on the pillars' role in the current context of online, digital, and blended learning; diverse contexts within which pillars of quality are mobilized; the extent to which our descriptions centered accessibility, equity, and inclusivity criteria; and actionability of the pillars for a range of stakeholders.

Literature Review

While online learning experts agree that equity is fundamental to quality online learning experiences, significant challenges remain when mobilizing this premise across contexts and for all stakeholders. Moodle, for instance, identified seven pillars of quality: resources, communication, collaboration, assessment, accreditation, reporting, and accessibility (2021). While these are significant elements of the online education experience for instructors, the descriptions are driven by the Moodle tool's features; for instance, Moodle emphasizes their tool's ability to assist with attendance taking and predictive analytics to identify at-risk students. While these are concerns for some instructors, they are less likely to represent quality learning experiences for students and may reinforce deficit-minded policies by characterizing certain students as "at risk." New America, on the other hand, also developed a peri-pandemic report, "Back to Basics: Quality in Digital Learning," which did not address how to mobilize equity in their indicator descriptions despite the authors' acknowledgment that "The equity gaps that persist across the higher education system are also prevalent across online classes" (n.p.). This highlights the importance of discussing equity as a foundational concept and the challenge of actuating equity in quality online learning experiences.

One of the best-known rubrics for assessing online course quality, Quality Matters (QM), provides a process that can guide online course design and assessment of its quality for instructors, instructional designers, and institutional decision-makers. One of QM's strengths is that they provide separate standards for a range of online learning contexts, including higher ed, K-12, and continuing and professional education. While their distinct rubrics account for a range of activities central to online learning and the range of stakeholders who make meaning through these educational experiences, the scope of their rubric is admittedly focused on one aspect of online course facilitation. According to QM, "While the QM model focuses primarily on course design, our members can leverage the QM process — along with QM resources and community members — to scale our model and apply it to all aspects of online learning" (Quality Matters, n.d.). QM, then, does not provide a model that captures a more holistic evaluation of quality in online learning.

As this range of rubrics indicates, one of the challenges of evaluating quality is the difficulty defining what quality means to a range of stakeholders and across contexts. Hafeez et al. (2022), for instance, identified four stakeholder groups that define quality differently (providers, or "funding agencies and the general public," students, employers, and administrators/instructors (376). They also defined four categories of quality classifications, including purposeful ("compliant with a given vision or mission"), exceptional ("educational institutions achieve differentiation and exclusivity"), transformative ("[p]ositive changes in learners' performance, as well as individual and professional ability"), and accountable (institutions are "held responsible to shareholders for making the best utilization of resources and delivering high-quality" education) (2022, p. 376). The lack of consensus Hafeez et al. identify is especially troubling because, as they note, quality standards are vital to sustainable development (p. 382). Alignment is needed, then, to ensure that all stakeholders, and especially students, are benefiting from their educational experiences in the long term.

In addition to this lack of consensus surrounding quality, we are concerned about the lack of attention to equity as a foundational element of any quality online, blended, or digital learning environment. The relationship between online learning and equity itself is fraught. On the one hand, "online learning has contributed significantly to student equity, by making it possible for a wider range of people to participate and succeed in HE" (Stone, 2022, p. 140). While this increased opportunity is promising, the COVID-19 pandemic highlighted the digital divide's ongoing presence as a barrier to success for many students (Kono and Taylor, 2021). As Kono and Taylor (2021) demonstrated, this suggests for educators and institutional decision-makers "the critical importance of extending culturally sustainable practices to all online learning environments in higher education as a way to mitigate equity issues related to the digital divide" (p. 151).

Overall, while we were guided in our process by the need to explicate the relationship between quality and equity in online, blended, and digital learning, the models we referenced and recent scholarship yielded some surprising takeaways. We were both heartened to see other organizations grappling with quality's complexity and challenged by a field-wide lack of actionable engagement with equity. We also found it interesting that other organizations were apparently struggling to articulate quality in a way that could be leveraged in a range of contexts/for all stakeholders.

Method

Case Study Method

At the inception of this inquiry, we sought to determine a research method that would allow us to closely examine the connection between the OLC Pillars of Quality and the advancement of quality and equity in digital learning broadly. Our work within the global non-profit organization Online Learning Consortium as researchers, educators, and leaders provided us with context for understanding the complex and diverse applications of quality and equity across a wide variety of contexts. As such, we selected a case study method for its ability to capture the multiple perspectives and sociocultural factors (Stake, 1995) that shape the instantiation and sustaining of quality and equity within online and blended learning. Lastly, we chose a case study method for its focus on providing benefit to relevant stakeholders as opposed to just promulgating findings for the sake of publication (Stake, 1978). By leveraging the case study method, we hoped to produce a series of findings that would surface new approaches to applying the pillars at the course, program, and institutional levels to improve student learning outcomes and equitable access to quality education within and across different digitally-mediated learning environments.

Ethnographically-Informed Methods

In addition to utilizing a case study method to answer our research questions, we also took an ethnographically-informed approach to our analysis process. Autoethnography was selected for inclusion in our research method because of its ability to serve as "process and product" (Ellis et al., 2011, p. 273) within a study, capturing sociocultural phenomena reflexively in the interpretation of individual and shared experiences (Adams et al., 2017; Ellis et al., 2011). We also designed a research method that was informed by portraiture, a method of inquiry that combines aestheticism and empiricism in the presentation of evidenced-based practices and phenomena (Lawrence-Lightfoot & Davis, 1997). Portraiture encourages the use of language that is inclusive and accessible, focusing on the good that exists within a study over merely citing pathology (Lawrence-Lightfoot & Davis, 1997). In line with the work to examine the pillars through a lens of equity, portraiture method allowed us to identify places where equity-neutral and deficit language would inhibit the adoption of the pillars across an inclusive array of cultural contexts. Lastly, we grounded this study in a sociocultural view of teaching and learning, framing our analysis of the OLC Pillars of Quality and their usage within a constructivist community of practice engaging in collaborative meaning-making and values-aligned action (Gee, 1999; Halliday, 1978; Street, 1984). Ultimately, this combination of research methods was utilized as a means of completing a cultural analysis within which we as researchers might help to instantiate new pathways to improving access to education by advancing quality and equity within online, blended, and digital learning environments.

Process

Our process was formulated by determining the most impactful ways we might interrogate our two research questions. In answering our first research question of how the OLC Pillars of Quality surface the relationship between quality and equity in online, blended, and digital learning, our team engaged in a deliberate and reflective process that sought to explore and recontextualize the pillars for our changed world and the needs of the field in redefining our learning futures. In line with the pillars situated as discreet, interconnected dimensions of quality, we wanted to interrogate how the pillar definitions described ensuring quality across a diverse set of contexts in a way that was inclusive and equitable. To accomplish this, we reviewed other quality frameworks for correlations, redundancies, and other similarities but found nothing similar to the OLC Pillars in function or goals. We then reflected on the pillar language for inclusivity using the instrument Applying Eight Equity Principles to

Solutions Network Assets Protocol (Bensimon et al, 2020), a tool that helped us to identify areas where the language of the pillars could be improved to better promote equity and inclusion in online, blended, and digital learning contexts.

Our inquiry continued by exploring our second research question - to determine how the OLC Pillars of Quality might be situated within practices related to supporting equitable and inclusive online, blended, and digital learning environments. We engaged in a thorough examination of the methods and examples used in the descriptions of the pillars, considering each approach and recommendation for its accessibility and inclusivity, and identifying places where the recommendations could be optimized to better support the adoption of the pillars across a diverse set of contexts. Through this process, we also identified areas where the examples could be broadened to honor differentiation in the roles of those engaging with the pillar definitions, making it more actionable and relevant for practitioners in the field. In addition to examining the examples within the pillar definitions, we also identified new needs for new, multimodal formats for presenting the pillars (i.e. playbooks, action guides) that would increase relevance, buy-in, and actionability.

Findings

The Complementary Nature of Quality and Equity

In completing our review of the OLC's Pillars of Quality, we observed a demonstrated need for differentiating between disparate definitions of online, blended, and digital learning to find one that embraced both quality and equity. In many cases, this involved being mindful of potential deficit language and framing. For instance, in our review of the OLC Access pillar, we preserved the emphasis on facilitating access throughout the student's lifecycle but shifted away from a model that would tout "equal access" (which risks making real barriers students face invisible) in favor of a model that actively centers inclusivity while removing barriers to student success and engagement. We more explicitly name populations likely to face such barriers due to discriminatory practices and reduce the emphasis on support services. This work is especially important now, as the pandemic exacerbated the digital divide through the shift to emergency remote teaching even as it created opportunities for more students to access quality education. We are also driven by the increased focus on equity and social justice within and outside of the classroom and our responsibility to provide actionable strategies for educators and students that can help them meaningfully engage in these conversations and develop pedagogies that are responsive to them.

Our review also highlighted our need for a set of guiding principles to support the variety of contexts within which instructors (broadly conceived) and learners seek to facilitate sustainable and equitable educational experiences. As we have noted in our review of the literature, we were surprised by the lack of frameworks to support this need, since most of the other pillars we referenced focused on higher education learning environments and emphasized the role that faculty and university decision-makers play and the ways in which they define quality. In our review of the OLC pillars, we recommended shifting language that emphasized higher education contexts, such as "student" and "faculty," to the more inclusive terms, "learner" and "instructor." In making this recommendation, we were particularly mindful of professional contexts and corporate training online learning experiences wherein these pillars might be deployed. We were also challenged to reconsider what "learning effectiveness" means when stakeholders (students, professionals, etc.) may have different goals for their learning experiences. We recommended changing language that focused on students receiving a high-quality education and toward a model of learning effectiveness that prioritizes learners "meeting articulated learning outcomes that result in them gaining meaningful and impactful competencies and skills." This approach encompasses a wider range of stakeholders, contexts, and, importantly, potential outcomes for learning.

We were pleased to find that our review of the pillars highlighted their ongoing relevance to our current work in addressing access to a quality and meaningful educational experience through the unique affordances of digital learning. Our pillar review provoked important questions about whether pillars of quality should remain constant or whether they should change over time. Do the pillars need to change when the higher education landscape shifts, and if so, how can we adjust the pillars quickly enough to keep up? Or, as we suspected, do we need to revise the pillars on a regular basis to ensure their framing and contextualization continue to meet the needs of the present while anticipating future challenges and trends? Despite some suggested phrasing changes (for instance, we suggested that Instructor Satisfaction and Student Satisfaction become Instructor Success and

Learner Success, respectively), the pillars themselves still instantiated quality online education while accounting for blended, hybrid, and digital learning contexts, as well.

Diverse Exemplars of Quality and Equity

In our exploration of our second research question, we sought to determine how the usage of the OLC Pillars of Quality might be contextualized within our current practices for designing, facilitating, and continuously improving equitable and sustainable education within digital learning. In following this line of inquiry and our subsequent analysis of the usage of the pillars across a manifold of sociocultural contexts, we determined that while the impact of the pillars in supporting the advancement of equitable digital learning was strong, this impact could be extended through the inclusion of a diverse set of exemplars as annotations to the pillar definitions. These exemplars would show that the pillar definitions were not meant to sit as a monolithic blueprint for quality online learning, offering rich and multifaceted applications of the pillars that would be actionable by institutions and stakeholders from a wide variety of contexts.

We also discovered that the language used within the pillar definitions could be broadened to be more inclusive of the entirety of the learner population, and not a subset of a privileged few. This was most evident in the definition of the pillar of scale, which surfaced a tension space within the field around historical views of the focus of online learning as the path to increased revenue, rather than the path to ubiquitous access to education and scale being an indicator of that inclusivity of learner populations. We also discovered an opportunity for the pillars to extend their accessibility through the usage of learner-centered language, both in the inclusion of examples that relate to increasing student agency, meaning-making, and personal goal setting, as well as acknowledging that those utilizing the pillars might not be teaching students in credit-bearing courses alone, but also faculty, staff, administrators, and participants in trainings and certifications. We noted a potential place for improvement in moving from language related to student and faculty satisfaction to defining learner and faculty success as a means of making these pillar definitions more inclusive of the effective practices needed to promote success as defined within unique organizational contexts rather than an individual's highly-personalized happiness with the learning environment independent of its efficacy or impact.

Lastly, we determined that extending the accessibility and strength of the pillars could be achieved by remixing the current format of the pillars as a list of static text-based definitions into a series of multimodal resources. Through a series of action guides, playbooks, or collections of portraits of usage across different institutions and contexts, stakeholders of all roles would be able to better apply the pillars to their daily work in advancing access to quality online, blended, and digital learning in sustainable and inclusive ways.

Conclusion

The OLC pillars have the ability to transform the ways in which we think about teaching and learning across a diverse set of sociocultural contexts. We as a field need to be paying attention to these frameworks and taxonomies and better understand how we can help each other and our students. We also need to regularly engage in inclusive review processes that ensure the usefulness of such frameworks for the communities we serve and their actionability in an ever-expanding range of educational contexts. As we consider how to meet the needs of the present while anticipating what is on the horizon, we are especially excited by the generative potential of these pillars as they elucidate challenges facing instructors, learners, and institutions and opportunities for sustainable development.

References

Acosta, A., Palmer, I., & Romo-González, L. (2021, July 13). *The five pillars of quality digital learning.* New America. https://www.newamerica.org/education-policy/reports/back-to-basics/

Adams, T.E., Ellis, C., & Jones, S.H. (2017). Autoethnography. *The International Encyclopedia of Communication Research Methods*, 1-11.

Bensimon, E.M., Chase, M.M., & Harper, S. (2020). *Applying eight equity principles to solutions network assets protocol.* Bensimon & Associates, USC Race and Equity Center.

Ellis, C., Adams, T.E., & Bochner, A.P. (2011). Autoethnography: An overview. *Historical social research/Historische sozialforschung*, 273-290.

Gee, J. (1999). *The new literacy studies and the "Social Turn."*

Hafeez, M., Naureen, S., & Sultan, S., 2022. Quality Indicators and Models for Online Learning Quality Assurance in Higher Education. *The Electronic Journal of e-Learning, 20*(4), 374-385.

Halliday, M.A.K. (1978). *Language as social semiotic: The social interpretation of language and meaning.* Maryland. University Park Press.

Kono, K. G., & Taylor, S. (2021). *Using an ethos of care to bridge the digital divide: Exploring faculty narratives during a global pandemic.* Online Learning, 25(1), 151–165. https://doi.org/10.24059/olj.v25i1.2484

Lawrence-Lightfoot, S., & Davis, J.H. (1997). *The art and science of portraiture.* Jossey-Bass.

Moodle. (2021, January 20). *7 pillars for quality education online.* https://moodle.com/news/7-pillars-for-quality-education-online/

Online Learning Consortium. (n.d.). *OLC quality scorecard suite.* https://onlinelearningconsortium.org/consult/olc-quality-scorecard-suite/

Quality Matters. (n.d.) *QM rubrics and standards.* https://www.qualitymatters.org/index.php/qa-resources/rubric-standards

Stake, R.E. (1978). The case study method in social inquiry. *Educational researcher*, 7(2), 5-8.

Stake, R.E. (1995). *The art of case study research.* Sage.

Stone, C. (2022). *From the margins to the mainstream: The online learning rethink and its implications for enhancing student equity.* Australasian Journal of Educational Technology, *38*(6), 139–149. https://doi.org/10.14742/ajet.8136

NEW MODELS OF HIGHER EDUCATION FOR LOW-INCOME COUNTRIES

Brian Mulligan, Education Futures, Ireland
Paul Press, Atlantic technological University, Sligo, Ireland
Colleen Fletcher, Mozambique

***Correspondence**: Brian Mulligan: brian.mulligan@gmail.com*

Abstract

In low-income countries, increasing access to higher education is particularly challenging. While tertiary education may boost a country's prosperity, the high cost of education, despite subsidies, remains a barrier to access. The digitisation of existing approaches to tertiary education is insufficient, and a more radical approach is needed.

The Atlantic Technological University has been working on two approaches that hold potential for addressing this challenge. A work-based degree in engineering has placed a student in Mozambique in a mining company, where they will learn the required practical engineering skills and study online. Although this approach will allow the student to earn an income as they study, the fees will still be significant as it is based on existing forms of online learning. Separately, the university is developing a 2-year low-cost Engineering programme based on free online content, modest payment for examinations, and supervision of a capstone project.

This paper focuses on the design of these programmes and the challenges involved. Attendees will learn how these new models of higher education for low-income countries could potentially address the cost barrier to access and significantly increase participation in tertiary education, leading to improved prosperity and economic growth.

Keywords:
low-cost higher education, low-income countries, work-based learning, self-directed learning, apprenticeship

The challenge of increasing access to higher education in low-income countries

Tertiary education is expensive. In the developed world this is unlikely to be sustainable. Demographic changes are likely to decrease enrollment levels but more significantly divert more private and public funds towards pensions and healthcare. However, it is a significantly bigger challenge in low-income countries.

It has been generally recognized that tertiary education is a necessary component of the economic development of low income countries (Margison 2016). However, given their economic situation they are unable to afford to provide mass access to tertiary education and training. Even when tertiary education is highly subsidised, as in Europe, students still have living expenses, ever increasing accommodation expenses, as well as expenses for books and other required learning resources. Added to this, they have the very significant opportunity cost of reducing, if not removing, their ability to work.

Could the problem in low-income countries be that they are copying an expensive educational model from the developed world, a model that emerged from universities in the Middle Ages? Copying this model puts low income countries in a dilemma. Because they are poor they cannot afford the expensive format used in the West, and because they cannot afford this they cannot provide tertiary education that is required for their economic development.

But does tertiary education need to be this expensive? Are there alternative models? Could learning technology be the key to making tertiary education more affordable, and thus massively increasing participation in low-income countries.

The Atlantic Technological University

The Atlantic Technological University is a new university located on the west of Ireland formed in 2022 from the merger of three Institutes of Technology. The Sligo campus, previously named Institute of Technology Sligo, has been working on a number of technology based solutions to the financial challenge of access to higher education that could be applicable in low-income countries. The potential for cost reduction in these two initiatives are based on three core ideas:

1. Integrating programmes with work allows students to "earn as they learn".
2. Online distance learning can significantly reduce costs in travel, accommodation and access to learning resources.
3. Independent study with "challenge examinations" for well motivated and capable students, can massively reduce tuition costs.

A Work-Based Degree in Engineering

Apprenticeships have been with us for some time. However, these are generally highly regulated and can be slow to evolve and exploit the potential of learning technologies. Rather than navigate the bureaucracy of apprenticeship regulation, the university launched in 2020 an ordinary degree in Mechatronic Systems Engineering, aimed at students in Ireland finishing secondary school, which copied many of the features of the apprenticeship model of education but also exploited the potential of learning technologies.

The young students recruited within Ireland onto this course were hired by manufacturing employers and required to work 24 hours per week. The students were required to carry out and report on certain specific tasks in the workplace, but beyond that (and unlike skills-based apprenticeships), because of the huge variety of manufacturing operations, employers were free to allocate tasks relevant to the nature of the processes in their own business. In this programme, the students receive one third of their credits for the evidence they produce of their learning in the workplace. For the other two thirds of their credits students attend regular online synchronous classes.

Even now in 2023, although it may be too early to definitively say how successful this approach has been, the initial signs are positive. Recruitment has been growing slowly but steadily. Employers have tended to be intrigued at first by the programme and then excited about the possibilities. They see this as a way to recruit young people locally that are likely to stay with the company and also as a way of addressing the lack of "work-readiness" of the campus graduates they usually recruit.

Secondary school students who are making their plans for after graduation tend to be somewhat puzzled by the idea, but many are extremely interested and to date there have been more applications from students than trainee positions within companies. However, interest from employers is growing steadily and the existing employers have expressed a moderately high level of satisfaction with their recruits. Because of this, the recruitment strategy adopted has been to firstly find suitable employers and then to recruit students from local secondary schools. It should also be noted that there has been significant interest from employees within manufacturing companies who have no previous engineering qualifications and this has helped quickly make the programme financially sustainable.

In 2022, a mining company in Mozambique expressed an interest in employing local young people and sponsoring them on the engineering programme. Having identified three potential trainees, one student reached a satisfactory level of English language and was accepted onto the programme. To date, his academic achievement has been good and his employer is very satisfied with his progress.

Challenges and Responses

Laboratories

The most obvious challenge in the delivery of a completely remote engineering programme is the access of students to laboratories for practical work. However, the institution had been delivering Mechatronic Engineering online within Ireland since 2006 and in that time had developed and sourced both simulations and remotely accessible equipment in order to minimise attendance on campus. In addition it had become apparent that the exposure that learners were getting to real equipment and processes in their workplaces was more valuable than the artificial experiences we could provide for them on campus. This work-based programme was launched in the first year of the Covid 19 pandemic, at which point it was decided that attendance at labs on campus was to be no longer required for work-based learners. Because the employer in Mozambique was able to demonstrate that they could expose the student to suitable control equipment, it was possible to allow that student on to the programme.

Fees

From the student's point of view this is a great opportunity to gain an otherwise unaffordable engineering degree. However, it does represent a significant investment for the employer both in terms of trainee supervision and tuition fees. Tuition fees for students from low-income countries have a low-level of subsidy from the Irish government and are normally approximately $9,000 per year. The employer considered this to be too expensive and because the university considered that exploring this model was valuable, reduced the fee to €2,000. However, the implication from this experience is that although a work-based degree could make engineering education more accessible for young people in the developing world, the high tuition fees will reduce the number of employers that are able to afford to take on trainees and thus massively reduce the number of traineeships available.

Skills and Work Supervision

Because the students recruited to this programme do not yet have any significant relevant knowledge or skills they are of limited value to the employer and require significant supervision. This again will reduce the attractiveness of the programme to employers.

To address the challenges described above another solution is being proposed.

Self Directed Learning

There are differing views on the success of MOOCs (Massive Open Online Courses). While they have achieved massive enrollment levels, completion levels are much lower and it is still unclear how such platforms can generate sufficient income to achieve financial sustainability. However, from these MOOCs and other initiatives we have learned much about at-scale provision and some closely linked models that exploit the cost reduction potential of scale have emerged.

Of particular note is the Georgia Tech masters degree in Computer Science. This programme, with a tuition cost of approximately $5,400 had an enrollment of over 12,000 learners in 2022 (Mendez 2022). Although not an openly accessible programme, it utilises many of the delivery and support approaches of MOOCs and places an emphasis on robust assessment.

Another noteworthy initiative is the University of the People (UoP). UoP delivers "tuition free" online degrees with no charge for instruction or books, only charging for assessment. It also, through philanthropic donations, organises scholarships for many who cannot afford the assessment fees. Accredited by the US Distance Education Accreditation Committee (DEAC) and with over 100,000 students in Business Administration, Computer Science, Health Science and Education, UoP appears to have been very successful at recruiting and graduating students (Coy 2022).

Inspired by these two models, the Atlantic Technological University is in the early stages of planning to create an "open" Higher Certificate (Associates Degree) in Mechatronic Engineering. This will use the model of free access to learning materials and payment for assessment.

Challenges and Responses

Cost of Content Creation

Traditionally the high cost of content creation has been a major barrier to entry into distance learning. However, the rise of "user generated" content has shown us that this is no longer necessarily true. In this project, content creation has been inspired by the original Kahn Academy videos and its many imitators on the web. Youtube has many channels of moderately good quality academic content for Engineering students, much of it published under Creative Commons licences. These videos can be produced very easily and with some relatively cheap recording facilities and simple, effective recording techniques, can be made to appear quite professional. In this institution we are training lecturers to simply create courses by both recording videos and curating them from the web. By adding self-test quizzes and peer assessments we can not only allow learners to gauge their own progress, but also monitor progress and issue certificates of completion.

Laboratories

Like the work-based degree described above, the development of practical skills is a challenge for remote students. However, unlike those work-based students, self-directed learners may not be in a related workplace thus not have exposure to real engineering equipment. Luckily, while many engineering activities require large expensive equipment, the key principles and practical skills in Mechatronics (physical devices, electronic control and software), can all be demonstrated at small scale using cheap equipment that can be purchased online. This can be augmented by online simulations which are widely available on the web.

Assessment

Four types of assessment will be used in this programme:

1. Unsupervised automated objective tests (quizzes)
2. Peer assessed assignments.
3. Supervised projects.
4. Proctored examinations.

While learning content can be made available for free, reliable assessment, which is crucial for certification cannot. Objective tests can be used to measure lower level learning outcomes at virtually no cost, but if the tests are not proctored they are not reliable indicators of achievement for certification purposes. However, they can be useful knowledge checks for the learners themselves.

Peer assessed assignments are another low-cost way of assessing performance and can test higher order outcomes. However, even though they are an excellent self-check for the learners, because the institution has no control over the assistance a learner might have available to them, they are not particularly reliable for the awarding of grades.

Supervised projects, as well as improving the learning experience of the students, are a more reliable way of measuring authentic learning. Because students are required to make interim submissions and will be interviewed on their submissions the opportunity for cheating will be much reduced. However, this is a relatively labour intensive form of assessment and to keep costs low, will be used sparingly in specific courses and also used in conjunction with peer assessment.

Although summative examinations are considered to be less authentic, proctored online examinations will form the most important part of assessment for accreditation because they are more reliable and cheaper to provide. Identity verification is also an important challenge for these examinations. It is expected that a solution similar to that used by online banking will be used.

Institutional Accreditation

Accreditation is expected to be the most significant challenge in developing this programme. Normally a programme with little or no learner support would not be acceptable, but this programme is specifically targeted at low-income students in low-income countries who cannot afford such support. Peer support will be facilitated at no cost, and there are many talented and well motivated students who can cope and even thrive in such a learning environment. In addition, certification can be justified on grounds of competency under Recognition of Prior Learning (RPL) policies. Such policies generally allow for students to prove they have specific knowledge or competency, regardless of how it was acquired.

Combining these two approaches

The main obstacles to the success of the Work Based Degree are the fees that are required to cover the online teaching methods and the challenge of creating enough suitable traineeship positions and particularly with employers who can afford to subsidise the full fees that need to be paid. While working with small scale kits is very useful in understanding engineering principles, real work experience creates engineers who are of much greater value to employers. By combining the low-cost two-year programme with the 3rd and 4th years in the workplace, we can address most of the challenges in both approaches..

The low-cost 2-year programme will allow students to start studying before they have a traineeship position and it can also, by shortening the length of the traineeship, reduce the costs to employers who take on trainees. For those who do not have positions, gradual accumulation of credits will allow students to gain skills and credibility that can help them get positions, even before they complete the programme. The skills developed and knowledge gained from the 2-year programme will make graduates much more valuable to employers and justify the creation of much more traineeship positions.

Summary

The cost of higher education, whether to the individual or the state, is an increasing challenge in the developed world. In low-income countries the challenge is even worse. Online Learning, Self-directed Learning and apprentice-style Work-Integrated Learning all have the possibility of reducing the cost of gaining skills, knowledge and qualifications. By adopting these approaches rather than campus based higher education, low-income countries may be able to achieve much higher levels of participation and a much higher rate. This in turn will increase prosperity and ability of governments to subsidise mass participation. At that point, such governments may choose which model is most appropriate for them.

References

Coy, P. (2022) "how can this Institution charge nothing for education", *New York Times*, February 16th, 2022, https://www.uopeople.edu/about/worldwide-recognition/media/how-can-this-university-charge-nothing-for-tuition/

Margison, S. (2016), "The worldwide trend to high participation higher education: dynamics of social stratification in inclusive systems", *Higher Education*, Vol 72, pp 413-424, June 2016. https://link.springer.com/article/10.1007/s10734-016-0016-x

Mendez, M.C. (2022) "Georgia Tech's Online Master's Becomes Even More Affordable", *The Report*, May 3rd, 2022, https://www.classcentral.com/report/georgia-tech-omscs-cost-decrease/

COMMUNITY CITIZEN INQUIRY: A TOOL FOR SUPPORTING CITIZENS, THE CASE OF NQUIRE

Eileen Scanlon, Christothea Herodotou, Kevin McLeod, Open University, UK

***Correspondence**: Eileen Scanlon: eileen.scanlon@open.ac.uk*

Abstract

Community citizen science inquiry is a combination of two ideas: first, citizen science inquiry (mass participation citizen science and learning to be a scientist through scientific inquiry, (Herodotou et al, 2017), and a concern to involve participation by the members of a community for community purposes. We describe the work we have done on this topic developing from our initial experiments in supporting inquiry learning with school children using technology and describing how this work has developed through conducting a number of studies involving students in a university technical college, and distance education students, then widened into investigation of the ideas with members of the public conducting citizen inquiries. These experiences have been supported by the development of the web platform nQuire (http://www.nquire.org.uk) which is now the basis of our work.

Our approach to citizen inquiry is driven by a concern for the nature of the participation from which members of the public can benefit and goes beyond involving people solely as volunteer data collectors. We report here on our experiences of the different types of inquiries or missions which have run on the platform since 2018, and the views of some participants on their involvement. We also discuss the issues in developing our vision of community citizen science inquiry and a potential centre for democratising research.

Keywords:

Citizen science, Inquiry learning, community learning

Introduction

nQuire is a web platform to conduct investigations; it builds on research work conducted at The Open University UK around community-led citizen science, citizen inquiry and public engagement with research. Everyone, whether researchers or scientists in academic and non-academic organizations, or members of the public can contribute to advancing science and can use scientific methods to produce and use research evidence as needed. Our contention is that engaging in science inquiry, to whatever extent, opens up the process of being a scientist to members of the public. We have facilitated this approach through the design of a set of web-based and mobile technologies over the past fifteen years. This line of research is particularly relevant and timely now for a variety of reasons. Citizen Science is a growing trend, but current approaches are often limited to recruiting members of the public only to take part in experiments that have been designed by scientists and contribute data as volunteers, for example, using volunteers to record water or air pollution in an area or identify astronomical events. Curtis in her thesis work (2017) noted the growing trend in online citizen science projects responding in part to the data deluge offering scientists both an opportunity and a challenge and which coincided with the availability of digital tools both for communication with others and for analysis of data. The move to online citizen science was particularly intriguing. Her particular interest was in the opportunities for participation and engagement of members of the public and their motivations for participation. One key feature was that, for volunteers, participating in online citizen science projects offers them an opportunity to become involved in authentic scientific research for altruistic purposes but also to learn more about science. Curtis writes that the volunteers she surveyed valued this aspect of their participation and comments

projects have enabled scientists to process large amounts of data, utilise the diversity of human pattern recognition and problem-solving skills, and on occasion, have resulted in contributions to knowledge (Lintott et al., 2009, Khatib et al., 2011, Lane et al., 2013, Schmitt et al., 2014) p.314.

She provides helpful guidance for scientists setting up such activities to be sustainable in terms of suggestions about sustaining participation, recognising the difficulties of the task. She noted a particular motivation for participation in projects with an outcome contributing to the development of science for altruistic purposes.

Another motivation she identified was some participants who were interested in learning more science and more about science.
Our overarching aim for contributing to the development of community citizen science inquiry is that we wish to work with individuals and communities with limited experience of research to establish how best to engage them in designing the process of designing and running a scientific investigation.

Inquiry learning and personal inquiry

Citizen science has been for a long time a special interest for researchers in educational technology at the United Kingdom Open University. Even in the early years of the University in the 1970s and 80s there was an interest in harnessing its large UK-wide student population in collecting data to involve them and engage them in community-based inquiries. UK-wide studies were conducted with the assistance of students monitoring SO_2 pollution across Britain, distribution of drosophila, peppered moths or similar. Results from students' data collection were shared (on forms returned to Milton Keynes by post) and developed into TV programs feeding back the national picture provided by the students. These TV programmes were broadcasted by the BBC along with other OU educational programmes.

More recently, our team developed a research interest in examining inquiry learning. Our focus was involving students in the scientific methods of data collection, interpretation and analysis. Inquiry learning approaches to teaching science and the literature discussed the benefits and challenges of involving students in this teaching method. The main challenge is developing appropriate support for students in the inquiry learning process. Our research originally focused on school-based science education but more recently on informal science learning experiences.

Our vision developed through this work has been to open up the processes of citizen science so that participants can be involved in more stages of the inquiry process and thereby:

- widen the benefit for participants
- develop understanding of the scientific inquiry process among the public
- bring evidence-based considerations into community inquiries
- lead to better understanding of contemporary relevant issues and scientific controversies.

In contemporary society there is a desperate need for increasing the public understanding and engagement in science as we have seen during the covid 19 pandemic, the ongoing climate crisis and campaigns of misinformation and fake news in relation to democratic citizenship. There are also direct benefits for education by connecting informal and formal learning in science and about science using inquiry learning.

Our project started with an educational challenge- the development of an approach to science inquiry for young people in secondary schools. Our platform, nQuire, was first developed as a system to support scripted personal inquiry among young people at school (Sharples et al., 2015). The project was built on the challenge of harnessing the benefits of inquiry learning while using contemporary means of technology support (Scanlon et al., 2012). Also, the project's emphasis on personal inquiry where importance was placed on students working on investigating issues of personal relevance and significance was key. We interpreted personal inquiry as inquiry potentially relevant to the participants themselves, their environment, or their community. The computer-based toolkit we produced was designed to guide school pupils while they conducted an inquiry from start to finish. These inquiries could involve classroom lessons and data collection, or other work conducted at after school clubs, at home, and outdoors in field sites or museums or libraries, most often requiring activity in at least three of these sites e.g., classroom, field work and home but also in several different configurations. We found that the toolkit was used successfully, and in particular '*effectively supported the transition between individual, group, and whole-class activities and supported learning across formal and informal settings'. (Sharples et al., 2015, p. 308)*

A key output of this first project was the design of the platform, nQuire, and an underlying model of the inquiry process - a pedagogical approach which underpinned it. This output was taken forward in several ways: as part of the development of the Open University's Open Science Laboratory with the Lab partially supported by a grant from the Wolfson foundation, and as part of a Nominet Trust funded project with Sheffield University Technical College. Our development of software to support our development of community citizen science inquiry occurred through the evolution of the various instantiations of nQuire (described variously as Activity Guides, nQuire-it, BBC Tomorrow's World nQuire).

A connection with Higher Education arose with the opportunity of working as part of the Open Science Laboratory a project supported by the Wolfson Trust. This opened up new possibilities for investigating inquiry learning with nQuire, extending the experience of using nQuire from within secondary education to undergraduate courses and university outreach activities. It also represented an opportunity to investigate citizen inquiry. As elements of the Open Science Laboratory were designed to include citizen science and adapted for access by the public, we were able to develop an activity. The Moon Rock Explorer as an example (Villasclaras-Fernandez et al., 2013). The Moon Rock Explorer was a prototype demonstrator and test-site for citizen inquiry. It provided a self-managed investigation into Moon geology for those with no previous knowledge of Moon rock or geology. A user accessed the system through a public URL and was presented with a video introduction to moon rock and an appeal to 'Investigate Moon Rock'. It had three features which extended the possibilities of using nQuire: a simplified representation of the inquiry features, integration with other scientific tools (the Virtual Microscope which was also available in the Open Science lab) and the addition of online communication tools.

Funding from the Nominet Trust allowed members of the nQuire team also to work with more teachers and pupils. Collaboration with Sheffield University Technology College, which specializes in creative technology design for children aged 14-19, allowed us to work with young people as full partners in design, implementation and testing in the nQuire: Young Citizen Inquiry project. Sheffield University Technical College (UTC) is a technology college specialising in project-based work in collaboration with industry. The outcome was the collaborative development of set of sensor tools on mobile devices (see Sharples et al., 2017) which would engage the students in practical science investigations. A design workshop with students aged 14-15 developed the initial interaction design and example investigations. Development of Sense-it (Sharples et al. 2017) then continued at The Open University (OU), with trials among OU staff members and with Sheffield UTC.

Sharples et al. (2015) wrote on this experience that typically
'an individual or group will initiate a new investigation (or 'mission') around a question or topic of interest or concern. They will encourage others of all abilities, including trained scientists, to join and contribute to the mission. All the data collected as part of the mission is made visible and available for download and sharing. As the mission progresses, the participants discuss the topic online, through comments and replies linked to the mission and each item of data, and attempt to reach a consensus about the findings. Social network features allow users to 'like' data items and be notified of comments and likes from other users. Themes (such as 'investigate the weather') can combine a set of missions with differing aims, methods and contributor. (p. 367)

This work developed alongside the work of a PhD student who was to investigate what was necessary to provide a community of practice round personally driven investigations or now called, missions (see Aristeidou et al., 2017).

This pattern of continuing work on inquiry and investigation came to the attention of the BBC who have had a long history of engaging the public in science via their Lab UK initiative (see BBC Lab UK - Wikipedia). An approach from people who had worked on Lab UK and the relaunch of an iconic BBC brand as Tomorrow's World led to a major investment by the BBC/OU partnership in the development of Tomorrow's World nQuire. This most recent version of the nQuire platform was supporting online science investigations. These allow the public to participate in science investigations linked to TV and radio broadcasts. This project led to a redesign of the nQuire tools aimed to engage members of the public in being fully engaged citizen scientists. That is, by involving them in designing experiments, recruiting participants, analysing findings and sharing results, we want to empower individuals or groups of citizens to design their own investigations, and in addition have experienced scientists offer support and assistance. This holds great potential as an approach as citizens can understand how science works, tackle problems in their communities or do investigations meaningful and relevant to themselves. The process of setting up an activity on nQuire means that they engage with the scientific method to set up an investigation. Our contention is that engaging in informal science activities may involve a process that can promote the development of critical thinking skills and argumentation. This is an important skill given the increasing demands on citizens to make sense of information for scientific claims and the possibility of misinformation and contested science in the public sphere.

The Tomorrow's World nQuire Project has developed a set of enabling technologies for supporting citizens' participation in scientific activities. In particular, the nQuire platform hosts at the moment, more than 200 investigations set by individuals, organisations and schools worldwide and more than 250,000 contributors. nQuire allows anyone to set up a new mission with mobile phones as data collectors, recruit other people to take part, and run a social network to discuss the data and restore results. This research connects to the mission of the Open University because it explores extending the involvement in citizen science projects to members of the public in terms of setting up missions, and in developing learning about science, and science concepts. We wish to work with members of the public in a variety of ways not just as data collectors, although recruitment to scientific endeavours is a valuable activity. We want to use our experience of the impact of involving people in personal inquiries.

Since the 2018 redesign of nQuire, 39 investigations have been conducted. The scale of the missions ranges quite widely with contributions from participants in individual missions ranging from 20 to 230K. Our largest mission was the BBC Garden Watch. Most of the missions have involved some scientific focus, for example, GardenWatch, birds, starling murmuration, pollinators (e.g., bees), mammals, worms, or climate related missions for example, heatwaves, climate anxiety, and other science topics such as astrobiology. Some missions were related to psychology, such as cognition, and the therapeutic value of sounds of nature, and some related to educational topics in particular on educational technology and online learning. Many of the missions involved academic researchers from a range of Universities, research organizations and charities.

Outcomes

We have captured the impact of using nQuire on learning and development, such as increased awareness and behavioural change, through a survey of 150 nQuire participants. This produced evidence of how participation in research activities via nQuire can enable life-long learning and achieve engagement with science (Herodotou et al., 2022). Herodotou writes: *'The main motivation for taking part in a scientific study on nQuire was to contribute to research and science (59%). A number of other participants participated because they believed that helping with science is important (13%) or had an a priori personal interest in the topic of the investigation (11%). 10% wanted to learn more about the topic of the investigation, 5% wanted to experience what is like to participate in a CCS project A majority of 48% said they know a little more about the topic of the mission, and 8% a lot more about it'. (p.15)*

However, there was less confidence in learning more than a little about a topic and in being interested in or confident in setting up their own missions. Herodotou et al. write:

'the transition from participating to creating scientific investigations is not a straightforward one; we observed a great majority of participants reporting that it is unlikely or highly unlikely that they would create their own mission. Amongst the factors explaining these perceptions were a lack of knowledge and skills for designing a study, a lack of support, and a lack of time'. (p. 17)

Conclusions

Our work has been to investigate inquiry learning and then to develop a distinctive approach to citizen science, community citizen science inquiry which is distinctive in privileging the idea of learning by engagement in such activity. The synergy of this activity of public engagement and public participation with the OU mission to be open to people, places, methods, and ideas is important to us. Having designed free online tools which are open and accessible to all, we have started to put in place an infrastructure which would empower citizens to set up their own research projects, an important enabler for digital citizenship. This facilitation of citizen engagement together with the potential to attract, inform and engage young people, or adult students by involving them in formal or informal inquiries has encouraged us to continue our exploration of this theme. We see how this approach can promote educational opportunities in line with the OU vision for social justice. We want to extend the reach of this initiative to many more people, including those from disadvantaged backgrounds.

We have described here how we take a democratic view of citizen science. We see members of the public as very important in the process, and in our work extend and encourage opportunities for involvement that are not limited to volunteering their time as data collectors, or being part of a crowdsourcing activity that is directed to addressing the questions of other scientists. This type of activity has its place obviously, and can lead to a sense of fulfilment by contributing to the creation of scientific knowledge, and as we saw in the work of Curtis, these activities can be motivating. However, as we have described here we see the potential benefits of citizen science approaches as being much more wide reaching than this. We are exploring the potential of a centre for democratising research connecting with our vision of opening up the research process to more people. This chimes with contemporary notions of participants as co-investigators.

To make progress with this ambition we need to develop our expertise in this area further. In terms of the findings of our survey of participants, despite some positive outcomes we have work to do to raise awareness of all the possibilities and the benefits of conducting community citizen inquiries. For individuals moving from the role of participant to creator of missions requires a better understanding of the potential role that using systems like nQuire can play in helping communities and individuals to collect evidence to underlie decision making in their com-unity. To successfully do so, we are exploring further the need for training to support the skills to design and carry out investigations.

References

Aristeidou, M., Sharples, M. & Scanlon, E. (2021). Technologies for citizen inquiry: participatory research in online communities. In: D. Burns, J. Howard, and S.M. Ospina. (Eds.), *The SAGE Handbook of Participatory Research and Inquiry*. London: SAGE Publications, pp. 496–512.

Curtis, V. (2018). *Online Citizen Science and the Widening of Academia: Distributed Engagement with Research and Knowledge Production*. Palgrave Studies in Alternative Education. Cham, Switzerland: Palgrave Macmillan

Herodotou, C., Sharples, M. and Scanlon, E. (Eds.) (2017). Citizen Inquiry: Synthesising Science and Inquiry Learning. Abingdon: Routledge.

Herodotou, C., Scanlon, E., & Sharples, M. (2021). Methods of promoting learning and data quality in citizen and Community Science *Frontiers in Climate*, 53.
Retrieved https://www.frontiersin.org/articles/10.3389/fclim.2021.614567/full [Open Access]

Herodotou, C., Sharples, M., & Scanlon, E. (Eds.). (2017). Citizen Inquiry: Synthesising Science and Inquiry Learning. Abingdon: Routledge

Herodotou, C., Twiner, A., Scanlon, E., McLeod, K., & Seale, J. (2022). From participants to creators: Considerations for community-led citizen science. In: *Proceedings of the 16th International Conference of the Learning Sciences* - ICLS 2022 (Chinn, C.; Tan, E.; Chan, C. and Kali, Y. eds.), International Society of the Learning Sciences, Hiroshima, Japan, pp. 11–18.

Scanlon, E., Anastopoulou, S. & Kerawalla, L. (2011). Inquiry learning reconsidered; contexts, representations and challenges. In: K. Littleton, E. Scanlon, and M. Sharples (Eds.), *Orchestrating Inquiry Learning*. Abingdon: Routledge

Scanlon, E., Herodotou, C., Sharples, M. & McLeod, K. (2020). *nQuire: citizens acting as scientists in massive open online learning.* In: L@S '20: Proceedings of the Seventh ACM Conference on Learning @ Scale, 12-14 Aug 2020, Virtual event, USA, ACM, pp. 257–260

Scanlon, E. & Herodotou, C. (2022). Advancing the Democratization of Research: Citizen Science. In: *Proceedings of the Ninth ACM Conference on Learning@ Scale* (pp. 280-283).

Scanlon, E., Anastopoulou, S. & Kerawalla, L. (2011). Inquiry learning reconsidered; contexts, representations and challenges. In: K. Littleton, E. Scanlon, and M. Sharples (Eds.), *Orchestrating Inquiry Learning*. Abingdon: Routledge

Scanlon, E., Woods, W. & Clow, D. (2014). Informal participation in science in the UK: identification, location and mobility with iSpot. *Journal of Educational Technology and Society,* 17(2) pp. 58–71.

Sharples, M., Aristeidou, M., Villasclaras-Fernández, E., Herodotou, C., & Scanlon, E. (2015). *Sense-it: a smartphone toolkit for citizen inquiry learning.* In The Mobile Learning Voyage-From Small Ripples to Massive Open Waters:

14th World Conference on Mobile and Contextual Learning, mLearn 2015, Venice, Italy, October 17-24, 2015, Proceedings 14 (pp. 366-377). Springer International Publishing.

Sharples, M., Aristeidou, M., Villasclaras-Fernández, E., Herodotou, C. & Scanlon, E. (2017). The Sense-it App: A Smartphone Toolkit for Citizen Inquiry Learning. *International Journal of Mobile and Blended Learning*, 9(2) pp. 16–38.DOI: https://doi.org/10.4018/IJMBL.2017040102

Sharples, M., Scanlon, E., Ainsworth, S., Anastopoulou, S., Collins, T., Crook, C., Jones, A., Kerawalla, L., Littleton, K., Mulholland, P. & O'Malley, C. (2015). Personal inquiry: orchestrating science investigations within and beyond the classroom. *Journal of the Learning Sciences*, 24(2) pp. 308–341.

Villasclaras-Fernandez, E., Sharples, M., Kelley, S .& Scanlon, E. (2013). *Supporting citizen inquiry: an investigation of Moon rock.* In: Scaling up Learning for Sustained Impact, Lecture Notes in Computer Science, Springer, pp. 383–395

Acknowledgements. We wish to acknowledge all members of the nQuire team past and present for their contributions over the years to the progress of citizen science inquiry and to acknowledge Professor Mike Sharples for his leadership and contribution..

.

DIGITAL SOVEREIGNTY OF OLDER CITIZENS FOR A SELF-DETERMINED USE OF PERSONAL HEALTH RECORDS: E-LEARNING DESIGN AND STUDY RESULTS FROM THE EPA-COACH PROJECT.

Ilona Buchem, Verena Kauth, Marcus Kirschen, Mona Katzer, Berlin University of Applied Sciences, Germany

***Correspondence**: Ilona Buchem: buchem@bht-berlin.de*

Abstract

Promoting digital literacy and digital sovereignty has become one of the key policies in Europe. Digital sovereignty has been defined as the ability to act and exercise freedom of choice in the digital world. While digital services and applications offer great opportunities for the older generations to live independently and communicate with family and friends, the digital sovereignty of citizens including older adults has become a concern of policy-makers. Hence fostering digital sovereignty has been seen as an important objective for a self-determined use of digital media including control over own data. This paper presents an approach to designing an e-learning application for senior learners, which is aimed at fostering the digital sovereignty of older citizens in using Personal Health Records (PHR) in Germany. This e-learning application, called ePA-Coach, is designed in a research project funded by the Federal German Ministry of Education and Research to offer an opportunity for citizens 65+ to acquire digital skills needed for the self-determined use of PHR. The paper presents the digital literacy framework for exercising digital sovereignty related to PHR, which was developed in the ePA-Coach project based on the European Digital Competence Framework. We describe how this framework was applied in the design of micro-learning units and combined with gamification techniques from the Octalysis framework. Finally, we outline results from two exploratory studies with older citizens which revealed strong preferences for design elements related to digital sovereignty such as choice and control of the learning progress.

Keywords:

Digital sovereignty, digital literacy, digital citizenship, personal health records (PHR), electronic health records (EHR), Digital Competence Framework (DigComp), micro-learning, senior learners, older citizens.

Introduction

Digital citizenship has been traditionally defined in relation to the opportunities and abilities for the use of technology with the aim of participation in society (Mossberger et al. 2007). While citizenship has focused on the relationship between citizens and the national state (Bennett, 2007), digital citizenship has emphasised individual choices and rights to participate in society, addressing the question of "how the digital facilitates new forms of participation" (Pangrazio & Sefton-Green, 2021, p. 18). From the perspective of the omnipresent "datafication" in the sense of "taking all aspects of life and turning them into data" (Cukier & Mayer-Schönberger, 2013), digital citizenship has been linked to digital literacy and its specific elements, such as (personal) data literacy, as a response to these socio-technological challenges (Pangrazio & Sefton-Green, 2021). Traditionally, data literacy emphasised normative descriptions of performance, evidence, skills, knowledge, attitudes, and behaviours, following influences from workforce demands (Pangrazio & Sefton-Green, 2021; Örtegren, 2022). Similarly in education, normative approaches to digital literacy have been common or even over-represented (Örtegren, 2022). In Europe, the "DigComp" framework (Digital Competence Framework) developed by the Joint Research Centre of the European Commission, has highlighted the use of digital technologies not only for work and learning but also for inclusion and participation in an increasingly digitalised society (Ferrari 2013; Redecker 2017). The "DigComp" framework defines "engaging in online citizenship" as one of the core dimensions of digital competence. Online citizenship means "to participate in society through online engagement, to seek opportunities for self-development and empowerment in using technologies and digital environments, to be aware of the potential of technologies for citizen participation" (Ferrari 2013, p. 5). In this sense, the "DigComp" framework has recognised that digital citizenship and participation in society have become a matter of competence.

It seems that in the face of the advances of digitalisation and datafication, the focus of digital literacy has shifted from mastery to sovereignty. The notion of "digital sovereignty" has been used in reference to the state, economic and individual levels (Pohle, 2020). Individual digital sovereignty has emerged as a response to concerns about citizens' control over their own data and has focused on empowering citizens to make use of digital technologies in a responsible and self-determined way (Pohle, 2020). Digital sovereignty goes beyond knowing how to download an app or use an online service and includes "the ability to assess the consequences of one's own online actions" (Stubbe, Schaat & Ehrenberg-Silies, 2019). Therefore, "the development of digital literacy in all stages of life has been seen as the basis for sovereign action in the digital world" (Pohle, 2020, p. 17).

While digital services and applications offer great opportunities for the older generations to live independently and communicate with family and friends, older adults also need to know how to use digital media in a self-determined way and understanding what happens with their data (Stubbe, Schaat & Ehrenberg-Silies, 2019). Promoting digital literacy and digital sovereignty of older citizens has entered policy-agendas in Europe. In 2022 the Council of Europe published "The Digital Era? Also my Era!", in which it calls for promoting digital literacy among senior citizens, to ensure equal access to digital services, provide training to navigate digital environments, and a range of measures for digital inclusion of older citizens (Hermans, 2022). While many spheres of life of older citizens have been impacted by digital technologies, information and services related to health (eHealth, mHealth) often play a central role. Numerous digital technologies and services have been developed to support healthcare-related activities such as diagnosis, consultation, treatment, documentation and communication with senior patients. The use of such digital health services is closely linked to digital literacy. Fostering digital literacy of older citizens, who may be less digitally experienced and competent, has become an important equity issue (Millard A, et al, 2018).

The introduction of Electronic Health Records (EHR) and Personal Health Records (PHR) has aimed to enhance digital health services. While the EHR has been used to increase the quality of healthcare and serve as digital repository with patients' information controlled by health organisations (e.g. hospitals, laboratories, clinics), the PHR has been used to enable citizens to store and manage their own health-related data and serve as health records controlled by the patient (Roehrs, 2017). EU member states have applied different legal approaches to the implementation and regulation of EHR/PHR. For example, in Germany, the Appointment Service and Supply Act (TSVG), requires health insurance funds to provide policy-holders with PHR (called elektronische Patientenakte, ePA) from 2021 onwards. In Germany, health insurance funds offer different PHR systems to their policy-holders and allow patients to electronically collect, manage and share health-related data, such as medical history, medication, treatment reports, and vaccinations[1]. PHR enables patients to choose whether to share or not to share their health data with healthcare stakeholders (Roehrs, 2017). By allowing patients to make decisions about their digital health records, PHR follows a patient-centric approach (Buchem et al., 2023). Key challenges in PHR adoption include concerns about privacy, security, insufficient measures for impaired people, usability issues, and unclear benefits (Segall et al, 2011; Taha et al., 2014; Roehrs, 2017; Poss-Doering et al., 2018).

Previous studies have shown that the use of the PHR requires a set of competencies ranging from the general capability to use digital technologies to the specific skills in the management of digital medical records according to regulations within a given national healthcare system (Day et al., 2012). For older citizens, who typically have less experience using digital technologies, using PHR may be a barrier to equal participation in the healthcare system (Gellner et al. 2021). The study by Taha et al. (2013) showed that both middle-aged adults (40-59 years) and older adults (60-85 years) experience difficulties in using PHR, such as managing common health tasks, reviewing and interpreting lab results, which is especially challenging for older adults with lower numeracy skills and less technology experience (Taha et al., 2013). Further studies pointed out that the needs of specific populations, including older adults, have to be taken into consideration when designing and deploying PHR. The study by Day et al. (2012) showed that computer and health literacy is one of the three key factors influencing how effectively patients are able to use PHR, the other two factors being an individual perception of convenience

[1] https://www.gesundheitsindustrie-bw.de/en/article/news/ehr-and-phr-digital-records-in-the-german-healthcare-system

and perceived transparency. Additionally, age-related changes in cognitive abilities, e.g. working memory, processing speed, and reasoning, may affect the ability of older adults to perform more complex PHR tasks (Taha et al., 2013). Since older generations usually have less experience in using digital technologies, the introduction of the EHR/PHR has called for measures aimed at fostering digital literacy and the digital sovereignty of older adults. Ensuring that older adults are given an opportunity to acquire the competencies necessary for a self-determined use of PHR is important from a societal perspective (Gellner, Kaiser & Buchem, 2021; Buchem, Kauth, Kirschen & Katzer, 2023). The UN Sustainable Development Goals, especially Goal 3.8 "Achieve universal health coverage, including financial risk protection, access to quality essential health-care services and access to safe, effective, quality and affordable essential medicines and vaccines for all"[2] are relevant for digital sovereignty in using PHR by older citizens.

The ePA Coach e-learning application presented in this paper aims to offer an opportunity for citizens 65+ to acquire digital skills needed for the use of PHR in Germany. The application was developed in the ePA-Coach project, a three-year R&D project funded by the German Federal Ministry of Research and Education. The ePA-Coach project aims to foster the digital sovereignty of older citizens in the context of PHR and to deliver an interactive learning application that allows senior learners to acquire digital competencies relevant to digital sovereignty in using PHR. Further sections present the competence framework developed in the ePA-Coach project with the aim of fostering the digital sovereignty of older citizens in using PHR, the design of the ePA-Coach application based on this competence framework, and the results from two exploratory studies with older citizens aimed at understanding which e-learning design elements are valued by senior learners and how these are related to digital sovereignty. The paper ends with conclusions and recommendations for further research.

Competence Framework for Digital Sovereignty

The digital competence framework developed in the ePA-Coach project is based on the European Digital Competence Framework, the "DigComp" framework (Vuorikari et al, 2022). The DigComp framework provides a frame of reference that can be adapted to the needs of different populations. The key five areas of competence are (1) Information and data literacy (the ability to search, evaluate, and manage digital information and data); (2) Communication & collaboration (the ability to communicate and collaborate effectively using digital technologies); (3) Digital content creation (the ability to create and edit digital content such as text, images, and video); (4) Safety (the ability to use digital technologies safely and protect personal data and privacy); (5) Problem-solving (the ability to use digital technologies to solve problems and make informed decisions). Each competence area includes several competencies subdivided into four levels: (1) Foundation; (2) Intermediate; (3) Advanced; (4) Highly Specialised. The digital competence framework in the ePA-Coach project adapted by the DigComp structure and defined five key competence areas in relation to the use of PHR by older citizens: (1) Basics & access (basic knowledge about PHR, registration, authorisation); (2) Handling of information & data (managing data, searching, filtering, deleting); (3) Communication & collaboration (exchanging health data with healthcare stakeholders, allowing and revoking access, authorising a representative); (4) Digital content creation (adding data and information to PHR); and (5) Safety (understanding PHR terms of use, declaration of consent, termination, revoking termination). The "problem-solving" competence area was addressed in the ePA-Coach framework by adding practical tasks across all five dimensions. Compared to the DigiComp framework, the number of levels was reduced to three (Beginner, Advanced, Expert) with the aim of reducing the complexity and enhancing understanding among senior learners. The three levels have been differentiated into complexity, autonomy, and cognitive levels (Figure 1). A detailed overview of the ePA-Coach competence framework was described by Gellner, Kaiser & Buchem (2021).

---

[2] https://www.un.org/sustainabledevelopment/health/

	Level 1 Beginner	Level 2 Advanced	Level 3 Expert
Complexity Level	low, basic and easy tasks	higher, clearly defined tasks	highest, best practices for given tasks
Autonomy Level	independant, with guidance if needed	independant, with minimum guidance	guiding others, adapting to others' needs
Cognitive Level	remember	understand and apply	apply

Figure 1. The structure of the ePA-Coach digital competence framework in the context of the PHR use.

The competence framework was then used to allocate and develop e-learning units at all three levels. There is a progression in the design, with the beginner units offering more theoretical information and tasks in the form of single/multiple choice, true/false, fill the blanks to sort the paragraphs questions, and the advanced units offering more complex and application-oriented exercises, for example in the form of embedded click dummies, which are used to practice real-life challenges related to the use of PHR. Similarly, the support in the units is scaffolded as the learner becomes increasingly confident in using the application. At the highest level (advanced), there is no help beyond the description of the scenario and it is possible for the learner to take the wrong path.

The design of learning activities at each level is informed by the Octalysis framework(Chou, 2019). The Octalysis framework defines eight core drives as fundamental types of motivations in both gamified and non-gamified contexts. The Octalysis framework suggests that these core drives motivate and engage individuals in various activities, including learning, and that designers and developers can use these core drives to create engaging and motivating learning experiences. Based on this approach and starting from an extensive literature review, followed by interviews with experts from the project team and the evaluation of preferences of senior learners, a senior-friendly gamification approach was developed to enhance motivation to learn and to use the ePA-Coach application. Figure 2 shows the final version of the Octalysis framework adjusted to the preferences of senior learners using values from the two exploratory studies described below.

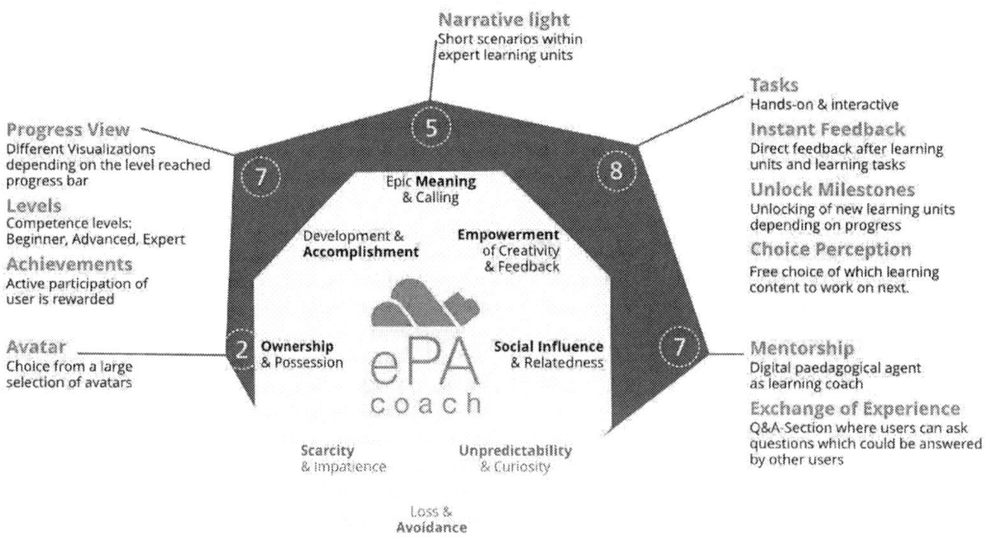

Figure 2. The Octalysis framework in the ePA-Coach project.

Overall, the ePA-Coach application was designed with a senior-friendly UX in mind by making the GUI very clear and senior-friendly, e.g. the interface has high contrasts, a larger, customisable font, and a clear typeface.

Design

The competence areas which are relevant to the ePA-Coach application were elaborated and prioritised with the help of the DigComp reference framework and the formulations were adapted to the context of ePA-Coach. Within the five competence areas, e-learning units were designed for the three levels, i.e. beginner, advanced, and expert. The entire program consists of 28 learning units, i.e. 12 beginner units, 11 advanced units, and 5 expert units. All units are designed as micro-learning units with micro-contents (Buchem & Hamelmann, 2010). Learners can freely choose what they want to learn next. The choice is only limited in that, within a competence area, all learning units of a competence level must first be completed in order to unlock the next level. Unlocking a level corresponds to the gamification techniques *Unlock Milestones* and *Levels* from the Octalysis framework. There are two ways to display competence areas in the ePA-Coach application – as clickable tiles with a progress bar (gamification technique *Progress View*) for the representation of the personal learning progress, or as a fictitious map (gamification technique *Narrative*) with marked locations for a competence area (Figure 3).

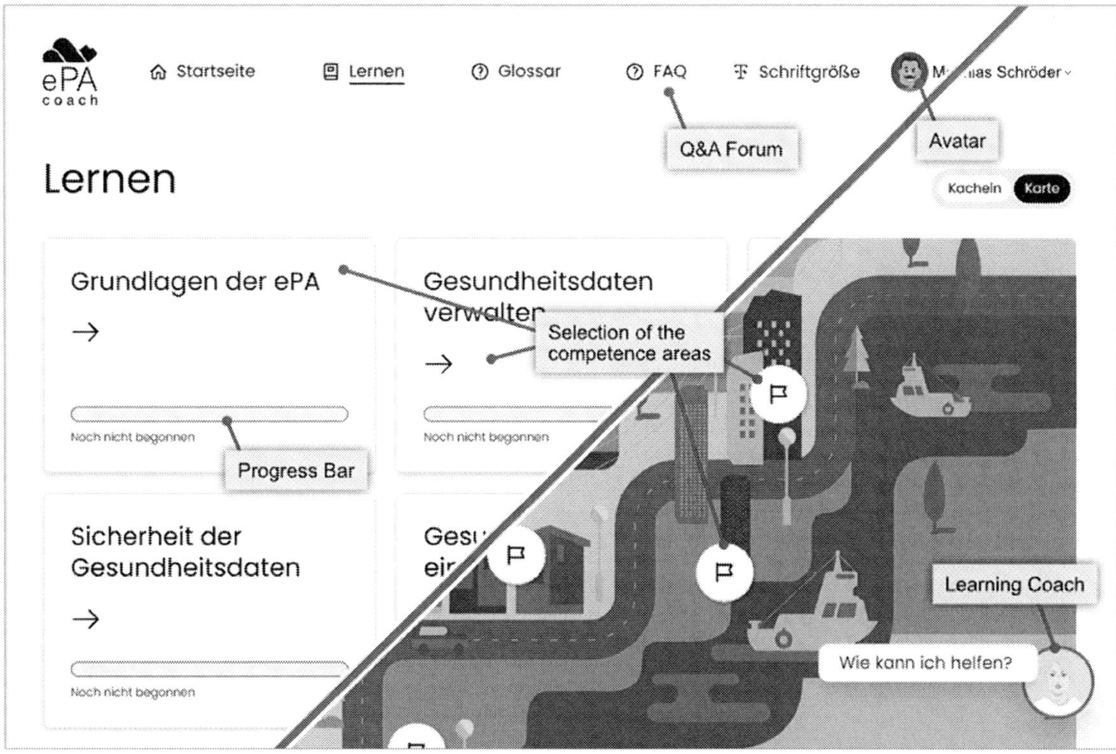

Figure 3. The ePA-Coach application, the learning area overview

As visualised in Figure 3 the basic design (left section) is oriented to the needs of senior learners, e.g. calm design, discreet use of colours, high contrasts, and a large and adjustable typeface. The element "avatar" can be selected by learners and used for interaction in the Q&A section. The AI-based "learning coach" (right, bottom section) is available to learners at all times and offers context-dependent assistance, and refers to appropriate resources, e.g. glossary.

The 28 learning units vary in complexity and are structured from general to specific, following the 3-level structure. Units at different levels were designed according to different instructional design models. *Beginner units* are based on the instructional design of *Nine Events of Instruction* by Gagné et al. (1992). Learning content is acquired independently by learners and consolidated with interactive exercises, such as single and multiple-choice, gap-filling texts, sorting tasks, and a final task. *Advanced* units are structured according to the *4C/ID* model by Kirschner et al. (2013). Here, practical learning tasks (gamification technique *Tasks)*, must be completed via simulations, which are implemented as click dummies with sub-tasks related to specific challenges. The support decreases with the growing complexity of the tasks (scaffolding). First learning tasks contain direct click instructions. Further tasks include only indirect instructions. The last tasks are completed with little support, in the form of hints. *Expert units* synthesise information from previous units and acquired knowledge is applied. This is done by first describing a scenario (gamification technique *Narrative)* and learners are challenged to apply previously acquired knowledge to solve more complex tasks in this scenario. In all learning units, knowledge and skills can be assessed and consolidated through learning tasks. These do not have any influence on the completion of a unit. Some tasks in the form of learning checks must be completed correctly in order to complete a unit and to increase progress in the competence areas. The gamification technique of *direct feedback* is applied to inform learners about their learning progress and possible difficulties. Learners can use a Q&A forum to share experiences with other learners (gamification technique *Exchange of Experience*). Active participation in the Q&A is rewarded (gamification technique *Achievements)* by ratings of answers by other learners.

Results

Based on the findings from two exploratory studies, the final e-learning concept and design were developed in several iterations. The recruitment of participants was primarily undertaken by the project partner Charité – Berlin University of Medicine, using an internal subject database, and with the help of stakeholders such as Berlin Senior Citizens' University and LMU Munich. The first study helped to gain insights into the assessment of the core drives proposed by Chou (2019). The results are based on the responses of a total of 41 senior learners aged 66 to 93 years old (average 74.7 years). The first study was conducted in May 2021. The second study provided insights into the perception of the ePA-Coach application, which was developed based on the iterated concept and taking into account results from the first evaluation. The evaluation began in June 2022 and ended in October 2022, resulting in 46 participants aged 65 to 88 years (average 73 years). Results from both studies were described in detail by Gellner and Buchem (2022) and Buchem et al. (2023). Here we outline results relevant to the discussion about digital sovereignty.

The results of the first study showed that the 41 senior participants perceived the following core drives as particularly motivating: *Development & Accomplishment* and *Empowerment of Creativity & Feedback.* These core drives are closely linked to digital sovereignty, such as development and empowerment. Core drives *Epic Meaning & Calling* and *Loss & Avoidance* was perceived as rather demotivating. Another aspect that emerged from the first study was related to how different gamification elements were perceived by older adults in the context of PHR. The results showed that *Instant Feedback* and *Practical Tasks* were perceived as most motivating, followed by *Unlock Milestones*, *Progress View*, *Levels*, and learning with a *Narrative.* Some of these elements are again closely related to digital sovereignty, especially in relation to controlling and monitoring own progress. The fourth main aspect examined in the first study was player types, which were derived from the *Gamification User Types Hexad Scale* by Marczewski (2015), which is a framework for understanding user motivations and it is based on six key motivational styles or player types. The study revealed that senior participants considered themselves to belong to *Free Spirit* and other intrinsic player types such as *Socialiser* and *Philanthropist.* These again closely correspond to the concept of digital sovereignty.

The results from the second study related to the design of the ePA-Coach application showed that the inclusion of *Instant Feedback* was valued highly by all 46 senior participants. The strong preference for this design feature was followed by the visualisation of the individual progress using the *Progress View* and the division of learning components into levels using *Steps & Levels.* The two latter gamification elements are connected to the core drive *Development & Accomplishment,* which was rated as the most motivating element, the same as in the first study. The second study revealed that the implementation of the core drive *Empowerment of Creativity & Feedback* received higher ratings than elements belonging to the core drive *Development & Accomplishment. Empowerment* included elements of *Instant Feedback, Unlocking Milestones*, *Practical Tasks,* and *Choice Perception.* Compared to these results, the core drive *Social Influence & Relatedness* was not perceived as valuable. This core drive included four elements: *Mentor* for learning support, *Experience Sharing* with other users, *Friendship* for adding acquaintances from real life as digital friends and seeing *Online Status*. All of these elements received neutral to negative ratings. Gamification elements belonging to the core drive *Ownership & Possession*, i.e. having your own *User Avatar* and *Action Reward* through unlocking more user avatars, also received low ratings. These results indicate that senior learners tend to value elements that enhance their individual digital sovereignty related to making choices, controlling and monitoring progress, and receiving instant feedback as opposed to social aspects related to friends, status, sharing or even mentoring.

Conclusions

This paper presented an e-learning design for enhancing the digital sovereignty of older citizens. This ePA-Coach e-learning application was designed to create an opportunity for citizens 65+ to acquire digital skills needed for the self-determined use of Personal Health Records (PHR) in the context of healthcare in Germany. The digital literacy framework for exercising digital sovereignty related to PHR was developed based on the European Digital Competence Framework and applied to design micro-learning units with micro-content using gamification techniques inspired by the Octalysis framework. The results from two exploratory studies with older citizens revealed strong preferences for design elements related to digital sovereignty. Senior learners perceived *intrinsic* core drives *Development & Accomplishment* and *Empowerment of Creativity & Feedback* with their different elements, such as free choice, hands-on tasks, instant feedback, unlocking milestones, progress view, levels, and achievements for active participation, to be particularly motivating. These results indicate that e-learning designs for senior learners, especially those aiming at enhancing digital sovereignty, should focus on creating possibilities of free choice, monitoring their own learning, hands-on practice, instant feedback, and meaningful achievements for active participation. In contrast, senior participants did not perceive *extrinsic* core drives related to the status, unpredictable tasks, and social influence as valuable. Our results also showed that support by a digital *Mentor* or coach received neutral ratings, indicating that senior participants felt somewhat ambivalent about this kind of support, again indicating a strong need for self-determined use. An interesting result is also the self-assessment of being an intrinsic player type (Free Spirit, Socialiser, Philanthropist) as opposed to extrinsic player types. Most participants perceived themselves to be *Free Spirits* who are characterised by the need for autonomy and freedom of choice, both in movement and in expression, which closely corresponds to the concept of digital sovereignty. Hence it can be concluded that senior learners tend to have a strong preference for different aspects related to digital sovereignty in relation to the design of e-learning. However, it must be emphasised that the results from both exploratory studies must not be generalised. Both studies have obvious limitations related to small sample sizes and the choice of participants from one country only. Future research with larger and international samples could explore in more detail, whether the need for digital sovereignty in e-learning applies to other populations of senior learners, and how this need can be achieved through the design of e-learning applications in eHealth/mHealth.

Acknowledgments

This publication was produced as part of the project ePA-Coach: Digital Sovereignty in the Context of the Electronic Patient File, founded by the Federal Ministry of Education and Research under the program Human-Technology Interaction for Digital Sovereignty. For more information, please visit https://technik-zum-menschen-bringen.de/projekte/epa-coach.

References

Buchem, I. & Hamelmann, H. (2010). Microlearning: a strategy for ongoing professional development. *eLearning Papers*, 21, September 2010 "Innovation in Lifelong Learning", pp. 1-15.

Buchem, I., Kauth V., Kirschen, M. & Katzer, M. (2023). *Designing E-Learning Activities for Senior Learners based on Core Drive Analysis Using Octalysis Gamification Framework: Results from the ePA-Coach Project.* Proceedings of the INTED 2023 Conference, Valencia, Spain.

Chou, Y. (2019). *Actionable Gamification: Beyond Points, Badges and Leaderboards.* CreateSpace Independent Publishing Platform.

Cukier, K. & Mayer-Schönberger, V. (2013). The Rise of Big Data. *Foreign Affairs*, 92(3), pp. 28-40.

Day, K., & Gu, Y. (2012). Influencing Factors for Adopting Personal Health Record (PHR). *Studies in health technology and informatics*, 178, pp. 39-44.

Ferrari, A. (2013). DIGCOMP: A Framework for Developing and Understanding Digital Competence in Europe, *Publications Office of the European Union*, Luxembourg.

Gellner, C. & Buchem, I. (2022). Evaluation of a gamification approach for older people in e-learning. *Proceedings of the 16th International Technology, Education and Development Conference (INTED)*, pp. 596-605.

Gellner, C., Kaiser, S. & Buchem, I. (2021). Entwicklung eines E-Learning-Konzepts zur digitalen Souveränität von Senioren im Kontext der elektronischen Patientenakte. In H.-W- Wollersheim, M. Karapanos, N. Pengel (Eds.). *Bildung in der digitalen Transformation*. Medien in der Wissenschaft, 78, pp. 161-167.

Gellner, C., Perotti, L., Koppenburger, A., Buchem, I., Dietrich, M. & Heimann-Steinert, A. (2021). Digital Literacy of Seniors in the Context of the Electronic Health Record, *Proceedings of the ICERI2021 Conference*, pp. 1297-1306, doi: 10.21125/iceri.2021.0374.

Hermans, A. (2022). Digital Era? Also My Era! Council of Europe, Information Society Department DGI (03). https://rm.coe.int/digital-literacy-for-seniors-print/1680a6ce9e

Marczewski, A. (2015). User Types HEXAD. In D. Diver (Eds.). *Even Ninja Monkeys Like to Play: Gamification, game thinking and motivational design* (pp. 65-80). Gamified UK.

Millard A, Baldassar, L. & Wilding, R. (2018). The significance of digital citizenship in the well-being of older migrants, *Public Health*, 158, pp. 144-148. The Royal Society for Public Health. Elsevier. doi: 10.1016/j.puhe.2018.03.005

Mossberger, K., Tolbert, C. J. & McNeal, R. S. (2007). *Digital Citizenship: The Internet, Society, and Participation*. Cambridge, MA: MIT Press. https://doi.org/10.7551/mitpress/7428.001.0001.

Örtegren, A. (2022), Digital Citizenship and Professional Digital Competence — Swedish Subject Teacher Education in a Postdigital Era. *Postdigit Sci Educ* 4, pp. 467–493, https://doi.org/10.1007/s42438-022-00291-7

Pangrazio, L. & Sefton-Green, J. (2021). Digital Rights, Digital Citizenship and Digital Literacy: What's the Difference?. *Journal of New Approaches in Educational Research*, 10(1), pp. 15-27.

Pohle, J. (2020). Digital sovereignty. A new key concept of digital policy in Germany and Europe. *Konrad-Adenauer-Stiftung e. V.*, Berlin.

Poss-Doering, R., Kunz, A., Pohlmann, S., Hofmann, H., Kiel, M., Winkler, E.C., Ose, D, & Szecsenyi, J. (2018). Utilizing a Prototype Patient-Controlled Electronic Health Record in Germany: Qualitative Analysis of User-Reported Perceptions and Perspectives. *JMIR Formative Research*, 2(2):e10411.

Redecker, C. (2017). European Framework for the Digital Competence of Educators: DigCompEdu. Luxembourg: *Publications Office of the European Union*. doi: 10.2760/159770

Roehrs A., da Costa C.A., Righi R.D. & de Oliveira K. S. (2017). Personal Health Records: A Systematic Literature Review. *Journal of Medical Internet Research*,19(1):e13, doi: 10.2196/jmir.5876.

Segall, N., Saville, J., L'Engle, P., Carlson, B., Wright, M.C., Schulman, K.A. & Tcheng, J.E. (2011). Usability evaluation of a personal health record, *Proceedings of the Annual Symposium* AMIA 2011, pp. 1233-42.

Stubbe, J., Schaat, S. & Ehrenberg-Silies, S. (2019). Digital souverän?: Kompetenzen für ein selbstbestimmtes Leben im Alter. Bertelsmann Stiftung, doi: 10.11586/2019035

Tondello, G. F., Wehbe, R.R., Diamond, L., Busch, M., Marczewski, A. & Nacke, L. E., (2016). The Gamification User Types Hexad Scale, *Proceedings of the 2016 Annual Symposium on Computer-Human Interaction in Play*, pp. 229–243, New York, NY, USA, doi: 10.1145/2967934.2968082.

Taha, J., Czaja, S.J., Sharit, J. & Morrow, D.G. (2013). Factors affecting usage of a personal health record (PHR) to manage health. *Psychology and aging*, 28(4), pp. 1124-39.

Vuorikari, R., Kluzer, S. & Punie, Y. (2022). DigComp 2.2: The Digital Competence Framework for Citizens - With new examples of knowledge, skills and attitudes, EUR 31006 EN, *Publications Office of the European Union*, Luxembourg, doi:10.2760/115376.

USING SHORT QUESTIONNAIRES TO SUPPORT STUDENTS' EMOTION AWARENESS AND REGULATION DURING AN ONLINE GROUP PROJECT

Jake Hilliard, Helen Donelan, Caroline Heaney, Karen Kear, Patrick Wong,
The Open University, United Kingdom

***Correspondence**: Jake Hilliard: jake.hilliard1@open.ac.uk*

Abstract

Over the past two decades, research has highlighted the profound influence emotions can have on students' learning, achievement, and wellbeing. Being able to successfully regulate one's emotions is now viewed as crucial when learning in educational settings. To support students with this process, a growing line of research has explored various ways of helping students understand and manage their emotions (e.g., via the use of digital tools aimed at helping students become more aware of their emotions and prompting ways to regulate these emotions). Despite this, limited research has been undertaken in online group learning settings, where students work remotely together as part of their course using collaborative communication tools. These learning contexts present unique challenges which can make emotion regulation more difficult than in face-to-face learning environments (e.g., delayed response times when communicating with peers and teachers and a reduced sense of how others are feeling, due to limited emotional cues when learning online). In this paper, we describe an approach used at the UK Open University (UKOU) to assist students' emotion awareness and regulation during a 9-week group project. This involves the use of short questionnaires which have been embedded into the Virtual Learning Environment (VLE) of a module. Since their inclusion, these questionnaires have been found to enhance emotional awareness in many students, as well as support the regulation of emotions in the group project. To conclude this paper, reflections on using the short questionnaires are discussed and implications for educators and institutions are identified.

Keywords: emotion, emotion regulation, emotion awareness, online group project, distance education.

Introduction

Emotions and their potential impacts on learning processes and human functioning have historically been ignored in educational settings (Artino & Naismith, 2015). However, in recent decades it has become increasingly apparent that emotions play a critical role in students' learning, achievement, and wellbeing (Pekrun et al., 2018). For instance, the experience of pleasant emotions, such as enjoyment, may: enhance a student's motivation to learn; foster the use of flexible learning strategies; and positively influence mental wellbeing. Conversely, the experience of unpleasant emotions, such as disappointment, may: reduce a student's task engagement; have damaging consequences on physical and mental health; and increase the chances of students dropping out of their course of study. Although the exact relationship between emotions and learning is complex and still not fully understood, it is evident that being able to successfully regulate one's emotions is a crucial process when learning (Jacobs & Gross, 2014).

Emotion regulation refers to the processes by which individuals influence the type, intensity, and duration of emotion they experience (Gross, 2015). Typically, this will involve trying to reduce the experience of unhelpful emotions and maintain or increase the experience of helpful emotions. For example, if a student is experiencing anxiety which is hindering their performance in an online group activity, they may try to reduce these feelings by thinking more positively or seeking social support from their teacher. On the other hand, if they are experiencing excitement which is facilitating their engagement, they may try to maintain this feeling by increasing their involvement in the task or sharing their feelings with other students in the group.

For students to successfully regulate their emotions, it is important that they are aware of, and understand, the emotions they are experiencing (Boden & Thompson, 2015). Research has shown that if students can adequately understand their emotions, they are more likely to engage in emotion regulation processes (Feldman Barrett et al., 2001) and are more prone to use adaptive emotion regulation strategies (i.e., those associated with beneficial outcomes) (Subic-Wrana et al., 2014). However, not all students are skilled at understanding and regulating their emotions, and many can find these processes extremely challenging (Harley et al., 2019). Finding ways to support students' emotional awareness and emotion regulation should, therefore, be an important consideration for educators (Coughlan et al., 2021; Järvelä et al., 2016).

Literature review

Emotions and online group learning

Investigation into the emotional experiences of students in online group activities is scarce. However, from the research that is available, it is evident that these learning environments can be highly emotionally charged, especially when they are linked to assessment (Hilliard et al., 2019). Previous research has highlighted that students experience a diverse range of emotional states when undertaking online group activities (Hilliard et al., 2019), but that feelings of anxiety and frustration are frequently experienced (Capdeferro & Romero, 2012; Hilliard et al., 2020). There may be many reasons for increased unpleasant emotions when undertaking online group activities. For instance, learning collaboratively can lead to conflict and tensions between group members (Hilliard et al., 2020). Study flexibility may also be reduced compared to working independently, due to the shared planning, discussion and creation often involved when working collaboratively. This can be challenging for students who learn online, as many may have chosen this mode of study in order to manage additional commitments (e.g., employment and caring responsibilities) and to have maximum study flexibility.

Emotion awareness and regulation in online group learning

Little is known about how and why students regulate their emotions in online group learning. When compared to face-to-face learning environments, online settings present novel challenges which can make emotion awareness and regulation more difficult (Marchand & Gutierrez, 2012). For example, in online environments, there are typically fewer opportunities for peer support compared to studying on a university campus (Barr, 2014). Response times when interacting with peers and teachers can also be delayed, as communication is often undertaken using text-based, asynchronous methods. Working online can also make it more challenging to be aware of, and understand, others' emotions due to limited emotional cues (Derks et al., 2008). This reduced visibility of emotional and affective experiences can limit the support offered to students that is often provided in face-to-face learning (e.g., by academic teaching staff and other students) (Barr, 2014).

Supporting students' emotion awareness and regulation when learning online

Over the last decade, researchers have started to explore various ways of helping students understand and manage their emotions when learning in both face-to-face and online settings. This has often used digital tools to help raise students' awareness of their own and other students' emotions, as well as to prompt and support emotion regulation (Coughlan et al., 2021; Feidakis et al., 2014; Järvelä et al., 2016; Lavoué et al., 2020). One example of such a tool is the Social Emotional Sampling Tool (SEST; see Webster, 2019 or Webster & Hadwin, 2013). This digital tool has been specifically developed for computer-supported collaborative learning activities and aims to support students' emotional awareness and regulation. More specifically, the SEST prompts students to assess their current emotional state (e.g., by asking them to identify an emotion they are experiencing and its cause) as well as plan ways to regulate their emotions.

Despite the growth of research exploring ways to support students' emotional awareness and regulation, there is still limited research which has been undertaken in naturalistic online group learning contexts. Gaining a greater insight would be of great value to educators and institutions who have adopted, or who are planning to adopt this pedagogical approach.

An approach used at the UK Open University

In this section, we describe an approach used at the UKOU to support students' emotion awareness and regulation during an assessed, online, group project. The assessed group project is part of a Level 2 undergraduate module in 'Communication and Information Technologies' and runs over a 9-week period. It requires students to work in teams of between 6 and 8 to design and build a website for a specific 'client' (e.g., the managers of a family-friendly hotel or community theatre), and then evaluate another group's work. To carry out the project, groups are provided with a version of WordPress for website development and an online forum on the VLE for group discussion. A student's overall grade is made up of both individual and group marks and the assignment contributes 1/6 of the overall module grade. Although groups can largely work how and when they want, there are several milestones during the project (as shown at the top of Figure 1).

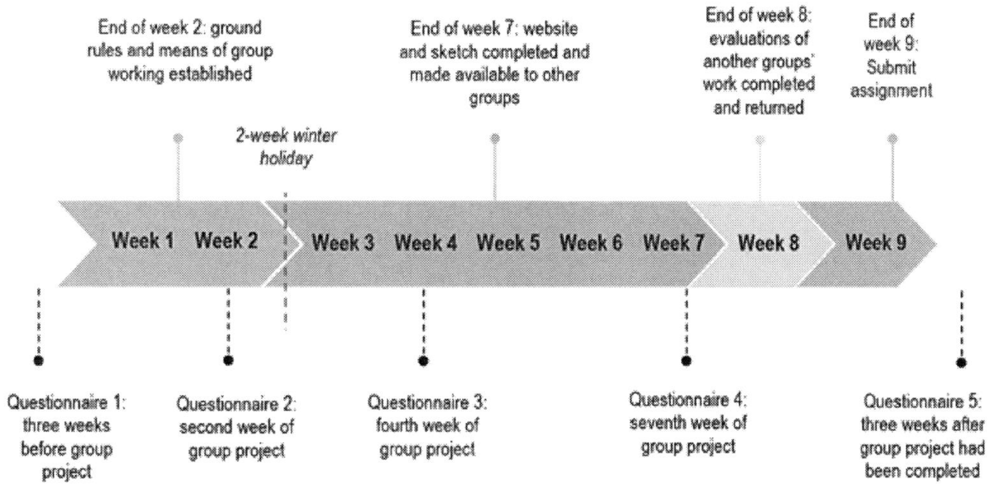

Figure 1. Milestones and timings of questionnaires through the group project.

To support the emotion awareness and regulation of students during the group project, five short questionnaires have been embedded into the weekly content of the module's VLE, with each questionnaire at a different point during the project. This type of questionnaire is known as 'real-time student feedback' at the UKOU and is used to gain information about students' experiences, with the intention of taking action to support students on a module. The timings of the questionnaires are shown at the bottom of Figure 1. The number and timings of questionnaires were agreed with the module team; the questionnaires were inserted at key time-points of the project without over burdening students during periods of heavy workload. It was considered important that questionnaires were placed before the project, at several points during it, and after it finished, so that students were supported at each stage.

Primarily, it was hoped that the questionnaires would: 1) allow students to reflect upon their feelings and help them understand the emotions they were experiencing; 2) prompt ways to regulate their emotions (if required); 3) support students' emotion management by providing positive, tailored feedback dependent on their questionnaire responses; and 4) allow module teams to implement actions/ interventions that would support students during the project, based on questionnaire responses (e.g., by alerting tutors to common issues faced by students or providing additional support to students via news items on the VLE). All responses to the five questionnaires are anonymous. Each questionnaire is open for two weeks; after this time, students are unable to access them. This is so that students' responses can be linked to specific stages of the collaborative project.

The first questionnaire (which is before the start of the group project) asks students about their initial feelings of undertaking the group project. Students respond by selecting one of three options: 'I am looking forward to it', 'I am uncertain about it', or 'I am very worried about it'. Based on their response, students are provided with tailored feedback aimed at acknowledging and supporting their feelings before starting the group project. An example of this is shown in Figure 2. Questionnaire 1 also asks students to reflect on why they are feeling the way they are, by responding in an open-ended textbox.

Feedback if students selected 'I am looking forward to it'

It's great that you are looking forward to taking part in the collaborative project! In the previous presentation, many students thought they gained a great deal from collaborating with other students.

Feedback if students selected 'I am uncertain about it'

It's OK to feel nervous about this activity. You can expect to encounter a few challenges but also benefit a great deal from collaborating with other students (some of them may feel as unsure as you are). You can also talk to your tutor and find help or advice on many aspects of your studies in the OU support area.

Feedback if students selected 'I am very worried about it'

Many students feel worried and anxious about taking part in collaborative activities. Although these feelings are often seen as negative, we've found that they can have positive impacts on participation and performance. For instance, these feelings may lead to increased effort and motivation levels and make students more proactive. We have also found that, although many students had worries before and during the collaborative activity, their reflections after the activity have been really positive.

If these feelings are very strong and persistent, and you think that they will make it hard for you fully take part in the activity, it is important that you get support. Your tutor will be able to give you help and advice, so do contact them. You can also find help or advice on many aspects of your studies in the OU support area.

Figure 2. Example feedback provided to students after indicating how they were feeling before the group project (questionnaire 1).

The remaining questionnaires (2-5) are primarily based on the SEST, although statements have been slightly adapted to reflect the specific learning context. Examples of the statements and responses included in these questionnaires are shown in Figure 3. These questionnaires prompt students to indicate an emotion they are currently experiencing in relation to the group project. Other questions ask about the cause and intensity of the emotion; goals and strategies for regulating the emotion; the student's perception of the overall group atmosphere; and their level of satisfaction with how things are going in the project. For these questionnaires, students receive tailored feedback after indicating their level of satisfaction with the group project.

In the final questionnaire (number 5), statements relate to emotion regulation goals and strategies are not included, and several statements and responses have been changed to past tense, as this questionnaire is undertaken after the group project has been completed. This questionnaire also asks students to respond to four Likert-type questions about whether the questionnaires have helped them become more aware of their emotions and have supported emotion regulation when undertaking the group project. For instance, students are asked: '*Did filling out the questionnaires help you regulate, or manage, your feelings in relation to the group project?*'.

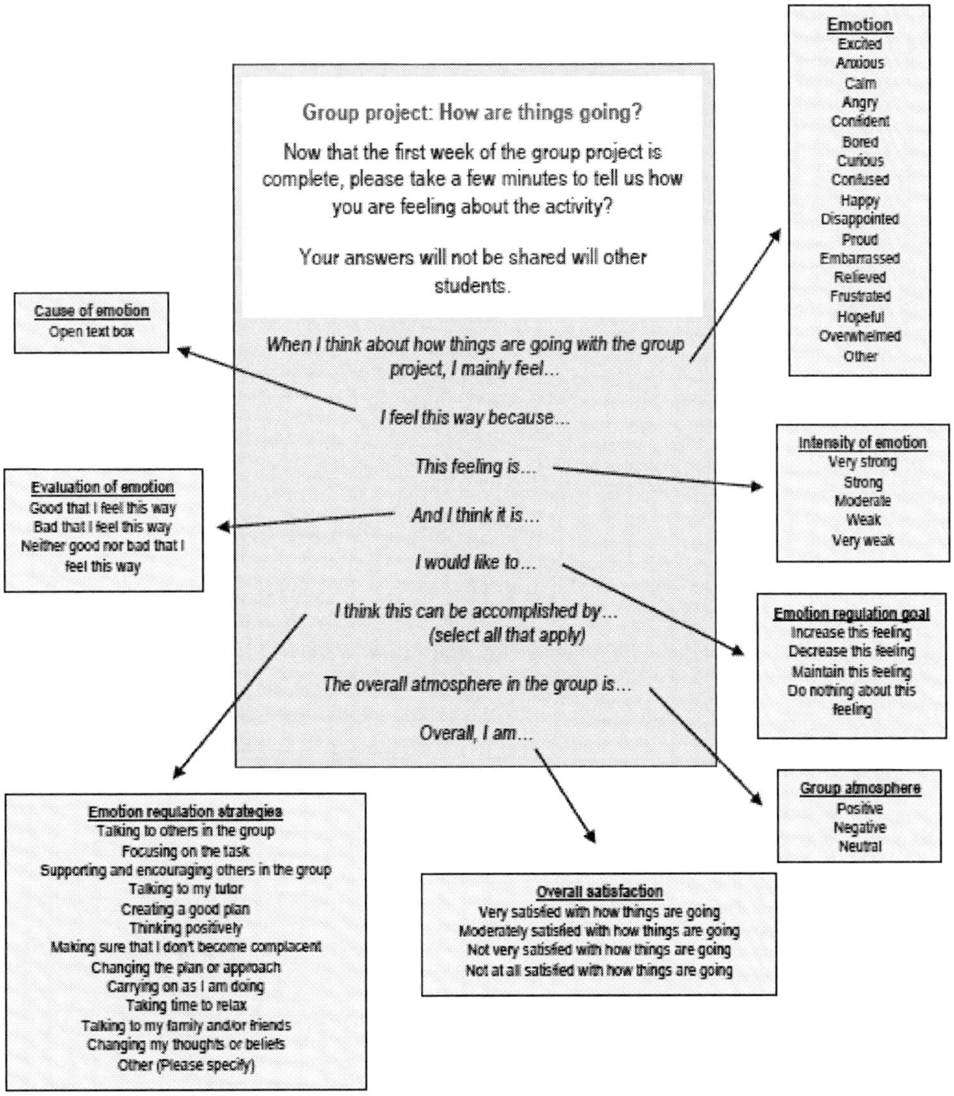

Figure 3. An example of the statements and responses included in questionnaires during the group project (questionnaires 2,3, and 4).

The questionnaires have now been embedded in the VLE pages of the module for three academic years. During this time, students' responses have highlighted that anxiety and frustration are by far the most reported emotions. Other commonly reported emotions include feeling confident, relieved, and hopeful. In relation to strategies students planned to use to regulate their emotions, talking to others in the group and focusing on the task were the most frequently selected. Other strategies that have been frequently reported include thinking positively and supporting and encouraging other group members.

Responses to questions in the final questionnaire also emphasised the usefulness of the questionnaires in supporting emotion awareness and regulation. When asked whether the questionnaires made students more aware of their emotions in relation to the group project, nearly half the respondents reported that they did (48.5% of the 379 respondents over the three years). When asked if questionnaires supported the regulation of emotions during the project, nearly a third of respondents (31.9%) reported that they did. Slightly over half of the respondents (54.6%) indicated that they have used strategies selected in the questionnaires to regulate their emotions. Furthermore, nearly half of the respondents (43.0%) indicated that the strategies listed in the questionnaires have prompted new ideas for how they could regulate their emotions during the group project.

Conclusions

The purpose of this paper was to describe an approach used to support students' emotion awareness and regulation during an online group project at the UKOU. The findings are encouraging, as they highlight the usefulness of the questionnaires in supporting emotion awareness and regulation in a naturalistic online group learning setting. This is important as research has shown that students who can sufficiently understand and manage their emotions will perform better academically (MacCann et al., 2020). Furthermore, being able to effectively regulate emotions has also been found to be associated with positive mental health and wellbeing (Zeidner et al., 2012).

The questionnaires described in this paper offer a practical and simple approach for supporting students' emotion awareness and regulation when learning collaboratively online: one which could easily be adopted by other educational institutions. Although the questionnaires have been specifically used for a group project in this context, the use of such questionnaires could be adapted to suit other learning situations, or could be used to support students' emotion awareness and regulation throughout their learning journey.

One of the key benefits of using the embedded VLE questionnaires is that students' responses are instantly available to module teams, providing real-time insight into students' feelings. This information can be used by educators to take quick action and apply interventions that can further support students. Future research is needed to explore how useful module teams find this information and what types of actions and interventions are used to support students, based on this information. For instance, educators may share certain anonymous data (e.g., of the types of emotions being experienced) with all students on the module to increase students' awareness of how other students are feeling about the project. Previous research (Hilliard et al., 2020) suggests that this may help reduce unpleasant feelings (such as anxiety, worry, and apprehension) in some students when learning collaboratively online, particularly in the early stages of the activities.

References

Artino, A. R., & Naismith, L. M. (2015). "But how do you really feel?" Measuring emotions in medical education research. *Medical Education, 49*(2), 140–142. https://doi.org/10.1111/medu.12642

Barr, B. (2014). Identifying and addressing the mental health needs of online students in higher education. , 17(2). *Online Journal of Distance Learning Administration, 17*(2).

Boden, M. T., & Thompson, R. J. (2015). Facets of emotional awareness and associations with emotion regulation and depression. *Emotion, 15*(3), 399–410. https://doi.org/10.1037/emo0000057

Capdeferro, N., & Romero, M. (2012). Are online learners frustrated with collaborative learning experiences? *The International Review of Research in Open and Distributed Learning, 13*(2), 26–44. https://doi.org/10.19173/irrodl.v13i2.1127

Coughlan, T., Lister, K., & Lucassen, M. (2021). Representing the unseen with "Our Journey": a platform to capture affective experiences and support emotional awareness in university-level study. *Journal of Formative Design in Learning*, 1–14. https://doi.org/10.1007/s41686-021-00055-9

Derks, D., Fischer, A. H., & Bos, A. E. R. (2008). The role of emotion in computer-mediated communication: A review. In *Computers in Human Behavior* (Vol. 24, Issue 3, pp. 766–785). https://doi.org/10.1016/j.chb.2007.04.004

Feidakis, M., Daradoumis, T., Caballé, S., & Conesa, J. (2014). Embedding emotion awareness into e-learning environments. *International Journal of Emerging Technologies in Learning (IJET), 9*(7), 39–46.

Feldman Barrett, L., Gross, J., Conner Christensen, T., & Benvenuto, M. (2001). Knowing what you're feeling and knowing what to do about it: Mapping the relation between emotion differentiation and emotion regulation. *Cognition & Emotion, 15*(6), 713–724. https://doi.org/10.1080/02699930143000239

Gross, J. J. (2015). Emotion regulation: Current status and future prospects. *Psychological Inquiry, 26*(1), 1–26. https://doi.org/10.1080/1047840X.2014.940781

Harley, J. M., Pekrun, R., Taxer, J. L., & Gross, J. J. (2019). Emotion regulation in achievement situations: An integrated model. *Educational Psychologist*, *54*(2), 106–126. https://doi.org/10.1080/00461520.2019.1587297

Hilliard, J., Kear, K., Donelan, H., & Heaney, C. (2020). Students' experiences of anxiety in an assessed, online, collaborative project. *Computers and Education*, *143*, 103675. https://doi.org/10.1016/j.compedu.2019.103675

Hilliard, Jake, Kear, K., Donelan, H., & Heaney, C. (2019). Exploring the emotions of distance learning students in an assessed, online, collaborative project. *Connecting through Educational Technology - Proceedings of the European Distance and E-Learning Network 2019 Annual Conference*, 251–259.

Jacobs, S. E., & Gross, J. J. (2014). Emotion regulation in education. In R. Pekrun & L. Linnenbrink-Garcia (Eds.), *International handbook of emotions in education* (pp. 183–201). Routledge.

Järvelä, S., Kirschner, P. A., Hadwin, A., Järvenoja, H., Malmberg, J., Miller, M., & Laru, J. (2016). Socially shared regulation of learning in CSCL: Understanding and prompting individual- and group-level shared regulatory activities. *International Journal of Computer-Supported Collaborative Learning*, *11*(3), 263–280. https://doi.org/10.1007/s11412-016-9238-2

Lavoué, E., Kazemitabar, M., Doleck, T., Lajoie, S. P., Carrillo, R., & Molinari, G. (2020). Towards emotion awareness tools to support emotion and appraisal regulation in academic contexts. *Educational Technology Research and Development*, *68*(1), 269–292. https://doi.org/10.1007/s11423-019-09688-x

MacCann, C., Jiang, Y., Brown, L. E. R., Double, K. S., Bucich, M., & Minbashian, A. (2020). Emotional intelligence predicts academic performance: A meta-analysis. *Psychological Bulletinulletin*, *146*(2), 150–186. https://doi.org/10.1037/BUL0000219

Marchand, G. C., & Gutierrez, A. P. (2012). The role of emotion in the learning process: Comparisons between online and face-to-face learning settings. *The Internet and Higher Education*, *15*(3), 150–160. https://doi.org/https://doi.org/10.1016/j.iheduc.2011.10.001

Pekrun, R., Muis, K. ., Frenzel, A. ., & Goetz, T. (2018). *Emotions at school*. Routledge.

Subic-Wrana, C., Beutel, M. E., Brähler, E., Stöbel-Richter, Y., Knebel, A., Lane, R. D., & Wiltink, J. (2014). How is emotional awareness related to emotion regulation strategies and self-reported negative affect in the general population? *PLoS ONE*, *9*(3), e91846. https://doi.org/10.1371/journal.pone.0091846

Webster, E. A. (2019). *Regulating Emotions in Computer-Supported Collaborative Problem-Solving Tasks*. University of Victoria.

Webster, E. A., & Hadwin, A. F. (2013). Regulating emotions during computer-supported collaborative problem solving. *Annual Conference of the Canadian Society for the Study of Education*.

Zeidner, M., Matthews, G., & Roberts, R. D. (2012). The emotional intelligence, health, and well-being nexus: What have we learned and what have we missed? *Applied Psychology: Health and Well-Being*, *4*(1), 1–30. https://doi.org/https://doi.org/10.1111/j.1758-0854.2011.01062.x

*** Formatting Issue - Best Available Paper/Graphic ***

OPEN EDUCATIONAL COURSES APRENDO+ BY NATIONAL AUTONOMOUS UNIVERSITY OF MEXICO (UNAM): ACHIEVEMENTS AND CHALLENGES

Leónides Villanueva-Gutiérrez, National Autonomous University of Mexico, Department of Educational Research, Center for Research and Advanced Studies, Lindsay Carrillo-Valdez, Department of Educational Research, Center for Research and Advanced Studies, Mexico

***Correspondence**: Lindsay Carrillo-Valdez: psiclcarrillovz@gmail.com*

Abstract

The National Autonomous University of Mexico has developed Aprendo+ open courses with the objective of offering the university community members and the general public the opportunity for the continuously updating knowledge or skills. In order to show the preliminary results of Aprendo+, we analize the metrics and platform reports for the 2018-2022 period. The results show that Aprendo+ has consolidated as a quality option for the continuously updating of the national and international university and non-university community. Being this a relatively new project, we found challenges related to information systematization, spreading and efficiency. To overcome these challenges will improve the content, reach and positive impact of Aprendo+ within the global community and its future.

Keywords:

Aprendo+, Open Educational Resources, Open Courses, Massive Online Open Courses

Introduction

This work has as precedent the "Building new spaces for education throughout life, Aprendo+ courses" conference, exposed by León-Martínez y Tapia-Rangel (2020) at the EDEN 2020 Annual Conference. In this work the authors exposed the general characteristics about their objectives, design and acceptance of the community towards the Aprendo+ Project developed by the National Autonomous University of Mexico (hereinafter UNAM). We are now focusing on showing the preliminary results given by the development of the Project emphasizing the achievements of the last 5 years as well as the upcoming challenges.

Open Educational Resources in the local and global context as precedents of Aprendo+.

The open educational resources are a variety of teaching and learning materials available for everyone, free usage and open licenses. This movement started locally in some American universities like The Massachusetts Institute (MIT), Harvard, Yale and Cambridge (Miranda & Tirado, 2012; Ramirez, 2013; Torres, 2021). Nowadays is a global movement (Brown et al, 2020) that summons and commits individuals, higher educational institutions and other organizations to create open and online courses that can be taken advantage by all people, breaking the physical classroom borders, as well as the frontiers between countries, sharing the educational resources through the web for global community capable of learning throughout life (Mihai, 2021).

Currently we find international experiences about the development of online massive courses. For example, some universities have come together to create projects of great importance like Mitx and Edx. besides, profit organizations such as Coursera and Udacity have developed a high offer of massive courses with a high student demand which has led to international recognition (Allen & Seaman, 2013; Sued, 2022).

We can find some platforms that have been able to establish themselves in Mexico, thanks to the great variety of courses and the design they use. MexicoX is the perfect example of this, a federal government effort to design courses focused on the professional development through a network between public universities, government institutions and civil society. Another example is Capacítate para el empleo by the Carlos Slim foundation. On its website, we can find a high offering of courses focused on training and development.

In this local and global context and in agreement with the Institutional Development Plans 2015-2019 and 2019- 2023 (National Autonomous University of Mexico [UNAM], 2020; National Autonomous University of Mexico. Coordination of the Open University, Educational Innovation and Distance Education [UNAM CUAIEED], 2023) that search the relevance of new courses that answer to the educational necessities of the population, support the creation of contents and its inclusion with the different university repositories, consolidate and increase UNAM national and international presence, the Open University and Distance Education Coordination (CUAED) created in 2015 the Aprendo+ plataform. The project (before called General Culture Courses) consists in the design of high quality, open and free massive courses which are focused on the people interested (university and non-university, local, national and worldwide) on updating the understanding and skills in their preferred fields of knowledge.

Aprendo+: Courses structure

The Aprendo+ educational offer is diverse, due to the join working between different schools and areas of the University for its development, where the most viable subjects are chosen to be developed in the courses. This offer has 78 different courses classified in four areas that are a part of the organizational structure of UNAM (UNAM, 2023). Those areas are: I) Physics, Mathematics Science and Engineering (7 courses); II) Biological, Chemical and Health Science (26 courses); III) Social Sciences (26 coursers); IV) Humanities and Arts (19 courses). Fields of knowledge 2 and 3 have the high offer while Area 1 showed the lowest offer (see Figure 1).

Figure 1.Distribution of the Aprendo+ courses by area.

The pedagogical offer is based on the explanation of specialized topics and content of each field of knowledge using the informal language, simple, clear, and casual instead of technical and formal language. The instructional sequences (Tobón-Tobón et al., 2010) for achieving the objectives are structured in 1) overall picture, 2) Units outlines, and 3) activities. On the overall picture describe the main structure of the course: the main objective of the course, number of units, type of activities, evaluation tools as well as the number of minimum hours that are required to conclude the course satisfactory. The units outlines include an introduction where the importance of the topics, the specific objective of each unit and the learning and self-evaluation activities of the course is explained. In the learning activities detailed instructions are given for solving exercises and task. The activities are accompanied by self-evaluation tools (questionnaires) that users can use as a guide for the solution of the activities and make a review about the general contents of the unit. At the end of the questionnaire, the platform shows general feedback that can help users identify areas of improvement.

The instructional design of the Aprendo+ courses provides two main characteristics, self-direct learning (Mihai, 2021) and flexibility. On one hand, the user can do the activities on its own without any help or guidance given that the activities and contents are congruent, offer all learning tools and clear instructions. On the other, given that there is no specific starting or closing schedule, the user has the freedom to choose between one or more courses at a time, start immediately, either, organize their personal and professional agenda and start later.

Methodology

A descriptive statistical analysis is presented from the metrics shown by the platform Aprendo+ (LMS Moodle) for the 2018-2022 period. Variables user-ID, course-ID, course name and email were used. Frequencies, percentages, percentage increase and in some cases average grades were obtained.

Results

Between 2018 and 2022, 1532690 subscriptions were registered for the platform courses. The 40.8% was completed, generating 626093 documentations of completion, while the 59.2% of the subscribed courses (906597) was left inconclusive (see Figure 2).

Figure 2. Completed and inconclusive course on Aprendo+ platform, 2018-2022.

The results shown next are focused on the statistics for the completed courses with the documentation of completion.

A total of 349369 that made the courses between 2018 y 2022 received the documentation of completion. Figure 3 shows sustained growth of the users who completed the courses between 2018 and 2020. From the 96 subscribed users in 2018, by 2019 58438 users registered with completed courses and documentation of completion, which shows an increase of 607.73%. By 2020 the number of users increased to 126738, a 116.88% increase in relation to 2019. In 2021 there was a decrease of users (79562) which shows a decrease of 37.22% in relation to 2020. Finally, in 2022 103812 users were registered (30.48% higher than the year before).

Figure 3. Number of users for Aprendo+ platform by year, 2018-2022

For the 626093 subscribed users that completed courses between 2018 and 2022 most of them used personal email accounts (53689 subscriptions), the rest used institutional email accounts (89104 subscriptions). Through the institutional email accounts, we can observe that firstly, users connected from different places of the world (203 countries). Second, as show in Figure 4, most of the users (71.73%) subscribed with educational accounts [domain
.edu (31%); .unam (3%); .ipn (1%); .uam (.07%) and others (37%)], from public and private college and university. The three main public Universities from México (UNAM, IPN y UAM), included the University where Aprendo+ platform resides (UNAM) shows the lowest number of subscriptions. Besides we found subscriptions with government accounts (25%) and government and non-government organization's accounts (3%).

Figure 4. Distribution of the subscriptions made with institutional email accounts, 2018-2022

According to the Figure 5, the field that shows the highest amount of completed courses with documentation of completion was Field 4, Humanities and Arts (209032 documentation of completion), followed by Field 1. Physics, Mathematics and Engineering (166080 documentation of completion), while Field 3. Social Science show the lowest documentation of completion (119392), followed by Field 2. Biological, chemical and health science (131589 documentación of completion).

Figure 5. Documentation of completion by field of knowledge, 2018-2022

According to the distribution of documentation of completion had per field of knowledge per year, Field 4. Humanities and Arts are steady with the highest number of completed courses and documentation of completion from 2018 to 2022 and Field 3. Social science showed the lowest number of completed courses since 2018. It is important to acknowledge that in 2020 (period of the social distancing due to pandemic) was the year with the highest number of completed courses and documentation of completion (see Figure 6).

Figure 6. Distribution of certification given by area per year 2018-2022

Finally, the Table 1 shows highlighted in green the 10 courses with the highest number of documentations of completion (completed courses) and highlighted in red the 10 courses with the lowest number of documentations of completion (completed courses). Most of the completed courses by users belong to fields 4 and 1. Unlike the courses with lower number of documentation of completion belong to fields 2 and 3. The amount of hours of the completed courses didn´t show a relation between the choice and duration of the course since it shows that the 10 most chosen courses demand a higher amount of hours to be completed (M = 19.1 hours) by the users compared to the average amount of time used by the users on least chosen courses (M = 16 hours).

Table 1: The 10 courses with higher documentation of completion and the 10 courses with the lowest documentation of completion. 2018-2022

Course name	Field of knowledg e	Hours	Documentation of completion
Orthography for beginners	4	20	94370
Basic tools of Microsoft Office 2010. Excel	1	30	83942
Basic tools of Microsoft Office 2010. Word	1	20	37232
How to control my stress? Attention to anxiety disorders	2	16	31604
Self-esteem: transcendence of life	4	13	26774
Basic tools of Microsoft Office 2010. PowerPoint	1	30	21771
Public speaking and presentations	4	20	16134
One, two, three... for human rights	3	2	13570
Learn to say no	2	10	13362
How to take advantage of Google's free tools	1	30	12915
UC science murals in Mexico City	4	6	784
I Quit Drugs Whenever I want! Drug Use and Its Effects	2	30	723
Myths and realities of the "Drive without alcohol" program (Breathalyzer)	3	10	558
I didn't crash, they hit me. Steps to follow in Mexico City	3	6	557
And how do you see it? Television critical reception	3	20	515
The mind fades: Dementias	2	7	324
Behavior and development problems in children and/or adolescents? Solution strategies to live better	2	30	321
Do you know what psychosis and schizophrenia are?	2	9	294
No more myths: healthy and responsible sexuality	2	30	284
What is epilepsy? Origin and treatment	2	12	211

Discussion

The objective of this paper was to show the preliminary results of the application of the open educational resources Aprendo+ developed by the UNAM, highlighting the achievements reached and challenges in the last five years (2018-2022). Therefor the research findings are discussed in two axes, on one side, the achievements and on the other the challenges and improvement measures.

Achievements

Aprendo+ and UNAM institutional goals

The creation of Aprendo+ courses on the four fields of knowledge, the steady increase in users, subscriptions and completed courses joined with users' diversity on educational level, institutions, countries of origin and more, shows that Aprendo+ is a key project for reaching the institutional goals established by the Institutional Development Plans (UNAM, 2020; UNAM CUAIEED, 2023) and to develop university extension mission.

Opportunities for the Self-directed learning

By its characteristics, the Aprendo+ courses give the users the opportunity to develop attitudes and abilities related to the self-directed learning (time organization, motivation, self-confidence, discipline, among others) and that according with Mihai (2021), become especially useful to improve learning through life and outside the institutionalized educational context. The simultaneous subscription to the Aprendo+ course, the amount of completed courses and the documentation of completion during the last five years shows evidence on the possibility of learning in an independent way by building personalized learning routes on different scenarios in which the user chooses what, when, and to what rhythm they want to learn.

Training for work: usage of software and soft abilities

The courses with the highest number of subscriptions and documentation of completion refer to the training and development of their topics, specifically with the usage of software and the improvement of soft abilities such as assertiveness, self-esteem, stress control, communication, and others. The finding above shows not only the main interest and preferences of the Aprendo+ users but also gives evidence the use of this open educational resource as an option for the personal and professional development.

Valuable resources during social distancing by COVID-19

During 2020 the platform showed the highest number of subscriptions, completed courses and generation of documentation of completion. Razo (2020) points out that the amount of time and available resources motivated a lot of the people to find new hobbies and learning options. With this, teachers, students and the public in general could identify the greatest potential of the Aprendo+ courses in order to learn something new and free during social distancing and temporarily closure of schools. This way Aprendo+ offer and the interest of people made the University to continue with its basic functions. Sánchez (2022) points out Aprendo+ as one of the main open educational resources that allowed the University to answer to the sanitary crisis under the phrase: "La UNAM no se detiene" (UNAM never stops).

Generation of the interdisciplinary work methodolgy and quality assurance.

Unlike other open educational projects, Aprendo+ work methodology is focus on the multi and interdisciplinary collaboration of specialist of different areas of knowledge. This methodology considers five important areas (Project Administration; Pedagogical Advisory and Instructional Design; Style Correction; Design and Visual

Communication, and System and Technological Software) and defines the processes and activities of each one to design and create the pedagogical contents, visual proposals and technological support for each one of the courses and to guarantee their quality.

Recognition of the University academics for the creation of the courses

One more achievement of this project is that university teachers identify the importance of attracting the public to the knowledge of each area. The teachers that participated in the design of Aprendo+ courses have been capable of creating original content with simple and attractive language that help to the accomplishment of the university extension.

Challenges

Courses for health education and prosocial behaviour

Aprendo+ courses with low registration and documentation of completion during the last five years are characterized for address topics related to the health, education and prosocial behaviour (Field 2). Both topics are sensitive due to the involvement of private people´s life. This does not mean we should not develop courses focused on health care, moreover on the post COVID-19 times. So, in order to improve Aprendo+ courses, it is important to solve two matters. The first has to do with the course's topics, contents and names, the second has to do with the distribution of information.

On the topics and contents, the challenge consists of selecting titles, topics and contents on health which are attractive, easy to understand and apply in daily life. It is unlikely that the title of a topic extremely specific like psychosis or schizophrenia becomes attractive for users not familiarized on mental health. Regarding to the spreading of the courses, the challenge consists in creating strategies that call potential users.

Dropout and terminal efficiency

Aprendo+ courses attract thousands of people who subscribe to the courses, but they interrupt them for different reasons. At Aprendo+ is extremely hard to calculate the dropout rate for the users can interrupt the course and take it back whenever it suits them best. However, we consider that time management and adaptability for online courses are the main reasons for not completing the courses. By not having a specific starting or closing schedule, users do the courses on the first weeks and then they interrupt them to do different activities. Such as for some inexperienced or non-motivated users, the lack of a guide or tutor to help solving doubts or to pressure to complete the course in addition to the lack of an official certification may lead to the dropout of the course. Therefore, we would have to implement new strategies that focused on the motivation of users like giving them micro credentials that support the abilities and knowledge acquired through the courses and that are useful in the work environment (Brown et al., 2020).

Systematization and processing of personal data

Currently, we do not ask for personal data on the platform with the purpose of avoiding legal requirements related to data protection. So the challenge consists of generating the proper conditions that allow them to collect and processing the personal data of the Aprendo+ users in order to get the learning metrics, feedback and improvement of the open resource. Through of data like age, gender, nationality, studies, country of residence, starting and ending date, number of subscribed users in a period of time, among others, we can define user profiles, identify needs and making decisions the Aprendo+ continuous improvement.

Measurement of the user satisfaction level

In order to improve the user experience, we need to develop a strategy to measure the satisfaction levels at the end of the course. This will help to identify the improvement areas for each one of the courses, the continuity of the learning objectives, contents, instructions and planned activities as well as to identify the users' interests in creating new courses.

*** **Formatting Issue - Best Available Paper/Graphic** ***

Diversification of the offer

We need to increase the learning offering, update periodically the course catalogue in all learning areas to the users in school as well as new users. We must increase the interest of academics of four fields of knowledge to design courses for Aprendo+. Therefore, it is a priority to measure the global impact of the platform and explore the possibility for the teachers to get digital badges as international creators of the open and high-quality educational resources.

Spreading

Aprendo+ is a project that has proven to be of a great reach and impact for learning throughout life, therefore we recommend to share the educational offer of this platform, through different media and institutional channels using wide reach campaigns like social media and gathering user reviews to motivate others.

Conclusion

The projects of the open educational resources based on clear, defined and interdisciplinary working methodologies represent quality options to get the knowledge into the global community who volunteer commitment to learning new skills or acquiring new knowledge, who incorporate continuous learning as part of their lifestyle. Aprendo+ is an example of what the universities can do to transcend and reinvent their spaces, times, ways of teaching and learning as well as to build a promising future for everyone.

References

Allen, I. E., & Seaman, J. (2013). *Changing course: Ten years of tracking online education in the United States.* Sloan Consortium.

Brown, M., McCormack, M., Reeves, J., Brooks, D. C., Grajek, S., Alexander, B., Bali, M., Bulger, S., Dark, S., Engelbert, N., Gannon, K., Gauthier, A., Gibson, D., Gibson, R., Lundin, B., Veletsianos, G. & Weber, N. (2020). *2020 Educause horizon report teaching and learning edition.* Educause.

León-Martínez, J, & Tapia-Rangel, E. (2020). Building new spaces for education throughout life, Aprendo+ courses. *Proceedings of the EDEN 2020 Annual Conference,* pp. 398-402. https://doi.org/10.38069/edenconf-2020-ac0038

National Autonomous University of Mexico. (2020). Plan de Desarrollo Institucional 2019-2023. https://www.rector.unam.mx/doctos/PDI2019-2023.pdf

National Autonomous University of Mexico. Coordinación de Universidad Abierta, Innovación Educativa y Educación a Distancia. (2023). Aprendo+. En línea de todo y para todos. https://aprendomas.cuaed.unam.mx/

Mihai, O. I. (2021, January). Self-education and lifelong learning. *Proceedings of the 8th International Conference on Education and Education of Social Sciences*, pp. 220-223. https://doi.org/10.51508/intcess.2021157

Miranda, A. & Tirado, F. (2012). Las nuevas universidades. El fenómeno de comunidades de aprendizaje en línea. *Revista de la Educación Superior, XLI*(4)(164), 9-33

Ramírez Montoya, M. S. (2013). Casos de formación e investigación en el área del movimiento educativo abierto en Latinoamérica: alcances, retos y oportunidades. In P. Canto (coords.), *Educación a distancia y tecnologías de la información y comunicación* (pp. 113-126). Unas letras industria editorial.

Razo, D. (2020). El renacimiento de los cursos en línea en la era del COVID-19. https://observatorio.tec.mx/edu-news/cursos-online-pospandemia/

Sánchez Mendiola, M. (2022). La Universidad Nacional Autónoma de México y la educación en la pandemia: respuestas, estrategias y retos. In R. J. Mercado del Collado & A. D. Otero Escobar (coords.), Háblame de TIC: Enseñanza remota de emergencia en la educación superior: ¿Base para la educación híbrida? (pp. 29-51). Brujas Editorial.

Seud, G. (2022). Coursera y la plataformización de la educación: operación de mercados, datificación y gobernanza. *Transdigital, 3*(5), 1-24. https://doi.org/10.56162/transdigital95

Tobón, S., Pimienta, J., & García, J. A. (2010). *Secuencias didácticas: aprendizaje y evaluación de competencias*. Pearson-Prentice Hall.

Torres Velandia, S. A. (2021). Recursos educativos abiertos y políticas institucionales en universidades públicas mexicanas: estudio de caso. *Revista Iberoamericana para la Investigación y el Desarrollo Educativo, 12*(22). https://doi.org/10.23913/ride.v11i22.865

WHAT DOES CBL, ESD AND SAP SPELL? ACTIVELY ENGAGED STUDENTS WHO LEARN. (THE BENEFITS OF USING A CHALLENGE BASED LEARNING (CBL), AN EDUCATION FOR SUSTAINABLE DEVELOPMENT (ESD) AND A STUDENT AS PARTNERS (SAP) APPROACH IN EDUCATION)

Monica Ward, DCU, Ireland

***Correspondence**: Monica Ward: monica.ward@dcu.ie*

Abstract

This paper looks at the integration of Challenge Based Learning (CBL), Education for Sustainable Development (ESD) and Student Partnership into a module underpinned by the Sustainable Development Goals (SDGs) for computing students. It provides a brief overview of Challenge Based Learning and outlines the three phases of the approach (Engage, Investigate and Act). It explains the approach to integrating Education for Sustainable Development (ESD) as a core element of the module, rather than an add-on element. It describes how the Students as Partners (SaP) approach was a key component of the module, whereby students were given the opportunity to choose the challenges they wished to address as well as submission formats. It shows how digital technologies underpinned the module to provide a coherent and beneficial learning experience for students. This paper highlights the feedback from students on this innovative approach to learning and some suggestions for others considering adopting this approach.

Keywords:

Challenge Based Learning, Education for Sustainable Development, Student Partnership, innovative teaching.

Introduction

Education should be informative, engaging and beneficial to learners, but it can be hard to achieve this for many reasons. Learners want active, authentic and meaningful learning experiences, but it can be difficult to provide them in certain traditional and institutional contexts. When things get innovative, things get messy and it can be difficult to envision how these innovations will work in practice. There are big challenges facing education - how to engage learners, how to ensure that they learn, how to enable them to become lifelong learners, how to ensure academic integrity in authentic and meaningful learning contexts. There are even bigger challenges facing society, including the need to address the Sustainable Development Goals (SDGs https://sdgs.un.org/goals). This paper provides an overview of how it is possible to give students creative, challenging and beneficial learning experiences with the use of digital technologies combined with a Challenge Based Learning (CBL) approach imbued with an Education for Sustainable Development (EDS) lens and having the students as active participants in their own learning. There are challenges but the opportunities outweigh them and it is worthwhile to adopt these innovative approaches for a better future from both an educational and sustainable perspective.

Background

Challenge Based Learning

Challenge Based Learning has been an approach that has been used since 2002 (Birol et al, 2002). While there is no one agreed definition, the definition by Malmqvist et al. (2015) encapsulates the essence of the approach. They define CBL as a learning approach where learning occurs via the identification, analysis and design of a solution to a sociotechnical problem. While there are some similarities, CBL differs from Project Based Learning and Problem Based Learning in that the solution is not known in advance, the process and not just the final product is important and there is an emphasis on sustainability. In their literature review of CBL, Gallagher and Savage (2020) identified eight characteristics of CBL. These are challenge definition, global themes, real-world challenges, technology, flexibility, multidisciplinary and innovation and creativity. Not all CBL experiences will have all of these characteristics, but most CBL experiences will include most of them as far as possible. One of the main CBL frameworks is the Challenge Learning Framework (Challenge Learning, 2018) which has three interconnected phases: Engage, Investigate and Act.

Education for Sustainable Development

2005-2014 was declared by the United Nations to be the Decade for Education for Sustainable Development (ESD). ESD encompasses the environment, economy and society. It aims to ensure that learners have the relevant knowledge, skills and dispositions and values to enable them to become active contributors to a more sustainable future. ESD is a complex topic and one that must take the local context and culture into consideration. Huckle and Wals (2015) report that the decade was idealistic and did not achieve what it set out to achieve. In some ways, this is to be expected, given the complexity of the topic. However, it is important to continue to integrate ESD into educational systems. McKeown et al. (2002) provide a very accessible overview of ESD. They outline the need to reorient education and the need to address knowledge, skills, perspectives, values, and issues in a formal curriculum.

Students as Partners

Students as Partners refers to activity engaging students in all aspects of the learning process from the design of the curriculum, how teaching and learning takes place and assessment design. Student choice and the concept of co-creation is very important. Mercer-Mapstone et al., (2017) provide a good overview of the topic of students as partners in Higher Education. Harrington et al. (2014) note that engaging students and staff effectively as partners in the learning process is one of the key issues facing higher education in the 21st century. Respect, reciprocity, and shared responsibility in learning and teaching are key principles in student partnership (Felten et al., 2014). One area of focus in the research literature to date is of student partnership activities at the undergraduate level, and focused on teaching and learning enhancement. Research shows that with a student partnership module, there is increased student engagement and self-efficacy and staff can gain new insights that can improve their teaching (Mercer-Mapstone et al., 2017). While it can be difficult to achieve full partnership across all aspects of teaching, learning and assessment, it is important to give students some control and ownership over their learning. The degree to which this is feasible and achievable will depend on the local context and is something that takes time to develop.

Methodology and Approach

Many modules are designed with the content as the main focus. This is understandable as the module designers are subject matter experts and their module is part of a larger programme that should deliver a comprehensive and coherent learning experience for students. "Content is king" is a phrase that comes to mind in this regard. It is not often that educators get a chance to develop a module from the beginning that focusses on combining innovative teaching approaches to create an enjoyable and beneficial sustainable development learning experience for students. The module [name redacted] is delivered to final year computing students and focusses on how technology can be used to address the SDGs. A student partnership approach underpinned the module, with students being given choice on the SDG they wanted to address as well as the regular discussions about the topics covered in the module. The module follows the three phases of CBL: Engage, Investigate and Act.

Challenge Based Learning – Engage Phase

In the Engage phase, students are introduced to the concept and approach of CBL, so that they can understand the unknown nature of the module. They learn about the SDGs, which they have not encountered before on their programme. They also learn about innovative and potentially disruptive technologies that could help to address the SDGs. Resources are provided on the VLE (Moodle) along with some HP5 quizzes for self-assessment. The Engage phase ends with a blitz where the students have a chance to select which SDG they want to focus on and a general subtopic within that goal that they would like to address. The board feature on Moodle is used to enable students to see what SDGs are popular with the class and to post some ideas of possible topics for investigation. The students self-coalesce in a group by the end of the blitz and this is their group for the rest of the module.

Challenge Based Learning – Investigate Phase

In the Investigate phase, the students have an opportunity to learn about emerging technologies that might be used to address their chosen SDG. There are master classes on a variety of topics, most of which are new to the students. These classes cover both technical and non-technical topics so students can consider the potential ethical, psychological and society impacts of any proposed technical solution. Some of the master classes are delivered online, and there is extensive use made of Moodle boards to showcase group progress and provide feedback on a weekly basis.

Challenge Based Learning –Act Phase

In the Act phase, students come up with their proposed solution. In this module, they have to produce an artefact for their chosen client. In an ideal scenario, there would be a real-world external client, but in this case, students decide who their real-world client would be. For example, a group looking at a technical solution to micro plastics in European waters, might have the European Commissioner for Environment, Oceans and Fisheries as their client. Students can decide what their artefact is, but in general, it is usually a project report. Some students also submit an infographic, a podcast or a video along with their report. Students also do an Interactive Oral assessment (Sotiriadou et al., 2020) at the end of the module, where they get to engage in a discussion with their real-world client (a role assumed by the module coordinator). Students are also required to submit a group technical report and an individual module reflection at the end of the module.

Digital Technology

Digital technology plays an important role in this module. It is used to provide access to resources, submission of assignments and live webinars throughout all phases of the module. Extensive use is made of Moodle boards which allow students to give their opinions on different topics and enable both the students and module coordinator to see progress across the semester. Vevox (vevox.com) is used for quizzes throughout the module to gauge students' knowledge before teaching a topic so that known areas are briefly reviewed and unknown areas are explored in greater depth. Vevox quizzes are also used to get anonymous student feedback at the midpoint of the module. Students work in groups in face-to-face sessions and online synchronously and asynchronously. They develop (digital) resources throughout the lifetime of the module and they use a range of digital tools and apps for regular group communication.

Results and Discussion

This module has been delivered twice, in 2021 and 2022. In both years, the module followed the engage, investigate and act phases of CBL. This module is an optional module for students and in both years around 80% of the students (36 and 42 respectively) have chosen the module. Many aspects of the module are novel for the students. They would not have experienced CBL before. Up to this point in their education, the students would only have been familiar with modules with known or expected solutions to assignments and assessments. The concept of an unknown solution can be challenging for them.

This module could not incorporate all aspects of ESD but there was a strong focus on the SDGs throughout the module. Somewhat surprisingly, they were unfamiliar with the SDGs. There is an image in the public's consciousness that 'young' people are very engaged with the issues surrounding climate change, but the experience to date on this module is that they are unaware of the other SDGs. The students would have mainly focussed on technical and information management topics in their education prior to this module. The incorporation of ethical, psychological and societal considerations into their (technical) recommendations was novel for the students.

On this programme, students have very limited choice over the modules they take and the topics of their assessments. This is one of the few modules where they can choose the topic and how they want to submit their work. Initially, students feel a bit uncertain about this, but it has worked well so far. Students are more invested in their learning and it is also more interesting for the other students and the module coordinator as they get to learn more about different topics.

Individual and Group Assessment

It is always important to have a balance between individual assessments and group assessments in a CBL module. Individual assignments enable the student to demonstrate their own knowledge and thinking on a particular topic. Group assignments are more natural in the CBL context as the students should all be working towards the same goal across the duration of the semester. There is always the issue of free riders in group activities and students who work hard on the group activity always feel aggrieved when those who have not contributed get the same marks as those who do. The regular weekly check-ins with the students and the record of their interactions with the VLE and other technology tools (e.g. Google docs) enabled the module coordinator to monitor individual student contributions to the group project. While most group members have received the same grade for group work, students have been given different marks for the group component when there was a lesser contribution from certain group members.

Student Feedback

Although the feedback from students in the first year of delivery (2021) was generally positive, the students said they would like more clarity at the start of the module, particularly in regards to assignments and the overall approach to assessment. Some of the issues relating to this stemmed from the fact that the module coordinator was new to the CBL approach and there was an evolving of expectations as the module progressed. This issue was addressed in the second delivery of the module (2022).

At the end of the module, students were asked to reflect on collaborative situations, CBL and assessment and feedback in the module. The feedback reported here is from the 2022 cohort, but the feedback from the 2021 cohort was broadly similar. 86% of the students (36 out of 42 students) did a reflection and most students submitted a report, while others submitted slides, podcasts, and videos. The students were honest and open - one student recorded three separate audio files, one for each component - the last one was around five minutes, the other two were almost 15 minutes each.

Students were happy to use technology for collaboration throughout the module. One student remarked that "... *sharing documents and presentations through google was how all of the projects were completed, this was incredibly helpful as everyone could work on their own time at their own pace.... we wouldn't have been able to complete our projects without them*". Students liked the CBL approach. They reported that "*A lot of college can be theory work, which is important to know but I think that a CBL approach is more beneficial when it comes to implementing knowledge from college into the real world and the workplace.*" . They also noted that it enabled them to "actively engage with their learning". One student said that CBL "*clearly facilitated the enrichment of my knowledge gained during my projects.*", while another noted that "*it encouraged me to think critically and creatively*".

In relation to assessment, the feedback from the students was also positive. Students reported that a closed-book, timed, invigilated exam would not have been appropriate for the module. According to one student, "*In my opinion, timed, closed-book exams are not a testament to what you learnt in a subject, given the pressure, nor would an exam indicate the personal impact the CBL had.*" and another student agreed with this sentiment - "*I also feel that continuous assessment provides a clearer and more accurate representation of my knowledge and understanding*". The positive benefits of Moodle boards were also noted by one student "[*the Moodle] boards ensured that our group engaged in discussions revolving around our topics. These discussions were often then brought to the class, where our lecturer could provide feedback that could help alter the direction of our project.*"

Staff

Mercer-Mapstone et al. (2018) note that often the literature on student partnership is student-focussed and there is a need for more research on the staff aspect. The experience of this module is that it is challenging, enlightening and invigorating for staff. Challenging because 'control' is shared between the academic and the students. Enlightening because it can show the academic what students can do when correctly supported. Invigorating because students' enthusiasm to learn can remind the academic of what education can be and re-invigorate their pedagogy of job philosophy.

Limitations

This module has only been delivered twice and there are elements that need to be enhanced in order for the module to be truly a CBL module. There are two main components that would strengthen the module. The first is the involvement of real-world stakeholders. Instead of the students producing their solution artefact for an external client that they will not actually interact with, it would be ideal if they could work with a real client who is intrinsically interested in the challenge. This is difficult to achieve and the issue of parity would be very important - would the students with an actual external stakeholder have an unfair advantage over students who did not? This would be something that needs to be addressed in future.

The second enhancement would be to include students from other disciplines into the module. In the two iterations to date, the students have all been from the same programme. However, it is planned that students from different disciplines will take the module in future years and it will be interesting to see how the students interact and learn together to produce their proposed solutions.

Suggestions

There are four main suggestions for others considering using this approach of combining a CBL, ESD and a Students as Partners approach in their teaching. The first is to familiarise oneself with the literature on CBL, learn from others who have used a CBL approach and decide on how best it will fit with the module in the local context. The second is to leverage the existing resources available in the institution and across academic networks, particularly in relation to speakers for the master classes. Many academics and researchers are happy to talk about their areas of expertise with students and this usually makes for an engaging and interesting learning experience. The third suggestion is to use technology extensively throughout the module - it makes things much easier for students and staff, it enhances flexibility and gives students the opportunity to learn key transversal and transferable skills in a safe environment. The fourth and final suggestion is to just go for it. It can be daunting for an academic who is used to having control over a module and being a subject matter expert, to cede control over to students and not know the answers to questions that students might ask. However, it can be a rewarding and rich experience. If the students are being asked to step into the unknown, the module coordinator should also walk with them on this journey.

Conclusion

People can sometimes feel deflated when they consider the challenges of the SDGs. Academics can feel overwhelmed at the difficulties in integrating ESD into their modules in an interesting and coherent manner. Experience to date indicates that staff are interested in this multifaceted approach, but they are slightly concerned about how to go about it and would like to learn more about a real world example. While there are limitations in this case study, it is important to show others what can be done and that it is possible to transform learning. The approach adopted in this case study to weave CBL, EDS and student partnership approaches into a beneficial and enjoyable learning experience for students and staff demonstrates the art of the possible in this space and interesting approaches for future education.

References

Birol, G., McKenna, A., Giorgio, T., & Brophy, S. (2002, June). Implementation of educational modules in a biotechnology course: *A challenge based education approach*. In 2002 Annual Conference (pp. 7-632).

Challenge Learning, 2018. *Challenge Based Learning Framework*. https://www.challengebasedlearning.org/framework/

Felten, P., Cook-Sather, A., & Bovill, C. (2014). *Engaging students as partners in learning and teaching: A guide for faculty*. John Wiley & Sons.

Gallagher, S. E., & Savage, T. (2020). Challenge-based learning in higher education: an exploratory literature review. *Teaching in Higher Education*, 1-23.

Harrington, K., Flint, A., & Healey, M. (2014). *Engagement through partnership: Students as partners in learning and teaching in higher education*. Other. Higher Education Academy, York, UK. http://repository.londonmet.ac.uk/5176/

Huckle, J., & Wals, A. E. (2015). The UN Decade of Education for Sustainable Development: business as usual in the end. *Environmental Education Research*, 21(3), 491-505.

McKeown, R., Hopkins, C. A., Rizi, R., & Chrystalbridge, M. (2002). *Education for sustainable development toolkit* (p. 2002). Knoxville: Energy, Environment and Resources Center, University of Tennessee.

Mercer-Mapstone, L., Dvorakova, S. L., Matthews, K. E., Abbot, S., Cheng, B., Felten, P., ... & Swaim, K. (2017). A systematic literature review of students as partners in higher education. *International Journal for Students as Partners*.

Sotiriadou, P., Logan, D., Daly, A. & Guest, R. (2020) 'The role of authentic assessment to preserve academic integrity and promote skill development and employability', *Studies in Higher Education*, 45(11), 2132-2148. 10.1080/03075079.2019.1582015

A TYPOLOGY FOR OER BUSINESS MODELS

Robert Farrow, The Open University, UK

Correspondence: *Robert Farrow: rob.farrow@open.ac.uk*

Abstract

This paper provides an update on activity in the innovation and business models strand of the ENCORE+ project. A range of business models that support or draw on open educational resources (OER) have been proposed. This paper reviews models that have been proposed (Tlili et al., 2020; Padilla Rodriguez et al., 2018; Belleflamme & Jacqmin, 2015; Ubachs & Konings, 2016; and Farrow, 2019) and suggests a synthesis into one typology of OER business models. The ENCORE+ OER Business Model Typology has been developed as part of a wider effort to understand and evaluate economically sustainable approaches to OER as well as to formulate OER value propositions for different stakeholders. In related work, a range of OER innovation case studies (N=48) are being prepared for publication. These will illustrate different instances of innovation with OER and show how OER actors understand their value proposition to different audiences.

Keywords:

Open Educational Resources (OER) – Open Educational Practices – (OEP) – Innovation – Evaluation – Business Models – Sustainability

Introduction

The European Network for Catalysing Open Resources in Education (ENCORE+, n.d.) is a pan-European Knowledge Alliance funded under the Erasmus+ programme. The project is running from 2021 to 2023 to support the modernisation of education in the European area through open educational resources (OER). OER are "teaching, learning and research materials in any medium, digital or otherwise, that reside in the public domain or have been released under an open license that permits no-cost access, use, adaptation and redistribution by others with no or limited restrictions" (UNESCO, n.d.).

One key strand ENCORE+ of work pertains to OER innovation and OER business models. ENCORE+ works with diverse stakeholder base to identify, synthesise and share strategies and business models across business and higher education. The pedagogical value of OER is now well established and OER can support improved learner performance and pedagogical innovation (Weller et al., 2015; Hilton, 2016); however, awareness of OER in the business world is very low and there are few business models that truly leverage the affordances of open licences (BizMOOC, 2019). This paper reports on the development of the conceptual framework being used in the ENCORE+ network to describe and discuss different approaches to OER business models and sustainability.

OER business models: the search for sustainability

Several recent papers and studies have articulated different archetypal business models for OER. This section describes outcomes from these studies. Konkol et al. (2021) recently wrote about OER business models and sustainability. They frame this in terms of what they call the paradox '"that generating revenue out of OER is not intended, but ignoring income can make OER unsustainable". This reflects the tension between traditional models based around competition and newer, "open" paradigms based around collaboration. Konkol et al. (2021) propose the following business models relevant to OER:

- The *Selling course experience model* or "Freemium" model where educational materials (e.g., slides, texts, data) are offered for free. Sustainability here is derived from income streams offered alongside this, such as answering questions, giving feedback on submissions, supervising research and examination, and certification.

- In the *Governmental model,* national and international governmental agencies provide funding for creating OER. This (along with philanthropy) is how a lot of OER has traditionally been funded but is rather dependent on the political and strategic priorities of those outside the business itself.

- Operating in a similar fashion but at a smaller scale, the *Institutional model* sees higher education providers set aside some part of their budget for OER programmes. This is often implemented in ways that are consistent with the philosophy of open, but again involves competition for scarce resources without much in the way of longer term capacity building. There is also the risk that strategic priorities can change quickly.

- The *Online Programme model* is realised by extending presence-based education to online or blended courses. This content is typically only accessed by registered students rather than being truly "open". This approach has perhaps become more common with the pivot to online education resulting from the Covid-19 pandemic.

- The *Substitution model* which sees cost savings from redundant services (e.g. obsolete systems) being redirected towards OER programmes.

- In the *Community-based model,* the members of an OER community or network collaboratively create and use OER. Revenue can be generated by hosting the required infrastructure or charging for related activity.

- The *Donations model* involves donations from, e.g., foundations, society, industry, government, or non-governmental agencies. This form of funding is very dependent on external sources and can be seen as a scaled down version of the philanthropic model with obvious risks – but could still work in the case of, for example, significant endowments.

- In the *Institutional subscriptions model,* the provider makes educational materials accessible to institutions who subscribed as paying members (Okoli and Wang, 2015). Individuals who are part of these institutions can access the materials.

- Along similar lines we have the *Sponsorship/Advertising model* which relies on generating revenue by exposing students to commercial messages. Perceived by many to be both unethical and antithetical to the goals of education, this model also raises questions about what is involved in the transaction between educator, learner and sponsor as well as the metrics by which success is evaluated.

- Perhaps somewhere between the community and revenue based models we find the *Membership model* which relies on organisations contributing to the university with money, services, and goods in exchange for privileges such as early access to roadmap decisions and code releases. This requires a good fit between the priorities of the university/business and those of the sponsor over time in order to be sustainable.

- The *Selling data model* generates revenue by selling data about the activities of those using a learning environment

- The *Consultancy, training, and support model* sees institutions offer professional services around the use of OER

- Finally we have the *Author pays model* where publishers generate revenue by charging content creators (as in the case of article processing charges, for instance). (Approaches like this have been seen to favour those who have access to funding and discriminate against less established professionals or those from areas where less funding is structurally available.)

Tlili et al. (2020) report on the outcomes of a Delphi study. They propose the following 10 OER Business Models:

- Through *Internal funding* of higher educational institutions
- Leveraging *Sustainable OER networks* to reduce costs
- Through *Public funding*
- Based on *Endowments and donations*
- Offering *Services to learners*
- Offering learning-related *Data to companies*
- Producing *OER on demand* as an area of entrepreneurship
- Relying on the voluntary efforts of *OER authors*
- Relying on other *Stakeholder communities* to provide labour or services

Belleflamme & Jacqmin (2015:155-162) suggest the essential features of six potential business models based around offering services around OER content:

- *Platformization* (e.g. MOOCs) facilitates interactions between stakeholders and subsides the participation of each side
- The *Certification model* sees charges made for certification of learning with OER. This retains the degree as the prestige qualification and makes evenues depend on completion, not enrolment.
- The *Freemium model* often sees free learning followed by paid content, and monetary benefits may be hard to calculate (Littlejohn & Hood, 2018:104).
- The *Advertising model* offers an online route to monetization but potentially at the cost of negative effects on learning; brand,
- A *Job matching model* could use user data to address asymmetry in job market information (c.f. GMV Conseil, 2018) although continuous monitoring raises privacy concerns and the approach is still largely unproven in practice.
- The *Subcontractor model* outsources some core HEI function to MOOC platform

Padilla Rodriguez et al. (2018:2) review five business models for MOOC

- *Integration with mainstream education* (supplementary courses; upselling; offering credits; additional services).
- A *Freemium approach* with charges for additional services such as examination.
- *Partnerships with enterprises* such as with a focus on human resource development)
- *Involvement of target audience* communities through peer assessment, moderation, support to reduce costs
- *Philanthropy* where funding is provided by charity/foundation/NGO/government

This page intentionally left blank.

ENCORE+ OER Business Model Typology

Existing attempts to describe OER business models are diffuse and unsystematic, with overlapping concepts. The introduction of a consistent typology is a route to amelioration and understanding (Doty & Glick, 1994) as well as consistent language and terminology (Grant & Booth, 2009). Typologies are typically formed by grouping cases into types on the basis of common features (Stapley et al., 2022). This process is grounded in deduction but inevitably involves some subjective judgement in cases where the features of cases are qualitative and interpretative.

The ENCORE+ project has rationalised the above into 14 types organised into 4 categories below. Models are distinguished according to four categories. These categories are characterised by the revenue sources associated with a set of models: external to an organisation; internal to an organisation; funded by community; or service based models. The proposed typology is a synthesis of Tlili et al., 2020; Padilla Rodriguez et al., 2018; Belleflamme & Jacqmin, 2015; Ubachs & Konings, 2016; and Farrow, 2019 in that it draws on the findings of these studies to determine a set of characteristics, then reconstructs these. This typology is rational and consistent, accommodating the types identified in the literature more simply and without contradiction. The typology is made available on an open licence for others to use and comprises part of the OER Innovation Evaluation Framework used in the ENCORE+ project.

Table 1: ENCORE+ OER Business Model Typology

Category	**Business Model**	**Description**
Externally funded	*Donations Model*	Funding from donations or grants, e.g., foundations, society, industry, non-governmental agencies
	Governmental Model	National and international governmental agencies providing funding for OER
	Sponsorship / Advertising Model	Generating revenue by exposing learners to commercial messages
Internally funded	*Institutional Model*	Higher education providers setting aside some part of their budget for OER programmes
	Substitutions Model	Cost savings from redundant services (e.g. obsolete systems) are redirected towards OER programmes
	Author pays Model	Publishers generate revenue by charging content creators
Community funded	*Community based*	Members of a community or network collaboratively create and use OER, generating revenue through services and/or infrastructure
	Membership Model	The Membership model relies on organizations contributing to the OER provider with money, services and/or goods

	Platformization	Organises stakeholders around a digital ecosystem, facilitating interaction and generating insights
Higher Education Service Models	*Data Exploitation Model*	Generates revenue by selling analytic data about the activities of those using a learning environment
	Dual-Mode University	Use of OER in an online course (e.g. Massive Open Online Course) to develop a distance learning or virtual university operation
	Freemium	Educational materials are offered for free and sustainability is derived from subsequent income streams offered alongside this (e.g. assessment or access to a larger curriculum)
	Online Programme	Extending presence-based education to online or blended courses
	Segmentation Model	Commercializing a service relating to OER (such as printing open textbooks; providing assessment or certification of learning)

Understanding OER Innovation

Another ENCORE+ activity strand has audited innovation related behaviours for a range of organisations that use OER. OER is of course an innovation in teaching and learning practice, but the practices associated with using OER can themselves be a foundation for further innovation (Coughlan et al., 2019). This potential is often overlooked for being highly contextual or marginal to the key focus of OER initiatives, yet the culture of innovation that exists alongside many OER projects and in the practice of open educators is a key attraction for many working in the field.

More than OER innovation 40 case studies have been prepared and a selection of these will be presented with a critical commentary in the summer of 2023. Alongside this, the related evaluation framework is being shared on an open licence for others to use and better understand the role of innovation in their own OER practice. The ENCORE+ OER Business Model Typology is part of the evaluation frameworks and data is being collected to map real life examples of each business model type. These achievements build on various aspects of theoretical work conducted in the last two years (Farrow & Granly, 2021; Farrow, 2022) as well as a series of face-to-face and online stakeholder events conducted within or as part of the ENCORE+ network.

References

Belleflamme, P. & Jacqmin, J. (2015). An Economic Appraisal of MOOC Platforms: Business Models and Impacts on Higher Education. *CESifo Economic Studies*, Volume 62, Issue 1, 1 March 2016, Pages 148–169, https://doi.org/10.1093/cesifo/ifv016

BizMOOC. Massive Open Online Courses for Business Learning. https://moocbook.pressbooks.com/

Coughlan, T., Pitt, R. & Farrow, R. (2019) Forms of innovation inspired by open educational resources: a post-project analysis. *Open Learning: The Journal of Open, Distance and e-Learning*, 34:2, 156-175. https://doi.org/10.1080/02680513.2018.1552579

Doty, D. H., & Glick, W. H. (1994). Typologies as a Unique Form of Theory Building: Toward Improved Understanding and Modeling. *The Academy of Management Review*, 19(2), 230–251. https://doi.org/10.2307/258704

ENCORE+ (n.d.). European Network for Catalysing Open Resources in Education. https://encoreproject.eu/

Farrow, R. (2022). A Framework for Understanding Innovation with OER. Open Education Global 2022. Université de Nantes, France. https://pretalx.com/oeglobal2022/talk/QYVRCM/

Farrow, R. (2019). Massive Open Online Courses for Employability, Innovation and Entrepreneurship: a Rapid Assessment of Evidence. EMC-LM Project. CC-BY 4.0. https://emc.eadtu.eu/images/publications_and_outputs/EMC-LM_WP1_REA_Report_v.1_web.pdf

Farrow, R. & Granly, J. (2021). Building the 21st Century OER Ecosystem. Open Education 2021. https://www.slideshare.net/robertfarrow/building-the-21st-century-oer-ecosystem

Geser, G., Schön, S., & Ebner, M. (2019). Business models for Open Educational Resources: how to exploit OER after a funded project? In *EdMedia+ Innovate Learning* (pp. 1537-1543). Association for the Advancement of Computing in Education (AACE).

Gilliot, J.-M. & Bruillard, É. (2018). Recherches actuelles sur les MOOC. Sciences et Technologies de l'Information et de la Communication pour l'Éducation et la Formation, ATIEF, 2018. https://hal-imt-atlantique.archives-ouvertes.fr/hal01802224/document

Grant, M.J. and Booth, A. (2009), A typology of reviews: an analysis of 14 review types and associated methodologies. *Health Information & Libraries Journal,* 26: 91-108. https://doi.org/10.1111/j.1471-1842.2009.00848.x

Hilton III, J. (2016). Open educational resources and college textbook choices: a review of research on efficacy and perceptions. *Educational Technology Research and Development.* http://link.springer.com/article/10.1007/s11423-016-9434-9/fulltext.html

King, M., Pegrum, M., & Forsey, M. (2018). MOOCs and OER in the Global South: Problems and Potential. *The International Review of Research in Open and Distributed Learning,* 19(5). http://www.irrodl.org/index.php/irrodl/article/view/3742

Konkol, M., Jager-Ringoir, K. & Zurita-Milla, R. (2021): Open Educational Resources – Basic concepts, challenges, and business models. Faculty of Geo-Information Science and Earth Observation (ITC), University of Twente. DOI: 10.5281/zenodo.4789124

Littlejohn, A. and Hood, N. (2018) *Reconceptualising Learning in the Digital Age: the (Un)democratising of Learning.* Singapore: Springer.

McAndrew, P. and Farrow, R. (2013). Open education research: from the practical to the theoretical. In: McGreal, Rory; Kinuthia, Wanjira and Marshall, Stewart eds. *Open Educational Resources: Innovation, Research and Practice.* Vancouver, Canada: Commonwealth of Learning and Athabasca University, pp. 65–78.

Padilla Rodriguez, B.C., Armellini, A. & de la Garza Escamilla, S.L. (2018). Sustainability of Massive Open Online Courses (MOOCs): Beyond Business Models. In T. Bastiaens, J. Van Braak, M. Brown, L. Cantoni, M. Castro, R. Christensen, G. Davidson-Shivers, K. DePryck, M. Ebner, M. Fominykh, C. Fulford, S. Hatzipanagos, G. Knezek, K. Kreijns, G. Marks, E. Sointu, E. Korsgaard Sorensen, J. Viteli, J. Voogt, P. Weber, E. Weippl & O. Zawacki-Richter (Eds.), *Proceedings of EdMedia: World Conference on Educational Media and Technology* (pp. 1641-1647). Amsterdam, Netherlands: Association for the Advancement of Computing in Education (AACE). https://www.learntechlib.org/primary/p/184391/

Rothe, H., Täuscher, K. & Basole, R. (2018). Competition between platform ecosystems: a longitudinal study of MOOC platforms. *Twenty-Sixth European Conference on Information Systems* (ECIS2018), Portsmouth, UK.

Slavova, M. (2017). Lessons Learned from the Development and Implementation of MOOC in Digital and Social Media Marketing. *Bulgarian Journal of Business Research* (22), pp.56-63. https://www.ceeol.com/search/article-detail?id=559144

Stapley, E., O'Keeffe, S., & Midgley, N. (2022). Developing Typologies in Qualitative Research: The Use of Ideal-type Analysis. *International Journal of Qualitative Methods*, 21. https://doi.org/10.1177/16094069221100633

Tlili, A., Nascimbeni, F., Burgos, D., Zhang, X., Huang, R., & Chang, T. W. (2020). The evolution of sustainability models for Open Educational Resources: insights from the literature and experts. *Interactive Learning Environments,* 1-16.

UNESCO (n.d.). Open Educational Resources. https://www.unesco.org/en/open-educational-resources?hub=785

Weller, M., de los Arcos, B., Farrow, R., Pitt, B., & McAndrew, P. (2015). The Impact of OER on Teaching and Learning Practice. *Open Praxis,* *7*(4), 351-361. doi:10.5944/openpraxis.7.4.227

STUDENT PERCEPTIONS OF THE FIRST DIGITAL BADGING EXPERIENCE AT COSTA RICA'S STATE UNIVERSITY OF DISTANCE EDUCATION

Mario Barahona Quesada, Universidad Estatal a Distancia, Costa Rica

Adriana Cascante-Gatgens, Universidad Estatal a Distancia, Costa Rica

Maynor Barrientos Amador, Universidad Estatal a Distancia, Costa Rica

Correspondence: *Mario Barahona Quesada:mbarahona@uned.ac.cr*

Abstract

This full paper shows the perception of a group of students at the Costa Rica's State University of Distance Education, UNED, who received their first digital badge after participating in a course/workshop aimed at developing basic research skills. The course/workshop was offered by UNED's Student Observatory based on its ***Guide for formative research***. A questionnaire was designed consisting of close-ended and open-ended items. The instrument was built upon researchers' main concerns and upon insights from other studies on this topic available in the literature. After a revision process, the final version of the questionnaire included six demographic variables and 40 items to delve into particular dimensions of the students' experience with digital badges and skill development. Results show a considerable positive impact of the course/workshop content, methodology, tasks and evidence required on the motivation of students toward the development of research skills; data also shows that the used and implementation of digital badges increased students understanding of the value and importance of skills for labour markets.

Keywords:

Digital badges; micro-credentialing; skill; distance education; research

Introduction

The increasing development of online education has a significant impact on traditional teaching models, the management of the academic offer or products and services in higher education institutions around the world, and on the not-always-clear traditional distinctions between formal, non-formal and informal learning (Brown et al. 2020; Brown et al., 2021). In addition, there have been a rapidly change in the nature of labour markets, a growing uncertainty in future employment outlooks within the framework of the Fourth Industrial Revolution, and negative effects on the economy caused by worldwide contingency measures against COVID-19. As a consequence, there have been an exponential demand for flexible, open and accessible mechanisms for the development and acquisition of new skills and training in emerging knowledge-oriented fields to satisfy the immediate requirements of different productive sectors (Orr, Pupinis and Kirdulytė 2020). At the international level, the systematic incorporation of micro-credentials to academic products and services in higher education has been seen as a promising alternative to traditional credentials and certifications to respond to current challenges and to contribute to the human and economic development of contemporary societies. However, there are still questions about what micro-credentials should be defined, what degree of endorsement do they receive from the different social actors, and what quality assurance processes support them (Orr, Pupinis and Kirdulyte 2020).

In December 2020, the European Commission published *A European approach to micro-credentials*, a document that constitutes a first step on the path towards the widespread adoption of micro-credentials by EU higher education institutions and the creation of an Area of European Education by the year 2025. According to this proposal, a micro-credential will be understood as scalable evidence of the results obtained throughout a short learning experience (European Commission 2020). Since 2021, a team of the Universidad Estatal a Distancia of Costa Rica (UNED) has been working in collaboration with the National Institute for Digital Learning (NIDL) of the University of the City of Dublin in Ireland on a joint agenda to develop a framework for UNED and Costa Rica compatible with the European approximation that will allow UNED to design, implement and use micro-credentials in the short, medium and long term. It is expected that this framework will have a positive influence on different dimensions of the institutional and national delivery of higher education, and will enable the active participation of UNED in the global discussion on the latest trends in distance education. Through the adoption of micro-credentials, UNED expects to strengthen its digital transformation process, to generate an innovative offer of services and products, to promote further collaboration and mobility between UNED and the European Education Area, and to provide open and flexible opportunities for updating, requalification and lifelong learning credentialing at a time when the country faces high rates of unemployment and inequality (OECD 2021a, 2021b), an urgent economic recovery (PEN 2021a) and its worst educational crisis in several decades (PEN 2021b).

As part of this work, a first experience of micro-credentialed skills development was carried out at UNED through the implementation of digital badges in order to develop learning about the design and issuing of digital badges with a group of students from the institution related to UNED's Student Observatory. This first experience was carried out as part of the course/workshop *Research Kit*, aimed mainly at UNED's students, with the objective to bring the participants closer to basic but key concepts of the research process and to help students develop research skills and abilities. The course/workshop, includes activities and tasks related to the first stages of a research project including theme choice, problem statement, search for academic literature in databases, research justification and background, and the statement of a research objective, from a formative research approach. The workshop course/workshop aims to develop specific skills based on declarative, procedural and attitudinal competencies described in the *Guide for formative research of the UNED's Student Observatory* (Aguzzi, 2021).

The course/workshop was offered in an online format, in synchronous sessions through the Zoom platform, and was supported by readings, complementary materials, and the development of specific tasks and evidence. This course/workshop lasted 6 sessions. The participants dedicated a total of 20 hours to develop all the activities proposed (12 hours of synchronous session and 8 hours of asynchronous work). Once they completed all the activities satisfactorily, and according to the established deadlines, the participants received a digital badge as a micro-credential for 20 hours.

The purpose of this full paper is to show the feedback of the participants in the first course/workshop in relation to the use of digital badges and the research-related skills they were able to developed.

Method

Participants

Eighteen online learners (16 women, 2 men) between ages 21 and 55 ($M = 34.56$, $SD = 9.32$), who earned digital badges after successfully completing the course/workshop *Research Kit* at UNED, voluntarily and anonymously participated in the study. Eight respondents were undergraduates studying Education ($n = 6$), Business ($n = 1$), or Police Science ($n = 1$), whereas the remaining 10 respondents were graduates pursuing degrees in Education ($n = 4$), Business ($n = 2$), Police Sciences ($n = 1$), Engineering ($n = 1$), Law ($n = 1$), or Natural Resource Management ($n = 1$). Participants were distributed all over the country; 7 of them were based in rural areas of Costa Rica and the other 11 were living in urban areas.

Instrument

To investigate participants' understanding and perceptions of digital badges and their perception of research skills development, a questionnaire was designed consisting of close-ended and open-ended items. The instrument was built upon our concerns as researchers and upon insights from other studies on this topic available in the literature (Hartnett, 2021; Iwata et al., 2019; Piedra, 2021; Zhou et al., 2019). After a revision process, the final version of the questionnaire included six demographic variables and 40 items to delve into particular dimensions of the students' experience with digital badges and research skills development.

Procedure

After successfully completing course/workshop *Research Kit* activities and receiving their corresponding digital badges, a request for voluntary participation was sent by email to the all the students. A total of 18 students anonymously self-completed the questionnaire, which was made available online through UNED's *Lime Survey* platform. The data collection period took place between March 20 and 25, 2023.

Data Analysis

Given our target population size (N = 18) and to improve interpretability, we report all the study results using the response frequencies for each question in the instrument.

Results

Assessment of the course/workshop Research Kit

When asked about their previous knowledge in relation to the research skills needed for the course/workshop, most students did not feel sure or felt that did not have any previous knowledge at all. However, after developing the different tasks and delivering all the evidence required, students felt more motivated toward research in general, and reported having enhanced their level of skill development.

Table 1: Attitudes towards the contents of the course/workshop *Research Kit*

Item	Yes	No	Not sure
Before participating in the Research Kit Workshop, did you have any knowledge about the effective choice of research topics?	4	4	10
Before participating in the Research Kit Workshop, did you have any knowledge about the correct approach to a research problem?	6	4	8
Before participating in the Research Kit Workshop, did you have any knowledge about the development of a justification for a research problem?	4	4	10
Before participating in the Research Kit Workshop, did you have any knowledge about the development of a background for a research problem?	6	5	7
Before participating in the Research Kit Workshop, did you have any knowledge about the effective search for bibliographic references in research?	4	2	12
Before participating in the Research Kit Workshop, did you have any knowledge about the correct approach to a research aim?	2	3	13
Do you consider that the evidence collection strategy used to assess your learning during the Research Kit Workshop were effective?	18	0	0

Note. $N = 18$.

Table 2: Motivation towards research skills development

Item	Highly motivated	Somewhat motivated	Poorly motivated
Did the activities carried out in each step of the *Research Kit* motivated you towards the development of research skills?	15	2	1

Note. $N = 18$.

Table 3: Perceived positive aspects of the course/workshop *Research Kit*

Positive aspects	n	%
Increase in motivation towards the research process	13	22.41
Increase in interest in participating in research experiences	13	22.41
Development of research skills not enhanced until that moment	12	20.69
The work methodology applied during the workshop	11	18.97
The reference material used during the workshop	9	15.52

Note. $N = 18$.

Most students reported positively on the quality of the course/workshop, and most of them highlighted the methodology used as innovative. They found the tasks required as effective and logically connected to the topics and skills developed.

Understanding of digital badges

Only two of the participants in the study had knowledge about digital badges and had earned at least one before taking the course/workshop *Research Kit*.

Future use of digital badges

When asked about the future use of the digital badges they have earned through the course/workshop, 14 students reported that they will include the badge into their CV or résumé; 11 respondents mentioned that they will include the link to the badge when applying for a job; 10 of them indicated that they will include the badge into their LinkedIn profile; 6 participants said that they will include the badge into their profile in other social networks (not LinkedIn); and 2 learners were unsure about how to use their digital badges in the future.

Table 4: Intended future uses for digital badges

Digital badge use	*n*	%
I will include the badge into my CV or résumé.	14	32.56
I will include the link to the badge when applying for a job.	11	25.58
I will include the badge into my LinkedIn profile.	10	23.26
I will include the badge into my profile in other social networks (not LinkedIn).	6	13.95
I am not sure about how I will use the badge.	2	4.65

Note. N = 18.

Impact of digital badges

On a 4-point scale, we asked participants about the degree of motivation and impact that they associate with this digital badging experience. The 18 learners mentioned they were highly (n = 14) or somewhat (n = 4) motivated during the course/workshop activities given the possibility to earn the digital badge. Furthermore, all students considered that the badge will have a major (n = 14) or moderate (n = 4) impact in their future academic or professional development.

Interest in earning further digital badges

All respondents indicated that they will be interested in earning new digital badges in the future. Eight students gave also additional reasons for their interest in digital badges, such as further personal and career development (n = 4), showcasing newly acquired skills (n = 3), or upskilling (n = 1).

Perceived value of digital badges

When asked about the strengths perceived in digital badges as proofs of learning outcomes, participants considered that digital badges increase motivation in the learning process (n = 15); interest in participating in learning experiences (n = 13); and that they allow recognition of digital learning (n = 13), skill development (n = 12), professional development (n = 10), academic achievements (n = 9), formal learning (n = 6), and non-formal learning (n = 1); and that they are easy to share (n = 11), to store (n = 10), and to showcase (n = 7).

Table 5: Perceived strengths of digital badges

Strength	n	%
Increase motivation in the learning process	15	14.02%
Increase interest in participating in learning experiences	13	12.15%
Allow recognition of digital learning	13	12.15%
Allow recognition of skills development	12	11.21%
Easy to share	11	10.28%
Easy to store	10	9.35%
Allow recognition of professional development	10	9.35%
Allow recognition of academic achievements	9	8.41%
Easy to showcase	7	6.54%
Allow recognition of formal learning	6	5.61%
Allow recognition of non-formal learning	1	0.93%

Note. N = 18.

Challenges for digital badges

Regarding the challenges that digital badges might face in the near future as proofs of learning outcomes, respondents indicated that they perceive, as major concerns, the lack of understanding (n = 12), formal recognition (n = 8), credibility (n = 7), regulation (n = 3), and visibility (n = 3). Additionally, some students mentioned that they prefer printed certificates (n = 2), that the use of digital badges seems inconsistent (n = 2), or that they simply don't know enough about the topic (n = 3).

Table 6: Perceived challenges for digital badges

Challenge	n	%
Lack of understanding	12	30.00%
Lack of formal recognition	8	20.00%
Lack of credibility	7	17.50%
Lack of regulation	3	7.50%
Lack of visibility	3	7.50%
I don't know	3	7.50%
Printed certification is preferable	2	5.00%
Inconsistent use	2	5.00%

Note. N = 18.

The data shows a considerable positive impact of the course/workshop content, methodology, tasks and evidence required on the motivation of students toward the development of research skills, and data also shows that the used and implementation of digital badges increased students understanding of the value and importance of skills for labour markets.

Discussion

This study shows the perception of a group of students at a Costa Rican distance higher education institution, who received their first digital badge after participating in a course/workshop aimed at developing basic research skills. The analysis shows the relevance of micro-credentials as a innovative way to bridge formative research, learning, and the generation of new skills in short learning experiences that are perceived as significant for the productive sectors (Brown et al. 2020; Brown et al., 2021; European Commission 2020 Orr, Pupinis and Kirdulyte 2020).

The findings shown in this study contribute to the current discussion in the field of online education, specifically, in distance teaching-learning models and the need to redefine conservative distinctions between formal and non-formal learning (Brown et al. 2020; Brown et al., 2021), particularly in the generation of new skills (Orr, Pupinis and Kirdulytė 2020). In addition, it is considered especially important to share empirically data related to experiences around micro-credentials in a Latin American context where the subject is relatively new and remains unexplored.

This study also shows how students perceived receiving the micro-credential as positive, and how they feel motivated to include their digital badges in their CV, and how they perceive that the skills that they developed in this short learning experience (European Commission 2020) and was certified with a micro-credential might help them get integrated into their labour field of interest. This perception is consistent with the practical incidence of the implementation of micro-credentials, not only in higher education institutions, but also in the different productive sectors where highly-trained students in various skills are required (Orr, Pupinis and Kirdulytė 2020). Students also reported positive comments regarding the development of skills in a virtual environment in the specific area of formative research. The students, at the beginning of the course, showed unsure or totally ignorant about the different stages of the research process and micro-credential; however, once the course/workshop was completed and the certification was obtained, the comments were very positive regarding the development of micro-credentialed certified research skills.

Finally, this study evidenced the lack of knowledge of the students who participated in this experience about micro-credentials, although students found themselves highly motivated with the integration of micro-credentials as a certifying strategy, and how micro-credentials were incorporated in a virtual environment together with the tasks required and specific skills developed. These results demonstrate the need to continue conducting research on the use, design and application of micro-credentials in the online and distance higher education and its incidence in teaching and skills development for labour markets.

References

Aguzzi, M. (2021). Guía para la investigación formativa del Observatorio Estudiantil UNED. Universidad Estatal a Distancia.

Brown, M., Nic Giolla Mhichíl, M., Beirne, E., & Costello, E. (Eds.). (2020). Proceedings of the 2019 ICDE World Conference on Online Learning (Vol. 1). Dublin City University. http://dx.doi.org/10.5281/zenodo.3804014

Brown, M., Nic Giolla Mhichíl, M., Mac Lochlainn, C., Pirkkalainen, H., & Wessels, O. (2021). Paving the road for the micro-credentials movement. European Consortium of Innovative Universities. https://doi.org/10.5281/zenodo.4438507

European Commission. (2020). A European approach to micro-credentials: Output of the micro-credentials higher education consultation group. https://op.europa.eu/en/publication-detail/-/publication/7a939850-6c18-11eb-aeb5-01aa75ed71a1

Hartnett, M. (2021). How and why are digital badges being used in higher education in New Zealand? Australasian Journal of Educational Technology, 37(3), 104-118. https://doi.org/10.14742/ajet.6098

Iwata, J., Wang, S., & Clayton, J. (2019). Students' perceptions about the use of digital badges in an online English terminology course: A three-year study. In F. Meunier, J. van de Vyver, L. Bradley, & S. Thouësny (Eds), CALL and complexity: Short papers from EUROCALL 2019 (pp. 199-205). Research-publishing.net. https://doi.org/10.14705/rpnet.2019.38.1009

Organization for Economic Cooperation and Development. (2021a). Income inequality [Indicador]. https://doi.org/10.1787/459aa7f1-en

Organization for Economic Cooperation and Development. (2021b). Unemployment rate [Indicador]. https://doi.org/10.1787/52570002-en

Orr, D., Pupinis, M. y Kirdulytė, G. (2020). Towards a European approach to micro-credentials: A study of practices and commonalities in offering micro-credentials in European higher education. European Commission. https://doi.org/10.2766/7338

Piedra, D. (2021). Exploring the perceived value of an open digital badge for virtual collaboration. Canadian Journal for New Scholars in Education, 12(2), 20-37. https://journalhosting.ucalgary.ca/index.php/cjnse/article/view/72596

Programa Estado de la Nación. (2021a). Informe Estado de la Nación 2021. http://hdl.handle.net/20.500.12337/8205

Programa Estado de la Nación. (2021b). Octavo Informe Estado de la Educación. http://hdl.handle.net/20.500.12337/8152

Zhou, L., Chen, L., Fan, Q., Ji, Y. (2019). Students' perception of using digital badges in blended learning classrooms. Sustainability, 11(7), Article 2151. http://dx.doi.org/10.3390/su11072151

PERSONALISED PRESENTATION OF MATHEMATICS FOR VISUALLY IMPAIRED OR DYSLEXIC STUDENTS: CHALLENGES AND BENEFITS

Muhammad H. Al Omoush and Tracey Mehigan, School of Computing, Dublin City University, Ireland

Correspondence: *Muhammad H. Al Omoush: muhammad.menazelalomoush2@mail.dcu.ie*

Abstract

Artificial Intelligence in Education (AIEd) has the potential to transform learning by providing personalised and adaptive environments and enabling more effective assessment and feedback (Luckin et al., 2016). Implementing AIEd has different challenges involving accommodating different learning styles, understanding how learners interact with tools, creating accessible technology for students with learning or sensory disabilities, and managing cognitive load and stress. The potential benefits of using AIEd for the personalised presentation supports inclusive learning environments, including improved understanding, accessibility to learning (Costas-Jauregui et al., 2021), reduced stress (Hsu et al., 2021), and cognitive load (Turan & Goktas, 2016), to improve mathematical understanding and student confidence. Neto et al. (2021) argue that the opportunity to utilise robots to enhance inclusive classroom experiences lies in their ability to utilise their physical attributes, multimodal feedback systems, customised social behaviours, and sensory functions. The potential benefits promote the development of inclusive and intelligent educational frameworks. In this paper, the authors examine the potential of using AIEd combined with robotics to provide a personalised learning framework for students with learning disabilities (e.g., dyslexia) and sensory disabilities (e.g., vision impairment/blindness). The paper will assess the challenges and benefits of the AIEd framework combined with robotics for inclusive mathematics education.

Keywords:

Artificial Intelligence in Education (AIEd), Universal Design for Learning (UDL), Virtual Reality/Augmented Reality (VR/AR), Human Computer Interaction (HCI), Robotics, Mathematics Education, Extensive Academic Emotion (EAE).

1. Introduction and Background

Mathematics education can be challenging for some students, particularly students with visual impairments or dyslexia. Traditional teaching methods often rely on visual cues, making it difficult for visually impaired students to understand mathematical concepts fully. While students with dyslexia experience challenges that include difficulties with reading, writing, spelling, and phonemic awareness (Lyon, Shaywitz, & Shaywitz, 2003). These difficulties can lead to academic and occupational struggles, as well as negative emotional outcomes such as low self-esteem and anxiety (Shehu, Zhilla, & Dervishi, 2015). In addition, they may also experience challenges with executive function, working memory, and attention (Sesma et al., 2009). These challenges can significantly impact mathematics education, so educators must be aware of them to provide appropriate support and accommodations.

1.1 A Framework for Inclusion: Promoting Disability Rights in Education in Ireland and Europe

The United Nations adopted the Convention on the Rights of Persons with Disabilities (CRPD) in 2006, and both Ireland and the European Union (EU) have ratified it (European Union, 2006). The CRPD aims to protect and promote the rights of persons with disabilities, including in education. In Ireland, the Disability Act 2005 provides a framework for providing services for people with disabilities, including in education. The act requires public bodies, including schools, to provide reasonable accommodations for people with disabilities (electronic Irish Statute Book, 2005). The Employment Equality Acts 1998-2015 and the Equal Status Acts 2000-2015 also prohibit discrimination against people with disabilities in employment and education (Government of Ireland, 2015a; Government of Ireland, 2015b). Additionally, the National Disability Inclusion Strategy 2017-2021 in

Ireland provides a framework for promoting the inclusion of people with disabilities in all aspects of life, including education (Gov.ie, 2017). These regulations and strategies demonstrate a commitment to promoting the inclusion of people with disabilities in education in Ireland and Europe and highlight the need to design inclusive educational frameworks.

2. Towards Establishing Effective Personalisation for the Presentation of Mathematics to Individual Learners

Universal Design for Learning (UDL) framework is based on designing educational materials and environments that are accessible and effective for all learners, regardless of their backgrounds or abilities. This includes providing multiple means of representation, expression, and engagement that allow students to access and interact with information in ways that work best for them (McKenzie & Dalton, 2020), which might mean providing materials in alternative formats, such as Braille or audio recordings, for visually impaired students. For dyslexic students, this might mean providing materials with alternative text formats or using assistive technology to support reading and writing. Using the UDL framework, educators can create more accessible and effective learning environments that benefit all students, including those with disabilities or learning differences.

Other inclusive educational programs that are effective in teaching mathematics to visually impaired and dyslexic students include the Sonification Sandbox and the MathTrax (Garcia et al., 2019). These systems also focus on providing multiple means of representation and engagement to support diverse learners. Choosing an inclusive educational framework ultimately depends on the student's needs, learning styles, available resources, and technology.

Humans process information in various ways, including through visual and verbal modalities and other cognitive factors such as personality traits. The Felder-Silverman Learning Style Model (FSLSM) and Myers-Briggs Type Indicator (MBTI) are two widely used models for understanding how people learn (Felder & Silverman, 1988; Myers & Briggs Foundation, 2019). The FSLSM identifies four dimensions of learning styles: sensing vs intuitive, visual vs verbal, active vs reflective, and sequential vs global. While the Myers-Briggs Type Indicator (MBTI) identifies four dichotomies of personality types, including extraversion vs introversion, sensing vs intuition, thinking vs feeling and judging vs perceiving. Both (FSLSM) and (MBTI) might help educators personalise the presentation of mathematics to individual learners (Adewale et al., 2019; Ivanov et al., 2019). Stein et al. (2019) argue that while the MBTI has the potential to aid educators in personalising instruction, it can be difficult to collect comprehensive and precise information about the personality types of individuals.

A study by Mehigan et al. (2011) found that eye-tracking technology can accurately identify learners' preferred processing styles and that different types of learners may benefit from different presentation formats. The study evaluated the findings using gaze patterns, heat maps, and fixation count. By identifying learners' preferred processing styles, educators and curriculum designers can tailor the presentation of mathematical content to suit the needs of individual learners better, potentially leading to more effective learning outcomes in UDL.

Robots have the potential to improve education. Salas-Pilco (2020) found that using robots in educational environments benefited learners. The study investigated the influence of robots on students' physical, social-emotional, and intellectual learning outcomes, where each student displayed distinct learning trajectories.

2.1 Cognitive load and stress affect learning and academic achievement in educational psychology

Research on academic emotions (AE) suggests that emotions play a critical role in how individuals experience cognitive load and stress (Pekrun, 2006; Pekrun et al., 2002). Negative emotions such as stress can cause external cognitive load as thoughts about emotions, emotion regulation processes, and learning tasks compete for working memory resources; positive emotions can also have the same effect (Oaksford et al., 1996).

Educators can reduce cognitive load and stress by implementing strategies that promote self-regulation and positive academic emotions, such as providing clear and structured learning materials, giving feedback that emphasises effort and improvement, and encouraging student autonomy and choice (Pascoe, Hetrick & Parker, 2019). AIEd frameworks can help students cope with increased cognitive load and stress management.

There has been an increasing focus on (AE) in the past few years. To further this concept, Mehigan, and Pitt (2019) suggest incorporating emotional factors from HCI research into the design of interactive systems, resulting in the concept of Extensive Academic Emotion (EAE). When examining the role of AIEd, the idea of (EAE) can potentially impact student engagement and achievement positively or negatively.

EAE can potentially improve learning outcomes and increase engagement by fostering positive academic emotions while decreasing cognitive load and stress. The use of Virtual Reality/Augmented Reality (VR/AR) and other HCI technologies can facilitate immersive and interactive learning experiences, aiding learners in developing a more comprehensive understanding of intricate concepts and in applying their knowledge in practical, real-world situations (Zhu, 2016).

3. Towards the Development of Technologies for the Inclusive Presentation of Mathematical Content

Traditional mathematical notation heavily relies on visual representations, which can be challenging for students with visual impairments (Máckowski et al., 2018). Dyslexic students may struggle to decode and comprehend written mathematical symbols and notation (Nieminen & Pesonen, 2019). Thus, developing technology that can present mathematical content in a way that is accessible to these learners is crucial.

The use of artificial intelligence (AI) in education has the potential to benefit all students, including visually impaired and dyslexic students. AI can provide alternative modalities for presenting information, such as graphics, animations, and tactile feedback (Mukhiddinov & Kim, 2021).

AI technologies can provide alternative means of accessing information through text-to-speech or speech-to-text conversion (Abhishek et al., 2022), enhancing mathematics education for visually impaired students. Additionally, robots could provide personalised and adaptive learning experiences tailored to each student's needs and abilities (Johal et al., 2018). For example, using a robot tutor has improved reading comprehension and fluency in dyslexic students (Belpaeme et al., 2018).

Robots are great for implementing new educational methods, such as teaching through exploration (Jamet et al., 2018) and personalising instruction using AI. That is due to the robots' physical embodiment, movement, voice, and vision capabilities, which have encouraged their adoption as assistive technology (Neto et al., 2021). According to (Daniela & Lytras, 2018), educational robots can have multiple benefits utilised to construct knowledge and an assistive aid for students who struggle in certain subject areas. Additionally, educational robots can potentially transform the classroom culture by fostering an inclusive learning environment where all students feel accepted and engaged.

(VR/AR) technologies can provide multisensory experiences that help students visualise, touch, and hear mathematical concepts, thereby enhancing the student's understanding and engagement with the subject matter (Lorusso et al., 2021; Donally, 2022), which can offer a promising approach to teaching Mathematics to blind and dyslexic students.

However, there are also potential challenges in using VR/AR technologies to teach mathematics to blind and dyslexic students. One challenge is the cost of the technology, which can be prohibitive for many schools and educational institutions (Vuorinen et al., 2018). Another challenge is the need for specialised software and training for teachers to use these technologies in the classroom effectively (Smith & Hattingh, 2020). Additionally, some students may experience discomfort or motion sickness when using VR/AR technologies, which can negatively impact their learning experience (Tychsen & Foeller, 2019). Despite these challenges, using VR/AR technologies in mathematics education holds excellent potential for providing personalised and inclusive learning experiences.

4. Understanding Learner Interaction with AIEd and Other Learning Technologies

Incorporating personalised delivery of mathematical education along with multimodal feedback and immersive environments can provide multiple benefits for students with dyslexia or visual impairments. These benefits may include the following:

- Inclusion:
  Multimodal feedback and immersive environments enable students with dyslexia or vision impairments to participate fully in mathematics classes, eliminating learning barriers, enhancing collaboration opportunities with other students and teachers, and promoting inclusivity.

- Improved learning, accessibility and understanding:
  Personalised interaction can enhance the accessibility for visually impaired students, enabling them to access information more easily and process it more effectively (Máckowski et al., 2018). Furthermore, it also provides multiple sensory channels for processing information and enables all students to engage with mathematical concepts more effectively.

- Reduced stress:
  Immersive environments can help to reduce stress and anxiety in students with dyslexia or vision impairments by creating a more relaxed and engaging learning environment (Hsu et al., 2021).

- Reduced cognitive load:
  Research has shown that learners' cognitive load and motivation can be affected by the design and usability of learning tools and requires a deep understanding of the learners' needs and preferences (Zhu & Simon, 1987). Multimodal feedback and immersive environments can help reduce cognitive load for students with dyslexia or vision impairments by presenting information clearly and concisely and enabling students to engage with concepts at their own pace (Turan & Goktas, 2016).

Creating a user-friendly AIEd system that includes all students in the learning process is crucial; this involves understanding the elements that affect users' interaction with the system, such as the content's suitability for the users' learning objectives and the user interface's overall quality (Holmes et al., 2022).

According to Roll and Wylie (2016), AI in education (AIEd) has made significant technological and theoretical progress, resulting in successful pedagogical outcomes. One notable application of AIEd is using intelligent tutors for personalised content delivery, feedback provision, and progress monitoring, as highlighted by Bayne (2015). Guan et al. (2020) suggest that AI can provide specialised support, bridge knowledge gaps, and enable instructors to deliver effective and efficient adaptive instruction.

Several aspects of education have included (AI), including curriculum development, personalised learning materials, evaluation, and teacher-student interaction. The advantages of interactive learning environments (ILEs) include monitoring and analysing students' progress, offering feedback, and facilitating effective engagement and interaction between students and teachers (Alam, 2021). Robots can be developed using (AI), computers, and integrated support equipment to enhance students' learning experiences. Collaborative robots (cobots) can work alongside human teachers to teach basic skills while adapting to each student's abilities (Timms, 2016).

Conclusion

The paper outlines insights into the challenges and benefits of implementing a combined framework of AIEd and robotics for the personalised presentation of mathematics. Additionally, the authors identify potential benefits and challenges of personalised presentation of mathematical equations with multimodal feedback and immersive environments for students with dyslexia or vision impairments. The paper explores the potential development of an AIEd framework and its implementation towards creating a holistic tool for developing an inclusive learning environment for mathematical education.

AI, VR, AR, and robotics could become increasingly essential in mathematics learning, providing students with more interactive and personalised ways to engage with mathematical concepts. However, these technologies pose several challenges, such as appropriate training for educators, equitable access to these resources, and concerns about privacy and data security. The future plans for integrating these technologies in mathematics education include using adaptive learning systems, personalised content, and more immersive learning experiences. These technologies can potentially revolutionise how we teach and learn mathematics. However, we must also address these challenges and ethical considerations.

Acknowledgement

This work was conducted with the financial support of the Science Foundation Ireland Centre for Research Training in Digitally-Enhanced Reality (d-real) under Grant No. 18/CRT/6224.

References

Abhishek, S., Sathish, H., K, A. K., & T, A. (2022, September 1). Aiding the Visually Impaired using Artificial Intelligence and Speech Recognition Technology. IEEE Xplore.

Adewale, O. S., Agbonifo, O. C., & Lauretta, O. (2019). Development of a myers-briggs type indicator based personalised e-Learning system. International Journal of Computer (IJC), 35(1), 101-125.

Alam, "Should Robots Replace Teachers? Mobilisation of AI and Learning Analytics in Education," 2021 International Conference on Advances in Computing, Communication, and Control (ICAC3), Mumbai, India, 2021, pp. 1-12.

Bayne, S. (2015). Teacherbot: Interventions in automated teaching. Teaching in Higher Education, 20(4), 455–467.

Belpaeme, T., Kennedy, J., Ramachandran, A., Scassellati, B., & Tanaka, F. (2018). Social robots for education: A review. Science Robotics, 3(21), east 5954.

Book (eISB), electronic I. S. (2005). electronic Irish Statute Book (eISB). Www.irishstatutebook.ie. https://www.irishstatutebook.ie/eli/2005/act/14/enacted/en/html

Costas-Jauregui, V., Oyelere, S. S., Caussin-Torrez, B., Barros-Gavilanes, G., Agbo, F. J., Toivonen, T., Motz, R., & Tenesaca, J. B. (2021). Descriptive Analytics Dashboard for an Inclusive Learning Environment. 2021 IEEE Frontiers in Education Conference (FIE).

Daniela, L., & Lytras, M. D. (2018). Educational Robotics for Inclusive Education. Technology, Knowledge, and Learning, 24(2), 219–225.

Donally, J. (2022). The immersive classroom: Create customised learning experiences with AR/VR. International Society for Technology in Education.

European Union. (2006). Convention on the Rights of Persons with Disabilities. https://www.un.org/development/desa/disabilities/convention-on-the-rights-of-persons-with-disabilities.html

Felder, R. M., & Silverman, L. K. (1988). Learning and teaching styles in engineering education. Engineering Education, 78(7), 674-681.

Garcia, B., Diaz-Merced, W., Casado, J., & Cancio, A. (2019). Evolving from xSonify: a new digital platform for sonorization. EPJ Web of Conferences, 200, 01013.

Gov.ie - National Disability Inclusion Strategy (2017-2021). (2017). Www.gov.ie. https://www.gov.ie/en/publication/8072c0-national-disability-inclusion-strategy-2017-2021/

Government of Ireland. (2015a). Employment Equality Acts 1998-2015. https://www.irishstatutebook.ie/eli/2015/act/25/enacted/en/html

Government of Ireland. (2015b). Equal Status Acts 2000-2015. https://www.irishstatutebook.ie/eli/2015/act/22/enacted/en/html

Guan, C., Mou, J., & Jiang, Z. (2020). Artificial intelligence innovation in education: A Twenty-year data-driven historical analysis. International Journal of Innovation Studies, 4(4), 134–147.

Holmes, W., & Tuomi, I. (2022). State of the art and practice in AI in education. European Journal of Education, 57, 542– 570.

Hsu, J. L., & Goldsmith, G. R. (2021). Instructor strategies to alleviate stress and anxiety among college and university STEM students. CBE—Life Sciences Education, 20(1), es1.

Ivanov, V., Dimitrov, L., Ivanova, S., & Olefir, O. (2019). Creativity enhancement method for STEM education. 2019 II International Conference on High Technology for Sustainable Development (HiTech).

Jamet, F., Masson, O., Jacquet, B., Stilgenbauer, J.-L., & Baratgin, J. (2018). Learning by Teaching with Humanoid Robot: A New Powerful Experimental Tool to Improve Children's Learning Ability. Journal of Robotics, 2018, 1–11.

Johal, W., Kennedy, J., Charisi, V., Park, H. W., Castellano, G., & Dillenbourg, P. (2018, March). Robots for Learning-R4L: Inclusive Learning. In Companion of the 2018 ACM/IEEE International Conference on Human-Robot Interaction (pp. 397-398).

Lorusso, M. L., Borasio, F., Da Rold, M., & Martinuzzi, A. (2021). Towards consensus on good practices for the use of new technologies for intervention and support in developmental dyslexia: A Delphi study conducted among Italian specialised professionals. Children, 8(12), 1126.

Luckin, R., Holmes, W., Griffths, M., & Forcier, L. B. (2016). Intelligence unleashed: An argument for AI in education. Pearson Education.

Lyon, G. R., Shaywitz, S. E., & Shaywitz, B. A. (2003). Defining dyslexia, comorbidity, teachers' knowledge of language and reading: A definition of dyslexia. Annals of Dyslexia, 53(1), 1-14.

M. Maćkowski, P. Brzoza, M. Zabka, and D. Spinczyk, "People, Multimedia platform for Mathematics´interactive learning accessible to blind," Multimed. Tools Appl., vol. 77, no. 5, pp. 6191–6208, 2018.

McKenzie, J. A., & Dalton, E. M. (2020). Universal design for learning in inclusive education policy in South Africa. African Journal of Disability, 9.

Mehigan, T. J., Barry, M., Kehoe, A., & Pitt, I. (2011). Using eye tracking technology to identify visual and verbal learners. 2011 IEEE International Conference on Multimedia and Expo.

Mehigan, T., & Pitt, I. (2019). Engaging learners through emotion in Artificially Intelligent environments. In EDULEARN19 Proceedings (pp. 5661-5668). IATED.

Mukhiddinov, M., & Kim, S.-Y. (2021). A Systematic Literature Review on the Automatic Creation of Tactile Graphics for the Blind and Visually Impaired. Processes, 9(10), 1726.

Myers & Briggs Foundation. (2019). The Myers-Briggs Type Indicator. https://www.myersbriggs.org/my-mbti-personality-type/mbti-basics/home.htm?bhcp=1

Neto, I., Nicolau, H., & Paiva, A. (2021). Community Based Robot Design for Classrooms with Mixed Visual Abilities Children. Proceedings of the 2021 CHI Conference on Human Factors in Computing Systems.

Nieminen, J., & Pesonen, H. V. (2019). Taking Universal Design Back to Its Roots: Perspectives on Accessibility and Identity in Undergraduate Mathematics. Education Sciences, 10(1), 12.

Oaksford, M., Morris, F., Grainger, B., & Williams, J. M. G. (1996). Mood, reasoning, and central executive processes. Journal of Experimental Psychology: Learning, Memory, and Cognition, 22(2), 476–492.

Pascoe, M. C., Hetrick, S. E., & Parker, A. G. (2019). The impact of stress on students in secondary school and higher education. International Journal of Adolescence and Youth, 25(1), 104–112.

Roll, I., & Wylie, R. (2016). Evolution and revolution in artificial intelligence in education. International Journal of Artificial Intelligence in Education, 26(2), 582–599.

Salas-Pilco, S. Z. (2020). The impact of AI and robotics on physical, social-emotional and intellectual learning outcomes: An integrated analytical framework. British Journal of Educational Technology.

Sesma, H. W., Mahone, E. M., Levine, T., Eason, S. H., & Cutting, L. E. (2009). The contribution of executive skills to reading comprehension. Child neuropsychology: a journal on normal and abnormal development in childhood and adolescence, 15(3), 232–246.

Shehu, A., Zhilla, E., & Dervishi, E. (2015). The impact of the quality of social relationships on self-esteem of children with dyslexia. European Scientific Journal, 11(17).

Smith, C., & Hattingh, M. J. (2020). Assistive Technologies for Students with Dyslexia: A Systematic Literature Review. Lecture Notes in Computer Science, 504–513.

Stein, R., & Swan, A. B. (2019). Evaluating the validity of Myers-Briggs Type Indicator theory: A teaching tool and window into intuitive psychology. Social and Personality Psychology Compass, 13(2), e12434.

Timms, M. J. (2016). Letting Artificial Intelligence in Education Out of the Box: Educational Cobots and Smart Classrooms. International Journal of Artificial Intelligence in Education, 26(2), 701–712.

Turan, Z., & Goktas, Y. (2016). The Flipped Classroom: instructional efficiency and impact of achievement and cognitive load levels. Journal of e-learning and knowledge Society, 12(4).

Tychsen, L., & Foeller, P. (2019). Effects of immersive virtual reality headset viewing on young children: Visuomotor function, postural stability, and motion sickness. American Journal of Ophthalmology.

Vuorinen, K., Erikivi, A., & Uusitalo-Malmivaara, L. (2018). A character strength intervention in 11 inclusive Finnish classrooms to promote social participation of students with special educational needs. Journal of Research in Special Educational Needs, 19(1), 45–57.

Zhu, K. (2016). Virtual reality and augmented reality for education. SIGGRAPH ASIA 2016 Symposium on Education: Talks.

Zhu, X., & Simon, H. A. (1987). Learning mathematics from examples and by doing. Cognition and Instruction, 4(4), 235–264

APPLICATION OF ESCO TO DOCUMENT LIFELONG LEARNING - CASE STUDIES IN GERMAN CONTINUING EDUCATION INSTITUTIONS

Jana Riedel; Lydia Stark, Jörg Neumann, TU Dresden, Germany

***Correspondence**: Jana Riedel: jana.riedel@tu-dresden.de*

Abstract

The rapidly changing labor market and the promotion of labor mobility lead to a demand for lifelong learning as well as the need for transparency and comparability of competencies. The application of skill classifications to describe competencies on educational certificates provides a way to document lifelong learning in a standardized way. In this paper, case studies regarding the application of the ESCO classification in three continuing education institutions are described. The results show that ESCO is a useful tool to document learning outcomes of continuing education courses in a comparable and transparent way but the mapping of competencies requires a lot of effort and differs in quality. The presented analysis identifies steps for further development of ESCO and for the change process when it comes to the standardized documentation of skills and competencies.

Keywords:

standardized skills description, ESCO, lifelong learning, labor mobility, continuing vocational education and training

Documentation of lifelong learning pathways via digital certificates

The global need for qualified workers in a rapidly changing labor market that includes new job profiles as well as new kinds of key skills and competencies regarding digitalization or sustainability creates a high demand for lifelong learning. At the same time, there is a variety of education and training opportunities that is not easy to evaluate or compare while assessing the suitability of employees for specific professional tasks or job profiles.

There are political initiatives to address this problem using standardized descriptions of occupations, skills and competencies or qualifications. Currently, these are mainly used to establish skills monitoring systems that provide information on labor market needs (Siekmann & Fowler, 2017). The classifications are intended to ensure statistical and research-based processes for decision-making on labor market strategies, but are not yet widespread in practice of the continuing education system.

In the project "MyEduLife" we assume that using standardized skills descriptions on educational certificates helps to enable the documentation of lifelong learning and to ensure a comparability and permeability in the continuing education and training system. For that purpose, we decided to use the European classification for Skills, Competences, Qualifications and Occupations (ESCO) that has been introduced by the European Commission to strengthen European labor market mobility and transparency (Europäische Kommission, 2019). In this paper, we describe the application of the ESCO classification in three German continuing education institutions. Case studies were conducted and accompanied the process of identifying relevant ESCO concepts to be used for standardized representation of learning outcomes on educational certificates.

Learning outcomes and standardized skills description in German continuing education and training

Regulations and standards in the field of continuing education and training in Germany

The German system of continuing education and training is regulated at the national level with different types of regulations for the various educational offers. The field of vocational continuing education and training is separated into further professional education and further vocational training, both of which have different regulatory conditions. On the one hand, further education courses aim to provide higher professional qualifications and are regulated by the state through so-called framework plans, which specify learning objectives, content and scope. There are around 400 state-regulated further education courses (Bundesinstitut für Berufsbildung, 2013). On the other hand, further training courses aim at maintaining and expanding existing skills to meet current occupational requirements and are developed based on market conditions without specific state regulations. In some cases, there are regulations by ordinance or professional associations that affect those further training courses instead.

Especially in the field of further education, there are changes in the respective regulations on learning objectives and content that are negotiated by the relevant federal ministries, the social partners, and the trade associations responsible for the respective occupation under the direction of the Federal Institute for Vocational Education and Training (BIBB) (Bundesinstitut für Berufsbildung, 2013).

So far, the German Federal Employment Agency (BA) provides a standard for the description of competencies using a specific classification called Dokumentationskennzahlen (DKZ, documentation indicators). This classification is specific for the German national system using own labels and description for competencies that may be acquired during continuing education programs. The DKZ is linked to ESCO through a mapping conducted by experts of the corresponding competencies to the ESCO-pillar of skills and competencies.

For the issuance of certificates, there are no regulations regarding the information contained. Therefore, it is not clear to what extend the more than 60,000 existing educational institutions (Schrader & Martin, 2021) provide information on learning outcomes and whether or not standards are applied.

Application of ESCO in German continuing education and training

The ESCO classification provides a structured vocabulary to describe occupations as well as knowledge and skills in a standardized way and is available in 27 different languages (including German). Since the beginning of this year it is available in version 1.1.1. The ESCO is organized along three pillars: occupations (based on ISCO-08), skills and competencies and qualifications, with the latter not being completed yet, due to conflicting national interests. There are connections between the pillar for occupations and the pillar for skills and competencies linking typical skills and competencies for every occupation.

The skills and competencies pillar is further structured by the categories knowledge, skills, languages and transversal skills. More than 13,000 entries, organized by hierarchical levels, are located in this pillar. The number of levels differs for each subcategory. It is possible to connect to the classification via API. The database can be searched via web interface as well.

The introduction of ESCO into the German system is viewed skeptically regarding the governance structures especially in terms of the development of curricula for continuing education and training (Annen et al., 2020). National systems cannot be affected by EU regulations due to the principle of subsidiarity and the prohibition of harmonization (Annen et al., 2020).

There have been project-based initiatives to apply ESCO for the documentation of learning outcomes (Rentzsch et al., 2020; TALQ, 2018) that already identified difficulties in practical applicability. This involves the level of detail of knowledge and skills, which is not of the same quality for all professions. The TALQ project used the occupation of stage technicians to show that sector-specific additions are necessary in order to make a realistic assessment of the knowledge and skills possessed by employees (TALQ, 2018). In the context of continuing academic education, existing learning objectives were successfully linked to ESCO entries using the example of continuing education courses in museum education, digital forensics, and nursing (Rentzsch et al., 2020). Nevertheless, more research is needed to assess the applicability of ESCO for a widespread practical use and acceptance to document learning outcomes.

Methods: case studies in vocational education and training institutions

Research Design

To answer our research questions "To what extent can ESCO be used to document learning outcomes accurately and meaningful?" (RQ1) and "How do education and training institutions assess the applicability and usefulness of the ESCO classification?" (RQ2) we conducted case studies in three continuing education and training institutions as testing partners. Relevant ESCO concepts for their specific courses in the fields of trading, welding and voltage switching were identified and the whole process of applying the standard was systematically documented and evaluated based on a document analysis of the results and a group discussion. Figure 1 illustrates the procedure of the scientific monitoring of the application process.

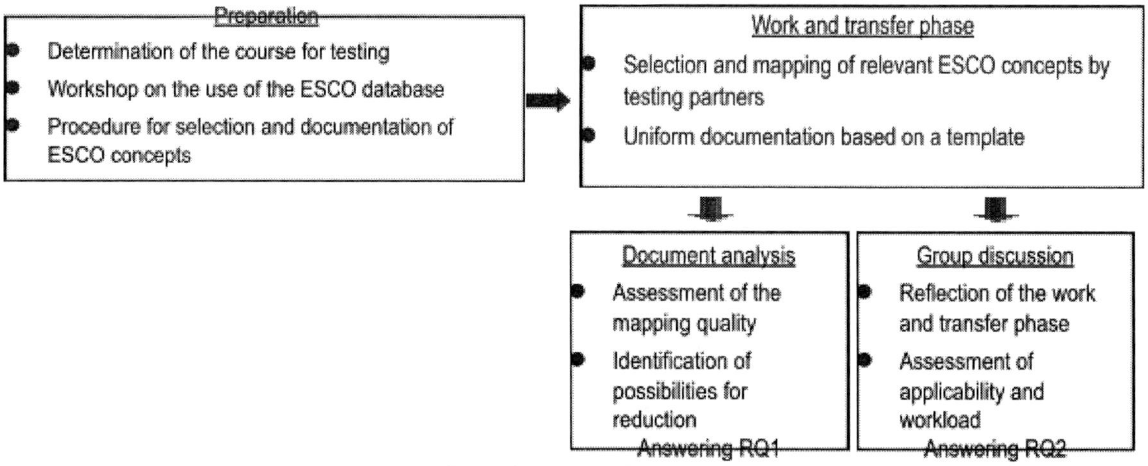

Figure 1. Research Design

Intervention

The application of ESCO for the documentation of learning outcomes on educational certificates was performed by the testing partners themselves. They are familiar with the respective educational content and are able to describe the contents, results and learning objectives of their continuing education programs in detail. Moreover, they are able to map ESCO concepts based on their adequate professional expertise. A joint preparatory workshop of 3.5h was held to introduce the procedure and ensure uniform documentation of the results. In this workshop, the courses suitable for the testing were determined and the testing partners were instructed on how to use the ESCO database.

Research and mapping of ESCO concepts was done manually by searching the public ESCO database for keywords or links between concepts of skills and/or occupations. For documentation purposes of the change process in the institutions, the testing partners were asked to fill in a template and provide information about (1) what information about the course content is currently shown on the certificate, (2) how this can be defined as a learning objective or learning outcome and (3) which equivalent can be found for this in the pillar of skills and competences of the ESCO database. Further, the testing partners were asked to document (4) any difficulties or specifics in applying the ESCO standard. It was possible to assign several ESCO concepts to one learning objective or one ESCO concept to several learning objectives.

The testing partners had approximately eleven weeks to complete the task (in addition to their regular work) with the possibility to receive help in case questions or uncertainties occurred. The scope of the task exceeded the time resources of the responsible persons, so that some of the completed templates could not be made available until 7 weeks later.

Document Analysis

The analysis of the documents created in the work and transfer phase was carried out by applying further criteria to qualitatively assess the respective mapping:

- Number of defined learning objectives
- Number of assigned ESCO concepts
- Number of ESCO concepts identified more than once (duplications)
- Assessment of mapping quality based on five evaluation levels:
    - 1 - exact match,
    - 2 - ESCO concept covers larger area than the originally defined learning objective
    - 3 - ESCO concept covers only part of the originally defined learning objective,

- 4 - no apparent match,
- 5 - the learning objective is too specific to identify a match for it in ESCO. Accordingly, no ESCO concept was assigned at this point, so this category refers to the learning objective instead.

- Classification of the ESCO concept within the ESCO hierarchy

The aim of a more detailed description of the identified ESCO concepts based on their classification in the ESCO hierarchy was to identify overlaps or focal points within the hierarchy in order to find out whether individual concepts can be grouped together for a clearer presentation on the educational certificates.

Group discussion

To answer RQ2, a group discussion was conducted with four leading questions that addressed the initial situation in the educational institutions and the application of the ESCO standard. The group discussion was analyzed according to the rules of structuring content analysis (Mayring, 1994) using MAXQDA software. The main categories were derived from the interview guideline and revised by inductively developed categories and subcategories. The following category system emerged, as shown in Table 1.

Table 1: Category system

deductive categories		inductive categories
actual situation	learning outcome documentation	certificates
		ESCO reference
ESCO application	challenges	missing prerequisites
		missing matches
		lack of orientation
		acceptance
	potentials	competence orientation
		benefit for others
	perspectives	alternatives
		transferability
		course planning and certificate organization
		assistance

Results: Opportunities and challenges of the ESCO standard

Mapping ESCO concepts to learning outcomes

The testing institutions chose different courses and used learning objectives on different levels (coarse vs. fine learning objectives) and from different sources (regulations vs. own definition). This approach led to different numbers and quality of learning objectives as well as mapped ESCO concepts. The detailed results are shown in Table 2.

Table 2: Number and quality of learning outcomes and ESCO concepts in the piloting courses (for categories of quality see chapter 2: Document analysis)

topic of the course	trading	welding	voltage switching
proficiency of learning objectives	state regulation	regulation by professional association	own formulation
level of learning objectives	coarse objective	fine objective	coarse objective
number of learning objectives	13	351	11
number of associated ESCO concepts	57	74	25
number of duplications in ESCO concepts	7	265	0
Mapping quality category 1	17 (29,8 %)	17 (22,7 %)	3 (12,0 %)

category 2	5 (8,8 %)	39 (52,0 %)	8 (32,0 %)
category 3	29 (50,9 %)	14 (20 %)	9 (36,0 %)
category 4	6 (10,5 %)	4 (5,3 %)	5 (20,0 %)
category 5*	0	35	2

*category 5 is related to the learning objective, not to the ESCO concept. Therefore, it is not included in the calculation of percentage.

None of the courses has a concordance concerning the number of learning objectives and the number of ESCO concepts. This means that there are no direct expressions of learning objectives in ESCO concepts, but there is the possibility to describe one learning objective using several ESCO concepts, at least for the two cases where coarse objectives were used for the mapping process. That is why, in these cases category 1 and category 3 allocations can be labeled good matchings.

For the 'trading' course, this means that 80 % of the identified ESCO concepts have a good quality, while there are 9 % that are even coarser and another 11 % that do not fit in terms of the definition of the learning objective. Here, the mapping is likely due to the detailed knowledge of the subject matter experts, who know that further knowledge and skills are to be expected behind the learning objective in the context of the specific training. In this case, using ESCO may allow for greater transparency about the actual contents of the educational courses.

Regarding the course 'voltage switching', learning outcomes were used for the mapping that were defined by the training institution itself. The quality of the allocations is rated less specific. Only 48 % of the identified concepts can be labeled good quality. In contrast, 20 % do not match the descriptions of the learning outcomes and 32 % are coarser than the learning outcome. In this case, the validity on an educational credential is weakened in that the ESCO concept promises a greater skill set than was taught in the continuing education course.

Differences regarding the quality of the allocations might have various reasons, such as the quality of the learning objectives or the type and subject of the education or training course, which have to be analyzed in further research.

The example of the 'welding' course shows that for learning objectives defined at a very detailed level hardly suitable ESCO concepts are mapped. Not only does the huge number of learning objectives create a high workload in the mapping process, but the descriptions also lead to a reduced number of relevant ESCO concepts and a large number of duplicates. Overall, 35 learning objectives could not be allocated at all and 52 % were brought to a coarser level. Nevertheless, the number of allocations rated good quality is similar to that of the course 'voltage switching' (43 %).

These findings confirm the findings from other projects (TALQ, 2018) that more sector-specific concepts may be needed to create good quality mapping. With this in mind, it can be assumed that the results rated 'good quality' regarding the course 'trading' are based on a better representation of this sector in the database. However, other explanations might apply to this fact as well, such as the source of the learning objectives, which were derived from a well-defined state regulation. Overall, there is still a need to improve the quality of allocations and to enable sector-specific extensions. Thus, the use of ESCO can be viewed as "different" and it depends on the acceptance of the users (training institutions, participants, employers) to what extent it is established in practical use to describe skills acquired in training.

Application and acceptance of the classification

The acceptance and willingness to adopt ESCO in the certification processes of continuing education and training has been analyzed by a group discussion about the application of ESCO. None of the three institutions had used descriptions of learning objectives in general or in a standardized way using ESCO before. Only in some cases they record some areas of action or course content on the corresponding certificates.

The presentation of the learning outcomes of the exemplarily selected further education offers with the competence descriptions of the ESCO classification turned out to be more difficult than expected, as the testing partners had to face several challenges in the process. Among other things, the transformation process was difficult because certain prerequisites for the description of competencies according to ESCO were not given on the part of the educational institutions. Moreover, the classification and competence descriptions of ESCO did not always match the actual circumstances in the educational institutions. Therefore, the allocations often are vague and inconclusive. The ESCO descriptions are only partially fitting and can be assigned to several given competencies or they do not reflect actual requirements of the professions and the competencies taught in the training and continuing education courses. In addition to these content-related challenges, it was also difficult to deal with the ESCO classification as a whole, which was expressed as a feeling of disorientation and a lack of acceptance. Due to the enormous amount of time and effort involved, ESCO is not perceived as practical and is rejected as a standard for competency documentation beyond the project context by the testing partners.

In addition to these challenges, potentials for the testing partners as well as for training participants and employers were identified as well. A detailed presentation of competencies for continuing education offerings increases the significance of certificates and in turn helps to place and advertise the offering to the target group. Based on the data, suggestions for further training or professional activities can be generated and comparisons with job vacancies are possible, which is also useful for participants and employers.

The general idea to use standardized descriptions for the documentation of learning outcomes is accepted by the testing partners. However, improvements regarding ESCO, such as supporting structures or technical and content improvements to the database, are needed to successfully apply this process to other courses as well. In this regard, the need for an AI-based system to suggest links to ESCO concepts was mentioned. The EU Commission is already developing such an AI-Tool with the expected release date in 2023.

Discussion: Next steps for change

The paper addresses the application of the ESCO classification to describe learning outcomes of continuing education programs in a standardized way, based on three case studies. It shows that the use of the ESCO may not only lead to a more transparent and comparable documentation of learning objectives, but can also improve the level of detail of the representation. While this approach is generally requested by the testing institutions, the use of the ESCO as a standardized way for describing learning outcomes is not accepted yet. The mapping effort seems to be too high and the mapping quality too low. Therefore, the continuing education institutions wish to have this process simplified and supported.

Furthermore, the testing shows that the use of broad objectives in defining learning outcomes and the use of predefined learning objectives can lead to a higher mapping quality. At the same time, sector-specific differences cannot be ruled out, so that demands for further development of the content of the ESCO classification remain. In this context, it should be examined to what extent a direct participation of sector experts can be facilitated. Further development of the ESCO - both in terms of content and in terms of possible application - seems desirable, since the potential of a standardized documentation of learning outcomes are manifold and have been confirmed by the testing institutions.

References

Annen, S., Mottweiler, H., & Lemouillour, I. (2020). ESCO als neues Instrument europäischer Berufsbildungs steuerung? Theoretische Einordnung und empirische Evidenz. *bwp@, 39*(Berufliche Bildung in Europa – 20 Jahre nach Lissabon und am Ende von ET 2020. Entwicklungen und Herausforderungen zwischen supranationalen Strategien und nationalen Traditionen). https://www.bwpat.de/ausgabe39/annen_etal_bwpat39.pdf

Bundesinstitut für Berufsbildung (Hrsg.). (2013). *Fortbildungsordnungen und wie sie entstehen*. Bundesinstitut für Berufsbildung. https://www.bibb.de/dienst/veroeffentlichungen/de/publication/download/7062

Europäische Kommission. (2019). *ESCO handbook. European Skills, Competences, Qualifications and Occupations*. https://ec.europa.eu/esco/portal/document/de/0a89839c-098d-4e34-846c-54cbd5684d24

Mayring, P. (1994). Qualitative Inhaltsanalyse. In A. Boehm, A. Mengel, & T. Muhr (Hrsg.), *Texte verstehen: Konzepte, Methoden, Werkzeuge* (Bd. 14, S. 159–175). UVK Univ.-Verl. Konstanz.

Rentzsch, R., Shajek, A., Vogel-Adham, E., & Hartmann, E. A. (2020). Standardisierung in der wissenschaftlichen Weiterbildung als ein Kernprozess der Professionalisierung. *ZHBW Zeitschrift Hochschule und Weiterbildung*, *2*, 19–26. HttPs://DOI.OrG/10.4119/zHWB-3411

Schrader, J., & Martin, A. (2021). Weiterbildungsanbieter in Deutschland: Befunde aus dem DIE-Weiterbildungskataster. *Zeitschrift für Weiterbildungsforschung*, *44*(3), 333–360. https://doi.org/10.1007/s40955-021-00198-z

Siekmann, G., & Fowler, C. (2017). *Identifying work skills: International approaches*. National Centre for Vocational Education Research. https://www.ncver.edu.au/research-and-statistics/publications/all-publications/identifying-work-skills-international-approaches

TALQ. (2018). *Final Report*. https://www.podiumtechnieken.be/wp-content/uploads/2018/05/TALQ_final-REPORT_december_04th.pdf

Acknowledgements

This work was supported by the German Federal Ministry of Education and Research for the project "MyEduLife – The blockchain as a tool for decentralised storage of individual continuing education biographies" under grant No. 21INVI02.

A SYSTEMATIC REVIEW OF CHINESE STUDENTS' ONLINE LEARNING EXPERIENCE IN HIGHER EDUCATION

Yiyi Mao and Kyungmee Lee, Lancaster University, United Kingdom

Correspondence: *Yiyi Mao: y.mao11@lancaster.ac.uk*

Abstract

The Covid-19 pandemic prompts an increasing number of university students to engage in online learning (OL). China is one of the countries that have experienced a radical shift in this sense. Before the pandemic, the online mode of university study was not recognised as a legitimate educational experience in China; thus, a small number of Chinese students engaged in online study. Subsequently, there is a relatively incomplete understanding of their OL experiences. Given the exponential expansion of OL in China during the pandemic, it would be a timely effort to synthesise knowledge on Chinese students' OL experiences. For that purpose, the present paper presents the results of a systematic literature review of 34 published journal articles concerning Chinese students' online study. The results give a deep insight into Chinese distance higher education from students' perspectives and call for more studies on the implications of relevant policy and cultural dimensions on Chinese students' online study journey.

Keywords:

Online learning; higher education; Chinese students; systematic literature review

Introduction

While Chinese higher education (HE) has a long history, lasting 3,000 years, distance higher education in China started late on a small scale. However, it is uptaking across China and is fast-increasing. The number of HE institutions providing distance online education programmes has increased from 4 universities in 1998 to 86 universities, including six open universities in 2021. During this period, a range of issues have been reported, such as inadequate technology infrastructure and professional support (Chen et al., 2016; Ting et al., 2018). Without having a chance to address those issues, the ongoing COVID-19 pandemic has led to an increasing number of Chinese college students participating in online learning (OL). The Ministry of Education (2020a) reported that 3.5 billion college students were involved in distance learning during the pandemic. As a result, more issues come up, such as low completion rates and decreased student motivation (Liu et al., 2020; Yang et al., 2021). In such a climate, a small group of researchers have investigated Chinese students' OL experiences (e.g. Chen et al., 2022). Nevertheless, there is a lack of in-depth understanding of Chinese students in online distance learning contexts, corresponding to the relatively short history of online distance education in China. Consequently, such a knowledge gap has created unhelpful stereotypes, assumptions, and biases against online Chinese students (Lee and Bligh, 2019). Therefore, it is a timely attempt to conduct a systematic review to display the current status of the scholarship in this field. The present authors have collected and reviewed the relevant literature to provide a deep insight into Chinese students' OL experiences—both perceived benefits and challenges in their experiences. The review aims to identify a gap in the literature that can be a useful departure point for future research and offer some practical recommendations for HE institutions and online distance educators to better design their online programmes.

The following research questions drive this review:

Q1. What are the geographical landscape, theoretical framework and research methods represented in previous studies?

Q2. What are the main topics of the previous studies?

Q3. What statements about Chinese students are represented in the previous studies?

Methodology

Using Scopus, the largest database of peer-reviewed literature (www.scopus.com), the authors selected 34 published journal articles from 177 items, with a strong connection to Chinese students' OL experiences. With the assistance of ATLAS.ti, a coding framework was developed, including the features of the selected studies, main topics, and characteristics of online Chinese students in the selected papers. The following part will present the results.

Results and discussion

The features of the selected studies

Among the 34 articles, more than half of them (n=18) focused on investigating Chinese learners' domestic online learning, with a handful of scholars (n=14) targeting overseas Chinese students' online study. Two publications compared the differences in online learning behaviours between Chinese students and students from other countries. In respect of theories used in the selected papers, theories related to learning and learners were most frequently adopted by previous scholars (26%, n=11). Then theories about culture and knowledge construction (24%, n=9) and technology-related theories (19%, n=8) were used in some selected articles. Notably, over a third of the studies did not explicitly mention any particular theories (31%, n=13). In addition, there was a good balance in methodological approaches (i.e., quantitative, qualitative, and mixed-method research) in the selected articles, with the quantitative approaches (n=14) used more frequently than the other two. However, there was a great variation in the authors' selection of specific research designs. The majority of researchers (n=22) employed a case study design in their studies while some scholars (n=8) selected a comparative design and cross-sectional design. Few scholars (n=4) adopted an experimental design and an action research design.

Discussion

Overall, we can conclude that the OL experiences of Chinese students have been relatively under-researched, as the small number of selected articles demonstrates. Especially given the large higher education system in China (also a large number of Chinese oversea students worldwide), 34 is a somewhat disappointing number when it comes to the studies concerning Chinese students' OL experiences at Chinese universities and foreign universities. This might be related to Chinese education policy. Until the pandemic, during which all face-to-face educational provisions were banned, the Ministry of Education (2020b) in China did not recognise distance learning as a legitimate medium of study. Due to the lack of government and social recognition of distance education degrees, Chinese students were unwilling to participate in distance learning programmes, leading to a lack of relevant research. Even though Chinese students have been allowed to stay in China during the pandemic, attending online courses offered by foreign universities, at the moment of the present review, there is still insufficient research outcome reporting Chinese students' online learning experiences.

While some of the reviewed articles use theories to guide their investigation, it is worth being aware that there are also a good number of studies investigating Chinese students' OL experiences without utilising any relevant theories. This is worrying because the low use of theories in relevant studies results in poor assumptions about online international students. Bligh and Lee (2020) argue that theory can facilitate researchers effectively challenge their prejudices and taken-for-granted presumptions to interpret and fathom the social phenomena under investigation in a more meaningful and comprehensive way, thereby advancing the technology-enhanced learning (TEL) field and its scholarship. Thus, it can be especially recommended to employ a range of theoretical frameworks to examine Chines students' behaviours and attitudes in online learning contexts.

Regardless of being well-balanced across the methodological approaches, a case study design is disproportionately employed by the majority of previous studies when it comes to specific research design. Yin (2009) believes that the case study method helps researchers effectively explore a complex social phenomenon and the dynamic cause-and-effect relationships underpinning the phenomenon. The 22 studies provide meaningful knowledge and understanding of online Chinese students and their experiences, yet the scholarship can benefit from utilising more diverse research designs. As Gorard (2013) criticises earlier, case studies often focus on collecting a limited dataset to simply and conveniently describe a concerning case, which aligns with major limitations (i.e., the limited data scope, small sample size) displayed by the selected papers (Cheng & Ding, 2021; Mikal et al., 2015). Therefore, future research can employ diverse research methodologies with extended scopes of data and topics, aiming to establish a complete account of Chinese students' OL experiences.

Focused topics of the previous studies

Even though the body of literature on Chinese students' OL experiences is not large, there is a diversity of research perspectives on the topic. Research on Chinese learners' OL experiences, whether for local students or overseas students, primarily concentrated on students' attitudes towards online classes (n=19), followed by students' perceptions of a range of OL technologies (n=15) and activities (n=15). Ten studies concerned how Chinese students learned specific learning subject knowledge online, with half of them focusing on language learning experiences. An equivalent number of scholars (n=10) explored various cultural matters that emerged in Chinese students in a cross-cultural OL context. Some researchers (n=7) assessed Chinese students' online learning strategies. A small number of individual studies examined Chinese students' online learning performances (n=5) and influencing factors (n=5).

Discussion

Evidently, the main topics of the selected papers are various. Here, students' attitude towards online learning is the spotlight in the reviewed publications. The previous studies provide conflicting explanations of Chinese students' perceptions of different aspects of online learning. Although Chinese students are generally satisfied with their OL experiences, they hold a conservative attitude toward the fully online and distance learning mode (Zhou et al., 2021; Zhu et al., 2009). This may simply be caused by Chinese students' unfamiliarity with online learning (or familiarity with on-campus learning), given that online distance education has been a relatively new phenomenon in China (Andersson & Grönlund, 2009). Therefore, the research on online Chinese students still needs more dynamics. We have also noticed that none of the previous studies looked into the impact of national and institutional policies that shaped and influenced Chinese students' online study experience. Given that a lack of government and social recognition of distance education has led to the slow development of online learning in China and the low participation rate among Chinese students in online HE, it may be necessary to investigate the impact of policy changes on students' online study experience, especially in the context of the post-pandemic.

The myths of Chinese cultures and Chinese learners

Generally speaking, the previous authors seldom used positive statements describing the characteristics of Chinese students and culture. In terms of cultural dimension, Chinese traditional culture was often described as authoritative (n=8), competitive (n=3), and face-saving (n=3), while it placed importance on collectivism (n=8) and harmony (n=4). Many scholars appraised Chinese education as teacher-driven instruction (n=5), authoritarian (n=1), achievement-focused (n=4), and spoon-fed education (n=1). Some authors showed rather neutral attitudes toward Chinese education, focusing on content-based instruction (n=3) and fundamental skills training (n=3). Conservative and silent students tended to be the dominant representation of Chinese students (n=10), followed by being afraid of losing face (n=4) and avoiding conflict (n=2). Five studies included positive statements about Chinese students' characteristics that Chinese students tended to be diligent, adaptive, and holistic learners. Likewise, an article complimented Chinese students genuinely searching for new knowledge. Nevertheless, there have been a greater number of negative statements about Chinese students' learning behaviours—being passive (n=9), pragmatic, and utilitarian (n=6), and seldom asking for teacher guidance (n=9). A lack of critical thinking among Chinese students was also mentioned in three studies.

Discussion

One admits that the small number of empirical studies, the monolithic research design and the limited theories used in the studies of Chinese students' OL journey have led to misconceptions about Chinese traditional culture along with the emergence of stereotypes and prejudices. Here, most studies attribute the negative aspects of Chinese culture and education to their traditional root in Confucianism. This notion is uncritically applied by some scholars (e.g. Nield, 2004; Du, 2016). Subsequently, Chinese students' characteristics and learning behaviours are also negatively regarded as the outcomes of such cultural and educational characteristics (e.g. Law et al., 2013; Windsor, 2021). Online international Chinese students are also considered in a fragile position when it comes to cultural adaptation (Yong, 2021). Although some other characteristics such as conforming to norms, pursuing high standards in their work, and valuing academic success are not necessarily negative traits, such statements are devised rather negatively in the reviewed articles. The stereotype of Chinese students as being conservative and silent is commonly observed across the reviewed articles, which we have found worrying. It is because these discourses disregard the diversity of cultures and student groups. Lee and Bligh (2019) question how these scholars were able to verify that the investigated Chinese students were from the same cultural background. They criticise these deficient narratives that fail to provide online educators with a balanced and sophisticated perspective. Most damaging, these narratives may strengthen online tutors' prejudices about different races and/or nationalities (ibid). Therefore, it is suggested that online learning studies should be conducted without presumptions about students' cultural backgrounds in case stereotypes and prejudice emerge.

Conclusion

This paper systematically searches, selects, and reviews previous research concerning Chinese students' online learning experience. Based on the review results, the present authors of the paper have argued that there is a significant gap in our understanding of Chinese students' online learning experiences. The gap has been driven both by the historical backdrops of the development of online distance education in China and by a range of limitations of previous studies. Most studies focus on Chinese students' attitudes towards online learning, but those studies do not investigate the impact of Chinese national and institutional policies on such attitudes. Especially the fast-changing government policies on online and distance education since the Covid-19 pandemic deserve some careful examination as they are likely to create both short-term and long-term effects on Chinese students' engagement with online learning. Perhaps more importantly, the present authors note that the characteristics of online Chinese students are considered predominantly negative, creating unhelpful and problematic stereotypes of Chinese students that fail to capture diversity among the large group. This calls for more in-depth and comprehensive research efforts in the field of online and distance education.

References

Andersson, A., & Grönlund, Å. (2009). A conceptual framework for e-learning in developing countries: A critical review of research challenges. *The electronic journal of information systems in developing countries*, 38(1), 1-16.

Bligh, B., & Lee, K. (2020). Debating the status of 'theory' in technology enhanced learning research: Introduction to the Special Inaugural Issue. *Studies in technology enhanced learning*, 1(1), 17-26.

Chen, H., Van Reyk, D., Reyna, J., & Oliver, B. G. (2022). A comparison of attitudes towards remote learning during the COVID-19 pandemic between students attending a Chinese and an Australian campus. *Advances in physiology education.*

Chen, L., Lin, S., & Zheng, Q. (2016). Opportunities and challenges of chinese distance education in the 'Internet+'Era. *Modern distance education research*, 1, 3-10.

Cheng, P., & Ding, R. (2021). The effect of online review exercises on student course engagement and learning performance: A case study of an introductory financial accounting course at an international joint venture university. *Journal of accounting education*, 54, 1-25.

Du, J. (2016). Predictors for Chinese students' management of study environment in online groupwork. *Educational psychology*, 36(9), 1614-1630. doi: 10.1080/01443410.2015.1036008.

Gorard, S. (2013). *Research design: Creating robust approaches for the social sciences.* Sage.

Law, D., Yip, J., Wong, C., & Cheung, M. C. (2013). Enhancing the process of idea generation in Hong Kong chinese university students: The fashion visual merchandising experience. *Art, design and communication in higher Education*, 12(1), 103-121.doi: 10.1386/adch.12.1.103_1.

Lee, K., & Bligh, B. (2019). Four narratives about online international students: A critical literature review. *Distance education*, 40(2), 153-169.

Liu, X., Zhou, J., Chen, L., Yang, Y., & Tan, J. (2020). Impact of COVID-19 epidemic on live online dental continuing education. *European journal of dental education*, 24(4), 786-789.

Mikal, J. P., Yang, J., & Lewis, A. (2015). Surfing USA: How Internet Use Prior to and During Study Abroad Affects Chinese Students' Stress, Integration, and Cultural Learning While in the United States. *Journal of studies in international education*, 19(3), 203-224. doi: 10.1177/1028315314536990.

Ministry of Education of the People's Republic of China (2020a). The total number of students in Chinese higher education reaches 40.2 million, ranking first in the world. http://www.moe.gov.cn/fbh/live/2020/52717/mtbd/202012/t20201204_503482.html. Accessed 10 Apr 2022.

Ministry of Education of the People's Republic of China (2020b). New policy for Chinese students studying abroad during the COVID-19 pandemic. http://www.moe.gov.cn/fbh/live/2020/52834/mtbd/202012/t20201223_507111.html. Accessed 10 Apr 2022. .

Nield, K. (2004). Questioning the myth of the Chinese learner. *International journal of contemporary hospitality Management*, 16(3), 189-196. doi: 10.1108/09596110410531186.

Ting, S. R., Smith, A. C., & Gomez, E. (2018). E-learning in China: Progress, challenges, and research issues. *Digital transformation and innovation in Chinese education*, 1-17.

Windsor, R. J. (2021). The effectiveness of an online grammar study scheme for Chinese undergraduate students. *Smart learning environments*, 8(1), 1-14.

Yang, X., Li, D., Liu, X., & Tan, J. (2021). Learner behaviors in synchronous online prosthodontic education during the 2020 COVID-19 pandemic. *The journal of prosthetic dentistry*, 126(5), 653-657.

Yin, R. K. (2009). *Case study research: Design and methods*. Sage.

Yong, S. (2021). A reflective commentary about teaching international non-accounting postgraduates amid COVID-19. *Pacific accounting review*, 33(5), 616-624. doi: 10.1108/PAR-09-2020-0156.

Zhou, S., Zhou, Y., & Zhu, H. (2021). Predicting Chinese University Students' E-Learning Acceptance and Self-Regulation in Online English Courses: Evidence From Emergency Remote Teaching (ERT) During COVID-19. SAGE Open, 11(4), doi: 10.1177/21582440211061379.Yong, S. (2021). A reflective commentary about teaching international non-accounting postgraduates amid COVID-19. *Pacific accounting review*, 33(5), 616-624. doi: 10.1108/PAR-09-2020-0156.

Zhu, C., Valcke, M., & Schellens, T. (2009). A cross-cultural study of online collaborative learning. *Multicultural education and technology journal*, 3(1), 33-46. 10.1108/17504970910951138.

What Future SkillS will be Needed for Future IT-Professionals? An Empirical Study

Ulf-Daniel Ehlers, Baden-Wurttemberg Cooperative State University, Germany

***Correspondence**: Ulf-Daniel Ehlers: ulf.ehlers@gmail.com*

Abstract

The currently EU-wide largest survey on the future of skills for Professionals in the IT sector reveals a new configuration in skill demands. The skill study differentiated between three sets of skills: Business, technical and Future Skills and surveyed IT and HR professionals from more than 300 organizations in 27 European member states to assess the importance of skills today and within the next three to five years. It took place in the Blockchain sector, which stands exemplary for digital transformation of economies. It turns out that participants attribute high to very high importance to Future Skills even when compared to technical and business skills. This brings up questions for new qualification pathways and strategies with a strong focus on Future Skills. The here presented study provides an in-depth analysis of surveys and research skill demands for IT professionals and an analysis of skill supply, which has been investigated through a multi-method and multi-stakeholder research design.

Keywords:

Empirical skills research, *Transversal skills, Future skills, IT professional, Skill intelligence, Skill mismatch.*

1. Introduction

Skill development is high on the agenda of regional, national, and institutional decision makers in policy and institutions and counts for large parts of a regions' innovation capacity and an individual's resilience against biographical risks.[1] A growing number of studies is investigating the efficiency and effectiveness of such skill development of educational systems world-wide (Ehlers, 2022). For higher education, the investigations claim a mismatch between what graduates are able to do and what society and the labour market expects them to be able to do. The latter being the ability to deal with a volatile, uncertain, complex, and ambiguous environment ahead. The phenomenon has recently been termed as "skill gap" in a so-called Delta Study by McKinsey involving more than 18,000 participants (NSDC, 2020). The skill gap concept is also expressed in individuals' perceptions: As biographies become increasingly flexible, individuals have a growing responsibility to develop individual competence strategies for their biographies at large. In this context, the fit between educational opportunities and occupational requirements must increasingly be prioritized and translated into individual learning and action strategies, in which "Future Skills" play an essential role (Ehlers, 2020).

While the skill debate is lead under various diverging flags and terminology, the Future Skills concept has now been precisely and operationally defined and conceptualized by Ehlers (2020, 2022) in the NextSkills Study resulting in 17 defined Future Skill profiles. The study is rooted in an analysis of the state of the art of research and is modelled on sociological theory, neo-institutionalism, and individualization approaches, involving educational theoretical approaches of action competences and new theories of organizational development (for a detailed account of research methodology and state of research on Future Skills see Ehlers, 2020). Section 3 describes the approach briefly.

The Future Skills model has been used as a basis for building a quantitative instrument to investigate IT professionals and human resource experts' opinions about the relevance of different skill sets in relation to Future Skills. The question being if what has been known as hard skills can be really understood as superior to so-called soft skills – or if on the contrary, the former soft skills are more relevant skills for the future. The quantitative study is part of a larger multi-part, multi-mix and multi-perspective study based on methods of the emerging field of labour market intelligence research (Brunner & Ehlers, 2021; Ehlers & Bonaudo, 2021). It has been conducted in 27 European member states and addressed to IT professionals and management staff in the

[1] The explicit focus of policy can be seen e.g. in the fact that 2023 has been declared the European Year of Skills (see European Commission, 2022).

IT sector. In addition to the analysis of skill demands, the study also investigates skill supply – looking at learning pathways for Future Skills in the IT sector through curricula analysis, expert interviews, as well as informal learning communities and fora.[2]

In section 2 we will explain our Future Skill concept and describe two other different sets of skills which have been used to define skill demands in the IT sector. In section 3 we will shortly describe the research methodology which has been followed to determine skill demands. We will also state the methodology used to analyze skill supply – although the results will not be part of this chapter. In section 4 we summarize the results of the skills demand analysis.

Overall, the studies reveal a gain in importance for Future Skills against other skill sets.

2. Skill Sets for the IT Professional of the Future: Beyond Technical and Business Skills.

For the study, three skill sets (see Fig.1) have been selected in order to investigate their future relevance for professionals in the IT industry: a set of Technical Skills, a second set of Business and Managerial Skills and a third set of Future Skills resulting from a large-scale future skill study.[3]

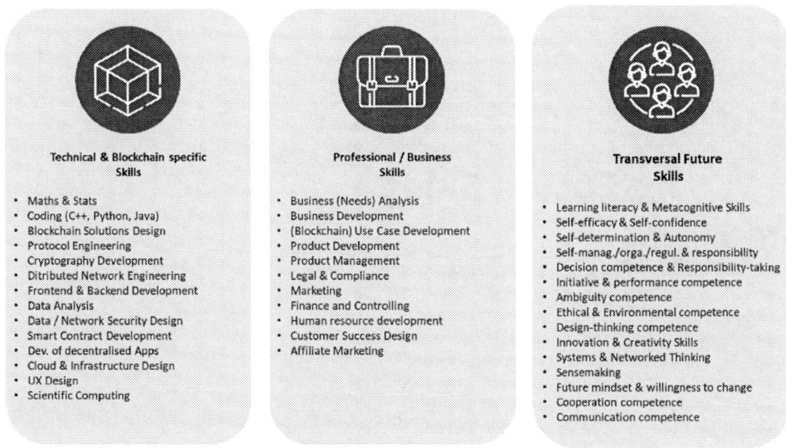

Figure 1 - List of Skills for future IT professionals

1 - Technical Skills (focus here on Blockchain) (Brunner & Ehlers, 2021): IT-specific skills relate to skills which are hard skills in the domain of digital technology and IT information technology development, informatics, programming, Distributed Ledger expertise, Blockchain security, Blockchain architecture, which in the core relate to domain-related knowledge, abilities, and attitudes of IT professionals

[2] The research has been conducted as part of the large-scale CHAISE Initiative together with 23 organisations from more than 16 European countries. CHAISE – being an acronym - stands for "A Blueprint for Sectoral Cooperation on Blockchain Skill Development".

[3] In a general understanding, we define "skills" as learnt or natural abilities of a person. Within the global debate on skills, talents, and competences, the discussion in literature is shifting to a more comprehensive concept of competences which includes skills and adds to it attitudes and knowledge (Erpenbeck et al., 2017, Ehlers 2020). The European Skills, Competences, Qualifications, and Occupations (ESCO) applies the same definition of "competence" as the European Qualification Framework (EQF). According to this framework, "competence means the proven ability to use knowledge, skills and personal, social and/or methodological abilities, in work or study situations and in professional and personal development." (ESCO, 2022).

2 - Professional / Business Skills (Brunner & Ehlers, 2021): Domain-related skills are defined by skills which are related to the field of profession of IT development but are comprised of skills which can be described or called complementing skills, like project management knowledge for IT and Blockchain-specific projects, business analysis skills for IT and Blockchain projects and alike

3 - Future Skills: Horizontal, transversal skills – often referred to as soft skills - are skills which enable professionals to act successfully in the changing and emergent environment of organizational future contexts. Research shows that these skills are of increasing importance (Ehlers, 2020) and the study is aimed to analyse the importance of these kind of skills for IT professionals in the Blockchain labour market development in Europe.

Figure 2 shows a summary of the 17 Future Skills.[4]

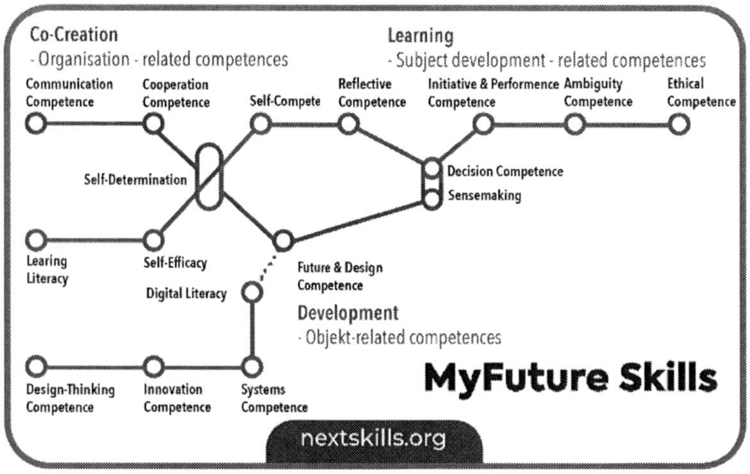

Figure 2 - Future Skills profiles (Ehlers, 2022)[5]

Future Skills is a concept which is directly connected to the former debate on key competences or 21st century skills (OECD, 2018; World Economic Forum, 2020) and which is now gaining increasing importance as a concept in educational policy and individuals' lives (Dettmers & Jochmann, 2021; Samochowiec, 2020). The importance of Future Skills has been stated in many studies both for the field of university graduates (Ehlers, 2020; Huber, 2016, 2019; Schlaeger & Tenorth, 2020; Wild et al., 2018) as well as for professionals in their jobs (Agentur Q, 2021; Dettmers & Jochmann, 2021; Stifterverband & McKINSEY, 2018), and also internationally (Ashoka & McKINSEY, 2018; McKinsey Global Institute, 2021; OECD, 2018; World Economic Forum, 2020). The body of studies indicates that research on Future Skills has established itself as a research field in its own right in recent years. Since 2016, 13 Future Skills studies are available within a Germany speaking context and at least 37 internationally. As a general trend, Future Skills concepts also include digital competencies, but place an emphasis on competencies of a transversal nature (e.g., ethical competence, dealing with ambiguity, etc.).

This also finds expression in the currently growing international field of research on Future Skills. Since 2015, there have been more than 37 international studies on Future Skills, with more to be published soon. Amongst them, the Organization for Economic Co-operation and Development (OECD) Skill Compass and concepts from the World Economic Forum which indicate a skills shift, which demand moving away from a knowledge based understanding of (higher) education to a multidimensional concept, including knowledge, but going beyond it towards so-called "key competencies" or transversal "Future Skills" (Ehlers, 2020; OECD, 2018; World Economic Forum, 2020).

3. Methodological Design

---

[4] The 17 Future Skills identified in the NextSkills study by Ehlers (2020) were combined into 15 for the CHAISE study after consolidations with blockchain and IT experts.

[5] An interactive Future Skills finder has been developed which can be accessed here: https://nextskills.org/future-skills-finder/

A variety of methodological approaches from the social sciences have been used for the study on Future Skills for IT professionals, contrasting the demand for skills with the supply for skills (Table 1). A number of different studies has been conducted in order to gain information about the demand of skills in the IT sector, as well as the supply (see Ehlers & Bonaudo, 2021). Amongst them, qualitative interviews with IT experts and training and education providers, job-ad analyses, community and fora analyses, and a Europe-wide skills survey (Brunner & Ehlers, 2021).

Table 1 - Research Flow and Data Collection

Research methods	Research activities	Data collected & analyzed
Quantitative standardized online survey	European Survey on Skills for IT professionals	304 Survey participants
Qualitative guideline-based interviews	In-depth expert interviews	36 interviews conducted (29 skill demand perspective & 7 skill supply perspective)
Qualitative document analysis	Job Ad analysis	459 Job ads collected[6] 314 analysed
Qualitative document analysis	Educational and training offerings with focus on Blockchain	133 Educational and training offerings collected[7] 120 analysed
Qualitative document analysis	Analysis of online fora and communities	17 Communities and fora analysed

For both perspectives – the skills demand as well as the skills supply – a number of data sources have been used.

Skills Demand

A detailed analysis of 314 job-ads collected from LinkedIn and further online job portals resulted in a description of preferred skills for job profiles. These data have been used to contextualize and define a Technical and a Business/ Managerial skill set. Together with the previously collected set of Future Skills, both the Technical and the Business skill set built the basis for designing the quantitative research questionnaire. More than 300 IT experts across 27 European countries rated the importance of the individual skill sets for three selected roles: architect, developer, and manager for the application context of the Blockchain sector. In addition, data from interviews of 28 IT experts have been collected to complement the data from the standardized surveys.

Skills Supply

For the skills supply perspective, 120 online training-offerings were simultaneously analysed according to the predefined skill set. In addition, 17 IT communities and forums were analysed according to skills and teaching methods. In order to get a more detailed insight into the training offered, 7 expert interviews were conducted with IT training providers, here with a focus on such forward-looking technologies like Blockchain.

4. Future Skills for IT Professionals

4.1 Overall Relevance of Future Skills

The quantitative data collected confirms that the Future Skills proposed in the NextSkills model are high on the agenda of IT professionals today and within the next three years. This holds true specifically if compared to skills sets on Technical Skills and Business Skills. The companies' assessment of how important transversal skills will be today and in the next 3 years shows that more than 90% of the respondents describe Future Skills today as either "somewhat important" or "very important". For the importance of Future skills in the next three years the vast majority (93%) of firms responded with either "very important" or "somewhat important".

Figure 3 provides an overview of the percentage of participants who describe each skill as important.

6 See registry of job ads: https://chaise-blockchainskills.eu/registry-of-blockchain-online-job-vacancies/

7 See registry of educational and training offerings: https://chaise-blockchainskills.eu/registry-of-blockchain-educational-and-training-offerings/

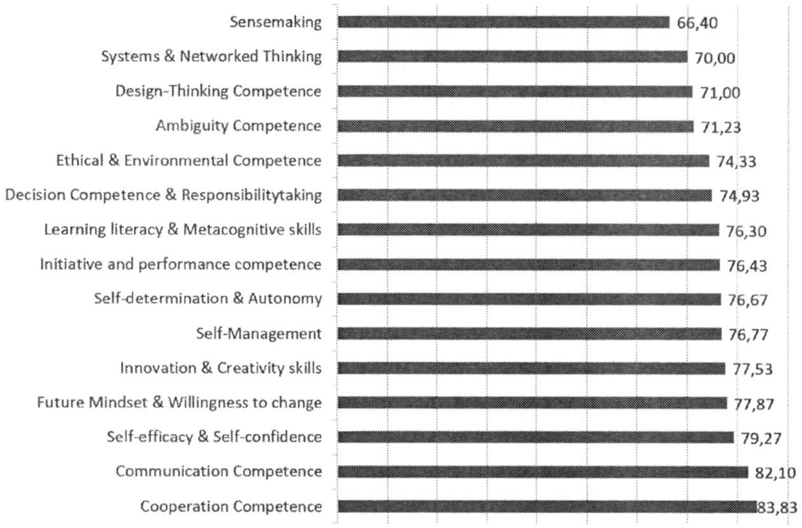

Figure 3 - Overview of the answers to the importance of the individual Future Skills[8]

As shown in figure 3 the most important Future Skills are cooperative competence (84%), communication competence (82,1%) and self-efficacy & self-confidence (79,3%). The following definitions and the definitions of the other skills can be found on nextskills.org:

- **Cooperation competence:** Cooperation competence as a Future Skill relates to the ability and disposition to cooperate and collaborate in (intercultural) teams either in face to-face or digitally supported interactions within or between organizations with the purpose of transforming differences into commonalities. Social intelligence, team-working competences, and consultation competence play a key role for this competence.
- **Communication competence:** Communication competence as a Future Skill entails not only language skills, but also discourse, dialogue, and strategic communication aspects, which – taken together – serve the individual to communicate successfully and in accordance with the respective situation and context, in view and empathy of her/his own and other's needs.
- **Self-efficacy & Self-confidence:** Self-efficacy as a Future Skill Profile refers to the belief and one's(self-) confidence to be able to master the tasks at hand relying on one's own abilities and taking over responsibility for one's decisions (Ehlers, 2020).

The following skills were described as important by fewer participants in the survey: Sensemaking (66.4%), Systems & Network Thinking (70%) and Design Thinking Competence (71%). These differences can all be explained by strong variations in the ratings of importance for each role profile. We will discuss these differences and possible explanations further in section 4.3.

The interest in Future Skills for individual job profiles is also highlighted in comparison to the importance rating of other skill sets, as shown in figure 4.

[8] In the EU Survey on Skills for IT professionals, 304 survey participants from IT industry have been asked for which of the three defined job profiles they consider the 15 Future Skills to be important (for more details on the survey see Brunner & Ehlers, 2021; Ehlers & Bonaudo, 2021). Figure 3 shows the average number of times participants rated the skills as important across all three roles.

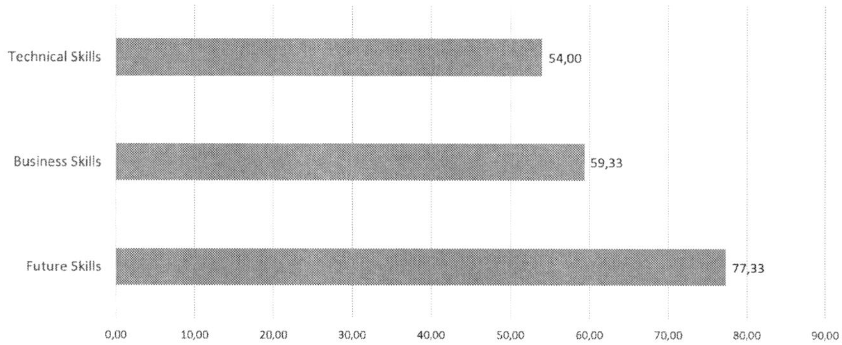

Figure 4 - Assessments of Importance of different Skill Sets

As can be seen in Figure 4, it is evident that Future Skills are regarded as very important skill sets across all job profiles. Even in a strongly IT-centric occupational field such as blockchain, they are rated more important than technical skills set. This indicates a clear skill shift from technical knowledge to Future Skills.

4.2 Comparing Importance of Different Skill Sets in IT Job Profiles

Skills are context bound and – for professionals - a particular skill gains its value through enabling professional performance, understood as successful action. While the general context of the study was aiming at defining skills for IT professionals at a general level, an additional analysis step has been undertaken: An analysis of the perceived skills requirements for certain role-profiles within the sector of IT professionals. The participants of the study were therefore additionally asked to relate the importance of skills to three different job role-profiles: Architect, Developer and Manager –all related to the sector of Blockchain. In the study, the three role-profiles are clearly described. (1) The IT or Blockchain Architect designs the multileveled architecture of a large IT or Blockchain system and software landscape and ensures the coherence of all aspects of a project as an integrated system. (2) The Developer role-profile codes applications, in our case Blockchain applications, and takes care of problem solving at the micro level. (3) The Manager of Blockchain applications and systems is tasked to track implementation progress, maintain close cooperation with business managers, and monitor the process quality to ensure that products meet their technical and business objectives. In a role-profile specific section of the study, participants have been asked to rate the important of the three different skills sets for the different role-profiles stated above.

304 participants from 13 countries took part in the survey, and rated different statements on a scale from very high to very low, depending on how important a skill is for the respective role. For the data evaluation, the highest two evaluation scores "very high" or "very important" and "somewhat high" or "somewhat important" were aggregated.

The data analysis shows that the skill set for Future Skills is the set rated with highest importance over all three role-profiles. Figure 5 gives an overview of the distribution of the importance of the different skills according to roles.

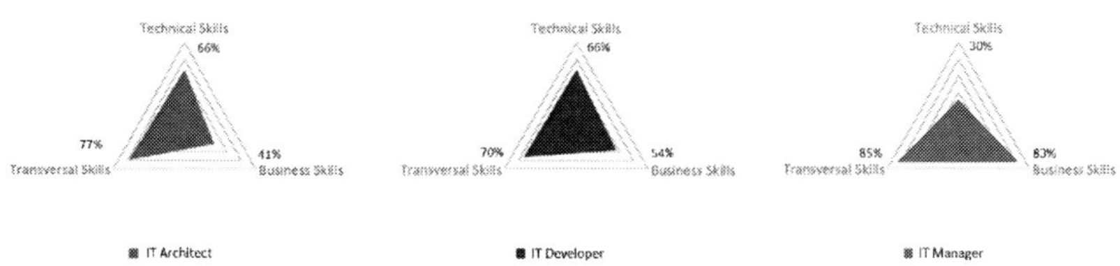

Figure 5 - Skill profiles per role for IT Professionals

Secondly, the analysis shows that the three skill sets used have a distinct importance and can be distinguished from each other. Thirdly, the analysis shows that professional roles do not rely on one competence profile only, but that domain specific skills and Future Skills complement each other in creating wholistic professional skill portfolios.

4.3 Future Skills in Comparison

In an additional step of analysis, the value and inner structure of the skill set of Future Skills has been questioned. The aim was to analyse which importance the participants attributed to each skill within the three-given role-profiles and to extract the inner Future Skill characteristic for each role-profile. An overview is given in fig. 6. While self-efficiency and self-determination are rated similarly important for all roles, there is a difference in skills such as creativity, system thinking, sensemaking, design thinking, future mindset, and ethical thinking. Here it can be seen that operational roles such as the Blockchain Developer are assigned a lower importance for some skills than the strategic roles of the Blockchain Architect or the Blockchain Manager. The Blockchain Manager, in his connecting role between the teams, has a strong focus on organization-related skills (cooperation, communication, sense making, etc.), while the Blockchain Architect has a stronger focus on object-related skills (system thinking, design thinking, innovation, etc.).

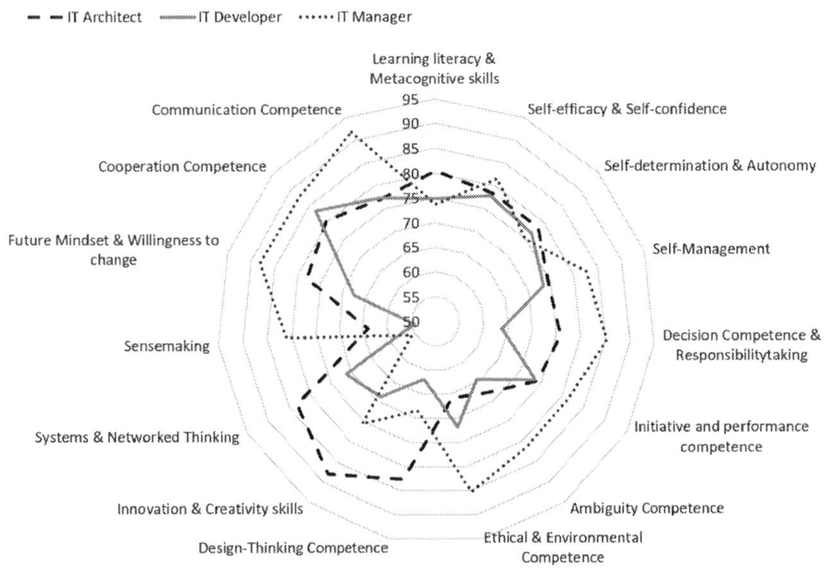

Figure 6 - Importance of Transversal Skills for different roles of IT professionals

A clear skill shift from so-called hard skills to transversal Future Skills can be observed in this area. IT professionals predominantly require transversal skills, which is also related to the many changes and innovations in the IT working environment. It requires professionals who can continuously adapt to their fast-moving environment. Transversal Future Skills are indispensable in this context.

As far as formal education is concerned, the interviewed experts (n=36) are divided. In many job-ads an academic education in the field of computer science or informatics is required, but some experts do not find traditional education particularly important and refer to short courses offered by numerous e-learning platforms such as Udemy and Cousera. On the other hand, these courses are also criticized for being too generic and superficial. In many cases they offer only a surface introduction to the topic. There is also a lack of face-to-face training sessions with supervision, which can be useful for practical training. To develop especially the missing Future Skills, it was clearly emphasized in the survey and in the interviews that training, and education programs should be as interactive as possible. The focus should be on practical application, dealing with real world problems, and working on concrete projects. But also, entrepreneurial skills and working in interdisciplinary teams were highlighted as important for the learning process. Especially in solution and use case design, extensive industry knowledge is a basic requirement. This rising demand of real-world use cases and practical learning shows the need for work-based oriented learning modules. Specialized knowledge of the basics of IT technologies should be taught as well as project-related skills. The involvement of experts and needs from the public sector and the economy offers further added value. However, self-learning in forums and via videos should also be encouraged, as future professionals need to continuously develop themselves on the job and should internalize this ability to self-learn in their formal education.

5. Summary and Conclusion

The study shows that higher education will have to move quite a bit from its current position. The new paradigm of higher education will have to be geared towards supporting the development of new and emerging skill needs and focus on learner agency. Learner agency refers to the feeling of ownership and control that learners have over their own learning (Schoon, 2018). When students believe their actions can make a difference, they become more confident, engaged, and effective learners. Every student can develop their agency – but they must be supported by their teachers and learning community to do so (Schoon, 2018).

The following conclusions can be drawn from the empirical research findings:

1. Skill profiles can be clearly defined: As shown in section 4.2 & 4.3, the different job profiles have different skill needs according to industry experts. Even in the case of Future Skills, a distinction can be made depending on the role which skills are rated as important.

2. Sectorial needs can be clearly described: By means of a targeted approach, it is possible to identify a clear sector need. The blockchain sector that is the focus here is still growing and yet job profiles can be clearly defined and distinguished from each other, and the respective need determined.

3. Future skills are on the rise: Future skills are not only described as increasingly important but exceed the importance of subject-specific skills for different role profiles (see section 4.1).

4. Method for skill analysis expert supported foresight procedures like Delphi studies and qualitative methods to avoid blind spot problems: In addition to the quantitative European-wide surveys and the analyses of job ads, forums and online courses, the expert interviews and focus groups provided important information on how the development of Future Skills can be promoted (see section 4.3).

5. Future Skills are in general important, but some can be identified as more important for certain job profiles than others: Job profiles that are more generalist or have more interfaces in collaboration with other people or departments show a higher rated need for Future Skills than job profiles that have more isolated areas of responsibility (see section 4.2).

The multi-method and multi-stakeholder approach in skill research in very dynamic fields of work, such as blockchain, provides a good information base for closing the skills gap. Especially between the advertisement in job ads, the discussion in online forums and the perspective assessment of blockchain experts, a lack of awareness for Future Skills in the high-tech community can be identified. Future Skills need to be codified in a way that is known to the general public in order to be properly used by recruiters in job ads and to find resonance in existing networks. The online communities are the first port of call for many blockchain enthusiasts, and this is where the topic of Future Skills should be addressed. Through better anchoring in formal education especially in ICT programs, more attention can be created for Future Skills. Furthermore, human resource managers should be educated about the importance of Future Skills. Higher education institutions and industry players should join forces and facilitate practice-oriented training in this area. In addition, there should be a regular exchange to prepare students with real world use cases for the new dynamic challenges of the working world.

References

Agentur Q. (2021). Future Skills: Welche Kompetenzen für den Standort Baden-Württemberg heute und in Zukunft erfolgskritisch sind. https://www.bw.igm.de/news/meldung.html?id=101055

Ashoka & McKINSEY. (2018). The Skilling Challenge - How to equip employees for the era of automation and digitization – and how models and mindsets of social entrepreneurs can guide us. https://www.ashoka.org/de-de/files/2018theskillingchallengeashokamckinseypdf

Brunner, M. & Ehlers, U.-D. (2021). Chaise - Blockchain skills for Europe: D2.5.1: Study on skills mismatches in the European Blockchain sector.

https://next-education.org/wp-content/uploads/2021/11/Chaise_WP2_D2.5.1_Study-on-Skill-Mismatch-in-the-blockchain-sector_v3.pdf

Dettmers, S. & Jochmann, W. (2021). Kienbaum & Stepstone Studie 2021: Future Skills - Future Learning. Stepstone, Kienbaum. https://media.kienbaum.com/wp-content/uploads/sites/13/2021/06/Kienbaum-StepStone-Studie_2021_WEB.pdf

Ehlers, U.-D. (2020). Future Skills: Lernen der Zukunft - Hochschule der Zukunft (1. Aufl.). Zukunft der Hochschulbildung - Future Higher Education. Springer Fachmedien Wiesbaden GmbH; Springer VS.

Ehlers, U.-D. (2022). Future Skills Compared: On the construction of a general framework model for future competencies in academic education. https://nextskills.org/wp-content/uploads/2022/07/2022-06-15-Future-Skills-Bildungsforschung_final_Vs_2ENG.pdf

Ehlers, U.-D. & Bonaudo, P. (2021). Chaise - Blockchain skills for Europe: D2.1.1: Research methodology to gather labour market intelligence and identify skills mismatches. https://next-education.org/wp-content/uploads/2023/01/CHAISE-WP2_D2.1.1_Research-Methodology-to-gather-labour-market-intelligence-and-identify-skills-mismatches_v3.pdf

Erpenbeck, J., Rosenstiel, L. von, Grote, S. & Sauter, W. (2017). Handbuch Kompetenzmessung: Erkennen, verstehen und bewerten von Kompetenzen in der betrieblichen, pädagogischen und psychologischen Praxis (3., überarbeitete und erweiterte Auflage). Schäffer-Poeschel Verlag.

ESCO. (2022). Competence. Europäische Kommission. https://ec.europa.eu/esco/portal/escopedia/Competence

European Commission. (2022, 12. Oktober). Commission kick-starts work on the European Year of Skills [Press release]. https://ec.europa.eu/social/main.jsp?langId=en&catId=89&newsId=10431&furtherNews=yes

Huber, L. (2016). „Studium Generale“ oder „Schlüsselqualifikationen“? Ein Orientierungsversuch im Feld der Hochschulbildung. Bildung und Schlüsselqualifikationen, 101–122.

Huber, L. (2019). "Bildung durch Wissenschaft" als Qualität des Studiums. Das Hochschulwesen, Artikel 67, 154–159.

ILO. (2017). Skill needs anticipation: Systems and approaches.: Analysis of stakeholder survey on skill needs assessment and anticipation. Geneva.

McKinsey Global Institute. (2021). DELTA: Foundational Skills for Citizens. https://www.mckinsey.com/industries/public-and-social-sector/our-insights/defining-the-skills-citizens-will-need-in-the-future-world-of-work

NSDC (Hrsg.). (2020). Global Skill Gap Report: Assessing Overseas Opportunities for Skilled Manpower from India. https://skillsip.nsdcindia.org/sites/default/files/kps-document/Global%20Skill%20Gap%20Report%2021April2020.pdf

OECD. (2018). The Future of Education and Skills: Education 2030. OECD. https://www.oecd.org/education/2030/E2030%20Position%20Paper%20(05.04.2018).pdf

OECD (Hrsg.). (2019). OECD Skills Strategy 2019: SKILLS TO SHAPE A BETTER FUTURE. https://www.oecd-ilibrary.org/docserver/9789264313835-en.pdf?expires=1673340365&id=id&accname=ocid56029192&checksum=4631D141B8717D5D3890C8FDDE1C3706

OECD (Hrsg.). (2021). OECD Skills Outlook 2021: LEARNING FOR LIFE. https://www.oecd-ilibrary.org/docserver/0ae365b4-en.pdf?expires=1673340542&id=id&accname=ocid56029192&checksum=B14744308AB7D4644198D1B92E365799

Samochowiec, J. (2020). Future Skills: Four scenarios for the world of tomorrow. GDI Gottlieb Duttweiler Institute. https://www.gdi.ch/sites/default/files/documents/2020-05/2020_e_future-skills_jacobsfoundation_summary.pdf

Schlaeger, J. & Tenorth, H.-E. (2020). Bildung durch Wissenschaft. Berliner Wissenschafts-Verlag.

Schoon, I. (2018). Conceptualising Learner Agency: A Socio-Ecological Developmental Approach. https://www.llakes.ac.uk/wp-content/uploads/2021/03/LLAKES-Research-Paper-64-Schoon-I.pdf

Stifterverband & McKINSEY. (2018). Future Skills: Welche Kompetenzen in Deutschland fehlen. https://www.stifterverband.org/medien/future-skills-welche-kompetenzen-in-deutschland-fehlen

Wild, S., Deuer, E. & Pohlenz, P. (2018). Studienerfolgsverständnis von hauptamtlichen Lehrkräften im Studienbereich Wirtschaft der Dualen Hochschule Baden-Württemberg (DHBW) – Ein Typisierungsversuch. Zeitschrift für

Evaluation - ZfEv(17 (2), 269–288.

World Economic Forum (Hrsg.). (2017). The Future of Jobs and Skills in Africa: Preparing the Region for the Fourth Industrial Revolution. https://www3.weforum.org/docs/WEF_EGW_FOJ_Africa.pdf

World Economic Forum (Hrsg.). (2020). The Future of Jobs Report 2020. https://www3.weforum.org/docs/WEF_Future_of_Jobs_2020.pdf

DISTANCE LEARNING AND ONLINE PEER TUTORING FOR BETTER DIGITAL EDUCATION ENVIRONMENTS: A POST-GRADUATE EXPERIENCE

Antonella Poce, University of Tor Vergata, Italy

Luca Contardi, Sapienza University, Italy,

Giulia Innocentini, University of Modena and Reggio Emilia, Italy

Maria Tolaini, University of Genova, Italy

Eliana Maria Torre, Sapienza University, Italy

Sabina Pirchi, University of Modena and Reggio Emilia, Italy

***Correspondence**: Antonella Poce: antonella.poce@uniroma2.it*

Abstract

This paper presents the results of qualitative research conducted on two post-graduate courses Museum Education and Advanced Studies in Museum Education (jointly University of Modena and Reggio Emilia and University of RomaTre) in the academic year 2021/2022. Students were involved in focus groups in order to enquire how digital transformation in education brought about by the COVID-19 pandemic can foster distance learning for better futures and help shape digital education environments that are accessible and equitable. Results show that the combination of technologies for distance learning and online peer tutoring can play a pivotal role in helping students develop their potential and build a sense of belonging, thus promoting their well-being.

Keywords:

Distance learning, peer tutoring, post-graduate courses, evaluation.

Introduction

In a period of great uncertainty such as the current one opened up by the COVID-19 pandemic, Education professionals must consider how best to deal with occurring changes. The digital transformation has been accelerated (or imposed) by the pandemic and it increasingly appears to be a significant opportunity that must be understood and addressed with the most appropriate methodological and research tools, in order to aim at and deliver on the promise for better futures for all.

The UN 2030 Agenda provides valuable guidelines in this regard. Goal 4, specifically dedicated to the field of education, states the need to ensure inclusive and equitable quality education and promote lifelong learning opportunities for all; it also recalls that providing it is fundamental to creating a peaceful and prosperous world. Goal 3, on the other hand, deals with good health and well-being, also aiming at the promotion of mental health well-being.

Digital transformation provides unprecedented opportunities for contact and training, also in the Creative Industries Education context (Poce *et al.*, 2021). However, more attention should be devoted to the digital sphere within the sector, not only with regard to the adoption of new digital technologies, but also in terms of digital skills and transverse competences professionals should possess (Poce, 2019). Nevertheless, within the cultural context transverse competencies and their development proved to be linked to people's well-being, considered in its multidimensional nature as comprised of many interrelated aspects (O'Brien & O'Shea, 2017; DES & NCCA, 2017). Therefore, new tools or new opportunities assured by the digital transformation, their positive effects, and new possible implementation must be taken into account and examined.

A useful tool for improving educational experiences, even more so in distance education (Valente, 2022), is peer tutoring. Peer tutoring is defined as an interaction between peers that leads to learning, i.e. a peer teaching activity in which students, adequately prepared for the purpose, provide help and support for the learning of others in an interactive, intentional, and systematic way (Topping, 1996; Topping, 2000). Studies conducted in the Italian context have highlighted the advantages of peer interaction, which favours and improves the learning process and experience (La Rocca, 2012). Moreover, among the positive effects observed also in distance learning, the creation of group bonds, and interactions that stimulate a sense of community, identity, and collectivity can be highlighted. (Poce *et al.*, 2022; Valente, 2022).

The study presented here involved students from two online post-graduate joint degree courses in Museum Education and Advanced Studies in Museum Education, both promoted by the Intellect Centre - Department of Education and Humanities, University of Modena and Reggio Emilia, jointly with the University of RomaTre, in the academic year 2021/2022. The courses, due to the COVID-19 pandemic in March 2020 underwent a transformation from blended to online teaching mode; moreover, peer tutoring was introduced from the academic year 2020-2021, in order to provide greater support to students (Poce et al., 2021).

Methodology

Research Questions

This research contribution inquires how digital transformation in education brought about by the COVID-19 pandemic can foster distance learning for better futures. Four research questions are set:

- How is students' well-being affected by the pandemic and the post-graduate course online attendance?
- How do technologies for distance learning affect students' motivation and learning process?
- What is the students' perceived usefulness of peer tutoring?
- Does the online peer tutoring service promote the development of students' transverse competences?

Participants

Five peer tutors and 34 students were involved. The former acted as researchers and were students attending the second year of the post-graduate course in Advanced Studies in Museum Education, who received special training to work as tutors. Their average age was 32 years old and they had a background in Western and Eastern history of art, archaeology, and museum activities. The interviewed students attended both post-graduate courses. All students had a similar profile: most of them fell in the 30-40 age range, with an average age of 35 years old; they all had a background in humanities, i.e. art, history, and archaeology, and were mainly employed in the cultural and educational sector.

Data Collection and Data Analysis

Peer tutors designed and carried out five focus groups targeted at students of both post-graduate courses, and then analysed the resulting data.

The focus group technique was employed because of its feasibility for deep data collection as it allows "more profound information than what can be obtained through interpersonal relationships" (Oprandi, 2000: 14). Peer tutors divided students into five small groups ensuring that each peer tutor was not interviewing their peer tutored group to avoid noble answers. Each focus group was one hour and a half long and was led on Teams by a peer tutor in charge of mediating and assisted by another peer tutor who took notes. Meetings were recorded and participants were informed of it as well as of the research purpose, the data processing, and the privacy policy. Table 1 summarises the structure of the focus groups.

Table 1: The structure of the focus groups

Section	Guiding questions
Well-being in relation to the COVID-19 pandemic and distance learning	How has the COVID-19 pandemic affected your well-being? How has attending the online post-graduate course affected your well-being?
Technologies for distance learning	What is your experience regarding the technologies for distance learning adopted for the post-graduate course? Did you experience Teams and Moodle before the post-graduate course?

Perception of the peer tutoring service	Have you used the peer tutoring service before this course? What are your impressions of this peer tutoring service? Do you think your expectations about peer tutoring are met? What do you think are the advantages and disadvantages of peer tutoring? Do you think the peer tutor is facilitating your learning?
Transverse competences promotion	Do you think that the online peer tutoring service is promoting your transverse skills? (i.e. Communication, Collaboration, Critical thinking, Divergent thinking)
Future implementations for distance learning	Do you think the peer tutoring service is fostering a sense of belonging? Do you think there are weaknesses in the way the online peer tutoring service is delivered? How could the online peer tutoring service be improved in order to better help future students?

The recordings were transcribed and the notes previously taken in relation to non-verbal aspects and group dynamics were inserted where relevant. Data were analysed following the guidelines elaborated by Hycner (1985).

Due to the students' similar profiles and the two post-graduate courses' analogous structure and delivery mode, results are discussed cumulatively for each section of the focus groups.

Results

Well-being in relation to the COVID-19 Pandemic and Distance Learning

Firstly, students were asked how the COVID-19 pandemic impacted their lives. 18 students confirmed the negative impact of the lockdowns and just 2 students took only advantage of it. Interestingly, 9 students admitted having mixed thoughts about it, as the event had partially positive repercussions. This result is somewhat related to the post-graduate courses: 29 students recognised the positive impact of the online courses on their lives, and 11 of these added that the fundamental element was the online delivery of the training offer.

The next question asked the students how the online post-graduate course affected their well-being. 12 students emphasised the importance of the course online delivery because it allowed them to participate without needing to commute. According to 2 students, the online delivery reassured them in anticipation of possible further lockdowns. 12 students benefitted from the course by investing time in their training and by reskilling. 4 students recognised the course as a chance to keep themselves busy.

These results suggest that, during such an uncertain time as the COVID-19 pandemic, technology has played a central role in increasing student well-being.

Technologies for Distance Learning

Concerning the technologies adopted for distance learning, students were asked about their own experiences, also regarding previous familiarity with digital tools. 25 students stated that they had not encountered any difficulties, finding them often intuitive, even when they had no previous experience with the platforms - Teams for synchronous lessons and Moodle for asynchronous activities.

Significantly, for those who claimed to have experienced an initial difficulty - 9 students - the intervention of the tutors proved crucial in overcoming it, thanks to the clarification and the technical support guaranteed. Tutee n° 15 explained: "I had never used Teams or Moodle, but [...] I found it quite intuitive right from the start. The initial lesson on how the platform works was enlightening. From there on everything went quite smoothly."

Moreover, 16 students believed they acquired new skills concerning the use of the technologies adopted. Student n° 36 claimed: "For me, they were extremely useful, I really learnt things that are useful for my job."

Digital technologies also allowed breaking out of the boundaries imposed by the pandemic and other factors, as expressed by some of the students (n° 33, n° 35): "The use of technology [...] allowed me to participate in this course; living in Milan I would have never been able to attend it otherwise"; "As I have difficulty commuting for health reasons, without these technologies I wouldn't have been able to do any of this at all".

These results show a widespread good mastery of the e-learning tools, as well as the effectiveness of the peer tutoring intervention in solving those cases in which the students encountered difficulties. Distance learning appears to be fundamental in guaranteeing learning opportunities for all. Furthermore, the use of digital tools led some of the students to improve their perception of the digital skills they possessed.

Perception of the Peer Tutoring Service

Students were initially asked if they have had peer tutoring experiences in previous training contexts and 25 answered that it was their first time.

27 students reported to have had positive first impressions of the service and only 4 found that their expectations were not met or partially missed. When asked about the advantages they identified them in: a constant presence for 16 and a liaison between students and lecturers for 7; their speed in responding for 22 and thoroughness for 3; the possibility of more informal communication for 11; a constant stimulus and encouragement for 3 and a way to network for 1.

In addition to this, the presence of the tutor also proved to be very useful during the lectures, as underlined by student n° 16: "I find tutors' mediation during the lessons very useful, because they make the different phases of the lesson clearer ".

The evidence of the usefulness and effectiveness of peer tutoring service was demonstrated by the first positive impressions and the advantages mentioned by the students. Student n° 7 observed: "I'm glad to be able to compare notes with a colleague because I believe that peer tutors are on the same level as us in terms of human experience and age, so in any case there is a strong exchange. So, let's say, that is the optimal solution".

Other students (n° 9 and n° 21) affirmed: "I am a very shy person, so knowing that on the other side there is a person who is more or less my age, who is having an experience like mine, was like a Linus blanket for me". "I think having a tutor is essential. [...] This is especially important when people like me, unable to follow most of the lessons, find themselves a bit lost."

These results show that peer tutoring is a valid and appreciated tool to offer a more effective and engaging educational experience to students.

Transverse Competences Promotion

When asked if peer tutors facilitated the development of their transverse competences, 17 students responded negatively, while 4 said they were uncertain. However, the answers to the following inputs that investigated the development of collaboration, critical thinking, divergent thinking, and communication showed that perhaps the initial question was not fully understood or that the concept of transverse competence was not clear. 3 of these 17 respondents stated that in fact collaboration (2 people) and critical thinking (1 person) had been facilitated by the peer tutors. In total, 13 students indicated one or more competences that, according to them, peer tutoring helped them develop. 10 people did not express their opinion on this matter.

Specifically, 9 people believed peer tutoring facilitated the implementation of divergent thinking. Student n°7 argued: "During the lectures, listening to a prompt from the tutor [...] helps you to think differently, which doesn't mean different from your own, but it's something additional [...] so in my opinion [this is a] very useful discussion." Student n° 29 felt that the peer tutors' involvement during classes: "stimulates me and [it] opens my mind a little more on some aspects that during the lecture I had not thought about".

Similarly, 9 people found their communication competence, especially with lecturers, improved as a result of the peer tutors' intervention. Student n° 30 explained that: "I was able to attend almost all the classes and I noticed how they [the peer tutors] helped me, because I could see that they would start asking questions right away; that made me feel a little more confident; so seeing them jumping in, I told myself let's jump in too".

6 students believed that critical thinking was facilitated and according to 2 people collaboration was similarly stimulated. Student n° 36 reported that: "The tutor asked us to help each other look for solutions to actual problems".

These results show that, when reflecting on each skill, not only most respondents identified improvements in their transverse competences but also provided insightful examples of how peer tutors supported them in developing them.

Future implementations for distance learning

Considering the question of whether the peer tutoring service fostered a sense of belonging, 4 students responded positively. Nevertheless, 12 felt the opposite: 2 students did not feel the need for it, while 10 believed that there weren't the conditions for it. However, when discussing the weaknesses of the peer tutoring service, only 1 student highlighted poor interaction between the tutor and the tutees, whereas 23 did not identify any weaknesses in the delivery of the peer tutoring service.

Concerning future opportunities to improve the peer tutoring service, 7 students considered it already adequate. 12 recommended creating regular opportunities for discussion. 8 stressed the importance of establishing relational connections and fostering a sense of belonging. 3 admitted that they could have used the service more. With particular reference to the online course delivery, 1 student expressed a desire to conduct in-person classes as well. Quite the opposite, 4 students emphasized the need to maintain the online delivery.

Conclusions

This study explored how digital technologies for distance learning and online peer tutoring can foster better futures for all. Previous research on the effectiveness of distance learning (Poce *et al.* 2021) and online peer tutoring (Poce *et al.* 2022) in the post-graduate courses under examination showed the need for further in-depth analyses, thus the adoption of the focus group approach. Although this method can lead to different outcomes depending on the participants' willingness to communicate and the group dynamics, and data gathered cannot be generalised due to the low number of study participants, results highlighted that technology and peer tutoring played a pivotal role in the students' learning process and motivation.

Students' well-being was positively affected by the attendance of the course. In such a time of uncertainty as the lockdowns, having the chance to keep busy, to receive adequate training, and to reskill was largely appreciated. In particular, technologies for distance learning ensured the delivery of the course regardless of the unfolding of the health emergency. Platforms such as Teams and Moodle allowed students and lecturers to break out of the boundaries imposed first by the pandemic and then by geographical or personal health reasons. This is the main reason students invested and engaged in a complex academic course. Overall, it appears that technology sustained students' learning path insofar as they already mastered or developed their digital skills.

Students found peer tutors especially helpful because of their constant presence and support both for technical aspects and during lectures, when they encouraged a dialogue between learners and presenters. No weaknesses were found in the delivery of the peer tutoring service, except for one person that highlighted poor interactions between the tutor and the tutees. Through their role as facilitators, peer tutors helped remove the barriers created by physical distance and influenced the behaviour of other students, encouraging them to develop their potential thus contributing to their well-being. Peer tutoring proved to be a positive, profitable and useful experience for the promotion of transverse competences, especially regarding divergent thinking and communication.

Students' suggestions for improvement will certainly be considered to further increase the quality of the distance education delivered in the context examined. Results show the need for further research in developing a sense of belonging. Therefore, more opportunities for group discussion will be created and the peer tutoring service will be enhanced, as they are linked with the development of a sense of belonging to a group (Delahunty *et al.*, 2014). In the upcoming years, the effectiveness of new technologies for distance education and further tutoring methodologies ought to be tested with the final objective to build digital education environments that are inclusive and equitable.

Authors' statement

The authors of the present paper contributed to the writing of this article as follows: A. Poce (Introduction, Conclusions); E. Torre (Methodology, which comprises the subparagraphs Research Questions, Participants, Data Collection and Data Analysis); G. Innocentini (Results. Well-being in relation to the COVID-19 Pandemic and Distance Learning, Future Implementations for Distance Learning); L. Contardi (Results. Technologies for Distance Learning); S. Pirchi (Results. Perception of the Peer Tutoring Service); M. Tolaini (Results. Transverse competences Promotion).

References

Delahunty, J., Verenikina, I. & Jones, P. (2014). Socio-emotional connections: identity, belonging and learning in online interactions. A literature reviews. *Technology, Pedagogy and Education, 23*(2), 243-265.

Department of Education and Skills & National Council for Curriculum and Assessment (2017). Junior Cycle Wellbeing Guidelines.

Hycner, R. H. (1985). Some Guidelines for the Phenomenological Analysis of Interview Data. *Human Studies*, 8, 278-303.

La Rocca, C. (2012). Il Peer Tutoring nell'Orientamente Universitario. Punti di forza e criticità. *Metis. Mondi Educativi. Temi, indagini, suggestioni, II*(1).

O'Brien, M. and O'Shea A. (2017). *A human development framework for orienting education and schools in the space of wellbeing*. NCCA, Dublin.

Oprandi, N. (2000). *Focus group. Breve compendio teorico-pratico*. Emme&erre, Padova.

Poce, A. (2019). Information and data literacy skills development in Creative Industries Adult Education: the Digiculture project. *Pedagogia Oggi, 17*(2), 184-201. doi: 10.7346/PO-022019-12.

Poce, A., Re, M. R., Valente, M., Amenduni, F. (2021). Redesigning post-graduate courses for future museum educators in time of a pandemic: an experience from University Roma Tre. *Proceedings of the EDEN Annual Meeting*, 107-115. doi:10.38069/edenconf-2021-ac0010

Poce, A., Re, M.R., Valente, M. (2022). Community Building in Post Pandemic Era: Peer Tutoring in Digital Learning Contexts for Soft and Professional Skills Enhancement. A Post-graduate Experience. In: Väljataga, T., Laanpere, M. (eds) Shaping the Digital Transformation of the Education Ecosystem in Europe. EDEN 2022. Communications in Computer and Information Science, vol 1639. Springer, Cham. https://doi.org/10.1007/978-3-031-20518-7_4

Topping, K. J. (1996). The effectiveness of peer tutoring in further and higher education: A typology and review of the literature. *Higher Education, 32,* 321-345.

Topping, K. J. (2000). Tutoring. Unesco International Academy of Education and International Bureau of Education.

Valente, M. (2022). Il tutoraggio tra pari in contesto universitario post-lauream: sollecitare le competenze trasversali e il Pensiero critico. In A. Poce & M. R. Re (Ed.), *Critical thinking between schools, universities and the workplace. Innovative learning experiences* (pp. 63-79). Edizioni Scientifiche Italiane.

MAPPING THE DROPOUT PHENOMENON FOR THE NEW DIGITAL CONTEXT

Berrin Cefa, University of Oldenburg, Germany

Olaf Zawacki-Richter, University of Oldenburg, Germany

***Correspondence**: Berrin Cefa Sari: berrin.cefa.sari@uni-oldenburg.de*

Abstract

Open, distance, and digital education (ODDE) has a long history concerning dropout. With the new reality of the digital age, the terminologies and concepts that have been long adopted are inevitably subject to change. To understand dropout in the digital transformation, it is important to take an evidence-based approach and examine the literature. Therefore, this study applies the steps of a systematic literature review to retrieve relevant articles on dropout since 2010 and conducts a content analysis via text mining. The results indicate that student dropout and retention declined in publication during the pandemic despite remaining one of the critical issues in higher education. The main concepts indicate that most of the dropout studies focus on comparisons between face-to-face and online modalities; the learning environment and engagement; and support and motivation.

Keywords:

Dropout, student retention, distance education, open education, online education

Introduction

Student attrition has been a major area of concern in higher education (HE) throughout the years and various theoretical models have explored the dimensions and factors that result in student retention or attrition (Rovai, 2003; Spady, 1970; Tinto, 1975). However, open and distance education, and subsequently online education, made the dropout phenomenon a central point because student-attrition rates have long been reported as higher than in face-to-face, on-campus education (Simpson, 2013; Smith, 2010). According to the traditional definiton, dropout is the failure of an individual to continue their engagement in the registered programme and disengagement from the academic institution as a result of socially and/or academicly unfavourable experiences (Tinto, 1975).

As the advancement of technology-driven education and the demand for HE continue to grow (Arnhold & Bassett, 2021), the context is subject to change, too. The long-established binary position of brick-and-mortar institutions versus distance education is becoming blurred as technology-driven education continues to advance. The rapidly increasing speed of technological development has made digital education, either online or technology-enhanced, a preferred option in higher education (Allen & Seeman, 2017). Online or distance learning has become a viable option for HE institutions looking for prevalence in more and wider student retainment (Nakamura, 2017). The Covid-19 pandemic has further propelled this trend and proved that teaching through online modalities is a resilient option amidst the crisis. Although there are numerous publications that report the difficulties and limits of online education, digital learning and new developments around generative AI technologies continue to reshape education.

Within this transformation, it is important to sustain the quality of higher education and improve student retention, which is one of the quality criteria of HE. However, it is questionable if the old definitions of retention and dropout are still valid in the current technological landscape. Facilitating up-to-date and valid terminology for the field of ODDE is highly important to explore current practices. To achieve this goal, it is crucial to attain an in-depth understanding of the dropout phenomenon first and map the phenomenon with evidence from the literature. This study serves as a preliminary analysis of a literature review corpus from 2010 onwards. The year 2010 was taken as a starting point for the spread of online education to wider communities through various advancements such as massive open, online courses (MOOCs) and open education resources (OER; Zawacki-Richter & Naidu, 2016).

Within the given frame, this study aims to map the dropout terrain according to the thematic clusters to answer the following questions:

- How are publications on dropout between 2010 and 2022 distributed according to years and journals?
- What is the thematic scope in the field of drop-out research and how do the themes relate to each other?

This study focuses on the reasons, factors, or results that affect dropout or student retention among undergraduate or master's level students. The exploration and mapping of how the dropout phenomenon is addressed in the literature is formed according to the PICO framework (Boland et al., 2017). The dropout context is framed with HE including any ODDE setting. MOOCs are excluded as long as they are not offered as a part of formal education.

Methodology

Method and Sample

Analyses of trends and conceptual themes are important to picture the progress of a certain phenomenon and make evidence-supported projections about the field of the studied subject (Lee et al., 2004). A good example of this is a content analysis by Zawacki-Richter and Naidu (2016), in which they map three decades of distance-education literature. Exploring the thematic clusters based on large body of texts enables a broad understanding of trends and themes within the field under investigation (Krippendorff, 2013). A crucial point of the method is the need for well-informed interpretation of the data. With this aim, this paper adopts content analysis of systematically selected literature on student dropout and retention between January 2010 and December 2022. Content analysis is a labour-intensive process as it requires the validation of codebooks, glossaries, and inter-rater reliability as these factors increase the risk of bias of the authors. Therefore, an automated content analysis tool, Leximancer, is used as the text mining tool. This text-mining approach has been used to decrease interpreter coding bias, generate automated semantic relations and outline the most-discussed themes in connection to the phenomenon under study.

As the reproducibility and replicability of such methods are crucial in research (Smith & Humphreys, 2006, p. 262) and as the articles assessed here are not limited to a single journal, the methods of a systematic review were adopted to form the data set. Systematic reviews have three main, consecutive steps, namely: a) identification of the major research publications, b) critical appraisal of the obtained studies, c) synthesis of findings in the final corpus based on the evidence (Gough et al., 2012). Such analyses can enrich the literature by providing information on the selected study field and guidance for future studies and directions (Petticrew & Roberts, 2008).

Data were retrieved from three databases of the educational technology field, namely Education Source, Scopus, and Web of Science, using the search string given in Table 1 and the inclusion and exclusion criteria given in Table 2.

Table 1

Search String

Concepts	Search terms with Boolean operators
Dropout	(dropout OR drop-out OR retention OR persistence OR attrition OR disengage*) N5 student*
Digital context	AND (online* OR distanc* OR blend* OR mobile OR technology-enhance*) N3 (learn* OR teach* OR study* OR studie* OR degree)
Higher education	AND "higher education" OR universit* OR college* OR "postsecondary education" OR "tertiary education" OR undergrad* OR postgrad*

Table 2

Inclusion and Exclusion Criteria

Inclusion	Exclusion
English	Not in English
Journal articles	Editorials, books, book chapters, conference proceedings, introductions, reviews, grey literature
Empirical research	Literature reviews, conceptional papers
Digital higher education, distance, open, online, hybrid, or blended learning	face to face only, MOOCs that are not a part of a formal university programme
Undergraduate students, master's students	K-12, PhD students, adult learners in lifelong learning programmes
Papers report on student retention, attrition, persistence, dropout	Papers report a sub-dimension of retention or dropout phenomenon without direct link to dropout or retention

The initial corpus after elimination of duplicates (N = 2426) was screened based on the abstracts. Before the abstract screening, inter-rater reliability between three raters was calculated (k = .70), resulting in good agreement. Of these abstracts screened, 669 articles were selected for full-text screening. Of these, the studies that were not retrieved for full texts (n = 33) were removed. After the final exclusion and inclusion assessment and further exclusions (n = 352), the abstracts of 287 studies were found eligible for this study and included for further analysis.

The titles and abstracts of the 287 included articles were used for text mining as they present the purpose, population, and main results of the studies in detail and in condensed form. As the data was extracted automatically from the original CSV file of the included studies, they were checked for and cleaned by removing stopwords as well as words, lexicons and/or expressions irrelevant to the analysis (e.g., automatic indication of copyright).

Limitations

This study is limited to journal articles, three databases, and English only publications. Although the selection of data was subject to wide inclusion of three big databases that include high ranking journals, the publication of journal articles is limited by the editorial processes and the scope of the journals. In addition, conference papers and book chapters were not included. MOOCs, unless a part of a formal degree programmes are also excluded from this study as the reasons for dropping out from MOOCs are diverse and may not show the same pattern of disengagement from institutional, formal-learning environments. Although Leximancer has been found to produce valid evidence for content analysis (e.g., Zawacki-Richter & Naidu, 2016), it "...is not a panacea and requires analytical sensitivity and judgment in its interpretation." (Harwood et al., 2015, p. 1041).

Findings and Discussion

Descriptive results

Figure 1 shows the trend of publications from 2010 to 2022:

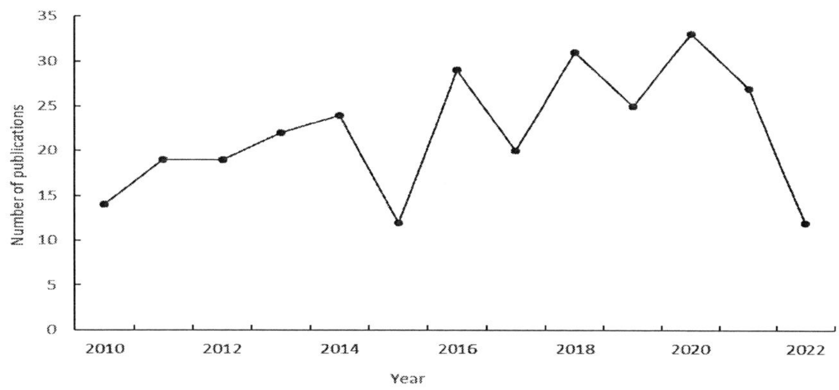

Figure 1. Publications per year

The publication trend per year reveals interesting results regarding its slightly fluctuating but generally increasing line until 2020. From the year 2020 on, there is a notable decline, which may be due to several reasons. The publication interest during the pandemic (2020-2022) may have shifted to more acute problems due to emergency remote teaching practices such as equality, inclusive education, and other constraints being experienced.

The included articles came from 133 different journals, with those contributing more articles from the field of ODDE. Online Journal of Distance Learning Administration ranks first (n = 12), followed by Online Learning (n = 10), Journal of Educators Online (n = 9), International Review of Research in Open & Distance Learning (n = 8), and Distance Education (n = 8). The list of the top ten journals is presented in Table 3.

Table 3

Number of included articles per journal

Journal	Number of Articles
Online Journal of Distance Learning Administration	12
Online Learning	10
Journal of Educators Online	9
International Review of Research in Open & Distance Learning	8
Distance Education	8
Computers & Education	7
Open Learning	7
American Journal of Distance Education	6
Internet & Higher Education	6
Journal of College Student Retention: Research, Theory & Practice	6

The majority of articles on drop-out and retention was published in journals with a management and institution focus. Based on the 3M-Framework, which groups research themes in three layers of micro, meso, and macro levels (Zawacki-Richter, 2009, Zawacki-Richter & Bozkurt, 2023), the dropout issue is considered on the meso-level of HE institutions. Drop-out and student retention rates are widely considered connected to institutional quality assurance and management strategies, which is also a meso-evel issue.

The scope of dropout phenomenon (2010 - 2022)

The first analysis was run for the whole corpus including all 287 papers based on titles and abstracts. Figure 2 displays the major themes and concepts covered in the articles published between 2010 and 2022.

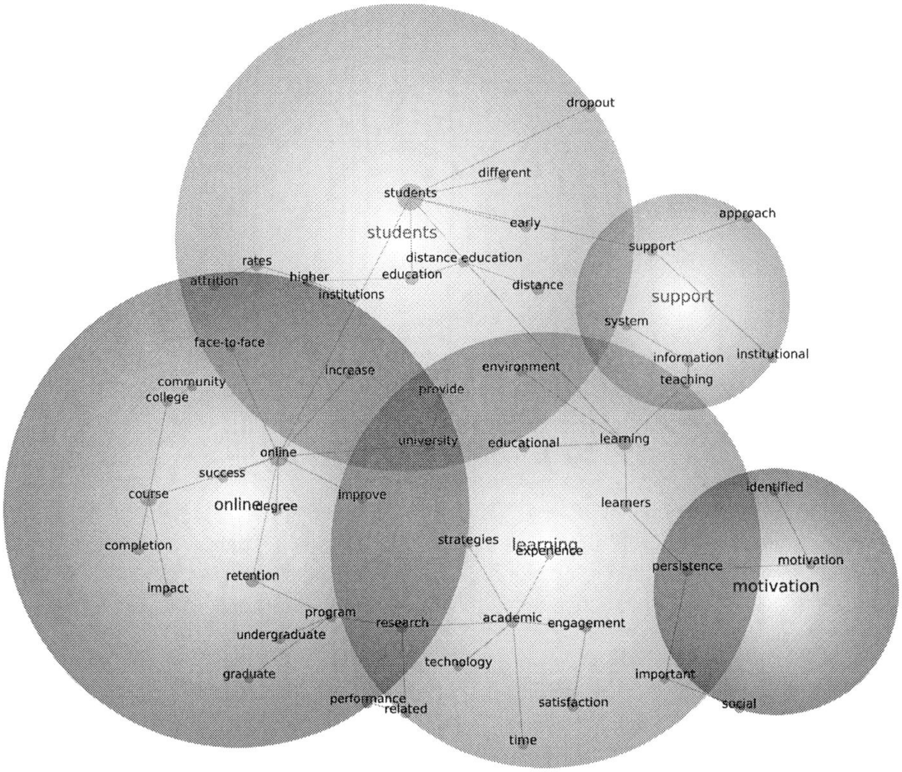

Figure 2. Concept map of the dropout phenomenon from 2010 to 2022 (N = 287)

The concept map shows five thematic regions that are named after the concept with the highest number of mentions in the corpus, namely: *students* (1238), *online* (968), *learning* (829), *support* (267), and *motivation* (125).

The thematic region of *students* covers three well-known facts in ODDE literature in general: 1) dropout rates are a major concern in distance education (see concept path *distance – education – higher – attrition*; Radovan, 2019; Xavier & Meneses, 2020); 2) as well as in online learning (*completion – course – success – online*); 3) often compared with face-to-face learning (Ashby et al., 2011; Ferguson, 2020). Many studies have compared and contrasted face-to-face education with online education (Clayton et al., 2010; Summers et al., 2005), despite the fact that the design quality of a course matters more than the mode of delivery (Matcha et al., 2020). The theme of *online* clearly indicates the link between success and course completion. This is a common approach to predicting dropout in online learning. When considering the development of higher education, the focus has tended to shift more towards graduation and course-completion rates as indicators of success, rather than the competencies that students achieve (Aljohani, 2016; Bodin & Orange, 2018).

The central thematic region of *learning* is the sole circle connecting all other four themes. Many factors of dropout based on Rovai's (2013) internal factors or Tinto's (1975) academic factors are highly dominant in this circle. For example, the relation of learning experience to academic strategies and engagement, and thus to satisfaction, is one highlight among the semantic connections (see concept path *satisfaction – engagement – academic – experience*). These are all linked to retention in online degrees. Whilst many studies discuss the vital mediator role of satisfaction and engagement for persistence in the corpus (e.g., Pechenkina, et al., 2017; Rahim, 2020), we must note the hazard of evaluating satisfaction based on course evaluations with superficial understanding of quality of online learning.

The concept map nicely underscores that student support is critical in ODDE (Brindley & Paul, 1996) with *support* as a thematic region of its own. The direct connection between *institutional*, *support*, and *students* indicates that researchers are dealing with institutional support systems in the publications. The *learning – environment* is connected to *information systems* through *teaching* in the *support* theme. Information systems include any medium such as learning management systems or dashboards that provide information about teaching and learning activities in the online environment. The corpus covers several examples on early warning systems (e.g., Bañeres et al., 2020; Kustitskaya, et al., 2022), the use of dashboards (e.g., Marshall, 2016); and predictive learning analytics (e.g., Herodotou, et al., 2020; Yasmin, 2013).

Finally, the concept of *motivation* is related to *persistence* in learning. Motivation may be due to internal or external factors of the individual learners (Price & Kadi-Hanifi, 2011). Thus, it is not directly linked to institutional measures of *support* in the concept map. Still, motivational intervention programs are in use through predictive learning analytics (e.g., Herodotou, et al., 2020). More importantly, *motivation* demonstrates the social interaction in the circle, which is highly motivational (Waite & Davis, 2006). Technology-enhanced media and digital learning tools have long enabled rich social-learning environments (Barlow, 2008; Price & Kadi-Hanifi, 2011).

Conclusion and future directions

This study analyzed the content of titles and abstracts of systematically collected journal articles with a text-mining tool and provided an overview of the themes, concepts, and semantic relations among the concepts..

The findings demonstrate that the dropout and student-retention literature discusses the high attrition rates in distance education, the common understanding of success as course completion, the need for support at the institutional level (*meso*) through information gathered at the teaching and learning (*micro*) level. The map also displays engagement, satisfaction, and academic strategies as topics related to retention.

This study contributes to ODDE literature by mapping the last thirteen years of publications gathered through three large databases that host high-quality, peer-reviewed journals and filtering the results to retention and dropout studies with replicable, reproducible data curation methods. However, there is still need for further research.

Student retention is considered a quality indicator (Burke, 2019) and being financially better for the institutions and government (Simpson, 2005). In addition to global crisis, new advances in the digital world are forcing HE to transform. These issues include, generative AI, advanced access to the technology in the global North, a growing digital divide between the Global South and North, and the need for effective teaching and learning strategies through hybrid learning environments. Further analysis and comparison studies should be conducted to see whether the trends in dropout research differ or vary based on a) period of time of the publications, b) digital divide-related research, and c) digital transformation-based research. Thus, a new understanding and problematization of dropout phenomenon should be developed and discussed.

References

Allen, I. E., & Seaman, J. (2017). Digital Learning Compass: Distance Education Enrollment Report 2017. Retrieved from https://files.eric.ed.gov/fulltext/ED580868.pdf.

Aljohani, O. (2016). A Review of the Contemporary International Literature on Student Retention in Higher Education. *International Journal of Education and Literacy Studies, 4*(1), 40-52.

Arnhold, N. & Bassett, R. M. (2021). *Steering tertiary education: Toward resilient systems that deliver for all.* Washington DC: World Bank.

Ashby, J., Sadera, W. A., & McNary, S. W. (2011). Comparing student success between developmental math courses offered online, blended, and face-to-face. *Journal of Interactive Online Learning, 10*(3), 128–140. https://www.scopus.com/inward/record.uri?eid=2-s2.0-84855766000&partnerID=40&md5=b41eb555c431319c49667b574a48e2f6

Bañeres, D., Rodríguez, M. E., Guerrero-Roldán, A. E., & Karadeniz, A. (2020). An early warning system to detect at-risk students in online higher education. *Applied Sciences (Switzerland), 10*(13), 1–28. https://doi.org/10.3390/app10134427

Barlow, T. (2008). Web 2.0: Creating a classroom without walls. *Teaching Science 54*(1), 46–8.

Berger, J., Blanco Ramírez, G., & Lyons, S. (2012). Past to present: A historical look at retention. College Student Retention: Formula for Student Success, 7–34.

Bodin, R., and S. Orange. 2018. Access and retention in French higher education: Student drop-out as a form of regulation. *British Journal of Sociology of Education, 39*(1), 126–43.

Boland, A., Cherry, M. G., & Dickson, R. (2017). *Doing a systematic review: A student's guide* (2nd edition). Thousand Oaks, CA: SAGE Publications.

Brindley, J. E., & Paul, R. (1996). Lessons from distance education for the university of the future. In R. Mills & A. Tait (Eds.), *Supporting the learner in open and distance learning* (pp. 43–55). Pitman Publishing.

Burke, A. (2019). Student retention models in higher education: A literature review. *College and University, 94*(2), 12-21.

Clayton, K.; Blumberg, F.; Auld, D.P. (2010). The relationship between motivation, learning strategies and choice of environment whether traditional or including an online component. *British Journal of Educational Technology, 41*, 349–364

Ferguson, S. (2020). Attrition in online and face-to-face calculus and precalculus courses: A comparative analysis. *Journal of Educators Online, 17*(1), 1–8. http://search.ebscohost.com/login.aspx?direct=true&db=eue&AN=142286978&site=ehost-live

Gough, D., Oliver, S., & Thomas, J. (Eds.). (2012). *An introduction to systematic reviews*. London; Thousand Oaks, Calif: SAGE

Harwood, I. A., Gapp, R. P., & Stewart, H. J. (2015). Cross-check for completeness: Exploring a novel use of Leximancer in a grounded theory study. *The Qualitative Report, 20*(7), 1029

Herodotou, C., Naydenova, G., Boroowa, A., Gilmour, A., & Rienties, B. (2020). How can predictive learning analytics and motivational interventions increase student retention and enhance administrative support in distance education? *Journal of Learning Analytics, 7*(2), 72–83. http://dx.doi.org/10.18608/jla.2020.72.4

Krippendorff, K. (2013). *Content analysis: An introduction to its methodology* (3rd ed.). Los Angeles, CA: Sage.

Lee, Y., Driscoll, M. P., & Nelson, D. W. (2004). The past, present, and future of research in distance education: Results of a content analysis. American Journal of Distance Education, 18, 225–241. doi:http://dx.doi.org/10.1207/s15389286ajde1804_4.

Marshall, J. (2016). Online course selection: Using course dashboards to inform student enrollment decisions. *Open Learning, 31*(3), 245–259. https://www.scopus.com/inward/record.uri?eid=2-s2.0-84986182693&doi=10.1080%2f02680513.2016.1227699&partnerID=40&md5=db793bdeede4e4d78194771472310e44

Matcha, W., Gasevic, D., Uzir, N. A. A., Jovanovic, J., Pardo, A., Lim, L., ... & Tsai, Y. S. (2020). Analytics of Learning Strategies: Role of Course Design and Delivery Modality. *Journal of Learning Analytics, 7*(2), 45-71.

Nakamura, M. (2017). The state of distance education in Japan. Quarterly Review of Distance Education, 18(3), 75–87.

Parr, C. (2013). MOOC Completion Rates 'Below 7 %'. Available at: http://www.timeshighereducation.co.uk/news/mooc-completion-rates-below-7/2003710.article.

Pechenkina, E., Laurence, D., Oates, G., Eldridge, D., & Hunter, D. (2017). Using a gamified mobile app to increase student engagement, retention and academic achievement. *International Journal of Educational Technology in Higher Education, 14*(1), 1–12. http://search.ebscohost.com/login.aspx?direct=true&db=eue&AN=124485246&site=ehost-live

Petticrew, M., & Roberts, H. (2008). *Systematic reviews in the social sciences: A practical guide*. Oxford, The UK: Blackwell Publishing.

Radovan, M. (2019). Should I stay, or Should I go? Revisiting Learner retention models in distance education. *Turkish Online Journal of Distance Education, 20*(3), 29–40. https://doi.org/10.17718/tojde.598211

Rahim, N. B. (2020). Improving Student Engagement and Behavioural Outcomes via Persistence among Distance Learners. *Akademika, 90*(2), 91–102.

Rovai, A. P. (2003). In search of higher persistence rates in distance education online programs. Internet and Higher Education, 6, 1-16. https://doi.org/10.1016/S1096-7516(02)00158-6

Simpson, O. (2005). The costs and benefits of student retention for students, institutions and governments. *Studies in Learning, Evaluation Innovation and Development, 2*(3), 34-43.

Simpson, O. (2013). Student retention in distance education: are we failing our students?. *Open learning: The Journal of Open, Distance and e-learning, 28*(2), 105-119.

Smith, A. E., & Humphreys, M. S. (2006). Evaluation of unsupervised semantic mapping of natural language with Leximancer concept mapping. *Behavior Research Methods, 38,* 262–279. doi:http://dx.doi.org/10.3758/BF03192778.

Smith B. (2010). E-learning technologies: A comparative study of adult learners enrolled on blended and online campuses engaging in a virtual classroom (Doctoral dissertation). Retrieved from ProQuest Dissertations and Theses database.

Spady, W. 1970. Dropouts from higher education: An interdisciplinary review and synthesis. *Interchange. 1*(1), 64–85.

Summers, J.J.; Waigandt, A.; Whittaker, T.A. A. (2005). Comparison of Student Achievement and Satisfaction in an Online Versus a Traditional Face-to-Face Statistics Class. *Innov. High. Educ.,29*, 233–250.

Tinto, V. 1975. Dropout from higher education: A theoretical synthesis of recent research. *The Review of Educational Research. 45*(1): 89–125.

Waite, S., & B. Davis. (2006). Developing undergraduate research skills in a faculty of education: Motivation through collaboration. *Higher Education Research and Development 25*(4). 403–19.

Xavier, M., & Meneses, J. (2020). *Dropout in online higher education: A scoping review from 2014 to 2018.* eLearn Center Universitat Oberta de Catalunya.

Zawacki-Richter, O. (2009). Research areas in distance education: A Delphi study. *The International Review of Research in Open and Distributed Learning, 10*(3). https://doi.org/10.19173/irrodl.v10i3.674

Zawacki-Richter, O., & Bozkurt, A. (2023). Research Trends in Open, Distance, and Digital Education. In O. Zawacki-Richter & I. Jung (Eds.), *Handbook of Open, Distance and Digital Education* (pp. 199–220). Springer Nature Singapore. https://doi.org/10.1007/978-981-19-2080-6_12

Zawacki-Richter, O., & Naidu, S. (2016). Mapping research trends from 35 years of publications in distance education. Distance Education, 37(3), 245–269. https://doi.org/10.1080/01587919.2016.1185079.

STUDENTS' DIGITAL COMPETENCIES IN REMOTE AND ONLINE HIGHER EDUCATION IN THE SECURITY AND DEFENCE FIELD

Marina Marchisio, Fabio Roman, Matteo Sacchet, Enrico Spinello, University of Turin, Italy

***Correspondence**: Matteo Sacchet: matteo.sacchet@unito.it*

Abstract

Using digital tools for teaching and learning has become quite common in the latest years: while already before the year 2020 their use had been constantly increasing, the breakout of the COVID-19 pandemic at the beginning of the current decade gave a strong impulse to their diffusion. This phenomenon has become enduring also now that the presence of the virus does no longer constitute an emergency, with a view that certain changes will become essentially permanent. The use of digital tools in teaching brings some advantages, for example by allowing to teach and learn at a distance, but also challenges, since moving from using PCs and other devices for everyday life to using them in educational contexts is less straightforward than expected. In this research, we analyse how students perceived higher education during the transition scenario implied by the pandemic, through a survey delivered to military and civilian students enrolled in security and defence studies, which investigates students feelings while undergoing relevant changes in their educational habits. From the analysis of the questionnaire, it resulted that students had trouble, among other things, relating with teachers and feeling the same intensity of engagement when unable to see them in person. This research is part of the activities of the European project DIGICODE, aimed at the improvement of education quality in security and defence by fostering the correct use of digital tools, and by developing the relative competencies in both students and teachers.

Keywords:

digital education, distance learning, online education, security and defence, student training

Introduction

International cooperation is pivotal in the security and defence contexts to stand together against today's threats. For the sake of cooperating skillfully and in the long run, it is better if military officers and civilians involved in the security and defence area cooperate early in their studies, for example when they are still students or in training (Marchisio & Spinello, 2021). This implies the use of appropriate tools allowing such a cooperation, such as e-learning, which nowadays provides a wide support to various teaching modalities: blended learning (Marchisio et al., 2022a), hybrid learning (Marchisio et al., 2022b), and more in general modalities which do not require a course to be taken purely online, allowing to strategically internazionalize the educational setting (Mihalova, 2006). While the diffusion of e-learning started with the computer and information revolution, being well under way during the 2010s, the event that caused a big leap forward in its use all around the world was the COVID-19 pandemic (Hodges et al., 2020). Inviting teachers, students, and more in general all the stakeholders to undergo specific training is important because it shows them how education is related to a peculiar use of the digital tools, which even people born in the computer age do not necessarily master in the best way possible before having acquired some appropriate expertise. The DIGICODE project implements this opportunity at European level, with the involvement of several nations like Bulgaria, Italy, Poland, and Romania. Its name stands for *Digital Competencies for Improving Security and Defence Education*, being an Erasmus+ Key Action 2 Strategic Partnership project, funded by the European Union. Its scope is to improve security and defence education, by benefitting from a didactic use of digital tools. In this paper, we are going to investigate the status of digital competencies of students before and during the COVID-19 pandemic by analyzing a questionnaire administered to students, asking them to rate several aspects such as: engagement, communication, development of digital competencies, and achievement of learning outcomes. Furthermore, we compare students' time management when working with computers and electronic devices. The sample is composed by Italian students enrolled in security and defence courses, which are cross-disciplinary studies strongly focused on international cooperation. A similar survey addressed to teachers has been already delivered and analyzed (Marchisio et al., 2022c), allowing us to set up comparisons between the two sides. The paper is structured as follows: Section 2 presents the state of the art, and Section 3 is devoted to the research question and the methodology. Section 4 reports all the results, while Section 5 sets up the relative discussion. Finally, some concluding remarks are reported in Section 6.

State of the art

Several recent studies addressed the opportunity of acquiring digital competencies in the security and defence setting. First, it is clear that digital tools provide the basis for e-learning, thus requiring all the stakeholders to be digitally competent, and in particular in relation with education. A criticality arises when these skills are overestimated, leading people to believe that what they know is sufficient to perform adequately, and that in case they need help, they will always be able to rely on others who know the tools better. This is a feeling spread among both students (Buffardi & Taddeo, 2017) and teachers (Tomczyk, 2021), which results in thinking that to acquire proper digital competencies is less important than it actually is. (Pinchuk & Prokopenko, 2021) analyzed the experience in modern educational approaches to STEM subjects in various countries: United States, Australia, China, Britain, Israel, Korea, and Singapore. This resulted in the possibility of implementing transdisciplinary integration while providing advanced training to the officers of the Armed Forces of Ukraine, the authors' native country. (Barron & Rowles, 2021) highlighted the importance of digital literacy also for specific military branches, such as Air Force. It has long been established that learning to use technology in general and learning to fine-tune it for education are quite different paths, since in the latter case the technical tools are the means rather than the scope (Goldin & Katz, 2009), implying the involvement of various other skills (Van Laar et al., 2017). A widely recognized criticality regards the fact that, albeit the competencies in digital fully fit into the *future skills* notion (Ehlers, 2020, and references therein), almost a half of Europeans lack even the basic skills, with a gender gap and a digital divide making the situation even worse, as per 2017 data (European Education Area, 2020). In 2020, the European Union published the Digital Education Action Plan (DEAP), outlining how digital competencies in education are strategic; it has been this declaration that inspired the outset of the DIGICODE project. In general, these skills are pivotal for addressing the challenges of educating sustainably (Mentsiev et al., 2022), fitting into the UN Sustainable Development Goals (United Nations, 2015).

Research question and methodology

We motivated our study with the need to give an answer to the following research question: *How did Italian students perceive higher education in a transition scenario requiring the use of digital skills, and how can these skills be improved?* The transition scenario is given by the disruptive changes in the use of digital tools in education provided by COVID-19 pandemic. This resulted in a survey in which both quantitative and qualitative aspects have been put under scrutiny, but here we focus on the former ones, since they are better suited for setting up a comparison between the situations before and during the COVID-19 pandemic. Furthermore, they also allow us to make a comparison between the students' and the teachers' perceptions, thus highlighting similarities and differences in how both stakeholders felt the scenario. We collected data from 361 Italian third year Bachelor students and Master students in Strategic Sciences, divided by age and gender as follows:

Table 0: Distribution of the students by age and gender

Age range	Females	Males	Did not specify
19-22 years old	29	84	0
23-25 years old	41	161	2
Over 25 years old	6	34	4

It must be noted that there is still a gender difference in the sample, but it is by now intrinsic in the current population of students, which is anyway representative. About 90% of them are military students, while the remaining 10% are civilians. They are almost equally divided between bachelor and master students, with a slight predominance of the former.

For the ratings, we set up a five-level Likert scale, in which 1 stands for the lowest score and 5 for the highest one; for the time spent, we used categorizations, in a case basically corresponding to the actual number of daily hours, in the other case encompassing reasonable ranges of weekly hours (e.g. "from 10 to 20 hours"). We analyzed the resulting numerical data both descriptively and inferentially, allowing on the one hand to clearly show the differences (if present), and on the other hand to state for them a solid significance under the statistical point of view.

Results

We compared pairs of questions investigating the situation before and during the COVID-19 pandemic, by means of Likert scales in Pairs 1-4, and categorical levels in Pairs 5-6. In the following tables, the word "before" stands for "before the pandemic, in a face-to-face context" while "during" stands for "during the pandemic, in emergency or online context".

Pair 1: how do you perceive your personal engagement?

Table 1: Rating of personal engagement by students

Engagement	Before	During	Difference
Very low (1)	5	9	+4
Low (2)	8	39	+31
Average (3)	64	116	+52
Good (4)	176	150	-26
Very good (5)	108	47	-61

Table 1 shows a diminution in how well students perceived their engagement in the pandemic setting: the generally lower scores, with 160 of them decreasing while only 44 of them increased (157 of them remained the same), are confirmed by observing that their average decreased from 4.04 (standard deviation: 0.83) to 3.52 (standard deviation: 0.94). Pairing data results in a differences' mean of -0.52 (standard deviation: 1.13), and inferential tests allow us to determine that this deterioration is statistically significant, resulting in the z-scores of a paired Wilcoxon signed-rank test and a paired t-test (both normally approximated) to be respectively 7.67 and 8.62, while it is general sufficient to have values higher than 3 in order to deem the variation significant. The practical consequence is that students found it difficult to engage remotely with the same intensity they were able to feel in classroom.

Pair 2: how do you rate your communication with teachers?

Table 2: Rating of communication with teachers

Communication	Before	During	Difference
Very low (1)	3	8	+5
Low (2)	12	43	+31
Average (3)	73	125	+52
Good (4)	187	147	-40
Very good (5)	86	38	-48

Table 2 shows again a diminution, this time concerning the quality of communication. 141 scores decreased, only 34 of them increased, and 186 of them did not change, resulting in the average falling from 3.94 (standard deviation: 0.80) to 3.45 (standard deviation: 0.91), being the differences' mean -0.49 (standard deviation: 1.03). Also here, z-scores allow us to state statistical significance, being them 7.92 for Wilcoxon and 9.02 for the t-test. This suggests that students had difficulties in feeling equally at ease in conferring with teachers at a distance rather than face-to-face, even if in general young people are more prone to communicate in ways that do not require the parts to be present in the same place and at the same time.

Pair 3: how do you rate your own development of digital competencies?

Table 3: Rating of development of digital competencies

Digital competencies	Before	During	Difference
Very low (1)	4	3	-1
Low (2)	19	10	-9
Average (3)	107	87	-20
Good (4)	172	197	+25
Very good (5)	59	64	+5

Contrarily to Tables 1-2, Table 3 shows an increment: 87 scores increased, 47 of them decreased, and 227 of them did not change, with the average rising from 3.73 (standard deviation: 0.84) to 3.86 (standard deviation: 0.76), and the differences' mean having the value 0.13 (standard deviation: 0.76). In this case, the z-scores are 2.90 for Wilcoxon and 3.17 for the t-test, so the variation is statistically significant with a p-value less than 0.01, but significance is lower than noticed for Pairs 1-2. This can be interpreted as the students developing some digital competencies because the situation required it, but doing it not necessarily uniformly, since a high number of students (more than the 60%), in fact, did not improve those competencies according to what they declared.

Pair 4: how do you rate your achievement of the learning outcomes?

Table 4: Rating of achievement of the learning outcomes

Learning outcomes	Before	During	Difference
Very low (1)	5	4	-1
Low (2)	10	10	0
Average (3)	95	105	+10
Good (4)	189	191	+2
Very good (5)	62	51	-11

In this case, Table 4 shows a basically balanced situation: 55 scores increased, 71 of them decreased, and 235 of them did not change, with the average moving from 3.81 (standard deviation: 0.80) to 3.76 (standard deviation: 0.77), thus varying of 0.05 (the standard deviation of the differences' mean is 0.84). These changes appear to be quite weak, and this is confirmed by the z-scores, being 1.41 for Wilcoxon and 1.13 for the t-test, thus deeming statistical insignificance (the p-value is higher than 0.05). The interpretation for this may concern the fact that students may have felt satisfied of what they were able to achieve as learners in the transition scenario, since after all the uncertainty could have resulted in even more difficulties.

Pair 5: how many hours per day do you spend on the PC for learning purposes?

Table 5: Daily time spent in front of a PC

Daily time in front of PC	Before	During	Difference
Less than 1 hour (1)	88	20	-68
About 2 hours (2)	114	42	-72
About 3 hours (3)	61	53	-8
About 4 hours (4)	30	54	+24
About 5 hours (5)	17	50	+33
6 hours or more (6)	17	108	+91

Here, we exclude from the analysis 34 students answering "It's hard to say" to the question relative to the pre-pandemic period, thus restricting (just slightly) our sample to 327 of them. The increments are prominent: the number of hours increased 225 times, while it decreased only 32 times (70 times it remained the same); the average augmented from 2.46 (standard deviation: 1.38) to 4.21 (standard deviation: 1.63), a jump of 1.75 (the standard deviation of the differences' mean is 1.98). The confirmation that z-scores can give is overwhelming: 11.80 for Wilcoxon and 16.73 for the t-test are the highest scores of all the pairs we considered. This means that most students required more time to spend in front of the PC, with the difference being considerable for several of them, albeit a minority did not require more time, some of them requiring even less time. The 30% of students requiring less or the same time reasonably used the PC enough already before the transition, an aspect related to the evidence the next pair of questions will show. It must be noted that these students used the PC enough, but not a lot before the pandemic, since there is a substantial uniformity with respect to the declared number of hours.

Pair 6: how much time per week do you spend studying for classes?

Table 6: Weekly time spent studying for classes

Weekly study time	Before	During	Difference

Less than 1 hour (1)	21	24	+3
From 1 to 4 hours (2)	113	102	-11
From 4 to 10 hours (3)	132	130	-2
From 10 to 20 hours (4)	64	74	+10
More than 20 hours (5)	31	31	0

In the last pair of questions, the situation is again balanced, with the category increasing 79 times and decreasing 75 times, along with 207 times in which it did not change. The increment of the average is from 2.92 (standard deviation: 1.03) to 2.96 (standard deviation: 1.05), resulting in a differences' mean of 0.04 (standard deviation: 1.02). As for the case of Pair 4, there is no significance in these modifications, a fact that z-scores indeed confirms by giving 0.83 for Wilcoxon and 0.78 for the t-test, implying a p-value higher than 0.05 and thus the inability to refuse the changes' insignificance (null hypothesis). Consequently, students did not feel the need to considerably increase the time they devoted to studying, by generally assuming they did it enough already before the COVID-19. It can be objected that how the scale is subdivided could affect these considerations, but the proximity of the numbers relative to increments and decrements would reasonably suggest the absence of a sound trend anyway.

Discussion

All these results can be related to the theoretical framework and the research questions. The averages' decrease in Pairs 1-2 (engagement and communication) and the increasing standard deviations suggest that diverse students react, at least up to a certain extent, differently to the challenges brought about by the pandemic, in part probably due to different starting conditions. Personalized learning paths could overcome diversity. A specific training to develop digital competencies, which are not uniform among students, could also be useful (Pair 3). It would have been reasonable to find increments in Pair 5, but trained students would consistently require less time to deal with technical matters, thus partially reducing the additional time they had to use the PC. Finally, the results shown in Pair 4 (learning outcomes) and Pair 6 (weekly study time) depict an already satisfactory situation, even if different students' engagement could improve the quality of the studying time. Another important aspect concerns the fact that it is also a matter of accommodation: it requires time to get used to changes, even if they are positive. In our context, this accommodation depends on how much students use technologies in education. It is clear that teachers should lead by example by using digital tools in the first instance. We can also compare the results just obtained with the analogous survey regarding teachers, depicted in (Marchisio et al., 2022c). Pairs 1-2 are strictly related with questions we asked teachers, namely those requiring them to rate the engagement of students (mirroring Pair 1), and the communication with students (mirroring Pair 2). In both cases, we see a statistically supported degradation of the ratings; this means that *both* sides shared the perception that students engaged with more difficulty, and that communication became more difficult in each direction, i.e. teachers communicated less easily with students and viceversa. A similar accordance concerns Pair 5, given that we asked teachers how many hours per day they spent at the PC for teaching (or preparing teaching) purposes. Both students and teachers experienced a sharp increase in the daily time they had to spend on computer for educational purposes, thus confirming the inevitability for each stakeholder of dealing with digital tools, by far more than what was required before. Pairs 3-4 are less related to the question we asked teachers; finally, with Pair 6 we return to a higher similarity, but if teachers required more time to perform their commitments, this is not true for students, since no statistically significant evidence occurred. This can be explained by the fact that it may be easier to adapt the learning to new scenarios rather than the teaching.

Conclusions and future works

This research gave us insights regarding how students changed their perception of higher education in the transition scenario implied by the COVID-19 pandemic. These modifications, due also to different perceptions in how they felt accommodated while undergoing relevant changes in their habits, have been related to practical consequences. They mainly consisted in difficulties in handling the didactic potential of digital tools (also here, with differences between students), a limitation that can be overcome by digitally competent teachers and organizations, making students acquire more specific competencies compared to those they already possessed. In addition, the delivery of interdisciplinary activities using digital tools and related innovative methodologies can help students have a broader vision of the matter. Some attempts have been done in two editions of the school "Systems for Command and Control in Security and Defence Field" in the framework of the DIGICODE project and the impact school design on teachers and school activities on students will be studied. An action of this kind is not exclusive to the security and the defence education, but given the internationality of this setting, implied by the needs of a wide collaboration against the threats in the present world, it constitutes a noteworthy context in which to apply it. As further future work, we can on the one hand extend the analysis to an international sample, after having disseminated the questionnaire among our foreign partners, and on the other hand repeat the study after proper intervention on programs and courses, looking for students' improvements.

Acknowledgment

The research activity described in this paper has been carried out inside the Erasmus+ Key Action 2 Strategic Partnership N. 2020-1-PL01-KA226-096192 "Digital Competences for Improving Security and Defence Education – DIGICODE".

References

Barron, A., & Rowles, P. (2021). Evaluation of digital literacy as an Air Force foundational competency. https://apps.dtic.mil/sti/pdfs/AD1143616.pdf

Buffardi, A., & Taddeo, G. (2017). The Web 2.0 Skills of Italian Students: An Empirical Study in Southern Italy. *Italian Journal of Sociology of Education*, *9*(1), 45-76.

Ehlers, U. D. (2020). *Future Skills – Future Learning, Future Higher Education*. Springer, Karlsruhe, Germany.

European Education Area (2020). Digital Education Action Plan. https://education.ec.europa.eu/document/digital-education-action-plan

Goldin, C. D., & Katz, L. F. (2009). *The Race between Education and Technology*. Harvard University Press, Cambridge, UK.

Hodges, C., Moore, S., Lockee, B., Trust, T., & Bond, A. (2020, March 27). The Difference Between Emergency Remote Teaching and Online Learning [Blog post]. https://er.educause.edu/articles/2020/3/the-difference-between-emergency-remote-teaching-and-online-learning

Marchisio, M., & Spinello, E. (2021). Internazionalization for enhancing the European Security and Defence Higher Education. *Proceedings of 15th International Conference on e-Learning* (*EL2021*), 99-106.

Marchisio, M., Remogna, S., Roman, F., & Sacchet, M. (2022a). Teaching Mathematics to Non-Mathematics Majors through Problem Solving and New Technologies. *Education Sciences*, 12, 34.

Marchisio, M., Rabellino, S., Roman, F., & Sacchet, M. (2022b). Valuable Features of Hybrid Teaching in a Higher Education Context. *Communications in Computer and Information Science*, 1639, 16-21.

Marchisio, M., Roman, F., Sacchet, M., & Spinello, E. (2022c). Teachers' perception of higher education in a transition scenario. *Proceedings of IEEE 46th COMPSAC Conference*, 139-144.

Mentsiev, A. U., Aygumov, T. G., & Yudina, A. M (2022). Digital skills development as a basis for sustainable education development. *AIP Conference Proceedings 2647*, 040085.

Mihalova, G. (2006). E-learning as internazionalization strategy in higher education. *Baltic Journal of Management*, *1*(3), 270-284.

Pinchuk, O., & Prokopenko, A. (2021). Actual areas of development of digital competence of officers of the Armed Forces of Ukraine. *Educational Dimension*, *5*(57), 89-108.

Tomczyk, L. (2021). Declared and Real Level of Digital Skills of Future Teaching Staff. *Education Sciences*, 11, 619.

United Nations (2015). The 2030 Agenda for Sustainable Development. https://sdgs.un.org/2030agenda

Van Laar, E., Van Deursen, A. J. A. M., Van Dijk, J., & De Haan, J. (2017). The relation between 21st-century skills and digital skills: A systematic literature review. *Computers in Human Behavior*, 72, 577-588.

AUTHOR INDEX